Accounting

The person that solves the pension crisis...

... may be sitting right in your classroom! Every one of your students has the potential to mak a difference. *WileyPLUS* gives you the technology you need to help them reach their full potential and experience the exhilaration of academic success that will last them a lifetime!

FOR INSTRUCTORS

WileyPLUS is built around the activities you perform in your class each day. With WileyPLUS you ca

Prepare & Present
Create outstanding class presentations using a wealth of resources such as PowerPoint™ slides, and figures and tables. You can even add materials you have created yourself.

Create Assignments
Automate the assigning and grading of homework or quizzes by using the question banks provided, or by writing your own.

Track Student Progress
Keep track of your students' progress and analyse individual a overall class results.

WileyPLUS is compatible with WebCT and Blackboard!

"WileyPLUS is a very powerful interactive resource"

Helen Iggulden,
University of Salford, UK

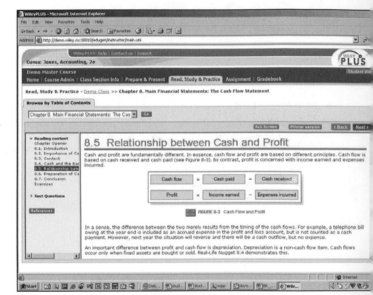

FOR STUDENTS

You have the potential to make a difference!
WileyPLUS is a powerful online system packed with features to help you make the most of your potential and get the best grade you can!

With WileyPLUS you get:

- A complete online version of your text and other study resources

- Problem-solving help, along with instant grading and feedback on your homework and quizzes

- The ability to track your progre and grades throughout the term

76% **of students surveyed said it made them better prepared for tests.***

* Based on a survey of 972 student users of *WileyPLUS*

Accounting

Second Edition

Michael Jones

School of Economics, Finance and Management
University of Bristol

John Wiley & Sons, Ltd

Copyright © 2006   by Michael Jones

Published by John Wiley & Sons Ltd, The Atrium, Southern Gate, Chichester, West Sussex PO19 8SQ, England

Telephone (+44) 1243 779777

Email (for orders and customer service enquiries): cs-books@wiley.co.uk
Visit our Home Page on www.wiley.com

Reprinted with corrections July 2006, August 2008, February 2010

Other Wiley Editorial Offices

John Wiley & Sons Inc., 111 River Street, Hoboken, NJ 07030, USA

Jossey-Bass, 989 Market Street, San Francisco, CA 94103-1741, USA

Wiley-VCH Verlag GmbH, Boschstr. 12, D-69469 Weinheim, Germany

John Wiley & Sons Australia Ltd, 42 McDougall Street, Milton, Queensland 4064, Australia

John Wiley & Sons (Asia) Pte Ltd, 2 Clementi Loop #02-01, Jin Xing Distripark, Singapore 129809

John Wiley & Sons Canada Ltd, 22 Worcester Road, Etobicoke, Ontario, Canada M9W 1L1

Wiley also publishes its books in a variety of electronic formats. Some content that appears in print may not be available in electronic books.

Library of Congress Cataloging-in-Publication Data

Jones, Michael.
  Accounting for non-specialists / Michael Jones. – 2nd ed.
      p. cm.
  Includes bibliographical references and index.
  ISBN 978-0-470-01779-1
 1. Accounting. I. Title.
  HF5635.J774 2006
  657 – dc22

                        2005024423

British Library Cataloguing in Publication Data

A catalogue record for this book is available from the British Library

ISBN-13: 978-0-470-01779-1 (PB)

Typeset in 10/13 Sabon by Laserwords Private Limited, Chennai, India
Printed and bound in Great Britain by TJ International Ltd, Padstow, Cornwall

Contents

About the Author

Michael Jones has taught accounting to non-specialists for 29 years, first at Hereford Technical College, then at Portsmouth Polytechnic (now University) and currently at School of Economics, Finance and Management, University of Bristol. He has taught financial accounting at all levels from GCSE level to final-year degree course. He has published over 140 articles in both professional and academic journals. These articles cover a wide range of topics such as financial accounting, the history of accounting and international accounting. The author's main research interest is in financial communication. He was formerly Professor of Financial Reporting at Cardiff Business School and Director of its Financial Reporting and Business Communication Unit. He is currently Professor of Financial Reporting at the School of Economics, Finance and Management, University of Bristol. Michael has one daughter, Katherine.

About the Book

Background

Accounting is a key aspect of business. All those who work for, or deal with, businesses, therefore, need to understand accounting. Essentially, understanding accounting is a prerequisite for understanding business. This book aims to introduce students to accounting and provide them with the necessary understanding of the theory and practice of financial and management accounting. The book, therefore, is aimed primarily at students studying accounting for the first time and seeks to be as understandable and readable as possible.

The Market

This book is intended as a primary text for students studying accounting for the first time: either those following an undergraduate degree in a business school or non-business studies students studying an accounting course. Thus, this includes students on both accounting and non-accounting degrees and also MBA students. The book therefore covers, for example, accountants, business, engineers, physicists, hotel and catering, social studies and media-study students. The text aims to produce a self-contained, introductory, one-year course covering the major aspects of accounting. However, it is also designed so that students can progress to more advanced follow-up courses in financial accounting or management accounting. The text is thus well-suited as an introduction for mainstream accounting graduates or MBA students as a basic text. In particular, MBA students should find the chapters on creative accounting, international accounting and strategic management accounting beneficial. The book should be particularly useful in reinforcing the fundamental theory and practice of introductory accounting.

Scope

The book sets down my acquired wisdom (such as it is) over 29 years and interweaves context and technique. It aims to introduce the topic of accounting to students in a student-friendly way. Not only are certain chapters devoted solely to context, but the key to each particular topic is seen as developing the student's understanding of the underlying concepts. This is a novel approach for this type of book.

The book is divided into 22 chapters within three sections. Section A deals with the context and techniques of basic financial accounting and reporting. Section B looks at the context of financial accounting and reporting. Finally, Section C provides an introduction to the context and techniques of management accounting.

Section A: Financial Accounting: The Techniques

In the first section, after introducing the context and background to accounting, the mechanics of financial accounting are explored, for example, bookkeeping and the preparation of financial statements (such as the profit and loss account and balance sheet). This section is presented using a tried and tested example, which starts from the accounting equation. A profit and loss account and balance sheet are then prepared. The section continues by explaining the adjustments to financial statements, different enterprises' financial statements, the cash flow statement and the interpretation of accounts.

Section B: Financial Accounting: The Context

The focus in this section is on exploring some wider aspects of external financial reporting. It begins by contextualising financial reporting by looking at the regulatory framework, measurement systems and the annual report. This is followed by an introductory overview of creative accounting and international accounting. This part of the book allows students to appreciate how accounting is rooted in a wider social and international context. Particularly novel is the inclusion of the regulatory framework, corporate governance, international accounting, and creative accounting. This material is included to give students a wider appreciation of accounting than is traditionally presented.

Section C: Management Accounting

This section begins with an exploration of the main concepts underpinning management accounting. Seven main areas are covered: costing, budgeting, standard costing, short-term decision making, strategic management accounting, capital investment and sources of finance. This section thus provides a good coverage of the basics of costing and management accounting as well as introducing strategic management accounting, a topic which has recently become more prominent. The aim of this section is to introduce students to a wide range of key concepts so that they gain a good knowledge base.

Coverage

The issues of double-entry bookkeeping, partnerships, manufacturing accounts, computers, internationalisation and the public sector are tricky ones for an introductory text. I have included double-entry bookkeeping, but tried to introduce a no-frills approach and focus on the essentials. This is because I strongly believe that double-entry bookkeeping is a fundamental stepping stone to understanding accounting. *The book is so designed that it is possible to miss out the detailed explanation of double-entry bookkeeping, but still follow the rest of the textbook*. This book, after much consideration, focuses on three types of business enterprise: sole traders, partnerships and limited companies. These three enterprises comprise the vast bulk of UK businesses. Indeed, according to the Office of National Statistics (2004), in the UK, 48 % of enterprises are companies, 22 % sole traders and 20 % partnerships. The sole trader is the simplest business enterprise. The earlier chapters in Section A, therefore, primarily focus on the sole trader to explain the basics. However, later chapters in Section A are more concerned with companies. A distinction is made throughout the book between the requirements of listed and non-listed companies.

Manufacturing accounts are excluded because I consider them unnecessarily complex for non-specialist students and also because of their diminishing importance within the UK economy. Indeed, in 2000, only 10 % of UK businesses were in production (Office for National Statistics, 2000). The impact of computers on accounting is covered in the text where appropriate. I consider that the widespread use of computers makes it even more important than before to understand the basics of accounting. Although the primary audience for this textbook is likely to be the UK, I have, where possible, attempted to 'internationalise' it. In fact, I have taught international accounting for 12 years. A synthesis of international accounting is thus provided in Chapter 14. However, I have also tried to integrate other international aspects into the book, for instance, drawing on the International Accounting Standards Board's Statement of Principles. A decision was taken at an early stage to focus on the private sector rather than the public sector. So when the terms company, firm, enterprise and organisation are used, sometimes interchangeably, generally they refer to private sector organisations. There is some coverage of public sector issues, but in general, students interested in this area should refer to a more specialised public sector textbook.

Special Features

A particular effort has been made to make accounting as accessible as possible to students. There are thus several special features in this book which, taken together, distinguish it from other introductory textbooks.

Blend of Theory and Practice

I believe that the key to accounting is understanding. As a result, the text stresses the underlying concepts of accounting and the context within which accounting operates. The book, therefore, blends practice and theory. Worked examples are supplemented by explanation. In addition, the context of accounting is explored. The aim is to contextualise accounting within a wider framework.

Novel Material

There has been a conscious attempt to introduce into the book topics not usually taught at this level, for example, regulatory framework, corporate governance, creative accounting, international accounting and strategic management accounting. The regulatory framework is introduced to give the students the context within which accounting is based. Corporate governance aims to set accounting within the wider relationship between directors and shareholders. Creative accounting, I have found, is an extremely popular subject with students and demonstrates that accounting is an art rather than a science. It is particularly topical, given the collapse of the US company Enron and other recent accounting scandals such as WorldCom, Xerox and Parmalat. Creative accounting also enables the behavioural aspects of accounting to be explored. International accounting allows students to contextualise UK accounting within a wider international setting. This is increasingly important with the growth in international trade. Finally, strategic management accounting is a growing area of interest to management accountants. Its inclusion in this book reflects this.

Interpretation

I appreciate the need for non-specialist students to evaluate and interpret material. There is thus a comprehensive chapter on the interpretation of accounts. Equally important, the book strives to emphasise why particular techniques are important.

Readable and Understandable Presentation

Much of my research has been into readable and understandable presentation. At all times, I have strived to achieve this. In particular, I have tried to present complicated materials in a simple way.

Innovative Presentation

I am very keen to focus on effective presentation. This book, therefore, includes many presentational features which aim to enliven the text. Quotations, extracts from newspapers and journals (real-life nuggets), and extracts from annual reports (the company camera) convey the day-to-day relevance of accounting. I also attempt to use realistic examples. This has not, however, always been easy or practical given the introductory nature of the material. In addition, I have attempted to inject some wit and humour into the text through the use of, among other things, cartoons and soundbites. The cartoons, in particular, are designed to present a sideways, irreverent look at accounting which hopefully students will find not only entertaining, but also thought-provoking. Finally, I have frequently used boxes and diagrams to simplify and clarify material. Throughout the text there are reflective questions (pause for thought). These are designed as places where students may pause briefly in their reading of the text to reflect on a particular aspect of accounting or to test their knowledge.

End-of-Chapter Questions and Answers

There are numerous questions and answers at the end of each chapter which test the student's knowledge. These comprise both numerical and discussion questions. The discussion questions are designed for group discussion between lecturer and students. At the end of the book an outline is provided to, at least, the first discussion question of each chapter. This answer provides some outline points for discussion and allows the students to gauge the level and depth of the answers required. However, it should not be taken as exhaustive or prescriptive. The other discussion answers are to be found on the lecturers' area of the website.

The answers to the numerical questions are divided roughly in two. Half of the answers are provided at the back of the book for students to practise the techniques and to test themselves. These questions are indicated by the number being in blue. The other numerical answers are to be found on the lecturer area of the website. A further extensive supplementary set of over 100 questions and answers is also available to lecturers on their website.

Websites

In addition to the supplementary questions, there are Powerpoint slides available on the lecturers' website. On the student's website, there are 220 multiple-choice questions (ten for each chapter) as well as 22 additional questions with answers (one for each chapter).

Includes Wiley Plus, which is a powerful online tool providing instructors and students with an integrated suite of teaching and learning resources, including an online version of the text, in one easy-to-use website.

Overall Effect

Taken together, I believe that the blend of theory and practice, focus on readable and understandable presentation, novel material, interpretative stance and innovative presentation make this a distinctive and useful introductory textbook. Hopefully, readers will find it useful and interesting! I have done my best. Enjoy!

Second Edition

The second edition has been extensively updated for new developments in accounting and to better reflect the nature of the book. The main changes are outlined below.

Title of the Book

The title of the book has been changed to reflect the nature of the book. Many accounting students and MBA students found the book useful and the title of Accounting for Non-specialists was on reflection considered to be too narrow.

New Developments

The book has been updated to reflect new developments in accounting such as the creation of the new UK Accounting Standards Setting Regime, the creation of limited liability partnerships, the change of certain accounting standards, and the evolving nature of the annual report.

International Financial Reporting Standards (IFRS)

The adoption of IFRS by European listed companies from 1st January 2005 has been fully reflected in this book. The book clearly distinguishes between listed companies that follow IFRS and non-listed companies that do not. This has necessitated extensive changes to Chapter 7 on partnerships and limited companies, Chapter 8 on cash flow statements and Chapter 9 on interpretation of accounts as well as Chapter 14 on international accounting. New formats have been used for the income statement and balance sheet of listed companies. In addition, the terminology has been changed to that used by IFRS. The updating of the book for IFRS has also enabled the book to be more international in outlook, examples of foreign companies such as Heineken, Nokia and Volkswagen have been used.

Performance Evaluation

It was considered that the topic of performance evaluation was neglected in the first edition. Therefore, in the second edition there is a substantive section now included in Chapter 17 which has been renamed 'Planning, Control and Performance' and now includes management control systems and responsibility centres.

Updating of Features

Key features of the book such as Real Life Nuggets, Soundbites and Company Cameras have, wherever possible, been updated.

Hopefully, these changes have improved the book!

Mike Jones
March 2006

Acknowledgements

In many ways writing a textbook of this nature is a team effort. Throughout the time it has taken to write this book I have consistently sought the help and advice of others in order to improve it. I am, therefore, extremely grateful to a great number of academic staff and students (no affiliation below) whose comments have helped me to improve this book. The errors, of course, remain mine.

Malcolm Anderson (Cardiff Business School)
Tony Brinn (Cardiff Business School)
Alex Brown
Peter Chidgey (BDO Binder, Hamlyn) Mark Clatworthy (Cardiff Business School)
Alpa Dhanani (Cardiff Business School)
Mahmoud Ezzamel (Cardiff Business School)
Charlotte Gladstone-Miller (Portsmouth Business School)
Paul Gordon (Heriot Watt University)
Tony Hines (Portsmouth Business School)
Deborah Holywell
Carolyn Isaaks (Nottingham Trent University)
Tuomas Korppoo
Margaret Lamb (Warwick Business School)
Andrew Lennard (Accounting Standards Board)
Les Lumsdon (Manchester Metropolitan University)
Claire Lutwyche
Louise Macniven (Cardiff Business School)
Neil Marriott (University of Glamorgan)
Howard Mellett (Cardiff Business School)
Joanne Mitchell
Peter Morgan (Cardiff Business School)
Barry Morse (Cardiff Business School)
Simon Norton (Cardiff Business School)
Phillip O'Regan (Limerick University)
David Parker (Portsmouth Business School)
Roger Pegum (Liverpool John Moores University)
Maurice Pendlebury (Cardiff Business School)
Elaine Porter (Bournemouth University)
Neil Robson (University of the West of England)

Julia Smith (Cardiff Business School)
Aris Solomon (University of Exeter)
Jill Solomon (Cardiff Business School)
Tony Whitford (University of Westminster)
Jason Xiao (Cardiff Business School)

This book is hopefully enlivened by many extracts from books, newspapers and annual reports. This material should not be reproduced, copied or transmitted unless written permission is obtained from the original copyright owner. I am, therefore, grateful to all those who kindly granted the publisher permission to reproduce the copyright material. This includes the following companies and plcs: AstraZeneca, Heineken, HBOS, Hyder, Laing, Nokia, Manchester United, Marks & Spencer, Rentokil, Rolls-Royce, J. Sainsbury, Tesco, Vodafone, Volkswagen and J.D. Wetherspoon. In addition, *Accountancy Age*, the *Economist, The Financial Times, The Guardian, Management Accounting*, the *New Scientist, Sunday Business, The Daily Telegraph* and *The Sunday Telegraph*. Each source is also specifically mentioned in the text.

Many of the Soundbites are drawn from the following texts. The full references are: H. Ehrlich (1998), *The Wiley Book of Quotations* (John Wiley & Sons, Inc., New York); R. Flesch (1959), *The Book of Unusual Quotations* (Cassell, London); J. Vitullo-Martin and J. Robert Moskin (1994), *The Executive's Book of Quotations* (Oxford University Press, New York); and E. Weber (1991), *The Book of Business Quotations* (Business Books, London).

Every effort has been made to trace the original copyright owner; if we have accidentally infringed any copyright the publishers offer their apologies.

I should also like to thank Steve Hardman and his team at John Wiley for their help and support. I am also very appreciative of the help and support of my partner, Jill Solomon. Finally, last but certainly not least, I should like to thank Jan Richards for her patience and hard work in turning my generally illegible scribbling into the final manuscript.

Dedication

I would like to dedicate this book to the following people who have made my life richer.

- My Father, Donald, who died in 2003
- My Mother
- My daughter, Katherine
- Tony Brinn (in memoriam)
- All my friends in Hereford, Cardiff and elsewhere
- All my colleagues
- And, finally, my past students!

Chapter 1

"One way to cheat death is to become an accountant, it seems. The Norfolk accountancy firm W.R. Kewley announces on its website that it was 'originally established in 1982 with 2 partners, one of whom died in 1993. After a short break he re-established in 1997, offering a personal service throughout.' He was, Feedback presumes, dead only for tax purposes."

New Scientist, 1 April 2000, p. 96

Learning Outcomes

After completing this chapter you should be able to:

✔ Explain the nature and importance of accounting.

✔ Outline the context which shapes accounting.

✔ Identify the main users of accounting and discuss their information needs.

✔ Distinguish between the different types of accountancy and accountant.

Introduction to Accounting

In a Nutshell

- *Accounting is the provision of financial information to managers or owners so that they can make business decisions.*

- *Accounting measures, monitors and controls business activities.*

- *Financial accounting supplies financial information to external users.*

- *Management accounting serves the needs of managers.*

- *Users of accounting information include shareholders and managers.*

- *Accounting theory and practice are affected by history, country, technology and organisation.*

- *Auditing, bookkeeping, financial accounting, financial management, insolvency, management accounting, taxation and management consultancy are all branches of accountancy.*

- *Accountants may be members of professional bodies, such as the Institute of Chartered Accountants in England and Wales.*

- *Although very useful, accounting has several limitations such as its historic nature and its failure to measure the non-financial aspects of business.*

Introduction

The key to understanding business is to understand accounting. Accounting is central to the operation of modern business. Accounting enables businesses to keep track of their money. If businesses cannot make enough profit or generate enough cash they will go bankrupt. Often accounting is called the 'language of business'. It provides a means of effective and understandable business communication. If you understand the language you will, therefore, understand business. However, like many languages, accounting needs to be learnt. The aim of this book is to teach the language of accounting.

Nature of Accounting

At its simplest, accounting is all about recording, preparing and interpreting business transactions. Accounting provides a key source of information about a business to those who need it, such as managers or owners. This information allows managers to monitor, plan and control the activities of a business. This enables managers to answer key questions such as:

- How much profit have we made?
- Have we enough cash to pay our employees' wages?
- What level of dividends can we pay to our shareholders?
- Should we expand our product range?

PAUSE FOR THOUGHT 1.1

Some Accounting Questions

You are thinking of manufacturing a new product, the superwhizzo. What are the main accounting questions you would ask?

....

The principal questions would relate to sales, costs and profit. They might be:

- What price are rival products selling at?
- How much raw material will I need? How much will it cost?
- How many hours will it take to make each superwhizzo and how much is labour per hour?
- How much will it cost to make the product in terms of items such as electricity?
- How should I recover general business costs such as business rates or the cost of machinery wearing out?
- How much profit should I aim to make on each superwhizzo?

In small businesses, managers and owners will often be the same people. However, in larger businesses, such as large companies, managers and owners will not be the same. Managers will run the companies on behalf of the owners. In such cases, accounting information serves a particularly useful role. Managers supply the owners with financial information in the form of a profit and loss account, a balance sheet and a cash flow statement. This enables the owners to see how well the business is performing. In companies, the owners of a business are called the shareholders.

Essentially, therefore, accounting is all about providing financial information to managers and owners so that they can make business decisions (see Definition 1.1). The formal definition (given below), although dating from 1966, has stood the test well as a comprehensive definition of accounting.

DEFINITION 1.1

Accounting

Working definition
The provision of information to managers and owners so that they can make business decisions.

Formal definition
'The process of identifying, measuring and communicating economic information to permit informed judgments and decisions by users of the information.'

American Accounting Association (1966), *Statement of Basic Accounting Theory*, p. 1

Importance of Accounting

Accounting is essential to the running of any business or organisation. Organisations as diverse as ICI, Barclays Bank and Manchester United football club all need to keep a close check on their finances.

At its simplest, money makes the world go round and accounting keeps track of the money. Businesses depend on cash and profit. If businesses do not make enough cash or earn enough profit, they will get into financial difficulties, perhaps even go bankrupt. Accounting provides the framework by which cash and profit can be monitored, planned and controlled.

Unless you can understand accounting, you will never understand business. This does not mean everybody has to be an expert accountant. However, it is necessary to know the language of accounting and to be able to interpret accounting numbers. In some respects, there is a similarity between learning to drive a car and learning about accounting. When you are learning to drive a car you do not need to be a car mechanic. However, you have to understand the car's instruments, such as a speedometer or fuel gauge. Similarly, with accounting, you do not have to be a professional accountant. However, you do need to understand the basic terminology such as income, expenses, profit, assets, liabilities, capital, and cash flow.

PAUSE FOR THOUGHT 1.2

Manchester United

What information might the board of directors of Manchester United find useful?

Manchester United is both a football club and a thriving business. Indeed, the two go hand in hand. Playing success generates financial success, and financial success generates playing success. Key issues for Manchester United might be:

- How much in gate receipts will we get from our league matches, cup matches and European fixtures?
- How much can we afford to pay our players?
- How much cash have we available to buy rising new stars and how much will our fading old stars bring us?
- How much will we get from television rights and commercial sponsorship?
- How much do we need to finance new capital expenditure, such as building a new stadium?

Financial Accounting and Management Accounting

A basic distinction is between financial accounting and management accounting. Financial accounting is concerned with information on a business's performance and is targeted primarily at those outside the business (such as shareholders). However, it is also used internally by managers. By contrast, management accounting is internal to a business and used solely by managers. A brief overview is provided in Figure 1.1.

Figure 1.1   Overview of Financial and Management Accounting

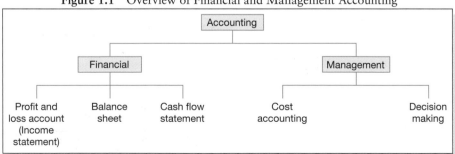

Financial Accounting

Financial accounting is the provision of financial information on a business's recent financial performance targeted at external users, such as shareholders. However, internal users, such as management, may also find it useful. It is required by law. Essentially, it is backward-looking, dealing with past events. Transactions are initially recorded using double-entry bookkeeping (see Chapter 3). Three major financial statements can then be prepared: the profit and loss account (also known as the income statement), the balance sheet and the cash flow statement (see Chapters 4–8). These are then interpreted using ratios (see Chapter 9) by users such as shareholders and analysts.

Management Accounting

By contrast, management accounting serves only the internal needs of the business. It is not required by law. However, all organisations generate some sort of management accounting: if they did not they would not survive long. Management accounting can be divided into cost accounting and decision making. In turn, cost accounting can be split into costing (Chapter 16) and planning, control and performance: budgeting (Chapter 17) and standard costing (Chapter 18). Decision making is divided into short-term decisions (Chapter 19) and long-term decision making (Chapters 20–21). In Chapter 22 both short-term and long-term sources of finance are considered.

> ## SOUNDBITE 1.1
>
> ### Investment Analysts
>
> 'Over-paid, under-qualified and inappropriately influential. That seems to be the conventional view of that rampaging beast, the city analyst.'
>
> *Source*: Damian Wild, *Accountancy Age*, 21 October 2004, p. 14

Users of Accounts

The users of accounting information may broadly be divided into insiders and outsiders (see Figure 1.2). The insiders are the management and the employees. However, employees are

Figure 1.2   Main Users of Accounting Information

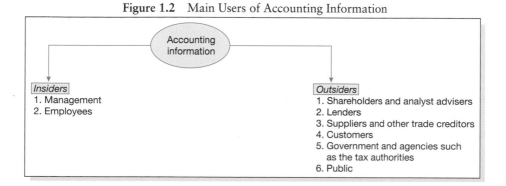

Accounting information

Insiders
1. Management
2. Employees

Outsiders
1. Shareholders and analyst advisers
2. Lenders
3. Suppliers and other trade creditors
4. Customers
5. Government and agencies such as the tax authorities
6. Public

also outsiders in the sense that they often do not have direct access to the financial information.

The primary user groups are the management and shareholders. Shareholders or investors are often advised by professional financial analysts who work for stockbrokers or big city investment houses. These financial analysts help to determine the share prices of companies quoted on the stock exchange. However, sometimes, they are viewed with mistrust (see Real-Life Nugget 1.1).

REAL-LIFE NUGGET 1.1

Financial Analysts

Working with analysts is a little like being a member of the Magic Circle or the freemasons – those who know how to perform these masterful sleights of hand or arcane rituals are forbidden from ever revealing them to outsiders. Of course, the alternative is that I can't reveal them because I don't understand them myself – I'll let you decide.

Source: Showbiz values come to the City, James Montier, *The Guardian*, 15 January 2000, p. 5. © Guardian Newspapers Limited 2000

The influence of other users (or stakeholders) is growing in importance. Suppliers, customers and lenders have a closer relationship to the company than the government and tax authorities, or the public.

These users all need accounting information to help them make business decisions. Usually, the main information requirements concern a company's profits, cash flow, assets and debt (see Figure 1.3).

Figure 1.3   User Information Requirements

User Group	Information Requirements
Internal Users	
1. Management	Information for costing, decision making, planning and control.
2. Employees	Information about job security and for collective bargaining.
External Users	
1. Shareholders and analyst advisers	Information for buying and selling shares.
2. Lenders	Information about assets and the company's cash position.
3. Suppliers and other trade creditors	Information about assets and the company's cash position.
4. Customers	Information about the long-term prospects and survival of the business.
5. Government and agencies such as tax authorities	Information to enable governmental planning. Information primarily on profits to use as a basis for calculating tax.
6. Public (e.g., individual citizens, or organisations such as Greenpeace)	Information about the social and environmental impact of corporate activities.

Shareholders, for example, require information so that they can decide whether to buy, hold or sell their shares. The information needs of each group differ slightly and, indeed may conflict (see Pause for Thought 1.3).

PAUSE FOR THOUGHT 1.3

Conflicting Interests of User Groups

Can you think of an example where the interests of users might actually conflict?

A good example would be in the payment of dividends to shareholders. The higher the dividend, the less money is kept in the company to pay employees or suppliers.

Another, more subtle, example is the interests of shareholders and analyst advisers. Shareholders own shares. However, they rely on the advice of analyst advisers such as stockbrokers. Their interests may superficially seem the same (e.g., selling underperforming shares and buying good performers). However, the analyst advisers live by the commission they make. It is in their interests to advise shareholders to buy and sell shares. Unfortunately, it costs money to buy and sell shares; therefore, this may not always be in the potential shareholders' best interests.

Accounting Context

It is important to realise that accounting is more than just a mere technical subject. Although it is true that at the heart of accounting there are many techniques. For example, as we will see in Chapter 3, double-entry bookkeeping is essential when preparing financial statements. However, accounting is also determined by the context in which it operates. Accounting changes as society changes. Accounting in medieval England and accounting today, for example, are very different. Similarly, there are major differences between accounting in Germany and in the United Kingdom. We can see the importance of context, if we look briefly at the effect of history, country, technology, and organisation (see Figure 1.4).

Figure 1.4 Importance of Accounting Context

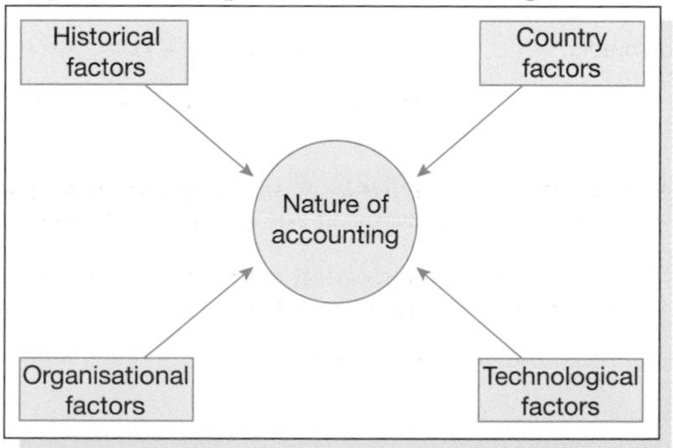

History

Accounting is an integral part of human society. Early societies had accounting systems which although appearing primitive to us today, served their needs adequately. The Incas in South America, for example, used knotted ropes, called quipus, for accounting. In medieval England notched sticks called tally sticks were used to record transactions.

Gradually, over time, human society became more sophisticated. A form of accounting called double-entry bookkeeping (every transaction is recorded twice) arose. Emerging from Italy in the fifteenth century, at the same time that Columbus discovered America, double-entry bookkeeping is now the standard way by which accounting transactions are recorded throughout the world.

> ### PAUSE FOR THOUGHT 1.4
>
> ## The Term 'Accounting'
>
> *Why is accounting so called?*
>
> ....
>
> It is believed that accounting derives from the old thirteenth-century word *aconter*, to count. At its simplest, therefore, accounting means counting. This makes sense as the earliest accountants would have counted sheep or pigs!

International Accounting

Double-entry bookkeeping, the profit and loss account and the balance sheet are now routine in most major countries. The International Accounting Standards Board (IASB) is also making great efforts to harmonise the disclosure and measurement practices of listed companies worldwide and publishes International Financial Reporting Standards (IFRS). However, there is still great diversity in the broader context in which accounting is carried out. Accounting in the UK, for example, is very different from accounting in France despite the fact that both countries are members of the European Union. Listed companies in both France and the UK, however, do have to follow IFRS. The UK prides itself on a flexible and self-regulated accounting system largely free of government control. By contrast, the French system is very standardised and largely government-controlled. In general, as Soundbite 1.2 shows, accounting plays an important role globally.

> ### SOUNDBITE 1.2
>
> 'We now operate in a global market-place, and this is driving the need for universal professional standards and the global qualifications that can deliver them'.
>
> *Source*: One World, One Revision, Chris Ward, *Accountancy Age*, 11 April 2005, p. 16

There are also clear differences between the UK and the US. For example, in the UK, there are Companies Acts, which apply to all UK companies whereas in the US only companies quoted on the stock exchange (i.e., listed companies) are subject to detailed and comprehensive Federal regulations. Also, US listed companies, unlike those in the UK, do not have to comply with IFRS. Unlisted companies are subject only to state regulations, which vary from state to state.

Technology

A rapid change which has affected accounting is computerisation. Up until the advent of computers, accounting was done manually. This was labour-intensive work. Each transaction was entered into the books twice using double-entry bookkeeping. The accounts were then prepared by hand. Similarly, costing, budgeting and decision making were all carried out manually.

Today, most businesses use computers. However, they must be used with caution. For the computer, GIGO rules. If you put garbage in, you get garbage out. To avoid GIGO, one needs to understand accounting. In fact, computerisation probably makes it more, rather than less, important to understand the basics.

Organisations

The nature of accounting will vary from business to business. It will depend on the structure of the business and the nature of the business activity.

Structure

If we take the accounts of the three types of business enterprise with which this book deals, a sole trader's accounts will normally be a lot simpler than those of either a partnership or a company. Sole traders generally run smaller, less complicated businesses (for example, a small butcher's shop). Partnerships are multi-owned businesses typically larger in size than sole traders. The sole traders' and partnerships' accounts will normally be less complicated than company accounts as they are prepared for the benefit of active owner-managers rather than for owners who do not actually run the business.

Nature of the Business

Every organisation is different. Consequently, every organisation's accounts will differ in certain respects. For example, property companies will own predominantly more land and buildings than non-property companies. Manufacturing companies will have more stock than non-manufacturing companies.

It is clear from Figure 1.5 that the nature of sales varies from business to business. In some businesses, a service is provided (e.g., bank, football club, insurance company and plumber).

Figure 1.5 Nature of Sales

Business	Nature of Main Sales
Bank	Interest received from customers
Football club	Gate receipts
Insurance company	Premiums received
Manufacturing company	Sales of goods to retailers
Plumber	Sales of services and other goods
Shop	Sales of goods to customers

The Company Camera 1.1 shows the sales (often termed turnover) of Manchester United plc, mainly gate receipts, television and merchandising, which are generated by entertaining its customers.

THE COMPANY CAMERA 1.1

Sales or Turnover

Turnover
Turnover, all of which arises from the Group's principal activity, can be analysed into its main components as follows:

	2004 £'000	2003 £'000
Matchday	61,206	70,593
Media	62,544	56,218
Commercial	45,330	46,190
	169,080	173,001

Turnover, all of which originates in the United Kingdom, can be analysed by destination as follows:

	2004 £'000	2003 £'000
United Kingdom	159,650	160,485
Rest of World	9,430	12,516
	169,080	173,001

Media income from European cup competitions is distributed by the Football Association and is therefore classified as being of United Kingdom origin and destination. Rest of World turnover includes an allocation of income receivable from Nike based on the geographical split of sales.

Source: Manchester United plc, 2004 Annual Report, p. 61

In other businesses, the sale is more tangible as goods change hands (for example, manufacturing companies and shops).

Overall, within the UK economy, services are becoming relatively more important and manufacturing industry is declining. In particular, there is an increase in information technology and knowledge-based industries. This trend is set to continue.

Types of Accountancy

We need to distinguish between the types of accountancy and the types of accountant. Accountancy refers to the process, while accountant refers to the person. In other words, accountancy is what accountants do! In this book, we primarily focus on bookkeeping, financial accounting and management accounting. However, accountants perform other roles such as auditing, financial management, insolvency, taxation and management consultancy. All of these are briefly covered below.

Auditing

Auditing is carried out by teams of staff headed by qualified accountants who are independent of the business. Essentially, auditors check that the financial statements, prepared by management, give a true and fair view of the accounts. Auditing is normally associated with company accounts. However, the tax authorities or the bank may request an audit of the accounts of sole traders or partnerships. For companies, auditors issue an auditor's report annually to shareholders. The Company Camera 1.2 provides an auditors' report for J. Sainsbury plc. This is issued after a thorough examination by the auditors of the accounting records and systems of the company. Auditors charge management an audit fee. For example, KPMG, a firm of auditors, charged HSBC Holdings £11.4 million in 2004 for auditing and consultancy services.

THE COMPANY CAMERA 1.2

Report of the Independent Auditors

Independent Auditors' report to the members of J. Sainsbury plc

We have audited the financial statements which comprise the Group profit and loss account, the balance sheets, the Group cash flow statement, the Group statement of total recognised gains and losses, the reconciliation of movements in equity shareholders' funds and the related notes, which have been prepared under the historical cost convention (as modified by the revaluation of certain fixed assets) and the accounting policies set out in the notes to the

THE COMPANY CAMERA 1.2 (*continued*)

financial statements. We have also audited the disclosures required by Part 3 of Schedule 7A to the Companies Act 1985 contained in the Directors' Remuneration report ('the auditable part').

Respective responsibilities of Directors and Auditors

The Directors' responsibilities for preparing the annual report and the financial statements in accordance with applicable United Kingdom law and accounting standards are set out in the Statement of Directors' responsibilities. The Directors are also responsible for preparing the Directors' Remuneration report.

Our responsibility is to audit the financial statements and the auditable part of the Directors' Remuneration report in accordance with relevant legal and regulatory requirements and United Kingdom Auditing Standards issued by the Auditing Practices Board. This report, including the opinion, has been prepared for and only for the Company's members as a body in accordance with Section 235 of the Companies Act 1985 and for no other purpose. We do not, in giving this opinion, accept or assume responsibility for any other purpose or to any other person to whom this report is shown or into whose hands it may come save where expressly agreed by our prior consent in writing.

We report to you our opinion as to whether the financial statements give a true and fair view and whether the financial statements and the auditable part of the Directors' Remuneration report have been properly prepared in accordance with the Companies Act 1985. We also report to you if, in our opinion, the Report of the Directors is not consistent with the financial statements, if the Company has not kept proper accounting records, if we have not received all the information and explanations we require for our audit, or if information specified by law regarding Directors' remuneration and transactions is not disclosed.

We read the other information contained in the annual report and consider the implications for our report if we become aware of any apparent misstatements or material inconsistencies with the financial statements. The other information comprises only the Operating and Financial Review, the Report of the Directors, the Statement of corporate governance and the unaudited part of the Remuneration report.

We review whether the Statement of corporate governance reflects the Company's compliance with the seven provisions of the Combined Code issued in June 1998 specified for our review by the Listing Rules of the Financial Services Authority, and we report if it does not. We are not required to consider whether the Board's statements on internal control cover all risks and controls, or to form an opinion on the effectiveness of the Group's corporate governance procedures or its risk and control procedures.

Basis of audit opinion

We conducted our audit in accordance with auditing standards issued by the Auditing Practices Board. An audit includes examination, on a test basis, of evidence relevant to the amounts and disclosures in the financial statements and the auditable part of the Directors' Remuneration report. It also includes an assessment of the significant estimates and judgments made by the Directors in the preparation of the financial statements, and of whether the accounting policies are appropriate to the Company's circumstances, consistently applied and adequately disclosed.

THE COMPANY CAMERA 1.2 (*continued*)

We planned and performed our audit so as to obtain all the information and explanations which we considered necessary in order to provide us with sufficient evidence to give reasonable assurance that the financial statements and the auditable part of the Directors' Remuneration report are free from material misstatement, whether caused by fraud or other irregularity or error. In forming our opinion we also evaluated the overall adequacy of the presentation of information in the financial statements.

Opinion

In our opinion:

- the financial statements give a true and fair view of the state of affairs of the Company and the Group at 27 March 2004 and of the profit and cash flows of the Group for the year then ended;
- the financial statements have been properly prepared in accordance with the Companies Act 1985; and
- those parts of the Directors' Remuneration report required by Part 3 of Schedule 7A to the Companies Act 1985 have been properly prepared in accordance with the Companies Act 1985.

PriceWaterhouseCoopers LLP
Chartered Accountants and Registered Auditors
London, 18 May 2004

Source: J. Sainsbury plc, Annual Report and Financial Statements, 2004, p. 21

Bookkeeping

Bookkeeping is the preparation of the basic accounts (bookkeeping is dealt with in more depth in Chapter 3). It involves entering monetary transactions into the books of account. A trial balance is then extracted, and a profit and loss account and balance sheet are prepared. Nowadays, most companies use computer packages for the basic bookkeeping function which is often performed by non-qualified accountants.

Financial Accounting

Financial accounting is a wider term than bookkeeping. It deals with not only the mechanistic bookkeeping process, but the preparation and interpretation of the financial accounts. For companies, financial accounting also includes the preparation of the annual report (a document sent annually to shareholders, comprising both financial and non-financial information). In orientation, financial accounting is primarily outward-looking and aimed at providing information for external users. However, monthly financial accounts are often prepared and used internally within a business. Within a company, financial accounting is usually carried out by a company's employees. Smaller businesses, such as sole traders, may use professionally-qualified independent accountants.

Financial Management

An area of growing importance for accountants is financial management. Some aspects of financial management fall under the general heading of management accounting. Financial management, as its name suggests, is about managing the sources of finance of an organisation. It may, therefore, involve managing the working capital (i.e., short-term assets and liabilities) of a company or finding the cheapest form of borrowing. These topics are briefly examined in Chapter 22. There is often a separate department of a company called the financial management or treasury department.

Insolvency

One of the main reasons for the rise to prominence of professional accountants in the UK was to wind up failed businesses. This is still part of a professional accountant's role. Professional accounting firms are often called in to manage the affairs of failed businesses, in particular to pay creditors who are owed money by the business.

Management Accounting

Management accounting covers the internal accounting of an organisation. There are several different areas of management accounting: costing (see Chapter 16), budgeting (see Chapter 17), standard costing (see Chapter 18), short-term decision making (see Chapter 19), strategic management accounting (see Chapter 20), capital investment appraisal (see Chapter 21), and management of working capital and sources of finance (Chapter 22). Essentially, these activities aim to monitor, control and plan the financial activities of organisations. Management uses such information for decisions such as determining a product's selling price or setting the sales budget.

Taxation

Taxation is a complicated area. Professional accountants advise businesses on a whole range of tax issues. Much of this involves tax planning (i.e., minimising the amount of tax that organisations have to pay by taking full advantage of the often complex tax regulations). This tax avoidance which operates within the law should be distinguished from tax evasion which is illegal. Professional accountants may also help individuals with a scourge of modern life, the preparation of their annual income tax assessment.

Management Consultancy

Management consultancy is a lucrative source of income for accountants (see Real-Life Nugget 1.2). However, as Soundbite 1.3 shows, management consultants are often viewed cynically. Management consultancy embraces a whole range of activities such as special efficiency audits, feasibility studies, and tax advice. Many professional accounting firms now make more money from management consultancy than from auditing. Examples of management consultancy are investigating the feasibility of a new football stadium or the costing of a local authority's school meals proposals.

SOUNDBITE 1.3

Management Consultancy

'[Definition of management consultancy] Telling a company what it should already know.'

The Economist (12 September 1987)

Source: *The Wiley Book of Business Quotations* (1998), p. 359

REAL-LIFE NUGGET 1.2

Management Consultancy

To be fair, many of these issues were problems of success. The accountancy industry had kick-started phenomenal growth and change in the management consultancy services it offered its client base. It was natural to sell those services to its existing clients who eagerly purchased the IT, strategy and financial management consultancy on top of the bog-standard audit and tax services.

Suddenly audit became the poor relation, both in terms of excitement and financial return.

Audit became a commodity and we all know what happens then – the product becomes devalued and the price goes down.

Source: How the Brits started the Rot, Peter Williams, *Accountancy Age*, 11 November 2004, p. 28

Types of Accountant

There are several types of accountant. The most high-profile are those belonging to the six professionally qualified bodies. In addition to these six accountancy bodies, there are other accounting associations, the most important of which is probably the Association of Accounting Technicians. The web addresses for these institutes are listed at the end of the chapter.

Professionally Qualified Accountants
Chartered Accountants

There are six institutions of professionally qualified accountants currently operating in the UK (see Figure 1.6). All jealously guard their independence and the many attempts to merge over the past few years have all failed (see Real-Life Nugget 1.3). 'It's like proposing that Manchester United and Manchester City merge, suggests one indignant ICAEW member, illustrating the strength of feeling' (Michelle Perry, *Accountancy Age*, 22 July 2004, p. 6).

Figure 1.6   Main UK Professional Accountancy Bodies

Body	Main Activities
Institute of Chartered Accountants in England and Wales (ICAEW)	Generally auditing, financial accounting, management consultancy, insolvency and tax advice. However, many work in industry.
Institute of Chartered Accountants in Ireland (ICAI)	Similar to ICAEW.
Institute of Chartered Accountants of Scotland (ICAS)	Similar to ICAEW.
Association of Chartered Certified Accountants (ACCA)	Auditing, financial accounting, insolvency, management consultancy, and tax advice. Many train or work in industry.
Chartered Institute of Management Accountants (CIMA)	Management accounting.
Chartered Institute of Public Finance and Accounting (CIPFA)	Accounting within the public sector and privatised industries.

REAL-LIFE NUGGET 1.3

Professional Accountancy Bodies

There have been several attempts to persuade the UK's accountancy bodies to merge over the past few years, all without much success. Six accountancy bodies is rather a lot and the government understandably gets exasperated from time to time by six (and sometimes seven) different responses to a consultation paper. But the bodies' members have consistently refused merger initiatives, always citing differing training requirements as a major consideration – and not without justification.

Source: Big Five Pressure Gets Results, Elizabeth Mackay, *Accountancy Age*, 9 March 2000, p. 18

There are three institutes of chartered accountants: the Institute of Chartered Accountants in England and Wales (ICAEW), the Institute of Chartered Accountants in Ireland (ICAI), and the Institute of Chartered Accountants of Scotland (ICAS). The largest of these three is the ICAEW. Its members were once mainly financial accountants and auditors, but now take part in a whole range of activities. Many leave the professional partnerships with which they train to join business organisations. In fact, qualifying as a chartered accountant is often seen as a route into a business career.

Association of Chartered Certified Accountants (ACCA)

The ACCA's members are not so easy to pigeonhole as the other professionally qualified accountants. They work both in public practice as auditors and as financial accountants. They also have an enormous number of overseas students. Many certified accountants train for their qualification in industry and never work in public practice.

Chartered Institute of Management Accountants (CIMA)

This is an important body whose members generally train and work in industry. They are found in almost every industry, ranging, for example, from coal mining to computing. They mainly perform the management accounting function.

Chartered Institute of Public Finance and Accountancy (CIPFA)

This institute is smaller than the ICAEW, ACCA or CIMA. It is also much more specialised with its members typically working in the public sector or the newly privatised industries, such as Railtrack. CIPFA members perform a wide range of financial activities within these organisations, such as budgeting in local government.

Second-Tier Bodies

The main second-tier body in the UK is the Association of Accounting Technicians. This body was set up by the major professional accountancy bodies. Accounting technicians help professional accountants, often doing the more routine bookkeeping and costing activities. Many accounting technicians go on to qualify as professional accountants.

The different accountancy bodies, therefore, all perform different functions. Some work in companies, some in professional accountancy practices, some in the public sector. This diversity is highlighted in an original way in Real-Life Nugget 1.4.

REAL-LIFE NUGGET 1.4

A Sideways Look at the Accounting Profession

Thus, to take parallels from the Christian church, we have:

- **the lay priest:** the accountant working for a company;
- **the mendicant priest:** the professional accountant in a partnership;
- **the monastic priest:** the banker, who, while not strictly an accountant, serves much the same ends in a separate and semi-isolated unit;
- **the father confessor:** the auditing accountant to whom everything is (officially) revealed, and who then grants absolution.

Source: Graham Cleverly (1971) *Managers and Magic*, Longman Group Ltd, London, p. 47

SOUNDBITE 1.4

Limitations of Traditional Accounts

'Non-financial items like business opportunities, management strategies and risks have a big effect on company performance and need to be reflected in company reports.'

Mike Starr, Chairman of American Institute of Certified Public Accountants. Committee on Enhanced Business Reporting.

Source: Consortium Urges Reporting Reforms, Nicholas Neveling, *Accountancy Age*, 17 February 2005, p. 11

Limitations of Accounting

Accounting, therefore, measures business transactions in numerical terms. It thus provides useful information for managers and other users of accounts. It is, however, important to appreciate certain limitations of accounting. First, accounting tends to measure the cost of past expenditures rather than the current value of assets. This is dealt with in more detail in Chapter 11. Second, traditional accounting does not capture non-financial aspects of business. Thus, if an industry pollutes the air or the water this is not recorded in the conventional accounts. Nor does traditional accounting measure the human resources of a business or its knowledge and skills base. The accounts can, thus, only give a partial picture of a business's activities.

Conclusion

Accounting is a key business activity. It provides information about a business so that managers or owners (for example, shareholders) can make business decisions. Accounting provides the framework by which cash and profit can be monitored and controlled. A basic distinction is between financial accounting (accounting targeted primarily at those outside the business, but also useful to managers) and management accounting (providing information solely to managers).

Accounting changes as society changes. In particular, it is contingent upon history, country, technology and the nature and type of the organisation. There are at least eight groups which use accounting information, the main ones being managers and shareholders. These user groups require information about, amongst other things, profits, cash flow, assets and debts. There are several types of accountancy and accountant. The types of accountancy include auditing, bookkeeping, financial accounting, financial management, insolvency, management accounting, taxation and management consultancy. The six UK professional accountancy bodies are the Association of Chartered Certified Accountants, the Chartered Institute of Management Accountants, the Chartered Institute of Public Finance and Accountancy, and the Institute of Chartered Accountants in England and Wales, the Institute of Chartered Accountants in Ireland

and the Institute of Chartered Accountants of Scotland. Although very useful, accounting has certain limitations, for example, its historic nature and its failure to measure non-financial transactions.

Websites

A list of useful websites is included below for students interested in a career in accounting and who wish to find out more information.

i) Accountancy Institutes

www.accaglobal.com	=	Association of Chartered Certified Accountants (ACCA)
www.cimaglobal.com	=	Chartered Institute of Management Accountants (CIMA)
www.cipfa.org.uk	=	Chartered Institute of Public Finance and Accounting (CIPFA)
www.icaew.co.uk	=	Institute of Chartered Accountants in England and Wales (ICAEW)
www.icai.ie	=	Institute of Chartered Accountants in Ireland (ICAI)
www.icas.org.uk	=	Institute of Chartered Accountants of Scotland (ICAS)
www.aat.co.uk	=	Association of Accounting Technicians (AAT)

ii) Accounting Firms

www.pwcglobal.com	=	PriceWaterhouseCoopers
www.ey.com	=	Ernst & Young
www.kpmg.com	=	KPMG
www.deloitte.com	=	Deloitte

Q&A   Discussion Questions

Questions with numbers in blue have answers at the back of the book.

Q1   What is the importance, if any, of accounting?

Q2   Can you think of three business decisions for which managers would need accounting information?

Q3   What do you consider to be the main differences between financial and management accounting?

Q4   Discuss the idea that as society changes so does accounting.

Q5   'Managers should only supply financial information to the 'current' shareholders of companies, no other user groups have any rights at all to information, particularly not the general public or government.' Discuss.

Section A

Financial Accounting: The Techniques

I n this section, we look at the accounting techniques which underpin the preparation and interpretation of the financial statements. Chapter 2 sets the scene for this section explaining the essential background. It deals with the nature and importance of financial accounting and introduces some of the basic concepts and terminology.

In these initial chapters, we focus primarily on the financial statements of the sole trader as these are the most straightforward. In Chapter 3, the key accounting techniques of the accounting equation, double-entry bookkeeping and the trial balance, are introduced. The double-entry section of this chapter is *self-contained and can be passed over by those students not wishing to study bookkeeping in depth*. In Chapters 4 and 5, the essential nature, function and contents of the profit and loss account and balance sheet are discussed. This will enable students more fully to appreciate the importance of the profit and loss account and balance sheet before their preparation from the trial balance is explained in Chapter 6. In Chapter 7, we prepare the profit and loss account (called income statement for listed companies) and balance sheet of partnerships and limited companies. The final two chapters look at the cash flow statement (Chapter 8) and the interpretation of accounts (Chapter 9) primarily from the perspective of limited companies. The cash flow statement is the third most important financial statement for a company. Finally, in Chapter 9 we look at 16 ratios commonly used to assess an organisation's performance. ∎

Chapter 2

"Living up to his reputation, he brooks no nonsense, adds no frills. A murmured thank you to the chair, then: 'Let us never forget that we are all of us in business for one thing only. To make a profit.' The hush breaks, the apprehension goes. Audibly, feet slide forward and chairs ease back. Orthodoxy has been established. The incantation has been spoken. No one is going to be forced to query the framework of his world, to face the terrible question, why?"

Graham Cleverly (1971), *Managers and Magic*, Longman, pp. 25–6

Learning Outcomes

After completing this chapter you should be able to:

✔ Explain the nature of financial accounting.

✔ Appreciate the basic language of accounting.

✔ Identify the major accounting conventions and concepts.

The Accounting Background

In a Nutshell

■ Financial accounting is about providing users with financial information so that they can make decisions.

■ Key accounting terminology includes income, expenses, capital, assets and liabilities.

■ The three major financial statements are the profit and loss account (also known as the income statement), the balance sheet and the cash flow statement.

■ The most widely agreed objective is to provide information for decision making.

■ The most important external users for companies are the shareholders.

■ Four major accounting conventions are entity, money measurement, historic cost and periodicity.

■ Four major accounting concepts are going concern, matching, consistency and prudence.

Introduction

Financial accounting is the process by which financial information is prepared and then communicated to the users. It is a key element in modern business. For limited companies, it enables the shareholders to receive from the managers an annual set of accounts which has been independently checked by auditors. For sole traders and partnerships, it allows the tax authorities to have a set of accounts which is often prepared by independent accountants. There are thus three parties to the production and dissemination of the financial accounts: the preparers, the users and the independent accountants. The broad objective of financial accounting is to provide information for decision making. Its preparation is governed by basic underpinning principles called accounting conventions and accounting concepts.

Financial Accounting

Once a year company shareholders receive through the post an annual report containing the company's annual accounts. These comprise the key financial statements as well as other financial and non-financial information. Sole traders and partnerships annually prepare a set of financial statements for the tax authorities. Managers will also use these financial statements to evaluate the performance of the business over the past year. The whole process is underpinned by a set of overarching accounting principles (i.e., accounting conventions and accounting concepts) and by detailed accounting measurement and disclosure rules.

Essentially, financial accounting is concerned with providing financial information to users so that they can make decisions. Definition 2.1 provides a more formal definition from the

DEFINITION 2.1

Financial Accounting

Working definition
The provision of financial information to users for decision making.

Formal definitions
'The objective of financial statements is to provide information about the financial position, performance and change in financial position of an enterprise that is useful to a wide range of users in making economic decisions.'

International Accounting Standards Board (2000), *Framework for the Preparation and Presentation of Financial Statements*

'The classification and recording of the monetary transactions of an entity in accordance with established concepts, principles, accounting standards and legal requirements and their presentation, by means of profit and loss accounts, balance sheets and cash flow statements, during and at the end of an accounting period.'

Chartered Institute of Management Accountants (2000), *Official Terminology*

International Accounting Standards Board (a regulatory body which seeks to set accounting standards which will be used worldwide) applicable to all commercial, industrial and business reporting enterprises as well as a fuller definition from the Chartered Institute of Management Accountants.

Financial accounting meets the common needs of a wide range of users. It does not, however, provide all the information users may need. An important role of financial accounting is that it shows the stewardship of management (i.e., how successfully they run the company). Shareholders may use this information to decide whether or not to sell their shares.

At a still broader level, accounting allows managers to assess their organisation's performance. It is a way of seeing how well they have done or, as Soundbite 2.1 shows, of keeping the score. The main financial statements for sole traders, partnerships and companies are the profit and loss account (or income statement) and the balance sheet. These contain details of income, expenses, assets, liabilities and capital. For companies (and often for other businesses), these two statements are accompanied by a cash flow statement,

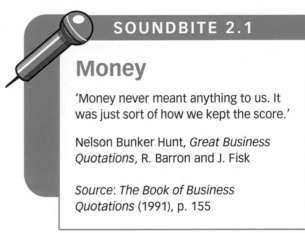

SOUNDBITE 2.1

Money

'Money never meant anything to us. It was just sort of how we kept the score.'

Nelson Bunker Hunt, *Great Business Quotations*, R. Barron and J. Fisk

Source: *The Book of Business Quotations* (1991), p. 155

which summarises a company's cash flows. Generally, the principal user is assumed to be the shareholder. These three statements are sent to shareholders once a year in a document called an annual report. However, managers need more detailed and more frequent information to run a company effectively. Monthly accounts and accounts for different parts of the business are, therefore, often drawn up.

PAUSE FOR THOUGHT 2.1

Annual Financial Accounts

Why do sole traders, partnerships and limited companies produce financial accounts?

There are several reasons. First, those running the business wish to assess their own performance and regular, periodic accounts are a good way to do this. Second, businesses may need to provide third parties with financial information. In the case of sole traders and partnerships, the tax authorities need to assess the business's profits. Bankers may also want regular financial statements if they have loaned money. Similarly, companies are accountable not only to their shareholders, but to other users of accounts.

Language of Accounting

Accounting is a language. As with all languages, it is important to understand the basics. Five basic accounting terms (income, expenses, assets, liabilities and capital or equity) are introduced here as well as the three main financial statements (profit and loss account, balance sheet and cash flow statement). These concepts are explained more fully later in the book.

Income

Income is essentially the revenue earned by a business. Sales is a good example. Income is income, even if goods and services have been delivered but customers have not yet paid. Income thus differs from cash received.

Expenses

Expenses are the costs incurred in running a business. Examples are telephone, business rates and wages. The nature of expenses varies from business to business. Real-Life Nugget 2.1 shows that the biggest expense for football clubs is their wages. Expenses are expenses, even if goods and services have been consumed but the business has still not paid for them. Expenses are, therefore, different from cash paid.

REAL-LIFE NUGGET 2.1

Football Club Expenses

Football clubs continue to spend most of their revenue on players' wages, but may end up paying them even more because of increased income from the new television deal.

Though revenue for all 20 Premiership clubs increased by 18% during the 1998–99 season, their total wage bill shot up by 31% to just over £397 m. Salary costs now account for more than 59% of the clubs' income, with Manchester United the highest payers.

According to the survey of Premiership finances by the accountants Deloitte and Touche, gate receipts still generate the bulk of club revenue but television money is catching up fast.

Source: TV deal to fuel Premiership wages hike, V. Chaudhary, *The Guardian*, 9 May 2000, p. 30. © Guardian Newspapers Limited 2000

Assets

Assets are essentially items owned (or leased) by the business which will bring economic benefits. An example might be a building or a stock of goods awaiting resale. Assets may be held for a long time for use in the business (such as motor vehicles) or alternatively be short-term assets (such as stock which is held for immediate resale). As Real-Life Nugget 2.2 shows, a solid asset base often underpins a successful company.

REAL-LIFE NUGGET 2.2

Assets

With assets of £2.6 billion and 2,300 staff, Pennon is a 'bog standard' utility with a waste disposal business bolted on the side. For investors this need not be a turn-off. Pennon generates oodles of cash relative to its size, and – like all utilities – gives most of it to shareholders in the form of dividends.

Source: Pennon's safe enough but doesn't hold water for growth prospects, Philip Aldrick, *Daily Telegraph*, 10 December 2004, p. 36

Liabilities

Liabilities are amounts the business owes to a third party. An example might be money owed to the bank following a bank loan. Alternatively, the company may owe money to the suppliers of goods (known as creditors).

Capital (Equity)

Capital is the assets of a business less its liabilities to third parties. Capital represents the owner's interest in the business. In effect, capital is a liability as it is owed by the business to the owner. Owners may be sole traders, partners or shareholders. A listed company's capital is termed equity.

Profit and Loss Account (Income Statement)

A profit and loss account or income statement, at its simplest, records the income and expenses of a business over time. Income less expenses equals profit. By contrast, where expenses are greater than income losses will occur. It is important (as Real-Life Nugget 2.3 shows) for even the world's largest companies to ensure that income (or revenue) exceeds expenses. The net profit (or net loss) in the profit and loss account is added (or subtracted) to capital in the balance sheet.

REAL-LIFE NUGGET 2.3

Revenues and Expenses

TROUBLED computer giant Compaq has warned of lower earnings from Europe amid growing concern about its key US direct-sales operation.

The world's second biggest computer company last week surprised markets when it forecast second-quarter losses, which are a result of higher expenses and lower-than-expected revenues.

Compaq is predicting losses of 15 cents a share, or $237 m, the first quarterly loss in eight years.

Source: Compaq's troubles mount, *Sunday Business*, 20 June 1999, p. 15

PAUSE FOR THOUGHT 2.2

Accounting Terms

Can you think of two examples of income, and three examples of expenses, assets and liabilities which a typical business might have?

....

These are many and varied. A few examples are given below:

Income	*Expenses*	*Assets*	*Liabilities*
Sales of goods	Telephone	Buildings	Bank loan
Sales of assets	Business rates	Motor cars	Creditors
Bank interest earned	Electricity	Furniture	Bills owing
	Repairs	Stock	
	Petrol consumed	Debtors	

The Company Camera 2.1 shows a reconstruction of the summary profit and loss account of Marks & Spencer plc. From The Company Camera 2.1 it can be seen that expenses are deducted from sales and other income to give profit before taxation. Once taxation and dividends have been deducted, we arrive at the retained profit (£289 million for 2004) and £261 million for 2003. The 2004 accounts of Marks & Spencer plc follow the format commonly used for sole traders, partnerships and non-listed companies. The 2005 accounts of Marks & Spencer will follow the format set out by the International Accounting Standards Board for listed companies. An example of these is given for the German car producer company Volkswagen in Appendix 2.2. This is prepared using a format where the total assets are totalled, these then equal total equity and liabilities. This approach is commonly used by non-UK companies under

THE COMPANY CAMERA 2.1

Marks & Spencer Summarised Company Profit and Loss Account

Marks & Spencer
Summary profit and loss account for the 53 weeks ended 3rd April 2004

	2004 £m	2003 £m
Sales	8,302	8,019
Add: Other income	(15)	27
	8,287	8,046
Less: Expenses	7,506	7,330
Profit before taxation	781	716
Taxation	(229)	(209)
Profit after taxation	552	507
Dividends	(263)	(246)
Retained Profit	289	261

Note: The profit and loss account has been simplified and reconstructed. The original summary profit and loss account can be found as Appendix 2.1 at the back of this chapter.

Source: Marks & Spencer, 2004, Annual Review and Summary Financial Statement, p. 20

International Financial Reporting Standards. UK companies more typically use a net assets approach as demonstrated in The Company Camera 7.4 by the British company AstraZeneca.

Balance Sheet

A balance sheet records the assets, liabilities and capital of a business at a certain point in time. Assets less liabilities will equal capital. Capital is thus the owners' interest in the business. The summary balance sheet for Marks & Spencer for 2004 is presented in The Company Camera 2.2. Here the assets are added together and then the liabilities are taken away. The net assets (i.e., assets less liabilities) equals the total capital employed by the business. A balance sheet in a listed company format following international accounting standards is presented for Volkswagen in Appendix 2.3.

THE COMPANY CAMERA 2.2

Illustration of a Summarised Company Balance Sheet

	As at 3 April 2004 £m	As at 29 March 2003 As restated £m
Fixed assets		
Tangible assets	3,497	3,435
Investments	10	30
	3,507	3,465
Current assets		
Stocks	398	362
Debtors	2,750	2,412
Cash and investments	720	472
	3,868	3,246
Current liabilities		
Creditors: amounts falling due within one year	(1,884)	(1,711)
Net current assets	1,984	1,535
Total assets less current liabilities	5,491	5,000
Creditors: amounts falling due after more than one year	(2,519)	(1,810)
Provisions for liabilities and charges	(49)	(186)
Net assets before net post-retirement liability	2,923	3,004
Net post-retirement liability	(469)	(896)
Net assets	2,454	2,108
Equity shareholders' funds	2,369	1,990
Non-equity shareholders' funds	85	118
Total shareholders' funds	2,454	2,108

Source: Marks & Spencer, 2004, Annual Review and Summary Financial Statement, p. 22

Cash Flow Statement

A cash flow statement shows the cash inflows and outflows of the business. The Company Camera 2.3 shows a summary cash flow statement for Marks & Spencer for 2004. All the cash flows from the day-to-day operations of the business (i.e., operating activities such as buying and selling goods or paying wages) are recorded. This gives a cash inflow from operating activities. Other cash flows (such as taxation and the payment of dividends) are then listed. Overall, Marks & Spencer has a negative cash outflow before funding (from external loans and so on) of £93 million in 2004. In Appendix 2.4, the cash flow statement for Volkswagen, a German listed company following international accounting standards, is presented.

THE COMPANY CAMERA 2.3

Illustration of a Summarised Company Cash Flow Statement

	53 weeks ended 3 April 2004 £m	52 weeks ended 29 March 2003 As restated £m
Operating activities		
Net cash inflow before exceptional items and contribution to the pension fund	**1,114**	1,188
Exceptional operating cash flows	**(48)**	(19)
Contribution to the pension fund	**(400)**	–
Cash inflow from operating activities	**666**	1,169
Dividend received from joint venture	–	8
Returns on investments and servicing of finance	**(49)**	(46)
Taxation	**(220)**	(217)
Capital expenditure and financial investment	**(294)**	(295)
Acquisitions and disposals	**51**	(39)
Equity dividends paid	**(247)**	(225)
Cash (outflow)/inflow before funding	**(93)**	355

Source: Marks & Spencer, 2004, Annual Review and Summary Financial Statement, p. 21

We will now look at three summary financial statements for a business called Gavin Stevens which we will meet in more depth in Chapter 3. Gavin Stevens runs a hotel and summary details of his income, expenses, assets, liabilities and capital are given below. At this stage, the financial statements for Gavin Stevens (Figure 2.1) and for Simon Tudent (Figure 2.2 on the following page) are drawn up using only broad general headings. More detailed presentation is covered in later chapters.

Figure 2.1   Preparation of Summary Profit and Loss Account, Balance Sheet and Cash Flow Statement for Gavin Stevens

Financial Information			
Income	£8,930	Liabilities	£1,350
Expenses	£5,600	Opening capital	£200,000
Assets	£204,680	Closing capital	£203,330
Cash inflows	£204,465	Cash outflows	£117,550

(i) Profit and Loss Account
Here we are concerned with determining profit by subtracting expenses from income. We call the profit, net profit.

	£
Income	8,930
Less: *Expenses*	5,600
Net Profit	3,330

(ii) Balance Sheet
Here we deduct the assets from the liabilities to give net assets. This represents the capital employed in the business.

	£
Assets	204,680
Liabilities	(1,350)
Net Assets	203,330

	£
Opening capital employed	200,000
Add: Profit	3,330
Closing capital employed	203,330

(iii) Cash Flow Statement

	£
Cash Inflows	204,465
Cash Outflows	(117,550)
Net cash inflow	86,915

We have a positive cash flow. In other words, our cash has increased by £86,915 over the year. Note that in accounting when figures such as liabilities and cash outflows are subtracted it is common to use brackets if the word 'less' is not used.

Student Example

In order to give a further flavour of the nature of the main accounting terms, this section presents the income and expenditure of Simon Tudent. Simon is a student.

Figure 2.2   A Student's Financial Statements

Simon has collected the following details of his finances for his last student year and possessions on 31 December. He has already divided them into income, expenses, assets and liabilities.

£

Income

Wages received from working in Student
Union (38 weeks at £25 per week)   950
Wages owing from Student
Union (2 weeks at £25 per week – also an
asset because he is owed it)   50

Assets

Second-hand car worth probably £700*
Cash at bank at start of year £2,500*
Computer worth about £150*
CD player worth about £200*
*All possessions at start of year.

Expenses

	£
Hall of residence fees	2,300
Money spent on books	200
Money spent on entertainment	500
Petrol used in car	300
Phone calls	50
Car repairs	200
General	150

Liabilities

Owes parents £150 for loan this year
Student loan from Government £3,000

Note: Simon's opening capital is simply his opening assets less any opening liabilities. For simplicity, we assume that they are worth the same as at the start and as at the end of the year (except for cash at bank).

....

From the information shown above, we can present three financial statements, shown below and on the next page.

1. A profit and loss account (strictly, for a student we should call this an income and expenditure statement).
2. A balance sheet (strictly, for a student we should call this an assets and liabilities statement).
3. A cash flow statement.

....

S. Tudent
Profit and Loss Account (Income and Expenditure) Year Ended 31 December

Income	£	£
Student union wages		1,000
(note: includes £50 owing)		
Less *Expenses*		
Hall of residence fees	2,300	
Books	200	
Entertainment	500	
Petrol	300	
Phone calls	50	
Car repairs	200	
General	150	3,700
Net Deficit		(2,700)

Note that this statement deals with all income and expenses *earned* and *incurred*, not just with cash paid and received. We deduct all the expenses from the income and ascertain that S. Tudent has a net deficit. In business, this would be called a net loss.

Figure 2.2   A Student's Financial Statements (*continued*)

S. Tudent
Balance Sheet (Assets and Liabilities) as at 31 December

Assets	£	£
Cash at bank		
(balance from cash flow statement)		2,900
Second-hand car		700
Computer		150
CD player		200
Owed by student union		50
		4,000
Liabilities		
Parental loan	(150)	
Government loan	(3,000)	(3,150)
Net assets		850

Capital Employed	£	
Opening capital employed	3,550*	Note: These two
Net deficit	(2,700)	figures balance
Closing capital employed	850	

*Opening possessions (£700 + £2,500 + £150 + £200)

We are simply listing the assets and liabilities. The assets less liabilities gives net assets. This also equals capital employed. The opening capital is simply opening assets less opening liabilities. Note that opening capital employed less the net deficit gives closing capital employed. A student loan is a liability because it is owed to the government. It is not income.

. . . .

S. Tudent
Cash Flow Statement Year Ended 31 December

	£	£
Bank balance at start of year		2,500
Add *Receipts*:		
Student loan	3,000	
Student Union	950	
Loan from parents	150	4,100
		6,600
Less *Payments*:		
Books	200	
Entertainment	500	
Petrol used	300	
Phone calls	50	
Car repairs	200	
General	150	
Hall fees	2,300	3,700
Bank balance at end of year (balancing figure)		2,900

Note that we are simply recording all cash received and paid. We were not given the closing bank figure. However, it must be £2,900: opening cash of £2,500 plus receipts of £4,100 gives £6,600 less £3,700 payments.

Student Loan

Students are often granted loans by the government. Why would a student loan from the government or a loan from one's parents be a liability, but a gift from parents be income?

....

This is because the loans must be repaid. They are, therefore, liabilities. When they are repaid, in part or in full, the liability is reduced. By contrast, a gift will be income as it does not have to be repaid.

Why is Financial Accounting Important?

Financial accounting is a key control mechanism. All businesses prepare and use financial information in order to help them measure their performance. It is also useful in a business's relationship with third parties. It enables sole traders and partnerships to provide accounting information to the tax authorities or bank. For the limited company, it makes company directors accountable to company shareholders. For small businesses, the accounts are normally prepared by independent qualified accountants. In the case of large businesses, such as limited companies, the accounts are normally prepared by the managers and directors, but then audited by professional accountants. Auditing means checking the accounts are 'true and fair'. This term 'true and fair' is elusive and slippery. It is probably best considered to mean faithfully representing the underlying economic transactions of a business.

The independent preparation and/or auditing of the financial accounts by accountants and auditors is an essential task in the protection of the users. The tax authorities need to ensure that the sole traders and partnership accounts have been properly prepared by an expert. Similarly, the shareholders need to have confidence that the managers have prepared a 'true and fair' account. For shareholders, this is particularly important as they are not directly involved in running the business. They provide the money, then stand back and allow the managers to run the company. So how can shareholders ensure that the managers are not abusing their trust? Bluntly, how can the shareholders make sure they are not being 'ripped off' by the managers. Auditing is one solution.

PAUSE FOR THOUGHT 2.4

Directors' Self-Interest

How might the directors of a company serve their own interests rather than the interests of the shareholders?

Both directors and shareholders want to share in a business's success. Directors are rewarded by salaries and other rewards, such as company cars, profit-related bonuses, or lucrative pensions. Shareholders are rewarded by receiving cash payments in the form of dividends or an increase in share price. The problem is that the more the directors take for themselves, the less there will be left for the shareholders. So if directors pay themselves large bonuses, the shareholders will get smaller dividends.

Accounting Principles

There are several accounting principles which underpin the preparation of the accounts. For convenience, we classify them here into accounting conventions and accounting concepts (see Figure 2.3). Essentially, conventions concern the whole accounting process, while concepts are assumptions which underpin the actual accounts preparation. There are four generally recognised accounting conventions and four generally recognised accounting concepts.

Figure 2.3   Accounting Principles

Accounting Conventions	*Accounting Concepts*
• Entity • Money measurement • Historic cost • Periodicity	• Going concern • Matching (or accruals) • Consistency • Prudence

Accounting Conventions

Entity

The entity convention simply means that a business has a distinct and separate identity from its owners. This is fairly obvious in the case of a large limited company where shareholders own the company and managers manage the company. However, for a sole trader, such as a small baker's shop, it is important to realise that there is a theoretical distinction between personal and business assets. The business is treated as a separate entity from the owner. The business's assets less third party liabilities represent the owners' capital.

Monetary Measurement

Under this convention only items which can be measured in financial terms (for example, in pounds or dollars) are included in the accounts. If a company pollutes the atmosphere this is not included in the accounts, since this pollution has no measurable financial value. However, a fine imposed for pollution is measurable and should be included in the accounts.

Historical Cost

Businesses may trade for many years. The historical cost convention basically states that the amount recorded in the accounts will be the *original* amount paid for a good or service. In some countries, such as the US, the historical cost convention is still very closely followed. Nowadays, in the UK, there are some departures. For example, many companies revalue land and buildings. This reflects the fact that they have increased in value. The Company Camera 2.4 shows that Tesco plc prepared its accounts using the historical cost convention.

THE COMPANY CAMERA 2.4

Historical Cost Convention

Basis of preparation of financial statements

These financial statements have been prepared under the historical cost convention, in accordance with applicable accounting standards and the Companies Act 1985.

Source: Tesco plc, 2004 Annual Report, p. 30

Periodicity

This simply means that accounts are prepared for a set period of time. Audited financial statements are usually prepared for a year. Financial statements prepared for internal management are often drawn up more frequently. This means, in effect, that sometimes rather arbitrary distinctions are made about the period in which accounting items are recorded.

Accounting Assumptions or Concepts

There are four generally recognised accounting concepts. The International Accounting Standards Board recognises two overriding underlying assumptions (going concern and accruals).

The UK Companies Act, however, recognises in addition two extra assumptions: consistency and prudence.

Going Concern

This concept assumes the business will continue into the foreseeable future. Assets, liabilities, income and expenses are thus calculated on this basis. If you are valuing a specialised machine, for example, you will value the machine at a higher value if the business is ongoing than if it is about to go bankrupt. If it were bankrupt the machine would only have scrap value. In Company Camera 2.5, we can see that J.D. Wetherspoon's directors have assured themselves that the company is a going concern.

THE COMPANY CAMERA 2.5

Going Concern Concept

The Directors have made enquiries into the adequacy of the company's financial resources, through a review of the company's budget and medium-term financial plan, including capital expenditure plans, cash flow forecasts and facilities available to the company, and have satisfied themselves that the company will continue in operational existence for the foreseeable future. For this reason, they continue to adopt the going concern basis in preparing the company's financial statements.

Source: J.D. Wetherspoon plc, 2004 Annual Report, p. 17

Matching

The matching concept (often known as the accruals concept) recognises income and expenses when they are accrued (i.e., earned or incurred rather than when the money is received or paid). Income is matched with any associated expenses to determine the appropriate profit or loss. A telephone bill owing at the accounting year end is thus treated as a cost for this year even if it is paid in the next year. If the telephone bill is not received by the year end, then the amount of telephone calls will be estimated.

Consistency

This concept states that similar items will be treated similarly from year to year. Thus consistency attempts to stop companies choosing different accounting policies in different years. If they do this, then it becomes more difficult to compare the results of one year to the next.

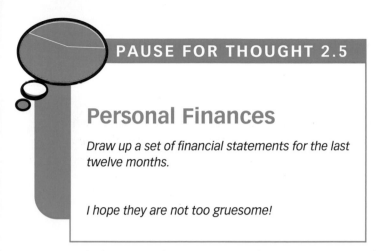

PAUSE FOR THOUGHT 2.5

Personal Finances

Draw up a set of financial statements for the last twelve months.

I hope they are not too gruesome!

Prudence

This is the most contentious of the four accounting concepts. Prudence introduces an element of caution into accounting. Income and profits should only be recorded in the books when they are *certain* to result in an inflow of cash. By contrast, provisions or liabilities should be made *as soon as they are recognised*, even though their amount may not be known with certainty. Prudence is contentious because it introduces an asymmetry into the accounting process. Potential incomes are treated differently from potential liabilities.

Conclusion

Financial accounting, along with management accounting, is one of the two main branches of accounting. Its main objective is to provide financial information to users for decision making. Shareholders, for example, are provided with information to assess the stewardship of managers so that they can then make decisions such as whether to buy or sell their shares. Understanding the accounting language is a key requisite to understanding accounting itself. Four accounting conventions (entity, money measurement, historical cost and periodicity) and four accounting concepts (going concern, matching, consistency and prudence) underpin financial accounting.

Q&A   Discussion Questions

Questions with numbers in blue have answers at the back of the book.

Q1 What is financial accounting and why is its study important?

Q2 'The objective of **financial statements** is to provide information about the **financial position, performance** and **change in financial position** of an enterprise that is useful to a wide range of **users** in making **economic decisions.**'

Discuss the key aspects *highlighted in bold* of this formal definition of the Objectives of Financial Statements as formulated by the International Accounting Standards Board in its *Framework for the Preparation and Presentation of Financial Statements*.

Q3 Sole traders, partnerships and limited companies all have different users who need financial information for different purposes. Discuss.

Q4 Classify the following as an income, an expense, an asset, or a liability:
(a) Friend owes business money
(b) Football club's gate receipts
(c) Petrol used by a car
(d) Photocopier
(e) Sales
(f) Telephone bill outstanding
(g) Long-term loan
(h) Cash
(i) Wages
(j) Capital

Q5 State whether the following are true or false. If false, explain why.
(a) Assets and liabilities show how much the business owns and owes.
(b) The profit and loss account shows the income, expenses and thus the net assets of a business.
(c) Stewardship is now recognised as the primary objective of financial accounting.
(d) When running a small business the owner must be careful to separate business from private expenditure.
(e) The matching and prudence accounting concepts sometimes conflict.

Q&A   Numerical Questions

Questions with numbers in blue have answers at the back of the book.

Q1 Sharon Taylor has the following financial details:

Sales	£8,000	Assets	£15,000
General expenses	£4,000	Liabilities	£3,000
Trading expenses	£3,000	Cash outflows	£12,000
Cash inflows	£10,000	Closing capital employed	£12,000
Opening capital employed	£11,000		

Required: Prepare Sharon Taylor's
(a) Profit and loss account
(b) Balance sheet
(c) Cash flow statement

Q2 Priya Patel is an overseas student studying at a British University. Priya has the following financial details:

	£		£
Tuition fees paid	6,840	Food paid	550
Hall of residence fees paid	2,000	General expenses paid	180
Money spent on books	160	Parental loan of £2,000 during year	
Money spent on entertainment	500		
Money earned at arts and		*State of affairs at the start of the year:*	
crafts bazaar	1,800	Cash at bank	8,600
Phone calls paid	100	Music system*	200
			* Still worth £200 at end of year.

Required: Priya's:
(a) Profit and loss account (income and expenditure account)
(b) Balance sheet (assets and liabilities)
(c) Cash flow statement

Appendix 2.1: Illustration of a Summarised Company Profit and Loss Account: Marks & Spencer plc 2004

SUMMARY PROFIT AND LOSS ACCOUNT

	53 weeks ended 3 April 2004			52 weeks ended 29 March 2003		
	Before exceptional items £m	Exceptional items £m	Total £m	Before exceptional items As related £m	Exceptional items £m	Total As related £m
Turnover – continuing operations	8,301.5	–	8,301.5	8,019.1	–	8,019.1
Operating profit – continuing operations	866.0	(42.1)	823.9	773.0	(43.9)	729.1
Profit on sale of property and other fixed assets	–	18.7	18.7	–	1.6	1.6
Net loss on sale/termination of operations	–	–	–	–	(1.5)	(1.5)
Net interest expense	(45.8)	–	(45.8)	(40.5)	–	(40.5)
Other finance (charges)/income	(15.2)	–	(15.2)	27.0	–	27.0
Profit/(loss) on ordinary activities before taxation	805.0	(23.4)	781.6	759.5	(43.8)	715.7
Taxation on ordinary activities	(242.0)	12.7	(229.3)	(217.9)	9.1	(208.8)
Profit/(loss) on ordinary activities after taxation	563.0	(10.7)	552.3	541.6	(34.7)	506.9
Minority interests (all equity)	–	–	–	0.4	–	0.4
Profit/(loss) attributable to shareholders	563.0	(10.7)	552.3	542.0	(34.7)	507.3
Dividends (including dividends in respect of non-equity shares)	(263.2)	–	(263.2)	(246.0)	–	(246.0)
Retained profit/(loss) for the period	299.8	(10.7)	289.1	296.0	(34.7)	261.3
Earnings per share			24.2p			21.8p
Adjusted earnings per share			24.7p			23.3p
Dividend per share			11.5p			10.5p

Source: Marks & Spencer, 2004 Annual Report, p. 26

Appendix 2.2: Illustration of a Limited Company's Balance Sheet

BALANCE SHEET FOR VOLKSWAGEN GROUP AS AT DECEMBER 31, 2004

€ million	Note	Dec. 31, 2004	Restated Dec. 31, 2003
Assets			
Non-current assets			
Intangible assets	11	7,490	7,145
Property, plant and equipment	12	23,795	23,852
Leasing and rental assets	13	8,484	8,450
Investment property	13	182	456
Investments in Group companies accounted for using the equity method	14	4,221	3,339
Other equity investments	14	293	304
Financial services receivables	15	22,762	20,840
Other receivables and financial assets	16	2,298	1,394
Deferred tax assets	17	2,056	1,583
		71,581	67,363
Current assets			
Inventories	18	11,440	11,670
Trade receivables	19	5,357	5,497
Financial services receivables	15	21,109	18,525
Current tax receivables	17	469	452
Other receivables and financial assets	16	3,862	3,955
Marketable securities	20	2,933	3,148
Cash and cash equivalents	21	10,221	7,536
		55,391	50,783
Total assets		**126,972**	**118,146**

BALANCE SHEET FOR VOLKSWAGEN GROUP AS AT DECEMBER 31, 2004 (*continued*)

€ million	Note	Dec. 31, 2004	Restated Dec. 31, 2003
Equity and Liabilities			
Equity	22		
Subscribed capital		1,089	1,089
Capital reserves		4,451	4,451
Retained earnings		18,325	18,219
Equity attributable to shareholders of Volkswagen AG		23,865	23,759
Minority interests		92	104
		23,957	**23,863**
Non-current liabilities			
Non-current financial liabilities	23	32,198	25,936
Other non-current liabilities	24	1,355	1,299
Deferred tax liabilities	25	2,251	2,154
Provisions for pensions	26	10,930	10,618
Provisions for taxes	25	2,065	1,378
Other non-current provisions	27	5,547	4,885
		54,346	**46,270**
Current liabilities			
Current financial liabilities	23	28,885	28,922
Trade payables	28	7,434	7,822
Current tax payables	25	57	25
Other current liabilities	24	6,303	5,315
Other current provisions	27	5,990	5,929
		48,669	**48,013**
Total equity and liabilities		**126,972**	**118,146**

Source: Volkswagen 2004, Annual Report, p. 41

Note: These results are prepared using International Financial Reporting Standards. The approach used here is to total the assets, these then equal total equity and liabilities. This approach is commonly used by non-UK companies. UK companies more typically use a net assets approach as demonstrated in The Company Camera 7.4 by the British company AstraZeneca.

Appendix 2.3: Illustration of a Limited Company's Income Statement (Profit and Loss Account)

INCOME STATEMENT OF THE VOLKSWAGEN GROUP
FOR THE PERIOD JANUARY 1 TO DECEMBER 31, 2004

€ million	Note	2004	Restated 2003
Sales revenue	1	88,963	84,813
Cost of sales	2	78,440	74,099
Gross profit		+10,523	+10,714
Distribution expenses		8,172	7,846
Administrative expenses		2,316	2,274
Other operating income	3	4,461	4,135
Other operating expenses	4	2,876	3,124
Operating profit		+1,620	+1,605
Share of profits and losses of Group companies accounted for using the equity method	5	+255	+511
Other financial result	6	−776	−762
Financial result		−521	−251
Profit before tax		+1,099	+1,354
Income tax expense	7	−383	−351
Current tax expense		−851	−623
Deferred tax income		+468	+272
Profit after tax	8	+716	+1,003
Minority interests	9	−39	−23
Profit attributable to shareholders of Volkswagen AG		+677	+980
Earnings per ordinary share (a)	10	+1.75	+2.54
Diluted earnings per ordinary share (a)	10	+1.75	+2.54
Earnings per preferred share (a)	10	+1.81	+2.60
Diluted earnings per preferred share (a)	10	+1.81	+2.60

Source: Volkswagen 2004, Annual Report, p.42.

Note: These accounts have been prepared using International Financial Reporting Standards. UK companies will generally follow a similar presentation.

Appendix 2.4: Illustration of a Limited Company's Cash Flow Statement

CASH FLOW STATEMENT FOR VOLKSWAGEN GROUP FOR THE PERIOD
JANUARY 1 TO DECEMBER 31, 2004

€ million	2004	Restated 2003
Cash and cash equivalents at beginning of period	7,536	2,987
Profit before tax	1,099	1,354
Income taxes paid	−21	−987
Depreciation and amortisation expense*	5,648	5,338
Amortisation of capitalised development costs	1,134	1,381
Impairment losses on equity investments*	62	6
Depreciation of leasing and rental assets and investment property*	1,774	1,508
Change in provisions	1,075	885
Loss on disposal of non-current assets	−21	70
Share of profit or loss of Group companies accounted for using the equity method	56	−72
Other noncash income/expense	−177	−442
Change in inventories	178	−1,109
Change in receivables (excluding financial services)	−4	−494
Change in liabilities (excluding financial liabilities)	691	933
Cash flows from operating activities	11,494	8,371
Acquisition of property, plant and equipment, and intangible assets	−5,550	−6,727
Additions to capitalised development costs	−1,501	−1,817
Acquisition of subsidiaries and other equity investments	−2,287	−356
Disposal of equity investments	1,045	–
Loans	−319	−67
Change in leasing and rental assets and investment property (excluding depreciation)	−1,942	−2,963
Change in financial services receivables	−4,801	−3,766
Proceeds from disposal of non-current assets (excluding leasing and rental assets and investment property)	276	232

CASH FLOW STATEMENT FOR VOLKSWAGEN GROUP FOR THE PERIOD
JANUARY 1 TO DECEMBER 31, 2004 (*continued*)

€ million	2004	Restated 2003
Cash flows from investing activities	−15,079	−15,464
Net cash flow	−3,585	−7,093
Change in investments in securities	280	229
Investing activities including investments in securities	−14,799	−15,235
Capital contributions	−	−
Dividends paid	−457	−539
Other changes in equity	7	−3
Proceeds from issue of bonds	13,718	−14,850
Repayment of bonds	−5,507	−3,871
Change in other financial liabilities	−1,437	954
Finance lease payments	−21	−27
Change in loans	−335	59
Cash flows from financing activities	5,968	11,423
Changes in cash and cash equivalents due to changes in the scope of consolidation	3	77
Effect of exchange rate changes on cash and cash equivalents	19	−87
Net change in cash and cash equivalents	2,685	4,549
Cash and cash equivalents at end of period	10,221	7,536
Cash and cash equivalents	10,221	7,536
Securities and loans	4,112	3,652
Gross liquidity	14,333	11,188
Total third-party borrowings	−61,083	−54,858
Net liquidity	−46,750	−43,670

*Offset with impairment reversals.

Source: Volkswagen 2004, Annual Report, p. 43

Note: These accounts have been prepared using International Financial Reporting Standards. UK companies will generally follow a similar presentation.

Chapter 3

Learning Outcomes

After completing this chapter you should be able to:

✔ Outline the accounting equation.

✔ Understand double-entry bookkeeping.

✔ Record transactions using double-entry bookkeeping.

✔ Balance off the accounts and draw up a trial balance.

Recording: Double-Entry Bookkeeping

In a Nutshell

- *Double-entry bookkeeping is an essential underpinning of financial accounting.*

- *The accounting equation provides the structure for double-entry.*

- *Assets and expenses are increases in debits recorded on the left-hand side of the 'T' (i.e., ledger) account.*

- *Income and liabilities are increases in credits recorded on the right-hand side of the 'T' (i.e., ledger) account.*

- *Debits and credits are equal and opposite entries.*

- *Initial recording in the books of account using double-entry, balancing off and preparing the trial balance are the three major steps in double-entry bookkeeping.*

- *The trial balance is a listing of all the balances from the accounts.*

- *The debits and credits in a trial balance should balance.*

Kissing Your Accountant

It has been a week for displays of affection in the market. The darlings of the entertainment industry have long been accustomed to hugging and kissing in public – anyone who has watched the Oscars ceremony knows this only too well. Now, this tendency towards overtly physical contact has spread into the financial world. The latest way to convey to the market that a deal is truly wonderful is for the leading figures to share a moment of intimacy.

The chief executives of Time Warner and AOL were photographed cuddling up after announcing their tie up. Chris Evans was even seen planting a smacker on his accountant after pocketing a cool £75 m, when Scottish Media Group bought out Ginger Productions. Of course, if I had made £75 m I might even be tempted to kiss my accountant – despite the fact that he still hasn't completed my income tax return and the January 31 deadline is getting ever closer.

Source: Showbiz values come to the City, James Montier, *The Guardian*, 15 January 2000, p. 31. © Guardian Newspapers Limited 2000

Introduction

Accounting is a blend of theory and practice. One of the key elements to understanding the practice of accounting is double-entry bookkeeping (see Definition 3.1). Although mysterious to the uninitiated, double-entry bookkeeping, in fact, is a mechanical exercise. It is a way of systematically recording accounting transactions into an organisation's accounting books.

Double-Entry Bookkeeping

Working definition
A way of systematically recording the financial transactions of a company so that each transaction is recorded twice.

Formal definition
'The most commonly used system of bookkeeping based on the principle that every financial transaction involves the simultaneous receiving and giving of value, and is therefore recorded twice.'

Chartered Institute of Management Accountants (2000), *Official Terminology*.

In a way it is like a business diary where all the financial transactions are recorded. Therefore, in essence, double-entry bookkeeping is the systematic recording of income, expenses, assets, liabilities and capital. For listed companies, capital is called equity. Double-entry bookkeeping's importance lies in the fact that the profit and loss account (known as income statement for a listed company) and balance sheet are prepared only after the accounting transactions have been recorded. The accounting equation and double-entry bookkeeping apply to all businesses. In this chapter, unless otherwise specified, the terminology used applies to sole traders, partnerships and non-listed companies.

The Accounting Equation

The reason why each transaction is recorded twice in the accounting books is not that accountants like extra work. In effect, it is a method of checking that the entries have been made correctly. At the heart of the double-entry system is the accounting equation. This starts from the basic premise that assets equal liabilities. It then logically builds up in complexity, as follows:

Step 1. **Assets = Liabilities**
    If there is an asset of £1, then somebody must be owed £1. This can either be a third party (such as the bank) or the owner of the business. There is thus a basic equality. For every asset, there is a liability.

Step 2. It should be appreciated that capital is a distinct type of liability because it is owed to the owner of a business. For a listed company, capital is known as equity. If we expand our accounting equation to formally distinguish between third party liabilities and capital we now have:
    Assets = Liabilities + Capital

PAUSE FOR THOUGHT 3.1

The Accounting Equation

John decides to start a business and puts £10,000 into a business bank account. He also borrows £5,000 from the bank. How does this obey the accounting equation?

. . . .

The asset here is easy. It is £15,000 cash. There is also clearly a £5,000 liability to the bank. However, the remaining £10,000, at first glance, is more elusive. A liability does, however, exist. This is because of the entity concept where the business and John are treated as different entities. Thus, the business owes John £10,000. We therefore have:

Asset		Liability		Capital
£15,000 in bank	=	£5,000 owed to bank	+	£10,000 owed to John

Where a business has a liability to its owner, this is known as capital.

In a sole trader, the capital is initially invested by the owner. In a company, like Manchester United (see The Company Camera 3.1), the capital or equity will have been invested by shareholders.

THE COMPANY CAMERA 3.1

Share Capital

	Group and Company	
	2004	2003
	£'000	£'000
Authorised:		
350,000,000 ordinary shares of 10 pence each	**35,000**	35,000
Allotted, called up and fully paid:		
	Number	£'000
At 1 August 2003	259,768,040	25,977
Shares issued during the period	2,419,588	242
At 31 July 2004	**262,187,628**	**26,219**

Share option schemes:

Note: Authorised share capital is the amount Manchester United is allowed to issue; allotted, called up and fully paid share capital is that actually issued.

Source: Manchester United plc, 2004 Annual Report, p. 75, note to the accounts 22

Step 3. **Assets = Liabilities + Capital + Profit**

When an organisation earns a profit its assets increase. Profit is on the same side as liabilities because profit is owed to the owner. Profit thus also increases the owner's share in the business. If a loss is made assets will decrease, but the principle of equality still holds.

Step 4. **Assets = Liabilities + Capital + (Income − Expenses)**

All we have done is broken down profit into its constituent parts (i.e., income less expenses). We have still maintained the basic equality.

Step 5. **Assets + Expenses = Liabilities + Capital + Income**

We have now rearranged the accounting equation by adding expenses to assets. We have still preserved the accounting equation.

Step 6. In accounting terms, **assets** and **expenses** are recorded using **debit entries** and **income, liabilities** and **capital** are recorded using **credit entries**. Each page of each book of account has a debit side (left-hand side) and a credit side (right-hand side). This division of the page is called a 'T' account, with debits being on the left and credits on the right. Thus:

'T' Account (ledger account)	
Assets and expenses on the left-hand side DEBIT	Incomes, liabilities and capital on the right-hand side CREDIT

PAUSE FOR THOUGHT 3.2

Illustration of Accounting Equation

A firm starts the year with £10,000 assets and £10,000 liabilities (£6,000 third party liabilities and £4,000 owner's capital). During the year, the firm makes £5,000 profit (£9,000 income, £4,000 expenses). Show how the accounting equation works.

	Accounting equation	*Transaction*
(1)	Assets = Liabilities	£10,000 = £10,000
(2)	Assets = Liabilities + Capital	£10,000 = £6,000 + £4,000
(3)	Assets = Liabilities + Capital + Profit	£15,000 = £6,000 + £4,000 + £5,000
(4)	Assets = Liabilities + Capital + (Income − Expenses)	£15,000 = £6,000 + £4,000 + (£9,000 − £4,000)
(5)	Assets + Expenses = Liabilities + Capital + Income	£15,000 + £4,000 = £6,000 + £4,000 + £9,000

'T' Account		'T' Account	
Assets + Expenses	Liabilities + Capital + Income	£15,000 + £4,000	£6,000 + £4,000 + £9,000

The 'T' account is central to the concept of double-entry bookkeeping. In turn, double-entry bookkeeping is the backbone of financial accounting. As Helpnote 3.1 shows, it is underpinned by three major rules.

HELPNOTE 3.1

Basic Rules of Double-Entry Bookkeeping

1. **For every transaction, there must be a *debit and a credit entry*.**

2. **These debit and credit entries are *equal* and *opposite*.**

3. **In the *cash book* all accounts *paid in* are recorded on the *debit* side, whereas all amounts *paid out* are recorded on the *credit* side.**

In practice, there are many types of asset, liability, capital, income and expense. Figure 3.1 provides a brief summary of some of these.

Figure 3.1   Summary of Some of the Major Types of Assets, Liabilities and Capital, Income and Expenses

Four Major Types of Items	1. **Assets** 2. **Liabilities and capital** 3. **Income** 4. **Expenses**

1. **Assets**
   Essentially items owned or leased by a business which will bring economic benefits. Two main sorts of tangible (i.e., assets with a physical existence):

I. *Fixed assets*
   These are infrastructure assets *not* used in day-to-day trading. They are assets in use usually over a long period of time.
   - i.   Motor vehicles
   - ii. Land and buildings
   - iii. Fixtures and fittings
   - iv. Plant and machinery

II. *Current assets*
   These are assets used in day-to-day trading
   - i.   Stock
   - ii. Debtors
   - iii. Cash

2. **Liabilities**
   Essentially these can be divided into:
   I. Short-term and long-term third party liabilities; and
   II. Capital which is a liability owed by the business to the owner.

I. *Third party liabilities*
   (a) *Short-term*
   - (i)   Creditors
   - (ii)   Bank overdraft
   - (iii) Proposed dividends
   - (iv) Proposed taxation (companies only)

   (b) *Long-term*
   - (i) Bank loan repayable after several years
   - (ii) Mortgage loan

II. *Capital*
   Capital is a liability because the business owes it to the owner. Owner's capital is increased by profit, but reduced by losses.
3. **Income**
   This is the day-to-day revenue earned by the business, e.g. sales.

4. **Expenses**
   These are the day-to-day costs of running a business, e.g. rent and rates, electricity, wages.

Figure 3.1 does not provide an exhaustive list of all assets and liabilities. For instance, it only deals with tangible assets (literally assets you can touch). It thus ignores intangible assets (literally assets you cannot touch) such as royalties or goodwill. However, for now, this provides a useful framework. Intangible assets are most often found in the accounts of companies and are discussed later. More detail on the individual items in Figure 3.1 is provided in later chapters.

PAUSE FOR THOUGHT 3.3

Debits and Credits

What do the terms 'debit' and 'credit' actually mean?

....

Debit and credit have their origins in Latin terms (*debeo*, I owe) and (*credo*, I make a loan). Debtor (one who owes, i.e., a customer) and creditor (one who is owed, i.e., a supplier) have the same origins. Over time, these terms have changed so that nowadays perhaps we have the following:

Debit   =   An entry on the left-hand side of a 'T' account. Records principally increases in either assets or expenses. However, may also record decreases in liabilities, capital or income.

Credit   =   An entry on the right-hand side of a 'T' account. Records principally increases in liabilities, capital or income. However, may also record decreases in assets or expenses.

HEALTH WARNING

Those students not wishing to gain an in-depth knowledge of double-entry bookkeeping can miss out pages 55–67.

Worked Example

If we now look at an example. Gavin Stevens has decided to open a hotel to cater for conferences and large functions.

1 January	G. Stevens invests £200,000 capital into a business bank account.	
2 January	Buys and pays for a hotel	£110,000
	Buys and pays for a second-hand delivery van	£3,000
	Buys cash purchases	£2,000
	Buys credit purchases from Hogen	£1,000
	Buys credit purchases from Lewis	£2,000
3 January	Returns goods costing £500 to Hogen	
3 January	Credit sales to Ireton £4,000 for a large garden party	
	Credit sales to Hepworth £5,000 for a business conference	
4 January	Pays electricity bill	£300
	Pays wages	£1,000
5 January	Ireton returns a crate of wine costing £70 to G. Stevens	
7 January	G. Stevens pays half of the bills outstanding and half of the debtors pay him	

It is now time to enter the transactions for Gavin Stevens into the books of account. This will be done in the next section. As Figure 3.2 shows, there are three main parts to recording the transactions (recording, balancing off and the trial balance).

Figure 3.2   Recording the Transactions

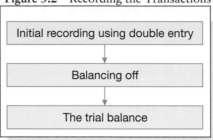

The bookkeeping role is an essential function of an accountant. It is a precursor of the arguably more challenging job of analysing and interpreting the information (see Real-Life Nugget 3.2).

Step 1   The Initial Recording Using Double-Entry Bookkeeping

The individual amounts are directly entered into two different ledger accounts, **one on each side**. Thus, on the 1st January we credit the capital account with £200,000, but debit the bank account with £200,000. This represents the initial £200,000 capital invested. We record three items (1) date of transaction, (2) **account** which is **equal and opposite** to complete the double-entry and (3) amount.

Each 'T' account (i.e., ledger page in the books of account) is treated separately. So that the transactions are easier to follow, each separate transaction is given a letter. Thus, the first transaction (investing £200,000 capital) is recorded as 'A' on the credit (i.e. right-hand side) in the capital account and also as 'A' on the debit (i.e. left-hand side) in the bank account (see Figure 3.3).

It must be remembered that all organisations will structure their accounts books in slightly different ways. In particular, very small businesses may not keep any proper books of accounts, just filing the original invoices and passing them on to their accountants. However, bigger businesses

Figure 3.3   Recording Gavin Steven's Entries Using Double-Entry Bookkeeping

Capital			Bank			
£		£	£		£	
	1 Jan. Bank	200,000 A	1 Jan. Capital	200,000 A	2 Jan. Hotel	110,000 B
			7 Jan. Ireton	1,965 M	2 Jan. Van	3,000 C
			7 Jan. Hepworth	2,500 N	2 Jan. Purchases	2,000 D
					4 Jan. Electricity	300 J
					4 Jan. Wages	1,000 K
					7 Jan. Hogen	250 O
					7 Jan. Lewis	1,000 P

Sales			Purchases			
£		£	£		£	
	3 Jan. Ireton	4,000 H	2 Jan. Bank	2,000 D		
	3 Jan. Hepworth	5,000 I	2 Jan. Hogen	1,000 E		
			2 Jan. Lewis	2,000 F		

Sales Returns			Purchases Returns			
	£	£		£		£
5 Jan. Ireton	70 L				3 Jan. Hogen	500 G

Electricity			Wages			
	£	£		£		£
4 Jan. Bank	300 J		4 Jan. Bank	1,000 K		

Hotel			Van			
	£	£		£		£
2 Jan. Bank	110,000 B		2 Jan. Bank	3,000 C		

Ireton (debtor)			Hepworth (debtor)			
	£	£		£		£
3 Jan. Sales	4,000 H	5 Jan. Sales returns	70 L	3 Jan. Sales	5,000 I	7 Jan. Bank	2,500 N
		7 Jan. Bank	1,965 M				

Hogen (creditor)			Lewis (creditor)			
	£	£		£		£
3 Jan. Purchases returns	500 G	2 Jan. Purchases	1,000 E	7 Jan. Bank	1,000 P	2 Jan. Purchases	2,000 F
7 Jan. Bank	250 O						

will keep day books (such as the sales day book and purchases day book) in which they will list their credit sales and credit purchases. Double-entry using day books is considered too complex for this book. Interested readers are referred to Alan Sangster and Frank Wood's *Business Accounting*.

HELPNOTE 3.2

Note that each entry in Figure 3.3 appears on both sides (i.e., as a debit and a credit, equal and opposite) of different accounts. For example, capital of £200,000 is a credit in the capital account of £200,000 and a debit in the bank account of £200,000. Each account represents one page. So, for example, the sales account has nothing on the left-hand side of the page.

In most businesses, the initial transactions are now recorded using a computer system. The individual ledger accounts are then stored in the computer. However, it is necessary to appreciate the underlying processes involved. These are now explained, both for Gavin Stevens and more generally.

If we look at the double-entry in terms of debit and credit for Gavin Stevens, we have the following, see Figure 3.4.

Figure 3.4   Debit and Credit Table for Gavin Stevens

Account	Debit	Credit
Capital	–	Liability to owner increases by £200,000
Bank	Assets increase through capital introduced and money from debtors	Assets decrease through payments to suppliers and payments of expenses
Sales	–	Income increases through credit sales £9,000
Purchases	Expenses increase through £2,000 cash purchases and £3,000 credit purchases	–
Sales returns	Income reduced when customers return £70 goods	–
Purchases returns	–	Expenses reduced when £500 goods returned to supplier
Electricity	Expenses increase by £300	–
Wages	Expenses increase by £1,000	–
Hotel	Assets increase by £110,000	–
Van	Assets increase by £3,000	–
Ireton	Asset of debtor increases by £4,000	Asset reduced by returns of £70 and receipt of £1,965
Hepworth	Asset of debtor increases by £5,000	Asset reduced by receipt of £2,500
Hogen	Liability decreases by payment of £250 and returns of £500	Liability to third party increases by creditor of £1,000
Lewis	Liability decreases by payment of £1,000	Liability to third party increases by creditor of £2,000

Step 2 Balancing Off

Helpnotes 3.3 and 3.4 provide a number of rules to guide us through double-entry bookkeeping. When all the entries for a period have been completed then it is time to balance off the accounts

HELPNOTE 3.3

Double-Entry Checks

Because of the way double-entry is structured, a number of rules can guide us when we make the initial entries.

1. Sales and purchases
   There will never be a debit in a sales account or a credit in a purchases account. Assets and liabilities never pass through these accounts

2. Returns
   Sales returns and purchases returns have their own accounts. You will never find a credit in a sales returns account or a debit in a purchases returns account

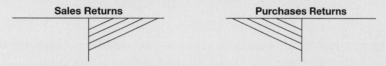

3. Assets and expenses
   When making the initial entries you never credit a fixed assets or expenses account

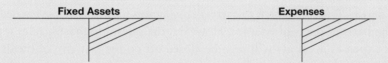

4. The bank account represents cash at bank. We always talk of cash received, and cash paid. Given the number of cash transactions the normal business conducts, there would normally be a separate cash book. The totals from the cash book would be summarised and then transferred to the bank account.

Bank account	
In	*Out*
Capital invested	Cash paid for purchases
Cash from sales	Cash paid for fixed assets such as cars
	Cash paid for expenses such as:
	Wages paid
	Rent paid
	Electricity paid
	Light and heat paid

Finally, if all else fails and you are still struggling with double-entry then Helpnote 3.4 may be useful.

HELPNOTE 3.4

The Bank Account

If you are having trouble remembering your double-entry, work back from the bank account; remember

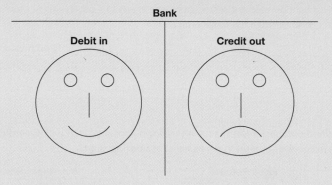

The smiling face represents money received so the business is better off. By contrast, the grumpy face represents money out, so the business is worse off.

and carry forward the new total to the next period. We are, in effect, signalling the end of an accounting period. It is convenient to carry all the figures forward. These carried forward figures will form the basis of the trial balance. However, the **sales, purchases, sales returns, purchases returns** and **expenses accounts** will then be **closed off** on the last day of the accounting period as they will **not** be carried forward to the next period. This is because in the next period all we are concerned with is that period's income and expenses. **The balance sheet items will be brought forward** on the first day of the new accounting period. This is because assets, liabilities and capital continue from accounting period to accounting period. Accounting periods may be weekly, monthly or annually. The aim of balancing off is threefold.

1. To prepare a trial balance from which we will prepare a balance sheet and trading, profit and loss account.
2. To close down income and expenses accounts which relate to the previous period.
3. To bring forward to the next period the assets, liabilities and capital balances.

First of all the accounts are balanced off. We then close off the revenue and expenses items to the trading account, and the profit and loss account. The trading account deals with purchases, purchases returns, sales and sales returns. The profit and loss account is concerned with expenses.

PAUSE FOR THOUGHT 3.4

The Trial Balance I

Why should the trial balance balance?

A trial balance is simply a list of all the balances on the individual accounts. If the double-entry process has been completed correctly, each debit will be matched by an equal and opposite credit entry. There will thus be equal amounts on the debit and credit sides. If the trial balance fails to balance – and it often will even for experts – then you know a mistake has been made in the double-entry process. You need, therefore, to find it. This process of trial and error is the reason why a trial balance is so called.

To illustrate balancing off we take three items from Gavin Stevens' accounts: sales (a trading account item), electricity (a profit and loss account item) and the bank account (a balance sheet item). We balance off after the first week. We will then draw up a trial balance.

1. **Trading account item**

Sales

	£		£
		3 Jan. Ireton	4,000
7 Jan. Bal. c/f	9,000	3 Jan. Hepworth	5,000
	9,000		9,000
7 Jan. Transfer to trading account	9,000	7 Jan. Bal. b/f	9,000

Note that the balance (bal.) would be carried forward (c/f) above the totals and brought forward (b/f) below them.

2. **Profit and loss account item**

Electricity

	£		£
4 Jan. Bank	300	7 Jan. Bal. c/f	300
	300		300
7 Jan. Bal. b/f	300	7 Jan. Transfer to profit and loss account	300

3. Balance sheet item

Bank

	£		£
1 Jan. Capital	200,000	2 Jan. Hotel	110,000
7 Jan. Ireton	1,965	2 Jan. Van	3,000
7 Jan. Hepworth	2,500	2 Jan. Purchases	2,000
		4 Jan. Electricity	300
		4 Jan. Wages	1,000
		7 Jan. Hogen	250
		7 Jan. Lewis	1,000
		7 Jan. Bal. c/f	86,915
	£204,465		£204,465
8 Jan. Bal. b/f	£86,915		

Note that there is no need to close off the bank account because it will be used at the start of the next period. However, note **the date is the starting date for the next period.**

NOW GO BACK TO THE DOUBLE-ENTRY STAGE ON PAGE 57 AND COMPLETE THE 'T' ACCOUNTS SHOWN THERE. MAKE SURE YOU UNDERSTAND HOW TO BALANCE OFF PROPERLY. THEN CHECK YOUR ANSWER WITH THE ANSWER BELOW ON PAGES 63 AND 64.

▷▷ HELPNOTE 3.5

Balancing Off

1. Always find which side has the greatest total (in the case below, £250)   (a)
2. Record the greatest total twice, once on the debit side and once   (b)
   on the credit side
3. Carry forward the balancing figure (bal. c/f)   (c)
4. Bring forward the balancing figure (bal. b/f)   (d)
5. For trading and profit and loss account items, only transfer the balance   (e)

In this case, we use a telephone account for period to 31 January.

Balancing off a telephone account

	£		£
1 Jan. Telephone	250 (a)	31 Jan. Bal. c/f	250 (c)
	250 (b)		250 (b)
31 Jan. Bal. b/f	250 (d)	31 Jan. Transfer to profit and loss account	250 (e)

The completed 'T' accounts are shown in Figure 3.5. The *balancing* off is shown in *italics* for ease of understanding. We have abbreviated balance brought forward (to Bal. b/f) and balance carried forward (to Bal. c/f), transfer to profit and loss account (to To P&L) and transfer to trading account (to To trading a/c). Note that balance sheet items brought forward (Bal. b/f) are brought forward on the first day of the new accounting period, i.e. 8th January.

Figure 3.5 Completed Double-Entry Bookkeeping Entries for Gavin Stevens

Capital

	£		£
7 Jan. Bal. c/f	*200,000*	1 Jan. Bank	200,000
	200,000		*200,000*
		8 Jan. Bal. b/f	*200,000*

Bank

	£		£
1 Jan. Capital	200,000	2 Jan. Hotel	110,000
7 Jan. Ireton	1,965	2 Jan. Van	3,000
7 Jan. Hepworth	2,500	2 Jan. Purchases	2,000
		4 Jan. Electricity	300
		4 Jan. Wages	1,000
		7 Jan. Hogen	250
		7 Jan. Lewis	1,000
		7 Jan. Bal. c/f	*86,915*
	204,465		*204,465*
8 Jan. Bal. b/f	*86,915*		

Sales

	£		£
7 Jan. Bal. c/f	*9,000*	3 Jan. Ireton	4,000
		3 Jan. Hepworth	5,000
	9,000		*9,000*
7 Jan. To trading a/c	*9,000*	*7 Jan. Bal. b/f*	*9,000*

Purchases

	£		£
2 Jan. Bank	2,000		
2 Jan. Hogen	1,000		
2 Jan. Lewis	2,000	*7 Jan. Bal. c/f*	*5,000*
	5,000		*5,000*
7 Jan. Bal. b/f	*5,000*	*7 Jan. To trading a/c*	*5,000*

Sales Returns

	£		£
5 Jan. Ireton	70	*7 Jan. Bal. c/f*	*70*
	70		*70*
7 Jan. Bal. b/f	*70*	*7 Jan. To trading a/c*	*70*

Purchases Returns

	£		£
7 Jan. Bal. c/f	*500*	3 Jan. Hogen	500
	500		*500*
7 Jan. To trading a/c	*500*	*7 Jan. Bal. b/f*	*500*

Electricity

	£		£
4 Jan. Bank	300	*7 Jan. Bal. c/f*	*300*
	300		*300*
7 Jan. Bal. b/f	*300*	*7 Jan. To P&L*	*300*

Wages

	£		£
4 Jan. Bank	1,000	*7 Jan. Bal. c/f*	*1,000*
	1,000		*1,000*
7 Jan. Bal. b/f	*1,000*	*7 Jan. To P&L*	*1,000*

Hotel

	£		£
2 Jan. Bank	110,000	*7 Jan. Bal. c/f*	*110,000*
	110,000		*110,000*
8 Jan. Bal. b/f	*110,000*		

Van

	£		£
2 Jan. Bank	3,000	*7 Jan. Bal. c/f*	*3,000*
	3,000		*3,000*
8 Jan. Bal. b/f	*3,000*		

Figure 3.5   Completed Double-Entry Bookkeeping Entries for Gavin Stevens (*continued*)

Ireton (debtor)				Hepworth (debtor)			
	£		£		£		£
3 Jan. Sales	4,000	5 Jan. Sales Returns	70	3 Jan. Sales	5,000	7 Jan. Bank	2,500
		7 Jan. Bank	1,965			7 Jan. Bal. c/f	2,500
		7 Jan. Bal. c/f	1,965		5,000		5,000
	4,000		4,000	8 Jan. Bal. b/f	2,500		
8 Jan. Bal. b/f	1,965						

Hogen (creditor)				Lewis (creditor)			
	£		£		£		£
3 Jan. Purchases Rets.	500	2 Jan. Purchases	1,000	7 Jan. Bank	1,000	2 Jan. Purchases	2,000
7 Jan. Bank	250			7 Jan. Bal. c/f	1,000		
7 Jan. Bal. c/f	250						
	1,000		1,000		2,000		2,000
		8 Jan. Bal. b/f	250			8 Jan. Bal. b/f	1,000

Note: We have closed off the trading and profit and loss accounts as at 7 January (sales, purchases, sales returns, purchases returns, electricity, wages) so that we can transfer these accounts to the trading and profit and loss account on that day. Balance sheet items are, however, brought forward on 8 January ready for the new period. In practice, we would probably not bring forward accounts with only one entry in, such as capital.

Step 3 Trial Balance

DEFINITION 3.2

Trial Balance

Working definition
A listing of debit and credit balances to check the correctness of the double-entry system.

Formal definition
'A list of account balances in a double-entry accounting system. If the records have been correctly maintained, the sum of the debit balances will equal the sum of the credit balances, although certain errors such as the omission of a transaction or erroneous entries will not be disclosed by a trial balance.'

Chartered Institute of Management Accountants (2000), *Official Terminology*.

The trial balance for Gavin Stevens may now be prepared. *Prepare your own answer before you look at the 'answer' shown in Figure 3.6.*

Figure 3.6   Gavin Stevens: Trial Balance as at 7 January

	Debit £	Credit £
Hotel	110,000	
Van	3,000	
Sales		9,000
Purchases	5,000	
Capital		200,000
Sales returns	70	
Purchases returns		500
Bank	86,915	
Electricity	300	
Wages	1,000	
Ireton	1,965	
Hepworth	2,500	
Hogen		250
Lewis		1,000
	210,750	210,750

SOUNDBITE 3.1

Trial Balance

'Nowadays, you hear a lot about fancy accounting methods, like LIFO and FIFO, but back then we were using the ESP method, which really sped things along when it came time to close those books. It's a pretty basic method: if you can't make your books balance you take however much they're off by and enter it under the heading ESP, which stands for Error Some Place.'

Sam Walton in *Sam Walton* p. 53

Source: *The Executive's Book of Quotations* (1994), pp. 3–4

Note that the **debit** items in Figure 3.6 are either **assets** or **expenses** and the **credit** items are either **income** or **liabilities.** This conforms to the accounting equation:

$$\text{Assets} + \text{Expenses} = \text{Liabilities} + \text{Capital} + \text{Income}$$

These balances are analysed for Gavin Stevens in Figure 3.7.

Figure 3.7   Analysis of Gavin Stevens' Trial Balance

Assets	Hotel, van, bank, debtors (Ireton, Hepworth)
Expenses	Purchases, sales returns, electricity, wages
Income	Sales, purchases returns
Liabilities	Creditors (Hogen, Lewis)
Capital	Capital

Essentially, the trial balance is a check on the accuracy of the double-entry process. If the double-entry has been done properly the trial balance will balance. If it does not, as Soundbite 3.1 on the previous page shows, there is an Error Some Place. Ideally, the books are then checked to find the error. Even when the trial balance balances, as Pause for Thought 3.5 shows, the accounts may not be totally correct.

PAUSE FOR THOUGHT 3.5

The Trial Balance II

If the trial balance balances that is the end of all my problems, I now know the accounts are correct. Is this true?

Unfortunately, this is not true! Although you can be happy that the trial balance does indeed balance, you must still be wary. There are several types of error (listed below) which may have crept in, perhaps at the original double-entry bookkeeping stage.

1. **Error of omission**
   You have omitted an entry completely. The trial balance will still balance, but your accounts will not be correct.
2. **Reverse entry**
   If you have completely reversed your entry and entered a debit as a credit, and vice versa, then your trial balance will balance, but incorrectly.
3. **Wrong amount**
   If the wrong figure (say £300 for the van instead of £ 3,000) was entered in the accounts, the books would still balance, but at the wrong amount.
4. **Wrong account**
   One of the entries might have been entered in the wrong account, for example, the van might be recorded in the electricity account.
5. **Compensating errors**
   If you make errors which cancel each other out, your trial balance will once more wrongly balance.

HEALTH WARNING

Those students who did not wish to gain an in-depth knowledge of double-entry bookkeeping can restart here.

Computers

Double-entry bookkeeping is obviously very labour-intensive. Computerised packages, such as *Sage*, are very popular. Normally, an entry is keyed into the bank account (e.g., hotel £110,000 or into a debtor's or creditor's account (e.g., sales to Ireton £4,000). The computer automatically completes the entries. Sales, purchases and bank transactions are standard and, therefore, only require one entry. For non-standard items both a debit and a credit entry is recorded. The computer, after all the transactions have been input, can produce a trial balance, a balance sheet and a trading and profit and loss account.

At first sight, therefore, computerised accounting packages which perform the double-entry transactions and then prepare the trading and profit and loss account and balance sheet would seem to be a gift from heaven. However, there are problems. The principal one is that, as many organisations have found to their cost, if you put rubbish into the computer, you get rubbish out. In other words, computer operators who are unskilled in accounting can create havoc with the accounts. To enter items correctly, it is necessary to have an understanding of the accounting process. Otherwise, disasters may occur with meaningless accounts. Therefore, unfortunately, understanding double-entry bookkeeping is just as important in this computer age.

Conclusion

The double-entry process is a key part of financial accounting. Without understanding double-entry it is difficult to get to grips with accounting itself. However, there is no need to be scared of double-entry. Essentially, it means that for every transaction which is entered on one side of a ledger account, an equal and opposite entry is made in another ledger account. These entries are called debit and credit. All the debits will equal all the credits. This is proved when the accounts are balanced off. The balance from each account is then listed in a trial balance. The trial balance shows that the double-entry process has been completed. However, a balanced trial balance does not necessarily guarantee that the double-entry has been correctly carried out (for example, there may be some errors of omission). Once the trial balance has been prepared it is possible to complete the trading and profit and loss account and balance sheet.

Q&A Discussion Questions

Questions with numbers in blue have answers at the back of the book.

Q1 Why is double-entry bookkeeping so important?

Q2 How do you think that the books of account kept by different businesses might vary?

Q3 Computerisation means that there is no need to understand double-entry bookkeeping. Discuss.

Q4 How much trust can be placed in a trial balance which balances?

Q5 Why are there usually more debit balances in a trial balance than credit balances?

Q6 State whether the following are true or false. If false, explain why.
    (a) We debit cash received, but credit cash paid.
    (b) Sales are debited to a sales account, but purchases are credited to a purchases account.
    (c) If a business purchases a car for cash we debit the car account and credit the bank account.
    (d) Purchases, hotel, electricity and wages are all debits in a trial balance.
    (e) Sales, rent paid and capital are all credits in a trial balance.

Q&A Numerical Questions

Questions with numbers in blue have answers at the back of the book.

Q1 From the following accounting figures show the six steps in the accounting equation: opening assets £25,000, opening liabilities £25,000 (£15,000 third party and £10,000 capital), profit £15,000 (income £60,000, expenses £45,000).

Q2 Show the debit and credit accounts of the following transactions in the ledger and what effect (i.e., income/decrease) they have on assets, liabilities, capital, income and expenses. The first one is done as an illustration.
    (a) Pay wages of £7,000

Debit effect	Credit effect
Wages: increases an expense	Bank: decreases an asset

    (b) Introduces £10,000 capital by way of a cheque.
    (c) Buys a hotel £9,000 by cheque.
    (d) Pays electricity £300.

(e) Sales £9,000 cash.

(f) Purchases £3,000 on credit from A. Taylor.

Q3 You have the following details for A. Bird of transactions with customers and suppliers.

(a) 1 June credit purchases of £8,000, £6,000 and £5,000 from Robin, Falcon and Sparrow, respectively.

(b) 4 June A. Bird returns goods unpaid of £1,000 and £2,000 to Robin and Falcon, respectively.

(c) 6 June A. Bird makes credit sales of £4,000, £7,000 and £6,000 to Thrush, Raven and Starling, respectively.

(d) 7 June Starling returns £1,000 goods unpaid which are faulty.

Required:

(i) Write up the relevant ledger accounts.

(ii) Balance off the accounts on 7 June for the trading and profit and loss account. Bring them forward on 7 June, however, there is no need actually to transfer them to the trading and profit and loss account.

(iii) Bring forward balances for assets and liabilities on 8 June.

Q4 Balance off the following four accounts at the month end. Transfer the balances for sales and purchases to the trading account.

(i) Sales

£		£
	8 June Bank	1,000
	9 June Brown	2,000

(ii) Purchases

£		£
1 June Bank	500	
30 June Patel	9,500	

(iii) Bank

£		£
3 June Cash 500	1 June Wages	800
Sales		
	7 June Rent	300
	8 June Purchases	200

(iv) R. Smith (debtor)

£		£
1 June Sales 800	3 June Sales	1,000
	Rets.	
	4 June Bank	3,000

Sales Rets. represents sales returns.

Q5 John Frier has the following transactions during a six month period to 30 June.

(a) Invests £10,000 on 1 January.

(b) Buys a motor van for £4,000 on 8 February by cheque.

(c) Purchases £8,000 goods on credit from A. Miner on 10 March.

(d) Pays A. Miner £3,000 on 12 April.

(e) Sells £9,000 credit sales to R. Army on 7 May.

(f) Receives £4,500 in cash on 10 June from R. Army.

Required: On 30 June prepare John Frier's:
  (i) Ledger accounts
 (ii) Trial balance after balancing off the accounts. Bring forward sales and purchases on 30 June, but there is no need to transfer the trading and profit and loss account items.

Q6 Katherine Jones sets up a small agency that markets and distributes goods. She has the following regular credit customers (Edwards, Smith and Patel) and regular suppliers of credit goods (Johnston and Singh). She has the following transactions in the first week of July.

1 July   Invests £195,000 capital into the business.
2 July   Buys some premises for £75,000 by cheque.
          Buys office equipment for £9,000 by cheque.
          Buys goods from Johnston for £3,000 and from Singh for £1,000, both are on credit.
          Cash purchases of £7,000.
3 July   Sales of £10,000, £9,000 and £7,000 are made on credit to Edwards, Smith and Patel, respectively.
4 July   Returns £500 goods unpaid to Johnston as they were damaged.
5 July   Pays bills for wages £4,000, electricity £2,000 and telephone £1,000.
7 July   Settles half of the outstanding creditors and receives half of the money outstanding from debtors.

Required: Prepare Katherine Jones':
  (i) Ledger accounts. Balance off the trading and profit and loss account items on 7 July. However, there is no need to transfer the trading and profit and loss account items.
 (ii) Trial balance after balancing off the accounts.

Q7 R. Poon was having a whale of a time trying to get a trial balance for his company Redwar. He had the following transactions during the month of May. He asks you to prepare the book entries and a trial balance.

1 May   Invests £8,000 in his business bank account.
2 May   Purchases £2,000 goods for cash from E. Skimo.
                  £4,000 of goods on credit from S. Eal.
                  £1,000 of goods on credit from P. Olar.
4 May   Sells £1,500 goods for cash to A.R.C. Tic.
                  £5,000 goods on credit to H. Unter.
                  £3,000 goods on credit to M. Dick.
7 May   M. Dick returns £2,000 goods unpaid saying that they were rotting.
8 May   R. Poon sends M. Dick's £2,000 goods (that he had originally purchased from S. Eal for £1,800) back unpaid because he can't stand the smell.
10 May   Purchases another £1,200 of goods on credit from S. Eal.
11 May   H. Unter buys on credit £1,600 of goods from R. Poon.

15 May   R. Poon receives bank interest of £250.
20 May   R. Poon pays S. Eal the amount owing.
20 May   R. Poon pays P. Olar £750.
21 May   R. Poon receives £2,000 from H. Unter.
21 May   R. Poon receives £800 from M. Dick.
31 May   R. Poon pays by cheque wages £800, rent £500, electricity £75, and stationery
£25.

Required: Prepare R. Poon's:
(i) Ledger accounts.
(ii) Trial balance after balancing off the accounts. Bring forward the trading and profit
and loss account items on 31 May, but there is no need actually to transfer the
trading and profit and loss account items.

Q8   Jay Shah has the following balances as at 31 December in his accounts.

	£		£
Capital	45,300	Purchases returns	500
Motor car	3,000	Bank	3,600
Building	70,000	Electricity	1,400
Office furniture	400	Business rates	1,800
A. Smith (debtor)	250	Rent	1,600
J. Andrews (creditor)	350	Wages	3,500
T. Williams (creditor)	550	Long-term loan	9,000
G. Woolley (debtor)	150	Sales	100,000
		Purchases	70,000

Required:
(i) Jay Shah's trial balance as at 31 December.
(ii) An indication of which balances are assets, liabilities, capital, income or expenses.

Q9   Mary Symonds, a management consultant has the following balances from the accounts
on 30 September.

	£		£
Office	80,000	Capital	28,150
Long-term loan	3,000	Electricity	1,600
Van	3,500	Telephone	3,400
H. Mellet (debtor)	650	Repairs	300
R. Edwards (debtor)	1,300	Business rates	900
P. Morgan (creditor)	1,400	Computer	3,000
Y. Karbhari (creditor)	600	Travel	4,000
Consultancy fees	70,000	Stationery	800
Cash at bank	3,700		

Required: Mary Symonds' trial balance as at 30 September.

Q10   The following trial balance for Rajiv Sharma as at 31 December has been incorrectly prepared. Prepare a correct version.

	£	£
Shop		55,000
Machinery	45,000	
Car		10,000
Sales	135,000	
Purchases	80,000	
Opening stock		15,000
Debtors		12,000
Creditors	8,000	
Long-term loan	16,000	
General expenses		300
Telephone	400	
Light and heat	300	
Repairs		400
	284,700	92,700

Required: A corrected trial balance as at 31 December.
Helpnote: If you rearrange the balances and the trial balance irritatingly still doesn't balance, remember capital.

Q11   Rachel Thomas's trial balance balances as follows:

	£	£
Sales		100,000
Shop	60,000	
Van	50,000	
Purchases	60,000	
Capital		172,800
Bank	100,000	
General expenses	1,000	
Return inwards	300	
Repairs	800	
A. Bright (debtor)	2,000	
B. Dull (creditor)		1,600
Telephone	300	
	274,400	274,400

Unfortunately, Rachel Thomas's bookkeeper was not very experienced. The following transactions were incorrectly entered.

(a) Purchase of a computer for £3,000 cash completely omitted.

(b) Credit sales of £800 to A. Bright forgotten.

(c) A photocopier worth £800 wrongly debited to the shop account.

(d) £300 credited to B. Dull's account should have been charged to A. Bright as it was a sales return.

(e) The van really cost £5,000, but had wrongly been recorded as costing £50,000 in both the van and bank accounts.

Required: A corrected trial balance as at 31 December.

Q12   Which of the following balances extracted from the books on 31 December would be used as a basis for next year's accounts?

	£		£
Capital employed	9,200	Debtors	700
Rent and rates	1,000	Creditors	1,400
Buildings	7,000	Bank	600
Telephone	1,500	Stock	1,300
Sales	100,000	Purchases	80,000
Computer	1,000		

Chapter 4

Learning Outcomes

After completing this chapter you should be able to:

✔ Explain the nature of the profit and loss account.

✔ Understand the individual components of the profit and loss account.

✔ Outline the layout of the profit and loss account.

✔ Evaluate the nature and importance of profit.

Main Financial Statements: The Profit and Loss Account (Income Statement)

In a Nutshell

- *One of three main financial statements.*

- *Consists of income, cost of sales and expenses.*

- *Cost of sales is essentially opening stock plus purchases less closing stock.*

- *Gross profit is sales less cost of sales.*

- *Net profit is income less cost of sales less expenses.*

- *Profit is determined by income earned less expenses incurred* not *cash received less cash paid.*

- *Profit is an elusive concept.*

- *Capital expenditure (i.e., on fixed assets such as property) is treated differently to revenue expenditure (i.e., an expense such as telephone).*

- *Profit is useful when evaluating an organisation's performance.*

Introduction

The profit and loss account is one of the three most important financial statements. Effectively, it records an organisation's income and expenses and is prepared from the trial balance. For companies, it is required by the Companies Act 1985. Profit and loss accounts seek to determine an organisation's profit (i.e., income less expenses) over a period of time. They are thus concerned with measuring an organisation's performance. Different organisations will have different profit and loss accounts. Indeed, they also have slightly different names. In this chapter, we focus on understanding the purpose, nature, contents and layout of the profit and loss account of the sole trader. The preparation of the profit and loss account of the sole trader from the trial balance is covered in Chapter 6. In Chapter 7 we investigate the preparation of the profit and loss accounts of partnerships and limited companies.

In this chapter, the term 'profit and loss account' is used except when we are *specifically* discussing the sole trader or a non-listed company. For sole traders, the more accurate term 'trading and profit and loss account' will be used. For listed companies, the term income statement as recommended by the International Accounting Standards Board is used and a different terminology is used for individual financial items. These terms are introduced in this chapter.

Context

The profit and loss account, along with the balance sheet and cash flow statement, is one of the three major financial statements. It is prepared from the trial balance and presents an organisation's income and expenses over a period of time. This period may vary. Many businesses prepare a monthly profit and loss account for internal management purposes. Annual accounts are prepared for external users like shareholders or the tax authorities. From now on we generally discuss a yearly profit and loss account. By contrast, the balance sheet presents an organisation's assets, liabilities and capital and is presented at a particular point in time. The cash flow statement shows the cash inflows and outflows of a business.

The major parts of the profit and loss account are:

$$\text{Income} - \text{Expenses} = \text{Profit}$$

As Soundbite 4.1 shows, profits are central to evaluating an organisation's performance. The profit figure is extremely important as it is used for a variety of purposes. It is used as an overall measure of performance and for more specific purposes, such as the basis by which companies distribute dividends to shareholders

SOUNDBITE 4.1

Profits

'You must deodorise profits and make people understand that profit is not something offensive, but as important to a company as breathing.'

Sir Peter Parker, quoted in the *Sunday Telegraph* (5 September 1976)

Source: *The Book of Business Quotations* (1991), p. 183

or as a starting point for working out taxation payable to the government. An organisation's profit performance is closely followed by analysts and by the press. In Real-Life Nugget 4.1, for example, there is discussion of Sage's 2000 financial results.

REAL-LIFE NUGGET 4.1

Profit Performance

HSBC Enters History Books with £10 Billion Profit

Banking group HSBC stepped into another row about profits yesterday when it announced the largest earnings in British corporate history, alongside bumper payouts for its top executives.

The company said it made pre-tax profits of £10 billion last year – 35pc more than in 2003 and higher than the £9.3 billion profits declared by oil giant Shell last month.

Source: Andrew Cave, *Daily Telegraph*, 1 March 2005, p. 38

Definitions

As Definition 4.1 indicates, a profit and loss account represents the income less the expenses of an organisation. Essentially, income represents money earned by the organisation (for example, sales), while expenses represent the costs of generating these sales (for example, purchases) and of running the business (for example, telephone expenses).

DEFINITION 4.1

Definition of a Profit and Loss Account (Income Statement)

Working definition
The income less the expenses of an organisation over a period of time, giving profit.
Formal definition
A key financial statement which represents an organisation's income less its expenses over a period of time and thus determines its profit so as to give a 'true and fair' view of an organisation's financial affairs.

Broadly, a working definition of income is the revenue earned by a business, while expenses are the costs incurred running a business. The International Accounting Standards Board formally defines income and expenses using the concept of an increase or a decrease in economic benefit. Incomes are thus increases in economic benefit (i.e., increases in assets or decreases in third party liabilities) which increase owner's capital. Expenses are decreases in economic benefit (i.e., decreases in assets or increases in third party liabilities) that decrease owner's capital. Both working and formal definitions are provided in Definition 4.2.

DEFINITION 4.2

Income

Working definition

Revenue earned by a business

Formal definition

'Increases in economic benefits during the accounting period in the form of inflows or enhancements of assets or decreases of liabilities that result in increases in equity.'

   International Accounting Standards Board (2000), *Framework for the Preparation and Presentation of Financial Statements*

Expenses

Working definition

Costs incurred running a business

Formal definition

'Decreases in economic benefits during the accounting period in the form of outflows or depletions of assets or incurrences of liabilities that result in decreases in equity.'

   International Accounting Standards Board (2000), *Framework for the Preparation and Presentation of Financial Statements*

PAUSE FOR THOUGHT 4.1

Limited Companies' Profit and Loss Account (Income Statement for Listed Companies)

Why do you think limited companies produce only abbreviated figures for their shareholders?

....

The answer to this is twofold. First of all, many limited companies are large and complicated businesses. They need to simplify the financial information provided. Otherwise, the users of the accounts might suffer from information overload. Second, for public limited companies, there is the problem of confidentiality. Remember that a company is owned by shareholders. Anybody can buy shares. A competitor, for example, could buy shares in a company. Companies would not wish to give away all the details of their sales and expenses to a potential competitor. They, therefore, summarise and limit the amount of information they provide. Limited companies, therefore, publicly provide abridged (or summarised) accounts rather than full ones using all the figures from the trial balance.

Layout

The profit and loss account is nowadays conventionally presented in a vertical format (such as in Figure 4.1 below). Here we begin with sales and then deduct the expenses. The 1985 Companies Act sets out several possible formats. For sole traders or partnerships, a full profit and loss account is sometimes prepared using all the figures from the trial balance. Often, however, the profit and loss account is presented in summary form, with many individual revenues and expenses grouped together. For companies presenting their results to the shareholders in the annual report, the exact relationship to the original trial balance is often unclear. Examples of Marks & Spencer plc and AstraZeneca plc profit and loss accounts (income statements) are given in The Company Cameras 2.1 (in Chapter 2) and 7.1 in Chapter 7 respectively.

Figure 4.1   Sole Trader's Trading and Profit and Loss Account

R. Beer		
Trading and Profit and Loss Account Year Ended 31 March 2010		
	£	£
Sales		100,425
Less *Cost of Sales*		
Opening stock	3,590	
Add Purchases	58,210	
	61,800	
Less Closing stock	2,200	59,600
Gross Profit		40,825
Add *Other Income*		2,000
Gaming machine		42,825
Less *Expenses*		
Wages	8,433	
Rates and water	3,072	
Insurance	397	
Electricity	2,714	
Telephone	292	
Advertising	172	
Motor expenses	530	
Darts team expenses	1,865	
Repairs and renewals	808	
Laundry	1,174	
Music and entertainment	3,095	
Licences	604	
Guard dog expenses	385	
Garden expenses	1,716	
Sundry expenses	1,648	
Accounting	800	
Depreciation	6,770	34,475
Net Profit		8,350

By contrast the trading and profit and loss account of the sole trader is more clearly derived from the trial balance. In this section we explain the theory behind this in more detail. In the following section the main terminology is explained. In order to be more realistic, we use the adapted trading and profit and loss account of a real person, a sole trader who runs a public house. This is presented in Figure 4.1.

The corresponding balance sheet for R. Beer is presented in the next chapter in Figure 5.2. In Chapter 6, we show how to prepare a trading and profit and loss account from the trial balance.

Main Components

Figure 4.2 shows the six main components of the trading and profit and loss account (sales, cost of sales, gross profit, other income, expenses and net profit) of a sole trader.

Figure 4.2   Overview of Trading and Profit and Loss Account

Sales
Less
Cost of Sales
Equals
Gross Profit
Add
Other Income
Less
Expenses
Equals
Net Profit

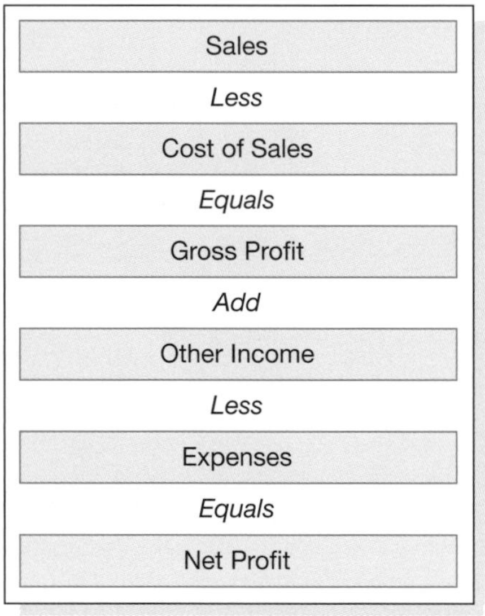

These six components are shown on the opposite page in Figure 4.3. In the first column, an overview definition is provided. This is followed by some general examples and then, whenever possible, a specific example. These components are then discussed in more detail in the text. The same order is used as for R. Beer's trading, and profit and loss account.

Figure 4.3   Main Components of the Trading and Profit and Loss Account

	Overview	General Examples	Specific Examples
Sales	Income earned from selling goods (may be reduced by sales returns, i.e. goods returned by customers)	Sales	e.g., Sales of beer
Cost of Sales	The items directly incurred in selling goods	1. Opening stock 2. Purchases (may be reduced by purchases returns, i.e., goods returned to supplier) 3. Closing stock	e.g., Barrels of beer a pub has at start of year e.g., Purchases of beer e.g., Barrels of beer a pub has left at end of year
Gross Profit	Sales less cost of sales	Measures gain of organisation from buying and selling	e.g., The direct profit a pub makes by reselling the beer
Other Income	Non-trading income which a firm has earned	1. Income from investments 2. Income from sale of fixed assets	e.g., Interest received from deposit account at bank e.g., Profit on selling a car for more than it was recorded in the accounts
Expenses	Items indirectly incurred in selling the goods	1. Light and heat 2. Employees' pay	e.g., Electricity e.g., Wages and salaries
Net Profit	Sales less cost of sales less expenses	Measures gain of organisation from all business activities	e.g., The profit a pub makes after taking into account all the pub's expenses

Sales

Generating sales is a key ingredient of business success. However, the nature of sales varies considerably from organisation to organisation. For companies, the words 'turnover' or 'revenue' are often used for sales. Essentially, sales is the income that an organisation generates from its operations. For example, Brook Brothers in Real-Life Nugget 4.2 sold clothes.

REAL-LIFE NUGGET 4.2

Sales
Thoughtless Thieves

In 1964 the lower Manhattan branch of Brook Brothers was robbed, and the thieves got away with clothes worth $200,000. One clerk remarked: 'If they had come during our sale two weeks ago, we could have saved 20 percent.'

Source: Peter Hay (1988), *The Book of Business Anecdotes*, Harrap Ltd, London, p. 100

These sales may be for credit or for cash. Credit sales create debtors, who owe the business money. Some businesses, such as supermarkets, have predominantly cash customers.

By contrast, manufacturing businesses will have largely credit customers. A further distinction is between businesses that primarily sell goods (e.g., supermarkets which supply food) and those which supply services (for example, a bank). Sales are very diverse. In the modern world, both developed and developing countries have varied businesses with varied sales.

The UK is an example of this (see Figure 4.4). It must be stressed that Figure 4.4 is for guidance only. The division between credit and cash, in particular, is very rough and ready.

Figure 4.4   Selected Industrial Sectors for 2004

Sector	Example of Sales	Credit/cash	Goods/services
Agriculture	Farm produce	Credit	Goods
Manufacturing	Manufactured goods	Credit	Goods
Construction	Buildings	Credit	Goods
Motor trades	New cars or car repairs	Cash and credit	Goods
Wholesale*	Food wholesaler*	Credit	Goods
Retail	Supermarket	Cash and credit card	Goods
Hotels and catering	Hotels	Cash and credit card	Services
Transport	Taxi fares	Cash	Services
Finance	Interest earned	Not applicable	Services
Property and business services	Rents	Cash and credit	Services

*Wholesale businesses act as middlemen between manufacturers and customers. They buy from manufacturers and sell on to retailers
Source: Size Analysis of United Kingdom Businesses, 2004, Office for National Statistics, Table B5.1

Sales are reduced by sales returns. These are simply goods which are returned by customers, usually because they are faulty or damaged. The Company Camera 4.1 demonstrates the sales for Manchester United.

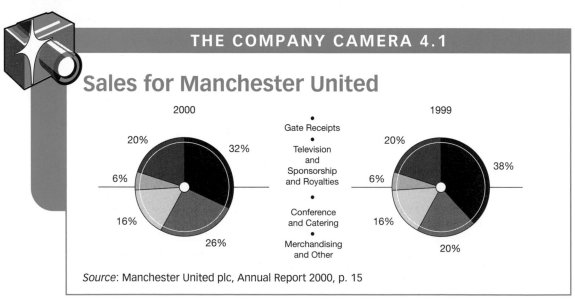

THE COMPANY CAMERA 4.1

Sales for Manchester United

2000

- Gate Receipts
- Television and Sponsorship and Royalties
- Conference and Catering
- Merchandising and Other

32% / 20% / 6% / 16% / 26%

1999

20% / 38% / 6% / 16% / 20%

Source: Manchester United plc, Annual Report 2000, p. 15

Cost of Sales

Cost of sales is essentially the expense of directly providing the sales. Cost of sales are normally primarily found in businesses which buy and sell goods rather than those which provide services. The main component of cost of sales is purchases. However, purchases are adjusted for other items such as purchases returns (goods returned to suppliers), carriage inwards (i.e., the cost of delivering the goods from the supplier), and, of particular importance, stock. In businesses that manufacture products, rather than buying and selling goods, the cost of sales is more complicated. It will contain, for example, those costs which can be directly related to manufacturing. The Company Camera 4.2 shows the cost of sales for J. Sainsbury plc, and Figure 4.5 presents a detailed example of cost of sales.

THE COMPANY CAMERA 4.2

Cost of Sales

Cost of sales consists of all costs to the point of sale including warehouse and transportation costs, all the costs of operating retail outlets and, in the case of Sainsbury's Bank plc, interest payable.

Source: J. Sainsbury plc Annual Report and Financial Statements 2004, p. 26

Figure 4.5   Cost of Sales

John Green, a retailer, runs a small business. He has the following details of a week's trading: Opening stock £2,000, carriage inwards £100, purchases £9,000, purchases returns £300, closing stock £3,800.
(i) What is his cost of sales? (ii) Why do we adjust for stock?

	£	£
Cost of Sales		
Opening stock		2,000
Add Purchases	9,000	
Less Purchases returns	300	
	8,700	
Add Carriage inwards	100	8,800
		10,800
Less Closing stock		3,800
		7,000

i.   Cost of sales is thus £7,000. Note that we have adjusted (i) for goods returned to the supplier £300, (ii) for carriage inwards which is the cost of delivering the goods from the supplier (i.e., like 'postage' on goods), and (iii) for closing stock.

ii. We need to match the sales with the actual cost directly incurred in generating them. Essentially, opening stock represents purchases made last period, but not used. They were not, therefore, directly involved in generating last period's sales. Similarly, closing stock represents this year's purchases which have not been used. They will, therefore, be used to generate the next period's, rather than this period's, sales.

Helpnote: When presenting cost of sales we subtract purchases returns and closing stock. We indicate this using the word 'less'. As a result, we do not put these figures in brackets.

Gross Profit

Gross profit is simply sales less cost of sales. It is a good measure of how much an organisation makes for every £1 of goods sold. In other words, the mark-up an organisation is making. Mark-ups and margins are discussed in Pause for Thought 4.2.

PAUSE FOR THOUGHT 4.2

Gross Profit

A business operates on a mark-up of 50 % on cost of sales. If its cost of sales was £60,000, how much would you expect gross profit to be?

....

	Mark-up %	£	Gross margin %
Sales	150	90,000	100
Cost of sales	100	60,000	67
Gross profit	50	30,000	33

Alternatively, a business might talk in terms of gross margin. This is a percentage of sales **not** of cost of sales. As we can see above, both mark-up and gross margin are different ways of expressing the same thing.

Businesses watch their cost of sales and their gross profit margins very closely. This is illustrated in The Company Camera 4.3 for Manchester United plc. Gross profit is determined in the trading account.

THE COMPANY CAMERA 4.3

Cost of Sales and Gross Margin

Cost of sales decreased by £3.8 million to £20.1 million as a result of the decrease in the number of home games and the cost of travel packages referred to above. The gross profit margin was 83 per cent compared to 78 per cent reflecting the improved sales mix with the higher margin television increasing and gate receipts decreasing.

Source: Manchester United plc, Annual Report 2000, p. 15

PAUSE FOR THOUGHT 4.3

Trading Account

What actually is the trading account and why is it so called?

....

The trading account is the initial part of the trading and profit and loss account. In other words, sales less cost of sales. As we can see below, it deals with the sales and purchases of goods and gives gross profit.

	£	£	£
Sales			100,000
Less Sales returns			10,000
			90,000
Less *Cost of Sales*			
Opening stock		8,000	
Add Purchases	50,000		
Less Purchases returns	4,000	46,000	
		54,000	
Less Closing stock		2,000	52,000
Gross Profit			38,000

It is termed a trading account because it gives details of an organisation's direct trading income (i.e., buying and selling goods) rather than non-trading income (e.g. bank interest) or expenses. Nowadays, because of the growth of businesses which have little stock (e.g., service companies), the trading account is becoming less important.

Other Income

This is basically income from activities other than trading. So it might be interest from money in a bank or building society (interest received). Or it might be dividends received from an investment or profit on sale of a fixed asset. In the case of the R. Beer example it was income from the gaming machine. Sometimes organisations report operating profits. Operating profit is concerned with trading activities (e.g., sales, purchases and expenses). Other income would be excluded.

Expenses

Expenses are many and varied. They are simply the costs incurred in meeting sales. Some examples of expenses are given below. However, the list is far from exhaustive.

- Accountants' fees (A)
- Advertising (S)
- Insurance (A)
- Light and heat (A)
- Petrol consumed (S)

- Sales commission (S)
- Business rates (A)
- Rent paid (A)
- Repairs and renewals (A)
- Telephone bill (A)

Often, these expenses are grouped into broad headings. For instance, in UK companies' published accounts, expenses are divided into selling and distribution costs (i.e., costs of marketing, delivering or distributing goods or services) and administrative costs (general running of the business). These categories are often very subjective. In the list above S = selling and distribution, and A = administrative.

Most expenses *are* a result of a cash payment (e.g., rent paid) or *will* result in a cash payment (e.g., rent owing). However, depreciation is a non-cash payment. It represents the expense of using fixed assets, such as motor vehicles, which wear out over time. The topic of depreciation is dealt with in more detail in Chapter 5.

Net Profit

Net profit is simply the amount left over after cost of sales and expenses have been deducted. It is a key method of measuring a business's performance. It is often expressed as a percentage of sales, giving a net profit to sales ratio.

Profit

The concept of profit seems a simple one, at first. Take a barrow boy, Jim, selling fruit and vegetables from his barrow in Manchester. If he buys £50 of fruit and vegetables in the morning and by the evening has sold all his goods for £70, Jim has made a profit of £20.

However, in practice profit measurement is much more complicated and often elusive. Although there are a set of rules which guide the determination of income and expenses, there are also many assumptions which underpin the calculation of profit. The main factors which complicate matters are:

- the matching concept
- estimation

- changing prices
- the wearing out of assets

Matching Concept

It is essential to appreciate that the whole purpose of the profit and loss account is to match **income earned** and **expenses incurred**. This is the matching concept which we saw in Chapter 2. **Income earned** and **expenses incurred** are not the same as **cash paid** and **cash received**. We have already seen that depreciation is a non-cash item. However, it is also important to realise that for many other income and expense items the **cash received and paid** during the year are **not the same as income earned and expenses incurred**. When we are attempting to arrive at income earned and expenses incurred we have to estimate certain items such as amounts owing (known as accruals). We also need to adjust for items paid this year which will, in fact, be incurred next year (for example, rent paid in advance).

Estimating

Accounting is often about estimation. This is because we often have uncertain information. For example, we may estimate the outstanding telephone bill or the value of closing stock.

Changing Prices

If the price of fixed assets, such as property, rises then we have a gain from holding that asset. Is this gain profit? Well, yes in the sense that the organisation has gained. But no, in that it is not a profit from trading. This whole area is clouded with uncertainty. There are different views. Normally such fixed asset gains are only included in the accounts when the fixed assets are sold.

Wearing Out of Assets

Assets wear out and this is accounted for by the concept of depreciation. However, calculating depreciation involves a lot of assumptions, for example, length of asset life.

Profit is thus contingent upon many adjustments, assumptions and estimates. All in all, therefore, the determination of profit is more an art than a science. It is true to say that different accountants will calculate different profits. And they might all be correct! It is, however, also true that despite the assumptions needed to arrive at profits, profits are a key determinant by which businesses of all sorts are judged. Real-Life Nugget 4.3, for example, shows press comment on football clubs.

REAL-LIFE NUGGET 4.3

Football Clubs' Profits
Football clubs' profits drop

Profits made by football clubs in the English Premiership more than halved during 1998/99, according to Deloitte & Touche. While average club income stood at a record-breaking £33.5 m, higher spending in the transfer market meant pre-tax profits shrunk by £22.7 m to £18.7 m compared to the previous season. Player transfer costs and in particular spiralling wages – which jumped by 31 % in the 1997/1998 season – were highlighted as the key to the profits slump.

Source: Accountancy Age, 11 May 2000, p. 3

Listed Companies

Listed companies in Europe follow International Financial Reporting Standards (IFRS). Under IFRS, the profit and loss account is called the income statement. There are also minor differences in presentation and terminology; for example, sales are conventionally termed revenues. The listed company is covered in depth in Chapter 7.

Capital and Revenue Expenditure

One example of the many decisions which an accountant must make is the distinction between capital and revenue expenditure. Capital expenditure is usually associated with balance sheet items, such as fixed assets, in other words, assets which may last for more than one year (e.g., land and buildings, plant and machinery, motor vehicles, and fixtures and fittings). By contrast, revenue expenditure is usually associated with profit and loss account items such as telephone, light and heat or purchases. This appears simple, but sometimes it is not. For example, to a student, is this book a capital or a revenue expenditure? Well, it has elements of both. A capital expenditure in that you may keep it for reference. A revenue expenditure in that its main use will probably be over a relatively short period of time. So we can choose! Often when there is uncertainty small-value items are charged to the profit and loss account. Interestingly, the WorldCom accounting scandal involved WorldCom incorrectly treating £2.5 billion of revenue expenditure as capital expenditure. This had the effect of increasing profit by £2.5 billion.

DEFINITION 4.3

Capital and Revenue Expenditure

Capital expenditure
A payment to purchase an asset with a long life such as a fixed asset.

Revenue expenditure
A payment for a current year's good or service such as purchases for resale or telephone expenses.

Limitations

So does the profit and loss account provide a realistic view of the performance of the company over the year, especially of profit? The answer is, maybe! The profit and loss account does list income and expenses and thus arrives at profit. However, there are many estimates which mean that the profit figure is inherently subjective. At the end of a year, for example, there is a need to estimate the amount of phone calls made. This brings subjectivity into the estimation of profit. Another example is that the loss in value of fixed assets is not accurately measured. Similarly, the valuation of stock is very subjective.

Interpretation

The profit and loss account, despite its limitations, is often used for performance comparisons between companies and for the same company over time. These performance comparisons can then be used as the basis for investment decisions. Profitability ratios are often used to assess a company's performance over time or relative to other companies (for example, profit is often measured against sales or capital employed). Ratios are more fully explained in Chapter 9.

Conclusion

The profit and loss account presents an organisation's income and expenses over a period. It allows the determination of both gross and net profit. In many ways, making a profit is the key to business success (as Soundbite 4.2 shows). Gross profit is essentially an organisation's profit from trading. Net profit represents profit after all expenses have been taken into account. It is

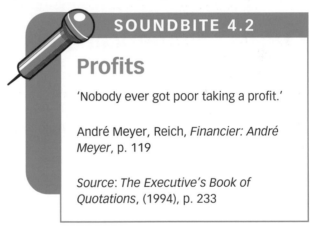

SOUNDBITE 4.2

Profits

'Nobody ever got poor taking a profit.'

André Meyer, Reich, *Financier: André Meyer*, p. 119

Source: The Executive's Book of Quotations, (1994), p. 233

important to realise that the profit and loss account is concerned with matching revenues earned with expenses incurred. It is not, therefore, a record of cash paid less cash received. Profit is not a precise absolute figure: it depends on many estimates and assumptions. However, despite its subjectivity, profit forms a key element in the performance evaluation of an organisation.

Q&A   Discussion Questions

Questions with numbers in blue have answers at the back of the book.

Q1   Why is the profit and loss account such an important and useful financial statement to such a variety of users?

Q2 'There is not just one profit there are hundreds of profits.' Do you agree with this statement, taking into account the subjectivity inherent in calculating profit?

Q3 The matching principle is essential to the calculation of accounting profit. Discuss.

Q4 Over time, with the decline of the manufacturing company and rise of the service company, stock, cost of sales and gross profit are becoming less important. Discuss.

Q5 State which of the following statements is true and which false? If false, explain why.
(a) Profit is income earned less expenses paid.
(b) Sales less cost of sales less expenses will give net profit.
(c) Sales returns are returns by suppliers.
(d) If closing stock increases so will gross profit.
(e) The purchase of a fixed asset is known as a capital expenditure.

Q&A   Numerical Questions

Questions with numbers in blue have answers at the back of the book.

Q1 Joan Smith has the following details from her accounts year ended 31 December 2009.

| Sales | £100,000 | Purchases | £60,000 | General expenses | £10,000 |
| Opening stock | £10,000 | Closing stock | £5,000 | Other expenses | £8,000 |

Required: Draw up Joan Smith's trading and profit and loss account for the year ended 31 December 2009.

Q2 Dale Reynolds has the following details from his accounts for the year ended 31 December 2009.

	£		£
Opening stock	5,000	Closing stock	8,000
Purchases	25,000	Purchases returns	2,000
Sales	50,000	Sales returns	1,000
Carriage inwards	1,000		

Required: Draw up Dale Reynolds trading account for the year ended 31 December 2009.

Q3 Mary Scott has the following details for the year to 31 December 2005.

	£		£
Sales	200,000	Income from investments	3,000
Opening stock	5,000	Wages	4,000
Purchases	100,000	Insurance	2,500
Closing stock	3,000	Electricity	3,500
Advertising	3,500	Telephone	4,000
Motor expenses	1,500	Purchases returns	1,000
Repairs	800	Sales returns	2,000
Sundry expenses	2,400		

Required: Draw up Mary Scott's trading and profit and loss account for the year ended 31 December 2005.

Q4 Given the following different scenarios, calculate sales, gross profit and cost of sales from the information available.

(a) Sales £100,000, gross margin 25 %.

(b) Sales £200,000, mark-up 30 %.

(c) Cost of sales £50,000, gross margin 25 %.

(d) Cost of sales £40,000, mark-up 20 %.

Chapter 5

Learning Outcomes

After completing this chapter you should be able to:

✔ Explain the nature of a balance sheet.

✔ Understand the individual components of a balance sheet.

✔ Outline the layout of a balance sheet.

✔ Evaluate the usefulness of a balance sheet.

Main Financial Statements: The Balance Sheet

In a Nutshell

- *One of three main financial statements.*

- *Consists of assets, liabilities and capital.*

- *Assets are most often fixed (e.g., land and buildings, plant and machinery, motor vehicles, and fixtures and fittings) or current (e.g., stock, debtors, cash).*

- *Liabilities can be current (e.g., trade creditors, short-term loans) or long-term (e.g., long-term loans).*

- *Listed companies have a special terminology and presentational format for the balance sheet.*

- *A sole trader's capital is capital plus profit less drawings.*

- *In modern balance sheets, a vertical format is most popular.*

- *A balance statement's usefulness is limited by missing assets and inconsistent valuation.*

- *Different business organisations will have differently structured balance sheets e.g., sole traders and limited companies.*

- *Balance sheets are used as a basis for determining liquidity.*

Introduction

The balance sheet, along with the profit and loss account and cash flow statement, is one of the most important financial statements. However, it is only in the last century that the profit and loss account has become pre-eminent. Before then, the balance sheet ruled supreme. The balance sheet is prepared from an organisation's trial balance. It consists of assets, liabilities and capital. For companies, it is required by the Companies Act 1985. Balance sheets seek to measure an organisation's net assets at a particular point in time. They developed out of concepts of stewardship and accountability. Although useful for assessing liquidity, they do not actually represent an organisation's market value. In this chapter, the primary focus will be on understanding the purpose, nature and contents of the balance sheet. The preparation of balance sheets of sole traders, partnerships and limited companies from the trial balance is covered, in depth, in Chapters 6 and 7, respectively. For listed companies, a different terminology and presentation is adopted. This is mentioned in this chapter, but dealt with in more depth in Chapter 7.

Context

The balance sheet is one of the key financial statements. It is prepared from the trial balance at a particular point in time, which can be any time during the year. The balance sheet is usually prepared for shareholders at either 31 December or 31 March. The balance sheet has three main elements: assets, liabilities and capital (known as equity for listed companies). Essentially, the assets less the third party liabilities (i.e., net assets) equal the owner's capital. Thus,

$$\text{Assets} - \text{Liabilities} = \text{Capital}$$

Alternatively:

$$\text{Assets} = \text{Liabilities} + \text{Capital}$$

The balance sheet and profit and loss account are complementary (see Figure 5.1). The profit and loss account shows an organisation's performance over the accounting period, normally

Figure 5.1 Comparison of Profit and Loss Account and Balance Sheet

	Profit and Loss Account (Income Statement)	Balance Sheet
Preparation source	Trial balance	Trial balance
Main elements	Income, expenses, profit	Assets, liabilities, capital
Period covered	Usually a year	A point in time
Main focus	Profitability	Net assets

a year. It is thus concerned with income, expenses and profit. A balance sheet, by contrast, is a snapshot of a business at a particular point in time. It thus focuses on assets, liabilities and capital. As Soundbite 5.1 shows, the balance sheet provides basic information which helps users to judge the value of a company.

Definitions

As Definition 5.1 shows a balance sheet is essentially a collection of the assets, liabilities and capital of an organisation at a point in time. It is prepared so as to provide a true and fair view of the organisation.

SOUNDBITE 5.1

Balance Sheets

'The market is mostly a matter of psychology and emotion, and all that you find in balance sheets is what you read into them; we've all guessed to one extent or another, and when we guess wrong they say we're crooks.'

Major L.L.B. Angas, *Stealing the Market*, p. 15

Source: *The Executive's Book of Quotations* (1994), p. 179

DEFINITION 5.1

Balance Sheet

Working definition
A collection of the assets, liabilities and capital of an organisation at a particular point in time.

Formal definition
'A statement of the financial position of an entity at a given date disclosing the assets, liabilities and accumulated funds such as shareholders' contributions and reserves prepared to give a true and fair view of the financial state of the entity at that date.'

Chartered Institute of Management Accountants (2000), *Official Terminology*

Broadly, assets are the things an organisation owns or leases; liabilities are things it owes. Assets can bring economic benefits by either being sold (for example, stock) or being used (for example, a car). Capital (sometimes known as ownership interest) is accumulated wealth. Capital is effectively a liability to the business because it is 'owed'

PAUSE FOR THOUGHT 5.1

Net Assets

If the assets were £20,000 and the liabilities to third parties were £10,000, what would (a) net assets and (b) capital be?

....

The answer would be £10,000 for both. This is because net assets equals assets less liabilities and capital equals net assets.

to the owner: Standard setters more formally define assets in terms of rights to future economic benefits and liabilities as obligations. Capital (ownership interest) is what is left over. In other words, assets less third party liabilities equal owners' capital.

By formally defining assets and liabilities, the balance sheet tends to drive the profit and loss account. In Definition 5.2 we present both formal and working definitions of assets, third party liabilities and capital (ownership interest).

DEFINITION 5.2

Assets

Working definition
Items owned or leased by a business.

Formal definition
'An asset is a resource controlled by the enterprise as a result of past events and from which future economic benefits are expected to flow to the enterprise.'

International Accounting Standards Board (2000), *Framework for the Preparation and Presentation of Financial Statements*

Liabilities

Working definition
Items owed by a business.

Formal definition
'A liability is a present obligation of the enterprise arising from past events, the settlement of which is expected to result in an outflow from the enterprise of resources embodying economic benefits.'

International Accounting Standards Board (2000), *Framework for the Preparation and Presentation of Financial Statements*

Capital (Ownership Interest or Equity)

Working definition
The funds (assets less liabilities) belonging to the owner(s).

Formal definition
'Equity is the residual interest in the assets of the enterprise after deducting all its liabilities.'

International Accounting Standards Board (2000), *Framework for the Preparation and Presentation of Financial Statements*

Layout

Traditionally, the balance sheet was always arranged with the assets on the right-hand side of the page and the liabilities on the left-hand side of the page. However, more recently, the vertical format has become most popular. For companies, the use of the vertical format was set out by the 1985 UK Companies Act. Examples of Marks & Spencer plc and AstraZeneca plc balance sheets are given in The Company Cameras 2.2 (in Chapter 2) and 7.4 (in Chapter 7), respectively. However, even organisations which are not companies now commonly use the vertical format. This sets out the assets and liabilities at the top. The capital employed is then put at the bottom. This modern format is the one which this book will use from now on. However, Appendix 5.1 (at the end of this chapter) gives an example of the traditional 'horizontal' format which readers may occasionally encounter.

In order to be more realistic, we use the adapted balance sheet of a real person, a sole trader who runs a public house. This is given in Figure 5.2. In Chapter 6, we show the mechanics of the preparation of the balance sheet from the trial balance. The purpose of this section is to explain the theory behind the presentation.

Figure 5.2 Sole Trader's Balance Sheet

	£	£	£
R. Beer			
Balance Sheet as at 31 March 2010			
Fixed Assets			
Land and buildings			71,572
Plant and machinery			3,500
Furniture and fittings			5,834
Motor car			3,398
Total fixed assets			84,304
Current Assets			
Stock	2,200		
Debtors	100		
Prepayments	50		
Bank	3,738		
Cash	340	6,428	
Current Liabilities			
Creditors	(3,900)		
Accruals	(91)		
Short-term loans	(1,000)	(4,991)	
Net current assets			1,437
Total assets less current liabilities			85,741
Long-term Creditors			(6,500)
Total net assets			79,241
Capital Employed			£
Opening capital			80,257
Add Net profit			8,350
			88,607
Less Drawings			9,366
Closing capital			79,241

Main Components

Figure 5.3 lists the main components commonly found in the balance sheet of a sole trader.

Figure 5.3   Main Components of the Balance Sheet

(Listed Companies Terminology in Brackets)	Overview	General Examples	Specific Examples
Fixed Assets (Property, plant and equipment)	Assets used to run the business long-term	1. Land and buildings 2. Plant and machinery 3. Fixtures and fittings 4. Motor vehicles	Public house, factory Lathe Computer, photocopier Car, van
Current Assets (i.e., short-term assets)			
(i) Stocks (Inventories)	Goods purchased and awaiting use or produced awaiting sale	1. Finished goods 2. Work in progress 3. Raw materials	Tables manufactured and awaiting sale Half-made tables Raw wood awaiting manufacture
(ii) Debtors (Trade Receivables)	Amounts owed to company	Trade debtors	Customers who have received goods, but not yet paid
(iii) Prepayments	Amounts paid in advance	Prepayments for services	Insurance prepaid
(iv) Cash and bank	Physical cash Money deposited on short-term basis with a bank	Cash in till Cash and bank deposits	Petty cash Current account in credit
Current Liabilities (i.e., amounts falling due within one year)			
(i) Creditors (Trade Payables)	Money owed to suppliers	Trade creditors	Amounts owing for raw materials
(ii) Accruals	Amounts owed to the suppliers of services	Accruals for services	Amounts owing for electricity or telephone
(iii) Loans	Amounts borrowed from third parties and repayable within a year	Short-term loans from financial institutions	Bank loan
Long-term Creditors (Non-current Liabilities)	Amounts borrowed from third parties and repayable after a year	Long-term loans from financial institutions	Loan secured, for example, on business property
Capital Employed (Equity)	Originally, the money the sole trader introduced into the business. Normally represents the net assets (i.e., assets less liabilities)	The capital at the start of the year and the capital at the end of the year are generally known as opening and closing capital	The opening and closing capital represent the opening and closing net assets
(i) Profit	The profit earned during the year	Taken from the profit and loss account, represents income less expenses	Net profit for year
(ii) Drawings	Money taken out of the business by the owner. A reduction of owner's capital	Living expenses	Owner's salary or wages

It provides some general examples and then, wherever possible, a specific example. The main components of the balance sheet are then discussed in the text. The same order is used as for R. Beer's balance sheet. Finally, in Figure 5.6 on page 103, we summarise the major valuation methods used for the main assets. An overview of the structure of the balance sheet is shown in Figure 5.4.

Figure 5.4   Overview of a Balance Sheet

Fixed Assets
Add
Current Assets less Current Liabilities
Equals
Total Assets less Current Liabilities
Less
Long-term Creditors
Equals
Total Net Assets
⇕
Opening Capital add Profit less Drawings equals Closing Capital

PAUSE FOR THOUGHT 5.2

Balance Sheets

Why does a balance sheet balance?

This is a tricky question! For the answer we need to think back to the trial balance. The trial balance balances with assets and expenses on one side and income, liabilities and capital on the other. Essentially, the balance sheet is a rewritten trial balance. It includes all the individual items from the trial balance in terms of the assets, liabilities and capital. It also includes all the income and expense items. However, all of these are included only as one figure 'profit' (i.e., all the income items less all the expense items). Incidentally, a balance sheet is probably called a balance sheet not because it balances, but because it is a list of all the individual balances from the trial balance.

Fixed Assets (Non-current Assets)

These are the assets that a business uses for its continuing operations. For listed companies, they are also known as non-current assets. There are generally recognised to be four main types of tangible assets (intangible assets, i.e. those which do not physically exist, are discussed in Chapter 7): land and buildings, plant and machinery, fixtures and fittings, and motor vehicles. For listed companies these are collectively called property, plant and equipment. Fixed assets are traditionally valued at historical cost. In other words, if a machine was purchased 10 years ago for £100,000, this £100,000 was originally recorded in the books. Every year of the fixed asset's useful life, an amount of the original purchase cost will be allocated as an expense in the profit and loss account. This allocated cost is termed depreciation. Thus, depreciation simply means that a proportion of the original cost is spread over the life of the fixed asset and treated as an annual expense. In essence, this allocation of costs relates back to the matching concept. There is an attempt to match a proportion of the original cost of the fixed asset to the accounting period in which the fixed assets were used up.

The most common methods of measuring depreciation are the straight-line method and the reducing balance method. The straight-line method is the one used in Figure 5.5. Essentially, the same amount is written off the fixed asset every year. With reducing balance, a set percentage is written off every year. Thus, if the set percentage was 20 %, then in Figure 5.5 £20,000 would be written off in year 1. This would leave a net book value of £80,000 (£100,000 − £20,000). Then 20 % of the net book value of £80,000 (i.e., £16,000) would be written off in year 2, and so on).

Figure 5.5   Illustrative Example on Depreciation

A machine was purchased 10 years ago for £100,000. Estimated useful life 20 years. We will assume the depreciation is equally allocated over 20 years. What would be the total depreciation (known as accumulated depreciation) after 12 years and at how much would the machine be recorded in the balance sheet?

Balance Sheet

Fixed Assets	Cost	Accumulated depreciation	Net book value
	£	£	£
Plant and machinery	100,000	(60,000)	40,000

In the balance sheet, the original cost (£100,000) is recorded, followed by accumulated depreciation (i.e., depreciation over the 12 years: 12 × £5,000 = £60,000). The term 'net book value' simply means the amount left in the books after writing off depreciation. It is important to note that the net book value does not equal the market value. Indeed, it may be very different. In the profit and loss account only one year' depreciation (£100,00 ÷ 20 years) of £5,000 is recorded each year.

Note: This topic is discussed more fully in Chapter 6.

Companies have great flexibility when choosing appropriate rates of depreciation. These rates should correspond to the lives of the assets. So, for example, if the directors believe the fixed assets have a life of five years they would choose a straight-line rate of depreciation of 20 %. The Company Camera 5.1 gives the rates of depreciation used by Manchester United plc. Interestingly, up until 1999 the club used the reducing balance method, which is relatively uncommon in the UK. However, it has now changed to the more conventional straight-line depreciation.

THE COMPANY CAMERA 5.1

Depreciation

Depreciation is provided on tangible fixed assets at annual rates appropriate to the estimated useful lives of the assets, as follows:

	Reducing Balance	Straight Line
Freehold land	Nil	Nil
Freehold buildings	1.33 %	75 years
Assets in the course of construction	Nil	Nil
Computer equipment and software	33 %	3 years
Plant and machinery	20 %–25 %	4–5 years
General fixtures and fittings	15 %	7 years

Tangible fixed assets acquired prior to 31 July 1999 are depreciated on a reducing balance basis at the rates stated above.

Tangible fixed assets acquired after 1 August 1999 are depreciated on a straight line basis at the rates stated above.

Source: Manchester United, 2004 Annual Report, p. 60

Finally, it is important to realise that nowadays, many businesses regularly revalue some fixed assets such as land and buildings every five years. Businesses can also revalue their fixed assets whenever they feel it is necessary (or, alternatively, devalue them if they have lost value). Where revaluations occur, the depreciation is based on the revalued amount.

Current Assets

Current assets are those assets which a company owns which are essentially short-term. They are normally needed to perform the company's day-to-day operations. The five most common forms of current assets are stocks, debtors, prepayments, cash and bank. For listed companies stocks and debtors are called inventories and trade receivables.

1. Stocks (Inventories)

Stocks are an important business asset. This is especially so in manufacturing businesses. Stocks or inventories can be divided into three categories: raw material stocks, work-in-progress stocks and finished goods stocks (see, for example, The Company Camera 5.2).

THE COMPANY CAMERA 5.2

Stocks (Inventories)

	2004 EURm	2003 EURm
Raw materials, supplies and other	326	346
Work in progress	477	435
Finished goods	502	388
Total	1,305	1,169

Source: Nokia, 2004, Annual Report, p. 25

Each category represents a different stage in the production process.

- *Raw material stocks*. These are stocks a company has purchased and are ready for use. A carpenter, for example, might have wood awaiting manufacture into tables.
- *Work-in-progress*. These are partially completed stocks, sometimes called stocks in process. They are neither raw materials nor finished goods. They may represent partly manufactured goods such as tables with missing legs. Some of the costs of making the tables should be included.
- *Finished goods stock*. This represents stock at the other end of the manufacturing process, for example, finished tables. Cost includes materials and other manufacturing costs (e.g., labour and manufacturing overheads).

Stocks at the year-end are often determined after a stock take. As Real-Life Nugget 5.1 shows, stocks or inventories can often represent a substantial percentage of a company's net assets. This is especially true for Corus, steelmakers, and Rolls-Royce, a manufacturing company. By contrast, Vodafone and J.D. Wetherspoon carry relatively little stock.

REAL-LIFE NUGGET 5.1

The Importance of Stock (Inventory) Valuation

Company	Inventory Value £m	Net Assets £m	Inventory ÷ Net Assets %
Tesco	1,199	7,990	15.0
Sainsbury	753	5,185	14.5
Corus	1,732	3,300	52.4
Marks & Spencer	398	1,985	20.0
Rolls-Royce	1,081	2,205	49.0
Vodafone	458	66,907	0.1
J.D. Wetherspoon	12	289	4.1

Source: 2004 Annual Reports

Generally, stock is valued at the lower of cost or net realisable value (i.e., the value it could be sold for). In the case of work-in-progress and finished goods, cost could include some overheads (i.e., costs associated with making the tables). In Chapter 16, we will look at several different ways of calculating cost (e.g., FIFO and AVCO).

Figure 5.6   Summary of the Valuation Methods Used for Fixed Assets and Stock

	Valuation method
Fixed Assets	Normally valued at historical cost, or revaluation less depreciation. Historical cost is the original purchase price of the asset. Revaluation is the value of the fixed assets as determined, usually by a surveyor, at a particular point in time.
Stock	Stock is generally valued at the lower of cost (i.e., what a business paid for it) and the amount one would realise if one sold it (called net realisable value). For a business with work-in-progress or finished goods stock, an appropriate amount of overheads is included

2. Debtors (Trade Receivables)

Debtors are sales which have been made, but for which the customers have not yet paid. If all transactions were in cash, there would be no debtors. Debtors at the year end are usually adjusted for those customers who it is believed will not pay. These are called bad and doubtful debts. Bad debts are those debts which will definitely not be paid. Doubtful debts have an element of uncertainty to them. Usually, businesses estimate a certain proportion of their debts as doubtful debts. These bad and doubtful debts are also included in the profit and loss account.

PAUSE FOR THOUGHT 5.3

Bad and Doubtful Debts

Can you think of any reasons why bad and doubtful debts might occur?

There may be several reasons, for example, bankruptcies, disputes over the goods supplied or cash flow problems. Most businesses constantly monitor their debtors to ensure that bad debts are kept to a minimum.

3. Prepayments

Prepayments are those items where a good or service has been paid for in advance. A common example of this is insurance. A business might, for example, pay £1,000 for a year's property insurance on 1 October. If the accounts are drawn up to 31 December, then at 31 December there is an asset of nine months' insurance (January–September) paid in advance. This asset is £750.

SOUNDBITE 5.2

Money

'They say money can't buy happiness, but it can facilitate it. I thoroughly recommend having lots of it to anybody.'

Malcolm Forbes (*Daily Mail*, 20 June 1988)

Source: *The Book of Business Quotations* (1991), p. 158

4. Cash and bank

This is the actual money held by the business. Cash comprises petty cash and unbanked cash. Bank comprises money deposited at the bank or on short-term loan. As Soundbite 5.2 shows, money has long been the topic of humour.

Current Liabilities

These are the amounts which the organisation owes to third parties. For a sole trader, there are two main types:

1. Creditors (Trade Payables)

These are the amounts which are owed to suppliers for goods received, but not yet paid (for example, raw materials). Like money, debts have often been a fertile subject for humourists (see Soundbite 5.3).

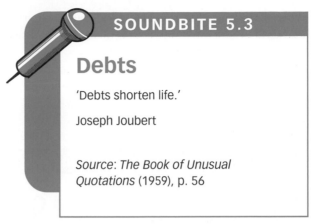

2. Accruals

Accruals is accounting terminology for expenses owed at the trial balance or balance sheet date. Accruals comply with the basic accounting concept of matching. In other words, because an expense has been incurred, but not yet paid, there is no reason to exclude it from the profit and loss account. Accruals are amounts owed, but not yet paid, to suppliers for services received. Accruals relate to expenses such as telephone or light and heat. For example, we might have paid the telephone bill up to 30 November. However, if our year end was 31 December then we might owe, say, another £250 for telephone. Importantly, accruals do **not** relate to purchases of trade goods owing: these are creditors.

3. Loans

Loans are the amounts which a third party, such as a bank, has loaned to the company on a short-term basis and which are due for repayment within one year.

The current assets less the current liabilities is, in effect, the operating capital of the business. It is commonly known as a business's working capital. Businesses try to manage their working capital as efficiently as possible (see Chapter 22). A working capital cycle exists (see Figure 5.7),

Figure 5.7   The Working Capital Cycle

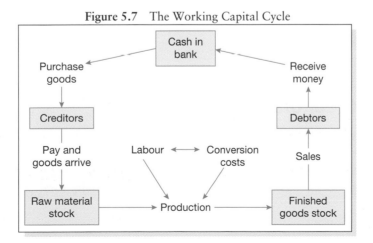

where cash is used to purchase goods which are then turned into stock. This stock is then sold and cash is generated. Successful businesses will sell their goods for more than their total cost, thus generating a positive cash flow.

In some cases, a business may have more current liabilities than current assets. Instead of being net current assets, this section becomes net current liabilities. This is the situation with Tesco in 2005, see The Company Camera 5.3.

THE COMPANY CAMERA 5.3

Current Assets and Current Liabilities

Current assets	£m	£m	£m	£m
Inventories	1,309	–	1,309	1,199
Trade and other receivables	1,002	(233)	769	811
Cash and cash equivalents	1,146	–	1,146	1,100
	3,457	(233)	3,224	3,110
Current liabilities				
Trade and other payables	(5,374)	417	(4,957)	(3,986)
Short-term borrowings	(477)	(5)	(482)	(847)
Current tax payable	(221)	–	(221)	(308)
	(6,072)	412	(5,660)	(5,141)
Net current liabilities	(2,615)	179	(2,436)	(2,031)

Source: Tesco, 2004/5 Restatement of Financial Information under International Financial Reporting Standards (IFRS), p. 7

Note: Special terminology is used for listed companies. Thus, inventories, trade receivables and trade payables are used for stocks, debtors and creditors, respectively.

Long-term Creditors

Long-term creditors (termed non-current liabilities for listed companies) are liabilities that the organisation owes and must repay after more than one year. The most common are long-term loans. The total assets of a business less current liabilities and long-term creditors give the total net assets of the business. Total net assets represent the total capital employed by a business.

Capital Employed (Equity)

For a sole trader the capital employed is opening capital plus profit less drawings. Thus for R. Beer it is:

	£
Opening capital	80,257
Add Profit	8,350
	88,607
Less Drawings	9,366
Closing capital	79,241

Opening capital is that capital at the start of the year (i.e., 1 April 2009). In essence, it represents the total net assets at the start of the year (i.e., all the assets less all the liabilities). If the business had made a loss, opening capital would have been reduced. It is important to realise that the profit (or loss) recorded under capital employed represents the net profit (or loss) as determined from the profit and loss account. It is, thus, a linking figure.

PAUSE FOR THOUGHT 5.4

Capital

A chip shop owner, B. Atter has opening capital of £19,500. His income is £100,000 and expenses are £90,000. He has taken out £15,000 to live on. His financial position has improved over the year. True or false?

Unfortunately, for B. Atter, the answer is false. If we quickly draw up his capital employed.

	£
Opening capital	19,500
Add Profit (i.e., income less expenses)	10,000
	29,500
Less Drawings	15,000
Closing capital	14,500

His capital has declined by £5,000 over the year.

Profit is the profit as determined from the profit and loss account (i.e., sales less purchases and expenses). Drawings is the money that R. Beer has taken out of the business for his own personal spending. Finally, closing capital is capital at the balance sheet date. It must be remembered at all times that:

$$\text{Assets} - \text{Liabilities} = \text{Capital}$$

Businesses need capital to operate. However, the capital needs to be used wisely (see Soundbite 5.4).

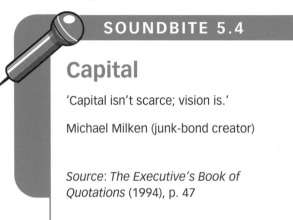

SOUNDBITE 5.4

Capital

'Capital isn't scarce; vision is.'

Michael Milken (junk-bond creator)

Source: *The Executive's Book of Quotations* (1994), p. 47

Limitations

To the casual observer, it looks as if the balance sheet places a market value on the net assets of the organisation. Unfortunately, this is wrong. Very wrong! To understand why, one must look at the major components of the balance sheet. The balance sheet is a collection of individual assets and liabilities. These individual assets and liabilities are not valued at a real-world, market value, so neither is the balance sheet as a whole. Taking the fixed assets, for example, only selected fixed assets are revalued. These valuations are neither consistent nor necessarily up-to-date. Also depreciation does not accurately measure the loss in value of fixed assets (nor is it supposed to). The balance sheet is thus a tangle of assets all measured in different ways.

PAUSE FOR THOUGHT 5.5

Financial Position

Angela Roll, a baker, has the following assets and liabilities. Fixed assets £59,000, current assets £12,000, current liabilities £8,000 and long-term creditors £7,000. Is it true that her total net assets are £50,000?

....

Actually, she is better off. They are £56,000:

	£	£
Fixed assets		59,000
Current assets	12,000	
Current liabilities	(8,000)	
Net current assets		4,000
Total assets less current liabilities		63,000
Long-term creditors		(7,000)
Total net assets		56,000

Another problem, especially for companies, is that significant assets are not shown on the balance sheets. All the hard work of an owner to generate sales and goodwill will only be recognised when the business is sold. Many key items that drive corporate value, such as know-how and market share, are also not recorded (see Real-Life Nugget 5.2). Neither is the value of human assets recorded! For example, what is the greatest asset of football clubs? You might think it was the footballers like David Beckham or Michael Owen. However, conventionally these players would not be valued as assets on the balance sheet unless they have been transferred from another club. Nor, in the case of zoos, would the animals bred in captivity be valued.

REAL-LIFE NUGGET 5.2

Missing Assets

In many respects, the current reporting model is more suited to a manufacturing economy than one based on services and knowledge. For example, it does a good job measuring historical costs of physical assets, like plant and equipment. But it ignores many of the key drivers of corporate value, such as know-how and market share. The result is incomplete, or distorted, information about a company's worth, and diminished relevance to investors.

Source: Dennis M. Nally, *The Future of Financial Reporting* (1999), International Financial Reporting Conference From Web http://www.amazon.co.uk/exec/abidos/ASIN

Interpretation

Given the above limitations, any meaningful interpretation of amounts recorded in balance sheets is difficult. However, there are ratios which are derived from the balance sheet which are used to assess the financial position of a business. These ratios are dealt with in more depth in Chapter 9. Here we just briefly comment on liquidity (i.e., cash position) and long-term capital structure.

The balance sheet records both current assets and current liabilities. This can be used to assess the short-term liquidity (i.e., short-term cash position) of a business. There are a variety of ratios such as the current ratio (current assets divided by current liabilities) and quick ratio (current assets minus stock then divided by current liabilities) which do this. In addition, the balance sheet records the long-term capital structure of a business. It is particularly useful in determining how dependent a business is on external borrowings. In Soundbite 5.5, for example, excessive borrowing created a balance sheet where there was negative net worth.

SOUNDBITE 5.5

Balance Sheet

'[MCI's balance sheet] looked like Rome after the Visigoths had finished with it. We had a $90-million negative net worth, and we owed the bank $100 million, which was so much that they couldn't call the loan without destroying the company.'

W.G. McGowgan, *Henderson Winners*, p. 187

Source: *The Executive's Book of Quotations* (1994), p. 81

Listed Companies

Listed Companies in Europe follow International Financial Reporting Standards. Their balance sheet is presented differently from that of sole traders, partnerships or non-listed companies. In particular, there is a different presentation and terminology. Several examples of listed companies balance sheets are given in this book (see, for example, Volkswagen in Appendix 2.2 and AstraZeneca in The Company Camera 7.4). They are all slightly different as there is no standardised format. A different terminology is also used. The main differences are listed in Figure 5.8. Listed companies are covered in more depth in Chapter 7.

Figure 5.8   Special Terminology for Listed Companies

Sole Traders, Partnerships, Non-Listed Companies	Listed Companies
Fixed Assets	Property, plant and equipment
Stocks	Inventories
Debtors	Trade receivables
Creditors	Trade payables
Capital	Equity
Long-term liabilities	Non-current liabilities

Conclusion

The balance sheet is a key financial statement. It shows the net assets of a business at a particular point of time. The three main constituents of the balance sheet are assets (fixed and current), liabilities (current and long-term) and capital. Normally a vertical balance sheet is used to portray these elements. The balance sheet itself is difficult to interpret because of missing assets and inconsistently valued assets. However, it is commonly used to assess the liquidity position of a firm.

 Discussion Questions

Questions with numbers in blue have answers at the back of the book.

Q1   The balance sheet and profit and loss account (income statement) provide complementary, but contrasting information. Discuss.

Q2   What are the main limitations of the balance sheet and how can they be overcome?

Q3   Is the balance sheet of any use?

Q4   Are the different elements of the balance sheet changing over time, for example, as manufacturing industry gives way to service industry?

Q5   State whether the following are true or false. If false, explain why.
(a) A balance sheet is a collection of assets, liabilities and capital.
(b) Stock, bank and creditors are all current assets.
(c) Total net assets are fixed assets plus current assets less current liabilities.
(d) Total net assets equal closing capital.
(e) An accrual is an amount prepaid, for example, rent paid in advance.

Q&A   Numerical Questions

Questions with numbers in blue have answers at the back of the book.

Q1   The following financial details are for Jane Bricker as at 31 December 2009.

	£		£
Capital 1 January 2005	5,000	Profit	12,000
Drawings	7,000		

Required: Jane Bricker's capital employed as at 31 December 2009.

Q2   Alpa Shah has the following financial details as at 30 June 2009.

	£		£
Fixed assets	100,000	Current liabilities	30,000
Current assets	50,000	Long-term creditors	20,000

Required: Alpa Shah's total net assets as at 30 June 2009.

Q3   Jill Jenkins has the following financial details as at 31 December 2005.

	£		£
Stock	18,000	Cash	4,000
Debtors	8,000	Creditors	12,000

Required: Jill Jenkins' net current assets as at 31 December 2005.

Q4   Janet Richards has the following financial details as at 31 December 2005.

	£		£
Land and buildings	100,000	Creditors	15,000
Plant and machinery	60,000	Long-term loan	15,000
Stock	40,000	Opening capital	200,000
Debtors	30,000	Net profit	28,000
Cash	20,000	Drawings	8,000
		Closing capital	220,000

Required: Janet Richards' balance sheet as at 31 December 2005.

Appendix 5.1: Horizontal Format of Balance Sheet

R. Beer's Balance Sheet as at 31 March 2010 (presented in horizontal format)

	£	£		£	£
Capital Employed			**Fixed Assets**		
Opening capital		80,257	Land and buildings		71,572
Add Profit		8,350	Plant and machinery		3,500
		88,607	Furniture and fittings		5,834
Less Drawings		9,366	Motor vehicles		3,398
Closing capital		79,241	Total fixed assets		84,304
Long-term loan		6,500			
		85,741			
Current Liabilities			**Current Assets**		
Creditors	3,991		Stock	2,200	
Loan	1,000	4,991	Debtors	100	
			Prepayments	50	
			Bank	3738	
			Cash	340	6,428
		90,732			90,732

Chapter 6

"Mr Evans was the chief accountant of a large manufacturing concern. Every day, on arriving at work, he would unlock the bottom drawer of his desk, peer at something inside, then close and lock the drawer. He had done this for 25 years. The entire staff was intrigued but no one was game to ask him what was in the drawer. Finally, the time came for Mr Evans to retire. There was a farewell party with speeches and a presentation. As soon as Mr Evans had left the buildings, some of the staff rushed into his office, unlocked the bottom drawer and peered in. Taped to the bottom of the drawer was a sheet of paper. It read, 'The debit side is the one nearest the window'."

R. Andrews, Funny Business, C.A. Magazine, April 2000, p. 26

Learning Outcomes

After completing this chapter you should be able to:

✔ **Show how the trial balance is used as a basis for preparing the financial statements.**

Preparing the Financial Statements

✔ Prepare the profit and loss account and the balance sheet.

✔ Understand the post-trial balance adjustments commonly made to the accounts.

✔ Prepare the profit and loss account and balance sheet using post-trial balance adjustments.

In a Nutshell

- *The trial balance when rearranged creates a profit and loss account and a balance sheet.*

- *The profit and loss account presents sales, cost of sales, other income and expenses.*

- *The balance sheet consists of assets, liabilities and capital.*

- *Sales less cost of sales less expenses gives net profit.*

- *Net profit is the balancing figure in the balance sheet.*

- *There are five main post-trial balance adjustments to the accounts: closing stock, accruals, prepayments, depreciation and doubtful debts.*

- *All five adjustments are made twice to maintain the double-entry: first, in the profit and loss account and, second, in the balance sheet.*

Introduction

A trial balance is prepared after the bookkeeping process of recording the financial transactions in a double-entry form. The bookkeeping stage is really one of aggregating and summarising the financial information. The next step is to prepare a profit and loss account and balance sheet from the trial balance. In essence, the profit and loss account sets out income less expenses and thus determines profit. Meanwhile, the balance sheet presents the assets and liabilities, including owner's capital. The two statements are seen as complementary. Chapters 4 and 5 discussed the nature and purpose of the profit and loss account and balance sheet. This present chapter looks at the mechanics of how we prepare the final accounts from the trial balance. It is thus a continuation of Chapter 3. These mechanics are the same for sole traders, partnerships and companies. However, listed companies (see Chapter 7) use a different format and terminology.

Main Financial Statements

Essentially, the two main financial statements rearrange the items in the trial balance. The profit for the year effectively links the profit and loss account and the balance sheet. In the **profit and loss account profit is income less expenses paid,** while in the **balance sheet, closing capital less drawings and opening capital give profit.** Looked at another way profit represents the increase in capital over the year. Profit is a key figure in the accounts and plays a vital part in linking the profit and loss account to the balance sheet. Profit is often reported graphically by companies in their annual reports. Rentokil Initial plc's profit figure is given in The Company Camera 6.1.

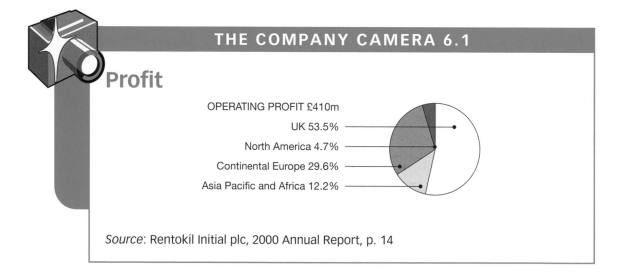

THE COMPANY CAMERA 6.1

Profit

OPERATING PROFIT £410m

UK 53.5%

North America 4.7%

Continental Europe 29.6%

Asia Pacific and Africa 12.2%

Source: Rentokil Initial plc, 2000 Annual Report, p. 14

Trial Balance to Profit and Loss Account and Balance Sheet

The elements of the trial balance need to be arranged to form the profit and loss account and balance sheet. Different organisations (for example, sole traders, partnerships and limited companies) all have slightly different formats for their balance sheets. However, the basic structure remains the same. For the sole trader, we normally refer to the trading and profit and loss account, rather than the profit and loss account. For illustrative purposes, we continue the example of Gavin Stevens, a sole trader, who is setting up a hotel. The format used here is that followed by most UK companies, except for listed companies, and broadly adheres to the requirements of the UK Companies Acts. There is *no prescribed format* for sole traders, therefore, *for consistency this book broadly adopts the format used by non-listed companies*. The individual items were explained in more detail in Chapters 4 and 5. It is worth pointing out that the cash flow statement is usually derived from the profit and loss account and balance sheet once they have been prepared and *not* from the trial balance (see Chapter 8).

Gavin Stevens, Continued

In Chapter 3, we prepared the trial balance. We now can use this to prepare the profit and loss account, and balance sheet. However, when we prepare the financial accounts we also need to collect information on the amount of stock held and on any expenses which are yet to be paid or have been paid in advance. In this example, we set out more details about stock, amounts owing for telephone and amounts prepaid for electricity in the notes to the trial balance. It is important to realise that none of these items have so far been entered into the books. We deal with these adjustments in more depth later in this chapter.

Gavin Stevens
Trial Balance as at 7 January

		Debit £	Credit £
Hotel		110,000	
Van		3,000	
Sales			9,000
Purchases		5,000	
Capital			200,000
Sales returns		70	
Purchases returns			500
Bank		86,915	
Electricity		300	
Wages		1,000	
Debtors	Ireton	1,965	
	Hepworth	2,500	
Creditors	Hogen		250
	Lewis		1,000
		210,750	210,750

Notes:
1. Gavin Stevens does not use all the catering supplies. He estimates that the amount of catering supplies left as closing stock is £50.
2. There is a special arrangement with the electricity company in which Gavin Stevens pays £300 in advance for a quarter. By 7 January he has used £50 which means he has prepaid £250. This is known as a prepayment.
3. There is a telephone bill yet to be received. However, Gavin Stevens estimates that he owes £100. This is known as an accrual.

We now prepare the trading and profit and loss account following the steps in Helpnote 6.1.

 HELPNOTE 6.1

Presentational Guide to the Four Steps (Given as A–D in Gavin Stevens' Trading and Profit and Loss Account)

In terms of presentation, we should note:

■ We must first determine cost of sales (Step A). This is, at its simplest, opening stock add purchases less closing stock. Purchases must be adjusted for purchases returns.

■ Sales less cost of sales gives gross profit (Step B). Sales must be adjusted for sales returns.

■ We list and total all expenses (Step C).

■ We determine net profit (Step D) by taking expenses away from gross profit.

Gavin Stevens
Trading and Profit and Loss Account for Week Ended 7 January

	£	£	£		
Sales			9,000		
Less Sales returns			70		
			8,930		
Less *Cost of Sales*					Trading account
Opening stock		–			
Add Purchases	5,000				
Less Purchases returns	500	4,500			
Less Closing stock		50	4,450	A	
Gross Profit			4,480	B	
Less *Expenses*					
Electricity		50			
Wages		1,000			Profit and loss account
Telephone		100	1,150	C	
Net Profit			3,330	D	

Points to notice:

1. All the figures are from the trial balance except for closing stock £50, electricity £50 and telephone £100 (from notes) and profit £3,330 (calculated).
2. The first part of the statement down to gross profit (B) (sales less cost of sales (A)) is called the trading account. It deals with sales and purchases. Essentially sales returns and purchases returns are deducted from sales and purchases, respectively. Stock is simply unsold purchases.
3. Gross profit (B) is sales minus cost of sales.
4. Net profit (D) is sales minus cost of sales minus expenses (C).
5. Net profit of £3,330 is also found in the balance sheet. It is the balancing item, simply income minus expenses.

We now prepare the balance sheet following the steps in Helpnote 6.2.

HELPNOTE 6.2

Presentational Guide to the Five Steps (Given as A–E in Gavin Stevens' Balance Sheet)

In terms of presentation, we should note:

■ All the fixed assets are added together (Step A).

■ Current assets less current liabilities are determined next (i.e., net current assets). This is often termed the working capital and represents the day-to-day trading resources of the business (Step B).

■ The total assets less current liabilities are determined (Step C).

■ If there are any long-term creditors these are deducted to arrive at total net assets (Step D).

■ Capital employed is determined. Effectively, net profit is added to opening capital to give closing capital (Step E).

Gavin Stevens
Balance Sheet as at 7 January

	£	£	£	
Fixed Assets				
Hotel			110,000	
Van			3,000	
			113,000	A
Current Assets				
Stock	50			
Debtors (£1,965 + £2,500)	4,465			
Electricity prepayment	250			
Bank	86,915	91,680		
Current Liabilities				
Creditors (£250 + £1,000)	(1,250)			
Telephone bill accrued	(100)	(1,350)		
Net current assets			90,330	B
Total net assets			203,330	C,D
Capital Employed			£	
Opening capital			200,000	
Add Net profit			3,330	
Closing capital			203,330	E

Points to notice:

1. All figures are from the trial balance except for closing stock £50, electricity prepayment £250, telephone bill (from notes) and profit £3,330 (balancing figure). Except for electricity all *these* figures are the same in the trading and profit and loss account. Electricity is different because in effect, we are splitting up £300. Thus:

Total paid £300 = £50 used up as an expense in the profit and
loss account, and
£250 not used up recorded as an asset in the
balance sheet.

2. Our statement is divided into fixed assets, current assets, current liabilities and capital employed.

3. The debtors are the trial balance figures for Ireton and Hepworth; the creditors those for Hogen and Lewis.

4. Our opening capital plus our net profit gives us our closing capital. In other words, the business owes Gavin Stevens £200,000 at 1 January, but £203,330 at 7 January.
5. Net profit of £3,330 is also found in the trading and profit and loss account. It is the balancing item. As we saw from Pause for Thought 6.1, the profit can be seen as the increase in net assets over the year. Or, alternatively, it can be viewed as assets less liabilities less opening capital.
6. The balance sheet balances. In other words total net assets equals closing capital.

PAUSE FOR THOUGHT 6.2

Accounting Equation and Gavin Stevens

How does the Gavin Stevens example we have just completed fit the accounting equation?

If we take our expanded accounting equation:

Assets + Expenses = Liabilities + Capital + Income

and rearrange it,

Assets − (Liabilities + Capital) = Income − Expenses

Now, if we substitute the figures from Gavin Stevens, we have:

Fixed assets (£113,000) + Current assets (£91,680) − (Current liabilities (£1,350) + Opening capital (£200,000)) = Income (£8,930) − (Cost of sales (£4,450) + Expenses (£1,150))

∴ £113,000 + £91,680 − (£1,350 + £200,000) = £8,930 − (£4,450 + £1,150)
∴ £204,680 − £201,350 = £8,930 − £5,600
∴ £3,330 = £3,330

The £3,330 represents net profit. This net profit, therefore, provides a bridge between the balance sheet and the profit and loss account.

Adjustments to Trial Balance

The trial balance is prepared from the books of account and is then adjusted for certain items. These items represent estimates or adjustments which typically do not form part of the initial double-entry process. Five of the main adjustments are *closing stock, accruals, prepayments, depreciation*, and *bad and doubtful debts*. The mechanics of their accounting treatment is discussed here. However, the items themselves are discussed in more depth in Chapters 4 and 5 on the profit and loss account and balance sheet.

Stock

Stock is an important asset to any business, especially manufacturing businesses. Stock control systems in large businesses can be very complex and sophisticated. In most sole traders and in many other businesses it is normal not to record the detailed physical movements (i.e., purchases and sales of stock). Stock is not, therefore, formally recorded in these organisations in the double-entry process. However, at the balance sheet date stock is valued. To maintain the double-entry, the asset of stock is entered twice: *first* in the trading part of the trading and profit and loss account; and *second*, in the current assets section of the balance sheet. These two figures for accounting purposes cancel out and thus the double-entry is maintained. Last year's closing stock figure becomes the current year's opening stock figure. The term inventory is usually used in listed company accounts.

Accruals

Accruals are the amounts we owe to the suppliers of services such as telephone or light and heat. In small businesses, accruals are normally excluded from the initial double-entry process. Accruals appear in the final accounts in two places. *First*, the amount owing is included in the profit and loss account under expenses. *Second*, a matching amount is included under current liabilities in the balance sheet. The double-entry is thus maintained. Figure 6.1 on the next page gives an example of accruals and prepayments (payments in advance for services).

Prepayments

Prepayments represent the amount paid in advance to the suppliers of services, for example rent paid in advance. In many ways prepayments are the opposite of accruals. Whereas accruals must be added to the final accounts to achieve the matching concept, a prepayment must be deducted. The amount paid in advance is treated as an asset which will be used up at a future date. It is therefore excluded from the accounts.

Figure 6.1 Accruals and Prepayments

From the following information calculate the trading and profit and loss, and balance sheet entries for:

1. Electricity

Mary Christmas has received three electricity bills for the year (£300, £400, £550). Another bill is due which is estimated at £600.

2. Rent

The quarterly rent for Mary Christmas's offices is £300 payable in advance. The first payment, when the business starts, is made on 1st January, the last on 31st December.

---

1. Electricity

Effectively, the total bill incurred for the year is the amount paid (£300 + £400 + £550) £1,250 and the amount due £600. Therefore, the total bill is £1,850; this is included in the profit and loss account. In the balance sheet, £600 is included.

2. Rent

The amount paid is 5 × £300 = £1,500.

However, only £1,200 relates to this year and should go in the trading and profit and loss account. The £300 balance is a prepayment in the balance sheet.

Trading and Profit and Loss Account		Balance Sheet	
Expenses	**£**	**Current Assets**	**£**
Electricity	1,850	Rent prepaid	300
Rent	1,200	**Current Liabilities**	
		Electricity owing	600

PAUSE FOR THOUGHT 6.3

Accruals and Prepayments

Can you think of four examples of accruals and prepayments?

. . . .

We might have, for example:

Accruals	*Prepayments*
Electricity owing	Rent paid in advance
Business rates owing	Prepaid electricity on metre
Rent owing	Prepaid standing charge for telephone
Telephone owing	Insurance paid in advance

Depreciation

As we saw in Chapter 5, fixed assets wear out over time and depreciation seeks to recognise this. Depreciation in the accounts is simply recording this – twice. *First*, a proportion of the original cost is allocated as an expense in the profit and loss account. *Second*, an equivalent amount is deducted from the fixed assets in the balance sheet (see Figure 6.2).

Figure 6.2   Example of Depreciation

A business has five assets shown at cost. Ten per cent of the original cost of each asset has been allocated as depreciation. Record the transactions in the accounts.

	£
Premises	80,000
Machine	75,000
Office furniture	12,000
Computer	1,500
Motor van	6,000

There are two parts to this. **First**, we record 10% of the original cost as an expense in the expenses section of the trading and profit and loss account.

Trading and Profit and Loss Account (Year 1)

Expenses	£
Depreciation on premises	8,000
Depreciation on machine	7,500
Depreciation on office furniture	1,200
Depreciation on computer	150
Depreciation on motor van	600

Second, we record the original cost, total depreciation (called accumulated depreciation) and net book value (original cost less depreciation) in the balance sheet. Note that accumulated depreciation is recorded in brackets – this shows it is being taken away.

Balance Sheet (Year 1)

Fixed Assets	£ Cost	£ Accumulated depreciation	£ Net book value
Premises	80,000	(8,000)	72,000
Machine	75,000	(7,500)	67,500
Office furniture	12,000	(1,200)	10,800
Computer	1,500	(150)	1,350
Motor van	6,000	(600)	5,400
	174,500	(17,450)	157,050

In next year's trial balance, the cost and accumulated depreciation figures would be recorded. The *accumulated depreciatio* is often called *provision for depreciation*. This example records only one year's depreciation. However, in future years, there will be more depreciation, which is why it is called accumulated depreciation.

In the following year, we also have 10% depreciation. The trading and profit and loss account is thus the same.

Trading and Profit and Loss Account (Year 2)

Expenses	£
Depreciation on premises	8,000
Depreciation on machine	7,500
Depreciation on office furniture	1,200
Depreciation on computer	150
Depreciation on motor van	600

In the balance sheet, however, we *add* this year's depreciation to the accumulated depreciation figure. We, therefore, have:

Balance Sheet (Year 2)

Fixed Assets	£ Cost	£ Accumulated depreciation	£ Net book value
Premises	80,000	(16,000)	64,000
Machine	75,000	(15,000)	60,000
Office furniture	12,000	(2,400)	9,600
Computer	1,500	(300)	1,200
Motor van	6,000	(1,200)	4,800
	174,500	(34,900)	139,600

In essence, we have merely added the two years' depreciation figures. Thus, for premises, our opening figure for accumulated depreciation was £8,000. We then added this year's depreciation to arrive at £16,000. The net book value is simply the residual figure.

For east of understanding these same figures are used in our comprehensive example, Live Wire, later in this chapter.

Rentokil Initial plc's fixed assets (as recorded in its 2004 balance sheet) are then given as an illustration in the Company Camera 6.2. As you can see, they can be quite complex.

THE COMPANY CAMERA 6.2

Fixed Assets

Tangible Fixed Assets	Land and Buildings	Plant, Equipment & Tropical Plants	Vehicles and Office Equipment	Total
	£m	£m	£m	£m
Consolidated				
Cost				
At 1st January 2004	311.4	665.8	361.9	1,339.1
Exchange adjustments	(0.5)	2.8	(0.4)	1.9
Additions at cost	10.8	138.9	45.0	194.7
On acquisition (note 31)	1.7	1.7	0.3	3.7
Disposal of businesses (note 32)	(3.0)	(1.3)	(4.2)	(8.5)
Disposals	(3.2)	(106.4)	(36.8)	(146.4)
At 31st December 2004	**317.2**	**701.5**	**365.8**	**1,384.5**
Aggregate depreciation				
At 1st January 2004	49.9	407.1	219.3	676.3
Exchange adjustments	(0.2)	1.7	(0.2)	1.3
Disposal of businesses (note 32)	(0.1)	(0.9)	(3.1)	(4.1)
Depreciation	5.2	122.2	37.1	164.5
Impairment losses (note 3)	9.3	–	–	9.3
Disposals	(1.2)	(104.9)	(32.4)	(138.5)
At 31st December 2004	**62.9**	**425.2**	**220.7**	**708.8**
Net book value at 31st December 2004	**254.3**	**276.3**	**145.1**	**675.7**
Net book value at 31st December 2003	**261.5**	**258.7**	**142.6**	**662.8**
Fixed assets held under finance leases:				
Cost	23.3	6.8	41.0	71.1
Aggregate depreciation	4.5	5.1	18.7	28.3
Net book value at 31st December 2004	**18.8**	**1.7**	**22.3**	**42.8**
Parent				
Cost				
At 1st January 2004	2.1	6.2	4.8	13.1
Additions at cost	–	0.1	2.0	2.1
Disposals	–	(0.2)	(1.4)	(1.6)
At 31st December 2004	**2.1**	**6.1**	**5.4**	**13.6**
Aggregate depreciation				
At 1st January 2004	1.1	4.2	3.2	8.5
Depreciation	0.1	–	1.3	1.4
Disposals	–	(0.1)	(1.2)	(1.3)
At 31st December 2004	**1.2**	**4.1**	**3.3**	**8.6**
Net book value at 31st December 2004	**0.9**	**2.0**	**2.1**	**5.0**
Net book value at 31st December 2003	1.0	2.0	1.6	4.6

THE COMPANY CAMERA 6.2 (*continued*)

	£m	£m	£m	£m
Fixed assets held under finance leases:				
Cost	–	–	1.2	1.2
Aggregate depreciation	–	–	0.6	0.6
Net book value at 31st December 2004	–	–	0.6	0.6

Source: Rentokil Initial plc, 2004 Annual Report, p. 56

Bad and Doubtful Debts

This is the last of the five adjustments. Bad and doubtful debts are also considered in Chapter 5 on the balance sheet. Essentially, some debts *may* not be collected. These are termed doubtful debts.

Other debts *will definitely not* be collected; they are called bad debts. The accounting entries to record this are in the profit and loss account as an expense and in the balance sheet as a reduction in debtors. Some businesses, such as building societies and banks, typically carry a high level of bad and doubtful debts. The Company Camera 6.3 shows the bad and doubtful debts for Vodafone, the UK mobile phone company.

THE COMPANY CAMERA 6.3

Doubtful Debts

Debtors are stated after allowances for bad and doubtful debts, an analysis of which is as follows:

	2004	2003	2002
	£m	£m	£m
Opening balance at 1 April	520	526	293
Exchange adjustments	(20)	17	29
Amounts charged to the profit and loss account	209	193	196
Acquisitions	11	2	108
Disposals	(21)	–	–
Debtors written off	(238)	(218)	(100)
Closing balance at 31 March	461	520	526

Source: Vodafone, 2004 Annual Report, p. 88

When considering the accounting treatment of bad and doubtful debts, it is crucial to distinguish between bad and doubtful debts.

1. Bad Debts

Bad debts are recorded as an expense in the profit and loss account and written off debtors in the balance sheet (see Figure 6.3).

Figure 6.3   Illustrative Example of Bad Debts

A business has debtors of £4,800, but estimates that bad debts will be £320.

Profit and Loss Account	£
Expenses	
Bad debts	320
Balance Sheet	
Current Assets	
Debtors less bad debts	
(£4,800 – £320)	4,480

For ease of understanding, these same figures are used in our comprehensive example, Live Wire, later in this chapter.

2. Provision for Doubtful Debts

A provision for doubtful debts is set up by a business for those debts it is dubious about collecting. This provision is *always* deducted from debtors in the balance sheet. However, only *increases or decreases* in the provision are entered in the profit and loss account. An *increase* is recorded as an *expense* and a *decrease* as an *income* (see Figure 6.4). *Where there are both bad and doubtful debts, the provision for doubtful debts is calculated first.*

Figure 6.4   Illustrative Example of Doubtful Debtors

A business has debtors of £4,800. There is a doubtful debt provision of 10% of debtors. Last year debtors were £2,400 and the doubtful debt provision was £240.

Profit and Loss Account	£
Expenses	
Increase in doubtful debt provision (£480 – £240)	*240*
Balance Sheet	
Current Assets	
Debtors less provision for doubtful debts	
(£4,800 – £480)	*4,320*

For ease of understanding, these same figures are used in our comprehensive example, Live Wire, later in this chapter.

It is now time to introduce some items commonly found in accounts. These are briefly explained in Figure 6.5. Mainly we focus on the accounts of a sole trader. Goodwill and other intangible assets such as brands (i.e., assets that we cannot touch) are discussed in more detail in Chapter 12.

SOUNDBITE 6.1

Debts

'A small debt makes a man your debtor, a large one makes him your enemy.'

Seneca (Ad Lucilium xix)

Source: *The Executive's Book of Quotations* (1994), p. 80

Figure 6.5 Introducing Common Items Found in the Final Accounts

Item	Explanation	Location
Bank overdraft	This is where the business owes the bank money. Too many students are in this position!	Balance sheet Current liabilities
Carriage inwards	This is usually found in manufacturing businesses. It is a cost of purchasing raw materials. It refers to the days when goods were brought in by horse-and-carriage.	Trading and profit and loss account Trading account Added to purchases
Carriage outwards	Similar to carriage inwards, except that it is an expense incurred by the business when selling goods.	Trading and profit and loss account Profit and loss account Expenses
Discount allowed	This is discount allowed by the business to customers for prompt payment. In other words, instead of paying, say £100, the customer pays £95. The sale of £100 is recorded as normal, but discount allowed is recorded separately.	Trading and profit and loss account Profit and loss account Expenses
Discount received	Similar to discount allowed. However, it is received by the business from the supplier for paying promptly. The business therefore, pays less. The purchase is recorded as normal, the discount received is recorded separately.	Trading and profit and loss account Proft and loss account Other income
Drawings	This is money which the sole trader or owner takes out for his or her living expenses. It is, in effect, the owner's salary. It is really a withdrawal of capital.	Balance sheet Capital employed *Note*: Do *not* put in expenses
Income receivable*	This is income which is received by the business from a third party. Examples, include dividends receivable from companies or interest receivable from the bank. Income received is a narrower term found in the cash statement.	Trading and profit and loss account Profit and loss account Other income
Interest payable*	This is the reverse of income receivable. It is interest payable by the business to outsiders, especially on bank loans. Interest paid is a narrower term found in the cash flow statement.	Trading and profit and loss account Profit and loss account Expenses
Long-term loan	This is a loan not repayable within a year. The loan may be with a bank or other organisation. Sometimes long-term loans are called debentures.	Balance sheet Long-term creditors

*Income receivable and interest payable are broader phrases than interest received and interest paid. They include interest earned yet to be received and interest incurred yet to be paid, respectively.

Comprehensive Example

We now close this chapter with a comprehensive example. This example includes most items normally found in the accounts of a sole trader. We use the example of a small engineering business run by Live Wire, which buys and sells electrical products. The trial balance is provided in Figure 6.6(a), and then in Figure 6.6(b) are the trading and profit and loss account, the balance sheet and the explanatory notes.

Figure 6.6   Worked Example of a Sole Trader's Accounts

(a)	Debit £	Credit £
Sales		250,000
Sales returns	800	
Purchases	100,000	
Purchases returns		600
Carriage inwards	200	
Carriage outwards	300	
Discounts allowed	150	
Discounts receivable		175
Dividends receivable		225
Interest receivable		100
Drawings	26,690	
Advertising	1,250	
Telephone	2,150	
Wages	27,000	
Electricity	3,700	
Business rates	1,500	
Travelling expenses	1,200	
Van repairs	650	
Petrol	3,800	
General expenses	1,200	
Insurance	1,500	
Premises at cost	80,000	
Accumulated depreciation as at 1 January 2009		8,000
Machine at cost	75,000	
Accumulated depreciation as at 1 January 2009		7,500
Office furniture at cost	12,000	
Accumulated depreciation as at 1 January 2009		1,200
Computer at cost	1,500	
Accumulated depreciation as at 1 January 2009		150
Motor van at cost	6,000	
Accumulated depreciation as at 1 January 2009		600
Opening stock	9,000	
Cash at bank	7,050	
Bank overdraft		3,600
Debtors	4,800	
Provision for doubtful debts as at 1 January 2009		240
Creditors		9,800
Long-term loan		15,600
Interest payable	1,150	
Capital		70,800
	368,590	368,590

Live Wire
Trial Balance as at 31 December 2009

Figure 6.6   Worked Example of a Sole Trader's Accounts (*continued*)

You have the following extra information:
(i)   Closing stock at 31 December 2009 was £8,600.
(ii) Of the insurance £500 was paid in advance.
(iii) Live Wire still owes £450 for the telephone.
(iv) Depreciation is charged at 10 % on the cost of the fixed assets (i.e., £8,000 for premises, £7,500 for machine, £1,200 for office furniture, £150 for computer and £600 for motor van). The accumulated depreciation is the depreciation charged to date.
(v)   Bad debts are £320. They have not yet been written off. The provision for doubtful debts has increased from £240 to £480 and is 10 % of debtors.

Required: Live Wire's Trading and Profit and Loss Account for year ended 31 December 2009 and Balance Sheet as at 31 December 2009

Live Wire

Trading and Profit and Loss Account Year Ended 31 December 2009

	£	£	£
Sales			250,000
Less Sales returns			800
			249,200
Less *Cost of Sales*			
Opening stock		9,000	
Add Purchases	100,000		
Carriage inwards	200		
	100,200		
Less Purchases returns	600	99,600	
		108,600	
Less Closing stock (Note 2)		8,600	100,000
Gross Profit			149,200
Add *Other Income*			
Discounts receivable		175	
Dividends receivable		225	
Interest receivable		100	500
			149,700
Less *Expenses*			
Carriage outwards		300	
Discounts allowed		150	
Advertising		1,250	
Telephone (Note 3)		2,600	
Wages		27,000	
Electricity		3,700	
Business rates		1,500	
Travelling expenses		1,200	
Van repairs		650	
Petrol		3,800	
General expenses		1,200	
Insurance (Note 4)		1,000	
Interest payable		1,150	
Depreciation (Note 5)			
Premises		8,000	
Machine		7,500	
Office furniture		1,200	
Computer		150	
Motor van		600	
Bad debts (Note 6)		320	
Doubtful debts (Note 7)		240	63,510
Net Profit			86,190

Figure 6.6   Worked Example of a Sole Trader's Accounts (*continued*)

(b)

Live Wire
Balance Sheet as at 31 December 2009

	£ Cost	£ Accumulated depreciation (Note 5)	£ Net book value
Fixed Assets			
Premises	80,000	(16,000)	64,000
Machine	75,000	(15,000)	60,000
Office furniture	12,000	(2,400)	9,600
Computer	1,500	(300)	1,200
Motor van	6,000	(1,200)	4,800
	174,500	(34,900)	139,600
Current Assets			
Stocks (Note 2)	8,600		
Debtors less bad and doubtful debts (Notes 6,7)	4,000		
Prepayments (Note 4)	500		
Cash at bank	7,050	20,150	
Current Liabilities			
Creditors	(9,800)		
Bank overdraft	(3,600)		
Accruals (Note 3)	(450)	(13,850)	
Net current assets			6,300
Total assets less current liabilities			145,900
Long-term Creditors			(15,600)
Total net assets			130,300
Capital Employed			£
Opening capital			70,800
Add Net profit			86,190
			156,990
Less Drawings			26,690
Closing capital			130,300

Notes:

1. All the figures in Live Wire's accounts, except for closing stock, telephone, insurance, depreciation, and bad and doubtful debts are as listed in the trial balance. The figures for profit and closing capital are calculated as balancing figures.
2. Closing stock of £8,600 is recorded in the trading account and in the balance sheet.
3. The telephone expense is adjusted for the £450 owing. In the profit and loss account, the expense increases to £2,600 (£2,150 + £450). In the balance sheet, the £450 owing becomes an accrual.
4. The insurance is adjusted for the £500 paid in advance. The expense in the profit and loss account thus becomes £1,000 (£1,500 − £500). The £500 is recorded as a prepayment in current assets in the balance sheet.
5. The depreciation for the year, which was the same as in Figure 6.2, has been recorded twice: *first* under expenses in the trading and profit and loss account, *second*, in the balance sheet under fixed assets. The double-entry is thus maintained.
6. The £320 for bad debts has been recorded twice: *first*, under expenses in the trading and profit and loss account, and, *second*, under current assets (debtors) in the balance sheet. The double-entry is thus completed (see also Figure 6.3).
7. Doubtful debts represents the increase in the provision for doubtful debts from £240 to £480. The increase of £240 is recorded twice. *First*, under expenses in the trading and profit and loss account, and, *second*, as part of the £480 deduction from debtors under current assets in the balance sheet. The double-entry is thus completed (see also Figure 6.4).

Conclusion

The two main financial statements – the trading and profit and loss account and the balance sheet – are both prepared from the trial balance. The trading and profit and loss account focuses on income, such as sales or dividends receivable, and expenses, such as telephone or electricity. The balance sheet, by contrast, focuses on assets, liabilities and owner's capital. In both financial statements, profit becomes the balancing figure.

After the trial balance has been prepared, the accounts are often adjusted for items such as closing stock, accruals (amounts owing), prepayments (amounts prepaid), depreciation (the wearing out of fixed assets), and bad and doubtful debts. In each case, we adjust the accounts twice: *first* in the trading and profit and loss account and *second* in the balance sheet. The double-entry and thus the symmetry of the accounts is thus maintained.

Q&A   Discussion Questions

Questions with numbers in blue have answers at the back of the book.

Q1   What is a sole trader and why is it important for the sole trader to prepare a set of financial statements?

Q2   'Profit is the figure which links the profit and loss account and the balance sheet.' Discuss.

Q3   Why do we need to carry out post-trial balance adjustments when we are preparing the final accounts?

Q&A   Numerical Questions

The numerical questions which follow are graded in difficulty. Those at the start are about as complex as the illustrative example, Gavin Stevens. They gradually become more complex, until the final questions equate to the illustrative example, Live Wire.

Questions with numbers in blue have answers at the back of the book.

Q1   Michael Anet has the following trial balance

M. Anet
Trial Balance as at 31 December 2009

	Debit £	Credit £
Hotel	40,000	
Van	10,000	
Sales		25,000
Purchases	15,000	
Capital		51,900
Bank	8,000	
Electricity	1,500	
Wages	2,500	
A. Brush (Debtor)	400	
A. Painter (Creditor)		500
	77,400	77,400

Required: Prepare Michael Anet's trading and profit and loss account for the year ended 31 December 2009 and balance sheet as at 31 December 2009.

Q2   Paul Icasso has the following trial balance.

P. Icasso
Trial Balance as at 31 March 2010

	Debit £	Credit £
Hotel	50,000	
Van	8,000	
Sales		35,000
Purchases	25,000	
Sales returns	3,000	
Purchases returns		4,000
Capital		60,050
Bank	9,000	
Electricity	1,000	
Advertising	800	
Debtors Shah	1,250	
Debtors Chan	2,250	
Creditors Jones		1,250
	100,300	100,300

Required: Prepare Paul Icasso's trading and profit and loss account for the year ended 31 March 2010 and a balance sheet as at 31 March 2010.

Q3 Rose Ubens, buys and sells goods. Her trial balance is presented below.

R. Ubens

Trial Balance as at 31 December 2009

	Debit £	Credit £
Opening stock	3,600	
Building	20,400	
Motor van	3,500	
Debtors	2,600	
Creditors		3,800
Cash at bank	4,400	
Electricity	1,500	
Advertising	300	
Printing and stationery	50	
Telephone	650	
Rent and rates	1,200	
Postage	150	
Drawings	7,800	
Capital		19,950
Sales		88,000
Purchases	66,000	
Sales returns	800	
Purchases returns		1,200
	112,950	112,950

Note:
1. Closing stock is £4,000

Required: Prepare Rose Ubens trading and profit and loss account for the year ended 31 December 2009 and a balance sheet as at 31 December 2009.

Q4 Clara Onstable has prepared her trial balance as at 31 December. She has the following additional information.
(a) She pays £240 rent per month. She has paid £3,600, the whole year's rent plus three months in advance.
(b) She has paid insurance costs of £480. However, she has paid £120 in advance.

Required: Prepare the extracts for the final accounts.

Q5   Vincent Gogh, a shopkeeper, has the following trial balance.

V. Gogh
Trial Balance as at 31 December 2009

	Debit £	Credit £
Sales		40,000
Sales returns	500	
Purchases	25,000	
Purchases returns		450
Opening stock	5,500	
Debtors	3,500	
Creditors		1,500
Cash at bank	1,300	
Long-term loan		3,700
Motor car	8,500	
Shop	9,000	
Business rates	1,000	
Rent	600	
Electricity	350	
Telephone	450	
Insurance	750	
General expenses	150	
Wages	10,500	
Drawings	12,900	
Capital		34,350
	80,000	80,000

You also have the following additional information.
1. Closing stock as at 31 December 2009 is £9,000.
2. V. Gogh owes £350 for electricity.
3. £200 of the rent is paid in advance.

Required: Prepare V. Gogh's trading and profit and loss account for the year ended 31 December 2009 and a balance sheet as at 31 December 2009.

Q6   Leonardo Da Vinci, who sells computers, has extracted the following balances from the accounts.

L. Da Vinci
Trial Balance as at 30 September 2009

	Debit £	Credit £
Sales		105,000
Sales returns	8,000	
Purchases	70,000	
Purchases returns		1,800
Opening stock of computers	6,500	
Drawings	8,500	
Debtors	12,000	
Creditors		13,000
Cash at bank	1,800	
Long-term loan		6,600
Discounts allowed	300	
Carriage inwards	250	
Business premises	18,000	
Motor van	7,500	
Computer	1,500	
Wages	32,500	
Electricity	825	
Telephone	325	
Insurance	225	
Rent	1,250	
Business rates	1,000	
Capital		44,075
	170,475	170,475

You have the following additional information.
1. Closing stock of computers as at 30 September 2009 is £7,000.
2. Da Vinci owes £175 for the telephone and £1,200 for electricity.
3. The prepayments are £25 for insurance and £250 for rent.

Required: Prepare Da Vinci's trading and profit and loss account for the year ended 30 September 2009 and a balance sheet as at 30 September 2009.

Q7   Helen Ogarth is preparing her accounts for the year to 31 December 2009. On 1 January 2009 she purchased the following fixed assets.

	£
Buildings	100,000
Machine	50,000
Motor van	20,000

She wishes to write off the following amounts for depreciation.

	£
Buildings	10,000
Machine	3,000
Motor van	2,000

Required: Prepare the appropriate extracts for the balance sheet and trading and profit and loss account.

Q8   Michael Atisse, a carpenter, has the following trial balance as at 31 December 2005.

	Debit £	Credit £
Work done		50,000
Purchases of materials	25,000	
Opening stock of tools	650	
Motor expenses	3,550	
Debtors	1,000	
Creditors		4,000
Cash at bank	3,600	
Long-term loan		16,800
Building at cost	52,300	
Motor car at cost	8,000	
Computer at cost	6,300	
Office equipment at cost	10,200	
Business rates	1,300	
Electricity	900	
Interest on loan	1,600	
Drawings	5,200	
Telephone	1,200	
Capital		50,000
	120,800	120,800

You have the following additional information.
1. Closing stock of tools   £4,500
2. Depreciation is to be written off the fixed assets as follows:

Buildings	£3,000
Motor car	£2,000
Computer	£1,400
Office equipment	£1,800

Required: Prepare M. Atisse's trading and profit and loss account for the year ended 31 December 2005 and the balance sheet as at 31 December 2005.

Q9   Clare Analetto, an antique dealer, has the following trial balance as at 31 December 2005.

	Debit £	Credit £
Sales		100,000
Sales returns	5,000	
Purchases	70,000	
Purchases returns		6,000
Opening stock of antiques	9,000	
Debtors	16,800	
Business rates	800	
Creditors		14,000
Cash at bank	17,100	
Long-term loan		12,000
Bank interest receivable		850
Rent	2,050	
Electricity	1,950	
Insurance	1,250	
Loan interest	1,200	
General expenses	1,025	
Motor van expenses	1,800	
Premises at cost	60,000	
Machinery at cost	16,500	
Office equipment at cost	1,750	
Motor car at cost	2,050	
Drawings	8,200	
Repairs to antiques	1,300	
Telephone	500	
Capital		85,425
	218,275	218,275

You also have the following notes to the accounts.
1. Closing stock of antiques is £7,000.
2. Depreciation for the year is to be charged at 2 % on premises, 10 % on machinery, 15 % on office equipment, and 25 % on the motor car.

Required: Prepare C. Analetto's trading and profit and loss account for the year ended 31 December 2005 and the balance sheet as at 31 December 2005.

Q10   Michelle Angelo has debtors of £40,000 at the year end. However, she feels that £4,000 are bad.

Required: Prepare the appropriate balance sheet and trading and profit and loss account extracts.

Q11   Simon Eurat, who runs a taxi business, has the following trial balance.

S. Eurat
Trial Balance as at 30 June 2005

	Debit £	Credit £
Cash overdrawn at bank		1,500
Long-term loan		3,550
Receipts		28,300
Diesel and oil	8,250	
Taxi repairs and service	3,950	
Radio hire	3,400	
Road fund licences	2,300	
Buildings at cost	68,000	
Taxis at cost	34,500	
Business rates	450	
Electricity	1,300	
Telephone	1,250	
Debtors	100	
Creditors for motor repairs		1,800
Insurance on buildings	1,300	
General expenses	850	
Drawings	9,600	
Bank interest	150	
Capital		103,250
Wages	3,000	
	138,400	138,400

You have the following additional information.
1. 10 % of the debtors are considered bad.
2. £800 of the insurance is prepaid.
3. There is £250 owing for electricity and £300 owing for telephone.
4. Depreciation on taxis is to be 25 % on cost and on buildings 2 % on cost.

Required: Prepare S. Eurat's trading and profit loss account for the year ended 30 June 2005 and balance sheet as at 30 June 2005.

Q12 Rebecca Odin has the following details of her fixed assets.

	Cost	Accumulated depreciation as at 31 December 2004
	£	£
Buildings	102,000	8,000
Machinery	65,000	6,500
Motor car	8,000	4,000
Computer	9,000	2,700

She charges depreciation at 2 % per annum on cost for buildings, 10 % per annum on cost for machinery, 25 % per annum on cost for the motor car and 15 % per annum on cost for the computer.

Required: Prepare the appropriate extracts for
(a) the balance sheet as at 31 December 2004.
(b) the trading and loss account for year ended 31 December 2005 and for the balance sheet as at 31 December 2005.

Q13   Deborah Urer owns a small bar. Her trial balance as at 30 June 2005 is set out below.

	Debit £	Credit £
Takings from sales		145,150
Purchases of beer, wine and spirits	83,250	
Discounts receivable		450
Dividends receivable		150
Drawings	26,400	
Advertising	3,600	
Motor expenses	1,750	
Telephone	2,800	
Electricity	1,250	
Insurance	1,900	
General expenses	2,250	
Repairs	350	
Premises at cost	20,340	
Accumulated depreciation as at 1 July 2004		6,300
Bar equipment at cost	8,200	
Accumulated depreciation as at 1 July 2004		2,500
Bar furniture at cost	5,600	
Accumulated depreciation as at 1 July 2004		1,800
Motor car at cost	3,600	
Accumulated depreciation as at 1 July 2004		2,000
Debtors	220	
Provision for doubtful debts		20
Loan interest	650	
Creditors		3,650
Cash at bank	4,350	
Long-term loan		6,500
Wages	2,560	
Business rates	2,450	
Opening stock	5,500	
Capital		8,500
	177,020	177,020

You also have the following additional information.
1. Closing stock is £6,250.
2. There is £200 owing for electricity and £300 of the insurance is prepaid.
3. Bad debts are £25.
4. The doubtful debt provision is to be increased to £25 on 30 June 2005.
5. There are the following depreciation charges:

    2 % on premises

    10 % on bar equipment and bar furniture

    25 % on motor car

Required: Prepare D. Urer's trading and profit and loss account for the year ended 30 June 2005 and the balance sheet as at 30 June 2005.

Q14   Bernard Ruegel has drawn up a trial balance which is presented below.

B. Ruegel
Trial Balance as at 30 September 2005

	Debit £	Credit £
Carriage inwards	350	
Carriage outwards	180	
Discounts allowed	80	
Discounts receivable		75
Sales		208,275
Sales returns	185	
Purchases	110,398	
Drawings	38,111	
Purchases returns		98
Interest receivable		790
Advertising	1,987	
Telephone	476	
Wages and salaries	10,298	
Electricity	1,466	
Rent	2,873	
Cash at bank	21,611	
Travelling expenses	1,288	
Van repairs	1,471	
Petrol	2,187	
Business rates	2,250	
General expenses	1,921	
Insurance	1,100	
Premises at cost	50,981	
Accumulated depreciation as at 1 October 2004		28,300
Machine at cost	21,634	
Accumulated depreciation as at 1 October 2004		8,200
Office furniture at cost	8,011	
Accumulated depreciation as at 1 October 2004		2,386
Computer at cost	2,980	
Accumulated depreciation as at 1 October 2004		1,200
Motor van at cost	2,725	
Accumulated depreciation as at 1 October 2004		1,725
Motor car at cost	5,386	
Accumulated depreciation as at 1 October 2004		1,980
Opening stock	11,211	
Loan interest	1,500	
Bank overdraft		8,933
Debtors	11,000	
Provision for doubtful debts		850
Creditors		4,279
Long-term loan		14,811
Capital		31,758
	313,660	313,660

You have the following extra information:

1. Closing stock is £13,206.
2. There are the following amounts owing: advertising £325, telephone £125, carriage outwards £20, general expenses £37, wages and salaries £560.
3. The following amounts are prepaid: travelling expenses £288, electricity £76, insurance £250.
4. It is business policy to treat 10 % of total debtors as doubtful.
5. There is a bad debt of £600.
6. It has been decided to write down the fixed assets to the following net book value amounts as at 30 September 2005.

	£
Premises	21,081
Machine	12,434
Office furniture	4,151
Computer	125
Motor van	275
Motor car	1,599

Required: Prepare, taking the necessary adjustments into account, the trading and profit and loss account for the year ended 30 September 2005 and the balance sheet as at 30 September 2005.

Chapter 7

"Corporation, [i.e. Company] n. An ingenious device for obtaining individual profit without individual responsibility."

Ambrose Bierce, *The Devil's Dictionary*, p. 29

Learning Outcomes

After completing this chapter you should be able to:

✔ Explain the nature of partnerships and limited companies.

✔ Outline the distinctive accounting features of partnerships and limited companies.

✔ Demonstrate how to prepare the accounts of partnerships and limited companies.

✔ Understand the differences between listed and non-listed companies.

Partnerships and Limited Companies

In a Nutshell

- *Sole proprietors, partnerships and limited companies are the main forms of business enterprise.*

- *A partnership is more than one person working together.*

- *Partnership accounts must share out the profit and capital between the partners.*

- *Sharing out profit, capital and current accounts are special partnerships features.*

- *A limited company is based on the limited liability of the shareholders (i.e., they lose only their initial investment if things go wrong).*

- *A limited company's special features are taxation, dividends and capital employed split between share capital and reserves.*

- *In company accounts it is common to find intangible assets (i.e. assets you cannot touch) such as goodwill or patents.*

- *Limited companies may be private or public.*

- *A listed company's accounts will follow International Financial Reporting Standards, have different formats and use different terminology.*

- *Annual reports are sent to shareholders. They are also increasingly put on a company's website.*

Introduction

The three most common types of business enterprise are sole traders, partnerships and public corporations. For example, in 2004, in the UK, there were 514,820 sole proprietors (or sole traders), 309,385 partnerships and 753,020 companies and public corporations (Office for National Statistics, 2004). Of these 1,256 were listed companies. So far, in this book, we have focused on sole traders. Sole traders are, typically, relatively small enterprises owned by one person. Their businesses and accounts tend to be less complicated than those of either partnerships or companies. They are thus ideal for introducing the basic principles behind bookkeeping and final accounts. In this chapter, we now look at the profit and loss accounts and balance sheets of partnerships and limited companies. The cash flow statements prepared by companies are covered in Chapter 8. Partnerships are normally larger than sole traders. However, basically their accounts are similar to those of the sole trader. This reflects the fact that partners, like sole traders, generally own and run their own businesses. For companies, however, the owners provide the capital, but the directors run the company. This divorce of ownership and management is reflected in the accounts of limited companies. In certain respects, particularly the capital employed, the accounts of limited companies thus appear quite different to those of partnerships and sole traders. These differences are heightened by the fact that from 1st January 2005 listed companies (i.e., companies quoted on a national stock exchange) in the UK and other European Union countries had to follow accounting standards set by the International Accounting Standards Board.

Context

In this section, we briefly set out the main features of sole traders, partnerships and limited companies. The main points are summarised in Figure 7.1 on the next page. In essence, the differences between these three types of business enterprise can be traced back to size and capital structure. In terms of size, sole traders are normally smaller than partnerships, which are usually smaller than companies. This greater size causes accounting to be more complicated for companies than for sole traders.

An important distinction between the three businesses is the capital structure. Sole traders and most partners own and run their businesses. They provide the capital, although they may borrow money. The main problem for partnerships is simply the fair allocation of both the capital and profit to the partners. For companies, the owners provide the capital whereas the directors run the company. The concept of limited liability for companies means that shareholders can only lose the money they initially invested.

Partnerships

Introduction

Partnerships may be seen as sole traders with multiple owners. Many sole traders take on partners to help them finance and run their businesses. As in all human relationships, when

Figure 7.1   Sole Traders, Partnerships, and Limited Companies Compared

Feature	Sole Traders	Partnerships	Limited Companies
Business			
(i) Owners	Sole traders	Partners	Shareholders
(ii) Run company	Sole traders	Partners	Directors
(iii) Statutory accounting legislation	No specific act	Partnership Act, 1890	Companies Acts
(iv) Number of owners	1	2–20 (but certain exceptions such as accountants, solicitors)	Private 1–50 Public 2 upwards
(v) Liability	Unlimited	Unlimited, except for limited partners	Limited
(vi) Number in UK* in 2004	514,820	309,385	753,020
(vii) Size of turnover in UK*	(a) 64 % under £100,000 (b) 1 % over £1 m	(a) 33 % under £100,000 (b) 7 % over £1 m	(a) 33 % under £100,000 (b) 22 % over £1 m
Accounting			
(i) Main external users of accounts	Tax authorities, bank	Tax authorities, bank	Tax authorities for small, private companies, shareholders for public companies
(ii) Main financial statements	Trading and profit and loss account and balance sheet	Trading, profit and loss and appropriation account and balance sheet	Profit and loss account (income statement), balance sheet and cash flow statement
(iii) Main differences in profit and loss account from sole trader	–	Appropriation account shares out profit	Appropriation account has dividends and taxation
(iv) Main differences in net assets from sole trader	–	None	Companies, when in groups, may have goodwill. They are also likely to have other intangible assets such as patents or brands. In current liabilities, there are proposed dividends (for non-listed companies only) and taxation payable
(v) Main differences in owners' capital from sole trader	–	Capital and current accounts record partners' share of capital invested and profit	Capital essentially divided into share capital and reserves

*From Office for National Statistics, Size Analysis of United Kingdom Businesses, 2004

partners are well-matched partnerships can prove very successful businesses. However, when they are ill-suited problems can occur (see Soundbite 7.1). Except for certain occupations (such as firms of accountants or solicitors) the maximum number of partners in the UK is 20. An important aspect of both sole traders and partnerships is that liability is generally unlimited. (There is an exception, if you are a limited partner. Limited partners can lose only the capital invested. However, they do not participate in running the company and there must be at least one unlimited liability partner.) In other words, if a business goes bankrupt the personal assets of the owners are *not* ring-fenced. Bankrupt partners may have to sell their houses to pay their creditors. Recently, however, for professional partnerships, particularly accounting partnerships, a new organisational form, the limited liability partnership (LLP), has been created. For these organisations, liability is capped.

Sole traders and partners prepare accounts for use in their own personal internal management, but also for external users, such as the tax authorities and banks. The key issue which underpins partnerships is how the partners should split any profits. The ratio in which the profits are split is called the profit sharing ratio or PSR.

The allocation of profits between the partners is presented in the appropriation account. The appropriation, or 'sharing out', account appears after the calculation of net profit. In other words, we add a section at the bottom of the sole trader's trading and profit and loss account. So we now have the trading and profit and loss and appropriation account.

REAL-LIFE NUGGET 7.1 (*continued*)

'Sometimes the occupation of persons harmonizes admirably with their surnames,' a nineteenth-century antiquarian continues:

Gin & Ginman are innkeepers; so is Alehouse; Seaman is the landlord of the Ship Hotel, and A. King holds the 'Crown and Sceptre' resort in City Road. Portwine and Negus are licensed victuallers, one in Westminster and the other in Bishopsgate Street. Mixwell's country inn is a well-known resort. Pegwell is a shoemaker, so are Fitall and Treadaway, likewise Pinch; Tugwell is a noted dentist; Bird an egg merchant; Hemp a sherriff's officer; Captain Isaac Paddle commands a steamboat; Mr. Punt is a favourite member of the Surrey wherry [rowing] club; Laidman was formerly a pugilist; and Smooker or Smoker a lime burner; Skin & Bone were the names of two millers in Manchester; Fogg and Mist china dealers in Warwick street: the firm afterward became Fogg & Son, on which it was naturally enough remarked that the 'son had driven away the mist.' Mr. I. Came, a wealthy shoemaker in Liverpool, who left his immense property to public charities, opened his first shop on the opposite side of the street to where he had started as a servant, and inscribed a sign: 'I CAME from over the way.'

Finally, Going & Gonne was the name of a well-known banking house in Ireland, and on their failure in business some one wrote:

> Going & Gonne are now both one
> For Gonne is going and Going's gone.

Source: Peter Hay (1988) *The Book of Business Anecdotes*, Harrap Ltd, London, pp. 119–20

The main elements of the basic appropriation account are salaries and the sharing of the profit. Salaries are allocated to the partners before the profit is shared out. Note that for partners, salaries are an appropriation *not* an expense. Figure 7.2 demonstrates the process.

Figure 7.2   Main Elements in the Appropriation Account

Main Elements	Explanation	Layout		
			£	£
Net Profit	Profit as calculated from trading and profit and loss account	Net profit before appropriation		18,000
Salaries	The amount which each partner earns must be deducted from net profit before profit sharing	Less: Salaries A	5,500	
		B	3,500	9,000
				9,000
Residual Profit	The profit share for each individual	Profit A	6,000	
		B	3,000	9,000

Two partners, A and B, share £18,000 net profit. The profit sharing ratio is 2:1. Their salaries are £5,500 and £3,500, respectively. The example is continued in Figure 7.3.

Partners' capital can be divided into two parts: capital accounts and current accounts. Each partner needs to keep track of his or her own capital.

PAUSE FOR THOUGHT 7.1

Partners' Profit Sharing

Why are profits not just split equally between partners?

Superficially, it might seem that the partners might just split the profit equally between them. So if a partnership of two people earns £30,000; each partner's share is £15,000. Unfortunately, life is not so simple! In practice, profit sharing is determined by a number of factors, such as how hard each partner works, their experience and the capital each partner has contributed. It might, therefore, be decided that the profit sharing ratio or PSR was 2:1. In this case, one partner would take £20,000; the second would take £10,000.

Capital Accounts

These accounts represent the long-term capital invested into the partnership by the individual partners. When new partners join a partnership it is conventional for them to 'buy their way' into the partnership. This initial capital introduction can be seen as purchasing their share of the net assets of the business they have joined. This initial capital remains unchanged in the accounts unless the partners specifically introduce or withdraw long-term capital. It represents the amount which the business owes the partners.

Current Accounts

In contrast to the capital accounts, current accounts are not fixed. Essentially, they represent the partners' share of the profits of the business since they joined, less their withdrawals. In basic current accounts, the main elements are the opening balances, salaries, profit for year, drawings and closing balances. These elements are set out in Figure 7.3. This continues Figure 7.2, with drawings of £12,000 for A and £10,000 for B. It is important to realise that the salaries are credited (or added) to the partners' current account rather than physically paid. The partners physically withdraw cash which is known as drawings. Drawings are essentially sums taken out of the business by the partners as living expenses.

Figure 7.3   Main Elements in Partners' Current Accounts

Main Elements	Explanation	Layout		
			A £	B £
Opening Balances	Amount of profits brought forward from last year. Normally a credit balance, and is the amount the business owes the partner	Opening balances	7,000	6,000
		Add:		
Salaries	The amount which the partners earn by way of salary	Salaries	5,000	4,000
Profit Share	Amount of the profit attributable to partner. Determined by profit sharing ratio	Profit	5,500	3,500
			17,500	13,500
Drawings	Amount the partners take out of the business to live on	Less:		
		Drawings	12,000	10,000
Closing Balances	The amount of profits carried forward to next year. This is usually the balance owed to the partner	Closing balances	5,500	3,500

PAUSE FOR THOUGHT 7.2

Debit Balances on Current Accounts

What do you think a negative or debit balance on a partner's current account means?

This means that the partner owes the partnership money! A current account represents the partner's account with the business. It is increased by or credited with (i.e., the business owes the partner money) the partner's salary and share of profit. The account is then debited (or reduced) when the partner takes money out (i.e., drawings). If the partner takes out more funds than are covered by the salary and profit share a debit balance is created. It is, in effect, like going overdrawn at the bank. A partner with a debit balance owes rather than is owed capital.

Partnership Example: Stevens and Turner

Let us imagine that Gavin Stevens has traded for several years. He has now teamed up with Diana Turner. Both partners have invested £35,000 capital. Their salaries are £12,000 for Stevens and £6,000 for Turner. Their current accounts stand at £8,000 (credit) Stevens, £9,000 (credit) Turner. They share residual profits in Steven's favour 2:1. Their opening trial balance is below.

Stevens and Turner: Partnership Trial Balance as at 31 December 200X

		£	£
Capital accounts	Stevens		35,000
	Turner		35,000
Current accounts	Stevens		8,000
	Turner		9,000
Drawings	Stevens	18,000	
	Turner	13,500	
Hotel		110,000	
Vans		30,200	
Opening stock		5,000	
Debtors		15,000	
Creditors			20,000
Bank		20,300	
Electricity		1,850	
Wages		12,250	
Telephone		350	
Long-term loan			50,000
Sales			270,000
Purchases		195,000	
Other expenses		5,550	
		427,000	427,000

Notes:

1. Closing stock is £10,000.
2. For simplicity, we are ignoring all other post-trial balance adjustments such as depreciation, bad and doubtful debts, accruals and prepayments.
3. Salaries are £12,000 for Stevens and £6,000 for Turner. These are 'notional' salaries in that the money is not actually paid to the partners. Instead it is credited to their accounts.

Using this trial balance we now prepare, in Figure 7.4, the trading and profit and loss and appropriation account and the balance sheet

Figure 7.4   Stevens and Turner Partnership Accounts Year Ended 31 December 200X

Stevens and Turner
Trading and Profit and Loss and Appropriation Account for Year Ended
31 December 200X

	£	£
Sales		270,000
Less *Cost of Sales*		
Opening stock	5,000	
Add Purchases	195,000	
	200,000	
Less Closing stock	10,000	190,000
Gross Profit		80,000
Less *Expenses*		
Electricity	1,850	
Wages	12,250	
Telephone	350	
Other expenses	5,550	20,000

Net profit before appropriation		60,000
Less Salaries:		
Stevens	12,000	
Turner	6,000	18,000
		42,000
Profits:		
Stevens	2	28,000
Turner	1	14,000
		42,000

Note: The net profit is calculated as for a sole trader. The profit is then shared out between the partners. This appropriation is shown between the asterisks.

Stevens and Turner
Balance Sheet as at 31 December 200X

	£	£	£
Fixed Assets			
Hotel			110,000
Vans			30,200
			140,200
Current Assets			
Stock	10,000		
Debtors	15,000		
Bank	20,300	45,300	
Current Liabilities			
Creditors	(20,000)	(20,000)	
Net current assets			25,300
Total assets less			
current liabilities			165,500
Long-term Creditors			(50,000)
Total net assets			115,500

	Stevens	Turner	
	£	£	£
Capital Employed			
Capital Accounts	35,000	35,000	70,000
Current Accounts			
Opening balances	8,000	9,000	
Add:			
Salaries	12,000	6,000	
Profit share	28,000	14,000	
	48,000	29,000	
Less Drawings	18,000	13,500	
Closing balances	30,000	15,500	45,500
Total partners' funds			115,500

Note: The total net assets part of the balance sheet is drawn up as for a sole trader. The capital and current accounts show the amounts due to the partners. They are distinctive to partnership accounts and are shown between the asterisks.

Limited Companies

The Basics

Limited companies are a popular form of legal business entity. As Real-Life Nugget 7.2 indicates, in actual fact, a 'company' does not physically exist. The essence of limited companies lies in the fact that the shareholders' (i.e., owners') liability is limited. This means that owners are only liable to lose the amount of money they have initially invested. For example, if a shareholder invests £500 in a company and the company goes bankrupt, then £500 is all the shareholder will lose. All the shareholder's personal possessions (for example, house or car) are safe! This is a great advantage over partnerships and sole traders where the liability is unlimited.

REAL-LIFE NUGGET 7.2

The Company

A second major feature of the orthodox creed is the ascription of supernatural existence to the 'company'. Objectively and rationally speaking, the 'company' does not exist at all, except in so far as it is a heterogeneous collection of people. In order to facilitate the mutual ownership and use of assets, and for other technical reasons, the corporation is treated in law as a person. It is a legal fiction, but a fiction nonetheless.

Source: Graham Cleverly (1971), *Managers and Magic*, Longman Group Limited, London, p. 31

PAUSE FOR THOUGHT 7.3

Limited Liability

For suppliers, and particularly lenders, limited liability can be bad news as their money may be less secure. Can you think of any ways they may seek to counter this?

A fact that is often overlooked is that in small companies limited liability is often not seen as a bonus to those who have close connections with the company. Suppliers may be less certain that they will be paid and bankers more worried about making loans. In many cases, unlimited liability is replaced by other control mechanisms. For example, suppliers may want to be paid in cash or have written guarantees of payment. Bankers will often secure their loans against the property of the business and, in many cases, against the personal assets of the owners. So the owners may not avoid losing their personal possessions in a bankruptcy after all.

The mechanism underpinning a limited liability company is the share. The total capital of the business is divided into these shares (literally a 'share' in the capital of the business). For instance, a business with capital of £500,000 might divide this capital into 500,000 shares of £1 each. These shares may then be bought and sold. Subsequently, they will probably be bought or sold for more or less than £1. For instance, Sheilah might sell 50,000 £1 shares to Mary for £75,000. There is thus a crucial difference between the face value of the shares (£1 each in this case) and their trading value (£1.50 each in this case). The face value of the shares is termed **nominal value**. The trading value is termed **market price**. If market price increases it is the individual shareholder *not* the company that benefits.

The risk for the shareholders is that they will lose the capital they have invested. The reward is twofold. First, shareholders will receive dividends (i.e., annual payments based on profits) for investing their capital. The dividends are the reward for investing their money in the company rather than, for example, investing in a bank or building society where it would earn interest. The second reward is any potential growth in share price. For example, if Sheilah originally purchased the shares for £50,000, she would gain £25,000 when she sold them to Mary.

It is important to realise that the shareholders own the company, they do not run the company. Running the company is the job of the directors. This division is known as the 'divorce of ownership and control'. In many small companies, however, the directors own most of the shares. In this case, although in theory there is a separation of ownership and control, in practice there is not.

There are two types of company in the UK. The private limited company and the public limited company. The main features are outlined in Figure 7.5.

Figure 7.5   Features of Private Limited Companies (Ltds) and Public Limited Companies (plcs) in the UK

Feature	*Private Limited Company*	*Public Limited Company*
Names	Ltd after company name	plc after company name
Number of shareholders	1 upwards	2 to unlimited
Share trading	Restricted	Unrestricted
Stock market listing	No	Usually
Authorised share capital	No minimum	At least £50,000
Size	Usually small to medium enterprises	Usually medium to large enterprises
Accounts	Follow National Standards	Follow International Accounting Standards

The essential difference is that private limited companies are usually privately controlled and owned whereas public limited companies are large corporations usually trading on the stock market. The major companies world-wide such as British Petroleum, Toyota and Coca-Cola are all, in essence, public limited corporations. (Even though laws vary from country to country, they are broadly equivalent.) In these large companies, the managers are, in theory, accountable to the shareholders. In practice, many commentators doubt this accountability.

There are several reasons why companies prepare accounts. First, the detailed accounts (normally comprising a profit and loss account (income statement), a balance sheet and cash flow statement) will be used by management for internal management purposes. They will often be prepared monthly. The published accounts which are sent to the shareholders will usually be prepared annually.

The second reason is to comply with the Companies Act 1985. This lays down certain minimum statutory requirements which are supplemented by accounting standards and stock exchange regulations. Companies following these accounting requirements will normally prepare and send their shareholders published accounts containing a profit and loss account (income statement), balance sheet and (except for small companies which are exempt) a cash flow statement. These account are prepared using a standardised format. For large companies, these accounts are sent out to shareholders as part of the annual reporting package. This is dealt with in detail in Chapter 12; however, it is briefly introduced later in this chapter. Companies, as part of their statutory reporting requirements, will also submit a set of accounts to the Registrar of Companies.

Third, as well as preparing accounts for shareholders, companies may also provide accounts to other users who have an interest in the company's affairs. Of particular importance is the role of corporation tax. The shareholder accounts are usually used as the starting point for assessing this tax, which was introduced in 1965, and is payable by companies on their profits. It is calculated according to a complicated, and often-changing, set of tax rules. 'Accounting' profit is usually adjusted to arrive at 'taxable' profit. Unlike partnerships and sole traders, who are assessed for income tax as individuals, companies are assessed for corporation tax as taxable entities themselves.

Finally, especially for large companies, there may be a wide range of potential users of the accounts such as employees, customers, banks and suppliers. Their information needs were discussed in Chapter 1. The accounts of medium and large companies are usually prepared by the directors and then audited by independent accountants. This is so that the shareholders and other users can be assured that the accounts are 'true and fair'. The auditors' report is a badge of quality.

PAUSE FOR THOUGHT 7.4

Abridged Company Accounts

Companies often prepare a full, detailed set of accounts for their internal management purposes. Why would they not wish to supply these to their shareholders?

....

For internal management purposes detailed information is necessary to make decisions. However, in the published accounts, directors are careful what they disclose. In a public limited company, anybody can buy shares and thus receive the published accounts. Directors do not wish to give away any secrets to potential competitors just because they own a few shares. In actual fact, the Companies Acts requirements allow the main details to be disclosed in a way that is sometimes not terribly informative.

A distinctive feature of many companies is that they are organised into groups. This book does not cover the preparation of group accounts (which are often complex and complicated and best left to more specialist textbooks). Interested readers might try Alexander and Britton (2004), *Financial Reporting*. For now we merely note that many medium and large companies are not, in fact, single entities, but are really many individual companies working together collectively. There is, usually one overall company which is the controlling company. This is further discussed in Chapter 12.

Distinctive Accounting Features

The essence of the profit and loss account of sole traders, partnerships and limited companies is the same. However, there are some important differences. In the case of a sole trader and partnerships the only important difference is that for partnerships the profit is divided (this is formally known as appropriated) between the partners. For limited companies, there is an abridged, standardised format set out by the 1985 Companies Act for non-listed companies. For listed companies, the format is similar, but is prepared under International Financial Reporting Standards. An illustration of the formats for the four business entities is given in Figure 7.6.

Figure 7.6 Differences between Profit and Loss Accounts of Sole Traders, Partnerships and Limited Companies

Sole Traders: Trading and Profit and Loss Account		Partnerships: Trading and Profit and Loss and Appropriation Account		Non-Listed Limited Companies: Profit and Loss Account		Listed Companies: Income Statement	
	£		£		£		£
Sales	200,000	Sales	200,000	Sales	200,000	Sales	200,000
Cost of Sales	(100,000)	Cost of Sales	(100,000)	Cost of Sales	(100,000)	Cost of Sales	(100,000)
Gross Profit	100,000	Gross Profit	100,000	Gross Profit	100,000	Gross Profit	100,000
Other Income	10,000	Other Income	10,000	Other Income	10,000	Other Income	10,000
	110,000		110,000		110,000		110,000
Expenses	(60,000)	Expenses	(60,000)	Expenses	(60,000)	Expenses	(60,000)
Net Profit	50,000	Net Profit	50,000	Profit before Tax	50,000	Profit before Tax	50,000
				Taxation	(20,000)	Taxation	(20,000)
		Partner A	25,000	Profit after Tax	30,000	Profit for the period	30,000
		Partner B	25,000	Dividends	(15,000)		
			50,000	Retained Profit	15,000		

Be careful of the limited companies' format. There are several possible variations and the examples in Figure 7.6 have been grossly simplified for comparison purposes. For listed companies, the profit and loss account is called the income statement. Note that for listed companies dividends are not recorded in the income statement.

The special nature of limited companies leads to several distinctive differences between the accounts of limited companies and those of sole traders and partnerships, both in the profit and loss account (income statement) and in the balance sheet. We now deal with four special features of a company: taxation, dividends, the balance sheet format and long-term capital. We also discuss intangible assets which can occur in the accounts of sole traders and partnerships, but are much more common in company accounts.

1. Taxation

As previously noted, companies pay corporation tax. As Soundbite 7.2 shows, taxation has never proved very popular. For companies, taxation is assessed on annual taxable profits. Essentially, these are the accounting profits adjusted to comply with taxation rules. The accounting consequences of taxation on the profit and loss account (income statement) and balance sheet are twofold.

SOUNDBITE 7.2

Taxation

'The art of taxation consists in so plucking the goose as to obtain the largest possible amount of feathers with the smallest possible amount of hissing.'

Jean-Baptiste Colbert

Source: *The Book of Business Quotations* (1998), p. 257

- In the profit and loss account (income statement), *the amount for taxation for the year is recorded*.
- In the balance sheet, under current liabilities, *the liability for the year is recorded as proposed taxation*.

2. Dividends

A reward for shareholders for the capital they have invested is the dividends they receive. The accounting treatment for dividends mirrors that of taxation in the case of non-listed companies.

- In the profit and loss account, record *all dividends for the year*.
- In the balance sheet, record *dividends proposed (i.e. final dividend) under current liabilities*.

Note that for listed companies **no** dividends are recorded in the income statement. In the balance sheet, only paid dividends are recorded and are deducted from shareholder's equity.

Many companies, like J. Sainsbury plc (the UK supermarket group) (see The Company Camera 7.1) pay interim dividends as payments on account during the accounting year and then final dividends once the accounts have been prepared and the actual profit is known.

THE COMPANY CAMERA 7.1

Dividends

The Directors recommend the payment of a final dividend of 11.36 pence per share (2003:15.58 pence). Subject to shareholders approving this recommendation at the Annual General Meeting (AGM), the dividend will be paid on 23 July 2004 to shareholders on the register at the close of business on 28 May 2004.

Source: J. Sainsbury plc, 2004 Annual Report, p. 8

It is important to note that for non-listed companies there is no direct record of taxation paid or dividends paid in the profit and loss account or balance sheet. Taxation paid and dividends paid, however, appear in the cash flow statement.

PAUSE FOR THOUGHT 7.5

Taxation and Dividends Paid

If you have details of the profit and loss charge for taxation and dividends and the opening and closing liabilities, how do you calculate the amount actually paid?

One becomes a detective. Take this example: opening taxation payable £800, closing taxation payable £1,000, profit and loss charge £3,000.

Our opening liability of £800 plus this year's charge of £3,000 equals £3,800. At the end of the year, however, we only owe £1,000. We must, therefore, have paid £2,800. This logic underpins the calculation of tax paid and dividends paid in the cash flow statement, covered in Chapter 8.

3. Balance Sheet Format

Essentially the balance sheet formats for sole traders, partnerships and non-listed limited companies are broadly the same except for owners' capital employed. However, listed companies follow a very different presentational format. Indeed, for listed companies there are a variety of formats. These can be categorised broadly as falling into (1) a total assets and a total equity and liabilities format followed by most European companies and (2) a net assets format followed by most UK companies. These different formats are outlined in Figure 7.7

Figure 7.7   Different Balance Sheet Structures for Sole Traders, Partnerships and Limited Companies

Sole Traders, Partnerships and Non-listed Companies	£	£	Listed Companies (1) Net Assets Format	£	Listed Companies (2) Assets and Liabilities Format	£
Fixed Assets		80,000	**ASSETS**		**ASSETS**	
Current Assets	80,000		**Non-Current Assets**	80,000	**Non-Current Assets**	80,000
Current Liabilities	(20,000)		**Current Assets**	80,000	**Current Assets**	80,000
Net Current Assets		60,000	*Total Assets*	160,000	*Total Assets*	160,000
Total Assets less						
Current Liabilities		140,000	**LIABILITIES**		**EQUITY AND**	
Long-term creditors		(20,000)			**LIABILITIES**	
Total Net Assets		120,000	**Current Liabilities**	(20,000)	Equity*	120,000
			Non-Current		**Non-Current Liabilities**	20,000
			Liabilities	(20,000)	**Current Liabilities**	20,000
			Total Liabilities	(40,000)		
			Net Assets	120,000		
Capital Employed*		120,000	Equity*	120,000	**Total Equity and**	160,000
			Approach used in this book for listed companies.		Liabilities	

Note: *A breakdown of the Capital Employed/Equity figure for the three business types is presented in Figure 7.10

UK listed companies prefer to subtract total liabilities from total assets to arrive at net assets which equals equity (Assets – Liabilities = Equity). By contrast, European listed companies prefer to record total assets and then to add equity to liabilities (Assets = Equity and Liabilities). Although the totals are different, the individual figures are the same. Examples of the two different approaches are given in the Company Camera 7.4 on page 173 (net assets approach) and Appendix 2.3 (total assets and total equity and liabilities approach). The situation is further complicated by the fact that instead of totalling all the assets and liabilities and then striking a balance, some UK companies present a net figure for net current assets. This is illustrated below.

	£	£
Non-current assets		80,000
Current assets	80,000	
Current liabilities	(20,000)	
Net current assets		60,000
Non-current liabilities		(20,000)
Net assets		120,000

In this book, from now on the net assets approach will be used for listed companies as followed by UK listed companies as presented in Figure 7.7. This is considered the simplest and easiest to understand.

4. Long-Term Capital

The long-term capital of a company can be categorised into share capital (comprising ordinary and preference shares) and loan capital (often called debentures). We can see the differences between these in Figure 7.8. This is portrayed diagrammatically in Figure 7.9.

Figure 7.8   Different Types of Long-Term Capital of a Company

Features	Ordinary Shareholders	Preference Shareholders	Debenture holders
Type of capital	Share	Share	Loan
Ownership	Own company	Do not own company	Do not own company
Risk	Lose money invested first	Lose money invested after ordinary shareholder	Often loans secured on assets
Reward	Dividends	Usually fixed dividends	Interest
Accounting treatment for non-listed companies	Under capital employed	Under capital employed	Deducted from net assets
Accounting treatment for listed companies	Under equity	Under equity	Under liabilities as a non-current liability

Figure 7.9   Long-Term Capital Structure of a Company

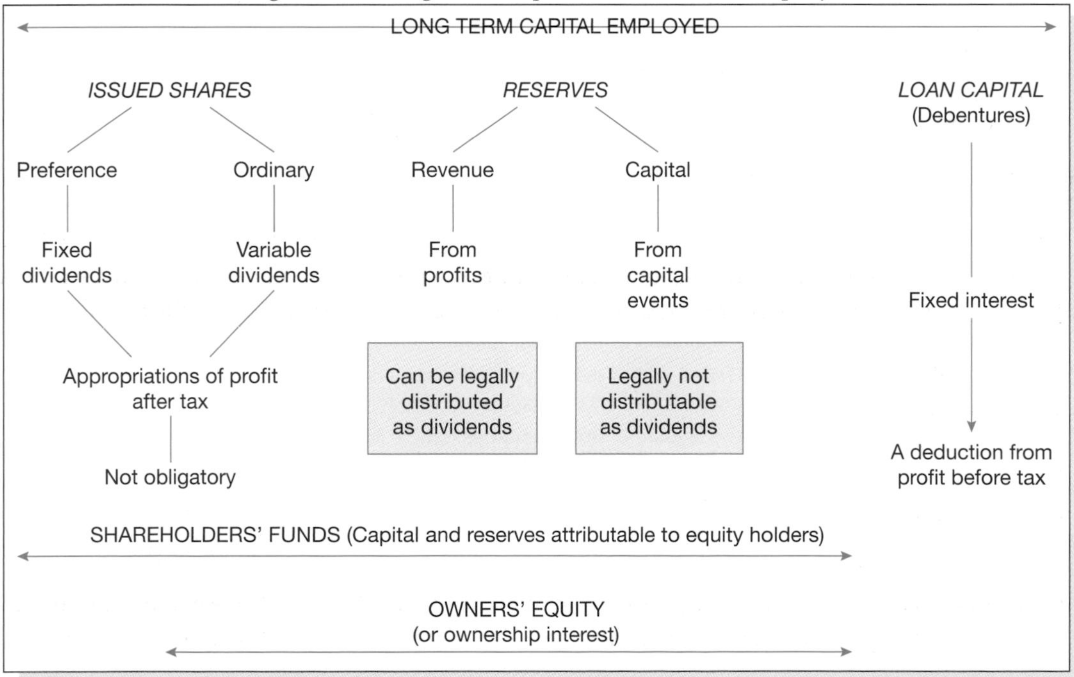

Essentially, ordinary shareholders own the company and, therefore, take the most risk and, potentially, gain the most reward. Preference shareholders normally receive a fixed dividend, whereas debenture holders receive interest. Debentures are long-term loans.

As Figure 7.10 below shows, the limited company's capital employed (equity) is presented differently from that of the sole trader or partnership. For a limited company, the capital employed (equity) is not adjusted for drawings. Excluding long-term capital, a company's capital employed (equity) is essentially represented by share capital and reserves. Unfortunately, there are many different types of share capital and reserves. Figure 7.11 below provides a quick overview of these.

Figure 7.10   Owner's Capital Employed for Sole Trader, Partnerships and Limited Companies

Sole Trader		Partnership		Limited Company	
	£		£		£
Opening capital	100,000	Capital Accounts	100,000	Share Capital	100,000
Add Net Profit	50,000	Current Accounts	20,000	Reserves	20,000
	150,000	Total partners'	120,000	Total shareholders'	120,000
Less Drawings	30,000	funds		Funds*	
Closing capital	120,000			*Total equity for a listed company	

Figure 7.11   Overview of the Main Terminology of a Limited Company's Share Capital and Reserves, and Loan Capital

Term	Explanation
Share Capital	The capital of the company divided into shares.
Authorised share capital	The amount of share capital that a company is allowed to issue to its shareholders.
Called-up share capital	The amount of issued capital that has been fully paid to the company by shareholders. For example, a share may be issued for £1.50 and paid in three equal installments. After two installments are paid the called-up share capital will be £1.
Issued share capital	The amount of share capital *actually* issued.
Ordinary (equity) share capital	The amount of share capital relating to the shareholders who own the company and are entitled to ordinary dividends.
Preference share capital	The amount of share capital relating to shareholders who are not owners of the company and are entitled to fixed dividends.
Market value	The value the shares will fetch on the open market. This may differ significantly from their nominal value.
Nominal value	The face value of the shares, usually their original issue price.

Figure 7.11 Overview of the Main Terminology of a Limited Company's Share Capital and Reserves, and Loan Capital (*continued*)

Term	Explanation
Reserves	The accumulated profits (revenue reserves) or capital gains (capital reserves) to shareholders.
Capital reserves	Reserves which are not distributable to shareholders as dividends, for example, the share premium account or revaluation reserve.
General reserve	A reserve created to deal with general, unspecified contingencies such as inflation.
Profit and loss account	The accumulated profits of a non-listed company.
Retained earnings	The accumulated profits of a listed company.
Revaluation reserve	A capital reserve created when fixed assets are revalued at more than the original purchase cost. The revaluation is a gain to the shareholders.
Revenue reserves	Reserves that are distributable to shareholders as dividends, for example, the profit and loss account, general reserve.
Share premium account	A capital reserve created when new shares are issued for more than their nominal value. For example, if shares were issued for £150,000 and the nominal value was £100,000, the share premium account would be £50,000.
Total shareholders' funds (Total equity)	The share capital and reserves which are owned by ordinary and preference shareholders. Total equity is used for a listed company.
Loan capital	Money loaned to the company by third parties. They are not owners of the company and are entitled to interest not dividends.
Debentures	Just another name for a long-term loan. Debentures may be secured or unsecured.
Secured and unsecured loans	Secured loans are loans which are secured on (or guaranteed by) the assets of the company. Unsecured loans are loans which are not secured on the assets.

Essentially, share capital represents the amount that the shareholders have directly invested. The amount a company is allowed (authorised share capital) to issue is determined in a company document called the Memorandum of Association. The amount actually issued is the issued share capital. It is important to emphasise that the face value for the shares is not its market value. If you like, it is like buying and selling stamps. The Penny Black, a rare stamp, was issued at one penny (nominal value), but you would have to pay a fortune for one today (market value). Shareholders' funds is an important figure in the balance sheet and is equivalent to total net assets (The Company Camera 7.2 shows the shareholders' funds for J.D. Wetherspoon).

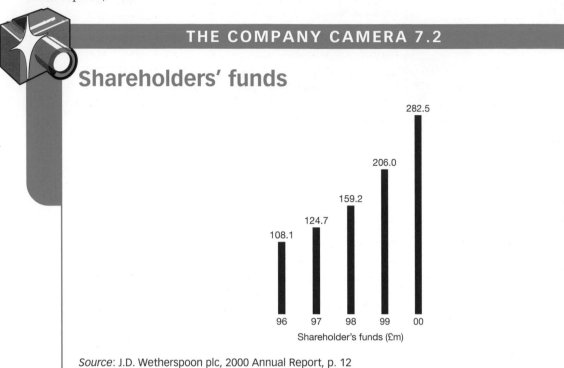

THE COMPANY CAMERA 7.2

Shareholders' funds

Shareholder's funds (£m)

Year	Value
96	108.1
97	124.7
98	159.2
99	206.0
00	282.5

Source: J.D. Wetherspoon plc, 2000 Annual Report, p. 12

Reserves are essentially gains to the shareholder. Capital reserves are gains from activities such as issuing shares at more than the nominal value (share premium account) or revaluing fixed assets (revaluation reserve). They cannot be paid out as dividends. By contrast, revenue reserves, essentially accumulated profits, are distributable.

PAUSE FOR THOUGHT 7.6

The Nature of Reserves

Can you spend reserves?

....

No! Reserves are not cash. Reserves are in fact liabilities which the business owes to the shareholders. They represent either accumulated profits (profit and loss account) or gains to the shareholders such as an issue of shares above the nominal value (share premium account) or the revaluation of fixed assets (revaluation account). Reserves are represented by assets. However, these assets may be fixed assets or current assets. They do not have to be cash, and, if they are not they obviously cannot be spent.

Intangible Assets

Intangible assets are literally fixed assets one cannot touch. As opposed to tangible fixed assets (plant, property and equipment) such as land and buildings, plant and machinery, fixtures and fittings and motor vehicles. They can occur in all businesses, but are most common in companies.

Intangible assets are increasing in value and frequency as organisations become more knowledge-based. As the old manufacturing firms which are heavily dependent on tangible fixed assets decline and the new information technology businesses arise, the balance of assets in companies changes. There are now many types of intangible assets, such as goodwill. Goodwill is covered in more depth in Chapter 12.

PAUSE FOR THOUGHT 7.7

Intangible Assets

Apart from goodwill, can you think of any other intangible assets?

....

There are many, but four of the most common are brands, copyright, patents and software development costs. Perhaps the most frequently occurring of these is patents. A patent is an intangible asset which represents the amount a firm has paid to register a patent or has paid to purchase a patent from another business or individual. A patent itself is the right of the patent's owner to exploit the invention for a period of time. Patents are recorded in the balance sheet under intangible assets.

Accounting Treatment
Profit and Loss Account

Essentially, the profit and loss account (income statement) is calculated as normal. We then have to appropriate (or distribute) the profit to the government by way of tax. In addition, non-listed companies distribute dividends to their shareholders. Listed companies' dividends are not recorded in the income statement. This is demonstrated in Figure 7.12.

Figure 7.12   Limited Companies' Appropriation Account Format

The profit and loss account was prepared as normal. The profit was £100,000. The tax for the year was £40,000 and dividends are £25,000.				
Unlisted Limited Co. Ltd **Profit and Loss Account (extract)**			**Listed Limited Co. Ltd** **Income Statement (extract)**	
		£		£
Profit before Taxation (calculated as normal)		100,000	*Profit before Taxation* (calculated as normal)	100,000
Taxation		(40,000)	Taxation	(40,000)
Profit after Taxation		60,000	*Profit for the year*	60,000
Dividends for year		(25,000)		
Retained Profit		35,000		

Balance Sheet

In the balance sheet, the main differences between a sole trader or partnership and a non-listed company are (i) that taxation payable and dividends payable are recorded under current liabilities; (ii) in the presentation of capital employed; and (iii) that limited companies are more likely than sole traders or partnerships to have intangible assets such as goodwill or patents. The current liabilities presentation is relatively straightforward, so only the capital employed format is presented here (see Figure 7.13).

Figure 7.13   Limited Companies' Capital Employed Format

Limited Co. Ltd has the following details of capital employed.			
Ordinary share capital	£100,000	Profit and loss	£15,000
Preference share capital	£50,000	Share premium account	£5,000
		Revaluation reserve	£6,000

	£	£
Share Capital and Reserves[1]		
Share Capital		
Ordinary share capital		100,000
Preference share capital		50,000
		150,000
Reserves		
Capital reserves		
Share premium account	5,000	
Other reserves		
Revaluation reserve	6,000	
Profit and loss account[2]	15,000	26,000
Total shareholders' funds[3]		176,000

For a listed company, there are certain changes in terminology.
1. Share capital and reserves becomes capital and reserves attributable to equity holders.
2. Profit and loss account becomes retained earnings.
3. Total shareholders' funds becomes total equity.

For a listed company, there is, in addition, as we saw in Figure 7.7, a different balance sheet presentation. In addition, under current liabilities, there would be no proposed dividends. There is also a different terminology (see Figure 7.14).

Figure 7.14   Different Terminology Used in Differing Businesses for Balance Sheets

Sole Traders, Partnerships and Non-listed companies	Listed Companies
Fixed Assets	Non-current assets
Tangible fixed assets	Property, plant and equipment
Stock	Inventory
Debtors	Trade receivables
Long-term liabilities	Non-current liabilities
Creditors	Trade payables
Capital	Equity

Intangible assets are recorded in the balance sheet under fixed assets (non-current assets). The more conventional fixed assets, such as land and buildings, are then recorded as tangible assets (property, plant and equipment).

Limited Company Example: Stevens, Turner Ltd

In order to demonstrate a more comprehensive example of the preparation of a limited company's accounts, we now turn again to the accounts of Gavin Stevens. When we last met Gavin Stevens he had formed a partnership with Diana Turner and they were trading as a partnership, Stevens and Turner (see Figure 7.4). We now assume that many years into the future the partnership has turned into a non-listed company. We will now prepare the company accounts (see Figure 7.15). **The distinctive elements of a limited company's account are bordered by asterisks.** It is important to realise that in this section we are preparing the **full accounts for internal management purposes.** In the following section, however, we show the published accounts of Stevens, Turner assuming they are a public limited company.

Stevens, Turner Ltd: Trial Balance as at 31 December 202X

	£000	£000
Ordinary share capital (£1 each)		300
Preference share capital (£1 each)		150
Share premium account		25
Revaluation reserve		30
General reserve		20
Profit and loss account as at 1 January 202X		50
Long-term loan		80
Land and buildings	550	
Patents	50	
Motor vehicles	50	
Opening stock	10	
Debtors	80	
Creditors		45
Bank	75	
Electricity	8	
Wages	50	
Telephone	7	
Sales		350
Purchases	150	
Loan interest	8	
Other expenses	12	
	1,050	1,050

Notes:

1. Closing stock is £25,000.
2. For simplicity, we are ignoring all other post-trial balance adjustments such as depreciation, bad and doubtful debts, accruals and prepayments.
3. The following are not recorded in the trial balance: (a) ordinary dividends payable £6,000; (b) preference dividends payable £3,000; (c) taxation payable £26,000.

4. Authorised ordinary share capital is £350,000; authorised preference share capital is £200,000.
5. Patents are included as an example of an intangible asset. They need to be recorded under fixed assets at the top of the balance sheet. Below these the other fixed assets are recorded as tangible assets.

Figure 7.15 Stevens, Turner Ltd: Accounts for Year Ended 31 December 202X

Stevens, Turner Ltd
Trading, Profit and Loss and Appropriation Account for Year Ended
31 December 202X

	£000	£000
Sales		350
Less *Cost of Sales*		
Opening stock	10	
Add Purchases	150	
	160	
Less Closing stock	25	135
Gross Profit		215
Less *Expenses*		
Electricity	8	
Wages	50	
Telephone	7	
Loan interest	8	
Other expenses	12	85
Profit before Taxation		130
Taxation[1]		(26)
Profit after Taxation		104
Ordinary dividends[1]		(6)
Preference dividends[1]		(3)
Retained Profit		95

Stevens, Turner Ltd
Balance Sheet as at 31 December 202X

	£000	£000	£000
Fixed Assets			
Intangible Assets			
Patents			50
Tangible Assets			
Land and buildings			550
Motor vehicles			50
Total fixed assets			650
Current Assets			
Stock	25		
Debtors	80		
Bank	75	180	
Current Liabilities			
Creditors	(45)		
Taxation payable[1]	(26)		
Dividends payable[1]	(9)	(80)	
Net current assets			100
Total assets less current liabilities			750
Long-term Creditors			(80)
Total net assets			670

Figure 7.15   Stevens, Turner Ltd: Accounts for Year Ended 31 December 202X *(continued)*

	£000	£000	£000
Share Capital and Reserves			
Share Capital		*Authorised*	*Issued*
Ordinary share capital		350	300
Preference share capital		200	150
		550	450
Reserves			
Capital reserves			
Share premium account		25	
Other reserves			
Revaluation reserve		30	
General reserve		20	
Opening profit and loss account	50		
Retained profit for year	95		
Closing profit and loss account		145	220
Total shareholders' funds			670

Note 1:
In this case, the amount payable equals the charge for the year. This will not always be so.

Limited Companies: Published Accounts

The internal company accounts are not suitable for external publication. The published accounts which are sent to shareholders are incorporated in a special document called an annual report and have several special features: they are standardised, abridged and have supplementary notes.

- *Standardised.* Published accounts use special Companies Acts' formats. In actual fact, these formats are broadly used throughout this book for consistency and to aid understanding.
- *Abridged.* The Companies Acts' formats mean that the details are summarised.
- *Supplementary notes.* Supplementary notes are used to flesh out the details of the main accounts.
- *Annual report.* In the case of public limited companies, an annual report is sent to shareholders. Increasingly, the annual report is also put onto a company's website. The website will include the financial statements, but also much more information. A separate chapter is devoted to the annual report (Chapter 12), given its importance, with Figure 12.4 providing some corporate Website addresses.

The Company Cameras 7.3 and 7.4 that follow on pages 172 and 173 show the income statement and balance sheet for A UK company, AstraZeneca. They have been prepared using International Financial Reporting Standards and using dollars rather than pounds.

The specific requirements for published company accounts are complex and beyond the scope of this book. All European listed companies must prepare their accounts in accordance

THE COMPANY CAMERA 7.3

Income Statement of a Public Limited Company

Consolidated Income Statement

For the six months ended 30 June	2005 $m	As restated 2004 $m
Sales	11,875	10,362
Cost of sales	(2,723)	(2,409)
Distribution costs	(104)	(86)
Research and development	(1,725)	(1,745)
Selling, general and administrative expenses	(4,236)	(4,165)
Other operating income	84	147
Operating profit	**3,171**	2,104
Finance income	316	272
Finance expense	(252)	(246)
Profit before tax	**3,235**	2,130
Taxation	(968)	(515)
Profit for the period	**2,267**	1,615
Attributable to:		
Equity holders of the Company	2,259	1,608
Minority interests	8	7
	2,267	1,615
Basic earnings per $0.25 Ordinary Share	$1.38	$0.95
Diluted earnings per $0.25 Ordinary Share	$1.38	$0.95
Weighted average number of Ordinary Shares in issue (millions)	1,634	1,684
Diluted average number of Ordinary Shares in issue (millions)	1,634	1,686
Dividends declared in the period	1,061	914

Source: AstraZeneca plc 2005. Half Year Results 2005, p.14
Helpnote: AstraZeneca's income statement is presented in summary, abridged form. The detail is in the attached notes (not shown here). This income statement was prepared under IFRS. However, as there is no mandated format other listed UK and European companies may use slightly different formats.

with International Financial Reporting Standards. The terminology and presentation of the accounts differs from that conventionally used for sole traders, partnerships and non-listed companies. However, Figure 7.16 on page 174 is a summary of what Stevens, Turner plc might look

THE COMPANY CAMERA 7.4

Balance Sheet of a Public Limited Company (net assets format)

Consolidated Balance Sheet

	30 June 2005 $m	As restated 31 Dec 2004 $m	As restated 30 June 2004 $m
Assets			
Non-current assets			
Property, plant and equipment	7,355	8,097	7,537
Goodwill and intangible assets	2,696	3,050	2,919
Other investments	221	262	133
Deferred tax assets	1,174	1,218	1,843
	11,446	12,627	12,432
Current assets			
Inventories	2,663	3,020	3,138
Trade and other receivables	4,926	4,771	4,701
Short term investments	398	1,167	2,573
Cash and cash equivalents	5,451	4,067	1,499
	13,438	13,025	11,911
Total assets	24,884	25,652	24,343
Liabilities			
Current liabilities			
Short term borrowings and overdrafts	(150)	(142)	(102)
Other creditors	(6,647)	(6,445)	(6,855)
	(6,797)	(6,587)	(6,957)
Non-current liabilities			
Loans	(1,163)	(1,127)	(1,097)
Deferred tax liabilities	(1,163)	(1,328)	(1,642)
Retirement benefit obligations	(1,803)	(1,761)	(1,508)
Provisions	(306)	(266)	(268)
Other liabilities	(82)	(86)	(68)
	(4,517)	(4,568)	(4,583)
Total liabilities	(11,314)	(11,155)	(11,540)
Net assets	13,570	14,497	12,803
Equity			
Capital and reserves attributable to equity holders			
Share capital	404	411	419
Share premium account	584	550	521
Other reserves	1,892	1,851	1,875
Retained earnings	10,597	11,592	9,892
	13,477	14,404	12,707
Minority equity interests	93	93	96
Total equity and reserves	13,570	14,497	12,803

Source: AstraZeneca plc, 2005. Half Year Results 2005, p.16

Helpnote: AstraZeneca's balance sheet is presented in summarised, abridged form. The detail is in the attached notes (not shown here). It will be noted that the assets and liabilities are totalled before arriving at net assets. Net assets equals total equity and reserves. However, as there is no mandated format other listed and European companies may use slightly different formats. In particular, most European listed companies total the assets and then total the equity and liabilities. In addition, it is possible using the net assets presentation to include current assets less current liabilities as a sub-total.

Figure 7.16   Stevens, Turner Ltd: Accounts Presented as Published Accounts of a Public Limited Company

Stevens, Turner plc
Income Statement Year Ended 31 December 202X

	£000
Sales[1]	350
Cost of Sales	(135)
Gross Profit	215
Administrative expenses	(85)
Profit before Taxation	130
Taxation	(26)
Profit for year[2]	104

Stevens, Turner plc
Balance Sheet as at 31 December 202X

	Notes	£000
ASSETS		
Non-current assets[3]		
Property, plant and equipment[3]	1	600
Goodwill and intangible assets		50
Current Assets		650
Inventory[3]		25
Trade receivables[3]		80
Bank		75
		180
Total Assets		830
LIABILITIES		
Current Liabilities[3]	2	(80)
Non-current liabilities[3]		(80)
Total Liabilities[3]		(160)
Net Assets		670
EQUITY[3]		£000
Capital and Reserves attributable to Equity Holders		
Called-up share capital	3	450
Share premium account		25
Other reserves	4	50
Retained earnings	5	145
Total Equity		670

Notes to the accounts	£000		£000
1. Property, Plant and Equipment		**3. Called-up Share Capital**[3]	
Land and buildings	550	Ordinary share capital	300
Motor vehicles	50	Preference share capital	150
	600		450
2. Current Liabilities		**4. Other Reserves**	
Trade receivables	45	Revaluation reserve	30
Taxation payable	26	General reserve	20
Ordinary dividends payable	6		50
Preference dividends payable	3	**5. Retained Earnings**	
	80	Balance as at 1 January 202X	50
		Retained profit for year	95*
		Balance as at 31 December 202X	145

* No dividends were paid during the year, so none are deducted here.

like. It is prepared using the same information presented in the trial balance for Stevens Turner Ltd., presented earlier in this chapter.

We have thus summarised the accounts of Stevens, Turner plc and supplemented them with notes to the accounts. The main figures can thus easily be identified. There are some points of interest, indicated by the superscript notes in Figure 7.16.

1. Sales may also be called 'turnover' or 'revenue'.
2. No dividends are shown in the income statement. Dividends paid are deducted from retained earnings. There are assumed to be none in this example. dividends payable are not recorded.
3. These are the terms used in published accounts. They are equivalent to the terms: fixed assets; property, plant and equipment; inventories; creditors: amounts falling due within one year; creditors: amounts falling due after one year and capital that we have used so far.
4. Called-up share capital has a technical meaning (see Figure 7.11). However, for convenience, it can be taken here as issued share capital.

Conclusion

Partnerships and limited companies are important types of business organisation. Partnerships are broadly similar to sole traders, except that there is the problem of how to divide the capital and profit between the partners. Limited companies, unlike partnerships or sole traders, are based on the concept of limited liability. The principal differentiating features in the accounts of companies are corporation tax, dividends and the division of capital employed into share capital and reserves. Limited companies may be either private limited companies or public limited companies. It is the latter which are quoted on the stock exchange. The presentation and format of public limited companies differs from that of the other types of business organisation.

Q&A   Discussion Questions

Questions with numbers in blue have answers at the back of the book.

Q1 Why do you think that three different types of business enterprise (sole traders, partnerships and limited companies) exist?

Q2 Discuss the view that the accounts of partnerships are much like those of sole traders except for the need to share out the capital and profit between more than one partner.

Q3 Distinguish between a private limited company and a public limited company. Is there any difference between the users of the accounts of each type of company?

Q4 Why is the distinction between capital and revenue reserves so important for a company?

Q5   State whether the following are true or false. If false, explain why.
     (a) Drawings are an expense recorded in the partners' trading, profit and loss and appropriation account.
     (b) Partner's current accounts report the yearly short-term movements in partners' capital.
     (c) The nominal value of a company's shares is the amount the shares will fetch on the stock market.
     (d) An unsecured loan is secured on specific assets such as the company's machinery.
     (e) Reserves can be spent on the purchase of fixed assets.

Numerical Questions

These questions are separated into those on (A) partnerships and (B) limited companies. Within each section, they are graded in difficulty.

Questions with numbers in blue have answers at the back of the book.

A Partnerships

Q1   Two partners, Peter Tom and Sheila Thumb, have the following details of their accounts for the year ended 31 December 2009.

			£	
Net profit before appropriation: £100,000	Capital accounts:	Tom	8,000	
Profit sharing ratio: 3 Tom, 1 Thumb		Thumb	6,000	
Salaries: Tom £10,000, Thumb £30,000	Current accounts:	Tom	3,000	cr
Drawings: Tom £25,000, Thumb £30,000		Thumb	1,000	dr

Required: Prepare the relevant trading, profit and loss and appropriation account, and balance sheet extracts.

Q2   J. Waite and P. Watcher's trial balance as at 30 November 2009 is set out below.

		£	£
Capital accounts:	Waite		88,000
	Watcher		64,000
Current accounts:	Waite	2,500	
	Watcher		12,000
Drawings:	Waite	13,300	
	Watcher	6,300	
Land and buildings at cost		166,313	
Motor vehicles at cost		65,000	
Opening stock		9,000	
Debtors		12,000	
Creditors			18,500
Bank		6,501	
Electricity		3,406	
Wages		14,870	
Telephone		1,350	
Rent and business rates		6,660	
Long-term loan			28,000
Sales			350,000
Purchases		245,000	
Interest on loan		2,800	
Other expenses		5,500	
		560,500	560,500

Notes:
1. Closing stock is £15,000.
2. Salaries are £18,000 for Waite and £16,000 for Watcher.
3. There is £300 owing for rent.
4. Depreciation for the year is £2,000 on land and buildings and £3,000 on motor vehicles. The business was started on 1 December 2008.
5. The split of profits is 3 Watcher: 2 Waite.

Required: Prepare the trading, profit and loss and appropriation account for year ended 30 November 2009 and the balance sheet as at 30 November 2009.

Q3 Cherie and Tony's trial balance as at 31 December 2005 is set out below.

		£	£
Capital accounts:	Cherie		30,000
	Tony		35,000
Current accounts:	Cherie		26,000
	Tony		18,500
Drawings	Cherie	21,294	
	Tony	18,321	
Land and buildings at cost		203,500	
Plant and machinery at cost		26,240	
Land and buildings accumulated depreciation as at 1 January 2005			12,315
Plant and machinery accumulated depreciation as at 1 January 2005			9,218
Debtors		18,613	
Creditors			2,451
Bank		25,016	
Electricity		1,324	
Wages		12,187	
Telephone		1,923	
Insurance		1,318	
Long-term loan			83,000
Sales			251,800
Sales returns		340	
Purchases		128,317	
Purchases returns			206
Other expenses		1,497	
Opening stock		8,600	
		468,490	468,490

Notes:
1. Closing stock is £12,000.
2. £197 of the other expenses was prepaid and £200 is owed for the telephone.
3. Salaries will be £12,000 for Cherie and £10,000 for Tony.
4. Depreciation is fixed at 2 % on the cost of land and buildings and 10 % on the cost of plant and machinery.
5. Profits are shared in the ratio 2 for Cherie and 1 for Tony.

Required: Prepare the trading, profit and loss and appropriation account for the year ended 31 December 2005 and the balance sheet as at 31 December 2005.

Q4 Sister and Sledge are trading in partnership, sharing profits and losses in the ratio of 2:1, respectively. The partners are entitled to salaries of Sister £6,000 per annum and Sledge £5,000 per annum. There is the following additional information.

(1) Stock as at 31 December 2005 was valued at £8,800.
(2) Staff salaries owing £290.
(3) Advertising paid in advance £200.
(4) Provision for bad and doubtful debts to be increased to £720.
(5) Provision should be made for depreciation of 2 % on land and buildings on cost, and for fixtures and fittings at 10 % on cost.

Trial Balance as at 31 December 2005

	£	£
Capital accounts:		
Sister		12,500
Sledge		5,000
Current accounts:		
Sister		1,500
Sledge	600	
Drawings:		
Sister	9,800	
Sledge	6,700	
Long-term loan		40,250
Land and buildings at cost	164,850	
Stock as at 1 January 2005	9,500	
Fixtures and fittings at cost	12,500	
Purchases	126,000	
Cash at bank	3,480	
Sales	305,400	
Trade debtors	9,600	
Carriage inwards	200	
Carriage outwards	300	
Staff salaries	24,300	
Trade creditors		26,300
General expenses	18,200	
Provision for bad and doubtful debts		480
Advertising	5,350	
Discounts receivable		120
Discounts allowed	350	
Rent and business rates	2,850	
Land and buildings accumulated depreciation as at 1 January 2005		9,750
Fixtures and fittings accumulated depreciation as at 1 January 2005		3,500
Electricity	4,500	
Telephone	5,720	
	404,800	404,800

Required: Prepare the trading and profit and loss and appropriation account for the year ended 31 December 2005 and the balance sheet as at 31 December 2005.

B Limited Companies

i Non-Listed Companies

Q5   Red Devils Ltd has the following extracts from its accounts.

Red Devils Ltd
Trial Balance as at 30 November 2009

	£	£
Gross profit for year		150,000
7% Debentures		200,000
6% Preference share capital (£150,000 authorised)		150,000
£1 Ordinary share capital (£400,000 authorised)		250,000
Share premium account		55,000
Fixed assets	680,900	
General expenses	22,100	
Directors' fees	19,200	
Debtors	4,700	
Bank	5,300	
Creditors		12,200
Profit and loss account as at 1 December 2008		9,000
General reserve as at 1 December 2008		11,000
Stock as at 30 November 2009	105,000	
	837,200	837,200

Notes:
1. An audit fee is to be provided of £7,500.
2. The debenture interest for the year has not been paid.
3. The directors propose the following:
    (a) A dividend of 10p per share (10%) on the ordinary shares
    (b) To pay the preference dividend
    (c) To transfer £3,500 to the general reserve (Note: transfers are recorded in the appropriation account)
4. Corporation tax of £17,440 to be provided on the profit for the year.

Required: Prepare for internal management purposes:
(a) The profit and loss account and appropriation account for the year ended 30 November 2009.
(b) The balance sheet as at 30 November 2009.

Q6   **Superprofit Ltd**

Trial Balance as at 31 December 2009

	£000	£000
Ordinary share capital		210
Preference share capital		25
Share premium account		40
Revaluation reserve		35
General reserve		15
Profit and loss account as at 1 January 2009		28
Long-term loan		32
Land and buildings	378	
Patents	12	
Motor vehicles	47	
Opening stock	23	
Debtors	18	
Creditors		33
Bank	31	
Electricity	12	
Insurance	3	
Wages	24	
Telephone	5	
Light and heat	8	
Sales		351
Purchases	182	
Other expenses	26	
	769	769

Notes (all figures in £000s):

1. Closing stock is £26.
2. The following had not yet been recorded in the trial balance:
    (a) Dividends payable on ordinary shares £9 and on preference shares £3
    (b) Taxation payable £13
    (c) Interest on long-term loan £4
    (d) Auditors' fees £2
    (e) The authorised share capital is ordinary share capital £250, preference share capital £50.
3. The business started trading on 1 January 2009. Depreciation for the year is £18 for land and buildings and £7 for motor vehicles.

Required: Prepare for *internal management purposes* the income statement for year ended 31 December 2009 and the balance sheet as at 31 December 2009.

ii Listed Companies

Q7   Lindesay Trading plc

Trial Balance as at 31 March 2006

	£000	£000
Ordinary share capital		425
Preference share capital		312
Share premium account		18
Revaluation reserve		27
General reserve as at 1 April 2005		13
Retained earnings as at 1 April 2005		17
Long-term loan		87
Land and buildings at cost	834	
Patents	25	
Motor vehicles at cost	312	
Opening inventory as at 1 April 2005	10	
Trade receivables	157	
Trade payables		93
Bank	186	
Electricity	12	
Wages and salaries	183	
Telephone	5	
Sales		1,500
Insurance	6	
Purchases	750	
Other expenses	125	
Land and buildings accumulated depreciation as at 1 April 2005		25
Motor vehicles accumulated depreciation as at 1 April 2005		88
	2,605	2,605

Notes (all figures in £000s):

1. Closing inventory is £13.
2. The following are not recorded in the trial balance:
   (a) Taxation payable £58.
3. Authorised share capital was £500 for ordinary share capital and £400 for preference share capital.
4. There was £45 owing for wages and salaries.
5. Debenture interest was £8.
6. Of the insurance £1 was prepaid.
7. The proposed auditors' fees are £3.
8. A transfer to the general reserve was made of £16.
9. Depreciation is to be £17 on land and buildings and £60 on motor vehicles.

Required: Prepare for *internal management purposes* the trading, profit and loss and appropriation account for the year ended 31 March 2006 and the balance sheet as at 31 March 2006. Lindesay Trading plc does not currently draw up its internal accounts using International Financial Reporting Standards preferring to use UK National Standards.

Q8 The following trial balance was extracted from the books of Leisureplay plc for the year ended 31 December 2005.

	£000	£000
Ordinary share capital (£1 each)		700,000
Preference share capital (£1 each)		80,000
Debentures		412,000
Retained earnings as at 1 January 2005		98,000
Share premium account		62,000
Revaluation reserve		70,000
General reserve		18,000
Freehold premises at cost	1,550,000	
Motor vehicles at cost	18,000	
Furniture and fittings at cost	8,000	
Freehold premises accumulated depreciation as at 1 January 2005		102,000
Motor vehicles accumulated depreciation as at 1 January 2005		9,350
Furniture and fittings accumulated depreciation as at 1 January 2005		1,100
Inventory as at 1 January 2005	5,000	
Cash at bank	183,550	
Provision for bad and doubtful debts		1,000
Purchases/sales	500,000	800,000
Trade receivables/payables	28,900	7,000
Sales returns/purchases returns	3,500	3,800
Carriage inwards	60	
Carriage outwards	70	
Bank charges	20	
Rates	4,280	
Salaries	5,970	
Wages	3,130	
Travelling expenses	1,980	
Preference dividends	5,000	
Ordinary dividends	25,000	
Discount allowed	20	
Discount received		15
General expenses	8,100	
Gas, electricity	9,385	
Printing, stationery	1,850	
Advertising	2,450	
	2,364,265	2,364,265

Notes (all figures are in 000s):
(a) Inventory as at 31 December 2005 is £12,000
(b) Depreciation is to be charged as follows:

   (i)   Freehold premises   2 % on cost
   (ii)   Motor vehicles   10 % on cost
   (iii) Furniture and fittings   5 % on cost

(c) There is the following payment in advance:
   General expenses   £500
(d) There are the following accrued expenses:
   Business rates   £300
   Advertising   £550
   Auditors' fees   £250
(e) Authorised ordinary share capital is £1,000,000 £1 shares, and authorised preference share capital is 100,000 £1 shares.
(f) Taxation has been calculated as £58,500.
(g) Debenture interest should be charged at 10 %.
(h) Provision for bad and doubtful debts is increased to £1,600 and a bad debt of £400 is to be written off.
(i) The ordinary and preference dividends should be deducted from retained earnings.

Required: Prepare for *internal management purposes* the income statement for Leisureplay plc for the year ended 31 December 2005 and balance sheet as at 31 December 2005 using International Financial Reporting Standards.

Q9   You have the following summarised trial balance for Stock High plc as at 31 March 2009. Further details are provided in the notes.

	£000	£000
Sales		1,250
Cost of sales	400	
Administrative expenses	200	
Distribution expenses	150	
Patents	50	
Land and buildings at cost	800	
Motor vehicles at cost	400	
Land and buildings accumulated depreciation as at 1 April 2008		140
Motor vehicles accumulated depreciation as at 1 April 2008		150
Long-term loan		60
Retained earnings as at 1 April 2008		36
Share premium account		25
Revaluation reserve		30
General reserve		25
Ordinary share capital		450
Preference share capital		100
Taxation paid	86	
Ordinary dividends paid	50	
Trade payables		12
Inventory as at 31 March 2009	20	
Trade receivables	100	
Cash	22	
	2,278	2,278

Notes (In £000s except for note 3):
1. At the balance sheet date £8 is owing for taxation.
2. Depreciation is to be charged at 2 % on cost for land and buildings (used for administration) and 20 % on cost for motor vehicles (used for selling and distribution).
3. Authorised share capital is 600,000 £1 ordinary shares and £150,000 £1 preference shares.

Required: Prepare the income statement for the year ended 31 March 2009 and the balance sheet as at 31 March 2009 as it would appear in the published account as prepared under International Financial Reporting Standards.

Chapter 8

"Cash is King. It is relatively easy to 'manufacture' profits but creating cash is virtually impossible."

UBS Phillips and Drew (January 1991).
Accounting for Growth, p. 32

Now, as you all know, profit and cash flow are not the same thing.

Indeed, many financial analysts believe that we should maximise cash flow, not profit.

However, the truth is we need to maximise profits, so that we can maximise our bonuses.

©MMI Mike Jones

Learning Outcomes

After completing this chapter you should be able to:

✔ Explain the nature of cash and the cash flow statement.

✔ Demonstrate the importance of cash flow.

✔ Investigate the relationship between profit and cash flow.

✔ Outline the direct and indirect methods of cash flow statement preparation.

Main Financial Statements: The Cash Flow Statement

In a Nutshell

- *Cash is key to business success.*

- *Cash flow is concerned with cash received and cash paid, unlike profit which deals with income earned and expenses incurred.*

- *Reconciling profit to cash flow means adjusting for movements in working capital and for non-cash items, such as depreciation.*

- *Large companies provide a cash flow statement as the third major financial statement.*

- *Sole traders, partnerships and small companies may, but are not required to, prepare a cash flow statement.*

- *The two ways of preparing a cash flow statement are the direct and the indirect methods.*

- *Most companies use the indirect method of cash flow statement preparation.*

- *Listed companies use a different format than other business organisations.*

Introduction

Cash is king. It is the essential lubricant of business. Without cash, a business cannot pay its employees' wages or pay for goods or services. As Real-Life Nugget 8.1 shows, at its most extreme, this can lead to a business's failure. A business records cash in the bank account in the books of account. Small businesses may sometimes prepare a cash flow statement directly from the bank account. More usually, however, the cash flow statement is prepared indirectly by deducing the figures from the profit and loss account and balance sheet. The cash flow statement, at its simplest, records the cash inflows and cash outflows classified under certain headings such as cash flows from operating (i.e., trading) activities. All companies (except small ones) must prepare cash flow statements in line with financial reporting regulations. However, some sole traders, partnerships and smaller companies also provide them, often at the request of their bank. As Real-Life Nugget 8.2 shows, banks are well aware of the importance of cash.

As well as preparing cash flow statements on the basis of past cash flows, businesses will continually monitor their day-to-day cash inflows and outflows. As we shall see in Chapter 17, they also prepare cash budgets which look to the future. Cash management, therefore, concerns the past, present and future activities of a business.

REAL-LIFE NUGGET 8.1

Cash Bloodbath

With last week's collapse of Boo.com – the first big liquidation of a dot.com company in Europe – the internet gold rush has taken on the appearance of a bloodbath.

The company's principal failing – and there were many, it was burning cash at a rate of $1m a week – was to forget that in the new economy the old rules still apply.

Source: *Accountancy Age*, 25 May 2000, p. 26

REAL-LIFE NUGGET 8.2

Cash Flow

Bankers *do* know about cash flow. They have to live with it on Friday, every Friday, in any number of companies up and down the country. Where there is insufficient cash to pay the wages, really agonising decisions result. Should the company be closed, with all the personal anguish it will cause, or should it be allowed to limp on, perhaps to face exactly the same agonising dilemma in as little as a week's time?

Source: B. Warnes (1984), *The Genghis Khan Guide to Business*, Osmosis Publications, London, p. 6

Importance of Cash

Cash is the lifeblood of a business. Cash is needed to pay the wages, to pay the day-to-day running costs, to buy stock and to buy new fixed assets. The generation of cash is, therefore, essential to the survival and expansion of businesses. Money makes the world go round! In many ways, the concept of cash flow is easier to understand than that of profit. Most people are more familiar with cash than profit. Cash is, after all, what we use in our everyday lives.

At its most stark, if a business runs out of cash it will not be able to pay its creditors and it will cease trading. As Jack Welch, a successful US businessman, has said, 'There's one thing you can't cheat on and that's cash and Enron didn't have any cash for the last three years. Accounting is odd, but cash is real stuff. Follow the cash' (*Guardian*, 27 February 2002, p. 23).

It is far easier to manipulate profit than it is to manipulate cash flow. This is highlighted by Real-life Nugget 8.3. Phillips and Drew, a firm of city fund managers (now called UBS Global Management), basically state that cash is essential to business success.

REAL-LIFE NUGGET 8.3

Importance of Cash

'In the end, investment and accounting all come back to cash. Whereas "manufacturing" profits is relatively easy, cash flow is the most difficult parameter to adjust in a company's accounts. Indeed, tracing cash movements in a company can often lead to the identification of unusual accounting practices. The long term return of an equity investment is determined by the market's perception of the stream of dividends that the company will be able to pay. We believe that there should be less emphasis placed on the reported progression of earnings per share and more attention paid to balance sheet movements, dividend potential and, most important of all, cash.'

Source: UBS Phillips and Drew (January 1991), *Accounting for Growth*, p. 1

Context

The cash flow statement is the third of the key financial statements which medium and large companies provide. It summarises the company's cash transactions over time. At its simplest, the cash flow is related to the opening and closing cash balances.

$$\text{Opening cash} + \text{Inflows} - \text{Outflows} = \text{Closing cash}$$

Cash inflows are varied, but may, for example, be receipts from sales or interest from a bank deposit account. Cash outflows may be payments for goods or services, or for capital expenditure items such as motor vehicles.

All *large* companies are required to provide a cash flow statement. There are two methods of preparation. The first is the **direct method**, which categorises cash flow by function, for example receipts from sales. A cash flow statement, using the direct method, can be prepared from

PAUSE FOR THOUGHT 8.1

Yes, But What Exactly is Cash?

Cash is cash! However, there are different types of cash, such as petty cash, cash at bank, bank deposit accounts, or deposits repayable on demand or with notice. How do they all differ?

....

The basic distinction is between cash and bank. However, the terms are often used loosely and interchangeably. Cash is the cash available. In other words, it physically exists, for example, a fifty pound note. Petty cash is money kept specifically for day-to-day small expenses, such as purchasing coffee. Cash at bank is normally kept either in a current account (which operates via a cheque book for normal day-to-day transactions) or in a deposit account (basically a store for surplus cash). Deposits repayable on demand are very short-term investments which can be repaid within one working day. Deposits requiring notice are accounts where the customer must give a period of notice for withdrawal (for example, 30 days).

the bank account and is the most readily understandable. The second method is the **indirect method.** This uses a 'detective' approach. It deduces cash flow from the existing balance sheets and profit and loss account and reconciles operating profit to operating cash flow. The cash flow statement, using the indirect method, is not so readily comprehensible. Unfortunately, this is the method most often used.

Cash and the Bank Account

As we saw in Chapter 4, cash is initially recorded in the bank account. In large businesses, a separate book is kept called the cash book. Debits are essentially good news for a company in that they increase cash in the bank account, whereas credits are bad news in that they decrease cash in the bank account. From the bank account it is possible to prepare a simple cash flow statement.

PAUSE FOR THOUGHT 8.2

Cash Inflows and Outflows

What might be some examples of the main sources of cash inflow and outflow for a small business?

....

Cash Inflow	Cash Outflow
Cash from customers for goods	Payments to suppliers for goods
Interest received from bank deposit account	Payments for services, e.g., telephone, light and heat
Cash from sale of fixed assets	Repay bank loans
Cash introduced by owner	Payments for fixed assets, e.g., motor vehicles
Loan received	Interest paid on bank loan

Let us take the example once more of Gavin Stevens' bank account (see Figure 8.1). As Figure 8.1 shows, we have essentially summarised the figures from the bank account and reclassified them under certain headings.

Figure 8.1   Simple Cash Flow Statement for Gavin Stevens

Taking Gavin Stevens' bank account:

Bank

	£		£
1 Jan. Capital	200,000	2 Jan. Hotel	110,000
7 Jan. Ireton	1,965	2 Jan. Van	3,000
7 Jan. Hepworth	2,500	2 Jan. Purchases	2,000
		4 Jan. Electricity	300
		4 Jan. Wages	1,000
		7 Jan. Hogen	250
		7 Jan. Lewis	1,000
		7 Jan. Bal. c/f	86,915
	204,465		204,465
8 Jan. Bal. b/f	86,915		

From the bank account, we can summarise the main cash flows and record them in a cash flow statement, as follows:

Gavin Stevens
Cash Flow Statement up to 7 January

	£	£
Opening Cash Balance		
Add *Inflows*		
Capital invested (1)	200,000	
Trading (2)	4,465	204,465
Less *Outflows*		
Capital expenditure (3)	113,000	
Trading (4)	4,550	117,550
Closing Cash Balance		86,915

Notes:
(1) Represents the initial capital investment. Often termed a 'financing' cash flow.
(2) Represents money received from debtors (Ireton £1,965 and Hepworth £2,500). Often termed cash flow from a 'trading' or 'operating' activity.
(3) Represents the purchase of fixed assets (hotel £110,000 and van £3,000). Often termed cash flow from 'investing' activities.
(4) Represents the money paid for goods and services (purchases £2,000, electricity £300, wages £1,000, Hogen £250, Lewis £1,000). Often termed cash flow from a 'trading' or 'operating' activity.

For sole traders and partnerships, there is no regulatory requirement for a cash flow statement in the UK. Small companies are also exempt. Many organisations do, nevertheless, prepare one. UK non-listed companies are regulated by an accounting standard, Financial Reporting Standard 1. However, UK listed companies, like all European listed companies, follow International Accounting Standard 7.

These standards lay down certain main headings for categorising cash flows (see Figure 8.2).

Figure 8.2   Main Headings for Cash Flow Statements

A Sole Traders, Partnerships and Non-Listed Companies	B Listed Companies	Simplified Meaning	Examples of Inflows	Examples of Outflows
Net Cash Flow from Operating Activities[1]	Cash flows from operating activities	Cash flows from the normal trading activities of a business	i. Cash for sale of goods	i. Payment for purchases of goods ii. Expenses paid
Returns on Investments and Servicing of Finance	i. **Cash flows from investing activities.** This covers interest received and dividends received. ii. **Cash flows from operating activities.** This covers taxation paid.	Cash received from investments or paid on loans	i. Interest received ii. Dividends received	i. Interest paid
Taxation	**Cash flows from operating activities**, covers taxation.	Cash paid to government for taxation	i. Taxation refunds	i. Taxation paid
Capital Expenditure and Financial Investment	Cash flows from investing activities.	Cash flows relating to the purchase and sale of i. fixed assets ii. investments	i. Receipts for sale of fixed assets, e.g., motor vehicles ii. Sale of investments	i. Payments for fixed assets, e.g., motor vehicles ii. Purchase of investments
Acquisitions and Disposals[2]	**Cash flows from investing activities**	Payments for the purchase or sale of other companies	i. Cash paid to buy another company	i. Cash received for sale of another company
Equity Dividends Paid		Dividends companies pay to shareholders	None	Dividends paid
Financing	**Cash flows from financing activities**	Cash flows relating to the issuing or buying back of shares or loan capital	Cash received from the issue of i. shares ii. loans	Cash paid to buy back i. shares ii. loans

1. Where cash flow is positive we use the term net cash inflow, where it is negative we use net cash outflow.
2. This item mainly applies to groups of companies. They are outside the scope of this chapter.

We use the headings in column A for sole traders, partnerships and non-listed companies. We use the three headings in the column B for listed companies: (1) Cash flows from operating activities (which covers flows from operating activities, taxation); (2) Cash flows from investing activities (which covers capital expenditure and financial investment, acquisitions and disposals, interest received and dividends received); and (3) Cash flows from financing activities. Unfortunately, these headings are very cumbersome and often lack transparency.

Relationship between Cash and Profit

Cash and profit are fundamentally different. In essence, cash flow and profit are based on different principles. Cash flow is based on cash received and cash paid (see Figure 8.3). By contrast, profit is concerned with income earned and expenses incurred.

Figure 8.3   Cash Flow and Profit

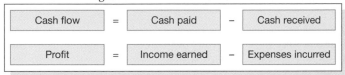

| Cash flow | = | Cash paid | − | Cash received |
| Profit | = | Income earned | − | Expenses incurred |

In a sense, the difference between the two merely results from the timing of the cash flows. For example, a telephone bill owing at the year end is included as an accrued expense in the profit and loss account, but is not counted as a cash payment. However, next year the situation will reverse and there will be a cash outflow, but no expense.

An important difference between profit and cash flow is depreciation. Depreciation is a non-cash flow item. Cash flows occur only when fixed assets are bought or sold. Real-Life Nugget 8.4 demonstrates this.

REAL-LIFE NUGGET 8.4

Cash Loss vs. Stated Loss

As always, there is the need to distinguish between a stated loss, per the profit and loss account, and a cash loss. One company the author handled was running at an apparently frightening loss of £25,000 per month, but on closer examination there was not too much to worry about. It had a £30,000 monthly depreciation provision. It was in reality producing a cash-positive profit of £5,000 per month. It had *years* of life before it. This gave all the time needed to get the operation right.

Source: B. Warnes (1984), *The Genghis Khan Guide to Business*, Osmosis Publications, London, p. 63

Figure 8.4 shows how some common items are treated in the profit and loss account and cash flow statement. Some items, such as sale of goods for cash, appear in both. However, amounts owing, such as a telephone bill, appear only in the profit and loss account. By contrast, money received from a loan only affects the cash flow statement.

Figure 8.4   Demonstration of How Some Items Affect the Profit and Loss Account and Some Affect the Cash Flow Statement

Transaction	In Profit and Loss Account	In Cash Flow Statement
i. Sale of goods for cash	Yes	Yes
ii. Sale of goods on credit	Yes	No
iii. Telephone bill for year owing	Yes	No
iv. Telephone bill for year paid	Yes	Yes
v. Cash purchase of fixed assets	No	Yes
vi. Profit on sale of fixed assets	Yes	No
vii. Cash from sale of fixed assets	No	Yes
viii. Money received from a loan	No	Yes
ix. Bank interest received for a year	Yes	Yes

Sometimes, a business may make a profit, but run out of cash. This is called overtrading and happens especially when a business starts trading.

PAUSE FOR THOUGHT 8.3

Overtrading, Cash Flow vs. Profit

A company, Bigger is Better, doubles its sales every month.

Month	1	2	3	4
	£000	£000	£000	£000
Sales	10	20	40	80
Purchases	(8)	(16)	(32)	(64)
Profit	2	4	8	16

It pays its purchases at once, but has to wait two months for its customers to pay for the sales. The bank, which has loaned £10,000, will close down the business if it is owed £50,000. *What happens?*

....

Month	1	2	3	4
	£000	£000	£000	£000
Cash at bank	10	2	(14)	(36)
Cash in	–	–	10	20
Cash out	(8)	(16)	(32)	(64)
Cash at bank	2	(14)	(36)	(80)

The result: Bye-bye, Bigger is Better. Even though the business is trading profitably, it has run out of cash. This is because the first cash is received in month 3, but the cash outflows start at once.

Preparation of Cash Flow Statement

In this section, we present the two methods of preparing cash flow statements (the direct and indirect methods). In Figure 8.5 a cash flow statement is prepared for a sole trader using the **direct method,** which classifies *operating* cash flows by function or type of activity (e.g., receipts from customers). In essence, this resembles the cash flow statement for Gavin Stevens in Figure 8.1. We assume a bank has requested a cash flow statement and that it is possible to extract the figures directly from the company's accounting records. We then present the cash flow statement for a company using the more conventional **indirect method** (see Figures 8.8 and 8.9 on pages 200 and 201). In this case, we derive the operating cash flow from the profit and loss account and balance sheets. Finally, in Figure 8.10, we prepare a cash flow statement using International Financial Reporting Standards with the same basic information that was in Figure 8.9.

Direct Method

This method of preparing cash flow statements is relatively easy to understand. It is made of functional flows such as payments to suppliers or employees. These are usually extracted from the cash book or bank account. Figure 8.5 on the next page demonstrates the direct method.

PAUSE FOR THOUGHT 8.4

Profit and Positive Cash Flow

If a company makes a profit, does this mean that it will have a positive cash flow?

....

No! Not necessarily. A fundamental point to grasp is that if a company makes a profit this means that its *assets will increase*, but this increase in assets *will not necessarily be in the form of cash*. Assets other than cash may increase (e.g., fixed assets, stock or debtors) or liabilities may decrease. This can be shown by a quick example. Noreen O. Cash has two assets: stock £25,000 and cash £50,000. Noreen makes a profit of £25,000, but invests it all in stock. We can, therefore, compare the two balance sheets.

	Before £	After £		Before £	After £
Stock	25,000	50,000	Capital	75,000	75,000
Cash	50,000	50,000	Profit	–	25,000
	75,000	100,000		75,000	100,000

There is a profit, but it does not affect cash. The increase in profit is reflected in the increase in stock.

We used the headings in Figure 8.2. The *net cash inflow from operating activities* represents all the cash flows relating to trading activities (i.e., buying or selling goods). By contrast, *returns on investments and servicing of finance* deals with interest received or paid, resulting from money invested or money borrowed. *Capital expenditure and financial investment* are concerned with the cash spent on, or received from, buying or selling fixed assets. Finally, *financing* represents a loan paid into the bank.

From Richard Hussey's cash flow statement it is clear that cash has increased by £66,400. However, the statement also clearly shows the separate components such as a positive operating cash flow of £59,150. By looking at the cash flow statement, Richard Hussey can quickly gain an overview of where his cash has come from and where it has been spent. The principles underlying the direct method of preparation are similar to those used in the construction of a cash budget (see Chapter 17).

Figure 8.5   Preparation of a Sole Trader's Cash Flow Statement Using the Direct Method

You have extracted the following aggregated cash figures from the accounting records of Richard Hussey, who runs a book shop. The bank has requested a cash flow statement. Prepare Hussey's cash flow statement for year ended 31 December 2009.

	£		£
Cash receipts from customers	150,000	Interest received	850
Cash payments to suppliers	60,000	Interest paid	400
Cash payments to employees	30,000	Cash from sale of	3,000
Cash expenses	850	motor car	
Loan received and paid into the bank	8,150	Payment for new motor car	4,350

Richard Hussey
Cash Flow Statement Year Ended 31 December 2009

	£	£
Net Cash Inflow from Operating Activities		
Receipts from customers	150,000	
Payments to suppliers	(60,000)	
Payments to employees	(30,000)	
Expenses	(850)	59,150
Returns on Investments and Servicing of Finance		
Interest received	850	
Interest paid	(400)	450
Capital Expenditure and Financial Investment		
Sale of motor car	3,000	
Purchase of motor car	(4,350)	(1,350)
Financing		
Loan	8,150	8,150
Increase in Cash		66,400

Indirect Method

The most common method of cash flow statement preparation is the indirect method. This method, which can be more difficult to understand than the direct method, has three steps.

- First, **we must adjust profit before taxation to arrive at operating profit.**
- Second, **we must reconcile operating profit to operating cash flow by adjusting for changes in working capital and for other non-cash flow items such as depreciation.** By adjusting the operating profit to arrive at operating cash flow, we effectively bypass the bank account. Instead of directly totalling all the operating cash flows from the bank account, we work indirectly from the figures in the profit and loss account and the opening and closing balance sheets. *This reconciliation is done either as a separate calculation or in the cash flow statement.*
- Third, **we can prepare the cash flow statement.**

These steps are outlined in Figure 8.6 and the direct and indirect methods are compared.

Figure 8.6   Comparison of Direct and Indirect Methods of Preparing Cash Flow Statements

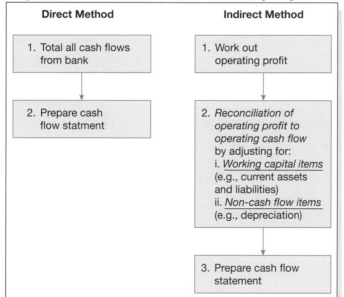

We will now look in more detail at the first two steps. Figure 8.8 illustrates them. We then work through a full example, Any Company Ltd, in Figure 8.9. This format has conventionally been used by all UK sole traders, partnerships and companies. However, as listed companies now follow IFRS we include an example, Any Company plc in Figure 8.10. Essentially, the method of preparation in the two figures is identical, but the presentation differs.

1. Calculation of Operating Profit by Adjusting Profit before Taxation

In the indirect method, we need to calculate operating cash flow (i.e., net cash flow from operating activities). To do this we need to first calculate operating profit so that we can reconcile operating profit to operating cash flow. Operating profit is calculated by *adjusting profit before taxation to operating profit*. The profit before tax figure must be adjusted by adding interest paid and deducting interest received, which are investment rather than operating items. (Strictly, these items are called interest payable and interest receivable, for simplicity we call them in this section interest paid and interest received: see Figure 6.5 for an explanation of this.) For listed companies, this adjustment is recorded under the heading *Net Cash Flow from Operating Activities*.

2. Reconciliation of Operating Profit to Operating Cash Flow

It is possible to identify two main types of adjustment needed to adjust operating profit to operating cash flow: (i) *working capital adjustments* and (ii) *non-cash flow items*, such as depreciation. It is important to emphasise that we need to consider operating cash flow and operating profit. The term 'operating' is used in accounting broadly to mean trading activities such as buying or selling goods or services. For listed companies, we start from profit before taxation not operating profit. Taxation paid is also deducted under *Net Cash Flow from Operating Activities*.

(i) Working Capital Adjustments   Effectively, working capital adjustments represent short-term timing adjustments between the profit and loss account and cash flow statement. They principally concern stock, debtors and creditors. Essentially, an increase in stock, debtors or prepayments (or a decrease in creditors or accruals) means less cash flowing into a business for the current year. For example, when debtors increase there is a delay in receiving the money. There is thus less money in the bank. By contrast, a decrease in stock, debtors or prepayments (or an increase in creditors or accruals) will mean more cash flowing into the business.

(ii) Non-Cash Flow Items   Two major items are depreciation and profit or loss on the sale of fixed assets. These two items are recorded in the profit and loss account, but not in the cash flow statement. **Depreciation** (which has reduced profit) must be **added back to profit** to arrive at cash flow. By contrast, **profit on sale of fixed assets** (which has increased profit) must be **deducted from profit** to arrive at *Operating Cash Flow*. Cash actually spent on purchasing fixed assets or received from selling fixed assets is included under *Capital Expenditure and Financial Investment* (or for listed companies *Cash Flows from Investing Activities*) in the cash flow statement.

Figure 8.7 provides examples of both working capital and non-cash flow adjustments.

Figure 8.7   Summary of Adjustments Made to Profit to Arrive at Cash Flow

Item	Effect on Cash Flow	Adjustment
i. Working Capital (Source: **Comparison of opening and closing balance sheets**) Increase in stock Increase in debtors Increase in prepayments Decrease in creditors Decrease in accruals	All of these **reduce** cash flow as more 'cash' is tied up in working capital (i.e., current assets less current liabilities)	**Deduct from profit** to arrive at cash flow
Decrease in stock Decrease in debtors Decrease in prepayments Increase in creditors Increase in accruals	All of these **increase** cash flow as less cash is tied up in working capital (i.e., current assets less current liabilities)	**Add to profit** to arrive at cash flow
ii. Non-Cash Flow Items (Source: **Profit and loss account**) Depreciation Loss on sale of fixed assets	Have **no effect** on cash flow, but were deducted from profit as expenses	**Add back to profit** to arrive at cash flow
Profit on sale of fixed assets	Has **no effect** on cash flow, but increased profit as other income	**Deduct from profit** to arrive at cash flow

Figure 8.8 on the next page now demonstrates the first two steps (calculation of operating profit and reconciliation of operating profit to operating cash flow). **The increases or decreases in working capital items are established by comparing the individual current assets and current liabilities in the opening and closing balance sheets.** By contrast, the **non-cash flow items (depreciation and profit on sale of fixed assets) are taken from the profit and loss account.**

Figure 8.8   Illustration of Profit Adjustments

Colette Ash has the following extracts from her business profit and loss account for year ending 31 December 2009 and the balance sheets as at 31 December 2008 and 31 December 2009. Reconcile her operating profit to her operating cash flow.

Profit and Loss Account	£	Balance Sheets	31.12.2008	31.12.2009
Profit before Taxation	95,000	**Current Assets**	£	£
After deducting:		Stock	4,000	5,300
Depreciation	3,000	Debtors	3,250	3,000
Interest paid	10,000	Prepayments	350	300
After adding:		Cash	6,300	10,500
Profit sale	1,000	**Current Liabilities**		
of fixed assets		Creditors	(1,850)	(1,750)
Interest received	5,000	Accruals	(650)	(700)

i. Calculation of Operating Profit

Before reconciling operating profit to operating cash flow, we must adjust our profit before taxation for interest paid and interest received which are investment rather than operating items. These items will appear in our cash flow statement as *returns on investments and servicing of finance*. Interest paid has already been deducted from our profit before taxation and interest received has already been credited to profit. We must reverse these entries. We, therefore, have

	£
Profit before Taxation	95,000
Add Interest paid	10,000
Less Interest received	(5,000)
Operating Profit	100,000

ii. Reconciliation of Operating Profit to Operating Cash Flow

We are now in a position to adjust the operating cash flow for all changes in working capital and for all non-cash flow items (i.e., depreciation and profit on sale of fixed assets).

C. Ash
Reconciliation of Operating Profit to Operating Cash Flow

	£	£
Operating Profit		100,000
Add:		
Decrease in debtors	250	
Decrease in prepayments	50	
Increase in accruals	50	
Depreciation	3,000	3,350
Deduct:		
Increase in stock	(1,300)	
Decrease in creditors	(100)	
Profit on sale of fixed assets	(1,000)	
		(2,400)
Net Cash Inflow from Operating Activities		100,950

The three-stage process is now illustrated in Figure 8.9, which shows the calculation of a cash flow statement for Any Company Ltd. The profit and loss accounts and balance sheets are provided. Then steps 1–3 which follow show how a cash flow statement would be prepared using the indirect method.

Figure 8.9   Preparation of the Cash Flow Statement of Any Company Ltd using the Indirect Method

Any Company Ltd
Profit and Loss Account Year Ended 31 December 2009 (extracts)

	£000
Profit before Taxation (see note below)	150
Taxation	(30)
Profit after Taxation	120
Dividends	(20)
Retained Profit	100

Note:
This is after having added interest received of £15 to profit and having deducted interest paid of £8 from profit.

Balance Sheets

	31 December 2008		31 December 2009	
	£000	£000	£000	£000
Fixed Assets				
Intangible Assets				
Patents		30		50
Tangible Assets				
Plant and machinery				
Cost	300		500	
Accumulated depreciation	(50)	250	(60)	440
Total fixed assets		280		490
Current Assets				
Stock	50		40	
Debtors	20		45	
Prepayments	25		30	
Cash	45	140	40	155
Current Liabilities				
Creditors	(35)		(15)	
Accruals	(5)	(40)	(10)	(25)
Net current assets		100		130
Total assets less current liabilities		380		620
Long-term Creditors		(80)		(110)
Total net assets		300		510
Capital and Reserves		£000		£000
Ordinary share capital		250		360
Profit and loss		50		150
Total shareholders' funds		300		510

Notes:
1. There are no disposals of fixed assets. Therefore, the increases in fixed assets between 2008 and 2009 are purchases of fixed assets.
2. Taxation and dividends in the profit and loss account equal the amounts actual paid. This will not always be so.

Figure 8.9   Preparation of the Cash Flow Statement of Any Company Ltd using the Indirect Method (*continued*)

Step 1: Calculation of Operating Profit

We need first to adjust net profit before taxation (£150) taken from profit and loss account, by adding back interest paid (£8) and deducting interest received (£15). These items are *investment* not operating flows. This is because we wish to determine operating or trading profit. Thus:

	£000
Net Profit before Taxation	150
Add Interest paid	8
Deduct Interest received	(15)
Operating Profit	143

Step 2: Reconciliation of Operating Profit to Operating Cash Flow

This involves taking the company's operating profit and then adjusting for:

(i). movements in working capital (e.g., increase or decreases in stock, debtors, prepayments, creditors and accruals).

(ii). non-cash flow items such as depreciation, and profit or loss on sale of fixed assets.

	£000	£000
Operating Profit		143
Add:		
Decrease in stock (1)	10	
Increase in accruals (1)	5	
Depreciation (2)	10	25
Deduct:		
Increase in debtors (1)	(25)	
Increase in prepayments (1)	(5)	
Decrease in creditors (1)	(20)	(50)
Net Cash Inflow from Operating Activities		118

(1) Represents increases, or decreases, in the current assets and current liabilities sections between the two balance sheets (i.e., movements in working capital).

(2) Difference in accumulated depreciation in the two balance sheets represents depreciation for year (i.e., represents a non-cash flow item).

Step 3: Cash Flow Statement Year Ended 31 December

This involves deducing the relevant figures in the cash flow statement by using the existing figures from the profit and loss account and the opening and closing balance sheets. We start from net cash inflow calculated in Step 2

	£000	£000
Net Cash Inflow from Operating Activities (see above)		118
Returns on Investments and Servicing of Finance		
Interest received (1)	15	
Interest paid (1)	(8)	7
Taxation		
Taxation paid (1)	(30)	(30)
Capital Expenditure and Financial Investment		
Patents purchased (2)	(20)	
Plant and machinery purchased (2)	(200)	(220)
Equity Dividends Paid (1)	(20)	(20)
Financing		
Increase in long-term creditors (2)	30	
Increase in share capital (2)	110	140
Decrease in Cash (2)		(5)
		£000
Opening Cash		45
Decrease in cash		(5)
Closing Cash		40

Notes:

1. Figure from profit and loss account.

2. Represents increase or decrease from balance sheets.

In Figure 8.10, the same figures are used for Any Company plc. However, the headings used are those prescribed by International Financial Reporting Standards. To simplify things, the terminology for a non-listed company is maintained. For example, stock not inventory is used.

Figure 8.10 Preparation of the Cash Flow Statement of Any Company plc using the Indirect Method

The figures are the same as in Figure 8.9, Any Company Ltd, but this time the headings for a Listed Company are used. Note that *Net Cash Inflow from Operating Activities* is calculated in the Cash Flow Statement itself.

Any Company plc
Cash Flow Statement Year Ended 31 December

	£000	£000
Cash Flows from Operating Activities		
Net Profit before Taxation		150
Add:		
Interest paid (1)	8	
Decrease in inventory (2)	10	
Increase in accruals (2)	5	
Depreciation (3)	10	33
Deduct:		
Interest received (1)	(15)	
Increase in debtors (2)	(25)	
Increase in prepayments (2)	(5)	
Decrease in creditors (2)	(20)	
Interest paid (1)	(8)	
Taxation paid (4)	(30)	(103)
Net Cash Inflow from Operating Activities		80
Cash Flows from Investing Activities		
Patents purchased	(20)	
Plant and machinery purchased	(200)	
Interest received	15	
Net Cash used in Investing Activities		(205)
Cash Flows from Financing Activities		
Increase in long-term creditors	30	
Increase in share capital	110	
Dividends paid	(20)	
Net Cash from Financing Activities		120
Net Decrease in Cash		(5)
		£000
Opening Cash		45
Decrease in Cash		(5)
Closing Cash		40

Notes
1. Interest paid is both added back and deducted under operating activities. However, interest received is deducted from operating activities, but then recorded as an inflow under investing activities. Note different treatment from a non-listed company where they are both recorded under *Returns on Investments* and *Servicing of Finance*.
2. These items are all movements in working capital.
3. Depreciation is a non-cash flow item.
4. Taxation paid is recorded under operating activities not under *Taxation* as per a non-listed company.

Helpnote:
The main differences between the two methods of presentation are that:
1. More detail is recorded under operating activities in the listed company method. In this category, we add interest paid and deduct interest received, interest paid and taxation paid. For a non-listed company, interest paid and interest received are recorded under *Investing Activities* and taxation paid under *Taxation*.
2. Under the listed company, there are only three headings not six as under the non-listed company format.

An example of a cash flow statement for AstraZeneca, a UK listed company, is given in Company Camera 8.1.

Cash Flow Statement in Listed Company Format

Consolidated Cash Flow Statement

For the six months ended 30 June	2005 $m	As restated 2004 $m
Cash flows from operating activities		
Profit before tax	3,235	2,130
Finance income and expense	(64)	(26)
Depreciation and amortisation	630	605
Decrease/(increase) in working capital	131	(378)
Other non-cash movements	45	84
Cash generated from operations	3,977	2,415
Interest paid	(13)	(19)
Tax paid	(810)	(713)
Net cash inflow from operating activities	3,154	1,683
Cash flows from investing activities		
Disposal of business operations	–	68
Movement in short term investments and fixed deposits	776	443
Purchases of property, plant and equipment	(411)	(583)
Disposals of property, plant and equipment	73	11
Purchase of intangible assets	(38)	(95)
Purchase of fixed asset investments	(6)	(7)
Interest received	88	86
Dividends paid by subsidiaries to minority interests	(5)	(5)
Dividends received	–	4
Net cash inflow/(outflow) from investing activities	477	(78)
Net cash inflow before financing activities	3,631	1,605
Cash flows from financing activities		
Proceeds from issue of share capital	34	72
Repurchase of shares	(1,182)	(968)
Increase in loans	–	731
Dividends paid	(1,079)	(897)
Movement in short term borrowings	10	(2)
Net cash outflow from financing activities	(2,217)	(1,064)
Net increase in cash and cash equivalents in the period	1,414	541
Cash and cash equivalents at beginning of the period	3,927	872
Exchange rate effects	(28)	(16)
Cash and cash equivalents at the end of the period	5,313	1,397
Cash and cash equivalents consists of:		
Cash and cash equivalents	5,451	1,499
Overdrafts	(138)	(102)
	5,313	1,397

Source: AstraZeneca, Half year results 2005, p.17.

All the adjusted figures, therefore, involved comparing the two balance sheets or taking figures direct from the profit and loss account. In Figures 8.9 and 8.10, the *dividends and taxation* in the profit and loss were *assumed to be the amounts paid*. This will not always be so. Where this is not the case, it is necessary to do some detective work to arrive at cash paid! This is illustrated for dividends paid and tax paid in Figure 8.11.

Figure 8.11 Deducing Cash Paid for Dividends or Tax – the Sherlock Holmes Approach

If we have only details of dividends payable or tax payable and the amount for the year, *we need to deduce dividends paid* or tax paid by a bit of detective work. For example, S. Holmes Ltd has the following information:

Profit and Loss Account (extracts)   **Balance Sheets (extracts)**

				2004	2005
	£			£	£
Tax	9,000	Tax payable		6,500	7,500
Dividends	4,000	Dividends proposed		4,000	5,000

How much did S. Holmes pay for dividends and taxation?

Effectively, we know the opening and closing amounts owing (i.e., accruals) and the profit and loss charge. The amount paid is the balancing figure.

	Opening accrual	+	Profit and loss	−	Amount paid	=	Closing accrual
∴ Tax:	£6,500	+	£9,000	−	£8,000	=	£7,500
Dividends:	£4,000	+	£4,000	−	£3,000	=	£5,000

Or for those who like 'T' accounts.

Tax or dividends account

	£		£
Amount paid	x	Opening accrual	x
Closing accrual	x	Profit and Loss	x
	x		x

Tax   Dividends

	£		£		£		£
Amount paid	8,000	Opening accrual	6,500	**Amount paid**	3,000	Opening accrual	4,000
Closing accrual	7,500	Profit and Loss	9,000	Closing accrual	5,000	Profit and Loss	4,000
	15,500		15,500		8,000		8,000

Thus tax paid = £8,000 and dividends paid = £3,000

Essentially, we find the total liability by adding the amount owing at the start of the year to the amount incurred during the year recorded in the profit and loss account. If we then deduct the amount owing at the end of the year, we arrive at the amount paid.

In Company Camera 8.2, J.D. Wetherspoon's 2004 cash flow statement is presented. Although Wetherspoon is a listed company, the cash flow statement was prepared before 2005 and can be treated as that applicable to non-listed companies. There was also a net investment in new pubs of £54.6 million (under net cash outflow from capital expenditure). Finally, Wetherspoon financed its operations mainly by bank loans of £47.9 million. Overall, Wetherspoon's cash decreased by £5.5 million. Wetherspoon also reports its free cash flow (£75.0 million). Essentially, this is a company's cash flow from ongoing activities excluding financing.

Cash flow statements provide important insights into a business's inflows and outflows of cash. From J.D. Wetherspoon's cash flow statement (see The Company Camera 8.2), for example, we can see that in 2004 there was a cash inflow from operating activities of £128.9 million.

THE COMPANY CAMERA 8.2

Cash flow statement for the year ended 25 July 2004

	Notes	2004 £000	2004 £000	2003 £000	2003 £000
Net cash inflow from operating activities	10	**128,874**	**128,874**	130,565	130,565
Returns on investments and servicing of finance					
Interest received		**20**	**20**	109	109
Interest paid		**(19,329)**	**(19,329)**	(21,251)	(21,251)
Refinancing costs paid		**(1,325)**		–	
Net cash outflow from returns on investment and servicing of finance		**(20,634)**		(21,142)	
Taxation					
Corporation tax paid		**(13,942)**	**(13,942)**	(10,277)	(10,277)
Capital expenditure and financial investment					
Purchase of tangible fixed assets for existing pubs		**(20,590)**	**(20,590)**	(15,896)	(15,896)
Proceeds of sale of tangible fixed assets		**7,891**		10,732	
Purchase of own shares for ESOP trust		–		(153)	
Purchase of own shares for Employee Share Incentive Plan		**(1,556)**		–	
Investment in new pubs and pub extensions		**(54,056)**		(77,275)	
Net cash outflow from capital expenditure and financial investment		**(68,311)**		(82,592)	
Equity dividends paid		**(7,322)**		(5,438)	
Net cash inflow before financing		**18,665**		11,116	
Financing					
Issue of ordinary shares		**1,219**		233	
Purchase of own shares		**(48,583)**		(17,369)	
Repayment of bank loans		**(25,000)**		(25,000)	
Advances under bank loans		**47,928**		32,527	
Advances under US senior loan notes		**271**		44	
Net cash (outflow) from financing		**(24,165)**		(9,565)	
Decrease/increase in cash	11	**(5,500)**		1,551	
Free cash flow	9		**75,033**		83,250
Cash flow per ordinary share	9		**37.5p**		38.8p

Source: J.D. Wetherspoon plc, 2004 Annual Report p. 21
Note: This cash flow statement was prepared by J.D. Wetherspoon before the company had to follow IFRS format for listed companies.

Most companies comment on their cash flow in their annual reports. Sainsbury's, for example, summarises its cash flow activities in The Company Camera 8.3.

THE COMPANY CAMERA 8.3

Net Cash Flow from Operating Activities

The Group's net debt has increased by £684 million during the year to £2,088 million of which £554 million relates to the purchase of IT assets through the acquisition of Swan.

Operating cash inflow remained strong at £847 million (2003: £1,070 million), but was lower than last year due to an adverse working capital movement. Working capital increased in the year by £221 million as a result of higher stock levels in Sainsbury's Supermarkets, due to the timing of Easter and the expansion of the General Merchandising activities. Creditors and other provisions have decreased due to lower incentive accruals and exceptional provisions required at the end of the year.

Source: Sainsbury's plc, Annual Report, 2004, p. 6

Conclusion

Cash and cash flow are at the heart of all businesses. Cash flow is principally concerned with cash received and cash paid. It can thus be contrasted with profit which is income earned less expenses incurred. Cash is initially entered into the bank account or cash book. Companies usually derive the cash flow statement from the profit and loss account and balance sheets, not the cash book. This is known as the indirect method of cash flow statement. The cash flow statement, after the profit and loss account and the balance sheet, is the third major financial statement. As well as preparing cash flow statements based on past cash flows, managers will constantly monitor current cash flows and forecast future cash flows. Cash is much harder to manipulate than profits. 'Accounting sleight of hand might shape profits whichever way a management team desires, but it is hard to deny that a cash balance is what it is. No more, no less.' (E. Warner, *Guardian*, 16 February 2002, p. 26).

Q&A   Discussion Questions

Questions with numbers in blue have answers at the back of the book.

Q1   At the start of this chapter, it was stated that 'cash is king' and that it is relatively easy 'to manufacture profits, but virtually impossible to create cash'. Discuss this statement.

Q2   What is the relationship between profit and cash flow?

Q3   The direct method of preparing the cash flow statement is the easiest to understand, but most companies use the indirect method. Why do you think this might be so?

Q4   Preparing a cash flow statement using the indirect method is like being an accounting detective. Discuss this view.

Q5   State whether the following are true or false. If false, explain why.
(a) Depreciation and profit from sale of fixed assets are both non-cash flow items and must be added back to operating profit to arrive at operating cash flow.
(b) Stock, debtors and fixed assets are all items of working capital.
(c) Decreases in current assets such as stock, debtors and prepayments must be added back to profit to arrive at cash flow.
(d) We need to adjust profit before taxation for non-operating items (such as interest paid or received) to arrive at operating profit for non-listed companies.
(e) The indirect method of cash flow statement is seldom used by large companies.

Q&A   Numerical Questions

These questions are designed to gradually increase in difficulty. Questions with numbers in blue have answers at the back of the book. The first seven questions relate to sole traders, partnerships and non-listed companies, therefore, the format as laid down in Financial Reporting Standard 1 should be used. In Question 8, which relates to a listed company, the format required under International Financial Reporting Standards should be used.

Q1   Bingo has the following items in its accounts:
(a) Dividends payable
(b) Cash from loan
(c) Sale of goods on credit
(d) Purchase of goods for cash
(e) Cash purchase of fixed assets
(f) Cash on sale of motor car
(g) Loan repaid

(h) Taxation payable
 (i) Receipts from share capital issue
 (j) Bank interest paid

Required: Are the above items recorded in the profit and loss account, the cash flow statement, or both? If these items appear in the cash flow statement, state which heading would be most appropriate when using the direct method (e.g., net cash inflow from operating activities).

Q2 The cash flows below were extracted from the accounts of Peter Piper, a music shop owner.

	£		£
Loan repaid	25,000	Purchase of office equipment	15,000
Sale of property	25,000	Interest paid	350
Interest received	1,150	Payments to suppliers	175,000
Payments to employees	55,000	Expenses paid	10,000
Receipts from customers	250,000		

Required: Prepare a cash flow statement using the **direct** method for the year ended 31 December 2009.

Q3 The *cash flows* below were extracted from the accounts of Picasso and Partners, a painting and decorating business.

	£		£
Bank interest paid	1,000	Purchase of a building	88,000
Loan received	9,000	Sale of office furniture	2,300
Cash for sale of a motor car	4,000	Payment for a motor car	12,000
Interest received	300		

Required: Prepare a cash flow statement under the **indirect** method for the year ended 31 December 2009. You know that the operating profit was £111,000 with £75,000 of working capital adjustments to be deducted and £15,000 of non-cash adjustments to be added back to arrive at operating cash flow. The operating profit has already been adjusted for the interest paid and received (so do not adjust again!).

Q4   Diana Rink Ltd, a chain of off-licences, has the following extracts from the accounts.

Profit and Loss Account   **Balance Sheets as at 31 December**

	£		2008 £	2009 £
Operating profit	95,000	**Current Assets**		
Depreciation for year	8,000	Stock	19,000	16,000
Profit on sale of	3,500	Debtors	10,000	11,150
fixed assets		Prepayments	5,000	3,500
		Cash	10,000	3,250
		Current Liabilities		
		Creditors	1,700	2,000
		Accruals	750	1,000

Required: Prepare a statement which reconciles operating profit to operating cash flow.

Q5   Brian Ridge Ltd, a construction company, has extracted the following *cash flows* from its books as at 30 November 2005.

	£		£
Operating profit	25,000	Interest paid	500
Increase in stock over year	3,500	Increase in long-term creditors	4,600
Increase in debtors over year	1,300	Purchase of plant and	18,350
Increase in creditors over year	800	machinery	
Depreciation for year	6,000	Share capital issued	3,200
Tax paid	23,500	Dividends paid	550
Interest received	3,000	Purchase of patents	1,650

Required: Prepare a cash flow statement using the indirect method. The operating profit has already been adjusted for the interest paid and received (so do not adjust again!).

Q6   You have the following extracts from the profit and loss account and balance sheets for Grow Hire Ltd, a transport company.

Grow Hire Ltd
Profit and Loss Account Year Ended 31 December 2009 (extracts)

	£000
Profit before Taxation (Note)	112,000
Taxation paid	(33,600)
Net Profit after Taxation	78,400
Dividends paid	(35,800)
Retained Profit	42,600

Note: After adding interest received £13,000 and deducting interest paid £6,500.

Q6   Grow Hire Ltd (*continued*)

Grow Hire Ltd
Balance Sheets as at 31 December

	2008		2009	
	£000	£000	£000	£000
Fixed Assets				
Intangible Assets				
Patents		8,000		42,200
Tangible Assets				
Land and buildings:				
Cost	144,000		164,000	
Accumulated depreciation	(28,000)	116,000	(44,000)	120,000
Total fixed assets		124,000		162,200
Current Assets				
Stock	112,000		110,000	
Debtors	18,000		11,000	
Cash	7,000		10,000	
	137,000		131,000	
Current Liabilities				
Creditors	(45,000)		(20,000)	
Accruals	(4,000)		(5,000)	
	(49,000)		(25,000)	
Net current assets		88,000		106,000
Total assets less current liabilities		212,000		268,200
Long-term Creditors		(16,000)		(28,000)
Total net assets		196,000		240,200
Capital and Reserves		£000		£000
Share capital		177,000		178,600
Profit and loss		19,000		61,600
Total shareholders' funds		196,000		240,200

There were no sales of fixed assets during the year.

Required: Prepare a cash flow statement using the indirect method for the year ended 31 December 2009.

Q7 You have the following information regarding dividends and taxation for Brain and Co., a software house.

Profit and Loss Account (Extract from Year to 31 December 2005)

	£
Profit before Taxation	106,508
Taxation	(51,638)
Profit after Taxation	54,870
Dividends	(27,329)
Retained Profit	27,541

Balance Sheets as at 31 December (Extracts)

	2004	2005
Current Liabilities	£	£
Tax payable	50,320	65,873
Dividends payable	23,100	29,400

Required: Calculate tax paid and dividends paid.

Q8 A construction company, Expenso plc, has the following summaries from the profit and loss accounts and balance sheets for the year ended 30 September 2009.

	£000
Sales	460,750
Cost of Sales	(328,123)
Gross Profit	132,627
Other Income	
Interest received	868
	133,495
Expenses includes interest	
paid £85,000	(123,478)
Profit before Taxation	10,017
Taxation	(3,005)
Profit for Year	7,012

Q8 Expenso plc (*continued*)

Expenso plc
Balance sheets as at 30 September

	2004 £000	2004 £000	2005 £000	2005 £000
ASSETS				
Non-current Assets				
Property, Plant and Equipment				
Land and buildings:				
Cost	20,000		26,000	
Accumulated depreciation	(7,000)		(8,000)	
Net book value	13,000		18,000	
Plant and machinery:				
Cost	25,000		30,000	
Accumulated depreciation	(8,500)		(10,000)	
Net book value	16,500	29,500	20,000	38,000
Intangible Assets				
Patents		4,000		4,500
Total non-current assets		33,500		42,500
Current Assets				
Inventory	2,800		6,400	
Trade receivables	3,200		4,500	
Cash	8,800	14,800	1,500	12,400
Total Assets		48,300		54,900
LIABILITIES				
Current Liabilities				
Trade payables	(4,600)		(5,000)	
Accruals	(400)		(350)	
Taxation	(4,200)		(3,200)	
	(9,200)		(8,550)	
Non-current Liabilities	(12,100)		(12,505)	
Total Liabilities		(21,300)		(21,055)
Net assets		27,000		33,845
EQUITY				
Capital and Reserves attributable to Equity Holders		£000		£000
Share capital		18,630		22,568
Retained earnings		8,370		11,277
Total Equity		27,000		33,845

Notes:
1. There were no sales of fixed assets during the year.
2. The dividends paid during the year were £4,105. They have been charged to retained earnings.

Required: Prepare a cash flow statement using the indirect method and using International Financial Reporting Standards for the year ended 30 September 2005.

Chapter 9

"More money has been lost reaching for yield than at the point of a gun."

Raymond Revoe Jr, *Fortune*, 18 April 1994, *Wiley Book of Business Quotations* (1998), p. 192

Interpretation of Accounts Learning Outcomes

After completing this chapter you should be able to:

✔ Explain the nature of accounting ratios.

✔ Appreciate the importance of the main accounting ratios.

✔ Calculate the main accounting ratios and explain their significance.

✔ Understand the limitations of ratio analysis.

Interpretation of Accounts

In a Nutshell

- *Ratio analysis is a method of evaluating the financial information presented in accounts.*
- *Ratio analysis is performed after the bookkeeping and preparation of final accounts.*
- *There are six main types of ratio: profitability, efficiency, liquidity, gearing, cash flow, and investment.*
- *Three important profitability ratios are return on capital employed (ROCE), gross profit ratio and net profit ratio.*
- *Four important efficiency ratios are debtors collection period, creditors collection period, stock turnover ratio and asset turnover ratio.*
- *Two important liquidity ratios are the current ratio and the quick ratio.*
- *Five important investment ratios are dividend yield, dividend cover, earnings per share (EPS), price earnings ratio, interest cover.*
- *Ratios can be viewed collectively using Z scores or pictics.*
- *For some, predominately non-profit oriented businesses, it is appropriate to use non-standard ratios, such as performance indicators.*
- *Four limitations of ratios are that they must be used in context, the absolute size of the business must be considered, ratios must be calculated on a consistent and comparable basis and international comparisons must be made with care.*

Introduction

The interpretation of accounts is the key to any in-depth understanding of an organisation's performance. Interpretation is basically when users evaluate the financial information, principally from the profit and loss account and balance sheet, so as to make judgements about issues such as profitability, efficiency, liquidity, gearing (i.e., amount of indebtedness), cash flow, and success of financial investment. The analysis is usually performed by using certain 'ratios' which take the raw accounting figures and turn them into simple indices. The aim is to try to measure and capture an organisation's performance using these ratios. This is often easier said than done!

Context

The interpretation of accounts (or ratio analysis) is carried out after the initial bookkeeping and preparation of the accounts. In other words, the transactions have been recorded in the books of account using double-entry bookkeeping and then the financial statements have been drawn up (see Figure 9.1). For this reason, the interpretation of accounts is often known as financial statement analysis. The financial statements which form the basis for ratio analysis are principally the profit and loss account (or income statement) and the balance sheet.

Figure 9.1   Main Stages in Accounting Process

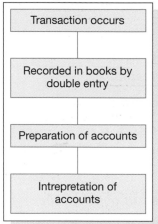

Overview

Two useful techniques, when interpreting a set of accounts, are (i) vertical and horizontal analysis, and (ii) ratio analysis. Vertical and horizontal analysis involve comparing key figures in the financial statements. In vertical analysis, key figures (such as sales in the profit and loss account and total net assets in the balance sheet) are set to 100 %. Other items are then expressed as a percentage of 100. In horizontal analysis, the company's profit and loss account (income statement) and balance sheet figures are compared across years. We return to vertical and horizontal analysis later in the chapter. For now, we focus on ratio analysis.

Broadly, ratio analysis can be divided into six major areas: profitability, efficiency, liquidity, gearing, cash flow and investment. The principal features are represented diagrammatically in Figure 9.3 on page 220, but set out in more detail in Figure 9.2 on the following page.

Figure 9.2   Principal Features of the Main Areas of the Interpretation of Accounts

Main Area	Main Source of Ratios	Main Ratios	Overview Definition
1. Profitability	Mainly derived from profit and loss account	1. Return on capital employed (ROCE)	$$\frac{\text{Profit before tax and loan interest}}{\text{Average capital employed}}$$
		2. Gross profit ratio	$$\frac{\text{Gross profit}}{\text{Sales}}$$
		3. Net profit ratio	$$\frac{\text{Net profit before tax}}{\text{Sales}}$$
2. Efficiency	Mixture of profit and loss account and balance sheet information	1. Debtors collection period*	$$\frac{\text{Average debtors}}{\text{Credit sales}}$$
		2. Creditors collection period*	$$\frac{\text{Average creditors}}{\text{Credit purchases}}$$
		3. Stock turnover ratio*	$$\frac{\text{Cost of sales}}{\text{Average stock}}$$
		4. Asset turnover ratio	$$\frac{\text{Sales}}{\text{Average total assets}}$$
3. Liquidity	Mainly from balance sheet	1. Current ratio	$$\frac{\text{Current assets}}{\text{Current liabilities}}$$
		2. Quick ratio*	$$\frac{\text{Current assets} - \text{stock}}{\text{Current liabilities}}$$
4. Gearing	Mainly from balance sheet	1. Gearing ratio	$$\frac{\text{Long-term borrowing}}{\text{Total long-term capital}}$$
5. Cash flow	Cash flow statement	1. Cash flow ratio	$$\frac{\text{Total cash inflows}}{\text{Total cash outflows}}$$
6. Investment	Mainly share price and profit and loss account information	1. Dividend yield	$$\frac{\text{Dividend per ordinary share}}{\text{Share price}}$$
		2. Dividend cover	$$\frac{\text{Profit after tax and preference shares}}{\text{Ordinary dividends}}$$
		3. Earnings per share	$$\frac{\text{Profit after tax and preference dividends}}{\text{Number of ordinary shares}}$$
		4. Price/earnings ratio	$$\frac{\text{Share price}}{\text{Earnings per share}}$$
		5. Interest cover	$$\frac{\text{Profit before tax and loan interest}}{\text{Loan interest}}$$

Note: For listed companies the ratios are essentially the same, but the terminology will be different for the four ratios with an asterisk. For example, the debtors collection period would be replaced by the trade receivables collection period. The definition would be: $\frac{\text{average trade receivables}}{\text{credit sales}}$

It is important to appreciate that there are potentially many different ratios. The actual ratios used will depend on the nature of the business and the individual preferences of users. The interpretation of accounts and the choice of ratios is thus inherently subjective. The ratios in Figure 9.3 have been chosen because generally they are appropriate for most businesses and are commonly used.

Figure 9.3 Main Ratios

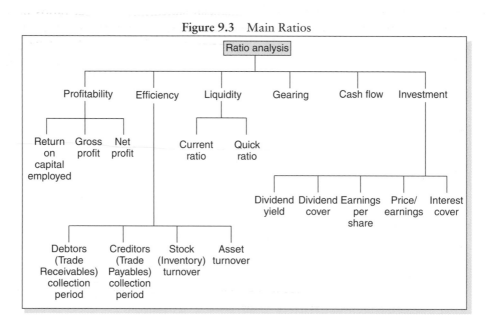

The 16 ratios, therefore, cover six main areas. Each of the above ratios can yield many more; for example, the gross profit ratio in Figure 9.2 is currently divided by sales. However, gross profit per employee (divide by number of employees) or gross profit per share (divide by number of shares) are also possible. The fun and frustration of ratio analysis is that there are no fixed rules. None of the ratios, except for earnings per share, is a regulatory requirement.

Importance of Ratios

Once the managers have prepared the accounts, then many other groups, such as investment analysts, will wish to comment on them. This is expressed in Soundbite 9.1. Different users will be interested in different ratios. For example, shareholders are primarily interested in investment ratios that measure the performance of their shares. By contrast, bankers and loan creditors may be interested primarily in liquidity (i.e., can the company repay its loan?). Ratios are important for three main reasons. First, they provide a quick and easily digestible snapshot of an organisation's achievements. It is much easier to glance at a set of ratios and draw conclusions from them than plough through the often quite complex financial statements. Second, ratios provide a good yardstick by which it is possible to compare one company with another (i.e., inter-firm comparisons) or to compare the same company over time (intra-firm comparisons). Third, ratio analysis takes account of size. One company may make more absolute profit than another. At first glance, it may, therefore, seem to be doing better than its competitor. However, if absolute size is taken into account it may in fact be performing less well.

PAUSE FOR THOUGHT 9.1

Ratios and Size

Two companies, David and Goliath, have net profits of £1 million and £100 million. Is it obvious that Goliath is doing better than David?

....

No! We need to take into account the size of the two businesses. David may be doing worse, but then again ... Imagine that David's sales were £5 million, while Goliath's sales were £5,000 million. Then, in £ millions,

	David			Goliath		
$\dfrac{\text{Net profit}}{\text{Sales}}$	$\dfrac{1}{5}$	=	20%	$\dfrac{100}{5,000}$	=	2%

Suddenly, Goliath's performance does not look so impressive. Size means everything when analysing ratios.

Closer Look at Main Ratios

It is now time to look in more depth at the main categories of ratio and at individual ratios. The ratios are mainly derived from the accounts of John Brown Ltd. Although John Brown is a non-listed limited company, many of the ratios are also potentially usable for partnerships or sole traders. They are also applicable to listed companies although as Figure 9.2 on page 220 shows the terminology is slightly different for some ratios. John Brown's financial statements are given at the back of this chapter as Appendix 9.1.

Some ratios (return on capital employed, debtors and creditors collection period, stock turnover and asset turnover) use average figures from two years' accounts. In practice, two years' figures are not always available. In this case, as for John Brown, the closing figures are used on their own. When this is done, then any conclusions must be drawn cautiously.

In order to place the interpretation of key ratios in context, I have, wherever the information was available, referred to figures calculated from the UK's top publicly quoted companies. This information was collected from Fame and Extel, two corporate databases, in July 2005. Where this information was not available I have used information from November 2001.

Profitability Ratios

The profitability ratios seek to establish how profitably a business is operating. Profit is a key measure of business success and, therefore, these ratios are keenly watched by both internal users, such as management, and external users, such as shareholders. There are three main profitability ratios (return on capital employed, gross profit ratio, and net profit ratio). The figures used are from John Brown Ltd (see Appendix 9.1).

(i) Return on Capital Employed

This ratio considers how effectively a company uses its capital employed. It compares net profit to capital employed. A problem with this ratio is that different companies often use different versions of capital employed. At its narrowest, a company's capital employed is ordinary share capital and reserves. At its widest, it might equal ordinary share capital and reserves, preference shares, long-term loans (i.e., debentures) and current liabilities. Different definitions of capital employed necessitate different definitions of profits.

The most common definition measures *profit before tax and loan interest* against *long-term capital* (i.e., ordinary share capital and reserves, preference share capital, long-term capital). Therefore, for John Brown we have:

$$\frac{\text{Profit before tax and loan interest}}{\text{Long-term capital (ordinary share capital and reserves, preference share capital and long-term loans)}} = \frac{50 + 10}{150 + 65 + 50 + 70} = \frac{60}{335} = 17.9\,\%$$

Essentially, the 17.9 % indicates the return which the business earns on its capital. The key question is: could the capital be used anywhere else to gain a better return? In this example, with only one year's balance sheet we can only take one year's capital employed. If we have an opening and a closing balance sheet, we can take the average capital employed over the two balance sheets.

(ii) Gross Profit Ratio

The gross profit ratio (or gross profit divided by sales) is a very useful ratio. It calculates the profit earned through trading. It is particularly useful in a business where stock is purchased, marked up and then resold. For example, a retail business selling car batteries (see Figure 9.4) may well buy the batteries from the manufacturer and then add a fixed percentage as mark-up. In the case of pubs, it is traditional to mark up the purchase price of beer by 100 % before reselling to customers.

Figure 9.4 Gross Profit Illustration

Snowfield batteries buys car batteries from a wholesaler for £40 each and resells them for £60 each. What will Snowfield's gross profit be?

It will simply be sales (£60) − purchases (£40) = gross profit (£20). Expressed as a percentage this is $\frac{20}{60}$ = 33.33%.

This is useful because Snowfield will know that its gross profit ratio should be 33.33%. If it is not, then there may be a problem, such as theft of stock.

In the case of John Brown, the gross profit is

$$\frac{\text{Gross profit}}{\text{Sales}} = \frac{100}{200} = 50\,\%$$

This is the *direct* return that John Brown makes from buying and selling goods.

(iii) Net Profit Ratio

The net profit ratio (or net profit divided by sales) is another key financial indicator. Whereas gross profit is calculated *before* taking expenses into account, the net profit ratio is calculated *after* expenses. This ratio may be calculated before or after taxation. For John Brown, the alternatives are:

$$\frac{\text{Net profit before taxation}}{\text{Sales}} = \frac{50}{200} = 25\,\%$$

$$\frac{\text{Net profit after taxation}}{\text{Sales}} = \frac{35}{200} = 17.5\,\%$$

The most popularly used alternative is net profit before taxation. This assumes that taxation is a factor that cannot be influenced by a business. This is the ratio which will be used from now on. As Real-Life Nugget 9.1 shows, most companies have traditionally, and still today, operate on net profit margins less than 10 %. Across the top UK 250 public limited companies this ratio was 11.4 % in July 2005.

REAL-LIFE NUGGET 9.1

Net Profit Margins

However as we have already said profits are only likely to be a comparatively minor factor in cash flow anyway. *After-tax* profits in even the most spectacularly successful company will rarely run at more than about 10 % of annual turnover and most companies will operate at well below this figure, say, 7 % or 8 % *before* tax.

Source: B. Warnes (1984) *The Genghis Khan Guide to Business*, Osmosis Publications, p. 66

Efficiency Ratios

The efficiency ratios look at how effectively a business is operating. They are primarily concerned with the efficient use of assets. Four of the main efficiency ratios are explained below (debtors collection period, creditors collection period, stock turnover, and asset turnover). The first two are related in that they seek to establish how long debtors and creditors take to pay. The figures used are from John Brown (see Appendix 9.1 at the end of this chapter).

(i) Debtors Collection Period (Trade Receivables Collection Period)

This ratio seeks to measure how long customers take to pay their debts. Obviously, the quicker a business collects and banks the money, the better it is for the company. This ratio can be worked out on a monthly, weekly or daily basis. This book prefers the daily basis as it is the most accurate method. The calculation for John Brown follows:

$$\text{Daily basis} = \frac{\text{Average debtors}}{\text{Credit sales per day}} = \frac{40}{200/365} = 73 \, \text{days} \; ?$$

It, therefore, takes 73 days for John Brown to collect its debts. It is important to note that 'credit' sales (i.e., not cash sales) are needed for this ratio to be fully effective. This information, although available internally in most organisations, may not be readily ascertainable from the published accounts. Normally, the average of opening and closing debtors is used to approximate average debtors. When this figure is not available (as in this case), we just use closing debtors. Across the top 250 UK plcs it took 52 days to collect money from debtors in July 2005.

(ii) Creditors Collection Period (Trade Payables Collection Period)

In many ways, this is the mirror image of the debtors collection period. It calculates how long it takes a business to pay its creditors. The slower a business is to pay the longer the business has the money in the bank! As with the debtors collection period, we can calculate this ratio either monthly, weekly or daily. Once more, we prefer the daily basis. This is calculated below for John Brown.

$$\text{Daily basis} = \frac{\text{Average creditors}}{\text{Credit purchases per day}} = \frac{50}{100/365} = 183 \text{ days}$$

It is usually not possible to establish accurately the figure for credit purchases from the published accounts. In John Brown, cost of sales is used as the nearest equivalent to credit purchases (remember that cost of sales is opening stock add purchases less closing stock). As with the debtors collection ratio, strictly we should use average creditors for the year (i.e. normally, the average of opening and closing creditors). If this is not available, as in this case, we use closing creditors.

It is often important to compare the debtors and creditors ratios. For John Brown, this is:

$$\frac{\text{Debtors collection period (in days)}}{\text{Creditors collection period (in days)}} = \frac{73 \text{ days}}{183 \text{ days}} = 0.40$$

In other words John Brown collects its cash from debtors in 40 % of the time that it takes to pay its creditors. The management of working capital is effective.

PAUSE FOR THOUGHT 9.2

Debtors and Creditors Collection Period

Businesses whose debtors collection periods are much less than their creditors collection periods are managing their working capital well. Can you think of any businesses which might be well placed to do this?

. . . .

Businesses which sell direct to customers, generally for cash, would be prime examples. Pubs and supermarkets operate on a cash basis, or with short-term credit (cheques or credit cards). Their debtor collection period is very low. However, they may well take their time to pay their suppliers. If they have a high turnover of goods, they may collect the money for their goods from customers before they have even paid their suppliers.

(iii) Stock Turnover Ratio (Inventory Turnover Ratio)

This ratio effectively measures the speed with which stocks move through the business. This varies from business to business and product to product. For example, crisps and chocolate have a high stock turnover, while diamond rings have a low turnover. Strictly this ratio compares cost of sales to average stock. Where this figure is not available, we use the next best thing, closing stock. Thus for John Brown, we have:

$$\frac{\text{Cost of sales}}{\text{Average stock}} = \frac{100}{60} = 1.66 \text{ times}$$

(iv) Asset Turnover Ratio

This ratio compares sales to total assets employed (i.e., fixed assets and current assets). Businesses with a large asset infrastructure, perhaps a steel works, have lower ratios than businesses with minimal assets, such as management consultancy or dot.com businesses. Once more, where the information is available, it is best to use average total assets. For John Brown, average total assets are not available, we therefore use this year's total assets:

$$\frac{\text{Sales}}{\text{Average total assets}} = \frac{200}{395} = 0.51 \text{ times}$$

In other words, every year John Brown generates about half of its total assets in sales. This is very low. There are many other potential asset turnover ratios where sales are compared to, for example, fixed assets or total net assets.

Liquidity Ratios

Liquidity ratios are derived from the balance sheet and seek to test how easily a firm can pay its debts. Loan creditors, such as bankers, who have loaned money to a business are particularly interested in these ratios. There are two main ratios (the current ratio and quick ratio). Once more we use John Brown (Appendix 9.1).

(i) Current Ratio

This ratio tests whether the short-term assets cover the short-term liabilities. If they do not, then there will be insufficient liquid funds immediately to pay the creditors. For John Brown this ratio is:

$$\frac{\text{Current assets}}{\text{Current liabilities}} = \frac{120}{60} = 2$$

In other words, the short-term assets are double the short-term liabilities. John Brown is well covered. Across the top 250 UK plcs, this ratio was 2.16 in July 2005. In other words, current assets were double current liabilities.

(ii) Quick Ratio

This is sometimes called the 'acid test' ratio. It is a measure of extreme short-term liquidity. Basically, stock is sold, turning into debtors. When debtors pay, the business gains cash. The quick ratio excludes stock, the least liquid (i.e., the least cash-like) of the current assets, to arrive at an immediate test of a company's liquidity. If the creditors come knocking on the door for their money, can the business survive? For John Brown we have:

$$\frac{\text{Current assets} - \text{stock}}{\text{Current liabilities}} = \frac{120 - 60}{60} = 1.0$$

For John Brown, the answer is yes. John Brown has just enough debtors and cash to cover its immediate liabilities. Across the top 250 UK plcs in July 2005 this ratio was 1.80.

Gearing

Like liquidity ratios, gearing ratios are derived from the balance sheet. Gearing effectively represents the relationship between the ordinary shareholders' funds and the debt capital of a company. Essentially, ordinary shareholders' funds represent the capital owned by the ordinary shareholders. By contrast, debt capital is that supplied by external parties (normally preference shareholders and loan holders).

So far, so good. However, the role of preference share capital and short-term liabilities is worth discussing. First, preference share capital is technically part of shareholders' funds, but preference shareholders **do not own** the company and usually receive a fixed dividend. We therefore treat them as debt. Second, current liabilities and short-term loans, to some extent, do finance the company. However, generally gearing is concerned with *long-term* borrowing. Figure 9.5 now summarises shareholders' funds and long-term borrowings.

Figure 9.5   Main Elements of the Gearing Ratio

Ordinary Shareholders' Funds	Long-term Borrowings
Ordinary share capital Share premium account Revaluation reserve General reserve Profit and loss account Other reserves	Preference share capital Long-term loans (i.e., long-term creditors, also known as debentures)

We can now calculate the gearing ratio for John Brown. The preferred method used in this book is to compare long-term borrowings to total long-term capital employed (i.e., ordinary shareholders' fund plus long-term borrowings). Thus we have for John Brown:

$$\frac{\text{Long-term borrowings}}{\text{Total long-term capital}} = \frac{\text{Preference share capital and debentures}}{\substack{\text{Ordinary share capital, profit and loss}\\\text{account and preference share capital and}\\\text{long-term loans (i.e., long-term creditors)}}}$$

$$= \frac{50 + 70}{150 + 65 + 50 + 70} = \frac{120}{335} = 36\%$$

In other words, 36 % (or 36 pence in every £1) of John Brown is financed by long-term non-ownership capital. Essentially, the more highly geared a company, the more risky the situation for the owners when profitability is poor. This is because interest on long-term borrowings will be paid first. Thus, if profits are poor, there may be little, if anything, left to pay the dividends of ordinary shareholders. Conversely, if profits are booming there will be relatively more profits left for the ordinary shareholders since the return to the 'borrowers' is fixed. When judging the gearing ratio, it is thus important to bear in mind the overall profitability of the business.

Cash Flow

The cash flow ratio, unlike the other ratios we have considered so far, is prepared from the cash flow statement, not the profit and loss account or balance sheet. There are many possible ratios, but the one shown here simply measures total cash inflows to total cash outflows. This is illustrated in Figure 9.6 (it is based on Figure 8.9 from Chapter 8, Any Company Ltd).

Figure 9.6   The Cash Flow Ratio

Any Company Ltd has the following cash inflows and outflows (in £000s).

	Inflows	Outflows
Net Cash Inflow from Operating Activities	118	
Returns on Investments and Servicing of Finance	15	8
Taxation		30
Capital Expenditure and Financial Investment		220
Equity Dividends Paid		20
Financing	140	
Totals	273	278

Therefore, our cash flow ratio is:

$$\frac{\text{Total cash inflows}}{\text{Total cash outflows}} = \frac{273}{278} = 0.98$$

To all intents and purposes, our total cash inflows thus match our total cash outflows.

Investment Ratios

The investment ratios differ from the other ratios, as they focus specifically on returns to the shareholder (dividend yield, earnings per share and price/earnings ratio) or the ability of a company to sustain its dividend or interest payments (dividend cover and interest cover). The ratios once more are calculated from John Brown (see Appendix 9.1). The first four ratios covered below are mainly of concern to the shareholders. The fifth, interest cover, is of more interest to the holders of long-term loans. Many companies give details of investment ratios in their annual reports. The Company Camera 9.1 shows the earnings per share, dividends per share and dividend cover for Manchester United from 2000 to 2004.

THE COMPANY CAMERA 9.1

Investment Ratios

Earnings per share (pence)	7.4	11.5	9.6	5.5	4.6
Dividends per share (pence)	2.65	4.00	3.10	2.00	1.90
Dividend cover (times)	2.8	2.9	3.1	2.8	2.4

Source: Manchester United plc, 2004 Annual Report, p. 81

(i) Dividend Yield

This ratio shows how much dividend the ordinary shares earn as a proportion of their market price. The market price for the shares of leading public companies is shown daily in many newspapers, such as (in the UK) the *Financial Times*, the *Guardian*, the *Telegraph* or *The Times*. Dividend yield can be shown as net or gross of tax (dividends are paid net after deduction of tax; gross is inclusive of tax). The calculation of gross dividend varies according to the tax rate and tax rules. For simplicity, we just show the *net* dividend yield.

For John Brown, the dividend yield is:

$$\frac{\text{Dividend per ordinary share}}{\text{Share price}} = \frac{£10m \div £150m}{£0.67} = \frac{0.067}{£0.67} = 10\%$$

The dividend yield is perhaps comparable to the interest at the bank or building society. However, the increase or decrease in the share price over the year should also be borne in mind. The return from the dividend combined with the movement in share price is often known as the total shareholders' return. Across the top 200 UK plcs in November 2001, the dividend yield ratio was 4.1%.

(ii) Dividend Cover

This represents the 'safety net' for ordinary shareholders. It shows how many times profit available to pay ordinary shareholders' dividends covers the actual dividends. In other words, can the current dividend level be maintained easily. For John Brown we have:

$$\frac{\text{Profit after tax and preference dividends}}{\text{Ordinary dividends}} = \frac{30}{10} = 3.0$$

Thus, dividends are covered three times by current profits. As The Company Camera 9.2 shows, J.D. Wetherspoon's dividend is well covered by profit available. Across the top 200 UK plcs in November 2001, dividend cover was 2.5.

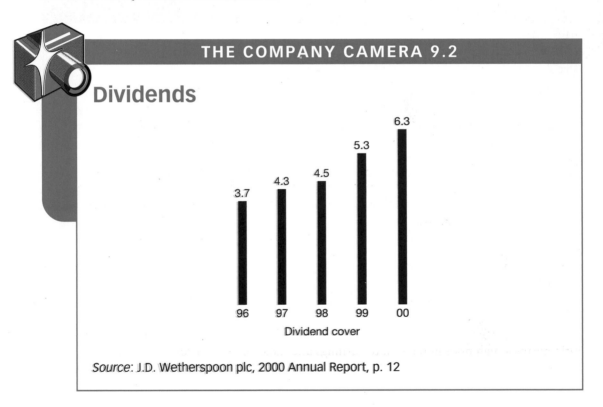

THE COMPANY CAMERA 9.2

Dividends

96: 3.7
97: 4.3
98: 4.5
99: 5.3
00: 6.3

Dividend cover

Source: J.D. Wetherspoon plc, 2000 Annual Report, p. 12

(iii) Earnings per Share (EPS)

Earnings per share (EPS) is a key measure by which investors measure the performance of a company. Its importance is shown by the fact that it is required to be shown in the published accounts of listed companies (unlike the other ratios). It measures the earnings attributable to a particular ordinary share. For John Brown it is:

$$\frac{\text{Profit after tax and preference dividends}}{\text{Number of ordinary shares}} = \frac{30}{150} = 20\text{p}$$

Each share thus earns 20 pence. Manchester United's EPS was 7.4p in 2004. As The Company Camera 9.3 shows, the number of ordinary shares is adjusted for the fact that some share options may be taken up to create new shares. This is called diluted EPS. Across the top 250 UK plcs in July 2005, EPS was 32.0 pence.

THE COMPANY CAMERA 9.3

Earnings per Share

10 Earnings per ordinary share

The calculation of earnings per share is based on the profit for the year and the weighted average number of ordinary shares in issue for the year of 260,734,479 (2003 259,276,711). Share options outstanding at each year end have no dilutive effect on basic earnings per share.

The calculation of diluted earnings per share is based on the profit for the year divided by the weighted average number of shares in issue, adjusted for the dilutive effect of outstanding share awards, being 262,189,660 (2003 259,992,683) shares.

Source: Manchester United plc, 2004 Annual Report, p. 64

(iv) Price/Earnings (P/E) Ratio

This is another key stock market measure. It uses EPS and relates it to the share price. A high ratio means a high price in relation to earnings and indicates a fast-growing, popular company. A low ratio usually indicates a slower-growing, more established company. If we look at John Brown, we have:

$$\frac{\text{Share price}}{\text{Earnings per share}} = \frac{67}{20} = 3.35$$

This indicates that the earnings per share is covered three times by the market price. In other words, it will take more than three years for current earnings to cover the market price. Across the top 200 UK plcs in November 2000, the P/E ratio was 36.

The P/E ratio is shown in the financial pages of newspapers along with dividend yield and the share price. In Real-Life Nugget 9.2, we show details from the *Guardian* for the aerospace and defence and automobiles sectors. This shows that the P/E ratio for aerospace and defence ranged from 13.9 to 21.5.

REAL-LIFE NUGGET 9.2

Share Price Details

London prices

52-WEEK			PRICE	CHANGE	YLD	P/E
HIGH	LOW	STOCK				
Aerospace & defence						
295.50	199.25	BAE Systems	292.25	+0.75	3.3	17.0
509.50	373.50	Chemring Group	508.00	−1.50	1.9	13.9
146.00	123.70	Cobham	138.75	−0.25	2.2	14.7
306.00	208.00	Meggitt	295.00	+1.25	2.4	18.8
312.00	223.38	Rolls-Royce	312.00	+1.25	2.6	21.5
961.00	9.13	Smiths Group	918.50	−0.50	3.0	20.7
829.50	617.00	Ultra Electronics	826.00	−3.50	1.7	18.8
495.00	377.50	†UMECO	495.00		2.7	17.5
357.00	255.25	†VT	331.00	−4.00	2.9	15.9
Automobiles						
283.00	187.50	Europen Motor	283.00	+5.50	3.4	8.2
268.75	202.00	GKN	264.00	−0.25	4.5	14.7
2092.00	1478.00	Inchcape	1957.00	−7.00	2.6	11.7
340.00	278.50	Lookers	316.50	+3.50	3.8	5.0
331.25	261.00	Pendragon	303.00	+1.75	3.4	9.5
552.50	413.00	Vardy (Reg)	557.50	−2.50	3.2	10.3
199.50	159.50	Wagon	165.50		5.6	–

Source: The Guardian, 26 July 2005

Explanation: The figures from left to right show the market capitalisation, the name of the share, the price on 26 July, the change since 25 July, the dividend yield and the P/E (price/earnings) ratio.

(v) Interest Cover

This ratio is of particular interest to those who have loaned money to the company. It shows the amount of profit available to cover the interest payable on long-term borrowings. Long-term borrowings can be defined as either preference shares and long-term loans or simply long-term loans. We will use only *long-term loans* here. This ratio is similar to dividend cover. It represents a safety net for borrowers. How much could profits fall before they failed to cover interest? However, it is worth pointing out that interest is paid out of cash, not profit. For John Brown, we have:

$$\frac{\text{Profit before tax and loan interest}}{\text{Loan interest}} = \frac{50 + 10}{10} = 6$$

Loan interest is thus covered six times (i.e., well-covered). Profits would have to fall dramatically before interest was not covered. Over the top 250 UK public limited companies in July 2005, this ratio was 23.56. Wetherspoon's interest cover is shown in Company Camera 9.4.

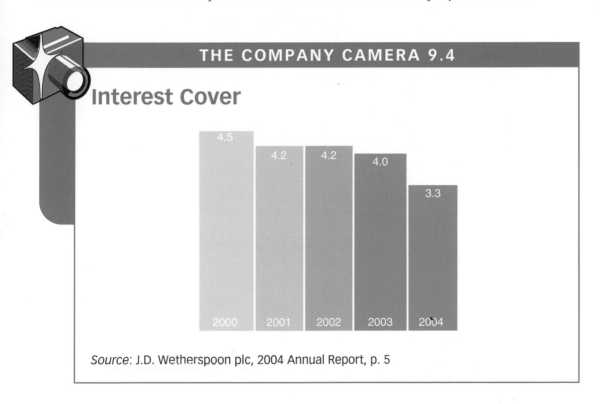

THE COMPANY CAMERA 9.4

Interest Cover

Year	Value
2000	4.5
2001	4.2
2002	4.2
2003	4.0
2004	3.3

Source: J.D. Wetherspoon plc, 2004 Annual Report, p. 5

Worked Example

Having explained the 16 ratios, it is now time to work through a full example. In order to do this, we use the summarised accounts of Stevens, Turner plc in Figure 9.7 (last seen in Chapter 7). Although adapted slightly, these are essentially the accounts in Figure 7.15. The main change is that there are now two years' figures and percentages.

Figure 9.7   Illustrative Example on Interpretation of Accounts

Summarised figures for Stevens, Turner plc 20X1 and 20X2					
	20X1	20X1	20X2	20X2	(Increase/decrease)
	£000	%	£000	%	%
Income Statements					
Sales (all credit)	350	100	450	100	+29
Cost of Sales (all credit)	(135)	(39)	(150)	(33)	+11
Gross Profit	215	61	300	67	+40
Loan interest	(8)	(2)	(10)	(2)	+25
Administrative expenses	(77)	(22)	(95)	(22)	+23
Profit before Taxation	130	37	195	43	+50
Taxation	(26)	(7)	(39)	(8)	+50
Profit for Year	104	30	156	35	+50
Balance Sheets					
ASSETS					
Non-current Assets					
Property, plant and equipment	600	90	611	75	+2
Intangible assets	50	7	250	31	+400
Total fixed assets	650	97	861	106	+32
Current Assets					
Inventory	25	4	42	5	+68
Trade receivables	80	12	38	5	−52
Bank	75	11	30	3	−60
	180	27	110	13	−39
Total Assets	830	124	971	119	+14
LIABILITIES					
Current Liabilities	(80)	(12)	(60)	(7)	−25
Non-current Liabilities	(80)	(12)	(100)	(12)	+25
Total Liabilities	(160)	(24)	(160)	(19)	–
Net Assets	670	100	811	100	+21
EQUITY	£000	%	£000	%	
Share Capital and Reserves attributable to Equity Holders					
Ordinary share capital (£1 each)	300	45	300	37	–
Preference share capital (£1 each)	150	22	150	18	–
	450	67	450	55	–
Reserves					
Share premium account	25	4	25	3	–
Revaluation reserve	30	4	30	4	–
General reserve	20	3	20	3	–
Retained earnings	154		301		
Less: Ordinary dividends	(6)		(12)		
Preference dividends	(3)		(3)		
	145	22	286	35	+97
Total Equity	670	100	811	100	+21
Market Price	£1		£1.50		

Vertical and Horizontal Analysis

Before calculating the ratios it is useful to perform vertical and horizontal analysis.

Vertical Analysis

Vertical analysis is where key figures in the accounts (such as sales, balance sheet totals) are set to 100 %. The other figures are then expressed as a percentage of 100 %. For example, cost of sales for 20X1 is 135, it is thus 39 % of sales (i.e., 135 of 350). Vertical analysis is a useful way to see if any figures have changed markedly during the year. Real-Life Nugget 9.3 presents a graph using vertical analysis for Tesco's 2004 results. In this case, total assets are shown as 100 %. In addition, Tesco's liquidity ratio (probably current ratio) and gearing are compared to that of other retailers.

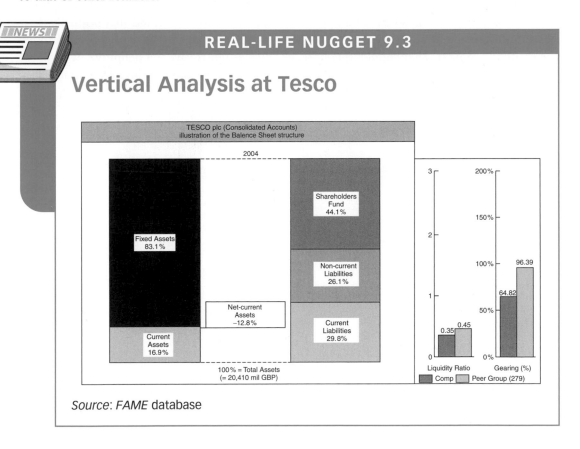

REAL-LIFE NUGGET 9.3

Vertical Analysis at Tesco

TESCO plc (Consolidated Accounts)
illustration of the Balance Sheet structure

2004

Fixed Assets 83.1%

Current Assets 16.9%

Net-current Assets −12.8%

Shareholders Fund 44.1%

Non-current Liabilities 26.1%

Current Liabilities 29.8%

100% = Total Assets (= 20,410 mil GBP)

Liquidity Ratio: 0.35, 0.45
Gearing (%): 64.82, 96.39

Comp / Peer Group (279)

Source: FAME database

In Stevens, Turner plc, in 20X2, we can see from the income statement that loan interest and administrative expenses represent 2 % and 22 % of sales, whereas in the balance sheet, in 20X2, tangible assets represent 75 % of total net assets. We need to assess whether or not these figures appear reasonable.

Horizontal Analysis

Whereas vertical analysis compares the figures within the same year, horizontal analysis compares the figures across time. Thus, for example, we see that sales have increased from £350,000 in 20X1 to £450,000 in 20X2, a 29 % increase. We need to investigate any major changes which look out of line. For example, why have there been so many changes in current assets: inventory, trade receivables, and cash have all changed markedly (i.e., inventory up 68 %, trade receivables down 52 %, and bank down 60 %)? These may represent normal trading changes, or then again....

Interpretation

We will now work through the various categories of ratio. We present them in tables and then make some observations. When reading these it needs to be borne in mind that normally these observations would be set in the context of the industry in which the company operates and in the economic context. They should, therefore, be taken as illustrative not definitive. We will use the available data. This is most comprehensive for 20X2 (as we can use the 20X1 comparative data).

(i) Profitability Ratios

Figure 9.8   Profitability Ratios for Stevens, Turner plc 20X1 and 20X2

Ratios	20X1	20X2
1. Return on Capital Employed		
$\dfrac{\text{Profit before tax and loan interest}}{\text{Average capital employed}^*}$	$\dfrac{130+8}{750^*}=18.4\%$	$\dfrac{195+10}{(911^*+750^{**})\div2}=24.7\%$
*(i.e. ordinary share capital and reserves, preference share capital and long-term capital, i.e. long-term creditors)	*(i.e., 300 + 25 + 30 + 20 + 145 + 150 + 80)	*(i.e., 300 + 25 + 30 + 20 + 20 + 286 + 150 + 100)
In 20X1, only one year-end figure is available.		*(i.e., 300 + 25 + 30 + 20 + 145 + 150 + 80)
2. Gross Profit Ratio		
$\dfrac{\text{Gross Profit}}{\text{Sales}}$	$\dfrac{215}{350}=61.4\%$	$\dfrac{300}{450}=66.7\%$
3. Net Profit Ratio		
$\dfrac{\text{Net profit before tax}}{\text{Sales}}$	$\dfrac{130}{350}=37.1\%$	$\dfrac{195}{450}=43.3\%$

Brief Discussion

Essentially, these profitability ratios tell us that Stevens, Turner plc's return on capital employed is running at between 18 % and 25 %, having increased over the year. This represents the return from the net assets of the company. Meanwhile, the business is operating on a high gross profit margin. This has also increased over the year. Finally, the net profit ratio has also increased, perhaps because the relative cost of sales has reduced.

(ii) Efficiency Ratios

Figure 9.9 Efficiency Ratios for Stevens, Turner plc 20X1 and 20X2

Ratios	20X1	20X2
1. Trade Receivables Collection Period		
$\dfrac{\text{Average trade receivables}}{\text{Credit sales per day}}$	$\dfrac{80^*}{350 \div 365} = 83$ days	$\dfrac{(80 + 38)^* \div 2}{450 \div 365} = 48$ days
	*only year-end figure available	*average of two year-end figures
2. Trade Payables Collection Period		
$\dfrac{\text{Average trade payables}}{\text{Credit purchases per day}^*}$	$\dfrac{80^*}{135 \div 365} = 216$ days	$\dfrac{(80 + 60)^* \div 2}{150 \div 365} = 170$ days
*in this case cost of sales	*only year-end figure available	*average of two year-end figures
3. Inventory Turnover Ratio		
$\dfrac{\text{Cost of sales}}{\text{Average inventory}}$	$\dfrac{135}{25^*} = 5.4$ times	$\dfrac{150}{(25 + 42)^* \div 2} = 4.48$ times
	*only year-end figure available	*average of two year-end figures
4. Asset Turnover Ratio		
$\dfrac{\text{Sales}}{\text{Average total assets}}$	$\dfrac{350}{50 + 600 + 180^*} = 0.42$ times	$\dfrac{450}{(50 + 250) + (600 + 611) + (180 + 110)/2^*} = 0.50$ times
(i.e., intangible, property, plant and equipment and current)	*the intangible assets, property, plant and equipment and current assets figures for 20X1	*the intangible assets, property, plant and equipment and current assets figures for 20X1 and 20X2 averaged (i.e. ÷ 2)

Brief Discussion

There have been substantial reductions in the trade receivables and trade payables collection periods. Trade receivables are now paid in 48 rather than 83 days. By contrast, Stevens, Turner pays its trade payables in 170 days not 216 days. By receiving money more quickly than paying it, Stevens, Turner is benefiting as its overall bank balance is healthier. However, it must be careful not to antagonise its suppliers as 170 days is a long time to withhold payment. Inventory is moving more slowly this year than last. However, each inventory item is still replaced $4^1/_2$ times each year. Finally, the asset turnover ratio is disappointing. Sales are considerably lower than total assets, even though there is some improvement over the year.

(iii) Liquidity Ratios

Figure 9.10   Liquidity Ratios for Stevens, Turner plc 20X1 and 20X2

Ratios	20X1	20X2
1. Current Ratio		
$\dfrac{\text{Current assets}}{\text{Current liabilities}}$	$\dfrac{180}{80} = 2.2$	$\dfrac{110}{60} = 1.8$
2. Quick Ratio		
$\dfrac{\text{Current assets} - \text{inventory}}{\text{Current liabilities}}$	$\dfrac{180 - 25}{80} = 1.9$	$\dfrac{110 - 42}{60} = 1.1$

Brief Discussion

There is a noted deterioration in both liquidity ratios. The current ratio has fallen from 2.2 to 1.8. Meanwhile, the quick ratio has declined from 1.9 to 1.1. While not immediately worrying, Stevens, Turner needs to pay attention to this.

(iv) Gearing Ratio

Figure 9.11   Gearing Ratio for Stevens, Turner plc 20X1 and 20X2

Ratio	20X1	20X2
$\dfrac{\text{Long term borrowings}^*}{\text{Total long} - \text{term capital}^{**}}$	$\dfrac{230^*}{750^{**}} = 30.7\%$	$\dfrac{250^*}{911^{**}} = 27.4\%$
*Preference shares and long-term loans (i.e., long-term creditors)	$^*150 + 80 = 230$	$^*150 + 100 = 250$
**Preference shares, long-term loans (i.e. long-term creditors), ordinary shares, share premium account, revaluation reserve, general reserve, retained earnings.	$^{**}150 + 80 + 300 + 25 + 30 + 20 + 145 = 750$	$^{**}150 + 100 + 300 + 25 + 30 + 20 + 286 = 911$

Brief Discussion

Gearing has declined over the year from 30.7% to 27.4%. In 20X2, 27.4 pence in the £ of the long-term capital employed is from borrowed money, rather than 30.7 pence last year. This improvement is due to the increase in retained profit during the year.

(v) Cash Flow Ratio

Figure 9.12   Cash Flow Ratio for Stevens, Turner plc 20X1 and 20X2

From the balance sheets and income statements in Figure 9.7, we can determine the cash flow statement. From this cash flow statement we can work out the cash inflows and cash outflows.

Stevens, Turner plc
Cash Flow Statement Year Ended 31.12.20X2

	£000	£000
Cash Flows from Operating Activities		
*Net Profit before Taxation and Loan Interest**		205
Add:		
Decrease in trade receivables	42	42
Deduct:		
Increase in inventory	(17)	
Decrease in trade payables	(20)	
Interest paid	(10)	
Taxation paid	(39)	(86)
Net Cash Inflow from Operating Activities		161
Cash Flows from Investing Activities		
Purchase of intangible assets	(200)	
Purchase of property, plant and equipment	(11)	(211)
Cash Flows from Financing Activities		
Increase in loan capital	20	
Dividends paid	(15)	5
Decrease in Cash		(45)
		£000
Opening Cash		75
Decrease in cash		(45)
Closing Cash		30

Therefore our cash flow ratio is:

	Cash Inflows	Cash Outflows
	£000	£000
Net Cash Inflow from Operating Activities	161	
Cash Flows from Investing Activities		211
Cash Flows from Financing Activities	5	
	166	211

$$\frac{\text{Total cash inflows}}{\text{Total cash outflows}} = \frac{166}{211} = 0.79.$$

More cash is flowing out than is flowing in. The main reason for this is the purchase of fixed assets.
*For simplicity, we assume no depreciation.

(vi) Investment Ratios

Figure 9.13   Investment Flow Ratios for Stevens, Turner plc 20X1 and 20X2

Ratios	20X1	20X2
1. Dividend Yield		
$\dfrac{\text{Dividend per ordinary share}^*}{\text{Share price}}$	$\dfrac{2^*}{100p} = 2\%$	$\dfrac{4^*}{150p} = 2.67\%$
*Net ordinary dividend by number shares	$^*6 \div 300 = 2p$	$^*12 \div 300 = 4p$
2. Dividend Cover		
$\dfrac{\text{Profit after tax and preference dividends}}{\text{Ordinary dividends}}$	$\dfrac{101}{6} = 16.8 \text{ times}$	$\dfrac{153}{12} = 12.8 \text{ times}$
3. Earnings per Share		
$\dfrac{\text{Profit after tax and preference dividends}}{\text{Number of ordinary shares}}$	$\dfrac{101}{300} = 33.7p$	$\dfrac{153}{300} = 51p$
4. Price/Earnings Ratio		
$\dfrac{\text{Share price}}{\text{Earnings per share}}$	$\dfrac{100}{33.7} = 3.0$	$\dfrac{150}{51} = 2.9$
5. Interest Cover		
$\dfrac{\text{Profit before tax and loan interest}}{\text{Loan interest}}$	$\dfrac{130 + 8}{8} = 17.2 \text{ times}$	$\dfrac{195 + 10}{10} = 20.5 \text{ times}$

Brief Discussion

The dividend yield is quite low at around 2 % to 3 %. However, it must be remembered that the share price has increased rapidly by 50p, and it is unusual to have strong capital growth and high dividends at the same time. Both dividend cover and interest cover are high. If necessary the company has the potential to increase dividends and interest. Earnings per share (EPS) has increased over the year and is now running at an improved 51 pence. It is this rise in EPS which may have fuelled the share price increase. The P/E ratio, however, is still very modest at 2.9.

Report Format

Students are often required to write a report on the performance of a company using ratio analysis. A report is not an essay! It has a pre-set style, usually including the following features:

- Terms of reference
- Heading
- Introduction
- Major sections
- Recommendations
- Appendix

Figure 9.14 illustrates a *concise* overall report on Stevens, Turner plc for 20X1 and 20X2.

Figure 9.14 Illustrative Report on Financial Performance of Stevens, Turner plc for 20X2

Report on the Financial Performance of Stevens, Turner plc Year Ended 20X2

1.0 Terms of Reference
The Managing Director requested a report on the financial performance of Stevens, Turner plc for the year ended 20X2 using appropriate ratio analysis.

2.0 Introduction
The income statement, balance sheet and cash flow data were used to prepare 16 ratios to assess the company's performance for 20X2. The 20X2 financial results were compared to those in 20X1. The underpinning ratios with their calculations are presented in the appendix. This report briefly covers the profitability, efficiency, liquidity, gearing, cash flow, and investment ratios.

3.0 Profitability
The company has traded quite profitably over the year. The return on capital employed and gross profit ratios have increased over the year from 18.4 % to 24.7 %, and from 61.4 % to 66.7 %, respectively. The net profit ratio improved from 37.1 % to 43.3 %. This ratio is extremely good.

4.0 Efficiency
The collection of money from trade receivables is still quicker than the payment of trade payables (48 days vs 170 days), which is good for cash flow. Both collection periods have declined over the year. The stock is turned over 4.48 times per year which is usual for this type of business. Finally, the asset turnover ratio appears quite low. However, once more this reflects the nature of the business.

5.0 Liquidity
Liquidity is an area to watch for the future. Both the current ratio and quick ratio have declined markedly over the year (from 2.2 to 1.8, and 1.9 to 1.1, respectively). While this is not immediately worrying, this ratio should not be allowed to slip any further.

6.0 Cash flow
The cash flow ratio is 0.84. More cash is flowing out than is coming in. The main reason appears to be the purchase of fixed assets.

7.0 Gearing
The dependence on outside borrowing has declined during the year from 30.7 % to 27.4 %. This is good news.

8.0 Investment
Both dividends and loan interest remain well-covered (respectively 12.8 times and 20.5 times). Overall, shareholders are receiving a good return for their investment. Share price has increased by 50 pence, which compensates for the low dividend yield of 2.67 %. The earnings per share remains a healthy 51p (up from 33.7p). Finally, the P/E ratio has remained steady at 2.9.

9.0 Conclusions
Overall, Stevens, Turner plc has had a good year in terms of profitability, investment performance, gearing, and efficiency ratios. The one area we really need to pay attention to is cash flow and liquidity. While not immediately worrying, this area should be carefully monitored.

Appendix 1 (Extract)

1. Return on capital employed	20X1			20X2		
$\dfrac{\text{Net profit before tax and loan interest}}{\text{Average capital employed}}$	$\dfrac{138}{750}$	=	18.4 %	$\dfrac{205}{830}$	=	24.7 %

Note: All the ratios are calculated in Figures 9.8 to 9.13.

A real report would be longer than this, but this report gives a good insight into the use of report format.

Holistic View of Ratios

So far we have looked at individual ratios. However, although useful, one ratio on its own may potentially be misleading or may even be manipulated through creative accounting. Therefore, there have been attempts to look at ratios collectively. Two main approaches are briefly discussed here.

1. The Z Score Model

The idea behind this model, which was first developed in the US, is to select ratios which when combined have a high predictive power. In the UK, an academic, Richard Taffler, developed the model using two groups of failed and non-failed companies. After a comprehensive study of accounts, he produced a model for listed industrial companies. This model proved successful in distinguishing between those companies which would go bankrupt and those companies which would not.

2. Pictics

Pictics are an ingenious way of presenting ratios. Essentially, each pictic is a face. The different elements of the face are represented by different ratios. Real-Life Nugget 9.4 demonstrates

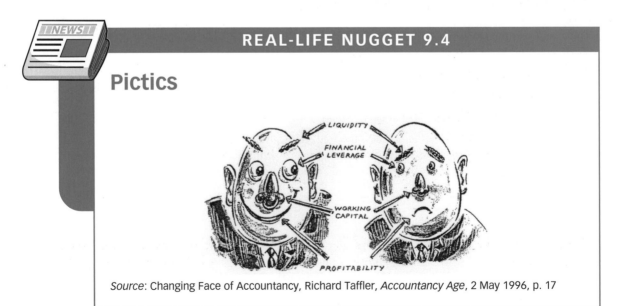

REAL-LIFE NUGGET 9.4

Pictics

Source: Changing Face of Accountancy, Richard Taffler, *Accountancy Age*, 2 May 1996, p. 17

two pictics. The face on the left represents a successful business while that on the right is an unsuccessful business. The size of the smile represents profitability while the length of the nose represents liquidity. Pictics are an easy way of presenting multi-dimensional information. Although it is easy to dismiss pictics as a joke, they have proved remarkably successful in controlled research studies.

Performance Indicators

The conventional mix of ratios may be unsuitable for some businesses, in particular those where non-financial performance is very important. Examples of such organisations include the National Health Service and the railways. Such businesses use customised performance measures often called performance indicators. For the National Health Service, indicators such as number of operations, or bed occupancy rate, may be more important than net profit.

PAUSE FOR THOUGHT 9.3

Performance Indicators

Which performance indicators do you think would be useful when assessing the performance of individual railway operating companies?

....

Potentially, there are many performance indicators. For example:

- Percentage of trains late
- Miles per passenger
- Volume of freight moved
- Passengers per train
- Number of complaints
- Number of accidents

Organisations like the rail companies need to balance financial considerations (such as making profits for shareholders) with non-financial factors (such as punctuality). As

Real-Life Nugget 9.5 shows, rail operating companies consider factors such as punctuality, passenger and train numbers as well as income from fares and subsidies.

REAL-LIFE NUGGET 9.5

Rail Companies Performance Indicators

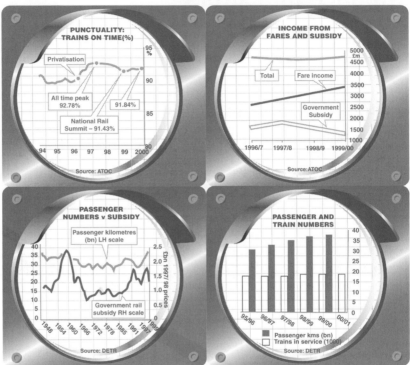

Source: Rail Companies in line for huge public handout, Arthur Leathley, *The Times*, 25 May 2000, p. 4

Limitations

Ratio analysis can be a useful financial tool. However, certain problems associated with ratio analysis must be appreciated.

1. Context

Ratios must be used in context. They cannot be used in isolation, but must be compared with past results or industry norms. Unless such a comparative approach is adopted ratio analysis is fraught with danger.

2. Absolute Size

Ratios give no indication of the relative size of the result. If net profit is 10 %, we do not know if this is 10 % of £100 or 10 % of £1 million. Both the ratio *and* the size of the organisation need to be taken into account.

3. Like with Like

We must ensure that we are comparing like with like. The accounting policies of different companies differ and this needs to be appreciated. If companies A and B, for example, use a different rate of depreciation then a net profit of 10 % for company A may equal 8 % for company B.

4. International Comparison

The comparison of companies in different countries is even more problematic than same-country comparisons. The economic and business infrastructure in Japan, for example, is very different from that in the US. Traditionally, this has led to the current ratio in the US being much higher than in Japan.

Despite the above limitations, ratios are widely used. As Real-Life Nugget 9.6 shows, even

REAL-LIFE NUGGET 9.6

Financial Ratios

Those of us with a grounding in accounting already know that financial information, although often (and naively) assumed to be precise, is necessarily based on significant assumptions and varying underlying principles. This means that accurate financial comparisons between companies (even those within the UK) cannot be made without a considerable amount of additional research and even restatement. In a cross-border analysis situation, the problem is further compounded by important accounting differences.

Despite this, traditional performance indicators such as profit margin, return on capital employed (ROCE), earnings per share (EPS) and the price earnings (P/E) ratio are widely published and used in decision making, often one suspects without any great attention being paid to what lies behind them. For example, banks, credit rating agencies, auditors, investment analysts, merger and acquisition teams and the financial press all use such financial ratios in their daily work.

Source: Financial Ratios: Can You Trust Them, M. Gardiner and K. Bagshaw, *Management Accounting*, September 1997, p. 30

though these accounting ratios are based on significant assumptions and varying underlying principles, they are still commonly employed by banks, credit rating agencies and other users.

Conclusion

Ratio analysis is a good way to gain an overview of an organisation's activities. There are a whole range of ratios on profitability, efficiency, liquidity, gearing, cash flow and investment. Taken together these ratios provide a comprehensive view of a company's financial activities. They are used to compare a company's performance over time as well as to compare different companies' financial performance. For certain businesses, particularly those not so profit-orientated, performance indicators provide a useful alternative. When calculating ratios care is necessary to ensure that the underlying figures have been drawn up in a consistent and comparable way. However, when used carefully, ratios are undoubtedly very useful.

Q&A   Discussion Questions

Questions with numbers in blue have answers at the back of the book.

Q1   What do you understand by ratio analysis? Distinguish between the main types of ratio analysis.

Q2   Do the advantages of ratio analysis outweigh the disadvantages? Discuss.

Q3   'Each of the main financial statements provides a distinct set of financial ratios.' Discuss this statement.

Q4   Devise a set of non-financial performance indicators which might be appropriate for monitoring:
(a) The Police
(b) The Post Office (now known as Royal Mail in the UK)

Q5   State whether the following are true or false? If false, explain why.

(a) Gross profit ratio $= \dfrac{\text{Gross profit}}{\text{Sales}}$

(b) Net profit ratio $= \dfrac{\text{Net profit after taxation}}{\text{Average capital employed}}$

(c) Current ratio $= \dfrac{\text{Current assets} - \text{stock}}{\text{Current liabilities}}$

(d) Debtors collection period $= \dfrac{\text{Debtors}}{\text{Credit sales per day}}$

(e) Asset turnover ratio $= \dfrac{\text{Sales}}{\text{Fixed assets}}$

(f) Dividend yield $= \dfrac{\text{Dividend per ordinary share}}{\text{Sales}}$

(g) Earnings per share $= \dfrac{\text{Profit after tax and preference dividends}}{\text{Number of ordinary shares}}$

Q&A Numerical Questions

Questions with numbers in blue have answers at the back of the book.

Q1 The information below is from the accounts of John Parry, a sole trader.

Trading and Profit and Loss Account Year Ended 31 December 2009

	£	£
Sales		150,000
Less Cost of Sales		
Opening stock	25,000	
Add Purchases	75,000	
	100,000	
Less Closing stock	30,000	70,000
Gross Profit		80,000
Less Expenses		30,000
Net Profit		50,000

Other information	31.12.2008	31.12.2009
	£	£
Total assets	50,000	60,000
Closing capital	300,000	500,000
Debtors	18,000	19,000
Creditors	9,000	10,000

Note: All of John Parry's sales and purchases are on credit.

Required: Calculate the following profitability and efficiency ratios:
(a) Return on capital employed
(b) Gross profit ratio
(c) Net profit ratio
(d) Debtors collection period
(e) Creditors collection period
(f) Stock turnover ratio
(g) Asset turnover ratio,

Q2 Henry Mellett has the following extracts from his balance sheet as at 31 March 2009.

	£
Current Assets	
Stock	18,213
Debtors	12,407
Cash	1,283
Current Liabilities	
Creditors	14,836
Long-term Creditors	30,000
Total net assets	150,000

Required: Calculate the following liquidity and gearing ratios:

(a) Current ratio

(b) Quick ratio

(c) Gearing ratio.

Q3 Jane Edwards Ltd has prepared her cash flow statement under the direct method. She has the following main cash flows.

	£		£
Cash from customers	125,000	Dividends paid	8,000
Cash paid to employees	18,300	Taxation paid	16,000
Cash paid to suppliers	9,250	Purchase of fixed assets	80,000
Issue of shares	29,000	Sale of fixed assets	35,000
Buy back loan	8,000		

Required: Calculate the cash flow ratio.

Q4 From the following information for Clatworthy plc calculate the investment ratios as indicated.

	£000
Sales	1,000
Profit before Taxation	750
(after charging loan interest of £40,000)	
Taxation	(150)
Profit for Year	600

Note: Preference dividends for the year were £20,000 and ordinary dividends were £40,000.

Market price ordinary shares £1.25. Number of ordinary shares in issue are 500,000.

Required:

(a) Dividend yield   (c) Earnings per share   (e) Interest cover.

(b) Dividend cover   (d) Price/earnings ratio

Q5   The abridged accounts for N.O. Hope plc are given below.

Income Statements	2004	2005
	£000	£000
Sales	400	440
Cost of Sales	(300)	(330)
Gross Profit	100	110
Administrative expenses	(15)	(25)
Distribution expenses	(5)	(10)
Profit before Taxation	80	75
Taxation	(16)	(15)
Profit for Year	64	60

Balance Sheets

ASSETS

Non-current Assets	£000	£000
Property, plant and equipment	120	235
Intangible assets	20	20
Total non-current assets	140	255
Current Assets		
Inventory	80	40
Trade receivables	40	20
Bank	20	10
	140	70
Total Assets	280	325

LIABILITIES

Current Liabilities	(70)	(75)
Non-current Liabilities	(20)	(40)
Total Liabilities	(90)	(115)
Net assets	190	210

EQUITY

Capital and Reserves attributable to Equity Holders	£000	£000
Share Capital		
Ordinary share capital (£1 each)	120	125
Preference share capital (£1 each)	17	17
	137	142
Reserves		
Capital reserves		
Share premium account	10	10
Revaluation reserve	10	10
Other reserves		
General reserve	8	8
Retained earnings	25	40
	53	68
Total Equity	190	210

Q5 N.O. Hope plc (*continued*)

1. Retained earnings were after taking dividends of £46,000 for 2004 and £45,000 for 2005 into account.

Required: Prepare a horizontal and vertical analysis. Highlight three figures that may need further enquiry.

Q6 The following two non-listed companies Alpha Industries and Beta Industries operate in the same industrial sector. You have extracted the following ratios from their accounts.

	Alpha	Beta
Return on capital employed	9%	20%
Gross profit ratio	25%	25%
Net profit ratio	7%	14%
Current ratio	2.1	1.7
Quick ratio	1.7	1.3
Price/Earnings ratio	4	8
Dividend cover	2	4

Required: Compare the financial performance of the two companies. All other things being equal, which company would you expect to have the higher market price?

Q7 Anteater plc has produced the following summary accounts.

Income Statement for the Year Ended 31 December 2009

	£000
Sales	1,000
Cost of sales	(750)
Gross Profit	250
Administrative expenses (includes debenture interest £3,000)	(120)
Distribution expenses	(30)
Profit before Taxation	100
Taxation	(20)
Profit for Year	80

Q7   Anteater plc (*continued*)

Balance Sheet as at 31 December 2009

	£000	£000
ASSETS		
Property, plant and equipment		420
Current Assets		
Inventory	40	
Trade receivables	50	
Cash	30	120
Total Assets		540
LIABILITIES		
Current Liabilities		(40)
Non-current Liabilities		(100)
Total Liabilities		(140)
Net Assets		400
Capital and Reserves attributable to Equity Holders		
Share Capital		£000
Ordinary share capital (£1 each)		300
Preference share capital (£1 each)		20
		320
Reserves		
Capital reserves		
Share premium account		10
Other reserves		
Retained earnings[1]		70
Total Equity		400

Share price £2.00.

[1]Preference dividends of £10,000 and ordinary dividends of £40,000 have been charged to retained earnings.

Required: From the above accounts prepare the following ratios:
(a) Profitability ratios
(b) Efficiency ratios
(c) Liquidity ratios
(d) Gearing ratio
(e) Investment ratios.

Q8 You are an employee of a medium-sized, light engineering company. Your managing director, Sara Potter, asks you to analyse the accounts of your company, Turn-a-Screw Ltd, with a competitor, Fix-it-Quick.

Profit and Loss Accounts Year Ended 31 December 2005

	Turn-a-Screw £000	Fix-it-Quick £000
Sales	2,500	2,800
Cost of Sales	(1,000)	(1,200)
Gross Profit	1,500	1,600
Administrative expenses (includes loan interest)	(900)	(1,170)
Distribution expenses	(250)	(200)
Profit before Taxation	350	230
Taxation	(76)	(46)
Profit after Taxation	274	184
Preference dividends	(30)	(20)
Ordinary dividends	(124)	(94)
Retained Profit	120	70

Balance Sheets as at 31 December 2005

	Turn-a-Screw £000	Turn-a-Screw £000	Fix-it-Quick £000	Fix-it-Quick £000
Fixed Assets				
Tangible assets		1,820		1,765
Current Assets				
Stock	120		115	
Debtors	100		115	
Cash	10		25	
	230		255	
Creditors: Amounts Falling Due within One Year	(190)		(225)	
Net current assets		40		30
Total assets less current liabilities		1,860		1,795
Creditors: Amounts Falling Due after More than One Year (10 % interest)		(250)		(400)
Total net assets		1,610		1,395

Q8 Turn-a-Screw Ltd (*continued*)

Capital and Reserves	£000	£000
Share Capital		
Ordinary share capital (£1 each)	850	860
Preference share capital (£0.50 each)	300	200
	1,150	1,060
	£000	£000
Reserves		
Capital reserves		
Share premium account	125	–
Other reserves		
Profit and loss account	335	335
Total shareholders' funds	1,610	1,395
Share price	£1.44	£1.00

Required: Using the accounts of the two companies calculate the appropriate:
(a) Profitability ratios
(b) Efficiency ratios
(c) Liquidity ratios
(d) Gearing ratio
(e) Investment ratios.
Briefly comment on your main findings for each category.

Q9 You have been employed temporarily by a rich local businessman, Mr Long Pocket, as his assistant. He has been told at the golf club that Sunbright Enterprises plc, a locally based company, would be a good return for his money. The last five years' results are set out below.

Profit and Loss Accounts Year Ended 31 December

	2001	2002	2003	2004	2005
	£000	£000	£000	£000	£000
Sales	1,986	2,001	2,008	2,010	2,012
Cost of Sales	(1,192)	(1,221)	(1,406)	(1,306)	(1,509)
Gross Profit	794	780	602	704	503
Expenses (including loan interest)	(633)	(648)	(487)	(606)	(437)
Profit before Taxation	161	132	115	98	66
Taxation	(32)	(26)	(23)	(19)	(13)
Profit for Year	129	106	92	79	53

Q9   Sunbright Enterprises plc (*continued*)

Balance Sheets as at 31 December

	2001 £000	2002 £000	2003 £000	2004 £000	2005 £000
ASSETS					
Non-current Assets					
Property, plant, and equipment	500	580	660	780	878
Current Assets					
Inventory	24	26	27	45	68
Trade receivables	112	120	121	130	134
Cash	25	24	30	21	9
	161	170	178	196	211
Total Assets	661	750	838	976	1089
LIABILITIES					
Current Liabilities	(83)	(90)	(111)	(126)	(210)
Non-current Liabilities (10 % interest)	(100)	(110)	(120)	(130)	(150)
Total Liabilities	(183)	(200)	(231)	(256)	(360)
Net Assets	478	550	607	720	729
EQUITY					
Capital and Reserves attributable to Equity Holders	£000	£000	£000	£000	£000
Share Capital					
Ordinary share capital (£1 each)	250	250	250	300	300
Preference share capital (£1 each)	88	88	88	100	100
	338	338	338	400	400
Reserves					
Capital reserves					
Share premium account	12	12	12	25	25
Other reserves					
Retained earnings	128	200	257	295	304
Total Equity	478	550	607	720	729
Share price	£1.10	£1.08	£1.07	£1.05	£0.95

Note: You have the following details of dividends over the last five years which have been deducted from the retained earnings.

	2001 £000	2002 £000	2003 £000	2004 £000	2005 £000
Preference dividends	(8)	(8)	(8)	(9)	(9)
Ordinary dividends	(25)	(26)	(27)	(32)	(35)

Required: Analyse the last five years' financial results for the company and calculate the appropriate ratios. Present your advice as a short report.
Note: Horizontal analysis, vertical analysis and a calculation of the cash flow ratio are not required.

Appendix 9.1: John Brown Ltd

John Brown Ltd has the following abridged results for the year ending 31 December 2009. The trading and profit and loss account is presented below and the balance sheet is presented on the next page.

John Brown Ltd
Trading and Profit and Loss Account Year Ended 31 December 2009

	£m	£m
Sales		200
Cost of sales		(100)
Gross Profit		100
Less *Expenses*		
General	40	
Loan interest	10	50
Profit before Taxation		50
Taxation		(15)
Profit after Taxation		35
Preference dividends (10 %)	(5)	
Ordinary dividends	(10)	(15)
Retained Profit		20

Appendix 9.1: John Brown Ltd (continued)

Balance Sheet as at 31 December 2009

	£m	£m	£m
Fixed Assets			275
Current Assets			
Stock	60		
Debtors	40		
Cash	20	120	
Current Liabilities			
Creditors	(50)		
Proposed dividends and tax	(10)	(60)	
Net current assets			60
Total assets less current liabilities			335
Long-term Creditors			(70)
Total net assets			265

	£m	£m
Capital Employed		
Capital and Reserves		
Share Capital		
Ordinary share capital (150m £1)		150
Preference share capital (50m £1)		50
		200
Reserves		
Other reserves		
Opening profit and loss account		50
Profit for year	15	
Closing profit and loss account		65
Total shareholders' funds		265

The market price of the ordinary shares was 67p.

Section B

Financial Accounting: The Context

I n Section A, we looked at the accounting techniques which underpin the preparation and interpretation of the financial statements of sole traders, partnerships and limited companies. These techniques do not exist in a vacuum. In this section, we examine five crucial aspects of the context in which these accounting techniques are applied.

Chapter 10 investigates the regulatory and conceptual frameworks within which accounting operates. The regulatory framework provides a set of rules and regulations which govern accounting. The conceptual theory is broader and seeks to set out a theoretical framework to underpin accounting. Then, in Chapter 11, the main potential alternative measurement systems which can underpin the preparation of accounts are laid out. This chapter shows how using different measurement systems can yield different profits and different balance sheet valuations.

The annual report, the main way in which public limited companies communicate financial information to their shareholders, is discussed in Chapter 12. This chapter outlines the nature, context and function of the annual report. Both the content and the presentation of the annual report are examined.

Finally, Chapters 13 and 14 investigate two interesting aspects of financial accounting: creative accounting and international accounting. Creative accounting explores the flexibility within accounting and shows how managers may manipulate financial information out of self-interest. Finally, Chapter 14 provides a broad international view of accounting. It shows that different countries have different accounting environments. Moreover, this chapter also shows the progress which has been made towards the harmonisation of accounting practices both in the UK and worldwide. In particular, the role of the International Accounting Standards Board is investigated. ■

Chapter 10

"Regulation is like salt in cooking. It's an essential ingredient – you don't want a great deal of it, but my goodness you'd better get the right amount. If you get too much or too little you'll soon know."

Sir Kenneth Berrill, *Financial Times* (6 March 1985)
Source: *The Book of Business Quotations* (1991), p. 47

Learning Outcomes

After completing this chapter you should be able to:

✔ **Outline the traditional corporate model.**

✔ **Understand the regulatory framework.**

✔ **Explain corporate governance.**

✔ **Understand the conceptual framework.**

Regulatory and Conceptual Frameworks

In a Nutshell

- *Directors, auditors and shareholders are the main parties in traditional corporate model.*

- *The regulatory framework provides a set of rules and regulations for accounting.*

- *At the international level, the International Accounting Standards Board provides a broad regulatory framework of International Accounting Standards. This applies to all European listed companies, including UK companies.*

- *In the UK, the two main sources of regulation are the Companies Acts and accounting standards.*

- *Financial statements must give a true and fair view.*

- *The UK accounting standard-setting regime operates under the Financial Reporting Council. It consists of the Accounting Standards Board, the Urgent Issues Task Force and the Financial Reporting Review Panel.*

- *Corporate governance is the system by which companies are directed and controlled.*

- *A conceptual framework is a coherent and consistent set of accounting principles which will help in standard setting.*

- *Some major elements in a conceptual theory are the objectives of accounting, users, user needs, information characteristics and measurement models.*

- *The most widely agreed objective is to provide information for decision making.*

- *Users include shareholders and analysts, lenders, creditors, customers and employees.*

- *Key information characteristics are relevance, reliability, comparability and understandability.*

Introduction

So far, we have looked at accounting practice – focusing on the preparation and interpretation of the financial statements of sole traders, partnerships and limited companies. In particular, we considered practical aspects of accounting such as double-entry bookkeeping, the trial balance, the profit and loss account (income statement), the balance sheet, the cash flow statement and ratio analysis. Accounting practice does not, however, take place in a vacuum. It is bounded both by a regulatory framework and a conceptual framework. These frameworks have grown up over time to bring order and fairness into accounting practice. They have been devised principally in relation to limited companies, but are also relevant to some extent to sole traders and partnerships.

The regulatory framework is essentially the set of rules and regulations which govern corporate accounting practice. At the international level, the regulatory framework is provided by the International Accounting Standards Board. This applies to all European listed companies, including UK companies. In the UK, regulations are set down mainly by government in Companies Acts and by independent private sector regulation in accounting standards. The conceptual framework seeks to set out a theoretical and consistent set of accounting principles by which financial statements can be prepared.

Traditional Corporate Model: Directors, Auditors and Shareholders

In the traditional corporate model there are three main groups. As Figure 10.1 shows, these three groups interact.

Figure 10.1   The Traditional Corporate Model

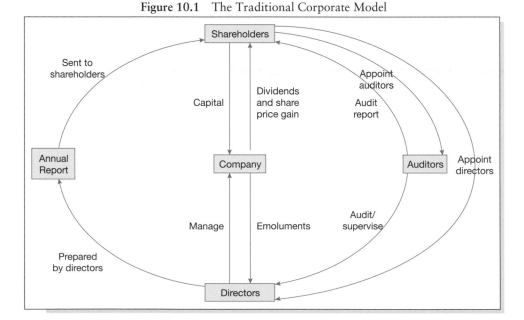

The directors are responsible for preparing the accounts – in practice this is usually delegated to the accounting managers. These accounts are then checked by professionally qualified accountants, the auditors. Finally, the accounts are sent to the shareholders.

1. Directors

The directors are those responsible for running the business. They are accountable to the shareholders, who in theory appoint and dismiss them. The relationship between the directors and shareholders is sometimes uneasy. The shareholders own the company, but it is the directors who run it. This relationship is often termed a 'principal–agent' relationship. The shareholders are the principals and the directors are the agents. The principals delegate the management of the company to directors. However, the directors are still responsible to the shareholders.

The directors are responsible for preparing the accounts which are sent to the shareholders. These accounts, prepared annually, allow the shareholders to assess the performance of the company and of the directors. They also provide information to shareholders to enable them to make share trading decisions (i.e., to hold their shares, to buy more shares or to sell their shares). As a reward for running the company, the directors receive emoluments. These may take the form of a salary, profit bonuses or other benefits in kind such as share options or company cars.

2. Auditors

Unfortunately, human nature being human nature, there is a problem with such arms-length transactions. In a nutshell, how can the shareholders trust accounts prepared by the directors? For example, how can they be sure that the directors are not adopting creative accounting in order to inflate profits and thus pay themselves inflated profit-related bonuses? One way is by auditing.

The auditors are a team of professionally qualified accountants who are *independent* of the company. They are appointed by the shareholders on the recommendation of the directors. It is their job to check and report on the accounts. This checking and reporting involves extensive work verifying that the transactions have actually occurred, that they are recorded properly and that the monetary amounts in the accounts do indeed provide a true and fair view of the company's annual accounts.

An audit (see Definition 10.1) is thus an independent examination and report on the accounts of a company.

The Audit

Working definition

An independent examination and report on the accounts.

Formal definition

The systematic independent examination of a business's, normally a company's, accounting systems, accounting records and financial statements in order to provide a report on whether or not they provide a true and fair view of the business's activities.

For their time and effort the auditors are paid often quite considerable sums. The auditors prepare a formal report for shareholders. This is part of the annual report. In The Company Camera 10.1 we attach an auditors' report prepared by PriceWaterhouseCoopers, the auditors of Rentokil, on Rentokil's 2004 accounts.

Report of the Auditors

Independent auditors' report to the members of Rentokil Initial plc

We have audited the financial statements which comprise the Consolidated Profit and Loss Account, the Balance Sheets, the Consolidated Cash Flow Statement, the Statement of Total Recognised Gains and Losses, the Reconciliation of Movement in Equity Shareholders' Funds and the related Notes which have been prepared under the historical cost convention and the accounting policies set out in the Statement of Accounting Policies. We have also audited the disclosures required by Part 3 of Schedule 7A to the Companies Act 1985 contained in the Remuneration Report ('the auditable part').

Respective responsibilities of directors and auditors

The directors' responsibilities for preparing the annual report and the financial statements in accordance with applicable United Kingdom law and accounting

THE COMPANY CAMERA 10.1 (*continued*)

standards are set out in the Statement of Directors' Responsibilities. The directors are also responsible for preparing the Remuneration Report.

Our responsibility is to audit the financial statements and the auditable part of the Remuneration Report in accordance with relevant legal and regulatory requirements and United Kingdom Auditing Standards issued by the Auditing Practices Board. This report, including the opinion, has been prepared for and only for the company's members as a body in accordance with Section 235 of the Companies Act 1985 and for no other purpose. We do not, in giving this opinion, accept or assume responsibility for any other purpose or to any other person to whom this report is shown or into whose hands it may come save where expressly agreed by our prior consent in writing.

We report to you our opinion as to whether the financial statements give a true and fair view and whether the financial statements and the auditable part of the Remuneration Report have been properly prepared in accordance with the Companies Act 1985. We also report to you if, in our opinion, the Report of the Directors is not consistent with the financial statements, if the company has not kept proper accounting records, if we have not received all the information and explanations we require for our audit, or if information specified by law regarding directors' remuneration and transactions is not disclosed.

We read the other information contained in the annual report and consider the implications for our report if we become aware of any apparent misstatements or material inconsistencies with the financial statements. The other information comprises only the Chairman's Statement, Chief Executive's Review, the Finance Director's Review, the Report of the Directors, the Audit Committee Report and the unaudited part of the Remuneration Report.

We review whether the corporate governance statement reflects the company's compliance with the nine provisions of the 2003 FRC Combined Code specified for our review by the Listing Rules of the Financial Services Authority, and we report if it does not. We are not required to consider whether the board's statements on internal control cover all risks and controls, or to form an opinion on the effectiveness of the company's or group's corporate governance procedures or its risk and control procedures.

Basis of audit opinion

We conducted our audit in accordance with auditing standards issued by the Auditing Practices Board. An audit includes examination, on a test basis, of evidence relevant to the amounts and disclosures in the financial statements and the auditable part of the Remuneration Report. It also includes an assessment of the significant estimates and judgements made by the directors in the preparation of the financial statements, and of whether the accounting policies are appropriate to the company's circumstances, consistently applied and adequately disclosed.

THE COMPANY CAMERA 10.1 (*continued*)

We planned and performed our audit so as to obtain all the information and explanations which we considered necessary in order to provide us with sufficient evidence to give reasonable assurance that the financial statements and the auditable part of the Remuneration Report are free from material misstatement, whether caused by fraud or other irregularity or error. In forming our opinion we also evaluated the overall adequacy of the presentation of information in the financial statements.

Opinion

In our opinion:

- the financial statements give a true and fair view of the state of affairs of the company and the group at 31st December 2004 and of the profit and cash flows of the group for the year then ended;
- the financial statements have been properly prepared in accordance with the Companies Act 1995; and,
- those parts of the Remuneration Report required by Part 3 of Schedule 7A to the Companies Act 1985 have been properly prepared in accordance with the Companies Act 1985.

PriceWaterhouseCoopers LLP
Chartered Accountants and
Registered Auditors
1 Embankment Place
London
WC2N 6RH
13th April 2005

Source: Rentokil, 2004 Annual Report, pp. 42–43

This auditors' report thus confirms that the directors of Rentokil have prepared a set of financial statements which have given a true and fair view of the company's accounts as at 31 December 2004. This is known as a clean or unqualified audit report. The shareholders of Rentokil can thus draw comfort from the fact that the auditors believe the accounts do give a true and fair view and faithfully reflect the economic performance of the company over the year.

3. Shareholders

The shareholders (in the US known as the stockholders) own the company. They have provided the share capital by way of shares. Their reward is twofold. First, they may receive an annual dividend which is simply a cash payment from the company based on profits. Second, they may benefit from any increase in the share price over the year. However, companies may make losses and share prices can go down as well as up, so this reward is not guaranteed. In the developed world, more and more companies are owned by large institutions (such as investment trusts or pension funds) rather than private shareholders.

The shareholders of the company receive an annual audited statement of the company's performance. This is called the annual report. It comprises the financial statements and also a narrative explanation of corporate performance. Included in this annual report is an auditors' report.

It is important to realise that shareholders are only liable for the capital which they contribute to a company. This capital is known as *share capital* (i.e., the capital of a company is divided into many shares). These shares limit the liability of shareholders and so we have limited liability companies. Shares, once issued, are bought or sold by shareholders on the stock market. This enables people, who are not involved in the day-to-day running of the business, to own shares. This division between owners and managers is often known as the divorce of ownership and control. It is a fundamental underpinning of a capitalist society.

PAUSE FOR THOUGHT 10.1

Risk and Reward

In the corporate model each of the three groups are rewarded for their contributions. This is called the 'risk and reward model'. Can you work out each group's risk and reward?

	Contribution (risk)	Reward
Shareholders	Share capital	Dividends and increase in share price
Directors	Time and effort	Salaries, bonuses, benefits-in-kind such as cars or share options
Auditors	Time and effort	Auditors' fees

Regulatory Framework

The corporate model of directors, shareholders and auditors is one of checks and balances. The directors manage the company, receive directors' emoluments and recommend the appointment of the auditors to the shareholders. The shareholders own the company, but do not run it, and rely upon the auditors to check the accounts. Finally, the auditors are appointed by shareholders on the recommendation of the directors. They receive an auditors' fee for the work they undertake when they check the financial statements prepared by managers.

PAUSE FOR THOUGHT 10.2

Checks and Balances

Is auditing enough to stop company directors pursuing their own interests at the expense of the shareholders?

....

Auditing is a powerful check on directors' self-interest. The directors prepare the accounts and the auditors check that the directors have correctly prepared them and that they give a 'true and fair' view. However, there are problems. The auditors, although technically appointed by the shareholders at the company's *annual general meeting* (i.e., a meeting called once a year to discuss a company's accounts), are recommended by directors. Auditors are also paid, often huge fees, by the company. The auditors do not wish to upset the directors and lose those fees. Given the flexibility within accounts, there are a whole range of possible accounting policies which the directors can choose. The regulatory framework helps to narrow this range of potential accounting policies and gives guidance to both directors and auditors. The auditors can, therefore, point to the rules and regulations if they feel that the directors' accounting policies are inappropriate. The regulatory framework is, therefore, a powerful ally of the auditor.

This system of checks and balances is fine, in principle. However, it is rather like having two football teams and a referee with no rules. The regulatory framework, in effect, provides a set of rules and regulations to ensure fair play. As Definition 10.2 shows, at the national level, these rules and regulations may originate from the government, the accounting standard setters or, more rarely, for listed companies, the stock exchange. The principal aim of the regulatory framework is to ensure that the financial statements present a true and fair view of the financial performance and position of the organisation.

DEFINITION 10.2

The National Regulatory Framework

Working definition
The set of rules and regulations which govern accounting practice, mainly prescribed by government and the accounting standard-setting bodies.

Formal definition
The set of legal and professional requirements with which the financial statements of a company must comply. Company reporting is influenced by the requirements of law, of the accounting profession and of the Stock Exchange (for listed companies).

Chartered Institute of Management Accountants (2000), *Official Terminology*

In most countries, including the UK, the main sources of authority for the regulatory framework are either via the government, through companies legislation, or via accounting standard-setting bodies through accounting standards. As Soundbite 10.1 suggests, there is a need not to overregulate. At the international level, there is now a set of International Accounting Standards (IAS) (also known as International Financial Reporting Standards (IFRS)) issued by the International Accounting Standards Board (IASB). The IASB is steadily growing in importance. Its standards are aimed primarily at large international companies (see Chapter 14 for a fuller discussion of IAS). European listed companies must comply with IAS.

> ### SOUNDBITE 10.1
>
> # Regulations
>
> 'If you destroy a free market you create a black market. If you have ten thousand regulations, you destroy all respect for the law.'
>
> Winston S. Churchill
>
> Source: *The Book of Unusual Quotations* (1959), pp. 240–241

Regulatory Framework in the UK

In the UK, there are two main sources of authority for regulation: the Companies Acts and accounting standards. There are some additional requirements from the Stock Exchange for listed companies, but given their relative unimportance, they are not discussed further here.

In the UK, as in most countries, the regulatory framework has evolved over time. As accounting has grown more complex, so has the regulatory framework which governs it. At first, the only requirements that companies followed were those of the Companies Acts. However, in 1970 the first accounting standards set by the Accounting Standards Steering Committee were issued. Today, UK companies must adhere both to the requirements of Company Acts and to accounting standards. For non-listed companies these are set by the Accounting Standards Board, for listed companies by the International Accounting Standards Board. The overall aim of this regulatory framework is to protect the interests of all those involved in the corporate model. Specifically, there is a need to provide a 'true and fair view' of a company's affairs.

True and Fair View

Section 226[2] of the 1985 Companies Act requires that 'the balance sheet should give a true and fair view of the state of affairs of the company as at the end of the financial year; and the profit and loss account shall give a true and fair view of the profit or loss of the company for the financial year.' The true and fair concept is thus of overriding importance. Unfortunately, it

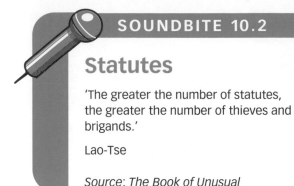

DEFINITION 10.3

Working Definition of a True and Fair View

A set of financial statements which faithfully, accurately and truly reflect the underlying economic transactions of an organisation.

is a particularly nebulous concept which has no easy definition. A working definition is, however, suggested in Definition 10.3 below. In essence, there is a presumption that the accounts will reflect the underpinning economic reality. Generations of accountants have struggled unsuccessfully to pin down the exact meaning of the phrase. In general, to achieve a true and fair view accounts should comply with the Companies Acts and accounting standards.

Occasionally, however, where compliance with the law would not give a true and fair view, a company may override the legal requirements. However, the company would have to demonstrate clearly why this was necessary.

Companies Acts

Companies Acts are Acts of Parliament which lay down the legal requirements for companies including regulations for accounting. There have been a succession of Companies Acts which have gradually increased the reporting requirements placed on UK companies. Initially, the Companies Acts provided only a broad legislative framework. However, later Companies Acts (CAs), especially the CA 1981, have imposed a significant regulatory burden on UK companies. The CA 1981 introduced the European Fourth Directive into UK law. Effectively, this Directive was the result of a deal between the United Kingdom and other European Union members. The United Kingdom exported the true and fair view concept, but imported substantial detailed legislation and standardised formats for the profit and loss account and balance sheets. The CA 1981, therefore, introduced a much more prescriptive 'European' accounting regulatory framework into the UK.

Accounting Standards

Whereas Companies Acts are governmental in origin, accounting standards are set by non-governmental bodies. Accounting standards were introduced, as Real-Life Nugget 10.1 indicates, to improve the quality of UK financial reporting.

REAL-LIFE NUGGET 10.1

Introduction of Accounting Standards

Inflation accounting was, in fact, only one part of a bigger move towards accounting standards – a move that was itself controversial. Standards had been proposed a few years earlier to limit the scope for judgement in the preparation of accounts. They were the profession's response to a huge City row when GEC chief executive Arnold Weinstock restated the profits of AEI, a company he had just taken over, from mega millions down to zero.

The City was outraged and demanded more certainty in accounts so it could have more faith in public profit figures.

Standards were the result and, though taken for granted now, many saw them as the death knell for the profession, precisely because they limited the scope for professional judgement. Many believed the profession had been permanently diminished when its ability to make judgements was curtailed.

Source: Demands for Change, Anthony Hilton, *Accountancy Age*, 11 November 2004, p. 25

At the international level, International Accounting Standards (IAS) are set by the International Accounting Standards Board. These are now mandatory for all European listed companies. The US market does not accept IAS at present without reconciliation to US GAAP. UK non-listed companies still follow UK accounting standards.

There are, as Figure 10.2 shows, three main constituents of the UK's accounting standards

Figure 10.2   UK's Regulatory Framework

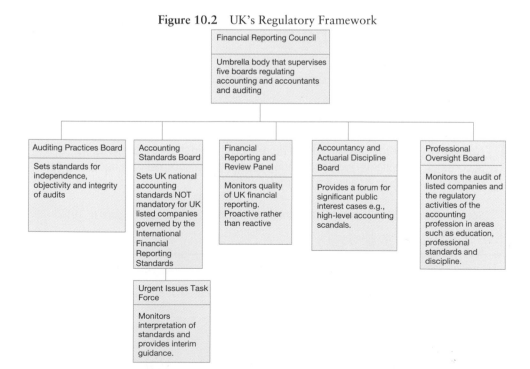

regulatory framework: the Accounting Standards Board (ASB), the Urgent Issues Task Force (UITF) and the Financial Reporting Review Panel (FRRP). They operate under the Financial Reporting Council. The current UK accounting standards regulatory framework was set up in 1990, but reorganised in 2004.

1. Financial Reporting Council (FRC)

The Financial Reporting Council is a supervisory body which ensures that the overall system is working. It supervises five boards including the Accounting Standards Board and the Financial Reporting Review Panel.

2. The Accounting Standards Board (ASB)

The Accounting Standards Board is the engine of the accounting standards process. The ASB has a full-time chairman and a full-time technical director plus eight part-time members.

In the UK, accounting standards are called Financial Reporting Standards (FRS). The ASB issues FRS which are applicable to the accounts of all non-listed UK organisations and are intended to give a true and fair view. These Financial Reporting Standards have replaced most of the Standard Statements of Accounting Practice which were issued from 1970 to 1990 by the ASB's predecessor, the Accounting Standards Committee. As Definition 10.4 shows, in essence, accounting standards are pronouncements which must normally be followed in order to give a true and fair view.

DEFINITION 10.4

Accounting Standards

Working definition
Accounting pronouncements which must be followed in order to give a true and fair view within the regulations.

Formal definition
'Accounting standards are authoritative statements of how particular types of transaction and other events should be reflected in financial statements and accordingly compliance with accounting standards will normally be necessary for financial statements to give a true and fair view.'

Source: Foreword to *Accounting Standards*, Accounting Standards Board, 1993, para. 16

Accounting standards are mandatory in that accountants are expected to observe them. They cover specific technical accounting issues such as stock, depreciation, and research and development. These standards essentially aim to improve the quality of accounting in the UK. They narrow the areas of difference and variety in accounting practice, set out minimum disclosure standards and disclose the accounting principles upon which the accounts are based. Overall, accounting standards provide a comprehensive set of guidelines which preparers and auditors can use when drawing up the financial statements.

3. Urgent Issues Task Force (UITF)

The Urgent Issues Task Force is the 'Flying Squad' of the standard-setting process. It works under the Accounting Standards Board. The development of standards takes time. The UITF, therefore, was set up to react quickly to new situations. Recommendations are made to curb undesirable interpretations of accounting standards or to prevent accounting practices which the ASB considers undesirable.

4. The Financial Reporting Review Panel (FRRP)

The FRRP investigates contentious departures from accounting standards. It is the 'detective' arm of the ASB. The FRRP questions the directors of the companies investigated. The last resort of the FRRP is to take miscreant companies to court to force them to revise their accounts. However, so far the threat of court action has been enough. The FRRP began as a reactive body only responding to complaints. However, recently the FRRP has become more proactive as Real-Life Nugget 10.2 explains.

REAL-LIFE NUGGET 10.2

FRRP

When it was set up in 1990 to deal with the scandals of the eighties, the government had decided that self-regulation was the best option. It is a strategy that Sir Bryan describes as highly successful 'because the people in the system knew they had to make it work because of the alternative'.

But since Enron, Parmalat et al, the pressure's on to up the ante. Enhancements include a new proactive approach to uncovering accounting cock-ups in the books of listed UK companies, with 300 sets of accounts slated for investigation by the Financial Reporting Review Panel (FRRP) this year.

Source: Insider, *Accountancy Age*, 1 April 2004, p. 15

In 2005, for example, the FRRP investigated the accounts of MG Rover. As Real-Life Nugget 10.3 shows this has triggered a government enquiry.

REAL-LIFE NUGGET 10.3

FRRP and MG Rover

The Phoenix Four, the Midlands businessmen behind the collapsed MG Rover Group, are to be investigated by the Department of Trade and Industry, which has set up an independent inquiry into the affairs of the former car maker.

The inquiry was announced yesterday by Alan Johnson, the Trade and Industry Secretary. He ordered the inquiry after receiving an initial report into the company's finances by the Financial Reporting and Review Panel (FRRP), part of the accountancy watchdog, the Financial Reporting Council.

A clean bill of health for MG Rover, and its associated companies, would have left the Government little choice but to close the case. But Mr Johnson said the FRRP report 'raises a number of questions that need to be answered'. He said the public interest demanded a more detailed account of what went on at MG Rover Group, which collapsed into administration in April with the loss of more than 5,000 jobs.

Source: Damian Reece, DTI Opens MG Rover Investigation, *Financial Times*, June 1 2005, p. 57. From Lexis-nexis.com

Corporate Governance

From the 1990s, corporate governance has grown in importance. Effectively, corporate governance is the system by which companies are directed and controlled (see Real-Life Nugget 10.4).

REAL-LIFE NUGGET 10.4

Corporate Governance

'Corporate governance is the system by which companies are directed and controlled. Boards of directors are responsible for the governance of their companies. The shareholders' role in governance is to appoint the directors and the auditors and to satisfy themselves that an appropriate governance structure is in place. The responsibilities of the board include setting the company's strategic aims, providing the leadership to put them into effect, supervising the management of the business and reporting to shareholders on their stewardship. The board's actions are subject to laws, regulations and the shareholders in general meeting.

Within that overall framework, the specifically financial aspects of corporate governance (the committee's remit) are the way in which boards set financial policy and oversee its implementation, including the use of financial controls, and the process whereby they report on the activities and progress of the company to the shareholders.'

Source: *Report of the Committee on the Financial Assets of Corporate Governance* (1992), Gee and Co., p. 15

The financial aspects of corporate governance relate principally to internal control, the way in which the board of directors functions and the process by which the directors report to the shareholders on the activities and progress of the company. These aspects have been investigated in the UK by several committees including the Cadbury Committee (1992), the Greenbury Committee (1995), the Hampel Committee (1998) and the Turnbull Committee (1999). In addition, since 2003 the Higgs, Smith, Turner and Walker Reports into corporate governance have been published.

The continuing interest in corporate governance arises in part for two reasons. First, there have been some unexpected failures of major companies such as Polly Peck, Maxwell Communications, Enron and Parmalat. Second, there have been extensive criticisms in the press of 'fat-cat' directors. These directors, often of privatised companies (i.e., companies which were previously state-owned and -run), are generally perceived to be paying themselves huge and unwarranted salaries.

As a result of the Cadbury Committee and other subsequent committees, there were attempts to tighten up corporate governance. In particular, there was a concern with the amount of information companies disclosed, with the role of non-executive directors (i.e., directors appointed from outside the company), with directors' remuneration, with audit committees (committees ideally controlled by non-executive directors which oversee the appointment of external auditors and deal with their reports), with relations with institutional investors and with systems of internal financial control set up by management.

In the annual report, companies now set out extensive details of directors' remuneration and disclose information about corporate governance. The auditors review these corporate governance elements to check that they comply with the principles of good governance and code of best practice as set out in the London Stock Exchange's rules. The Company Camera 10.2 presents part of J.D. Wetherspoon's statement on internal control. The directors acknowledge their responsibility to establish controls such as those to protect against the unauthorised use of assets.

THE COMPANY CAMERA 10.2

Internal Control

Corporate governance

The directors acknowledge their responsibility for the company's system of internal control, which can be defined as the controls established in order to provide reasonable assurance that the assets have been protected against unauthorised use, that proper accounting records have been maintained and that the financial information which is produced is reliable. Such a system can, however, provide only reasonable and not absolute assurance against material misstatement or loss. The directors recognise that, in attaining long-term shareholder value, they are responsible for providing a return which is consistent with a responsible

THE COMPANY CAMERA 10.2 (*continued*)

assessment and mitigation of risks. The key procedures in place to enable this responsibility to be discharged are as follows:

- A comprehensive budgeting process is in place, with a detailed operating plan for twelve months and a mid-term financial plan, both approved by the board. Business results are reported weekly for key items and monthly in full and compared with budget. Forecasts are prepared regularly throughout the year, for review by the board.
- Clearly defined authority limits and controls are in place over cash-handling, purchasing commitments and capital expenditure.
- A retail audit function monitors the control of cash, stock and operating procedures, in operating units. A separate internal audit function also looks at the overall business risks facing the company and reviews general business processes.
- Complex treasury instruments are not used. Decisions on treasury matters are reserved for the board.
- The directors confirm that they have reviewed the effectiveness of the system of internal control.

Source: J.D. Wetherspoon, 2004 Annual Report, p. 18

DEFINITION 10.5

Conceptual Framework

The development of a coherent and consistent set of accounting principles which underpin the preparation and presentation of financial statements.

Conceptual Framework

Since the 1960s, standard-setting bodies (such as the Financial Accounting Standards Board (FASB), in the USA, the International Accounting Standards Board (IASB) and the Accounting Standards Board in the UK) have sought to develop a conceptual framework or statement of principles which will underpin accounting practice. As Definition 10.5 shows, the basic idea of a conceptual framework is to create a set of fundamental accounting principles which will help in standard setting.

A major achievement of the search for a conceptual theory has been the emergence of the decision-making model. As Real-Life Nugget 10.5 sets out, there is a need to provide decision-useful information to investors. The five essential elements of a conceptual framework are broadly agreed by all three major standard-setting bodies: objectives, users, user needs, information characteristics and measurement rules. These elements are briefly discussed below.

REAL-LIFE NUGGET 10.5

Conceptual Framework

First – and of fundamental importance – all involved in global financial reporting must have a common mission or objective. At the heart of that mission is a conceptual framework which must focus on the investor, provide decision-useful information, and assure that capital is allocated in a manner that achieves the lowest cost in our world markets. I believe we all have an understanding and acceptance of providing decision-useful information for investors, but not all standard setters and not all standards yet reflect that mission.

Source: International Accounting Standards Board, IASC Insight, p. 12

1. Objectives

Both the US Financial Accounting Standards Board (FASB) and the International Accounting Standards Board (IASB) broadly agree that 'The objective of financial statements is to provide information about the financial position, performance and changes in financial position of an enterprise that is useful to a wide range of users in making decisions' (*Framework for the Preparation and Presentation of Financial Statements*, IASB, 1999, para. 12). This is widely known as the decision-making model (see Figure 10.3). In other words, the basic idea of accounting is to provide accounting information to users which fulfils their needs, thus enabling them to make decisions. Encompassed within this broad definition is the idea that financial statements show how the managers have accounted for the resources entrusted to them by the shareholders. This accountability is often called stewardship. To enable stewardship and decision making, the information must have certain information characteristics and use a consistent measurement model.

Figure 10.3   Decision-Making Model

In the UK, the ASB has developed a Statement of Principles. In its latest version, the Statement takes a broader definition of the objectives of financial reporting than either the FASB or the IASB. 'The objective of financial statements is to provide information about the reporting entity's financial position, performance and changes in financial position that is useful to a wide range of users for assessing the stewardship of the entity's management and for making economic decisions' (Accounting Standards Board, *Statement of Principles*, 1999). Thus, the ASB sees the *objective of financial reporting* to be (i) the *stewardship of management*, and (ii) *making economic decisions*.

Stewardship and decision making are discussed in more depth in Chapter 12. However, at this stage it is important to introduce them. Stewardship is all about accountability. It seeks to make the directors accountable to the shareholders for their stewardship or management of the company. Corporate governance is one modern aspect of stewardship. Decision making, by contrast, focuses on the needs of shareholders to make economic decisions, such as to buy or sell their shares. As performance measurement and decision making have grown in importance so has the profit and loss account. In a sense, decision making and stewardship are linked, as information is provided to shareholders so that they can make decisions about the directors' stewardship of the company.

Essentially, stewardship and decision making are user-driven and take the view that accounting should give a 'true and fair' view of a company's accounts. By contrast, the public relations view suggests that there are behavioural reasons why managers might seek to prepare accounts that favour their own self-interest. Self-interest and 'true and fair' may well conflict. In this section, we focus only on the officially recognised roles of accounting (stewardship and decision making). Discussion of the public relations role and the conflicting multiple accounting objectives is covered in Chapter 12.

PAUSE FOR THOUGHT 10.3

Stewardship and Decision Making

Why are assets and liabilities most important for stewardship, but profits most important for decision making?

Stewardship is about making individuals accountable for assets and liabilities. In particular, stewardship focuses on the physical existence of assets and seeks to prevent their loss and/or fraud. Stewardship is, therefore, about keeping track of assets rather than evaluating how efficiently they are used.

Decision making is primarily concerned with monitoring performance. Therefore, it is primarily concerned with whether or not a business has made a profit. It is less concerned with tracking assets.

2. Users

The main users are usually considered to be the present and future shareholders. Indeed, shareholders are the only group required by law to be sent an annual report. Shareholders comprise individual and institutional shareholders. Besides shareholders, there are a number of other users. Those identified by the International Accounting Standards Board include:

- lenders, such as banks or loan creditors
- suppliers and other trade creditors
- employees
- customers
- governments and their agencies, and the
- general public.

In addition to this list we can add:

- academics
- management
- analysts and advisers, and
- pressure groups such as Friends of the Earth.

Broadly, we can see that this list is the same as that discussed in Chapter 1. In Chapter 1, however, we distinguished between internal users (management and employees) and external users (the rest).

Generally the accounts are pitched at the shareholders. Satisfying their interests is generally thought to cover the main concerns of the other groups. The annual report adopts a general purpose reporting model. This provides a comprehensive set of information targeted at all users. It does not, therefore, specifically target the needs of one user group.

3. User Needs

User needs vary. However, commonly users will want answers to questions such as:

- How profitable is the organisation?
- How much cash does it have in the bank?
- Is it likely to keep trading?

In order to answer these questions, users will need information on the profitability, liquidity, efficiency and gearing of the company. This is normally provided in the three key financial statements: the profit and loss account (income statement), the balance sheet and the cash flow statement. Users will also be interested in the softer, qualitative information provided, for example, in accounting narratives such as the chairman's statement.

4. Information Characteristics

In order to be useful to users, the financial information needs to possess certain characteristics. Both the International Accounting Standards Board and the UK's Accounting Standards Board focus on four principal characteristics: relevance, reliability, comparability and understandability. It is helpful to classify these characteristics into those relating to content (relevance and reliability) and those relating to presentation (comparability and understandability) (see Figure 10.4).

Figure 10.4   Overview of Information Characteristics

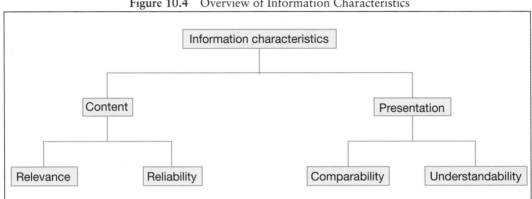

A. Content

Relevance   Relevant information affects users' economic decisions. Relevance is a prerequisite of usefulness. Examples of relevance are information that helps to predict future events or to confirm or correct past events. The relevance of financial information in the financial statements crucially depends on its materiality. If information is immaterial (i.e., will not affect users' decisions), then, in practice, it does not need to be reported.

Reliability   Reliable information is free from material error and is unbiased. Like relevance, reliability is a predeterminant of usefulness. Five characteristics underpin reliability. First, reliable information is representationally faithful (i.e., it validly describes the underlying events). The information must be free from material error. Second, information should reflect the substance of economic reality not just its legal form. For example, a leased asset is included on a balance sheet even though the company leases, but does not own the asset. Third, reliable information must be neutral, i.e., not biased. Fourth, reliable information must be prudent and not deliberately overstate assets or income, or understate liabilities or expenses. And, finally, information must be complete.

B. Presentation

Comparability   Accounts should be prepared on a consistent basis and should disclose accounting policies. This will then allow users to make inter-company comparisons and intra-company comparisons over time.

Understandability   Information that is not understandable is useless. Therefore, information must be presented in a readily understandable way. In practice, this means conveying complex information as simply as possible rather than 'dumbing down' information. Whether financial information is understandable will depend on the way in which it is characterised, aggregated, classified and presented.

The IASB and ASB recognise that trade-offs are inevitable where conflicts arise between relevance, reliability, comparability and understandability. For example, out-of-date information may be useless. Therefore, some detail (reliability) may be sacrificed to speed of reporting (relevance). In addition, the benefits derived from information should exceed the costs of providing it.

PAUSE FOR THOUGHT 10.4

Critics of the Conceptual Framework

The conceptual framework has been criticised for not achieving very much and being a social document rather than a theory document. What do you think these criticisms mean and are they fair?

....

The conceptual framework has brought into being the decision-making model. However, there is little agreement on the appropriate measurement model for accounting. In other words, should we continue to use historical cost or should we move towards some alternative measurement model that perhaps accounts for the effects of inflation? Critics have seen this failure to agree on a measurement model as a severe blow to the authority of the conceptual framework. In addition, there is concern that the conceptual framework has not really developed a theoretically coherent and consistent set of accounting principles at all. These critics argue that the conceptual framework is primarily descriptive – just describing what already exists. A descriptive framework is not a theoretical framework. Finally, some critics argue that the real reason for the search for a conceptual framework is to legitimise and support the notion of a standard-setting regime independent of government. The conceptual framework should thus be seen as a social document which supports the existence of an independent accounting profession.

5. Measurement Model

The objectives, users, user needs and information characteristics have proved relatively easy to agree upon. However, the choice of an appropriate measurement model for profit measurement and asset determination has caused much controversy. The measurement basis that underpins financial statements remains a modified form of historical cost. In other words, income, expenses, assets and liabilities are recorded at the date of their original monetary transaction. Unfortunately, although historical cost is relatively well-understood and easy to understand, it understates assets and overstates profits, especially in times of inflation. Most commentators agree that historical cost, therefore, is flawed. However, there is no consensus on a suitable replacement. The alternative measurement models are more fully discussed in Chapter 11.

Conclusion

In order to appreciate accounting practice properly, we need to understand the regulatory and conceptual frameworks within which it operates. These frameworks were primarily devised for published financial statements, such as those in the corporate annual report. The regulatory framework is the set of rules and regulations which governs corporate accounting practice. The International Accounting Standards Board sets International Accounting Standards. These are followed by all European listed companies, including UK companies. The two major strands of the UK's regulatory framework are the Companies Acts and accounting standards. The UK's accounting standards regulatory framework consists of four elements: the Financial Reporting Council, the Accounting Standards Board, the Urgent Issues Task Force and the Financial Reporting Review Panel. Corporate governance is the system by which companies are governed.

A conceptual framework is an attempt to create a set of fundamental accounting principles which will help standard-setting. A major achievement of the search for a conceptual framework has been the emergence of the decision-making model. The essence of this is that the objective of financial statements is to provide financial information useful to a wide range of users for making economic decisions. A second objective is to provide financial information for assessing the stewardship of managers. In order to be useful, this information must be relevant, reliable, comparable and understandable. Although there is general agreement on the essentials of a decision-making model, there is little consensus on which measurement model should underpin the decision-making process.

Selected Reading

The references below will give you further background.

They are roughly divided into those on the regulatory framework and those on the conceptual framework.

Regulatory Framework

Bartlett, S.A. and M.J. Jones (1997), Annual Reporting Disclosures 1970–90: An Exemplification, *Accounting, Business and Financial History*, Vol. 7, No. 1, pp. 61–80.

This article looks at how the accounts of one firm, H.P. Bulmers (Holdings) plc, the cider makers, were affected by changes in the regulations from 1970 to 1990.

Blake, J. and H. Lunt (2001), *Accounting Standards*, Financial Times/Prentice Hall.

A good, easy-to-digest, student-orientated guide to the main standards.

Solomon, J.F. and A. Solomon (2003), *Corporate Governance and Accountability*, John Wiley and Sons, Chichester.

Provides an overview of corporate governance.

The Combined Code (1998), London Stock Exchange, June.

This provides a comprehensive set of recommendations arising from the various corporate governance reports (i.e., Cadbury, Greenbury, Hampel). UK-listed companies now follow these.

The Financial Aspects of Corporate Governance (The Cadbury Committee Report) (1992), Gee and Co.

The first, and arguably the most influential, report into corporate governance. Authoritative.

UK GAAP (2000), Ernst and Young, Butterworth.

Provides a very comprehensive guide to UK and IAS standards as well as to the ASB's *Statement of Principles*. This guide is updated annually.

Conceptual Framework

Outlines of Potential Conceptual Frameworks by Professional Bodies

Accounting Standards Board (1999), Statement of Principles, *Accountancy*.

This synopsis offers a good, quick insight into current thinking in the UK about a conceptual theory.

Accounting Standards Setting Committee (ASSC) (1975), *The Corporate Report* (London).

A benchmark report which outlined the Committee's, at the time groundbreaking, thoughts about the theory of accounting. Easy-to-read.

Financial Accounting Standards Board (FASB) (1978), *Statement of Financial Accounting Concepts No. 1, Objectives of Financial Reporting by Business Enterprises* (Stanford, FASB).
Offers an insight into the US view of a conceptual theory.

International Accounting Standards Board (IASB) (2000), *Framework for the Preparation and Presentation of Financial Statements* in International Accounting Standards, 2000.
A very influential document outlining the IASB's views.

Critical Theorists

As well as the conventional view of the conceptual theory, many observers are critical of the whole process. Two are given below.

Archer, S. (1993), 'On the Methodology of a Conceptual Framework for Financial Accounting. Part 1: An Historical and Jurisprudential Analysis', *Accounting, Business and Financial History*, Vol. 3, No. 1, pp. 199–227.
Easier to read than Hines, below. It sees the conceptual framework as legitimating the accounting standard process rather than being a primarily theory-driven document.

Hines, R.D. (1991), 'The FASB's Conceptual Framework, Financial Accounting and the Maintenance of the Social World', *Accounting, Organizations and Society*, Vol. 16, No. 4, pp. 313–331.
A very challenging read. It presents an unorthodox outlook on the whole conceptual framework project.

Q&A Discussion Questions

Questions with numbers in blue have answers at the back of the book.

Q1 What is the role of directors, shareholders and auditors in the corporate model?

Q2 What is the decision-making model? Assess its reasonableness.

Q3 Discuss the view that if a regulatory framework did not exist it would have to be invented.

Q4 Companies often disclose 'voluntary' information over and above that which they are required to do. Why do you think they do this?

Q5 What is a conceptual framework and why do you think so much effort has been expended to try to find one?

Chapter 11

"What is a Cynic? A man who knows the price of everything and the value of nothing."

Oscar Wilde, Lady Windermere's Fan (1892)
Wiley Book of Business Quotations (1998), p. 349

Learning Outcomes

After completing this chapter you should be able to:

✔ Explore the importance of accounting measurement systems.

✔ Critically evaluate historical costing.

✔ Investigate the alternatives to historical costing.

Measurement Systems

In a Nutshell

- *Measurement systems determine asset valuation and profit measurement.*

- *The capital maintenance concept is concerned with maintaining the capital of a company.*

- *Historical cost, which records items at their original cost, is the most widely used measurement system.*

- *Current purchasing power adjusts historical cost for changes in the purchasing power of money (e.g., inflation).*

- *Replacement cost is based on the cost of replacing assets.*

- *Realisable value is based on the orderly sale value of the assets.*

- *Present value is based on the present value of the discounted net cash inflows of an asset.*

- *Exceptions to historical cost are the valuing of stock at the lower of cost or net realisable value or, in the UK, the revaluation of fixed assets.*

Introduction

Measurement systems underpin not only profit, but also asset valuation. Essentially, a measurement system is the way in which the elements in the accounts are valued. Traditionally, historical cost has been the accepted measurement system. Incomes, expenses, assets and liabilities have been recorded in the accounting system at cost at the time that they were first recognised. Unfortunately, historical cost, although easy to use, has several severe limitations; for example, it does not take inflation into account. However, although the limitations of historical cost accounting are well known, accountants have been unable to agree on any of the main alternatives such as current purchasing power, replacement cost, realisable value or present value.

SOUNDBITE 11.1

Measurement

'What you measure is what you get.'

Robert S. Kaplan and David P. Norton, *Harvard Business Review*, January–February, 1992

Source: *The Wiley Book of Business Quotations* (1998), p. 295

Overview

Measurement systems are the processes by which the monetary amounts of items in the financial statement are determined. These systems are fundamental to the determination of profit and to the measurement of net assets. In essence, the measurement system determines the values obtained. Potentially, there are five major measurement systems: historical cost, current purchasing power, replacement cost, realisable value and present value (see Figure 1.1).

Figure 11.1   The Alternative Measurement Systems

Measurement System	Explanation	Capital Maintenance System
Historical Cost Systems		
i. Historical cost	Monetary amounts recorded at the date of original transaction.	Financial capital maintenance.
ii. Current purchasing power	Historical cost adjusted by general changes in purchasing power of money (e.g., inflation), often measured using the retail price index (RPI).	Financial capital maintenance.
Current Value Systems		
i. Replacement cost	Assets valued at the amounts needed to replace them with an equivalent asset.	Physical capital maintenance.
ii. Realisable value	Assets valued at the amount they would fetch in an orderly sale.	Physical capital maintenance.
iii. Present value	Assets valued at the discounted present values of future cash inflows.	Physical capital maintenance.

Measurement systems are underpinned by the idea of capital maintenance (see Figure 11.2). Capital maintenance determines that a profit is made only after capital is maintained. This capital can be monetary (monetary capital maintenance) or physical (physical capital maintenance).

Figure 11.2   Capital Maintenance Concepts

What exactly is a capital maintenance concept and why is it important?

. . . .

A capital maintenance concept is essentially a way of determining whether the 'capital' of a business has improved, deteriorated or stayed the same over a period of time. There are two main capital maintenance concepts (*financial capital maintenance* and *physical capital maintenance*). **Under financial capital maintenance we are primarily concerned with monetary measurement, in particular, the measurement of the net assets.** This is true using both historical cost and current purchasing power. For example, under *historical cost* the capital maintenance unit is based on actual monetary units (i.e., actual pounds in the UK). Under *current purchasing power*, it is actual pounds adjusted by the rate of inflation. In both cases, if our closing net assets (as measured in £s) are higher than our opening net assets we make a profit. **Under physical capital maintenance, the physical productive capacity (i.e., operating capacity of the business) must be maintained.** For example, can we still produce the same amount of goods or services at the end of a period as we could at the start? We maintain the operating capacity in terms of *replacement costs, realisable values* or *present values* (i.e., discounted future cash inflows). For example, under replacement costs, we are concerned with valuing the operating capacity of the business at the replacement cost of individual assets and liabilities.

Historical cost and current purchasing power both stem from the normal bookkeeping practice of recording transactions at the date they occur in monetary amounts. For current purchasing power, these amounts are then adjusted by the general changes in the purchasing power of money. Under both measurement systems the concern is to maintain the monetary amount of the enterprise's net assets. In both cases, we are therefore concerned with financial capital maintenance.

Replacement cost, realisable value and present value are sometimes known as current value systems. They seek to maintain the physical (or operating) capital of the enterprise. The three systems differ in how they seek to do this. Replacement cost measures assets at the amount it would cost to *replace* them with an equivalent asset. Realisable value (also known as net realisable value or settlement value) measures assets at their sale value. Present value measures the business at the present discounted values of future net cash inflows. These three current value systems can be combined into a 'value to the business' model. A new measurement system that has recently grown in influence is fair value. This is sometimes known a Mark-to Market model as it seeks to capture an asset's market value. It is most usually associated with valuing complex financial instruments such as those used by financial institutions. A detailed description of fair value and the value to the business model (sometimes called current value accounting) is beyond the scope of this book.

It is, however, important to realise two fundamental points. First, historical cost still remains the most common measurement basis adopted by enterprises. Second, although historical cost is much criticised, there is no consensus about which measurement system, if any, should replace it. Disagreement on measurement systems is where attempts to arrive at a consensual conceptual theory have all floundered.

Measurement Systems

In this section, we have discussed two of the most important measurement systems: historical cost and replacement cost. Readers interested in the other three measurement systems are referred to more advanced texts such as Geoffrey Whittington's *Inflation Accounting: An Introduction to the Debate*.

Historical Cost

Historical cost has always been the most widely used measurement system. Essentially, transactions are recorded in the books of account at the date the transaction occurred. This original cost is maintained in the books of account and not updated for any future changes in value that might occur. To illustrate, if we paid £5,000 for a building in 1980, this will be the cost that is shown in the balance sheet when we prepare our accounts in 2006. This is even when the building has increased in value to say £20,000 through inflation. The depreciation will be based on the original value of the asset (i.e., £5,000 not £20,000).

The main strength of historical cost is that it is objective. In other words, you can objectively verify the original cost of the asset. You only need to refer to the original invoice. In addition, historical cost is very easy to use and to understand. Finally, historical cost enables businesses to keep track of their assets.

There is, however, one crucial problem with historical cost. It uses a fixed monetary capital maintenance system, which does not take inflation into account. This failure to take into account changing prices can cause severe problems. In particular, as Soundbite 11.2 shows, it may not accurately value a company's worth.

SOUNDBITE 11.2

Historical Cost Accounting's Limitations

'Historical cost-based financial reporting is not the most efficient way of reflecting a company's true value.'

Mike Starr, Chairman of American Institute of Certified Public Accountants Committee on Enhanced Business Reporting

Source: Nicholas Neveling, Consortium urges Reporting Reforms, *Accountancy Age*, 17 February 2005, p. 11

Replacement Cost

Replacement cost attempts to place a realistic value on the assets of a company. It is concerned with maintaining the operating capacity of a business. Essentially, replacement cost asks the question: what would it cost to replace the existing business assets with identical, equivalent assets at today's prices?

Replacement cost is an alternative method of measuring the assets and profits of a business rather than principally a method of tackling inflation. In the Netherlands, replacement costing has been successfully used by many businesses, such as Heineken. As The Company Camera 11.1 shows, Heineken values its tangible fixed assets at replacement cost based on expert valuation. Indeed, the problem for the Dutch is not so much the difficulties of using replacement cost, but of convincing the rest of the world that it is a worthwhile system.

PAUSE FOR THOUGHT 11.1

Historical Cost and Asset-Rich Companies

The balance sheets of asset-rich companies, such as banks, may not reflect their true asset values, if prepared under historical cost accounting. Why do you think this might be?

....

If we take banks and building societies as examples of asset-rich companies, these businesses have substantial amounts of prime location fixed assets. Almost in every town, banks occupy key properties in central locations. These properties were also often acquired many years ago, indeed possibly centuries ago. Using strict historical cost, these buildings would be recorded in the balance sheet at very low amounts. This is because over time money values have changed. If a prime site was purchased for £1,000 in 1700 that might have been worth a lot then. Today, it might be worth say £400 million. Thus, fixed assets will be radically understated, unless revalued.

THE COMPANY CAMERA 11.1

Replacement Cost and Heineken

Tangible Fixed Assets (Property, Plant and Equipment)

Except for land, which is not depreciated, tangible fixed assets are stated at replacement cost less accumulated depreciation. The following average useful lives are used for depreciation purposes:

Buildings	30–40 years
Plant and equipment	10–30 years
Other fixed assets	5–10 years

The replacement cost is based on appraisals by internal and external experts, taking into account technical and economic developments. Other factors taken into account include the experience gained in the construction of breweries throughout the world. Grants received in respect of investments in tangible fixed assets are deducted from the amount of the investment. Projects under construction are included at cost.

Source: Heineken, 2004 Annual Report, pp. 84–85

The main problem with replacement cost is that, in practice, it is often difficult to arrive at an objective value for the replacement assets. However, in many cases specific indices are available for certain classes of assets, allowing more accurate valuations.

Deficiencies of Historical Cost Accounting

Figure 11.3 shows how historical cost accounting can give a misleading impression of the profit for the year and of the value of assets in the balance sheet. In particular, strictly following historical cost will have the effect of:

(i) encouraging companies to pay out more dividends to shareholders than is wise,

Figure 11.3   The Deficiencies of Historical Cost Accounting

A company's only asset is a building, purchased 10 years ago for £20,000. The replacement cost for an equivalent building is now £200,000. The company, which deals only in cash, has profits of £10,000 per annum, it distributes 50% of its profits as dividends. The asset is written off over 20 years.

(i) Historical Cost Accounts in Year 10

Profit and Loss Account	£	Balance Sheet	£
Profit before depreciation	10,000	**Fixed Assets**	20,000
Depreciation	(1,000)	Accumulated depreciation	(10,000)
	9,000	Total fixed assets	10,000
Dividends	(4,500)	Cash	55,000
Retained Profit	4,500	Net assets	65,000

(a) Over the first ten years, the company's profits, or as it only deals in cash, cash flow is £100,000. It has paid out £45,000 in dividends leaving £55,000 cash in the company. This looks healthy.
(b) The shareholders are happy receiving an annual dividend.
(c) Return on capital employed (taking closing net assets) is:

$$\frac{£9,000}{£65,000} = 13.8\%$$

Everything, therefore, seems pretty good. *Unfortunately, the company has only £65,000 in net assets which is not enough to replace the fixed assets which will cost £200,000!*

(ii) Replacement Cost Accounts in Year 10

Profit and Loss Account	£	Balance Sheet	£
Profit before depreciation	10,000	**Fixed Assets**	200,000
Depreciation	(10,000)	Accumulated depreciation	(100,000)
	–	Total fixed assets	100,000
		Cash	100,000
		Net assets	200,000

(a) In this case, the company makes no profit because the increased depreciation has wiped out all the profits. There is no profit out of which to pay dividends. If the company had paid out dividends during the 10 years it would have no money left to replace the fixed assets.
(b) The net worth has risen considerably. This is a plus for the company. However, not paying out dividends is a considerable minus.
(c) There is no return on capital employed!
Suddenly, everything appears less rosy. *However, the firm can continue in business because it can just about replace its fixed assets* (in actual fact, its net assets equals the amount needed to replace the fixed assets). This assumes that the building could be sold for £100,000!

(ii) making companies appear more profitable than they really are, and,

(iii) impairing the ability of companies to replace their assets.

In practice, many UK companies now use a modified form of historical cost accounting. This involves revaluing fixed assets, often every five years. Depreciation is then based on the revised valuation. However, in other countries, such as the US, Germany and France, there is still rigid adherence to historical cost.

Illustrative Example of Different Measurement Systems

In Figure 11.4, we pull together some of the threads and show how the valuation of an individual asset can vary considerably depending upon the chosen measurement system.

Figure 11.4   Example of Different Measurement Systems

JoJo bought a van two years ago for £10,000. She expects to keep the van for five years. The used van guide states the van is now worth £2,500. Replacement cost for a van in a similar condition is £4,000. The future net cash flows will be £4,000 for the next three years (assume the cash flows occur at the end of the year) and she can borrow money at 10%. The retail price index was 100 when the van was bought and it is 120 now.

	Appropriate value £
Historical Cost	
We base our calculations on the original historical cost of £10,000.	
Using straight-line depreciation (£10,000 ÷ 5) = £2,000 p.a.	
Thus, £10,000 – £4,000 (two years' depreciation)	6,000
Current Purchasing Power	
We base our calculation on the original historical cost less depreciation.	
In the calculation above, this was £10,000 – £4,000 = £6,000*. We then	
adjust this for inflation. This is measured using the retail price index,	
which has increased from 100 to 120.	
$£6,000 \times \dfrac{Closing\ RPI}{Opening\ RPI} \left(\dfrac{120}{100}\right)$	7,200
Realisable Value	
In this case, our calculations are based upon the amount of money we	
would receive for the van if we sold it.	
Used van guide	2,500
Replacement Cost	
In this case, we base our calculations on the amount it would cost	
to replace the van with a similar asset in a similar condition.	
Similar value asset	4,000
Present Value	
Here, we are interested in looking at the future cash flows generated	
by the asset. We then discount them back to today's value (see Chapter 21	
for further information about discounting).	

£	Discount Factor*	£
4,000	0.9091	3,636
4,000	0.8264	3,306
4,000	0.7513	3,005
		9,947

            9,947

*10% interest discounted back, assumes cash flow is on the last day of each year.

We can, therefore, see that different measurement systems give different asset valuations. There are thus five different valuations ranging from £2,500 to £9,947.

	£
• Historical cost	6,000
• Current purchasing power	7,200
• Realisable value	2,500
• Replacement cost	4,000
• Present value	9,947

It is important to note that, in practice, each measurement system itself could potentially yield many different asset valuations, depending on the underlying assumptions and estimations. For example, present value is crucially dependent on the estimated discount rate (10 %), the estimated future cash flows (£4,000), and the timing of those cash flows.

Real Life

The merits of historical cost accounting and the advantages and disadvantages of the competing alternative measurement systems have been debated vigorously for at least 40 years. However, with some rare exceptions, most companies worldwide still use historical cost.

This is not to say that experimentation has not occurred. In the Netherlands, for example, Philips, one of the world's leading companies, used replacement cost accounting for over a generation. Finally, Philips abandoned replacement cost, not because of replacement cost's inadequacies, but because of the failure of international financial analysts to understand Philips accounts. Today, there are still companies in the Netherlands, such as Heineken, which use replacement cost. In the UK too, there were a few companies, usually ex-privatised utilities with extensive infrastructure assets, such as British Gas, which until recently used replacement costs.

In both the UK and the US in the 1970s, there were serious attempts to replace historical cost accounting initially with current purchasing, but later with current value accounting (a mixture of the three current value systems). These methods were thought to be superior to historical cost accounting when dealing with inflation, which was at that time quite high. They were also believed to provide a more realistic valuation of company assets. In the end these attempts failed. The reasons for their failure were quite complex. However, in general, accountants preferred the objectivity of a tried-and-tested, if somewhat flawed, historical cost system to the subjectivity of the new systems. In addition, rates of inflation fell.

The role of accounting measurement in the recent global credit crunch has aroused a lot of attention. This is particularly the role of fair value. When the value of financial assets declined then their fair value reduced and so did the valuation of the companies. Whereas some onlookers felt that accounting measurement was only measuring what had happened, others felt that accounting measurement had contributed to the economic problems by eroding company value.

Although the backbone of the accounts is historical cost, there is some limited use of alternative measurement systems (see Figure 11.5). In addition, in the UK, many companies revalue their fixed assets every five years. This is particularly common in companies that have many fixed assets, such as hotel chains. However, this periodic revaluation of fixed assets means that UK accounts are prepared on a different basis to those in countries, such as France or the US, where periodic revaluations are not permitted.

Figure 11.5   Use of Alternative Measurement Systems

'The measurement basis most commonly adopted by enterprises in preparing their financial statements is historical cost. This is usually combined with other measurement bases. For example, inventories [i.e. stocks] are usually carried at the lower of cost and net realisable value, marketable securities may be carried at market value and pension liabilities are carried at their present value. Furthermore, some enterprises use the current cost basis as a response to the inability of the historical cost accounting model to deal with the effects of changing prices of non-monetary assets.'

Source: International Accounting Standards Board (2000), *Framework for the Preparation and Presentation of Financial Statements*, para. 101

Conclusion

Different measurement systems will give different figures in the accounts for profit and net assets. The mostly widely used measurement system, historical cost, records and carries transactions in the accounts at their original amounts. Historical cost, however, does not deal well with changes in asset values resulting from, for example, inflation. There are four other main measurement systems (current purchasing power, replacement cost, realisable value, present value). Current purchasing power adjusts historical cost for general changes in the purchasing power of money. Replacement cost records assets at the amounts needed to replace them with equivalent assets. Realisable value records assets at the amounts they would fetch in an orderly sale. Finally, present value discounts future cash inflows to today's monetary values. Although historical cost is the backbone of the accounting measurement systems, there are departures from it, such as the valuation of stock at the lower of cost or realisable value. In particular, in the UK, many companies revalue their fixed assets. The role of fair value in the credit crunch has been hotly debated.

Selected Reading

The topic of accounting measurement systems can be extremely complex. The first two readings below have been deliberately selected because they are quite accessible to students. Students wishing for a fuller insight into the debate are referred to the book by Geoffrey Whittington below.

1. Accounting Standards Steering Committee (1975), *The Corporate Report*, Section 7, pp. 61–73.
   Although now 30 years old, this report provides a very good, easy-to-read, introduction to the topic.
2. International Accounting Standards Board (IASB) (2000) 'Framework for the Preparation and Presentation of Financial Statements', in *International Accounting Standards* (2000), paras. 99–110.
   It presents more modern thinking on the topics and is reasonably easy-to-follow.

For the Enthusiast

Whittington, G. (1983), *Inflation Accounting: An Introduction to the Debate* (Cambridge University Press).
   For students who enjoy a challenge. Gives a thorough grounding in the inflation debate, which is at the heart of choosing different measurement systems.

Q&A   Discussion Questions

Questions with numbers in blue have answers at the back of the book.

Q1 'Accounting measurement systems are the skeleton of the accounting body.' Critically evaluate this statement.

Q2 Why is historical cost still so widely used, if it is so deeply flawed?

Q3 What is the difference between a financial capital maintenance concept and a physical capital maintenance concept?

Q4 Why do many UK companies revalue their fixed assets? How might this affect profit? Why is this practice unusual internationally?

Chapter 12

"It is a yearly struggle: the conflict between public relations experts determined to put a sunny face on somewhat drearier figures, and those determined to tell it like it is, no matter how many 'warts' there are on the year's story. The annual report is a vital instrument designed – ideally – to tell the story of a company, its objectives, where the company succeeded or failed, and what the company intends to do next year."

Kirsty Simpson (1997), 'Glossy, expensive and useless', *Australian Accountant*, September, pp. 16–18

Learning Outcomes

After completing this chapter you should be able to:

✔ Explain the nature of the annual report.

✔ Outline the multiple, conflicting objectives of the annual report.

✔ Discuss the main contents of the annual report.

✔ Evaluate how the annual report is used for impression management.

The Annual Report

In a Nutshell

- *The annual report is a key corporate financial communication document.*

- *It is an essential part of corporate governance.*

- *It serves multiple, and sometimes conflicting, roles of stewardship/accountability, decision making and public relations.*

- *It comprises key audited financial statements: profit and loss account (i.e., income statement), balance sheet, and cash flow statement.*

- *It normally includes at least 22 identifiable sections.*

- *It also includes important non-audited sections such as the chairman's statement.*

- *Most important companies provide group accounts.*

- *Goodwill is an important intangible asset in many group accounts.*

- *Managers use the annual report for impression management.*

Introduction

The annual report is well-entrenched as a core feature of corporate life. This yearly-produced document is the main channel by which directors report corporate annual performance to their shareholders. All leading companies worldwide will produce an annual report. In the UK, both listed and unlisted companies produce one. Many other organisations, such as the British Broadcasting Corporation, now also produce their own versions of the annual report. Indeed, the Labour Government produced the first governmental annual report in 1998. Traditionally, the annual report was a purely statutory document. The modern annual report, however, now has multiple functions, including a public relations role. Modern reports comprise a mixture of voluntary and statutory, audited and unaudited, narrative and non-narrative, financial and non-financial information. They are also governed by a regulatory framework which includes Companies Acts and accounting standards. The modern annual report has become a complex and sophisticated business document. In particular, European listed companies now follow International Financial Reporting Standards. As most publicly available annual reports are those of listed companies, the terminology laid down by the IASB will be used in this chapter. In particular, we will use income statement rather than profit and loss account.

Definition

In essence, an annual report is a document produced to fulfil the duty of the directors to report to shareholders. It is produced annually and is a mixture of financial and non-financial information. As Definition 12.1 shows, it is a report containing both audited financial information and unaudited, non-financial information.

DEFINITION 12.1

Annual Report

Working definition
A report produced annually by companies comprising both financial and non-financial information.

Formal definition
A document produced annually by companies designed to portray a 'true and fair' view of the company's annual performance, with audited financial statements prepared in accordance with company legislation and other regulatory requirements, and also containing other non-financial information.

Context

The annual report has evolved over time into an important communications document, especially for large publicly listed companies. The earliest annual reports arose out of the need to make directors accountable to their shareholders. The main financial statement was the balance sheet. In order to ensure that the financial statements fairly represented corporate performance, the annual report was audited. The annual report, therefore, has always played a key role in the control of the directors by the shareholders. The central role of the annual report in external reporting can be seen in Figure 12.1.

Figure 12.1 The Annual Report

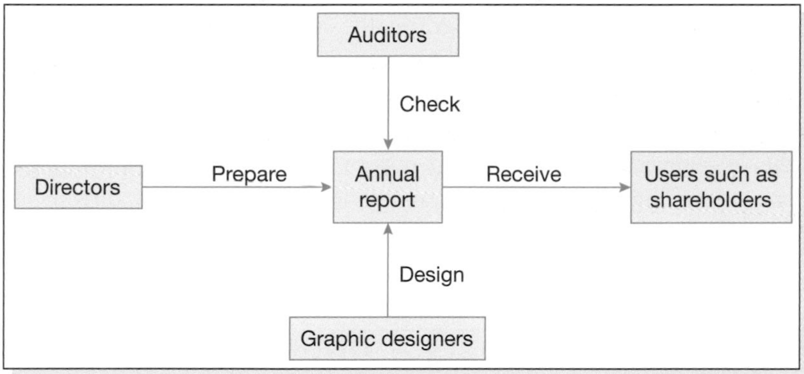

In essence, the directors are responsible for the preparation of the financial statements from the accounting records. The actual preparation is normally carried out by accounting staff. An annual report is then compiled, often with the help of a company's public relations department and graphic designers. These graphic designers are responsible for the layout and design of the annual report (providing, for example, colourful graphs and photographs). The annual report's financial content is then audited and disseminated to the main users, principally the shareholders. As discussed in Chapter 10, much of the annual report is mandated by a regulatory framework consisting principally of the requirements of the Companies Acts and accounting standards.

Multiple Roles

The annual report is a social as well as a financial document. Therefore, as society evolves, so does the annual report. The earliest annual reports were stewardship documents. Today's annual report is much more complex, being an amalgam of stewardship and accountability, decision making and public relations. These concepts are discussed below. The first two roles are those traditionally recognised by standard setters. However, the public relations role is more driven by preparer self-interest.

(i) Stewardship and Accountability

Effectively, stewardship involves the directors reporting their actions to the shareholders. This reflects the origins of financial reporting. In the middle ages, the stewards who managed the estates used to render an annual account of the master's assets (for example, livestock and cereals) to the lord of the manor. The main aim of the accounts, or annual statement, was thus for the lord of the manor to keep a check on the steward's activities. In particular, there was a concern that the steward should not defraud the lord of the manor. An important aspect of stewardship is this accountability. Accountability is traditionally seen as referring to the control and safeguarding of the assets of a company.

Gradually, as the economy became more sophisticated so did the accountability mechanisms. At first, there was a rudimentary statement of assets and liabilities, showing how much the organisation owned and was owed. This gradually evolved into the modern balance sheet. However, the fundamental aim was still to account for the assets and liabilities of the organisation. Accountability tended to diminish in importance with the rise of decision making.

An important modern aspect of stewardship is corporate governance. Essentially, in both Europe and the US, several well-publicised corporate financial scandals (e.g., Polly Peck, Maxwell) led to a growing concern with monitoring the activities of directors. In addition, the privatisation of the utilities created considerable concern over the salaries of so-called 'fat-cat directors'. Real-Life Nugget 12.1 discusses this issue. The committees which looked at

REAL-LIFE NUGGET 12.1

Directors' pay

Alex Brummer
Financial Editor

The call by Stephen Byers for world class salaries for world class performance is a terrific slogan. The trouble is that it fits only a handful of the executives and companies in the Guardian's pay survey. Of the 35 or so directors in the million-pounds-plus pay club only a handful – such as those at the drugs companies SmithKline Beecham and Glaxo Wellcome – deliver a world class product. Others such as Royal & Sun Al-liance, headed by Bob Mendelsohn, who took home £2.4m last year, just about register in Britain, certainly not on the global stage. As for the remuneration committees which sanctioned increases of 26% in directors' wage packets – in a year when trading profits went up just 6.9% – they should (if world class per-

formance really counted) all be fired. But the timid Byers, clearly fearful of up-setting pals in the boardroom, could not bring himself to say anything which might smack of controversy. Nevertheless, there are some areas of merit in what he has to say, if only he would show a sense of determination. It is ludicrous that some four years after Sir Richard Greenbury first exposed the excesses and unfairness in the system, ministers still creep through the undergrowth for fear of disturbing the big beasts. The disclosure principle has been around for quite a time but annual reports tend to obscure rather than clar-ify. There is a lack of clear tables showing the comparators used, there is no descr-iption of differences of opinion within remun eration committees. If it is possible for members of the Bank of England monetary policy committee to express their views publicly on some-thing as critical as interest rates, why not some better disclosure of remuneration committee voting patterns?

Source: The Guardian, 20 July 1999. © Guardian Newspapers Limited 2000

corporate governance in the 1990s all stressed the role that corporate financial communication could play in increasing directors' accountability to shareholders. The accounting scandals such as Enron and WorldCom in the US and Parmalat in Italy have reawakened interest in corporate governance. There has been increasing concern with auditor independence and the need for effective audit committees.

PAUSE FOR THOUGHT 12.1

'Fat Cat' Directors

There has been a great furore about the salaries of 'fat-cat' directors. What justification do you think they tend to give for their salaries? What do their critics argue?

....

The directors' view

Conventionally, directors argue that they are doing a complex and difficult job. They are running world-class businesses and they, therefore, need to be paid world-class salaries. They also create and add shareholder value because of increased share prices and, therefore, they deserve to be well paid.

The critics' view

Yes, but if the directors are paid on the basis of performance, then we would expect them *not* to get big bonuses when their organisations are doing less well. However, generally this does not happen. Also, much of the increase in share prices that directors ascribe to themselves is caused by a general rise in the stock market.

(ii) Decision Making

In the twentieth century, decision making has increasingly replaced stewardship as the main role of accounting. This reflects wider developments in society, business and accounting. In particular, decision making is associated with the rise of the modern industrial company. Industrialisation led to increasingly sophisticated businesses and to the creation of the limited liability company with its divorce of ownership and control. Shareholders were no longer involved in the day-to-day running of the business. They were primarily interested in increases in the value of their share price and in any dividends they received. These dividends were based on profits. Consequently, the income statement became more important relative to the balance sheet. The primary interest of shareholders shifted from cash and assets to profit. Thus, performance measurement and decision making replaced asset management and stewardship as the prime objective of financial information.

PAUSE FOR THOUGHT 12.2

Engines of Capitalism

Limited liability companies have been called the engines of capitalism. Why do you think this is so?

....

Effectively, limited liability companies are very good at allowing capital to be allocated throughout an economy. There are several advantages to investors. First, they can invest in many companies not just one. Second, they can sell their shares very easily, assuming a buyer can be found. Third, they stand to lose only the amount of capital they have originally invested. Their personal assets are thus safe.

These new shareholder concerns were officially recognised by two reports in the 1960s and 1970s in the US and the UK. Both reports, *A Statement of Basic Accounting Theory* (American Accounting Association, 1966) in the US and *The Corporate Report* (Accounting Standards Steering Committee, 1975) in the UK, proved turning points in the development of accounting. Before then stewardship had been the generally acknowledged role of accounting. After them, decision-usefulness was generally recognised as the prime criterion. In a sense, decision making and stewardship are linked, for shareholders need to make decisions about how well the directors have managed the company.

In a nutshell, the purpose of the annual report was recognised to be:

> 'to communicate economic measurements of and information about the resources and performance of the reporting entity useful to those having reasonable rights to such information'. (*The Corporate Report*, 1975, para. 3.2)

The decision-making model had been born!

As Definition 12.2 shows, the modern objective of accounting is still recognised as providing users with information so that they can make decisions.

DEFINITION 12.2

Decision-Making Objective of Annual Report

Working definition
Providing users, especially shareholders, with financial information so that they can make decisions such as buying or selling their shares.

Formal definition
'The objective of financial statements is to provide information about the financial position, performance and changes in financial position of an enterprise that is useful to a wide range of users in making economic decisions.'

Source: International Accounting Standards Board (2000), *Framework for the Preparation and Presentation of Financial Statements*

For the shareholder, these economic decisions might involve the purchase or sale of shares. Other users will have different concerns. For example, banks might be principally interested in whether or not to lend a company more money.

(iii) Public Relations Role

The public relations role reflects the annual report's development over the last 20 years as a major marketing tool. Company management has come to realise that the annual report represents an unrivalled opportunity to 'sell' the corporate image. In part, this only reflects human nature. We all wish to look good. It is a rare person who never attempts to massage the truth, for example, at a job interview. The public relations role of annual reports does, however, provoke strong reactions by some commentators (see Real-Life Nugget 12.2).

REAL-LIFE NUGGET 12.2

Public Relations and the Annual Report

'Queen Isabella was said to have washed only three times in her life, and only once voluntarily. That was when she was married. The other two times were at her birth and death. No wonder Columbus left to discover a new world. Why this olfactory analysis of history? Because this is the time of year when we are inundated with corporate annual reports, and in most of them the letter to the shareholders smells as wretched as Queen Isabella must have.

One of the sad truths about malodorous things is that people tend to get used to them in time. But I'll never become accustomed to the public-relations pap I read in most annual reports. Every year tens of thousands of stale, vapid, and uninspired letters to shareholders appear in elaborate annual reports. They are printed on expensive paper whose gloss and sheen are exceeded only by the glitzy words of the professional PR writer who ghosted the message. They will be read by shareholders who don't understand them – or believe them. Quite often they are hype. Sometimes they are dull. Some are boastful, others apologetic. And they are generally ambiguous.'

Source: Sal Marino, *Industry Week*, 5 May, 1997, p. 12

Conflicting Objectives

The standard-setting organisations generally only recognise the first two objectives of financial statements (also by implication of annual reports): stewardship and decision making. In effect, these two objectives clash with the public relations role. This is because the stewardship and decision-making roles rely upon the notion of providing a neutral and objective view of the company. However, the public relations view is where managers seek to present a favourable, not a neutral, view of a company's activities. This causes stress, particularly if a company did not perform as well as market analysts had predicted. In these cases, as we see in Chapter 13, there is great pressure for the company management to indulge in such impression management.

Main Contents of the Annual Report

Every annual report is unique. Ranging usually from about 30 to 60 or more pages, a company's report presents a variety of corporate financial and non-financial information. The traditional financial statements (e.g., balance sheet, income statement (i.e., profit and loss account) cash flow statement) and accompanying financial information (e.g., notes to accounts) are normally audited. Other parts, such as the chairman's statement, are not. However, most auditors are reluctant to let directors make statements that are blatantly inconsistent with the audited accounts. In addition, the report is a mixture of voluntary and mandatory (i.e., prescribed by regulation) information, and narrative and non-narrative information. In Figure 12.2, the main sections of a typical annual report are outlined. Although based on UK financial reporting practice, in the main these sections are also found in most European listed companies.

Figure 12.2   Main Sections of a Typical Annual Report

Section	Audited Formally	Narrative (N) Non-Narrative (NN)	Mandatory (M) Voluntary (V)
1. Income Statement	Yes	NN	M
2. Balance sheet	Yes	NN	M
3. Cash flow statement	Yes	NN	M
4. Statement of total recognised gains and losses	Yes	NN	M
5. Note on historical cost profits and losses	Yes	NN	M
6. Reconciliation of movements in shareholders' funds	Yes	NN	M
7. Accounting policies	Yes	N	M
8. Notes to the accounts	Yes	N	M
9. Principal subsidiaries	Yes	N	M
10. Business Review	No	N	V
11. Chairman's statement	No	N	V
12. Directors' report	No	N	M
13. Review of operations	No	N	V
14. Social and environmental accounting statement	No	N	V
15. Statement of corporate governance	No	N	M
16. Directors' Remuneration Report	No	N	M
17. Auditors' report	Not applicable	N	M
18. Statement of directors' responsibilities for the financial statements	No	N	M
19. Shareholder information	No	N	V
20. Highlights	No	NN	V
21. Historical summary	No	NN	V
22. Shareholder analysis	No	NN	V

A growing trend is for companies to produce multiple reports. Some companies produce an annual report which contains only financial statements aimed at sophisticated investors and another report entitled 'Annual Review' which contains simplified financial information and discussion. Companies also may produce separate environmental, corporate responsibility or sustainability reports. In addition, many companies produce web-based financial information. For simplicity, however, we assume for the rest of this chapter that a company produces only the traditional annual report.

The main sections of the annual report can be divided into audited and non-audited statements. These are shown in Figure 12.3 and discussed below. In the text various illustrative figures are included from the annual report of Tesco, a UK listed company, and from the annual report of the Finnish listed company, Nokia.

Figure 12.3   Overview of the Annual Report

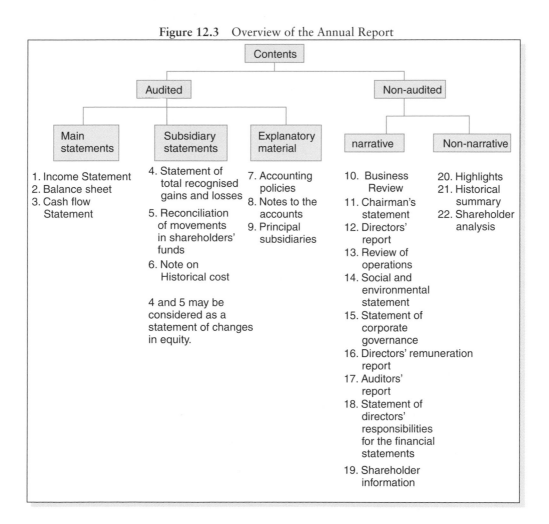

The Audited Statements

Nine audited financial sections are normally included by most UK companies in their annual reports. The first three (the income statement (see Chapter 4), the balance sheet (see Chapter 5) and the cash flow statement (see Chapter 8)) have already been covered in depth earlier. They are, therefore, only lightly touched on here. The remaining audited statements are all comparatively recent. They can be divided into subsidiary statements and explanatory material. All the sections are presented in a relatively standard way, following guidance laid down in the Companies Acts and accounting standards.

Main Statements

1. Income Statement or Profit and Loss Account   The income statement is widely recognised as the primary financial statement. It focuses on the revenue earned and expenses incurred by the business during the accounting period. Importantly, this is not the same as cash received and cash paid. European listed companies follow guidelines for the income statement as laid down by IAS 1 *Presentation of Financial Statements*. UK non-listed companies follow UK Financial Reporting Standard 3, *Reporting Financial Performance*. An illustration of the income statement for AstraZeneca is given in The Company Camera 7.3 in Chapter 7 on page 172.

2. Balance Sheet   Nowadays, the balance sheet is often seen as of secondary importance to the income statement as a decision-making document. It focuses on assets, liabilities and shareholders funds (i.e., capital employed) at a particular point in time (the balance sheet date). The balance sheet, along with the income statement, is prepared from the trial balance. The balance sheet is commonly used to assess the liquidity of a company, whereas the income statement focuses on profit. An illustration of the balance sheet for AstraZeneca is given in the Company Camera 7.4 in Chapter 7 on page 173.

3. Cash Flow Statement   Unlike the previous two statements, which use the matching basis and are prepared from the trial balance, the cash flow statement is usually prepared by deduction from the income statement and balance sheets. It is a relatively new statement, for example, introduced in the UK in 1991. The objective of the cash flow statement is to report and categorise cash inflows and outflows during a particular period.

Subsidiary Statements

4. Statement of Total Recognised Gains and Losses (STRGL)   This is another comparatively recent statement. The STRGL begins with the profit for the year taken from the income statement. It then deals with *non-trading gains and losses* traditionally taken to reserves not to the income statement. The STRGL attempts to highlight all shareholder gains and losses and not just those from trading. These gains and losses might, for example, be surpluses on property revaluation. Alternatively, as in the case of Tesco in 2004 (see The Company Camera 12.1), there may be a loss on foreign currency net investments.

THE COMPANY CAMERA 12.1

Statement of Total Recognised Gains and Losses

53 weeks ended 28 February 2004

	Group		Company	
	2004 £m	2003 £m	2004 £m	2003 £m
Profit for the financial year	1,100	946	771	618
(Loss)/gain on foreign currency net investments	(157)	22	(2)	–
Total recognised gains and losses relating to the financial year	943	968	769	618

Source: Tesco plc, 2004 Annual Report, p. 27

5. Reconciliation of Movements in Shareholders' Funds   This statement highlights major changes to the wealth of shareholders. These include profit (or loss) for the year, annual dividends and new share capital. As Tesco's reconciliation shows (see Company Camera 12.2 on the next page), they can also include loss on foreign currency net investments. As an alternative to the STRGL and the Reconciliation of Movements in Shareholders' Funds, companies may present a Statement of Changes in Equity.

THE COMPANY CAMERA 12.2

Reconciliation of Movements in Shareholders' Funds

53 weeks ended 28 February 2004

	Group		Company	
	2004 £m	2003 £m	2004 £m	2003 £m
Profit for the financial year	1,100	946	771	618
Dividends	(516)	(443)	(516)	(443)
	584	503	(255)	(175)
(Loss)/gain on foreign currency net investments	(157)	22	(2)	–
New share capital subscribed less expenses	844	421	869	433
Payment of dividends by shares in lieu of cash	158	40	158	40
Net addition to shareholders' funds	1,429	986	1,280	648
Opening shareholders' funds	6,516	5,530	3,257	2,609
Closing shareholders' funds	7,945	6,516	4,537	3,257

Source: Tesco plc, 2004 Annual Report, p. 27

6. Note on Historical Cost Profits and Losses   If the accounts are prepared under the historical cost convention then the original cost of assets is recorded in the accounts. However, sometimes assets, particularly fixed assets, will be revalued. These assets are not then included in the accounts at their original purchase price. Depreciation on the revalued fixed assets will then be more than on the original cost. This note records any such differences caused by departures from the historical cost convention.

Explanatory Material

7. Accounting Policies   Companies must describe the accounting policies they use to prepare the financial statements. The flexibility inherent within accounting means that companies have a choice of accounting policies in areas such as foreign currencies, goodwill, pensions, sales and inventories. Different accounting policies will result in different accounting figures. Nokia's policy on inventories is given as an illustration (see The Company Camera 12.3). It is clearly stated that inventories are valued at the lower of cost and net realisable value.

THE COMPANY CAMERA 12.3

Policy on Inventories

Inventories are stated at the lower of cost or net realisable value. Cost is determined using standard cost, which approximates actual cost, on a first in first out (FIFO) basis. Net realisable value is the amount that can be realised from the sale of the inventory in the normal course of business after allowing for the costs of realisation.

Source: Nokia, 2004 Annual Report, p. 15

---

8. Notes to the Accounts   These notes provide additional information about items in the accounts. They are often quite extensive. For example, in Tesco's 2004 annual report the main three financial statements take up three pages, but the 34 notes take up a further 24 pages. These notes flesh out the detail of the three main financial statements. They cover a variety of topics. For example, the first six Tesco notes cover prior year adjustment, segmental analysis, operating profit, employee profit-sharing, profit on ordinary activities before taxation, and employment costs. The notes to accounts can be crucial. 'The numbers are just part of the story. The balance sheet is just a snapshot. It captures some of the picture but not all of it so that's why the notes to the accounts are important' (Jill Treanor, *The Guardian*, March 6, 2000, p. 28).

9. Principal Subsidiaries   Most large companies consist of many individual companies arranged as the parent (or holding company) and its subsidiaries. Collectively, they are known as groups (see later in this chapter for a fuller explanation of groups). In the case of a group, there will be a listing of the parent (i.e., main) company's subsidiary companies (i.e., normally those companies where over 50 % of the shares are owned by the parent company) and associate companies (normally where between 20 % and 50 % of shares are owned by the parent company).

The Operating and Financial Review (OFR)

The recent independent Company Law Review (CLR) stated that requiring an operating and financial review (OFR) 'would improve the quality, usefulness and relevance of information available to the markets, and to everyone with an interest in the company'.

Investors and others need better information on intangible assets, such as employees' skills and on forward-looking issues such as the company's strategies and the opportunities, risks and uncertainties it faces.

Source: Jacqui Smith, *Accountancy Age*, 13 May 2004, p. 12

The Non-Audited Sections

The amount of non-audited information in annual reports has mushroomed over the last 30 years. It has caught even experienced observers by surprise (see, for example, Real-Life Nugget 12.4).

The Mushrooming Importance of Non-Audited Information

'In this survey we are interested in the pages outwith the statutory financial statements ... What surprised us was that the "narrative" pages exceeded or equalled the number in the statutory financial statements in half of our survey companies' annual reports.'

Source: Arthur Andersen (1996), *What's the Story*, p. 5

The non-audited information is extremely varied, but can be broadly divided into narrative and non-narrative information. The *narrative* information consists mainly of the chairman's statement, the directors' report, the operating and financial review, and the auditors' report. By contrast, the *non-narrative* information mainly comprises the highlights and the historical summary. Although these sections are not audited, the auditor is required to review the non-narrative information to see if there are material misstatements or material inconsistencies with the financial statements. If there are, the auditors consider whether any information needs to be amended. Unfortunately, all this is very subjective and, in reality, little guidance is given to auditors.

Narrative Sections

10. Business Review   The operating and financial review (OFR) represented a major innovation in UK financial reporting. For the first time, regulators formally recognised the importance of qualitative, non-financial information. It enabled companies to provide a formalised, structured and narrative explanation of financial performance. The ASB introduced the OFR as a voluntary statement in 1993. It has two parts: first, the operating review which discusses items such as a company's operating results, profit and dividends; second, the financial review which covers items such as capital structure and treasury policy. The OFR aims to provide investors with more relevant information. In an interesting example of government interference in UK accounting, the government in November 2005 decided to abolish the proposed mandatory status of the OFR. It has been replaced with a European piece of legislation the Business Review.

11. Chairman's Statement   This is the longest-established accounting narrative. It is provided voluntarily by nearly all companies. The chairman's statement provides a personalised overview of the company's performance over the past year. Most chairman's statements cover strategy, the financial performance and future prospects. It is also traditional for the chairman to thank the employees and retiring directors.

PAUSE FOR THOUGHT 12.3

Auditing the Accounting Narratives

What difficulties do you think an auditor might have if called upon to audit the narrative sections of the annual report, such as the chairman's statement?

....

The main difficulty is deciding how to audit the written word. Usually, auditors audit figures. They can thus objectively trace these back to originating documentation. The problem with accounting narratives is that they are very subjective. How do you audit phrases such as 'We have had a good year' or 'Profit has increased substantially'?

12. Directors' Report   The directors' report is prescribed by law. Its principal objective is to supplement the financial information with information that is considered vital for a full appreciation of the company's activities. Items presented here (or elsewhere in the accounts – an increasingly common practice) might include any changes in the company's activities, proposed dividends, and charitable and political gifts.

13. Review of Operations   This section forms a natural complement to the chairman's statement. Whereas the chairman provides the overview, the chief executive reviews the individual business operations, often quite extensively. Normally, the chief executive discusses, in turn, each individual business or geographical segment.

14. Social and Environmental Accounting Statement   A growing number of companies are reporting social and environmental, social responsibility or sustainability information. For example, over 70 % of the UK's top 350 listed companies report such information. This information is largely voluntary. Increasingly, companies are producing separate stand-alone environmental reports or sustainability reports. However, they may also include sections in their annual report. For example, J.D. Wetherspoon's in 2004 included a corporate social responsibility section in its 2004 annual report.

15. Statement of Corporate Governance This statement arise out of the drive to make directors more accountable to their shareholders. The corporate governance statement is governed by stock market requirements. The issues usually covered are risk management, treasury management, internal controls, going concern and auditors. A major objective is to present a full and frank discussion of the directors' remuneration. Contained within this section is often a Directors' Remuneration Report. However, growing numbers of companies record this separately.

SOUNDBITE 12.1

Sustainability Information

'Accounting mechanisms have not, for the moment at least, kept pace with our requirements for sustainability information.'

Prince Charles

Source: *Accountancy Age*, 2 June 2005, p. 12

16. Directors' Remuneration Report This includes details of directors' pay. It may include details of the remuneration committee, the remuneration policy and the main components of the directors' pay (for example: basic salary, incentives, bonuses, share options, and performance-related pay). There is also a graph showing the company's total shareholder return with an appropriate stock market index (see Company Camera 12.4 for Tesco plc's 2004 performance graph).

THE COMPANY CAMERA 12.4

PERFORMANCE GRAPH

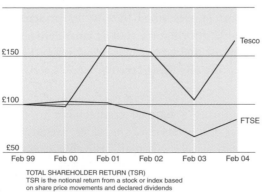

PERFORMANCE GRAPH The Group's total shareholder return performance (i.e. share price movements plus dividends reinvested) over the last five financial years relative to the FTSE 100 index of companies is show below. This index has been selected to provide an established and broad-based comparator group of retail and non-retail companies of similar scale to Tesco, against which the Group's TSR performance can be measured

TOTAL SHAREHOLDER RETURN (TSR)
TSR is the notional return from a stock or index based on share price movements and declared dividends

TESCO PLC 35

Source: Tesco plc, 2004, Annual Review and Summary Financial Statement, p. 35

17. Auditors' Report   The audit is an independent examination of the financial statements. An example of an auditors' report for Nokia, a Finnish company, is given in The Company Camera 12.5. An example of a UK company's audit report is given for Rentokil in The Company Camera 10.1.

THE COMPANY CAMERA 12.5

Independent Auditors' Report

To the shareholders of Nokia Corporation

We have audited the accounting records, the financial statements and the administration of Nokia Corporation for the year ended December 31, 2004. The financial statements prepared by the Board of Directors and the President include the report of the Board of Directors, consolidated financial statements prepared in accordance with International Financial Reporting Standards (IFRS), and parent company financial statements prepared in accordance with prevailing regulations in Finland. Based on our audit we express an opinion on the consolidated financial statements and on the parent company's financial statements and administration.

We conducted our audit in accordance with Finnish Generally Accepted Auditing Standards. Those standards require that we plan and perform the audit in order to obtain reasonable assurance about whether the financial statements are free of material misstatement. An audit includes examining, on a test basis, evidence supporting the amounts and disclosures in the financial statements, assessing the accounting principles used and significant estimates made by the management, as well as evaluating the overall financial statements presentation. The purpose of our audit of the administration has been to examine that the Chairman and the other members of the Board of Directors and the President have complied with the rules of the Finnish Companies' Act.

Consolidated financial statements

In our opinion, the consolidated financial statements prepared in accordance with International Financial Reporting Standards give a true and fair view of the consolidated results of operations as well as of the financial position. The financial statements are in accordance with prevailing regulations in Finland and can be adopted.

Parent company's financial statements and administration

The financial statements have been prepared in accordance with the Finnish Accounting Act and other rules and regulations governing the preparation of financial statements in Finland. The financial statements give a true and fair view, as

THE COMPANY CAMERA 12.5 (*continued*)

defined in the Finnish Accounting Act, of the parent company's result of operations, as well as the financial position. The financial statements can be adopted and the Chairman and the other members of the Board of Directors and the President of the parent company can be discharged from liability for the period audited by us. The proposal by the Board of Directors concerning the disposition of the profit for the year is in compliance with the Finnish Companies' Act.

Espoo, January 27, 2005

PricewaterhouseCoopers Oy
Authorized Public Accountants

Eero Suomela
Authorized Public Accountant

Source: Nokia, 2004 Annual Report, p. 53

Companies are legally required to publish the auditors' report. In essence, the report states whether the financial statements present a 'true and fair view' of the company's activities over the previous financial year. It sets out the respective responsibilities of directors and auditors as well as spelling out the work carried out to arrive at the auditors' opinion.

The auditors' report thus outlines the respective responsibilities of directors and auditors, the basis of the audit opinion and how the auditors arrived at their opinion. Pricewaterhouse-Coopers, the auditors of Nokia, are one of the world's leading auditing partnerships.

18. Statement of Directors' Responsibilities for the Financial Statements   This statement (see The Company Camera 12.6) was introduced because of a general misconception by

THE COMPANY CAMERA 12.6

Directors' Responsibilities for the Preparation of the Financial Statements

The directors are required by the Companies Act 1985 to prepare financial statements for each financial year which give a true and fair view of the state of affairs of the company and the Group as at the end of the financial year and of the profit or loss for the financial year.

THE COMPANY CAMERA 12.6 (*continued*)

The directors consider that in preparing the financial statements on pages 26 to 55 the company and Group have used appropriate accounting policies, consistently applied and supported by reasonable and prudent judgements and estimates, and that all accounting standards which they consider to be applicable have been followed.

The directors have responsibility for ensuring that the company and Group keep accounting records which disclose, with reasonable accuracy at any time, the financial position of the company and Group and which enable them to ensure that the financial statements comply with the Companies Act 1985.

The directors are responsible for the maintenance and integrity of the Annual Review and Summary Financial Statement and Annual Report and Financial Statements published on the Group's Corporate website. Legislation in the UK concerning the preparation and dissemination of financial statements may differ from legislation in other jurisdictions.

The directors have general responsibility for taking such steps as are reasonably open to them to safeguard the assets of the Group and to prevent and detect fraud and other irregularities.

Source: Tesco plc, 2004 Annual Report, p. 24

the general public of the purpose of an audit compared with the actual nature of an audit as understood by auditors. The directors must spell out their responsibilities which include (i) keeping proper accounting records; (ii) preparing financial statements in accordance with the Companies Act 1985; (iii) applying appropriate accounting policies; and (iv) following all applicable accounting standards.

19. Shareholder Information   Companies increasingly include a variety of shareholder information. This might, for example, include a financial calendar, share price details, shareholder analysis (see item 22) or notice of the AGM. The information may be narrative or non-narrative in nature.

Non-Narrative Sections

20. Highlights   This very popular feature normally occurs at the start of the annual report, often accompanied by graphs of selected figures. This section provides an at-a-glance summary of selected figures and ratios.

In Tesco's report (The Company Camera 12.7), for example, group sales, group profit, profit before tax, earnings per share and dividends per share are the financial ratios highlighted. The financial highlights may be seen as an abridged version of the historical summary.

THE COMPANY CAMERA 12.7

Financial Highlights

Group Sales	UP **11.9 %**
Group profit before tax	UP **12.0 %**
Earnings per share	UP **11.1 %**
Dividend per share	UP **11.2 %**

Source: Tesco plc, 2001 Annual Report, p. 1

21. *Historical Summary*   The historical summary is a voluntary recommendation of the stock exchange. Indeed, in the UK, it is one of the very few regulations set out by the stock exchange. Usually, companies choose to present five years of selected data from both the balance sheet and profit and loss account.

22. *Shareholder Analysis*   In many ways this item supplements item 19, shareholder information. It provides detailed analysis of the shareholders, for example, by size of shareholding.

These 22 items are by no means exhaustive, for example, J.D. Wetherspoon's plc, the pub chain, provides a list of its Directors, officers and advisers.

Presentation

The style of the annual report is becoming much more important. Companies are increasingly presenting key financial information as graphs rather than as tables. This information is voluntary and generally often supplements the mandatory information. Many companies use graphs to provide oases of colour and interest in otherwise dry statutory documents. In many cases, the graphs are presented at the front along with the highlights. Tesco, for example, in

1999 provided five-year graphs of group sales, group operating profit, earnings per share, and operating cash flow and capital expenditure (see The Company Camera 12.8).

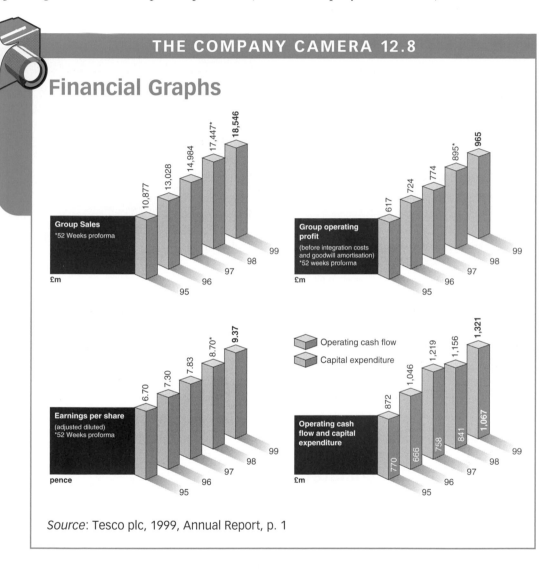

THE COMPANY CAMERA 12.8

Financial Graphs

Group Sales
*52 Weeks proforma

£m

10,877 · 13,028 · 14,984 · 17,447* · 18,546
95 · 96 · 97 · 98 · 99

Group operating profit
(before integration costs and goodwill amortisation)
*52 weeks proforma

£m

617 · 724 · 774 · 895* · 965
95 · 96 · 97 · 98 · 99

Earnings per share
(adjusted diluted)
*52 Weeks proforma

pence

6.70 · 7.30 · 7.83 · 8.70* · 9.37
95 · 96 · 97 · 98 · 99

Operating cash flow
Capital expenditure

Operating cash flow and capital expenditure

£m

Operating cash flow: 872 · 1,046 · 1,219 · 1,156 · 1,321
Capital expenditure: 770 · 666 · 758 · 841 · 1,067
95 · 96 · 97 · 98 · 99

Source: Tesco plc, 1999, Annual Report, p. 1

Photographs are also common in annual reports. These may be of employees or products. However, often they act as 'mood music' with no obvious relationship to the actual content of the report.

The increased use of the Internet provides many opportunities for companies to present their annual reports on their websites. Many companies are now experimenting with this new presentational format, often using varied presentational methods. Figure 12.4 gives some well-known company websites and students are encouraged to visit them.

Figure 12.4   Well-Known Company Websites

Internet Address	Description
(a) Information on Companies	
http://www.bized.ac.uk	Case studies, annual reports and company information on all top 100 UK companies
http://www.reportgallery.com.bigaz.htm	Annual reports of US firms
companiesonline.com	List of 100,000 USA companies
http://www.ukdirectory.com	UK websites by sector
http://www.ukplus.co.uk	Searchable directory of UK websites
(b) 10 Company Web Sites	
http://www.bp.com	British Petroleum
http://www.bt.com	British Telecom
http://www.british-airways.com	British Airways
http://www.glaxowellcome.com	Glaxo Wellcome
http://www.marks-and-spencer.co.uk	Marks & Spencer
http://www.manutd.com	Manchester United
http://www.sainsburys.co.uk	Sainsbury's
http://www.sb.com	Smithkline and Beecham
http://www.tesco.co.uk	Tesco
http://www.vodafone.co.uk	Vodafone

Source: PC Guide 2: *The Internet Guide*, Mark Goode, 2004

Group Accounts

Subsidiary and associated companies

An interesting feature of most of the world's largest companies is that they are structured as groups. It is the annual reports of these groups of companies such as Vodafone, Toyota or Wal-Mart that are most often publicly available. A group of companies is one where one or more companies is owned or controlled by another. In many cases, these groups are extremely complex and complicated involving many hundreds of subsidiary and associated companies. At its simplest, *subsidiaries* are normally companies where the parent (i.e., top group company) owns more than 50 % of shares and *associates* are companies where the parent owns 20–50 % of shares. The formal definitions (see Definition 12.3 on the next page) provided by the Accounting Standards Board (ASB), the International Accounting Standards Board (IASB) and the Companies Act are expressed in considerably more complex language.

DEFINITION 12.3

1. Subsidiary company

Working definition

A company where more than half the shares are owned by another company or which is effectively controlled by another company, or is a subsidiary of a subsidiary.

Formal definition

A subsidiary is an enterprise that is controlled by another enterprise. Control is presumed to exist when the parent owns, directly or indirectly through subsidiaries, more than one half of the voting power of an enterprise unless, in exceptional circumstances, it can be clearly demonstrated that such ownership does not constitute control. Control also exists even when the parent owns one half or less of the voting power of an enterprise when there is:

(a) power over more than one half of the voting rights by virtue of an agreement with other investors;
(b) power to govern the financial and operating policies of the enterprise under a statute or an agreement;
(c) power to appoint or remove the majority of the members of the board of directors or equivalent governing body; or
(d) power to cast the majority of votes at meetings of the board of directors or equivalent governing body.

Source: International Accounting Standards Board, International Accounting Standard 27, Scope of Consolidated Financial Statements, paras 6 and 12

2. Associated company

Working definition

A company in which 20–50% of the shares are owned by another company or one in which another company has a significant influence.

Formal definition

An associate is an enterprise in which the investor has significant influence and which is neither a subsidiary nor a joint venture of the investor. If an investor holds, directly or indirectly through subsidiaries, 20% or more of the voting power of the investee, it is presumed that the investor does have significant influence, unless it can be clearly demonstrated that this is not the case. Conversely, if the investor holds, directly or indirectly through subsidiaries, less than 20% of the voting power of the investee, it is presumed that the investor does not have significant influence, unless such influence can be clearly demonstrated. A substantial or majority ownership by another investor does not necessarily preclude an investor from having significant influence.

Source: International Accounting Standards Board, 2000, IAS 28, Accounting for Investments in Associates, paras 3 and 4

Group accounts are prepared using special accounting procedures, which are beyond the scope of this particular book (interested readers could try Elliot and Elliot, *Advanced Financial Accounting and Reporting*, or Alexander and Britton, *Financial Reporting*). In essence, the group income statement and group balance sheet attempt to portray the whole group's performance and financial position rather than that of individual companies.

Thus, in Figure 12.5, the group comprises seven companies. Company A is the parent company and owns over 50 % of companies B and C, making them subsidiaries. Company B also owns more than 50 % of the shares of companies B1 and B2. Companies B1 and B2 thus become sub-subsidiaries of Company A. These four companies (B, C, B1 and B2) are therefore consolidated as subsidiaries using normal accounting procedures. In addition, an appropriate proportion of companies D and E are taken into the group accounts since these two companies are associates as between 20 % and 50 % of the shares are held. Overall, therefore we have the aggregate financial performance of the whole group. One group set of financial statements is prepared. It is these group accounts that are normally published in the annual report.

Figure 12.5   Example of Group Structure

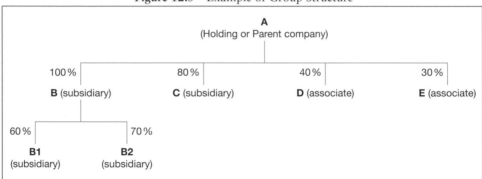

PAUSE FOR THOUGHT 12.4

Group Accounts

Nowadays, most leading companies must prepare group accounts. Can you think of any problems they might encounter?

There are many! Many companies will have hundreds of subsidiaries. All the information must be supplied to head office. At head office, it must all be collected and collated. Different subsidiaries may have different year-end accounting dates, operate in different countries using different accounting policies and different currencies. Some of the subsidiaries will have been acquired or sold, or the shareholdings of the parent company will have changed, during the year. All these are potential problems.

Goodwill

Goodwill is a particular feature of group companies. Goodwill is known as an intangible asset (i.e., one that you cannot touch). Goodwill, in accounting terms, is only recognised when one company takes over another. It represents the purchase price less the amount paid for the net assets (i.e., the value placed on the earnings power of a business over and above its net assets value). This can often be quite considerable. In other words, when the market values of the real world meet the historical costs of the accounting world there is a valuation gap. That gap is termed goodwill. European listed companies follow International Financial Reporting Standard 3 which states that goodwill is shown as an asset on the balance sheet. It is then reviewed every year to see if the goodwill has lost value. If it has lost value this value will be written off to the income statement. The annual review is called an impairment test. For UK non-listed companies, the UK standard requires a different treatment. The preferred treatment is that companies should write off goodwill to the profit and loss account annually over a period of up to 20 years. This process of writing off goodwill is called amortisation. It is similar to depreciation. Non-listed companies are also permitted, if they can make a case, to write off goodwill over a period of greater than 20 years or even not at all.

Impression Management

Managers have significant incentives to try to influence the financial reporting process in their own favour. These incentives may be financial and non-financial. Financially, managers may be keen, for example, to maximise their own remuneration. If remuneration is based on profits, they may seek to adopt accounting policies that will increase rather than decrease profits. In non-financial terms, managers, like all human beings, will try to portray themselves in a good light. This may result, for example, in managers selectively disclosing only positive features of the annual performance.

PAUSE FOR THOUGHT 12.5

Impression Management

Can you think of any non-accounting situations where human beings indulge in impression management?

There are many, just to take two: interviews and dating. At an interview, normal, sane candidates try to give a good impression of themselves in order to get the job. This may involve trying to stress their good points and downplay their bad points. When dating, you try to look good to impress your partner. Once more, most normal people will try to present themselves in a favourable light. You want to impress your dates not repel them.

In this section, three illustrative examples of impression management are discussed: creative accounting, narrative enhancement and use of graphs.

Creative Accounting

Creative accounting will be dealt with more fully in Chapter 13. Put simply, creative accounting is the name given to the process whereby managers use the flexibility inherent within the accounting process to manipulate the accounting numbers. Flexibility within the accounting system is abundant. By itself, flexibility allows managers to choose those accounting policies that will give a true and fair view of the company's activities. However, there are also opportunities for managers to choose policies which portray themselves in a good light. The worst excesses are covered by the regulatory framework. To see how the flexibility within accounting can alter profit, we take inventory (stock) and depreciation as examples.

Inventory (Stock)

In accounting terms

$$\text{Assets} - \text{Liabilities} = \text{Equity(Capital)}$$

In other words, if assets increase so will equity or capital. As capital, at its simplest, is accumulated profits, if we increase inventory we will increase accumulated profits. Inventory is an easy asset to manipulate, if we wish to increase our profits. We could, for example, do an extremely thorough stocktake at the end of one year, recording and valuing items which normally would have been overlooked.

PAUSE FOR THOUGHT 12.6

Inventory and Creative Accounting

A company has one asset inventory. Its abridged balance sheet is set out below.

	£		£
Inventory	50,000	Equity	30,000
		Profit	20,000
	50,000		50,000

If the company revalues its inventory to £60,000, what will happen to profit?

The answer is that profit increases by £10,000, as the new balance sheet shows.

	£		£
Inventory	60,000	Equity	30,000
		Profit	30,000
	50,000		60,000

Depreciation

Depreciation is the expense incurred when non-current assets such as plant and machinery are written down in value over their useful lives. Unfortunately, estimates of useful lives vary. For example, if an asset has an estimated useful life of five years then depreciation, using a straightline basis, would be 20 % per year. If the asset's estimated useful life was ten years, depreciation would be 10 % per year. In other words, by extending the useful life, we halve the depreciation rate and halve the amount that is treated as an expense in the income statement. Managers can thus alter profit by choosing a particular rate of depreciation. They would argue that they are more fairly reflecting the useful life of the asset.

Narrative Enhancement

Narrative enhancement occurs when managements use the narrative parts of the annual report to convey a more favourable impression of performance than is actually warranted. They may do this by omitting key data or stressing certain elements. Many companies stress, for example, their 'good' environmental performance. Indeed, social and environmental disclosures are nowadays exceedingly common. Since such disclosures are voluntary and reviewed rather than audited, there is great potential for companies to indulge in narrative enhancement. This can be seen from Real-Life Nugget 12.5.

REAL-LIFE NUGGET 12.5

Environmental Accounting

An interesting example of narrative measurement is given by Craig Deegan and Ben Gordon. They studied the environmental disclosure practices of Australian corporations. The number of positive and negative words of environmental disclosure in annual reports from 1980 to 1991 are recorded for 25 companies. They find:

	1980	1985	1988	1991
Mean positive disclosure	12	14	20	105
Mean negative disclosure	0	0	0	7

They conclude:

'The environmental disclosures are typically self-laudatory, with little or no negative disclosures being made by all firms in the study.'

Source: Craig Deegan and Ben Gordon (1996), *Accounting and Business Research*, p. 198

Graphs

Graphs are a voluntary presentational medium. Used well they are exceedingly effective. However, they also present managers with significant opportunities to manage the presentation of the annual report. For example, a variety of research studies show that managers are exceedingly selective in their use of graphs. They tend to display time-series trend graphs when performance is good, with these graphs presenting a rising trend of corporate performance. By contrast, when the results are poor, graphs are omitted.

Even when included, there is a potential for graphical misuse. For example, graphs may be (and often are) drawn with non-zero axes that enhance the perception of growth. Or graphs may simply be drawn inaccurately. Currently, graphs are not regulated, therefore companies are free to use them creatively.

An interesting example is shown in The Company Camera 12.9. These five graphs represent the financial performance of Polly Peck just before the company collapsed into bankruptcy. Although not inaccurately drawn, they do present a very effective, and misleading, display. Who could guess that this company was about to fail?

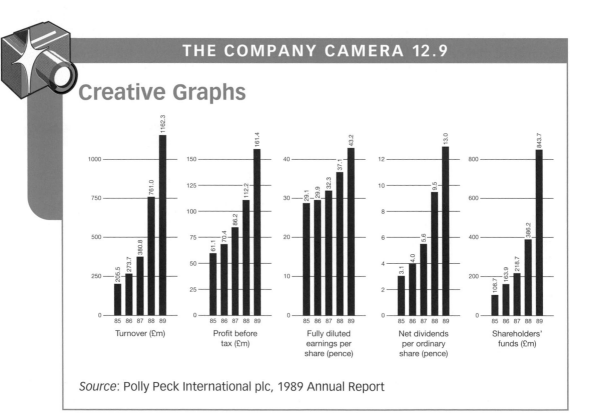

THE COMPANY CAMERA 12.9

Creative Graphs

Source: Polly Peck International plc, 1989 Annual Report

Conclusion

The annual report is a key part of the process by which managers report to their shareholders. It is central to the corporate governance process. There are three overlapping objectives: stewardship and accountability, decision making and public relations. The annual report is built around three core audited financial statements: the income statement, the balance sheet and the cash flow statement. However, in the UK another six important audited financial statements are normally present: statement of total recognised gains and losses; reconciliation of movements in shareholders' funds; note on historical cost profits and losses; accounting policies; notes to the accounts; and the principal subsidiaries. Most large companies comprise groups consisting of subsidiary and associated companies. The main accounts are therefore group accounts.

The modern annual report also consists of non-audited sections. These can be divided into narratives and non-narratives. In the UK, the ten narratives comprise the chairman's statement, the operating and financial review, the directors' report, the review of operations, the social and environment statement, the statement of corporate governance, the directors' remuneration report, the auditors' report, the statement of directors' responsibilities for the financial statements and shareholder information. The three non-narratives are the highlights, the historical summary and the shareholder analysis. As well as these sections, the modern annual report commonly uses graphs and photographs to enhance its presentation. Managements face many incentives to influence the financial reporting process in their favour. This can be done, for example, through creative accounting, narrative enhancement or the use of graphs.

Selected Reading

Unfortunately, there is no one book or article which really covers the modern annual report. Readers are referred to the following three sources which cover some valuable material.

1. Arthur Andersen (1996), '*What's the Story: A Survey of Narrative Reporting in Annual Reports*', London.
   This publication takes a good look at the rapid growth of the narrative parts of the annual report.
2. Deegan, C. and Gordon, B. (1996), 'A study of environmental disclosure practices of Australian companies', *Accounting and Business Research*, Vol. 26, No. 5, pp. 187–99.
   This article provides an interesting insight into how individual companies accentuate the good news and downplay bad news of their environmental activities.
3. Coopers and Lybrand, *Form and Content of Company Accounts* (1986) A good overview of legislation which governs the preparation of the financial statements. A handy reference item to the Companies Act 1985.

4. McKinstry, S. (1996) 'Designing the annual reports of Burton plc from 1930 to 1994', *Accounting, Organizations and Society*, Vol. 21, No. 1, pp. 89–111.
This rather heavyweight article looks at how one company's annual reports have changed over time, concentrating particularly on the public relations aspects.

Q&A   Discussion Questions

Questions with numbers in blue have answers at the back of the book.

Q1   Explain the role that the annual report plays in the corporate governance process.

Q2   Evaluate the stewardship/accountability, decision making and public relations roles of the annual report and identify any possible conflicts.

Q3   In your opinion what are the six most important sections of the annual report. Why have you chosen these sections?

Q4   Why do companies prepare group accounts?

Q5   What do you understand by the term 'impression management'? Why do you think that managers might use the annual report for impression management?

Chapter 13

"Every company in the country is fiddling its profits. Every set of published accounts is based on books which have been gently cooked or completely roasted. The figures which are fed twice a year to the investing public have all been changed to protect the guilty. It is the biggest con trick since the Trojan Horse."

Ian Griffiths (1986), *Creative Accounting*, Sidgwick and Jackson, p. 1

Learning Outcomes

After completing this chapter you should be able to:

✔ Explain the nature of creative accounting.

✔ Outline the managerial incentives for creative accounting.

✔ Demonstrate some common methods of creative accounting.

✔ Understand the real-life relevance of creative accounting.

Creative Accounting

In a Nutshell

- *Creative accounting involves managers using the flexibility within accounting to serve their own interests.*

- *The regulatory framework tries to ensure that accounts correspond to economic reality.*

- *Management will indulge in creative accounting, inter alia, to flatter profits, smooth profits or manage gearing.*

- *Income, inventory, depreciation, interest payable, and brands can all be managed creatively.*

- *In extreme cases, such as Parmalat, Polly Peck, WorldCom or Enron creative accounting can contribute to bankruptcy.*

- *Several well-known publications, in particular, Accounting for Growth, have documented actual cases of creative accounting.*

- *Companies can also creatively manage the published version of their accounts through, for example, creative graphics.*

- *Regulators, such as the International Accounting Standards Board, try to curb creative accounting. This creates a creative accounting 'arms race'.*

Introduction

Creative accounting became a hot topic in the late 1980s. Attention was drawn, by commentators such as Ian Griffiths (author of *Creative Accounting*), to how businesses use the flexibility inherent in accounting to manage their results. In itself, flexibility is good because it allows companies to choose accounting policies that present a 'true and fair view'. However, by the judicious choice of accounting policies and by exercising judgement, accounts can serve the interests of the preparers rather than the users. Creative accounting is not illegal but effectively, through creative compliance with the regulations, seeks to undermine a 'true and fair view' of accounting. Creative accounting can involve manipulating income, expenses, assets or liabilities through simple or exceedingly complex schemes. The current regulatory framework can partially be seen as a response to creative accounting. It attempts to ensure that accounting represents economic reality and presents a true and fair view of the company's activities. However, new regulations bring new opportunities for creative compliance and thus creative accounting. As Real-Life Nugget 13.1 shows, even well-known companies are accused of questionable accounting. Enron, once the seventh biggest US company, which went into liquidation in 2001 is believed to have indulged in creative accounting. Other US companies such as WorldCom have been involved in accounting scandals in which creative accounting has played a contributory role. Creative accounting also seems to have played an important role in banking failures in the recent credit crunch.

REAL-LIFE NUGGET 13.1

Microsoft and Cookie Jar Accounting

The Securities Exchange Commission (SEC), which has been cracking down on so-called 'cookie-jar' accounting, has mounted a probe of Microsoft's accounting for financial reserves . . .

The SEC customarily does not comment on its investigations. Microsoft, however, in an apparent attempt to prevent bad publicity and any negative effect on its stock price, recently revealed the existence of the probe in a conference call with analysts and reporters . . .

. . . Cookie-jar accounting is the practice of hiding assets in reserves when times are good so that they can be used as a fallback when times are bad. It is not illegal as such but the SEC is, nevertheless, adamant that there are limits beyond which a company cannot go. Specifically, the SEC has been targeting questionable accounting for restructuring charges and restructuring reserves. 'Some companies like the idea so much that they establish restructuring reserves every year', said Walter Schuetze, Chief of the SEC's enforcement division, in a recent speech.

Source: Microsoft faced with SEC accounting probe, J.R. Peterson, *The Accountant*, July 1999, p. 1
Helpnote: Cookie jar accounting is so called because you are hiding assets away when times are good, ready to use them when times are bad. It is thus 'saving up for a rainy day'.

Definition

Creative accounting is a slippery concept, which evades easy definition. As Definition 13.1 shows, there arc perhaps three key elements in creative accounting: flexibility, management of the accounts and serving the interests of managers.

DEFINITION 13.1

Creative Accounting

Working definition
Using the flexibility within accounting to manage the measurement and presentation of the accounts so that they serve the interests of the preparers.

Formal definition
'A form of accounting which, while complying with all regulations, nevertheless gives a biased impression (generally favourable) of the company's performance.'

Source: Chartered Institute of Management Accounting (2000), *Official Terminology*

(i) Flexibility

Accounting is very flexible. There are numerous choices, for example, for measuring depreciation, valuing inventory or recording sales. This flexibility underpins the idea that the financial statements should give a 'true and fair view' of the state of affairs of the company and of the profit. Accounting policies should thus, in theory, be chosen to support a true and fair view. In many cases they are, but the flexibility within accounting does sometimes enable managers to present a more favourable impression of the company's performance than is perhaps warranted. Indeed, within accounting there is a continuum (see Figure 13.1).

Figure 13.1 Flexibility within Accounting

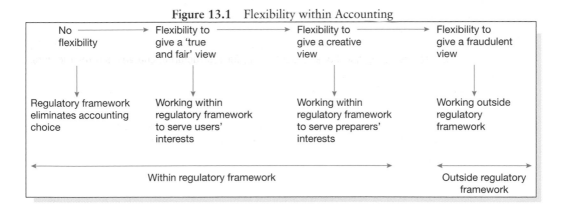

This continuum starts with a completely standardised accounting system. This gives way to flexibility so as to present a true and fair view. Next we have flexibility to account creatively. Finally, there is fraud, which involves non-compliance with the regulations rather than 'bending' them. In Soundbite 13.1, Zero Mostel seems to be urging Bloom to adopt practices that appear more fraudulent than creative. In the US, for example, WorldCom has been accused of fraudulently overstating profits by $3.8 bn (*Financial Times*, 26 June 2002, p. 1). In Italy, Parmalat Italy's eighth largest company in 2003 has been the centre of a corporate scandal. Executives fraudulently used a forged Bank of America document to vouch for $5 billion in assets and claimed the company had sold enough milk to Cuba to provide every Cuban with 55 gallons of milk for the year (Christopher Erdmann, The Parmalat Scandal: Italy's Enron, 2004).

(ii) Management of the Accounts

Unfortunately, in practice, the directors may choose accounting policies more to fulfil managerial objectives than to satisfy the requirements of users for a 'true and fair' view. Accounting thus becomes a variable to be managed rather than an instrument for providing true and fair information.

(iii) Interests of Managers

Accounting theory suggests that the aim of the accounts is to provide financial information to users so that they can make decisions. However, creative accounting privileges the interests of managers. Users *may*, indeed, benefit from creative accounting, but managers *will* definitely benefit.

Managerial Motivation

Managers have incentives to adopt creative accounting. Essentially, managers are judged, and rewarded, on the performance of their companies. It is, therefore, in managers' interests that their companies meet expectations. For example, if managers have profit-related bonuses, it makes sense for them to maximise their profits so they get bigger bonuses. Other managerial incentives might be the ownership of shares and share options, the need to smooth profits or to manage gearing.

Shares and Share Options

Managers may own shares. They also may have share options which allow them to buy shares today at a set price and then sell them for a higher price at a future date. If the stock market expects a certain amount of profit from a company, then managers may wish to adopt creative accounting to deliver that profit. Otherwise, the share price will fall and the managers will lose out.

Profit Smoothing

The stock market prefers a steady progression in earnings to an erratic earnings pattern. Companies with erratic earnings typically have lower share prices than those with steadier performances. Their lower share price makes these companies more vulnerable to takeover than companies with smoother profit trends. Managers of companies that are taken over may lose their jobs. Therefore, managers have incentives to smooth profits. Current shareholders are also likely to benefit from profit smoothing as the share price remains high.

PAUSE FOR THOUGHT 13.2

Profit Smoothing

Two firms (A and B) in the same industry have the following profit trends. Which do you think might be favoured by the stock market?

Years	1	2	3	4
	£m	£m	£m	£m
A	1	2	4	8
B	4	(1)	15	(3)

At first glance, A looks the better bet. Its profits steadily rise, doubling each year. However, company B, whose profit are irregular, actually makes the same cumulative profits as A (i.e., £15 m). Overall, the stock market will probably favour A with its steady growth. Indeed, in year 4, company A might even be able to make a successful bid for B! Company A's share price at that date will probably be much higher than company B's.

Manage Gearing

As well as managing profits, companies have incentives to manage gearing or conceal debt. Companies may wish to borrow money. However, existing borrowers may put restrictions on the amount of any new debt that can be raised. Managers may attempt to circumvent these restrictions using creative accounting. Enron, for instance, attempted to conceal the amount of debt it possessed.

The managerial incentives vary from firm to firm. For example, in some regulated industries (such as gas or water), managers may actually wish to reduce sales and profits so as to stop the government putting price restrictions on them. However, the key point about managerial incentives is that they encourage managers to serve their own or the company's interests rather than present a true and fair view of the company's performance.

SOUNDBITE 13.2

Restating your Figures

'The easiest way to do a snow job on investors (or on yourself) is to change one factor in the accounting each month. Then you can say, "It's not comparable with last month or last year. And we can't really draw any conclusion from the figures".'

Robert Townsend, *Up the Organization* (Knopf, 1970).

Source: *The Wiley Book of Business Quotations* (1998), p. 89

Methods of Creative Accounting

There are innumerable methods of creative accounting. These arise mainly from the flexibility of accounting and the existence of so many acceptable accounting policies. If you change your accounting policies, you will change your results. Indeed, as Robert Townsend suggests in Soundbite 13.2, one easy way of creative accounting is continually to change your accounting policies. In the US, WorldCom, which collapsed in 2002, was accused of repeatedly restating its accounts. However, the consistency concept does to some extent limit companies' abilities to do this.

Many creative accounting procedures are complex and often undetectable to the analyst. In this section, we will look at five of the more straightforward techniques. The aim is to give some illustrative examples rather than to present a comprehensive list. The worst excesses of creative accounting have been curbed by accounting rules and regulations that have been developed to try to ensure that the accounts correspond to economic reality. In many cases, some of the techniques listed will be used by management taking advantage of accounting's flexibility to give a true and fair view of the company's activities. In other cases, these techniques will be used creatively. To the onlooker it is generally difficult to distinguish these two contrasting uses. Motivation is the key distinguishing feature. Where managers attempt to serve their own interests rather than present a true and fair view, creative accounting is occurring.

Those readers who wish a more in-depth look at the subject are referred to Ian Griffiths, *New Creative Accounting* or Terry Smith's *Accounting for Growth*.

(i) Inflating Income

The problem is that sales recognition is not as precise as cash flow (see Real-Life Nugget 13.2). When should we recognise a sale as a sale? This may, at first, seem a silly question. However, the date of sale is not always obvious. For example, is it when (i) we dispatch goods to a customer, (ii) we invoice the customer, or (iii) we receive the money? Nor-

REAL-LIFE NUGGET 13.2

Income Recognition

'Once it is accepted that actual cash flows do not present a true and fair view of the company's performance, then the door marked creativity is pushed wide open. As long as a company can justify with a degree of reasonableness that its income recognition policy is soundly based then it has *carte blanche* to do pretty much what it likes.'

Source: Ian Griffiths (1995), *New Creative Accounting*, p. 16

mally, it is when we invoice the customer. However, in complex businesses there is often a fair degree of latitude about sales recognition. If you take a big construction project (like Multiplex's building of Wembley Stadium), for example, when should you recognise sales and take profits? There are rules to help in profit determination, but these rules still permit a good deal of flexibility.

Another troublesome area associated with income recognition is warranty provision (i.e. setting aside money to deal with customer returns). You can deal with this, in advance, and estimate a provision or deal with it on an actual return-by-return basis. Moreover, warranties can be treated as a reduction in sales or as an expense. The differing treatments can result in differing profits.

PAUSE FOR THOUGHT 13.3

Income Recognition

I was once involved in auditing a company selling agricultural machinery like combine harvesters. The company's year end was 30 June. Farmers wanted the machinery invoiced in March, but would pay in August when the machinery was delivered. Why do you think the farmers wished to do this and what income recognition policy was best for the company?

Essentially, this arrangement benefited both the company and the farmers. The company would take its sales in March, arguing this was the invoice date. The sales thus appeared before the June year end. The farmer would treat the purchase in March so that they could set off the machinery against taxation. As the tax year runs from April 6 to April 5, the farmers would hope to receive the capital allowances in one tax year, and pay for the machinery in the next tax year. Everybody was happy.

(ii) Inventory or Stock

Inventory provides a rich area for the creative accountant. The key feature about inventory is that if you increase your inventory you increase your profit (see Figure 13.2). The beauty of inventory is also that, in many businesses, inventory is valued once a year at an annual stock-take. When carrying out these stock-takes, it is relatively easy to take an optimistic or a pessimistic view of the value of inventory.

Figure 13.2   Inventory (Stock) as an Example of Creative Accounting

If there is only one asset, inventory, worth say £10 million, then if equity is £5 million and this year's profit is £5 million, then we have balance sheet A:

Balance Sheet A

	£m		£m
Equity	5	Inventory	10
Profit	5		
	10		10

The company could:

(1) adopt a more generous inventory valuation policy, perhaps by lowering the provisions for obsolete inventory (increases inventory by £0.5 million),
(2) do a particularly rigorous stock-take (increases inventory by £1.0 million undiscovered inventory). The balance sheet now looks like balance sheet B.

Balance Sheet B

	£m		£m
Equity	5.0	Inventory	11.5
Profit	6.5		
	11.5		11.5

Hey presto! We have increased our profits by £1.5 million.

(iii) Depreciation

Depreciation is the allocation of the cost of fixed assets over time. It is an expense recorded in the income statement. If the amount of depreciation changes then so will profit. The depreciation process is subject to many estimations, such as the life of the asset, which may alter the depreciation charge. A simple example is given in Figure 13.3 below. In essence, lengthening expected lives boosts profits while reducing them reduces profits. If management lengthens the assets' lives because it judges that the assets will last longer, this is fair enough. If the motivation, however, is to boost profits then this is creative accounting.

Figure 13.3   Depreciation

A business makes a profit of £10,000. It has £100,000 worth of fixed assets. Currently it depreciates them straight line over 10 years. However, the company is thinking of changing its depreciation policy to 20 years straight line. Will this affect profit?

	Original policy	New policy
	£	£
Profit before depreciation	10,000	10,000
Depreciation	(10,000)	(5,000)
Profit after depreciation	–	5,000

The answer is yes. By changing the depreciation policy, profit has increased by £5,000. In fact, the company looks much healthier.

The pace of technological change creates shorter asset lives. It would be assumed, therefore, that most companies would reduce their expected asset lives. However, as UBS Phillips and Drew point out below, in Real-Life Nugget 13.3, this is not necessarily so.

REAL-LIFE NUGGET 13.3

Change of Depreciation Lives

'Most changes in depreciation policies tend to be a lengthening of the expected lives rather than a shortening. Indeed it is difficult to identify any UK company which has recently reduced the depreciation life of any of its assets which has been of significance in terms of depressing reported profits. This is despite a general perception that many mechanical assets' true life expectations are shortening.'

Source: UBS Phillips and Drew (1991), *Accounting for Growth*, p. 11

Finally, Smith (1992) draws attention to British Airports Authority's (BAA) decision to lengthen its terminal and runway lives. Runway lives lengthened from 23.5 years in 1990 to 100 years in 1998. Annual depreciation was thus reduced.

(iv) Capitalisation of Costs such as Interest Payable

The capitalisation of costs involves the simple idea that a debit balance in the accounts can either be an expense or an asset. Expenses are deducted from sales and reduce profit. Assets are capitalised. Fixed assets are particularly important in this context. Only the depreciation charged on fixed assets is treated as an expense and reduces profit. Therefore, it will often benefit companies to treat certain expenses as fixed assets.

An example of this is interest costs. Where companies borrow money to construct fixed assets, they can argue, and often do, that interest on borrowing should be capitalised. However, some commentators such as Phillips and Drew find this a dubious practice (see Real-Life Nugget 13.4). Indeed, Phillips and Drew point out that some UK companies would actually make a loss, not a profit, if they did not capitalise their interest. In the US, WorldCom improperly capitalised huge amounts of expenses.

REAL-LIFE NUGGET 13.4

Capitalisation of Costs

'Virtually every UK listed property company, with the notable exception of Land Securities, makes use of capitalised interest (and often other costs as well) to defer the P&L impact of developments. While commercial property prices were rising rapidly, investors and banks did not worry about the amount of interest being capitalised. However, in more difficult property market conditions, such as those at present, the substantial difference between profits and cash flow caused by the significant capitalisation of costs can become critical in investment terms.

Often, there is clear justification for capitalising interest when it relates to a [sic] asset being constructed for use in the company's line of business, such as a supermarket, an aircraft or a new factory. The justification becomes much less convincing when the asset is being built for sale, such as property development and house building, for instance.'

Source: UBS Phillips and Drew (1991), *Accounting for Growth*, p. 10

(v) Brands

Brand valuation is a contentious issue within accounting. Some companies argue that it is appropriate to value brands so as better to reflect economic reality. By contrast, other observers believe that valuing brands is too subjective and judgemental and that the real motive behind brand valuation is for companies to boost asset values on the balance sheet. Brand accounting is a relatively new phenomenon in the UK. The idea is that, in many cases, brands are worth incredible amounts of money (think, for example, of Guinness or Kit Kat). Indeed, it is estimated that Coca-Cola's brand name adds £2 bn additional value to the company per year (Fiona Gilmore, *Accountancy Age*, May 2001).

Traditionally, brands have not formally been recognised as assets. However, from the mid-1980s, UK companies such as Grand Metropolitan and Cadburys started to include brands in their balance sheets. These brands are an asset and help to boost the assets in the balance sheet. They are *not* amortised (i.e. written off).

Traditional accountants are still suspicious of brands. This is because they are difficult to measure and, in essence, they are subjective. The situation in the UK is, therefore, something of an uneasy compromise. Acquired brands can be capitalised (i.e., included in the balance sheets). However, companies are not permitted to capitalise internally-generated brands. Overall, some companies capitalise their brands and some do not. There is also a great variety of ways in which brands are valued. In other words, there is great potential for creativity.

SOUNDBITE 13.3

Grasping Reality

'Some have suggested that Rolls-Royce accounts are fine because they meet with UK GAAP accounting rules, but let's remember that Enron complied with US rules. The question is whether you get a grasp of reality from the accounts, and I don't know that you do.'

Source: *The Guardian*, 12 February 2002, p. 23, Terry Macalister quoting Terry Smith of Collins Stewart brokers

Example

In order to demonstrate that creative accounting can make a difference, an example, Creato plc, is presented in Figure 13.4 on the next page. Adjustments are made for income, inventory, depreciation and the capitalisation of interest.

Figure 13.4   Example of Creative Accounting

Creato plc

Income Statement for Year Ended 31 December 2009

	Notes	£000	£000
Sales	1		100
Less *Cost of Sales*			
Opening inventory		10	
Add Purchases		40	
		50	
Less Closing inventory	2	15	35
Gross Profit			65
Less *Expenses*			
Depreciation	3	12	
Interest payable	4	15	
Other expenses		43	70
Loss for year			(5)

Notes

1. Creato has a prudent income recognition policy, a less conservative one would create an additional £10,000 sales.
2. Closing inventory could be valued, less prudently, at £18,000.
3. Depreciation is charged over five years; a few competitors charge depreciation over ten years even though this is longer than the realistic expected life.
4. £10,000 of the interest payable is interest on borrowings used to finance a new factory.

....

If we indulge in a spot of creative accounting we can transform Creato plc's income statement.

Creato plc

Income Statement for Year Ended 31 December 2009

		£000	£000
Sales	1		110
Less *Cost of Sales*			
Opening inventory		10	
Add Purchases		40	
		50	
Less Closing inventory	2	18	32
			78
Gross Profit			
Less *Expenses*			
Depreciation	3	6	
Interest payable	4	5	
Depreciation on capitalised interest payable	4	1	
Other expenses		43	55
Profit for year			23

Notes

1. We can simply boost sales by £10,000 and be less conservative.
2. If we value closing inventory at £18,000, this will reduce cost of sales, thus boosting gross profit.
3. By doubling the life of our property, plant and equipment, we can halve the depreciation charge.
4. If we have borrowed the money to finance property, plant and equipment, then we can capitalise some of the interest payable. Interest payable thus reduces from £15,000 to £5,000. We assume here that we will then depreciate this capitalised interest over ten years (this company's new policy for property, plant and equipment). Thus, we are charging £1,000 depreciation on the capitalised interest payable. We thus boost profit by £9,000 (i.e., £10,000 saved less £1,000 extra depreciation).

Hey presto! We have transformed a loss of £5,000 into a profit of £23,000.

Real Life

It should be stressed that creative accounting is very much a real-life phenomenon. Extensive research has demonstrated its existence. Of particular interest are two empirical studies: *Accounting for Growth* and *Company Pathology*. Although dating from the 1990s, these studies, which have not been repeated more recently, demonstrate quite clearly the existence of creative accounting. *Accounting for Growth* was published twice: first, by fund managers, UBS Phillips and Drew in 1991 as a report and second by Terry Smith in 1992 as a book. It caused considerable controversy – in fact, it resulted in Terry Smith, one of the analysts responsible for the research, leaving UBS Phillips and Drew. Essentially, as Real-Life Nugget 13.5 shows, UBS Phillips and Drew wished to draw attention to the recent growth in creative accounting.

REAL-LIFE NUGGET 13.5

Growth in Innovative Accounting

'The last ten years has been a time of major innovation as far as accounting techniques are concerned. Complex adjustments relating to acquisitions, disposals and many other transactions have become commonplace with the ultimate goal being to report continuous growth in earnings per share. The task now facing fund managers is to cut through the accounting camouflage in order to interpret the underlying trends. The penalty for getting the analysis wrong is the risk of substantial share price underperformance and in extreme cases, total loss.'

Source: UBS Phillips and Drew (1991), *Accounting for Growth*, p. 1

PAUSE FOR THOUGHT 13.4

Accounting for Growth

In their report, UBS Phillips and Drew identified the innovative accounting practices used by 185 UK companies. Why do you think this caused such a storm?

Before *Accounting for Growth* was published, there was much speculation about creative accounting. However, there was little systematic evidence. The Phillips and Drew report identified 165 leading companies (out of 185 they investigated) which had used at least one innovative accounting practice. It named names! The speculation turned into reality. The companies named were unhappy. As some of them were clients of UBS Phillips and Drew, some of the companies felt let down. The result of the storm was that Terry Smith left UBS Phillips and Drew and published his book, *Accounting for Growth*, on his own.

UBS Phillips and Drew analysed 185 UK listed companies. They identified 11 innovative (i.e., creative) accounting practices and drew up an accounting health check. They found that 165 companies used at least one innovative accounting practice, 17 used five or more and three used seven (see Real-Life Nugget 13.6). Interestingly, two of the high-scoring companies subsequently went bankrupt: Maxwell Communications and Tiphook.

REAL-LIFE NUGGET 13.6

High Scores in Health Check

Companies using the most accounting techniques in Phillips and Drew's 'Health Check'

Company	Sector	Frequency
British-Aerospace	Engineering	7
Maxwell	Media	7
Burton Group	Stores	7
Dixons	Stores	6
Cable and Wireless	Telephone networks	6
Blue Circle	Building materials	5
TI Group	Engineering	5
Bookers	Food manufacturing	5
Asda	Food retailer	5
Granada	Leisure	5
Next	Stores	5
Sears	Stores	5
LEP	Business services	5
Laporte	Chemicals	5
British Airways	Transport	5
Tiphook	Transport	5
Ultramar	Oils	5

Source: Accounting for Growth: Surviving the Accounting Jungle, M.J. Jones, *Management Accounting*, February 1992, p. 22

In *Company Pathology*, County NatWest Woodmac studied 45 'deceased' companies from 1989–90. They drew attention to questionable accounting practices, such as the capitalisation of interest. In only three out of the 45 cases did the audit report warn of the impending disaster. In only two out of the 45 cases did the pre-collapse turnover fall. Finally, in only six out of 45 cases did the last reported accounts show a loss. As Real-Life Nugget 13.7 on the next page shows, the report was often quite scathing. However, in the UK, given the active attention paid by the Accounting Standards Board to curbing creative accounting since the 1990s, many of the worst abuses have now been curtailed.

REAL-LIFE NUGGET 13.7

Analysis of Failed Companies

'A downturn in earnings per share is a lagging rather than a leading indicator of trouble. Accounting Standards give companies far too much scope for creative accounting. One set of accounts were described by an experienced and well qualified fund manager as "*a complete joke*". Auditors' reports seldom give warning of impending disaster.'

Source: County NatWest Woodmac (1991), *Company Pathology*, p. 4

Case Studies

(i) Polly Peck

An interesting example of a spectacular company collapse where creative accounting was present is Polly Peck. Polly Peck's demise is well-documented not only in Terry Smith's *Accounting for Growth*, but also in Trevor Pijper's *Creative Accounting: The Effect of Financial Reporting in the UK*.

Essentially, Polly Peck was one of the fastest expanding UK firms in the 1990s. It was headed by a charismatic chairman, Asil Nadir. It started off in food and electronics, and expanded rapidly. County NatWest Wood Mackenzie calculated that in the year to November 1989, Polly Peck's shares had grown faster than any other UK company. The 1989 results were full of optimism. For example, profit before tax had increased from £112 million to £161 million.

Indeed, the optimism was continued in the 1990 interim results. Eleven days after their publication, and six day before the collapse, Kitcat and Aitken (city analysts) reported that profits would increase substantially.

The collapse of Polly Peck cannot be attributed solely to creative accounting. There was fraud and deception and, in addition, there was the blind faith of bankers and shareholders. The signs were there for those who wished to look. For example, debt rose from £65.9 million in 1985 to £1,106 million in 1989. However, creative accounting did play its part in two key areas. First, Polly Peck capitalised the acquired brands, such as Del Monte, and thus strengthened its balance sheet. Second, and more seriously, the company indulged in currency mismatching. As explained in Figure 13.5 on the next page. This flattered Polly Peck's profit and loss account at the expense of seriously damaging its balance sheet.

Figure 13.5   Polly Peck's Currency Mismatching

> Polly Peck borrowed in Swiss francs, a strong currency,
> and paid back a low rate of interest. These borrowings
> were invested in Turkey, which had a weaker currency.
> Polly Peck was paid a high rate of interest.
> Unfortunately, however, the Turkish dinar depreciated
> against the Swiss franc. This meant that Polly Peck
> made capital losses of £44.7 million in 1989 on its
> borrowings. Meanwhile, its profit and loss had been
> flattered by £12.5 million (£68.1 million received less
> £55.6 million paid) because of the high rate of interest
> on the dinar deposits as compared with the low interest
> on the matched Swiss franc borrowings.

(ii) Enron

The spectacular collapse of Enron in December 2001 has brought creative accounting once
more back on the agenda, centre stage. Enron, at one time, was the seventh biggest US company.
However, from August 2000 its share price began to fall as a result of doubts about the strength
of its balance sheet and significant sales of shares by managers. Enron's main business was
to supply and make markets in oil and gas throughout the world. Enron first made gains on
investments in technology and energy businesses followed by losses. Following these losses,
Enron built up huge debts which have been estimated at $80 billion. From the accounts it was
not obvious that these liabilities existed. They were buried in rather complex legal jargon (see
The Company Camera 13.1).

THE COMPANY CAMERA 13.1

Extract from Enron's Notes to the Accounts

Enron is a guarantor on certain liabilities of unconsolidated equity affiliates and
other companies totalling approximately $1,863 million at December 31, 2001,
including $538 million related to EOTT trade obligations [EOTT Energy Partners]. The
EOTT letters of credit and guarantees of trade obligation are secured by the assets
of EOTT. Enron has also guaranteed $386 million in lease obligations for which it has
been indemnified by an 'Investment Grade' company. Management does not
consider it likely that Enron would be required to perform or otherwise incur any
losses associated with the above guarantees. In addition, certain commitments have
been made related to capital expenditures and equity investments planned in 2001.

Source: Enron, Annual Report (2000), Notes to the Accounts, p. 48

In order to manipulate income, to avoid reporting losses and keep its debts off the group's balance sheet, Enron set up special purpose entities (SPEs). Under US regulations if the SPEs were not controlled by Enron and if outside equity capital controlled at least 3 % of total assets then Enron would not have to bring the SPEs into its group accounts. It would thus not disclose its debts. Investors would not therefore realise the net indebtedness of the company. Many SPEs appear not to have been incorporated into the group accounts quite legally. However, in other cases it is alleged that control was held by Enron not by third parties and that Enron had provided third parties with funds so that the 3 % was not truly held independently. If this is the case, there was prima facie false accounting and questions began to be raised about the role of Arthur Andersen, the company's auditors. Arthur Andersen have also been accused of shredding documents relating to Enron. The role of the auditors as independent safeguards of the investors appears to have broken down. Finally, it has been reported in the press that Enron was receiving up-front payments for the future sales of natural gas or crude oil and effectively treating loans as sales.

Overall, therefore, Enron demonstrates that even well-known companies still indulge in creative accounting. In Enron's case, however, like that of Polly Peck, the borderline between creative accounting and fraud became blurred.

(iii) Banks

The role of creative accounting in the recent bank failures worldwide has caught the attention of many commentators. Banks, in particular, used many complex financial instruments such as derivatives and Collaterised Mortgage Obligations (CMO) where groups of mortgages are bundled together and sold on to third parties. It is not necessary to go into the details here, indeed, some of the creative instruments were so complex that the Board of Directors often did not understand them. However, the end result was that the accounts often became very difficult to understand. In many cases, substantial liabilities were kept off the balance sheet.

Creative Presentation

As well as creative accounting, companies can present their accounts in a flattering way. One of the ways they can do this is by using graphs. For example, they may use graphs only in years when the company has made a profit (the graph will show a rising trend). Alternatively, graphs may be deliberately drawn so as to exaggerate a rising trend. This may, for example, be done by using a non-zero axis. An example of creative graphical presentation is shown on the next page in Real-Life Nugget 13.8. In particular, it should be noted that the earnings per share graph is inconsistent with the other three. It is for three years not four and has a non-zero axis. The overall result is that it perhaps presents a more favourable view of the company's results than would otherwise be warranted.

Creative Graphs: T.I.P. Europe plc, 1989 Annual Report

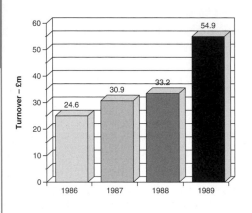

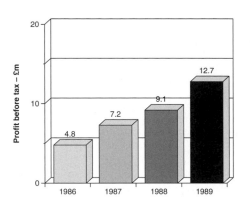

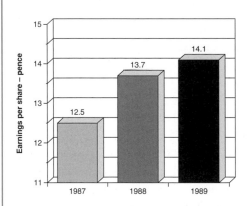

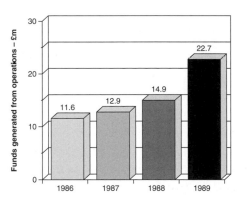

Source: Vivien Beattie and Michael Jones (1992), *The Communication of Information Using Graphs in Corporate Annual Reports*, ACCA Research Report, p. 65

Controlling Creative Accounting

One of the key objectives of the UK's Accounting Standards Board, which was set up in the 1990, was to control creative accounting. This is shown in the Financial Reporting Council's *The State of Financial Reporting – a Review* (1991) (paras 2.1 and 2.2) – see Real-Life Nugget 13.9. The International Accounting Standards Board also shares this concern.

REAL-LIFE NUGGET 13.9

Regulatory Response to Creative Accounting

'The corporate confidence developed during the 1980s boom, the associated readiness by banks to lend and by companies to borrow, the growth of innovative accounting practices (e.g. off balance sheet financing and the development of hybrid financial instruments) sometimes designed solely to avoid an increase in reported company gearing, coupled with a framework of accounting standards that was being outpaced by such developments, have made the recession which followed a correspondingly more chastening experience for bankers, creditors and shareholders, as well as for financial reporting itself.

The existence of weaknesses in the arrangements for formulating and securing compliance with accounting standards was well recognised long before the boom declined into recession.'

Source: Trevor Pijper (1993), *Creative Accounting: The Effect of Financial Reporting in the UK*, p. 15

Since 1990, there has been a concerted attempt by regulators to curb creative accounting. Undoubtedly, they have made substantial progress in many areas. Companies now have much less scope for creativity, for example, when dealing with leased assets. However, it is often a case of two steps forward, one step back. Indeed, there is a continuing battle between the regulators and creative accountants. Some merchant banks actively advise companies on 'creative compliance'. There is an evolving pattern of creative compliance from avoidance, to rules, back to avoidance. Atul Shah documents this using the case of complex convertible securities issued by listed UK companies. He concludes: '[r]egulators were slow to respond, and when they did make pronouncements, companies once again circumvented the rules with the help of various professionals. A "dialectic of creativity" is created, from avoidance to rules to avoidance again' (Shah, 1998, p. 36). This continual struggle between companies and regulators causes a creative accounting 'arms race'. In the US, after Enron and WorldCom, for example the Sarbenes-Oxley Act in the US introduced substantial new legislation.

Conclusion

Creative accounting emerged into the limelight in the 1980s. However, it is still alive and kicking today. As the collapse of Enron in 2001 clearly demonstrated. Managers have incentives to manage their accounting profits so that they serve managerial, rather than shareholder, interests. This is possible because of the extreme flexibility within accounting. There are numerous methods of creative accounting: some are extremely complex and others very simple. When used excessively, creative accounting can be positively dangerous; for example, it has contributed to corporate collapses. The regulators attempt, through accounting standards, to curb creative accounting. However, there is an ongoing battle as companies seek ways around the regulations.

Selected Reading

1. *Accounting for Growth*
   This report was a real accounting bombshell. It documents the use by 185 UK companies of 11 innovative accounting practices. The original report (see (a) below) was issued by UBS Phillips and Drew. Then Terry Smith published (b) below after he left UBS Phillips and Drew. Those who can't get hold of the original report/book, or who want a quick summary, could try Jones (c).
   (a) UBS Phillips and Drew (1991), *Accounting for Growth*.
   (b) Smith, T. (1992), *Accounting for Growth* (Century Business).
   (c) Jones, M.J. (1992), 'Accounting for growth: Surviving the accounting jungle', *Management Accounting*, February pp. 20–22.
2. County NatWest WoodMac (1991), *Company Pathology*.
   This report provides an interesting study into creative accounting by 45 companies.
3. Griffiths, I. (1986) *Creative Accounting* (Sidgwick and Jackson) and (1995) *New Creative Accounting* (Macmillan). Both very good reads which provide a journalist's view of the debate.
4. Pijper, T. (1993) *Creative Accounting: The Effect of Financial Reporting in the UK* (Macmillan). Another good overview of creative accounting.
5. Shah, A.K. (1998) 'Exploring the influences and constraints on creative accounting in the United Kingdom', *The European Accounting Review*, Vol. 7, No.1, pp. 83–104.
   This article provides a good insight into the evolving struggle between regulators and creative accountants.

Q&A   Discussion Questions

Questions with numbers in blue have answers at the back of the book.

Q1 What is creative accounting? And why do you think that it might clash with the idea that the financial statements should give a 'true and fair view' of the accounts?

Q2 Does creative accounting represent the unacceptable face of accounting flexibility?

Q3 Why do you think that there are those strongly in favour and those strongly against creative accounting?

Q4 What incentives do managers have to indulge in creative accounting?

Q5 Will creative accounting ever be stopped?

Q6 You are the financial accountant of Twister plc. The managing director has the following draft accounts. She is not happy.

Twister plc: Draft Income Statement Year Ended 30 June 2005

	Notes	£000	£000
Sales 1		750	
Less: *Cost of Sales*			
Opening inventory		80	
Add Purchases		320	
		400	
Less Closing inventory	2	60	340
Gross Profit			410
Less *Expenses*			
Depreciation	3	60	
Interest payable	4	30	
Other expenses		332	422
Net Loss			(12)

Notes

1. The company's sales policy is to record sales prudently, one month after invoicing the customer so as to allow for any sales returns. If the company recorded sales when invoiced, this would increase sales by £150,000.
2. This is a prudent valuation, a more optimistic valuation gives £65,000.
3. Depreciation is currently charged on fixed assets over ten years. This is a realistic expected life, but a competitor charges depreciation over 15 years.
4. Half the interest payable relates to the borrowing of money to finance the construction of fixed assets.

   Required: Using the accounts, and the notes above, present as flattering a profit as you can.

Chapter 14

"Whether we are ready or not, mankind now has a completely integrated financial and informational market place capable of moving money and ideas to any place on this planet in minutes."

W. Wriston, *Risk and Other Four-letter Words*, p. 132.
The Executive's Book of Quotations (1990), p. 150

Learning Outcomes

After completing this chapter you should be able to:

✔ **Explain and discuss the main divergent forces.**

✔ **Understand the macro and micro approaches to the classification of international accounting practices.**

✔ **Understand the accounting systems and environments in France, Germany, the UK and the US.**

✔ **Examine the convergent forces upon accounting, especially harmonisation in the European Union and standardisation through the International Accounting Standards Board.**

International Accounting

In a Nutshell

- *Global trade and investment make national accounting very constrictive.*

- *Divergent forces are those factors that make accounting different in different countries.*

- *The main divergent forces are: objectives, users, sources of finance, regulation, taxation, the accounting profession, spheres of influence and culture.*

- *Countries can be classified into those with macro and micro accounting systems.*

- *France and Germany are macro countries with tight legal regulation, creditor orientation and weak accounting professions.*

- *The UK and the US are micro countries, guided by the idea of fair presentation, with influential accounting standards, an investor-oriented approach and a strong accounting profession.*

- *Internationalisation causes pressure on countries to depart from national standards.*

- *The three main potential sources of convergence internationally are the European Union, the International Accounting Standards Board through International Financial Reporting Standards (IFRS) and US standards.*

Introduction

Increasingly, we live in a global world where multinational companies dominate world trade. The world's stock exchanges are active day and night. Accounting is not immune from this globalisation. There is an increasing need to move away from a narrow national view of accounting and see accounting in an international context. The purpose of this chapter is to provide an insight into these wider aspects of accounting. In particular, we explore the factors that cause accounting to be different in different countries, such as objectives, users, regulation, taxation and the accounting profession. Accounting in several important countries (France, Germany, the UK and the US) is also explored. Finally, this chapter looks at the international pressures for convergence towards one universal world accounting system. In essence, therefore, the aim of this chapter is to provide a brief overview of the international dimension to accounting.

Context

Perhaps surprisingly, given the variety of peoples and cultures throughout the world, the fundamental techniques of accounting are fairly similar in most countries. In other words, in most countries businesses use double-entry bookkeeping, prepare a trial balance and then a profit and loss account (income statement) and balance sheet. This system of accounting techniques was developed in Italy in the fifteenth century and spread around the world with trade.

However, the context of accounting in different countries is very different and causes transnational differences in the measurement of profit and net assets. The differences between countries are caused by so-called 'divergent forces', such as objectives, users, sources of finance, regulation, taxation, accounting profession, spheres of influence and culture. These divergent forces, which are examined in more detail in the next section, cause accounting in the UK to be different to that in, say, France or the US.

These international accounting differences caused few problems until the globalisation of international trade. However, with the rise of global trade and the erosion of national borders (see Soundbite 14.1), the variety of world accounting practices has been seen by many as a significant problem, particularly for multinational companies.

For large multinational companies, it is cheaper and easier to have just one set of world accounting standards. This is the aim of the International Accounting Standards Board (IASB). Meanwhile,

---

SOUNDBITE 14.1

National Boundaries

'National borders are no longer defensible against the invasion of knowledge, ideas, or financial data.'

Walter Wriston, *Risk and Other Four-Letter Words*, p. 133

Source: *The Executive's Book of Quotations* (1994), p. 202

within Europe there is pressure to harmonise accounting to create one set of Europe-wide standards. These pressures for the harmonisation and standardisation of accounting are called 'convergent forces'. In essence, therefore, these divergent and convergent forces pull accounting internationally in different directions. Large global corporations, such as Glaxo-Wellcome, Microsoft, Nokia and Toyota, dominate world trade. As Real-Life Nugget 14.1 shows, the sales of many of these corporations are greater than the gross national product of many countries. The sales of Mitsubishi and Mitsui in 1995 were greater than the GDP of countries such as Turkey, Thailand, Denmark, Hong Kong or Norway. In fact, only 23 countries in the world had a gross domestic product which exceeded the sales of either of these two companies. The situation today is likely to be relatively unchanged.

REAL-LIFE NUGGET 14.1

The World's Top Economic Entities

Country/company by GDP/sales   (Dollars Bn.)

1.	United States	7100
2.	Japan	4964
3.	Germany	2252
4.	France	1451
5.	United Kingdom	1095
24.	Mitsubishi (Japan)	184
25.	Mitsui (Japan)	181
26.	Itochu (Japan)	169
27.	Turkey	169
28.	General Motors (US)	169
29.	Sumitomo (Japan)	168
30.	Marubeni (Japan)	161
31.	Thailand	160
32.	Denmark	156
33.	Hong Kong	142
34.	Ford Motors (US)	137
35.	Norway	136

Source: FT Profile, Copyright Financial Times Information. It's bigger than Turkey, Thailand or Denmark – but it's not a country, Simon Caulkin, The Management Column, *Observer*, March 1998, p. 9

Divergent Forces

Divergent forces are those factors that cause accounting to be different in different countries. These may be internal to a country (such as taxation system) or external (such as sphere of influence). There is much debate about the nature and identity of these divergent forces. For example, some writers exclude objectives and users. Each country has a distinct set of divergent forces and the relative importance of each divergent force varies between countries. These divergent forces are interrelated. The main divergent forces discussed in this chapter are shown in Figure 14.1.

Figure 14.1   The Divergent Forces that Determine National Accounting Systems and Environments

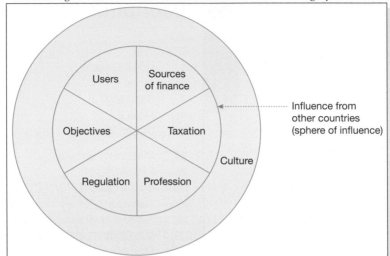

(i) Objectives

The objectives of an accounting system are a key divergent force. There are two major objectives: economic reality, and planning and control. The basic idea behind economic reality is that accounts should provide a 'true and fair' view of the financial activities of the company. The UK holds this view. The US takes a similar view: 'present fairly . . . in accordance with generally accepted accounting principles (GAAP)'. However, in the US there is a stronger presumption than in the UK that following GAAP will present a fair view of the company's activities. The 'true and fair' concept is basically linked to the underlying idea that the purpose of accounting is to provide users with financial information so that they can make economic decisions.

In contrast to economic reality, planning and control places more emphasis on the provision of financial information to government. Accounting in countries such as France and Germany is more concerned with collecting statistical and regularised information for comparability and planning. For example, in France accounting is seen as promoting national economic and fiscal planning. In France and Germany, the concept of a true and fair view is incorporated in national law. Unlike in the UK, this is more narrowly interpreted as compliance with the regulations.

(ii) Users

Users and objectives are closely interrelated. Users are also linked closely to another divergent force, sources of finance. In some countries, such as the UK and the US, shareholders are the main users of accounts. In the UK, institutional investors (such as insurance companies and pension firms) dominate, while in the US the role of the private individual is comparatively more important. When shareholders dominate, the accounting system focuses on profitability and the profit and loss account (income statement) becomes the main financial statement. However, recently standard setters have moved towards a balance sheet approach.

PAUSE FOR THOUGHT 14.1

Users

If the main users of accounts are banks rather than shareholders, how will that affect the items in the financial statements which they scrutinise?

Bankers essentially lend companies money and are concerned about two main things: loan security and loan repayments. They are, therefore, likely to focus on the balance sheet, particularly on assets, gearing and liquidity. They will wish to make sure that any assets on which the loans are secured have not been sold or lost value. They will investigate the gearing ratios to see that the company has not taken on too many additional loans. In addition, they will scrutinise the amount of cash and the liquidity ratios to ensure that there is enough cash to pay the loan interest.

Shareholders invest their capital and look for a return. They will, therefore principally be concerned with the profit and loss account. In particular, they will look at earnings, earnings per share, dividends and dividend cover. They will wish to be assured that the company is profitable and will remain profitable.

In other countries, such as France and Germany, the power of the shareholder is less. In France, for example, the users of accounting are more diverse, ranging from the government for economic planning, to the tax authorities for fiscal planning, to the banks. In Germany, the main users are the tax authorities and the banks. In France and Germany, the users are generally relatively more concerned about liquidity and the balance sheet than in the UK and the US. However, in both France and Germany, as more multinational companies are listed, the power of the shareholder is increasing.

(iii) Sources of Finance

A key question for any company is how to finance its operations. Apart from internally generated profits, there are two main sources: equity (or shareholder) finance and debt (or loan) finance. In some countries, such as the UK and the US, equity finance dominates. In other countries, for example, France and Germany, there is a much greater dependence on debt finance. The relative worldwide importance of the stock exchange (where equity is traded and raised) can be seen in Figure 14.2.

Figure 14.2   Relative Strength of Selected Major Stock Exchanges as at February 2003

Country	Exchange	Domestic Companies	Market Capitalisation
		No.	£bn
Australia	Australia	1,353	382
Canada	Toronto	1,252	606
France	Paris (Euronext)	737	928
Germany	Deutsche Borse	706	655
China	Hong Kong	973	462
Japan	Tokyo	2,134	2,042
UK	London	2,392	1,630
US	New York	1,885	8,543
	NASDAQ	3,176	1,978

Summarised from *Comparative International Accounting*, C. Nobes and R.H. Parker (2004), p. 12

The presence of a strong equity stock market leads countries to have an investor and an economic reality orientated accounting system. There is a focus on profitability and the importance of auditing increases. By contrast, a strong debt market is associated with the increased importance of banks.

(iv) Regulation

By regulation, we mean the rules that govern accounting. These rules are primarily set out by government as statute or by the private sector as accounting standards (see Chapter 10 for more detail on the UK). The balance and interaction between statutory law and standards within a particular country is often subtle. The regulatory burden is usually significantly greater for public listed companies than for smaller non-listed companies.

In the UK and the US, for example, accounting standards are very important. However, whereas in the UK there are Companies Acts applicable to all companies, in the US, the Securities Exchange Commission, an independent regulatory organisation with quasi-judicial powers, regulates the listed US companies. Other US companies are regulated by state legislation, which is often minimal.

In some countries, such as France and Germany, accounting standards are not very important. Indeed, France has no formal standard-setting body equivalent to the UK's Accounting Standards Board, while Germany only set up a standard-setting organisation in 1999. In France and Germany accounting regulation originates from the government. In Germany, by way of a Commercial Code and in France, by way of a comprehensive government manual for accounting.

(v) Taxation

Strictly, the influence of taxation is part of a country's regulatory framework. However, as the relationship between accounting and taxation varies significantly between countries, it is discussed separately here. Essentially, national taxation systems may be classed as 'independent' of, or 'dependent' on, accounting. In independent countries, such as the UK, the taxation rules and regulations do not determine the accounting profit. There are, in effect, two profits (calculated quite legally!) – one for tax and the other for accounting. The US uses a broadly independent tax system. However, there is a curious anomaly. If US companies wish to lower their taxable profits, they can use the Last-in-First-out (LIFO) method of stock or inventory valuation (which usually values stock lower than alternative stock valuation methods, and thus lowers profits). (See Chapter 16 for a fuller discussion of LIFO.) However, these companies *must* also use this method in their shareholder accounts.

In France and Germany, however, for individual companies accounting profit is dependent upon taxable profit. In effect, the rules used for taxation determine the rules used for accounting. Accounting, therefore, becomes a process of minimising tax paid rather than showing a 'true and fair view' of the company's financial activities. However, group accounts in France and Germany can be prepared using international principles as tax is calculated on individual company, rather than group accounts.

(vi) Accounting Profession

Accounting professions worldwide vary considerably in their size and influence. In the UK and US accountants play an important interpretive and judgemental role. Although accounting standards are independently set, qualified accounting professionals generally constitute the majority of the members of the accounting standards boards. In France and Germany, professionally qualified accountants have far less influence on accounting. There is less flexibility in the accounting rules and regulations and less need for judgement.

Figure 14.3 shows the age and size of some professional accountancy bodies. In the UK and the US, the accounting profession is very strong and influential. In the US, for example, in 2003 there were about 328,000 Certified Public Accountants (CPA). By contrast, in Germany, there were only 11,000 *Wirtschaftsprüfer*, the German equivalent of the CPA.

Figure 14.3   Age and Size of Selected Professional Accountancy Bodies

Country	Body	Founding Date of Original Body	Approximate Membership (000) in 2003
Australia	Australian Society of Certified Practising Accountants	1952 (1886)	97
	Institute of Chartered Accountants in Australia	1928 (1885)	34
Canada	Canadian Institute of Chartered Accountants	1902 (1880)	68
France	Ordre des Experts Comptables	1942	16
Germany	Institut der Wirtschaftsprüfer	1932	11
Japan	Japanese Institute of Certified Public Accountants	1948 (1927)	13
Netherlands	Nederlands Instituut van Register Accountants	1895	13
New Zealand	New Zealand Society of Accountants	1909 (1894)	27
United Kingdom and Ireland	Institute of Chartered Accountants in England and Wales	1880 (1870)	124
	Institute of Chartered Accountants of Scotland	1951 (1854)	15
	Association of Chartered Certified Accountants	1939 (1891)	95
	Institute of Chartered Accountants in Ireland	1888	13
United States	American Institute of Certified Public Accountants	1887	328

Note: Dates of earliest predecessor bodies in brackets.

Source: Nobes, C. and Parker, R. (2004), *Comparative International Accounting*, Table 1.2 (abridged), p. 6

(vii) Spheres of Influence

Accounting is not immune from the wider forces of economics and politics. Many countries' accounting systems have been heavily influenced by other countries. The UK, for example, imported double-entry bookkeeping from Italy in the fifteenth century. It then exported this to countries such as Hong Kong, India, Kenya, Malaysia, Nigeria and Singapore. These countries still follow a model inherited from the UK. The UK also originally exported its accounting system to the US. However, from the early 1900s, the US has influenced the UK rather than vice versa. Overall, it is perhaps possible to identify three broad spheres of influence: the UK, the US and the continental European. Currently, the UK is being influenced by both the US and the more prescriptive continental European model.

(viii) Culture

Culture is perhaps the most elusive of the divergent forces. Hofstede, in *Culture's Consequences* (Sage, 1980), defines culture as 'the collective programming of the mind which distinguishes the members of one human group from another'. Building on the work of Hofstede, accounting researchers have sought to establish whether culture influences accounting. For example, do the French or the British have a collective culture which influences accounting? Using such concepts as professionalism, uniformity, conservatism and secrecy, they have found some, if not overwhelming, support.

Classification

Accounting researchers have sought to classify national accounting systems using, for example, divergent forces, cultural characteristics, and accounting measurement and disclosure practices. A useful classification system is described by Nobes (1983). Broadly, his system classifies countries as either having macro or micro accounting systems. Figure 14.4 uses the divergent forces to summarise the major national characteristics of macro and micro countries. It can thus be seen that macro countries, such as France and Germany, are typified by governmentally-orientated systems where the influence of tax is strong, but that of the accounting profession is weak. Meanwhile, micro countries, such as the UK and the US, are typified by investor-orientated systems where tax influence is weak, but the influence of the accounting profession is strong.

Figure 14.4   Main National Characteristics of the Macro and Micro Classification

Divergent Force	Macro	Micro
Objectives	Planning and control	Economic reality
Users	Government, banks, tax	Shareholders
Sources of Finance	Banks	Stock exchange
Regulation	Government, relatively prescriptive	Private sector, relatively flexible
Taxation	Dominant, dependent system	Subordinate, independent system
Accounting Profession	Weak, uninfluential	Strong, influential
Spheres of Influence	Continental	UK, US
Examples	France, Germany	UK, US

Country Snapshots

Every country's accounting system and environment is a unique mixture of divergent forces. In this section, we look at the accounting systems and environments of four important developed countries: France, Germany, UK and the US. The aim is to provide a quick overview of the distinctive natural characteristics of each country's accounting systems.

France

The French accounting system is often cited as a good example of a standardised accounting system. It thus contrasts with the UK and US systems. Essentially, the French accounting system was introduced in order to provide the government with economic information for planning and controlling the French economy. The French system centres around *Le Plan Comptable Générale* (General Accounting Plan). This sets out a uniform system of accounting to be used throughout France. Of special interest is a chart of accounts where each item in the accounts is given a number. These numbers can then be used to aggregate items from different companies. Overall, *Le Plan Comptable Générale* resembles a comprehensive accounting manual which French companies follow.

In addition to *Le Plan Comptable Générale*, there are various detailed accounting and taxation laws. The role of taxation is particularly important. In essence, tax law drives accounting law. Standish (in Nobes and Parker, 2000, p. 205) comments:

> 'An enterprise wishing to take advantage of various tax concessions must accordingly enter the relevant tax assessable income or tax deductible charges in its accounts as if valid for tax purposes, even if the effect is to generate assets or liabilities that do not conform to the accounting criteria for asset and liability recognition and measurement'.

The accounting profession in France is much smaller than in the UK and US. There were 16,000 professional accountants in 2003 (Nobes and Parker, 2004, p. 6). Compared with other countries, the profession is not influential. There are, for example, no accounting standards in France comparable to those in the UK and US.

However, accounting in France has changed and is still changing rapidly (see Soundbite 14.2). For many years, French companies have been permitted to use non-French accounting principles. Many large French groups, therefore, used US accounting principles or International Accounting Standards (IAS). From 2005, French listed companies like all EU listed companies use IFRS in their group accounts. However, individual company accounts must still be prepared using French principles.

SOUNDBITE 14.2

France

'We're [France] somewhere between the United States and Germany on transparency, probably closer to US practices and certainly less able than German business to hide systematic abuses. We're going toward the US model, but it's going to take several years more.'

Alan Minc quoted in *International Herald Tribune* (October 10, 1996)

Source: *The Wiley Book of Business Quotations* (1998), p. 158

Germany

Germany has traditionally had a relatively distinctive accounting system (see Real-Life Nugget 14.2). Essentially, it is very prescriptive, government controlled and creditor orientated. Currently, there is no comprehensive body of accounting standards. The main regulations are contained in the Companies Acts, Commercial Code and Publication Law. These laws set out very detailed regulations.

REAL-LIFE NUGGET 14.2

German Accounting System

'Traditionally, German accounting has followed a relatively distinct path. Germany, along with France, has always represented a continental accounting tradition based on a creditor rather than a shareholder approach. The Franco-German approach is in direct contrast to the Anglo-Saxon view of accounting. This latter view, typified by UK/US accounting, espouses an economic reality, user-based approach, with the main user being the shareholder.'

Source: Germany: An Accounting System in Change, M.J. Jones, *Accountancy International*, August 1999, pp. 64–65

The measurement systems underpinning German accounting have traditionally been seen as very conservative. This is especially so when compared with UK accounting policies. For instance, as Real-Life Nugget 14.3 shows, in 1997 Rover, the UK car maker, would have made a profit of £147 m under UK rules. Under German rules it reported a loss of £363 m. Taxation law also dominates accounting, for example, expenses are only allowable for tax if they are deducted in the financial accounts.

REAL-LIFE NUGGET 14.3

German Accounting Rules

By Gavin Hinks

Rover accounts drawn up according to UK accounting rules show the car manufacturer lost considerably less in the lead up to last week's controversial sale than the figure reported in BMW's accounts.

The figures show that for the year ending December 1998, Rover lost around £160 m less than that stated in accounts drawn up under harsher German accounting standards.

According to UK accounts, Rover made losses of £509 m in 1998. But BMW accounts show the company lost £670 m.

REAL-LIFE NUGGET 14.3 (*continued*)

As morale plummeted at Rover's Longbridge works following the threat of thousands of job losses as a result of the sale to venture capital company Alchemy, a spokesman said the trend of lower losses in the company's UK accounts continued into 1999.

Last year, when controversy over Rover first appeared, *Accountancy Age* revealed the discrepancy between the two sets of accounts. An analysis of four years' of figures, from 1994 to 1997, revealed Rover had actually made a profit of £147 m according to UK rules while the German books stated a loss of £363 m.

Under German accounting policies investments are depreciated faster, there are more possibilities for making provisions and there are different rules for the valuation of stocks.

BMW was expected to move to International Accounting Standards which may have improved the position of Rover, but BMW this week refused to comment on which accounting standards are now being used.

Reading University Professor Chris Nobes, a member of the International Accounting Standards committee, said the problem was not unique to Rover. 'Normal German practice is more conservative than Britain's,' he added.

Chemical companies like Bayer and Hoechst, and Deutsche Bank, have moved away from German standards but the number switching is small. Lufthansa and Volkswagen use German standards.

Alchemy, the buyer of Rover, is certain to use UK accounting standards when dealing with its new purchase.

Source: *Accountancy Age*, 23 March 2000, p. 9

The German accounting profession is very small. In 2003, there were only 11,000 German professionally qualified accountants (Nobes and Parker, 2004, p. 6). Although small, the German profession is very well qualified. However, in Germany most accounting developments originate from the government rather than from the accounting profession.

By international standards, the German stock market is comparatively small. Its total market capitalisation is only about half that of the UK's. German industry is financed principally by banks. The focus of German accounting, therefore, has traditionally been on assets rather than profit.

SOUNDBITE 14.3

Germany

'Their people would come here and put down our people, our work ethic. I had a little problem with that. I finally slammed my door shut and told my German counterpart that I didn't need him telling us how good he was and how weak we were. We never had any problems after that.'

Time (9 October 1989)

Source: *The Wiley Book of Business Quotations* (1998), p. 294

However, German accounting, like French accounting, has changed rapidly. Listed German companies, like listed French companies, use IFRS to prepare their group accounts. This internationalism of German accounting started in the 1990s. In 1990, no German companies were listed in the US. However, Daimler Benz caused a minor sensation in Germany by listing on the US exchange in 1993. Since then German companies have increasingly used US or International Accounting Standards. In Germany, in 2005, a German Financial Reporting Enforcement Panel was established to monitor the reporting standards of German companies.

The UK

The UK is still an important player in accounting worldwide. However, it is no longer the world leader. The current UK system contains elements of US and Continental European accounting. The generally recognised objective of accounting in the UK is to give a 'true and fair view' of a company's financial activities to the users, most notably the shareholders. There are two sources of regulation: company law and accounting standards. Company law, which now includes the European Fourth and Seventh Directives, sets out an increasingly, prescriptive accounting framework. The financial reporting standards, set by the Accounting Standards Board, provide guidance on particular accounting issues. They are followed by UK non-listed companies which constitute the vast bulk of UK companies. Uniquely, the UK has a Financial Reporting and Review Panel, which investigates companies suspected of non-compliance with the standards. The UK, therefore, has an unusual mix of regulations. UK listed companies now follow IFRS for their group accounts.

The accounting profession in the UK is very influential and accounting in the UK is a relatively high status profession. It is also very fragmented, comprising the Institute of Chartered Accountants in England and Wales (ICAEW), the Institute of Chartered Accountants of Scotland, the Institute of Chartered Accountants in Ireland, the Association of Chartered Certified Accountants, the Chartered Institute of Management Accountants and the Chartered Institute of Public Finance and Accountancy. The ICAEW is the largest body numbering 124,000 professionally qualified accountants in 2003 (see Figure 14.3).

PAUSE FOR THOUGHT 14.2

Unique Features of UK Accounting System

Every country's accounting system and environment is unique. Can you think of three features of the UK's accounting and environment which contribute, in combination, to the uniqueness of the UK's accounting system?

There are many special features in the UK's system. Some of the main ones are listed below.

- Combination of a 'true and fair view' with Companies Acts, UK accounting standards and IFRS.
- The fragmentation of the accounting profession into six institutes.
- The dominance of the institutional investor in the stock market.
- The Financial Reporting Review Panel's role as guardian of good accounting practice.
- The ability of UK non-listed companies to depart from historical cost by revaluing their fixed assets.
- The ability of companies to capitalise their goodwill in the balance sheet and not necessarily write it off to the profit and loss account.

The main users of accounts in the UK are the shareholders. In particular, in the UK, institutional investors dominate. The stock market is very active and its market capitalisation is very high. Unlike most other countries, there is a separation between accounting profit and taxable profit. In essence, there are two distinct bodies of law. Certainly, taxable profit does not determine accounting profit.

The US

The US dominates world accounting. Most important developments in accounting originate in the US. A particular feature of the US environment is the position of the Securities Exchange Commission (SEC). The SEC was set up in the 1930s after the Wall Street crash of 1929. It is an independent regulatory institution with quasi-judicial powers. Listed US companies have to file a detailed annual form, called the 10-K with the SEC. The SEC also supervises the operation of the US standard-setting body, the Financial Accounting Standards Board (FASB). This body has been designated by the American Institute of Certified Public Accountants (AICPA) as the US's standard-setting body.

FASB is the most active of the world's national standard-setting bodies. The members of FASB have to sever their prior business and professional links. FASB has published over 150 standards. It is supported by the Emerging Issues Task Force, which examines new and emerging accounting issues. The US accounting standard-setting model proved the blueprint for the current UK system. Unlike France, Germany and the UK, US listed companies follow their own national standards rather than IFRS.

US listed companies are thus well regulated. However, curiously for the mass of US companies, which are not listed, there may be very few accounting or auditing requirements. Company legislation is a state not a federal matter. Each state, therefore, sets its own laws.

The accounting profession in the US is both numerous and influential. There were 328,000 members of AICPA in 2003 (see Figure 14.3). Most of the world's leading audit firms have their head offices in the US.

The objective of accounting in the US is generally recognised as being to provide users with information for decision making. Most of the finance for US industry is provided by shareholders. Unlike in the UK, the majority of shareholders in the US are still private shareholders. The market capitalisation of the US stock market is the greatest in the world. Many of the world's largest companies such as Microsoft or The General Electric Company are US. The high-quality financial information produced by US financial reporting standards is often argued to help the efficiency of the US stock market. However, in 2001 and 2002 a series of high-profile accounting scandals involving companies such as Enron, WorldCom and Xerox have led to a questioning of the quality of US accounting and auditing standards.

Real-Life Nugget 14.4 shows the connection between US capital markets and financial reporting standards.

In the US, as the aim of the accounts is broadly to reflect economic reality: the tax and accounting systems are generally independent. There is, however, one curious exception: last-in first-out (LIFO) stock (inventory) valuation. Many US companies adopt LIFO in their taxation accounts as it lowers their taxable profit. However, if they do so, federal tax laws state they must also use LIFO in their financial accounts. However, since LIFO stock values are generally old and out of date, this fails to reflect economic validity (see Chapter 16 for more on LIFO).

Convergent Forces

Convergent forces are pressures upon countries to depart from their current national standards and adopt more internationally-based standards. Convergent forces thus oppose divergent forces. The advantage of national standards is that they may reflect a particular country's circumstances. Unfortunately, the disadvantage is that they impair comparability between countries and are a potential barrier to international trade and investment.

PAUSE FOR THOUGHT 14.3

Pressures for Convergence

How might national accounting standards prove a barrier for a multinational company, such as Glaxo-Wellcome, or a large institutional investor, such as Aberdeen Asset Management?

. . . .

The world of trade and investment is now global. Companies such as Glaxo-Wellcome will, therefore, trade all over the world and have subsidiaries in numerous countries. They will sometimes have to deal with accounting requirements in literally hundreds of countries. To do this takes time, effort and, more importantly, money. If there was one set of agreed international accounting standards, this would make the life of many multinationals easier and cheaper.

Large institutional investors will also be active in many countries. For them, there is a need to compare the financial statements of companies from different countries. For example, an institutional investor, such as Aberdeen Asset Management, may wish to achieve a balanced portfolio and invest funds in the motor car industry. It would wish to compare companies such as BMW in Germany, Fiat in Italy, General Motors in the US and Toyota in Japan. To do this effectively, there is a need for comparable information. A common set of international accounting standards would provide the comparable information.

There are three main potential sources for the convergence of accounting worldwide: the European Union (EU), the International Accounting Standards Board (IASB) and the United States. The process of convergence through the EU is normally termed *harmonisation*, while that through the IASB is called *standardisation*.

European Union (EU)

The European Union is concerned with harmonising the economic and social policies of its member states. Accounting represents part of the economic harmonisation within Europe. In countries such as France and Germany, accounting regulation has always been seen as a subset of a more general legal regulation. Differences in accounting between member states are seen as a barrier to the harmonisation of trade.

The main legal directives affecting accounts are the Fourth Directive and the Seventh Directive. The Fourth Directive is particularly important to the UK. It is based on the German Company Law of 1965. The Fourth Directive ended up as a compromise between the traditional UK and the Franco-German approaches to accounting. The UK approach was premised on flexibility and individual judgement. By contrast, the continental approach set out a prescriptive and detailed legal framework. In the end, the Fourth Directive married the two approaches.

The UK for the first time accepted a standardised format for presenting company accounts and much more detailed legal regulation. However, France and Germany agreed to incorporate into law the British concept of the presentation of a true and fair view.

At one time, the European Union appeared to be developing its own standards. However, it has now thrown its weight behind IFRS. These are now required to be used by the 9,000 European listed companies for their group accounts.

SOUNDBITE 14.4

Different Accounting Standards

Different accounting standards are a drag on progress in much the same way as diverse languages are an inconvenience. Unlike creating a world language, creating one set of standards is achievable. Apart from the potential savings for companies with diverse international structures, complying with an internationally understood accounting paradigm opens up a wider investment audience.

Source: Talking the Same Language, Clem Chambers, *Accountancy Age*, 3 February 2005, p. 6

International Accounting Standards Board (IASB)

The International Accounting Standards Committee (IASC) was founded in 1973 by Sir Henry Benson to work for the improvement and harmonisation of accounting standards worldwide. Originally, there were nine members: Australia, Canada, France, Germany, Japan, Mexico, the Netherlands, the UK and Ireland, and the US. Member bodies were the national professional bodies of different countries. The IASC grew rapidly and, in 2001, 150 countries were members. The member bodies used their best endeavours to ensure that their countries followed International Accounting Standards (IAS). These were subsequently called International Financial Reporting Standards (IFRS). The IASC was reconstituted as the International Accounting Standards Board (IASB) in 2001 (to simplify matters we generally use IASB for both IASC and IASB throughout this book).

At first, the IASB merely codified the world's standards. After this initial step, the IASB began to work towards the improvement of standards. The IASB set out a restricted number of options within an accounting standard from which companies could then choose. Up until the mid-1990s, it is fair to say that the IASB made only limited progress. A threefold differentiation in the IASB's impact is possible: lesser developed countries, European countries and capital market countries. Lesser developed countries, such as Malaysia, Nigeria and Singapore, adopted IFRS because doing so was cheaper than developing their own standards. In Continental Europe, the IFRS were seen both as a problem and a solution. They were a problem in that generally IFRS were seen to adopt a primarily investor-orientated approach to accounting which conflicted with the traditional Continental European tax-driven, creditor-based model. They were a solution in that IFRS were preferable to US standards. Increasingly, in the early 1990s, French and German companies adopted US standards. Karl Van Hulle, Head of the EU's Accounting Unit commented in 1995, 'It would be crazy for Europe to apply American standards, as it would be crazy for the Americans to apply European standards. We ought to develop those standards which we believe are the best for us or for our companies'. Finally, for capital market countries such as the UK and the US, the IFRS were generally already similar to the national standards. Even so, there was a great reluctance, particularly by the US, to accept IFRS.

A breakthrough agreement came in 1995. IOSCO (The International Organisation of Securities Commissions), the body which represents the world's stock exchanges, agreed that when the IASB had developed a set of core standards it would consider them for endorsement and would recommend them to national stock exchanges as an alternative to national standards. The advantage to IOSCO was that there would be a common currency of standards which could be used internationally. In particular, there was the hope that non-US companies could trade on the New York Stock Exchange without having to use US Generally Accepted Accounting Principles (GAAP) or provide a reconciliation to US GAAP. The IASB subsequently experienced severe problems compiling a set of core standards. However, by 2000 these were in place. The importance of the IASB is shown in Real-Life Nugget 14.5.

REAL-LIFE NUGGET 14.5

Why IFRSs? Why now?

'The effective functioning of capital markets is essential to our economic well-being. In my view, a sound financial reporting infrastructure must be built on four pillars: (1) accounting standards that are consistent, comprehensive, and based on clear principles to enable financial reports to reflect underlying economic reality; (2) effective corporate governance practices, including a requirement for strong internal controls, that implement the accounting standards; (3) auditing practices that give confidence to the outside world that an entity is faithfully reflecting its economic performance and financial position; and (4) an enforcement or oversight mechanism that ensures that the principles as laid out by the accounting and auditing standards are followed.

'As the world's capital markets integrate, the logic of a single set of accounting standards is evident. A single set of international standards will enhance comparability of financial information and should make the allocation of capital across borders more efficient. The development and acceptance of international standards should also reduce compliance costs for corporations and improve consistency in audit quality.'

At the start of the new Millennium, three developments substantially enhanced the power of the IASB. First, in 2000 IOSCO allowed its members to use IFRS standards. Second, the IASC was reconstituted as the IASB in 2001 with a new chairman, Sir David Tweedie. The four main elements were: the IASC Foundation, the IASB, the Standards Advisory Council and the Standing Interpretations Committee. The IASC Foundation appoints the IASB, raises money and acts in a supervisory role. The IASB sets the IFRS. The Standards Advisory Council gives general advice and guidance to the IASB. Finally, the Standing Interpretations Committee interprets current IFRS, but also issues guidance on other accounting matters. The third important development was the decision in June 2000 by the European Union that all EU listed companies would follow IFRS from 2005.

These three developments considerably enhanced the power of the IASB. By 2009, 110 countries required the use of IFRS for all listed companies and 80 countries required their use by unlisted companies. The web addresses of some of these companies as well as the IASB website are given in Figure 14.5.

Figure 14.5   Some Useful Web Addresses for Companies using International Financial Reporting Standards

Company	Nationality	Website	Sector
Gucci	Dutch	Gucci.com	Leather, Fashion
Lufthansa	German	Lufthansa.com	Airlines
Nestle	Swiss	Nestle.com	Food and Drink
Nokia	Finnish	Nokia.com	Mobile Phones
Novartis	Swiss	Novartis.com	Drug Manufacturing
Puma	German	Puma.com	Sportswear
SAS	Danish	SASgroup.net	Airlines
Swatch	Swiss	Swatch.com	Watches
UBS	Swiss	UBS.com	Banking
Volkswagen	German	Volkswagen.com	Car Manufacturing

Many of the IFRS were revised in 2003 and 2004. In 2009, there were 39 IFRS in existence. There are, in addition, many interpretations (guidance documents) as well as the IASB's *Framework for the Preparation and Presentation of Financial Statements*. This framework defines the objectives of financial statements, the qualitative characteristics of financial statements and the basic elements and concepts of financial statements.

A consistent problem for the IASB has been the attitude of the US. Traditionally, the US has been reluctant to adopt IFRS. Although in principle, the US favours world standards, it has several concerns about IFRS. It feels they are not as rigorous as US standards and is also worried about their enforcement. However, the shortcomings of US accounting standards revealed by recent US accounting scandals have made the IAS potentially more attractive to US regulators. In October 2003, a joint convergence project was begun by the IASB and the FASB. The aim of this project is to eliminate differences between the standards set by the IASB and FASB. Short-term convergence projects are set to be completed by 2008 with a decision by the US on convergence scheduled for 2011.

PAUSE FOR THOUGHT 14.4

US Acceptance of IAS Standards

Cynics argue that it is in the US's interests deliberately to delay accepting International Accounting Standards. Why do you think this might be?

....

US standards are probably the most advanced of any country in the world. The US is also the richest country in the world and a source of potential capital for companies from other countries. To gain access to US finance, many overseas companies list on the US Stock Exchange. However, to do this they must adopt US standards or provide reconciliations to US standards. As time passes, more foreign companies adopt US standards. Cynics, therefore, believe that the US may be playing a waiting game. The longer the US delays approving IAS, the more foreign companies will list on the US exchange. These cynics argue, therefore, that it is in the US's interests to delay accepting IAS.

From a UK perspective, the Accounting Standards Board, which sets standards for UK domestic non-listed companies, has accepted, in principle, the need for eventual international harmonisation. The current policy is to depart from an international consensus only when there are particular legal or tax difficulties or when the UK believes the international approach is wrong. Recently, the ASB has made important efforts to harmonise UK and IAS standards in key areas such as goodwill, taxation and pensions. The UK is also harmonising its accounting practices with those currently used in the US.

US Standards

There is still the possibility that if the SEC refuses to endorse the IFRS, US standards will become a substitute for worldwide accounting standards. More and more companies worldwide are being listed in the US. The advantage of using US standards is that this enables non-US companies to list on the New York Stock Exchange. This is the world's largest stock exchange and a ready source of capital. Currently, these companies have to reconcile their earnings and net assets to US GAAP if they use IFRS or their own national standards.

Conclusion

Different countries have different accounting environments. These accounting environments are determined by divergent forces, such as objectives, users, sources of finance, regulation, taxation, the accounting profession, spheres of influence and culture. These divergent forces are interrelated and the mix of divergent forces is unique for each country. Countries can be classified as having macro or micro accounting systems. In macro countries, such as France or Germany, the emphasis is on tight legal regulation, with a creditor orientation and a weak accounting profession. By contrast, in micro countries such as the UK and the US, there is a focus on regulation via standards rather than the law and an overall investor-orientated approach with a strong accounting profession.

The great variety of accounting systems worldwide impedes the growth in world trade. Consequently, there are pressures for countries to depart from purely nationally-based accounting. The pressures result from the growth in multinational companies and in cross-border trade and investment. These convergent forces thus counteract the divergent forces.

At the European level, the European Union works towards the harmonisation of accounting practices. On the global level, the International Accounting Standards Board sets International Financial Reporting Standards. Having made a slow start, the IASB is now gathering momentum. There is now an agreement by the International Organisation of Securities Commission that its members are allowed to use IFRS when listing on individual exchanges. However, the US Securities and Exchange Commission still has reservations. In Europe listed companies must now use IFRS.

Selected Reading

1. Books

International Accounting is blessed with some very good, comprehensive books. As International Accounting is continually changing, it is always necessary to check that you have the latest edition.

Nobes, C.W., and R.H. Parker (2004), *Comparative International Accounting* (Eighth Edition), (Prentice Hall International: London).

This is the longest standing of the books. Nobes and Parker write some of the chapters themselves, but there are also useful chapters by other authors, especially Klaus Langer on Germany.

Roberts, C., P. Weetman and P. Gordon (2002), *International Financial Accounting: A Comparative Approach* (Financial Times Management: London).

This book provides a comprehensive coverage of the issues in this chapter.

Walton, P., A. Haller, and B. Raffournier (1998), *International Accounting*, (International Thompson Business Press: London).

Once more this is a useful book. Each chapter is written by a specialist.

2. Articles

Students may find the following three articles provide a reasonable coverage of the International Accounting Standards Board and Germany, respectively.

Jones, M.J. (1998), 'The IASB: Twenty-five years old this year', *Management Accounting*, May, pp. 30–32.

Jones, M.J. (1999), 'Germany: An accounting system in change', *Accountancy International*, August, pp. 64–5.

Nobes, C.W. (1997), 'German Accountancy Explained', *Financial Times Business Information*, London.

The key article on the micro–macro classification of accounting systems is listed below. Also there is a useful chapter in Nobes and Parker (2004).

Nobes, C.W. (1983), 'A judgmental international classification of financial reporting practices', *Journal of Business Finance and Accounting*, Spring, pp. 1–19.

Q&A   Discussion Questions

Questions with numbers in blue have answers at the back of the book.

Q1   Why is the study of international accounting important?

Q2   What are the main divergent forces and which are the most important?

Q3   Compare and contrast the main features of the Anglo-American and continental accounting systems.

Q4   Taking any one country, rank the divergent forces in order of importance.

Q5   Has the UK more in common with the US than with France?

Q6   Will the convergent forces outweigh the divergent forces?

Section C

Management Accounting

S o far, we have looked at financial accounting. Financial accounting is much more publicly visible than management accounting. Management accounting takes place within businesses and is essential to the running of a business. It can be usefully divided into (1) cost accounting, which includes costing (Chapter 16), and planning, control and performance (Chapters 17 and 18), and (2) decision making (Chapters 19–22).

This section investigates some major issues involved in management accounting. In Chapter 15, a brief introduction into the nature of management accounting is provided. Much of the terminology is introduced and an overview of the rest of the book is provided. Chapters 16, 17 and 18 look at cost accounting, one of the two main streams of management accounting. In Chapter 16, the role of costing in stock valuation and pricing is investigated. The cost allocation process is then outlined together with the use of different costing methods in different industries. Both traditional absorption costing and the more modern activity-based costing are discussed. Chapters 17 and 18 look at planning, control and performance. Chapter 17 sets out the cost control technique of budgeting. The different types of budget are also briefly discussed. Responsibility accounting is also discussed. Then in Chapter 18 standard costing is explored. The individual variances are explained and a worked example is shown.

Chapters 19–22 look at the decision-making aspects of management accounting. Chapter 19 investigates the managerial techniques (such as break-even analysis and contribution analysis) used for short-term operational decision making. Then Chapter 20 looks at the relatively new management accounting topic of strategic management accounting. This shows how management accounting influences strategic business decisions. In Chapter 21, we investigate capital budgeting. This chapter investigates the different techniques (such as payback and discounted cash flow) used to evaluate long-term investment decisions. Finally, Chapter 22 investigates two aspects of both internal and external sources of finance: short-term financing via the efficient management of working capital and long-term financing such as share capital and loan capital.

As most businesses are sole traders, partnerships or non-listed companies we use the accepted terminology for these businesses. However, when we are specifically referring to listed companies we use terminology as laid down by the International Accounting Standards Board in International Financial Reporting Standards. ∎

Chapter 15

"Jones was loyal to his staff, and diplomatic, but clearly had been bewildered by what he found when he arrived. 'Well, we've only just got an audited balance sheet for 1998', he said, 'We just don't have any contemporary operating or financial data on which to make management decisions in this airline at the moment. It's the old garbage-in, garbage-out syndrome.'"

Graham Jones commenting on the Greek airline company, *Olympic Airlines*
Source: Icarus Descending, Matthew Gwyther, *Management Today*, January 2000, pp. 52–53

Learning Outcomes

After completing this chapter you should be able to:

✔ Explain the nature and importance of management accounting.

✔ Outline the relationship between financial accounting and management accounting.

✔ Explain the main branches of cost accounting and decision making.

Introduction to Management Accounting

✔ Discuss cost minimisation and revenue maximisation.

✔ Understand some of the major terms used in management accounting.

In a Nutshell

■ *Management accounting is the provision of accounting information to management to help with costing, with planning, control and performance and with decision making.*

■ *Whereas the main focus of financial accounting is external, management accounting is internally focused.*

■ *Management accounting has its origins in costing; however, nowadays costing is less important as new areas such as strategic management accounting develop.*

■ *Management accounting can be broadly divided into cost accounting (costing; planning, control and performance) and decision making (short-term and long-term).*

■ *Costing consists of recovering costs for pricing and for the valuation of stock.*

■ *Planning, control and performance consists of planning and controlling future costs using budgeting and standard costing as well as evaluating performance.*

■ *Decision making involves short-term decision making, strategic management accounting, capital budgeting and sources of finance.*

■ *Traditionally, management accounting has been criticised for focusing on minimising costs rather than maximising revenue.*

Introduction

Management accounting is concerned with the internal accounting within a business. Essentially, it is the provision of both financial and non-financial information to managers so that they can manage costs and make decisions. In many ways, therefore, management accounting is less straightforward than financial accounting. Management accounting varies markedly from business to business and management accountants, in effect, carry around a toolkit of techniques, their 'tools of the trade'. The purpose of this section is to try to explain these techniques and to fit them into an overall picture of management accounting.

PAUSE FOR THOUGHT 15.1

Management Accounting

Why do you think management accounting is so called?

....

Management accounting is a relatively new term and has been in widespread use only since the 1950s. The term combines management and accounting. It suggests that accountants have a managerial role within the company. They are, in effect, more than just a functional specialist group. The term management accounting has come, therefore, to represent all the management and accounting activities carried out by accountants within a business. This involves not only costing, and planning, control and performance but also managerial decision making.

Context

The management accountant works within a business. The focus of management accounting is thus internal rather than external. In this book, we simplify the formal definition (see Definition 15.1 on the next page) and take the purpose of management accounting as being to provide managers with accounting information in order to help with costing, with planning, control and performance and with decision making. As the formal, official definition shows, management accounting concerns business strategy, planning and control, decision making, efficient resource usage, performance improvement, safeguarding assets, corporate governance and internal control.

Management Accounting

Working definition

The provision of financial and non-financial information to management for costing, for planning, control and performance, and for decision making.

Formal definition

'The application of the principles of accounting and financial management to create, protect, preserve and increase value so as to deliver that value to the stakeholders of profit and not-for-profit enterprises, both public and private. Management accounting is an integral part of management, requiring the identification, generation, presentation, interpretation and use of information relevant to:

- formulating business strategy;
- planning and controlling activities;
- decision making;
- efficient resource usage;

- performance improvement and value enhancement;
- safeguarding tangible and intangible assets;
- corporate governance and internal control.'

Source: Chartered Institute of Management Accounting (2000), *Official Terminology*

In essence, costing concerns (1) setting a price for a product or service so that a profit is made and (2) arriving at a correct valuation for stock. Planning, control and performance involves planning and controlling future costs using budgeting and standard costing as well as performance evaluation. Decision making involves managers solving problems using various problem-solving techniques.

PAUSE FOR THOUGHT 15.2

Problem Solving

Can you think of five problems the management accountant may need to solve?
The list is potentially endless. However, here are ten.

....

1. What products or services should be sold?
2. How much should be sold?
3. Should a product be made in-house or bought in?
4. Should the firm continue manufacturing the product?
5. At what level of production will a profit be made?
6. Which products or services are most profitable?
7. How can the firm minimise its working capital?
8. How can the firm maximise revenue?
9. Which areas should the firm diversify into?
10. Should new finance be raised via debt or equity?

Relationship with Financial Accounting

The orientation of management accounting is completely different to that of financial accounting. As Figure 15.1 shows, financial accounting is concerned with providing information (such as the balance sheet and profit and loss account) to shareholders about past events. Management accountants will also be interested in such information, often on a monthly basis.

Figure 15.1   Relationship between Financial and Management Accounting

Financial Accounting	*Management Accounting*
1. Aims to provide information principally for external users, such as shareholders. 2. Concerned with recording information using double-entry bookkeeping. 3. Works within a statutory context. 4. Main statements are balance sheet and profit and loss account (income statement). 5. Basically looks back to the past. 6. The end product is the annual reporting package in a standardised format.	1. Aims to provide information for internal users such as management. 2. Not so concerned with recording. Information is needed for costing, for planning, control and performance, for decision making etc. 3. There is no statutory context. 4. Not so concerned with preparing these financial statements. 5. Looks to the future. 6. Different businesses produce very different management information.

However, management accountants will also require a broader range of internal management information for costing, for planning, control and performance, and for decision making. Importantly, whereas financial accounting works within a statutory context, management accounting does not. Management accounting is thus much more varied and customised than financial accounting.

Financial accounting, in fact, has influenced the development of management accounting. Management accounting emerged much later than financial accounting. Indeed, early management accountants were primarily cost accountants (see Figure 15.2).

Figure 15.2 The Cost Accountant

'The cost accountant is essentially a practical man and it is important for the registered student to have first-hand experience of works and factory practice and routine, including, for example, the following: operation of various machines; shop floor organisation; purchase; storage and control of materials; design, planning and progress of work; inspection; work study; maintenance; warehousing and distribution.'

Source: The Cost Accountant, December 1957, p. 280. As cited in P. Armstrong and C. Jones (1992), *Management Accounting Research*, pp. 53–75

Armstrong and Jones (1992) argue that management accountants have been involved in a 'collective mobility' project where cost accountants have redefined themselves as management accountants dealing with wider management accounting and strategic management issues. In part, this has been an attempt to move away from costing, which was perceived as low status, and to emulate the Institute of Chartered Accountants in England and Wales, which was considered as high status.

Perhaps because of its comparatively humble origins, management accounting has often been seen as subservient to financial accounting. Johnson and Kaplan (1987) argued in *Relevance Lost* that most management accounting practices had been developed by 1925 and that since then there has been comparatively little innovation. Under this view, management accounting has major problems. In particular, product costing is distorted, decision-making information becomes unreliable and management accounting reflects external reporting requirements rather than modern management needs.

Opinions differ on the current relevance of management accounting. However, it is true that management accounting has struggled to adapt to changes in the business environment. In particular, it has been relatively slow to adapt to the decline of manufacturing industry and the rise of service organisations (see Figure 15.3). These difficulties are likely to be exacerbated by the rise of knowledge-based companies. Management accounting is also struggling to adapt to globalisation and technological change. As we will see, however, new management techniques have arisen (such as activity-based costing, strategic management accounting and just-in-time stock valuation) which seek to address the criticisms of management accounting.

Figure 15.3   Service Industries

'There are many service organisations which do not have finished good stocks or work-in-progress. They require management accounting information to ascertain the cost of each service and its contribution to total company profits. These organisations do not have to conform to any financial accounting requirements for the purpose of tracing costs to various services. Nevertheless, most service organisations adopted traditional product cost accounting techniques based on arbitrary overhead allocation, to trace costs to the different business segments.'

Source: Drury, C. (1996), *Cost and Management Accounting*, pp. 833–34

Overview

The diversity of management accounting makes if difficult to separate out individual strands. However, this book broadly splits management accounting into two.

1. **Cost Accounting.** This involves:
    (i)   *Costing* (recovering costs as a basis for pricing and for stock valuation), and
    (ii) *Planning, control and performance* (i.e., planning and controlling future costs using budgeting and standard costing).
2. **Decision Making.** This involves:
    (i)   *Short-term decision making* (such as break-even analysis, contribution analysis and the efficient management of working capital), and
    (ii) *Long-term decision making* (i.e., strategic management accounting, capital budgeting, and management of sources of long-term finance).
These two major areas are shown in Figure 15.4 on the next page.

The major areas shown in Figure 15.4 are discussed briefly below and then more fully discussed in the chapters that follow. Key terms that underpin management accounting are introduced. These new terms are highlighted in **bold** in the text and a full definition is then provided

Figure 15.4 Overview of Management Accounting

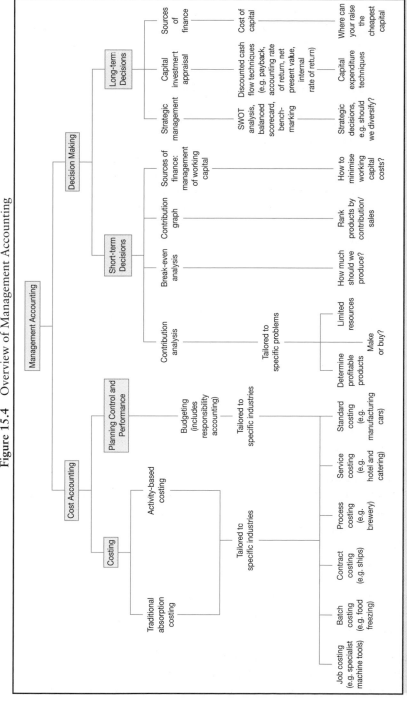

in Definitions 15.2 (below) and 15.3 (on page 386), which follow the same order as in the text. These terms are more fully discussed later in the book.

Cost Accounting

Costing (Chapter 16)

Costing has its origins in manufacturing industry. The basic idea underpinning costing is cost recovery (i.e. the need to recover all the **costs** of making a product into the price of the final product). Broadly, cost recovery is achieved using a technique called **total absorption costing**. Total absorption costing seeks to recover both **direct costs** and **indirect costs** into a product or service. This form of costing thus seeks to establish the total costs of a product so that they can be recovered in the final selling price. As well as costing for pricing, costing is used for stock valuation. In this case, either **absorption costing** or **marginal costing** is used.

Different industries will have different costing systems. For example, medicinal tablets will necessitate batch processing, while shipbuilding uses contract costing. A more modern technique called activity-based costing is often used.

Planning, Control and Performance (Chapters 17 and 18)

Planning, control and **performance** aims to control current costs and plan for the control of future costs as well as evaluating performance. Two essential **management control systems** (i.e. systems that provide information for managerial planning, control and performance evaluation are budgeting and standard costing.

- *Budgeting* (Chapter 17). Budgeting involves setting future targets. Actual results are then compared with these budgeted results. Any differences will be investigated. Budgets may be used as part of responsibility accounting. In such systems, a distinction is often made between **controllable costs** and **uncontrollable costs**.
- *Standard costing* (Chapter 18) is a standardised version of budgeting. Standard costing involves using preset costs for direct labour, direct materials and overheads. Actual costs are then compared with the **standard costs**. Any **variances** are then investigated.

DEFINITION 15.2

The Basic Building Blocks of Management Accounting: Some Key Cost Accounting Terms

i Costing

Cost. A cost is simply an item of expenditure (planned or actually incurred).

Total absorption costing. This form of costing is used to recover all the costs (both direct and indirect) incurred by a company into the price of the final product or service.

DEFINITION 15.2 (*continued*)

Direct costs. Direct costs are those costs that can be directly identified and attributed to a product or service, for example, the amount of direct labour that is incurred making a product. Sometimes these costs are called *product costs*.

Indirect costs. Indirect costs are those costs that cannot be directly identified and attributed to a product or service, examples are administrative, selling and distribution costs. These costs are totalled and then recovered into the product or service in an indirect way. For example, if there were £10,000 administrative costs and 10,000 products, each product might be allocated £1 of administrative costs. Indirect costs are often called *overheads* or *period costs*.

Absorption costing. Absorption costing is the form of costing used for valuing stock for external financial reporting. It recovers the costs of all the overheads that can be directly attributed to a product or service. However, unlike marginal costing, which can sometimes be used for stock valuation, it includes both fixed and variable production overheads.

Marginal costing. Marginal costing excludes fixed costs from the costing process. It focuses on sales, variable costs and contribution. Fixed costs are written off against contribution. It can be used for decision making or for valuing stock. When valuing stock only variable production overheads are included in the stock valuation. (See Definition 15.3 for explanations of *fixed costs, variable costs* and *contribution*.) Marginal costing is called contribution analysis when used for decision making.

ii Planning, Control and Performance Evaluation
Controllable costs. Costs that a manager can influence and that the manager can be held responsible for.

Uncontrollable Costs. Costs that a manager cannot influence and that the manager cannot be held responsible for.

Standard costs. Standard costs are individual cost elements (such as direct materials, direct labour and variable overheads) which are estimated in advance. Normally, the quantity and the price of each cost element is estimated separately. Actual costs are then compared with standard costs to determine variances.

Variances. Variances are the difference between the budgeted costs and the actual costs in both budgeting and standard costing. These variances are then investigated by management.

Decision Making

Decision making involves choosing between alternatives. When making a choice it is essential to consider only those costs that are relevant to the actual decision, i.e., *relevant costs*.

Short-Term Decisions (Chapter 19)

In many ways, distinguishing between short-term, operational decisions and long-term strategic decisions is somewhat arbitrary. However, it proves a useful basic distinction. Short-term decisions are dealt with in Chapter 19 and the first part of Chapter 22. Long-term decisions are covered in Chapters 20–21 and in the second half of Chapter 22.

SOUNDBITE 15.1

Choice or Deciding

'The art of management is about choice.'

G. Richard Thoman, *Business Week* (9 December 1996)

Source: *The Wiley Book of Business Quotations* (1998), p. 295

Businesses face many short-term decisions. Essentially, as Soundbite 15.1 shows, decision making is about choice. Businesses need to make numerous decisions.

For example, should a business make a product itself or buy in the product? Should a business continue making or providing a product or service? At what price will a product break even (i.e., make neither a profit nor a loss)? These decisions are solved using various problem-solving techniques such as break-even analysis and contribution analysis. In such short-term decisions, it is essential to distinguish between **fixed costs** and **variable costs**.

A key aspect of short-term decision making is contribution. Contribution is sales less variable costs. In other words, fixed costs are excluded. Contribution is at the heart of two common management accounting techniques: **break-even analysis** and **contribution analysis**. This area of management accounting is sometimes called **cost-volume-profit analysis**.

DEFINITION 15.3

The Basic Building Blocks of Management Accounting: Some Key Decision-Making Terms

Short-Term Decisions

Fixed costs. Fixed costs are those costs that *will not vary* with production or sales (for example, insurance) in an accounting period. They will not, therefore, be affected by short-term decisions such as whether or not production is increased.

Variable costs. Variable costs, however, *will vary* with production and sales (for example, the metered cost of electricity). Short-term decision making is primarily concerned with variable costs. Sales less variable costs gives *contribution*, a useful concept in short-term decision making.

Break-even analysis. Break-even analysis involves calculating the point at which a product makes neither a profit nor a loss. Fixed costs are divided by the contribution per unit (i.e. sales less variable costs divided by number of products). This gives the break-even point.

DEFINITION 15.3 (*continued*)

Contribution analysis. When there is more than one product, this technique is useful in determining which product is the most profitable. It compares the relative contribution of each product. This can also be called cost-volume-profit analysis.

Long-Term Decisions
Discounted cash flow. Discounted cash flow discounts the future expected cash inflows and outflows of a potential project back to their present value today. Decisions can then be made on whether or not to go ahead with the project.

Strategic Management Accounting (Chapter 20)

Whereas costing represents the oldest branch of management accounting, strategic management accounting represents the newest. Strategic management accounting represents a response to criticisms that management accounting is outdated and lacking in innovation. Using strategic management accounting, the management accountant relates the activities of the firm to the wider external environment. Strategic management is thus concerned with the long-term strategic direction of the firm.

PAUSE FOR THOUGHT 15.3

Cost Accounting and Management Accounting

A distinction is sometimes made between cost accounting and management accounting. What do you see as the essential difference?

Management accounting has its origins in cost accounting. However, gradually cost accounting and management accounting have been seen as distinct. Cost accounting is seen, at its narrowest, as focusing on cost collection and cost recovery and more widely as cost recovery and control. However, management accounting is viewed as a much broader term which not only encompasses cost accounting, but also involves decision making and, more recently, strategic management accounting. Cost accounting is thus typically portrayed as routine and low-level, whereas management accounting is seen as a higher-level activity.

Capital Investment Appraisal (Chapter 21)

Capital budgeting involves the financial evaluation of future projects. This evaluation is carried out by using various techniques such as payback, the accounting rate of return, net present value and the internal rate of return. Under net present value and the internal rate of return, the technique of **discounted cash flow** analysis is used.

Sources of Finance (Chapter 22)

The topic of business finance is immense. The aspects covered in this book are the financing of the business in the short and the long term. This covers both the internal generation of funds and the raising of external finance. In the short term, the management of working capital involves the management accountant in a series of short-term decisions about the optimal level of stock and debtors. Meanwhile, the long-term financing of the business involves the choice between internal financing through retained profits and external financing through either leasing, loans or share capital.

PAUSE FOR THOUGHT 15.4

Short-Term vs Long-Term Decisions

What do you think are the essential differences between short-term and long-term decisions?

....

Short-term decisions are operational, day-to-day decisions which typically involve the firm's internal environment. For example, what quantity of a particular product should we make or what should be the price of a particular product.

By contrast, long-term decisions are strategic, non-operational decisions. These typically involve a firm's external environment. So, for example, they may involve the need to diversify or the need to make acquisitions and disposals. Alternatively, they might evaluate whether a long-term capital investment is worthwhile.

Cost Minimisation and Revenue Maximisation

The management accountant can make a business more efficient through cost minimisation or revenue maximisation. Cost minimisation attempts to reduce costs. This may be achieved by tight budgetary control or cutting back on expenditure.

Some authors argue strongly that management accounting needs to refocus on revenue maximisation. In part, revenue maximisation is achieved through the new focus on strategic management accounting which looks outwards to the external environment rather than inwards. Substantial opportunities arise to adopt new techniques such as customer database mining. This latter technique looks at customer databases and seeks to extract from them customer data which will expand the business's revenue.

SOUNDBITE 15.2

Sales Maximisation

'Legend tells of the traveller who went into a county store and found the shelves lined with bags of salt. "You must sell a lot of salt", said the traveller, "Nah", said the storekeeper. "I can't sell no salt at all. But the feller who sells me salt – boy, can *he* sell salt".'

Martin Mayer, *The Bankers*, 1974

Source: *The Executive's Book of Quotations* (1994), p. 255

Management accountants have often been criticised for being overly concerned with cost cutting (see, for example, Lesley Jackson, H.P. Bulmer Holding plc's UK Finance Director, in Real-Life Nugget 15.1).

REAL-LIFE NUGGET 15.1

Cost minimisation

Jackson's time as general commercial manager gave her the opportunity to look at a business from a different angle. She says it made her a better accountant.

'A lot of accountants tend to look at cost minimalisation and low risk. They tend to have a more conservative mindset. I became slightly more maverick in this sense,' she says.

It was this broader outlook on business and varied skills-sets that gave Jackson the edge over other candidates for the role at Bulmers.

Source: Brewing up a Profit, Michelle Perry, *Accountancy Age*, 3 May 2001, p. 20

Use of Computers

The theory and practice of management accounting is shown in the next seven chapters. In practice, for most of the techniques shown, in practice, a dedicated computer program would be used. Alternatively, a spreadsheet could be set up so as to handle the calculations. These programs enable complicated and often complex real-life situations to be modelled. However, it is essential to be able to appreciate which figures should be input into the computer. As Peter Williams states.

'While it may be possible for any company with a PC to produce a set of management information using relatively low-cost accounting software, there is no guarantee that the output will be true and fair.'

Accountancy Age, 2 March, 2000, p. 23

Conclusion

Management accounting is the internal accounting function of a firm. It can be divided into cost accounting (costing; planning, control and performance) and decision making (short-term and long-term). In costing, the two main aspects are pricing and stock valuation. In planning, control, and performance budgeting and standard costing are used. Decision making has four main strands: short-term decision making; strategic management accounting; capital budgeting; and sources of finance. Management accountants are increasingly moving away from costing towards new areas such as strategic management accounting. In effect, this reflects the decline of manufacturing industry in developed countries.

Selected Reading

Armstrong, P. and C. Jones (1992), 'The decline of operational expertise in the knowledge-base of management accounting: An examination of some post-war trends in the qualifying requirements of the Chartered Institute of Management Accountants', *Management Accounting Research*, Vol. 3, pp. 53–75.
    An interesting look at how the management accounting profession has gradually changed over time. Originally concerned with costing, it now has a much wider focus.
Drury, C. (2005), *Management and Cost Accounting* (Thomson Learning: London). This is a comprehensive text on management and cost accounting. Once students have mastered the basics, this represents a good book for future reading.
Johnson, T. and R.S. Kaplan (1987), *Relevance Lost: The Rise and Fall of Management Accounting* (Harvard University Press).
    A benchmarking book which triggered a relook at management accounting. After this book a new management accounting emerged consisting of topics such as activity-based costing and strategic management accounting.
Kaplan, R.S. (1984), 'Yesterday's accounting undermines production', *Harvard Business Review*, July/August, pp. 95–101.
    This provides a good overview of the problems with traditional management accounting.

Q&A   Discussion Questions

Questions with numbers in blue have answers at the back of the book.

Q1   What are the main branches of management accounting and what are their main functions?

Q2   Why do you think that management accounting has been so keen to lose its costing image?

Q3   What are the following types of cost and why are they important?
(a)   Direct cost
(b)   Indirect cost
(c)   Fixed cost
(d)   Variable cost
(e)   Standard cost

Q4   The management accountant has been described as a professional with a toolkit of techniques. How fair a description do you think this is?

Q5   Why have management accountants been criticised for being cost minimisers and how might they be revenue maximisers?

Q6   State whether the following statements are true or false. If false explain why.
(a) The two main branches of management accounting are cost accounting and decision making.
(b) Total absorption costing is where all the overheads incurred by a company are recovered in the valuation of stock.
(c) The difference between absorption costing and marginal costing as a form of costing for stock valuation is that absorption costing includes direct materials, direct labour and all production overheads. By contrast, marginal costing only includes direct materials, direct labour and all *variable* production overheads. Marginal costing, therefore, excludes fixed production overheads.
(d) Strategic management accounting is concerned principally with short-term operational decisions.
(e) Discounted cash flow discounts the future expected cash flows of a project back to their present-day monetary values.

Chapter 16

Learning Outcomes

After completing this chapter you should be able to:

✔ Explain the nature and importance of costing.

✔ Discuss the process of traditional costing.

✔ Understand the nature of activity-based costing.

✔ Distinguish between different costing systems.

✔ Discuss target costing.

Costing

In a Nutshell

- *Costing is a subset of cost accounting and is used as a basis for stock valuation and for cost-plus pricing.*

- *There are direct costs and indirect costs or overheads.*

- *The six stages in traditional cost recovery are (1) recording costs, (2) classifying costs, (3) allocating indirect costs to departments, (4) reapportioning costs from service to productive departments, (5) calculating an overhead recovery rate, and (6) absorbing costs into products and services.*

- *Activity-based costing is a sophisticated version of cost recovery which uses cost allocation drivers based on activities to allocate costs.*

- *Different industries have different costing methods such as job costing, batch costing, standard costing, contract costing, process costing and service costing.*

- *Non-production overheads are included in cost-plus pricing, but not in stock valuation.*

- *In stock valuation, either all production costs (absorption costing) or only variable production costs (marginal costing) can be allocated.*

- *Target costing, developed by the Japanese, is based on market prices and set at the pre-production stage.*

- *Companies in trouble often cut costs, such as labour costs, in order to improve their profitability.*

Introduction

Management accounting can be broadly divided into cost accounting and decision making. In turn, cost accounting has two major strands: (1) costing, and (2) planning, control and performance. Costing involves ascertaining all the costs of a product or service so as to form the basis for pricing and for stock valuation. The first management accountants were essentially cost accountants. Their job was to make sure that manufactured products were priced so as fully to recover all the costs incurred in making them. This process of recording, classifying, allocating the costs and then absorbing those costs into individual products and services still remains the basis of cost recovery. However, the traditional methods of cost recovery were geared up for manufacturing industries and assumed that overhead costs were relatively small. The decline of manufacturing industry, the increasing importance of overhead costs, and the rise of service industries has caused a need to rethink some of the basics of cost recovery. In particular, the technique of activity-based costing has gained in popularity.

Importance of Cost Accounting

Cost accounting is a common term used to embrace both costing, and planning, control and performance. Definition 16.1 shows two formal definitions of cost accounting. The first is by

DEFINITION 16.1

Cost Accounting

Working definition
The determination of actual and standard costs, budgeting and standard costing.

Formal definition

1. 'The classification, recording and appropriate allocation of expenditure in order to determine the total cost of products or services.'

This earlier definition by ICMA is a good description of cost recovery.

2. 'The establishment of budgets, standard costs and actual costs of operations, processes, activities or products; and the analysis of variances, profitability or the social use of funds. The use of the term 'costing' is not recommended except with a qualifying adjective, e.g. standard costing.'

This CIMA (2000) definition embraces both cost accounting, and planning, control and performance.

the Institute of Cost and Management Accountants (ICMA), the predecessor body of the author of the second definition, the Chartered Institute of Management Accountants (CIMA). It is interesting to see that the definition has widened considerably. In particular, the more recent CIMA definition now explicitly mentions budgeting and standard costing.

In this book, we take cost accounting to involve two main parts. The first is costing, which is the process of determining the actual costs of products and service. This usually looks to the past. And, the second is costing for planning, control and performance where expected costs are determined for future periods either through budgeting or standard costing.

Costs are the essential building blocks for both financial and management accounting. In costing, costs represent *actual* items of expenditure. In budgeting and standard costing, costs represent *future* (expected) items of expenditure. Costs represent a major building block of management accounting. In financial accounting, it is important to match costs against revenue to determine profit.

An important part of this matching process in manufacturing industry is the allocation of production costs to stock. Either all production costs (absorption costing) or variable production costs (marginal costing) can be allocated. Sometimes marginal costing is termed variable costing. In Figure 16.1, we use absorption costing, in which all the production costs are allocated to stock. These costs will be included in the cost of opening stock in the next accounting period and then matched against sales to determine profit. Later on, in Figure 16.12, both absorption and marginal costing are shown for comparative purposes.

Figure 16.1   Allocation of Costs to Stock Using Absorption Costing

Stockco manufactures only toys. The direct costs of manufacturing 1,000 toys is £1,000. Total production overheads for the toys (for example, factory light and heat) are £500. At the end of the year 200 toys are in stock. What is the cost of the closing stock?

	1,000 units £	Per unit £
Direct costs	1,000	1.00
Production overheads	500	0.50
	1,500	1.50

The closing stock is thus 200 @ £1.50 = £300

Another extremely important function of costing is as a basis for pricing. The selling price of a product is key to making a profit. In many businesses, the fundamental economic law is that the cheaper the price of the goods, the more goods will be sold. This sentiment is expressed in Real-Life Nugget 16.1.

REAL-LIFE NUGGET 16.1

Pricing Policy

Retailing used to be so simple. If shopkeepers wanted to increase sales, they cut their prices, putting their goods within reach of people who previously could not afford them.

In developed countries, as incomes have risen, higher prices have become more affordable. But if retailers thought the need for discounting would fade, they were wrong.

Source: Marketing Value for Money, Richard Tomkins, *Financial Times*, 14 May 1999

In practice, there are two methods of pricing: market pricing and cost-plus pricing. In market pricing, the focus is external. The prices charged by competitors are examined together with the amount that customers are willing to pay. In cost-plus pricing, by contrast, the focus is internal. The total costs of making the product are established (i.e., all the direct costs and all the indirect costs or overheads) and then a profit percentage or profit mark-up is added. When setting prices, companies will bear in mind both the costs of making the product and also the amount for which competitor products are selling. At certain times firms will adopt different pricing strategies. For example, a company may discount its prices to boost sales.

PAUSE FOR THOUGHT 16.1

Cost-Plus Pricing

What is the purpose of cost-plus pricing and how can it prove dangerous in a competitive market?

Cost-plus pricing seeks to recover all the overheads into a product or service. However, it is only as good as the method chosen to recover the overheads, and the estimates made. The problem is that prices are often set by the market rather than by the company. A company may determine the cost of a product and then its selling price. However, in a competitive market, this price may be higher than competitors' prices or be more than customers wish to pay. When adopting cost-plus pricing it is always important to perform a reality check and ask: can we really sell the product or service at this price? In practice, therefore, it is advisable to use both cost-plus pricing and market pricing together.

In general, companies strive to keep their costs as low as possible. Those companies that can do this, such as Wal-Mart, the American retailer that purchased Asda, have a key competitive advantage (see Real-Life Nugget 16.2).

Types of Cost

A cost is simply an amount of expenditure which can be attributed to a product or service. It is possible to distinguish between two main types of cost: **direct costs** and **indirect costs**. Direct costs are simply those that **can** be directly attributed to a product or service. Indirect costs are those that **cannot** be directly attributed. Indirect costs are also known as overheads. In manufacturing industry, direct costs have declined over time while indirect costs have risen. This makes costing more difficult. Figures 16.2 (below) and 16.3 on page 399 demonstrate two cost structures, for

Figure 16.2   Cost Structure for a Manufactured Product (for Example, a Computer)

	£	Examples
Direct materials	50*	Plastics, steel
Direct labour	120*	Manufacturing labour
Direct expenses	10*	Royalties
Prime Cost	180	
Production overheads	60†	Supervisors' wages
Production Cost	240	
Administrative overheads	50†	Staff costs, office expenses
Selling and distribution overheads	60†	Advertising
Total Cost	350	
Profit	50	
Selling Price	400	

*Direct costs, i.e. those that can be directly attributed to the product
†Indirect costs, i.e. those that cannot be directly attributed to the product

a manufactured product and for a service product, respectively. In both cases, we are totalling all our costs so that we can recover them into the final selling price. This is known as **total absorption costing**. This should be distinguished from absorption costing and marginal costing which, as we have just discussed, are used for stock valuation not for pricing.

Essentially, a proportion of the cost of the manufactured product can be directly attributed. The direct materials are those such as the plastic, steel and glass that are actually used to make the product. The direct labour is the labour cost actually incurred in making the product. The direct expenses are royalties paid per product manufactured. These three costs (direct materials, direct labour and direct expenses) are known as the **prime cost. The remaining costs are all overheads**. The production overheads are those associated with the production process. Examples are supervisors' wages or the electricity used in the factory area. By contrast, administrative overheads (for example, staff costs, office expenses, accountants' fees) and selling and distribution overheads (for example, transport and advertising) are incurred outside the production area. An essential element of costing is that as we move further away from the direct provision of a product or service it becomes more difficult to allocate the costs fairly. Thus, it is easiest to allocate the direct costs, but most difficult to allocate the administrative costs. The Company Camera 16.1 provides an example of administrative overheads for the HBOS, a bank.

SOUNDBITE 16.1

Costs

'I haven't heard of anybody who wants to stop living on account of the cost.'

Ken Hubbard

Source: R. Flesch (1959) *The Book of Unusual Quotations*, p. 51

THE COMPANY CAMERA 16.1

Administrative Expenses

	Notes	2004 £million	2003 £million
Administrative expenses (excluding exceptional items) includes			
Staff costs	4	1,875	1,755
Property rentals		149	145
Hire of equipment		40	35

Source: HBOS, Annual Report and Accounts 2004, p. 10

In Figure 16.3, we use the example of a computer helpline, which callers phone to receive advice. In this case, the only direct costs will probably be direct labour. The administrative, selling and distribution costs will be proportionately higher. The key problem in cost recovery is thus how to recover the overheads. Direct costs can be directly allocated to a cost unit (i.e., an individual product or service unit, such as a customer's phone call). However, indirect costs have to be totalled and then divided up amongst all the cost units. This is much more problematic.

Figure 16.3 Cost Structure for a Service Product (for Example, the Cost per Customer Call for a Computer Helpline)

	£	Examples
Direct labour	4*	Telephone operator
Prime Cost	4	
Administrative expenses	5†	Management, office expenses
Selling and distribution costs	4†	Advertising, marketing
Total Cost	13	
Profit	2	
Selling Price	15	

*Direct costs, i.e. those that can be directly attributed to the service
†Indirect costs, i.e. those that cannot be directly attributed to the service

PAUSE FOR THOUGHT 16.2

Manufacturing a Television

From the following information can you work out the cost and selling price of each television using total absorption costing?

....

(i) *Direct materials £25; direct labour £50; direct expenses £3 per television.*
(ii) *£18,000 production overheads; £14,000 administrative expenses; and £15,000 selling and distribution costs.*
(iii) *1,000 televisions produced. Profit mark-up of 20% on total cost.*

We would thus have:	£
Direct materials	25
Direct labour	50
Direct expenses	3
Prime Cost	78
Production overheads (N1)	18
Production Cost	96
Administrative expenses (N1)	14
Selling and distribution costs (N1)	15
Total Cost	125
Profit (20% × £125, i.e. 20% mark-up on cost)	25
Selling Price	150

Traditional Costing

The aim of costing is simply to recover (also known as 'to absorb') the costs into an identifiable product or service so as to form the basis for pricing and stock valuation. In pricing, all the overheads are recovered. For stock valuation, only those overheads directly related to the production of stock can be recovered (i.e., direct costs and attributable production overheads). In the next two sections, we look at total absorption costing for pricing, using traditional costing and activity-based costing. In traditional cost recovery or cost absorption, there are six major steps. We will then look at activity-based costing, which is a more modern way of tackling cost recovery. Both traditional total absorption costing and activity-based costing can be used in manufacturing or non-manufacturing industries.

In manufacturing industry, total absorption costing means recovering all the costs from those departments in which products are manufactured (*production departments*) and from those that supply support activities such as catering, administration, or selling and distribution (*service support departments*) into the cost of the end product. In service industries, we recover all the costs from those departments that deliver the final service to customers (*service delivery departments*) and from the *service support departments*. We set out below the six steps for recovering costs into products (see Figure 16.4 on the next page). Diagrammatically, this process is illustrated in Figure 16.5 on the next page. **However, exactly the same process would be used for recovering costs into services.**

Figure 16.4   Six Steps in Traditional Total Absorption Costing

1. Record all the costs.
2. Classify all the costs.
3. Allocate all the indirect costs to the departments of a business.
4. Reallocate costs from service support departments to production departments.
5. Calculate an overhead recovery rate.
6. Absorb both the direct costs and the indirect costs (or overheads) into individual products.

Figure 16.5   Diagrammatic Representation of Traditional Total Absorption Costing

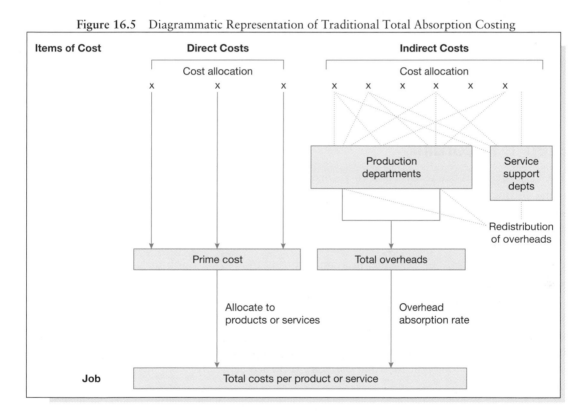

In essence, businesses need to make a profit. Revenue from sales, therefore, needs to exceed the total costs incurred in making a product. Businesses are thus very keen to ascertain their costs so that they can set a reasonable price for their products. Sometimes, especially for long-term contracts or one-off jobs, this can prove very difficult. For example, Cardiff's Millennium stadium, although a triumph of construction, was a financial disaster for John Laing (see Real-Life Nugget 16.3).

Step 1: Recording

The first step in cost recovery is to record all the costs. It is important to appreciate that many businesses have integrated financial accounting and management accounting systems. There is thus no need to keep separate records for both financial accounting and management accounting.

Direct costs, such as direct materials and direct labour, can be directly traced to individual products or services. For example, in manufacturing industries, a job may have a job card on which the direct material and direct labour incurred is recorded.

Indirect costs, such as rent or administrative costs, are much more difficult to record. There are two main problems: estimation and total amount. The first problem is that it is unlikely that the actual costs will be known until the end of a period. Transport costs, for example, may be known only after the journeys have been made. They will, therefore, have to be estimated. The second problem is that the total costs are recorded centrally. They must then be allocated to products.

Step 2: Classification

This involves categorising and grouping the costs before allocating them to departments. We may, for example, need to calculate the total rent or total costs for light and heat.

Step 3: Allocate indirect costs to departments

Direct costs can be directly traced to goods or services. For overheads, the process is indirect. The key to overhead allocation is to find an appropriate basis for allocation. These are called allocation bases or cost drivers. Figure 16.6 shows some possible allocation bases for various types of cost.

Figure 16.6   Departmental Allocation Bases

Types of Cost	Possible Allocation Bases
Power	Number of machine hours
Depreciation, insurance	Value of fixed assets
Canteen, office expenses	Relative area of floor space
Rent, business rates, light and heat	Number of employees

Step 4: Reallocate service support department costs to production departments

Once all the costs are allocated, we must reallocate them to the production departments. This is because we need to recover these costs into *specific products* which are *made* only in the *production departments*.

Step 5: Overhead recovery rate

Once we have allocated our costs to production departments, we need to absorb these costs into the final product. We must choose a suitable recovery rate. The choice of rate reflects the nature of the activity and could be any of the following (or even others):

- Rate per unit
- Rate per direct labour hour
- Rate per machine hour
- Rate per £ materials
- Rate per £ direct labour
- Rate per £ prime cost

Figure 16.7 illustrates this process

Figure 16.7   Overhead Recovery Rate

A firm has £12,000 indirect costs in department F. It also has the following data available:

	£	
Direct materials	30,000	240,000 units produced
Direct labour	70,000	6,000 direct labour hours are used
Prime Cost	100,000	50,000 machine hours are used

Calculate the various overhead recovery rates discussed above in step 5.
The various overhead recovery rates are:

1.	Per unit	$=$	$\dfrac{£12,000}{240,000}$	$=$	£0.05 per unit
2.	Per direct labour hour	$=$	$\dfrac{£12,000}{6,000}$	$=$	£2.00 per labour hour
3.	Per machine hour	$=$	$\dfrac{£12,000}{50,000}$	$=$	£0.24 per machine hour
4.	Per £ material	$=$	$\dfrac{£12,000}{30,000}$	$=$	£0.40 per £ material
5.	Per £ labour	$=$	$\dfrac{£12,000}{70,000}$	$=$	£0.17 per £ labour
6.	Per £ prime cost	$=$	$\dfrac{£12,000}{100,000}$	$=$	£0.12 per £ prime cost

In practice, only one of these six overhead recovery rates would be used, most likely direct labour hours.

Step 6: Absorption of costs into products

Once we have calculated an absorption rate we can absorb our costs. In practice, there will be many products of varying size and complexity. Figure 16.8 illustrates how we would now recover our costs into products.

Figure 16.8   Recovery into Specific Jobs

If, for example, the following Job X007 was one of the 200,000 units produced and we recover our overheads *per direct labour hour* then we might have the following situation.

Job X007		£
Direct materials	(10 kilos at £2)	20
Direct labour	(12 hours at £12)	144
Prime Cost		164

The direct materials are directly recovered into the job; we must now recover the indirect costs. We recover into our product 12 hours at £2.00 per hour (as calculated in Figure 16.7) = £24.00.

Our total cost is therefore	£
Prime Cost	164
Overheads	24
Total Cost	188
Profit: 25 % mark-up on cost	47
Selling Price	235

Comprehensive Example

In Figure 16.9, a comprehensive example of cost recovery looks at all six steps in the cost recovery process.

Figure 16.9 Comprehensive Cost Recovery Example

Millennium plc has the following three departments:

    A. Production
    B. Production
    C. Service support

Type of Cost	Proposed Basis of Apportionment	£
Rent and business rates	Floor area	4,000
Repairs and maintenance	Amount actually spent	1,000
Canteen	Number of employees	500
Depreciation	Cost of fixed assets	2,100
		7,600

It is estimated that:

  (i) Department A has a floor area of 4,000 sq.ft., Department B has a floor area of 3,000 sq.ft., and Department C has a floor area of 1,000 sq.ft.
 (ii) The following direct labour hours will be used: A (2,000 hours), B (3,000 hours), and C (300 hours)
(iii) Department A has 50 employees, Department B 30 employees and Department C 20 employees
 (iv) Department A has machinery costing £15,000, Department B has £25,000 machinery and Department C has £30,000 machinery
  (v) The wage rates are £11 per hour for A, £12 per hour for B, and £10 per hour for C
 (vi) Repairs are to be A £200; B £300; C £500.

It is estimated that 70% of Department C's facilities are used by Department A, and 30% by Department B, and that C's direct material and direct labour for the year will be £3,000 and £1,500. The overheads will be recovered by reference to the amount of direct labour hours used. Profit is to be at 25% on cost.

. . . .

Millennium plc wishes to prepare a quotation for the following job C206.

Direct material	£400
Direct labour	Department A 20 hours
	Department B 10 hours

We have already recorded (step 1), and classified (step 2) our information so the next stage (step 3) is to allocate our indirect costs (i.e. overheads) to departments.

Step 3: Overhead Allocation to Departments

Type of Cost	Allocation	Total £	A £	B £	C £
C's direct labour	Traced directly	3,000			3,000
C's direct material	Traced directly	1,500			1,500
Rent and business rates (calculation shown below in Helpnote point 1)	Area (4,000: 3,000: 1,000)	4,000	2,000	1,500	500
Repairs and maintenance	Actual	1,000	200	300	500
Canteen	No. of employees (50: 30: 20)	500	250	150	100
Depreciation	Cost of fixed assets (15,000: 25,000: 30,000)	2,100	450	750	900
Total		12,100	2,900	2,700	6,500

Figure 16.9   Comprehensive Cost Recovery Example (*continued*)

Helpnotes:

1. The allocations for each type of cost are made by allocating each cost across the departments in proportion to the total cost. For example, the rent and business rates total area is 8,000 sq.ft. Thus:

   A $(4,000/8,000) \times £4,000 = £2,000$.

   B $(3,000/8,000) \times £4,000 = £1,500$, and

   C $(1,000/8,000) \times £4,000 = £500$

2. We must include our direct labour and direct materials for Department C in our calculations of the overhead absorption rate because although direct for Department C, they are indirect for Departments A and B, which are the production departments.

Step 4: Reallocate Service Support Department Costs to Production Departments

The next stage is to reallocate the service support department costs to the production departments. Since 70 % of C is used by A, and 30 % by B, it is only fair to reallocate them in this proportion.

	Total £	A £	B £	C £
Total overheads	12,100	2,900	2,700	6,500
Reallocation %		70 %	30 %	(100 %)
		4,550	1,950	(6,500)
New total	12,100	7,450	4,650	

If there were more service support departments, we would have to continue to reallocate the costs until they were all absorbed into production departments. In this case the allocation is finished.

Step 5: Calculate an Overhead Recovery Rate

It is now time to work out an overhead recovery rate.

	Total £	A £	B £
Total overheads	12,100	7,450	4,650
Direct labour hours		2,000	3,000
Recovery rate		3.73	1.55

Step 6: Absorption of Costs into Products

Finally, we must absorb both our direct and indirect costs into our products as a basis for pricing.

Job C206

		£
Direct labour	A. 20 hours at £11	220.00
	B. 10 hours at £12	120.00
Direct material		400.00
Prime Cost		740.00
Overheads	A. 20 hours at £3.73	74.60
	B. 10 hours at £1.55	15.50
Total Cost		830.10
25 % mark-up on cost		207.52
Selling Price		1037.62

Total absorption costing (as we have just demonstrated in Figure 16.9) is where we try to recover all our overheads (direct and indirect) into a product or service. It forms the basis of job, contract, batch, process and service costing.

PAUSE FOR THOUGHT 16.3

Traditional Product Costing

Traditional product costing usually uses either direct machine hours or direct labour hours to determine its overhead recovery rate. Can you see any problems with this in a service and knowledge-based economy?

....

In manufacturing industry, products are made intensively using machines and direct labour. It makes sense, therefore, to recover overheads using those measures. However, in service industries or knowledge-based industries, products or services may have very little direct labour input and do not use machines. The financial services industry or Internet companies, for example, have very few industrial machines or direct labour. In this case, machine hours and labour hours become, at best, irrelevant and, at worst, very dangerous when pricing goods or services. In these and other industries new methods of allocating cost are necessary. The stimulus to find these new methods has led to the development of activity-based costing. This seeks to establish activities as a basis for allocating overheads.

Activity-Based Costing

Traditional total absorption costing was developed in manufacturing industries. In these industries, there are usually substantial quantities of machine hours or direct labour hours. These volume-related allocation bases are used to allocate overheads. However, recently traditional absorption costing has been criticised for failing to respond to the new post-manufacturing industrial environment and for lacking sophistication. Allocation using direct cost bases often, therefore, fails to reflect the true distribution of the costs. It is argued that this leads to inaccurate pricing.

Activity-based costing aims to remedy these defects. It is based on the premise that activities that occur within a firm cause overhead costs. By identifying these activities, a firm can achieve a range of benefits, including the ability to cost products more accurately. Essentially, activity-based costing is a more sophisticated version of the traditional product costing system. There is a six-stage process (see Figure 16.10 overleaf).

Figure 16.10 Six Steps in Activity-Based Costing

1. Record all the costs.
2. Classify all the costs.
3. Identify activities.
4. Identify cost drivers and allocate overheads to them.
5. Calculate activity-cost driver rates.
6. Absorb both the direct costs and indirect costs into a product or service.

We will now work through these six steps. The process is portrayed graphically in Figure 16.11.

Figure 16.11 Diagrammatic Representation of Activity-Based Costing

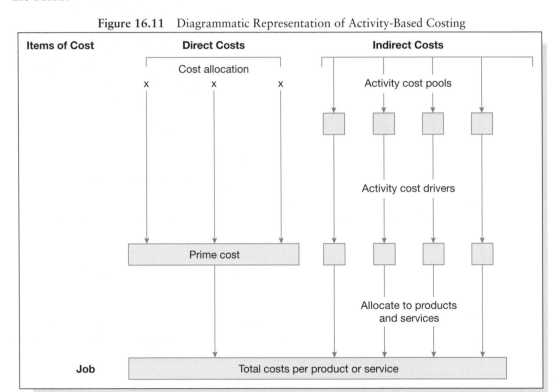

Steps 1 and 2

The first two steps are the same as for traditional costing.

Step 3: Identify activities

The firm identifies those activities that determine overhead costs. Production is one such activity.

Step 4: Identify cost drivers and allocate appropriate overheads to them

Activity-based accounting seeks to link cost recovery to cost behaviour. Activity-cost drivers determine cost behaviour. Activity-cost drivers for a production department, for example, might be the number of purchase orders, the number of set-ups, maintenance hours, the number of inspections, the number of despatches, machine hours or direct labour hours.

Step 5: Calculate activity-cost driver rates

Here, for each activity driver we calculate an appropriate cost driver rate. This is the total costs for a cost driver divided by the number of activities. An example might be £2,000 total costs for material inspections divided by 250 material inspections.

Step 6: Absorb both direct and indirect costs into a product or service

This process is similar to traditional product costing. The total costs are allocated to products using activity cost drivers; they are then divided by the number of products.

In Figure 16.12 an activity-based costing example is given for Fireco. This has two products

Figure 16.12   Activity-Based Costing Example

Fireco has the following costs: for setting up machinery £8,000, for ordering material £3,000, for inspecting the material £2,000 and sales ledger expenses £8,000. Selling price is cost plus 25%. There is also the following information:

	A £	B £
Direct materials	8,000	7,000
Direct labour	10,000	15,000
Number of set-ups	20	30
Number of purchase orders	4,000	1,000
Number of inspections	100	150
Number of sales invoices processed	7,000	3,000
Number of products	16,000	10,000

What would be the activity-cost driver rates, total cost and selling price?

As we have already completed steps 1–4 (recording, classifying, and identifying cost drivers with associated overheads), we can proceed to step 5, calculating the activity cost-driver rates.

Step 4: Calculation of Activity-Cost Driver Rates

Activity	Set-ups	Purchase orders	Inspections	Sales invoices
Cost	£8,000	£3,000	£2,000	£8,000
Cost driver	50 set-ups	5,000 purchase orders	250 inspections	10,000 sales invoices
Cost per unit of cost driver	£160	£0.60	£8.00	£0.80

Figure 16.12   Activity-Based Costing Example (*continued*)

Here we simply divided the total costs of each activity by the total number of the activities. There are, for example, 20 set-ups for A and 30 set-ups for B making 50 set-ups in total. We divide this into the total cost of £8,000 to arrive at £160 per set-up.

Step 6: Absorb both the Direct and Indirect Costs into the Products

Activity	Set-ups	Purchase orders	Inspections	Sales	Total costs*
A	20 × £160 = £3,200	4,000 × £0.60 = £2,400	100 × £8.00 = £800	7,000 × £0.80 = £5,600	£12,000
B	30 × £160 = £4,800	1,000 × £0.60 = £600	150 × £8.00 = £1,200	3,000 × £0.80 = £2,400	£9,000
Total	£8,000	£3,000	£2,000	£8,000	£21,000

Here, we multiplied the cost per unit of cost driver by the number of cost drivers. For example, we have 20 set-ups (i.e., number of cost drivers) for A and 30 set-ups (i.e., number of cost drivers) for B. Each set-up costs £160 (i.e., cost per unit of cost driver).

	A £	B £
Total overhead costs*	12,000	9,000
Number of products	16,000	10,000
Overhead per product	£0.75	£0.90

Here, we took the total overhead costs for A (£12,000) and for B (£9,000) and divided by the number of products to arrive at the overhead per product. We can now prepare the product cost statements for products A and B. Direct materials and direct labour are calculated by dividing the total costs for each product by the total number of products (i.e., for A's direct materials, we divide £8,000 by 16,000 products).

	A Product cost £	B Product cost £
Direct materials	0.50	0.70
Direct labour	0.62	1.50
Prime Cost	1.12	2.20
Overheads	0.75	0.90
Total Cost	1.87	3.10
Profit (25% mark-up on cost)	0.47	0.78
Sales Price	2.34	3.88

(A and B) and four activity-cost drivers have been identified (set-ups, purchase orders, inspections and sales invoices.

Activity-based costing is thus a more sophisticated version of traditional product costing. It can give more accurate and reliable information. It also significantly increases the company's ability to manage costs and is suitable for both manufacturing and service companies. However, importantly, it involves much more time and effort to set up than traditional product costing and may not be suitable for all companies.

Costing for Stock Valuation

Non-Production Overheads

It is important to distinguish between costing as a basis of pricing, which we have just looked at, and costing as the basis for stock valuation. The key difference is in the treatment of non-production overheads.

PAUSE FOR THOUGHT 16.4

Non-Production Overheads

Why are administrative, sales and marketing costs not included as overheads in stock valuation?

....

The problem of non-production overheads is a tricky one. The administrative, sales and marketing costs, for example, are required when calculating the total cost of a product as a basis for pricing. However, they should not be included when calculating a stock valuation. The reason is that these costs are not incurred in actually making the product. It would, therefore, be incorrect to include them in the cost of the product. These non-production costs are often called period costs. This is because they are allocated to the **period** *not* the **product**.

When valuing stock it is permissible to include production overheads, but not non-production overheads. However, for cost-plus pricing we need to take into account all overheads. These include non-production overheads such as sales, administrative and marketing expenses. As Figure 16.13 on the next page shows, there can be quite a difference.

Different stock valuation measures: FIFO, LIFO, AVCO

The inclusion of production overheads in finished goods stock is one key problem in stock valuation. Another difficulty, which primarily concerns raw material stock, is the choice of stock valuation methods. There are three main methods: FIFO, LIFO and AVCO. All three are permitted in management accounting and for stock valuation in the financial accounts in the US. However, in the UK only FIFO and AVCO are permitted for stock valuation in financial accounting.

Figure 16.13   Costing for Stock Valuation and for Cost-Plus Pricing

A product has the following cost structure. 100,000 products are manufactured.

	Stock valuation (Marginal costing)	Stock valuation (Absorption costing)	Cost-plus pricing (Total absorption costing)
	£000	£000	£000
Direct materials	10	10	10
Direct labour	25	25	25
Prime Cost	35	35	35
Variable production overheads	10	10	10
Fixed production overheads	–	5	5
Total Production Costs	45	50	50
Administrative costs			10
Marketing costs			8
Sales costs			7
Total Cost			75
Profit: 33.3% mark-up on cost			25
Selling Price			100

At what value should each item be recorded in stock and what is the selling price per item?

i. *Stock* using marginal costing

$$\frac{£45,000}{100,000} = 0.45\text{p}$$

ii. *Stock* using absorption costing

$$\frac{£50,000}{100,000} = 0.50\text{p}$$

iii. *Selling price* using total absorption costing

$$\frac{£100,000}{100,000} = £1.00$$

Helpnote: Using **marginal costing,** only the **variable production overheads** that can be attributed are included in the stock valuation. In **absorption costing,** we include **all the production overheads.** It is absorption costing that is used for stock valuation in *financial reporting.* In **total absorption costing,** we recover **all the costs** into the product's final selling price.

Stock valuation is not quite as easy as it may at first seem. It depends on which assumptions you make about the stock sold. Is the stock you buy in first, the first to be sold (first-in-first out (FIFO))? Or is the stock you buy in last, sold first (last-in-first-out (LIFO))? If the purchase price of stock changes then this assumption matters.

In Figure 16.14, we investigate an example of the impact that using FIFO or LIFO has upon the valuation of raw materials stock. We also include a third method, AVCO (average cost), which takes the average purchase price of the goods as their cost of sale.

Figure 16.14   FIFO, LIFO and AVCO Stock Valuation Methods

Stockco purchases its stock on the first day of the month. It starts with no stock. Its purchases and sales over the first three months are as follows:

		Kilos	*Cost per kilo*	*Total cost*
January 1	*Purchases*	*10,000*	*£1.00*	*£10,000*
February 1	*Purchases*	*15,000*	*£1.50*	*£22,500*
March 1	*Purchases*	*20,000*	*£2.00*	*£40,000*
		45,000		*£72,500*
March 30	*Sales*	*(35,000)*		
March 30	*Closing stock*	*10,000*		

What is the closing stock valuation using FIFO, LIFO and AVCO?

. . . .

(i) **FIFO:** Here, the first stock purchased is the first sold. The 35,000 kilos sold therefore, used up all the January stock (10,000 kilos), and the February stock (15,000 kilos), and (10,000 kilos) of the March stock. We, therefore, have left in stock 10,000 kilos of material valued at the March purchase price of £2.00 per kilo. Closing stock is, therefore, $10,000 \times £2 = £20,000$.

(ii) **LIFO:** Here the last stock purchased is assumed to be the first to be sold. The 35,000 kilos sold, therefore, used up:

20,000	kilos from March
15,000	kilos from February
35,000	

We, therefore, have remaining 10,000 kilos from January at £1 per kilo $= £10,000$.

(iii) **AVCO:** Here the stock value is pooled and the average cost of purchase is taken as the cost of the goods sold. We purchased 45,000 kilos for £72,500 (i.e. £1.611 per kilo). The cost of our stock, is therefore, $10,000$ kilos $\times$ average cost $£1.611 = £16,110$.

We can, therefore, see that our *stock valuations* vary considerably.

	£
FIFO	20,000
LIFO	10,000
AVCO	16,110

It should be appreciated that stock valuation is distinct from physical stock management. In most businesses, good business practice dictates that you usually physically issue the oldest stock first (i.e., adopt FIFO). However, in stock valuation you are allowed to choose what is acceptable under the regulations.

PAUSE FOR THOUGHT 16.5

FIFO, LIFO and AVCO and Cost of Sales

Do you think that using a different stock valuation method in Figure 16.14 would affect cost of sales or profit?

....

Yes!! Whichever valuation method is used, both cost of sales and profit are affected. Essentially, the cost of purchases will be split between stock and cost of sales.

	Total cost	Cost of sales	Stock
	£	£	£
FIFO	72,500	52,500 (N1)	20,000
LIFO	72,500	62,400 (N2)	10,000
AVCO	72,500	56,390 (N3)	16,110

			£
(N1) FIFO represents:	January	10,000 kilos at £1.00	10,000
	February	15,000 kilos at £1.50	22,500
	March	10,000 kilos at £2.00	20,000
			52,500

			£
(N2) LIFO represents:	February	15,000 kilos at £1.50	22,500
	March	20,000 kilos at £2.00	40,000
			62,500

			£
(N3) AVCO represents:		35,000 kilos at £1.611	56,390

Profit is affected because if cost of sales is less, stock, and thus profit, is higher and vice versa. In this case, using FIFO will show the greatest profit as its cost of sales is lowest. LIFO will show the lowest profit. AVCO is in the middle!

Different Costing Methods for Different Industries

So far we have focused mainly on allocating costs to individual jobs in manufacturing. However, job costing is not appropriate in many situations. Different industries have different costing problems. To solve these problems different types of costing have evolved. In order to give a flavour of this, we look below at four industries (see Figure 16.15).

Figure 16.15   Overview of Different Industries' Costing Methods

	Industry	Costing Method
1	Manufacturing in batches	Batch costing
2	Shipbuilding	Contract costing
3	Brewery	Process costing
4	Hotel and catering	Service costing

1. Batch Costing

Batch costing is where a number of items of a similar nature are processed together. There is thus not one discrete job. Batch costing can be used in a variety of situations, such as manufacture of medicinal tablets.

Figure 16.16   Batch Costing

A run of 50,000 tablets are made for batch number x1.11. There are 2,000 defective tablets and 50 tablets per box. Overheads are recovered on the basis of £6 per labour hour. The material was 3 kg at £5.00 per kg, and labour rate A 6 hours at £9.00, and rate B 7 hours at £10.00.

The costing statement might look as follows:	£
Direct materials (3 kg at £5.00)	15.00
Direct labour (13 hours: A 6 at £9	54.00
B 7 at £10)	70.00
Prime Cost	139.00
Overheads (13 hours at £6)	78.00
Total Cost	217.00
Boxes (48,000 ÷ 50)	960
Cost per box	22.6p

2. Contract Costing

A contract can be looked at as a very long job, or a job lasting more than one year. It occurs in big construction industries such as shipbuilding and aircraft building. A long-term contract extends over more than one year and creates the problem of when to take profit. If we have a three-year contract do we take all our profit at the start of our contract, at the end, or equally throughout the three years?

The answer has gradually evolved over the years, and there are now certain recognised guidelines for taking a profit or loss. Generally, losses should be taken as soon as it is realised they will occur. By contrast, profits should be taken so as to reflect the proportion of the work carried out. This is shown in The Company Camera 16.2, which shows John Laing's accounting policy for long-term contracts.

THE COMPANY CAMERA 16.2

Long-Term Contracts

Profits on long-term contracts are calculated in accordance with industry standard accounting practice and do not therefore relate directly to turnover. Profit on current contracts is only taken at a stage near enough to completion for that profit to be reasonably certain. Provision is made for all losses incurred to the accounting date together with any further losses that are foreseen in bringing contracts to completion.

Source: John Laing plc, Annual Report 2003, p. 67

In practice, allocating profits can be very complex. We will use a simplified formula: **Profit to be taken = %contractcomplete × total estimated contract profit × 2/3**. Usually, the customer and the supplier will negotiate and set a price for a contract in advance. Figure 16.17 provides an illustrative example.

Figure 16.17   Contract Costing

O&P Ferries requires a new ferry to be built. It asks Londonside Shipbuilders for a quotation. Londonside looks at its costs and decides that the ship will cost £4 million direct materials, £4 million direct labour and £5 million indirect overheads. They then quote O&P Ferries £19 million for the job. The aim to complete the job in 3 years. Londonside therefore estimate a £6 million profit (£19 million less £13 million). When should they take the profit?

Figure 16.17   Contract Costing (*continued*)

The answer is that the situation is reviewed as the contract progresses, and profit taken according to the formula given earlier. For example, if we have the following costs:

In £ millions	Year 1		Year 2		Year 3	
	£	£	£	£	£	£
Contract Price (Remains fixed)		19		19		19
Costs Incurred to Date						
Direct materials	2		3		5	
Direct labour	2		2		5	
Indirect overheads	2		3		6	
Total costs incurred to date	6		8		16	
Estimated future costs	8		5		–	
Total Costs (estimated and incurred)		14		13		16
Estimated Profit		5		6		3
% Contract complete		6/14ths		8/13ths		Complete

At the end of year 3 the contract is finished, therefore, the estimated profit will be the actual profit.

So if we apply our formula we can see how it works:

	% contract complete	×	Total estimated contract profit	×	$\frac{2}{3}$		This year's profit £	Total estimated profit to date £
Year 1	$\frac{6}{14}$	×	£5m	×	$\frac{2}{3}$ = £1.43m		£1.43m	£1.43m
Year 2	$\frac{8}{13}$	×	£6m	×	$\frac{2}{3}$ = £2.46m		£1.03m	£2.46m

We take an additional £1.03 million in year 2 (i.e., the profit to date, £2.46m, less year 1's profit, £1.43m).

| **Year 3** | | | | | | | £0.54m | £3.0m |

In year 3, we know the actual profit is £3 million. We can therefore take all the profit not taken so far. This is £3 million – £2.46 (already taken) = £0.54 million.

3. Process Costing

Process costing is used in industries with a continuous production process, e.g., beer brewing. Products are passed from one department to another, and then processed further. At any one point in time, therefore, many of the products will only be partially complete. To deal with this problem of partially completed products, the concept of equivalent units has developed. At the end of a process if we partially finish units then we take the percentage of completion and convert to fully completed equivalent units. If, for example, we have 1,000 litres of beer that are half way through the beer-making process this would equal 500 litres fully complete (i.e., there would be the equivalent of 500 litres).

Figure 16.18   Process Costing

A firm manufactures beer. There are two processes A and B. There are 1,000 litres of opening stock of beer for process B, the fermentation stage (the product has already been through process A). They are 50% complete. During the year 650 litres are finished and transferred (i.e., completed). The closing work in progress consists of 800 litres, 75% completed. The costs incurred in that process during that year are £15,000.

To find out the cost per litre, we must first find out how many litres are effectively produced during the period. We can do this by deduction. First of all we can establish the total stock that was completed by the end of the year. This will equal the stock we have finished and transferred (650 litres) plus the closing stock (800 litres, 75% complete, equals 600 litres). From this 1,250 litres we need to take the opening stock (1,000 litres, 50% complete, equals 500 litres). We have, therefore, our effective production of 750 litres.* The cost is then £15,000 divided by the 750 equivalent litres, equals £20 per litre

	Equivalent litres
Finished and transferred	650
Closing stock (800 × 75%)	600
Total completed	1,250
Opening stock (1,000 × 50%)	(500)
*Effective production	750

Therefore, using 'equivalent' litres our cost per litre for process B is:

$$\frac{£15,000}{750} = £20$$

4. Service Costing

Service costing concerns services such as canteens. In large businesses, for example, canteens might be run as independent operating units that have to make a profit. The cost of a particular service is simply the total costs for the service divided by the number of services provided. Service costing uses the same principles as job costing.

Figure 16.19   Service Costing for Canteens

A canteen serves 10,000 meals: 6,000 are roast dinners and 4,000 salads. The roast dinners are bought in for £2.50 each and the salads for £1.25. The canteen costs are £1,000. They are apportioned across the number of meals served. What is the cost of each meal?

	Roast Dinners £	Salads £
Bought-in price	2.50	1.25
Overheads per meal $\left(\dfrac{£1,000}{10,000} = 0.10p\right)$	0.10	0.10
	2.60	1.35

Target Costing

So far we have focused principally on cost-plus pricing. However, the Japanese have introduced a concept called target costing, which focuses on market prices. Essentially, a price is set with reference to market conditions and customer purchasing patterns. A target profit is then deducted to arrive at a target cost. This target cost is set in order to allow a company to achieve a certain market share and a certain profit. The target profit is set before the product is manufactured.

The costs are then examined and re-examined in order to make the target cost. Often this is done by breaking down the product into many individual components and costing them separately. The product may be divided into many functions using 'functional analysis'. Functions may include attractiveness, durability, reliability, and style among other things. Each function is priced. Target costing may also be used in conjunction with life cycle costing. Life cycle costing (see Chapter 20) involves tracing all the costs of a product over their entire life cycle. Target costing will be the first stage in this process.

Cost-Cutting

A final key reason why it is essential for a business to have a good knowledge of its costs is for cost-cutting. As we mentioned in Chapter 15, the two major ways to improve profitability are by improving sales or by cutting costs. Whereas improving sales is a long-term solution, cost-cutting is a short-term solution. It is particularly useful when a business is in trouble. By announcing cost-cutting measures, the business signals to the City and to its investors that it is serious about improving its profitability. Unfortunately, one of the most important elements of most companies costs is labour. Therefore, companies often shed labour. When doing this companies may run into trouble with trade unions or with politicians. Centrica's reduction of the number of staff in its gas showrooms is a good example of this (see Real-Life Nugget 16.4).

REAL-LIFE NUGGET 16.4

Cutting Labour Costs

Centrica, Britain's largest gas retailer, plans to axe almost 1,500 jobs in its underper-forming high street energy stores, drawing the wrath of unions who claimed the act was a 'betrayal of staff'.

The company said it would close its 243 British Gas Energy Centres and incur £60 m in costs to be charged this financial year.

Centrica chief executive Roy Gardner revealed the operating losses for those stores had grown to an estimated £25 m in the June half, compared with £33 m for the whole 1998 year.

Source: Centrica Faces Anger over Store Job Cuts, Anne Hyland, *Daily Telegraph*, 20 July 1999

As an alternative to cutting labour costs, companies sometimes attempt to cut other costs such as training or research and development. By doing this, companies may sacrifice long-term profitability for short-term profitability.

Conclusion

Costing is an important part of management accounting. It involves recording, classifying, allocating and absorbing costs into individual products and services. Cost recovery is used to value stock by including production overheads and for cost-plus pricing by determining the total costs of a product or service. Traditionally, overheads have been allocated to products or services primarily using volume-based measures such as direct labour hours or machine hours. However, more recently, activity-based measures such as number of purchase orders processed have been used. Different industries use different costing systems such as batch costing, contract costing, process costing and service costing. Target costing, based on a product's market price, has been developed in Japan. Businesses in trouble often cut costs, such as labour, in order to try to improve their profitability.

Q&A Discussion Questions

Questions with numbers in blue have answers at the back of the book.

Q1 What is costing and why is it important?

Q2 Compare and contrast the traditional and the more modern activity-based approaches to costing.

Q3 Overhead recovery is the most difficult part of cost recovery. Discuss.

Q4 Target costing combines the advantages of both market pricing and cost-plus pricing. Discuss.

Q5 State whether the following statements are true or false. If false, explain why.
  (a) A cost is an actual past expenditure.
  (b) When recovering costs for pricing we use total absorption costing. However, for stock valuation we use absorption costing or marginal costing.
  (c) When using traditional total absorption costing it is important to identify activity cost drivers.
  (d) In batch costing if we had 100 units that were 50 % complete this would equal 50 equivalent units.
  (e) In stock valuation, marginal costing is normally used in valuing stock in financial reporting.

Q&A Numerical Questions

Questions with numbers in blue have answers at the back of the book.

Q1 Sorter has the following costs:

(a)	Machine workers' wages	(i)	Depreciation on office furniture
(b)	Cost clerks' wages	(j)	Computer running expenses for office
(c)	Purchase of raw materials	(k)	Loan interest
(d)	Machine repairs	(l)	Auditors' fees
(e)	Finance director's salary	(m)	Depreciation on machinery
(f)	Office cleaners	(n)	Advertising costs
(g)	Delivery van staff's wages	(o)	Electricity for machines
(h)	Managing director's car expenses	(p)	Bank charges

Required: An analysis of Sorter's costs between:

(i)	Direct materials	(iv)	Administrative expenses
(ii)	Direct labour	(v)	Selling and distribution costs
(iii)	Production overheads		

Q2   Costa has the following costs:

	£
Salaries of administrative employees	90,800
Wages of factory supervisors	120,000
Computer overhead expenses	
($^2/_3$ in factory, $^1/_3$ in administration)	9,000
Interest on loans	3,000
Wages: selling and distribution	18,300
Salaries: marketing	25,000
Royalties	3,600
Raw materials used in production	320,000
Depreciation: Machinery used for production	8,000
Office fixtures and fittings	4,200
Delivery vans	3,500
Buildings ($^1/_2$ factory; $^1/_4$ office; $^1/_4$ sales)	10,000
Labour costs directly connected with production	200,000
Other production overheads	70,000
Commission paid to sales force	1,200

Required: A determination of Costa's:
(i)   prime cost
(ii) production cost
(iii) total cost

Q3   Makemore has three departments: Departments A and B are production and Department C is a service support department. It apportions its overheads as follows (see brackets):

		£
Supervisors' salaries	(number of employees)	25,000
Computer advisory	(number of employees)	18,000
Rent and business rates	(floor area)	20,000
Depreciation on machinery	(cost)	21,000
Repairs	(actual spend)	4,000
		84,000

You have the following information:
(a) Department A 1,000 employees, B 2,000 employees, C 500 employees.
(b) Department A 10,000 sq.feet, B 6,000 sq.feet, and C 4,000 sq.feet.
(c) Department A machinery costs £30,000, B machinery costs £15,000.

(d) Repairs are £2, 800, £1,100 and £100, respectively, for departments A, B and C.

(e) Department C's facilities will be reallocated 60 % for A and 40 % for B.

(f)

	Department A	Department B
Direct labour hours	80,000	40,000
Machine hours	100,000	200,000

Required: An apportionment of the overheads to products A and B

 (i) using direct labour hours, and

(ii) using machine hours.

Q4 Flight has two products, the 'Takeoff' and the 'Landing'. They go through two departments and incur the following costs:

		Takeoff		Landing	
Dept. A –	Direct labour	10 hours	£10 per hour	9 hours	£7 per hour
	Direct materials	10 kilos	£5 per kilo	7 kilos	£12 per kilo
Dept. B –	Direct labour	8 hours	£12 per hour	5 hours	£8 per hour
	Direct materials	5 kilos	£15 per kilo	6 kilos	£10 per kilo

Takeoff's indirect overheads are absorbed at £7 per labour hour for Dept. A and £5 per hour Dept. B.

Landing's indirect overheads are absorbed at £6 per labour hour for Dept. A and £4 per hour for Dept. B.

Selling price is to be 20 % on cost.

Required: The prices for which Flight should sell 'Takeoff' and 'Landing'.

Q5 An up-market catering company, Spicemeals, organises banquets and high-class catering functions. A particular function for the Blue Devils university drinking club has the following costs for 100 guests.

100 starters	at	£1.00 each	
50 main meals	at	£3.00 each	
50 main meals	at	£2.50 each	
200 sweets	at	£1.50 each	
200 bottles of wine	at	£5.00 each	
100 coffees	at	£0.20 each	

Direct labour:	Supervisory	8 hours	at	£15.00
	Food preparation	30 hours	at	£8.00
	Waitressing	200 hours	at	£5.00

Overheads relating to this job based on total hours are recovered at £1.10 per hour. There are £180,000 general overheads within the business and about 300 functions. Profit is to be 15 % on cost.

Required: The price Spicemeals should charge for this function and the amount for each guest.

Q6　A medicinal product 'Supertab' is produced in batches. Batch number x308 has the following costs:

Direct labour: Grade	1	200 hours	at	£5.00
	2	50 hours	at	£8.00
	3	25 hours	at	£15.00
Direct materials: Type	A	10 kilos	at	£8.00
	B	5 kilos	at	£10.00
	C	3 kilos	at	£15.00

Production overheads are based on labour hours at £3 per hour. 20,000 tablets are produced, but there is a wastage of 10 %. Non-production overheads are £15,000 for the month. There are usually 250 batches produced per month. There are 50 tablets in a container. The selling price will be 25 % on cost.

Required: What is the selling price of each container?

Q7　Dodo Airways has agreed a tender for a new aircraft at £20 m. The company making the product has the following cost structure for this long-term contract.

	Tender		Year 1		Year 2		Year 3	
	£m	£m	£m	£m	£m	£m	£m	£m
Sales price		20		20		20		20
Direct materials	3		1		2		4.5	
Direct labour	8		2		5		8.0	
Overheads	4	15	1	4	2	9	4.5	17
Profit		5		16		11		3
Estimated costs to complete				12		7		–

Required: What is the profit Dodo should take every year? Use the formula given in this chapter (see page 416).

Q8 Serveco is a home-service computer company. There are two levels of computer service offered: basic and enhanced service. You have the following details on each.

	Basic	Enhanced
Total basic call out time	25,000 hours	37,500 hours
Total travelling time	25,000 hours	5,000 hours
Parts serviced/replaced	50,000	100,000
Technical support (mins)	75,000	100,000
Service documentation (units)	100,000	25,000
Number of call outs	50,000	10,000

You have the following costs:

	Basic	Enhanced	Total
Basic computer operatives' labour	£20 per hour	£25 per hour	
Spare parts installed			£100,000
Technical support cost			£125,000
Service documentation cost			£300,000

Serveco requires a profit mark-up of cost plus 25 %.

Required: Calculate an appropriate standard call out charge for the basic and enhanced services using activity-based costing.

Q9 A company, Rugger, manufactures two products: the Try and the Conversion. The company has traditionally allocated its production overhead costs on the basis of the 100,000 direct hours used in the manufacturing department. Direct labour costs £5 per hour. The company is now considering using activity-based costing. Details of the overheads and cost drivers are as follows:

Production Overheads	Total Cost (£)	Cost Driver	Total
(a) Manufacturing	10,000	Assembly-line hours	100,000 hours
(b) Materials handling	60,000	Number of stores notes	1,500 notes
(c) Inspection	40,000	Number of inspections	600 inspections
(d) Set-ups	5,000	Number of set-ups	500 set-ups

You have the following information about the products.

	Try	Conversion
Number of units	15,000	2,500
Assembly-line hours (direct labour) per unit	6 hours	4 hours
Direct materials per unit	£8	£100
Number of stores notes	600	900
Number of inspections	257	343
Number of set-ups	200	300

Required: Calculate a product cost using
(i)   traditional total absorption costing, recovering overheads using direct labour hours;
(ii) activity-based costing, and then
(iii) comment on any differences.

Chapter 17

"The budget is God."

Slogan at Japanese Company, Topcom (*Economist*, January 13, 1996)
***Source*: *The Wiley Book of Business Quotations* (1998), p. 90**

Learning Outcomes

After completing this chapter you should be able to:

✔ **Explain the nature and importance of budgeting.**

✔ **Outline the most important budgets.**

✔ **Prepare the major budgets and a master budget.**

✔ **Discuss the behavioural implications of budgets.**

Planning, Control and Performance: Budgeting

In a Nutshell

- *The two major branches of cost accounting are costing, and planning, control and performance.*

- *Budgeting is a key element of planning, control and performance.*

- *Budgets are ways of turning a firm's strategic objectives into practical reality.*

- *Most businesses prepare, at the minimum, a cash budget.*

- *Large businesses may also prepare a sales, a debtors and a creditors budget.*

- *Manufacturing businesses may prepare a raw materials, a production cost, and a finished goods budget.*

- *Individual budgets fit into a budgeted trading and profit and loss account and a budgeted balance sheet.*

- *Budgeting has behavioural implications for the motivation of employees.*

- *Some behavioural aspects of budgets are spending to budget, padding the budget and creative budgeting.*

- *Responsibility accounting may involve budget centres and performance measurement.*

Introduction

Cost accounting can be divided into costing, and planning, control and performance. Budgeting and standard costing are the major parts of planning, control and performance. Budgeting, or budgetary control, is a key part of businesses' planning for the future. A budget is essentially a plan for the future. Budgets are thus set in advance as a way to quantify a firm's objectives. Actual performance is then monitored against budgeted performance. For small businesses, the cash budget is often the only budget. Larger businesses, by contrast, are likely to have a complex set of interrelating budgets. These build up into a budgeted trading and profit and loss account, and budgeted balance sheet. Although usually set for a year, budgets are also linked to the longer-term strategic objectives of an organisation.

Management Accounting Control Systems

A business needs systems to control its activities. Budgeting and standard costing are two essential management control systems that enable a business to run effectively. They represent an assemblage of management accounting techniques which enable a business to plan, monitor and control ongoing financial activities. A particular aspect of a management accounting control system is that it is often set up to facilitate performance evaluation. Performance evaluation involves evaluating the performance of either individuals or departments. A key facet of performance evaluation is whether it is possible to allocate responsibility and whether the costs are controllable or uncontrollable.

Nature of Budgeting

In many ways, it would be surprising if businesses did not budget. For budgeting is part of our normal everyday lives. Whether it is a shopping trip, a university term or a night out on the town, we all generally have an informal budget of the amount we wish to spend. Businesses merely have a more formal version of this 'informal' personal budget.

PAUSE FOR THOUGHT 17.1

Personal Budgets

You are planning to jet off for an Easter break in the Mediterranean sun. What sort of items would you include in your holiday budget?

....

There would be a range of items, for example,

- transport costs to and from the airport
- cost of flight to Mediterranean
- cost of hotel
- cost of meals

- spending money
- entertainment money
- money for gifts

All these together would contribute to your holiday budget.

Planning, control and performance is one of the two major branches of cost accounting. This is shown in Figure 17.1. Standard costing is, in reality, a more tightly controlled and specialised type of budget. Although often associated with manufacturing industry, standard costs can, in fact, be used in a wide range of businesses.

Figure 17.1   Main Branches of Cost Accounting

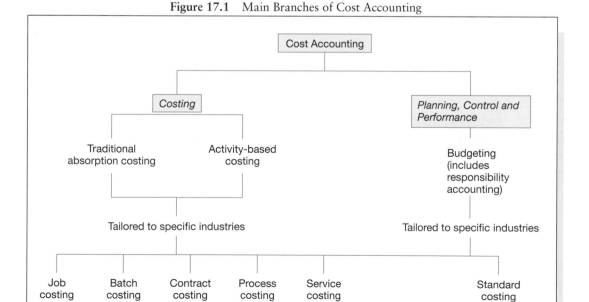

Budgeting can be viewed as a way of turning a firm's long-term strategic objectives into reality. As Figure 17.2 shows, a business's objectives are turned into forecasts and plans. These plans are then compared with the actual results and performance is evaluated.

Figure 17.2   The Budgeting Process

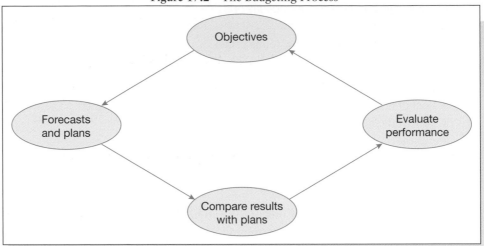

In small businesses, this process may be relatively informal. However, for large businesses there will be a complex budgeting process. The period of a budget varies. Often there is an annual budget broken down into smaller periods such as months or even weeks.

As Definition 17.1 shows, a budget is a quantitative financial plan, which sets out a business's targets.

DEFINITION 17.1

Budget

Working definition
A future plan which sets out a business's financial targets.

Formal definition
'A quantitative statement, for a defined period of time, which may include planned revenues, expenses, assets, liabilities and cash flows. A budget provides a focus for the organisation, aids the co-ordination of activities, and facilitates control.'

Source: Chartered Institute of Management Accountants (2000), *Official Terminology*

Four major aspects of budgets are planning, coordinating, motivation and control. Budgets, therefore, combine both technical and behavioural features. Budgets can be used for performance evaluation. These behavioural aspects and performance evaluation are discussed more fully later in the chapter.

(i) Planning

This involves setting out a comprehensive plan appropriate to the business. For small businesses, this may mean a cash budget. For larger businesses, there will probably be a formalised and sophisticated budgeting system.

(ii) Coordinating

A key aspect of the budgetary process is that it relates the various activities of a company to each other. Therefore, sales are related to purchases, and purchases to production. The business can be viewed as an interlocking whole.

(iii) Motivation

By setting targets the budget has important motivational aspects. If the targets are too hard, they can be demotivating. If too easy, they will not provide any motivation at all.

(iv) Control

This is achieved through a system of making individual managers responsible for individual budgets. When actual results are compared against target results, individual managers will be asked to explain any differences (or variances). The manager's performance is then evaluated. Budgets, as Real-Life Nugget 17.1 shows, are an indispensable form of administrative control. Formal performance evaluation mechanisms such as responsibility accounting are often introduced.

REAL-LIFE NUGGET 17.1

Budgeting

Budgeting now occupies a central position in the design and operation of most management accounting systems. Almost regardless of the type of organisation, the nature of its problems and the other means for influencing behaviour, the preparation of a quantitative statement of expectations regarding the allocation of the organisation's resources tends to be seen as an essential, indeed indispensable, feature of the battery of administrative controls. Nevertheless, despite its wide acceptance, budgeting remains one of the most intriguing and perplexing of management accounting procedures.

Source: A. Hopwood (1974), *Accounting and Human Behaviour*, p. 39

In large businesses, budgets are generally set by a budgetary committee. This will normally involve managers from many different departments. The sales manager, for example, may provide information on likely future sales, which will form the basis of the sales budget. However, it is important that individual budgets are meshed together to provide a coordinated and coherent plan. As Soundbite 17.1 shows, the starting point for this year's budget is usually last year's budget. A form of budgeting called *zero based budgeting* assumes the activities are being incurred for the first time. The budgetary process is normally ongoing, however, with meetings during the year to review progress against the current budget and to set future budgets.

SOUNDBITE 17.1

Last Year's Budget

'The largest determining factor of the size and content of this year's budget is last year's budget.'

Aaron Wildavsky, The Politics of the Budgetary Process, 1964

Source: The Executive's Book of Quotations (1994), p. 39

Although budgets are set within the business, external factors will often constrain them. A key external constraint is demand. It is futile for a company to plan to make ten million motorised skateboards if there is demand for only five million. Indeed, potential sales are the principal factor that limits the expansion of many businesses. Usually, the sales budget is determined first. Some businesses employ a *materials requirement planning* (MRP) system. Based on sales demand, MRP coordinates production and purchasing to ensure the optimal flow of raw materials and optimal level of raw material stocks. Another important budgetary constraint in manufacturing industry is production capacity. It is useless planning to sell ten million motorised skateboards if the production capacity is only five million. A key element of the budgetary process is thus harmonising demand and supply.

Nowadays, it is rare for businesses not to have budgets. As Figure 17.3 shows, budgets have many advantages. The chief disadvantages are that budgets can be inflexible and create behavioural problems. Budgets can be inflexible if set for a year. It is common to revise budgets regularly to take account of new circumstances. This is easier when they are prepared using spreadsheets. The behavioural problems may be created, for example, when individuals attempt to manipulate the budgeting process in their own interest. This is discussed later.

Figure 17.3   The Benefits of Budgeting

- Strategic planning can be more easily linked to management decisions
- Standards can be set to aid performance evaluation
- Plans can be set in financial terms
- Managers can be made responsible for budgets
- Budgets encourage cooperation and coordination

Cash Budget

The cash budget is probably the most important of all budgets. Almost all companies prepare one. Indeed, banks will often insist on a cash budget before they lend money to small businesses. For a sole trader, the cash budget is often as important as the trading and profit and loss account and balance sheet. It reflects the need to balance profitability and liquidity. There are similarities, but also differences, between the cash budget and the cash flow statement that we saw in Chapter 8.

PAUSE FOR THOUGHT 17.2

Budgets

Budgets are often said to create inflexibility as they are typically set for a year in advance. Can you think of any ways to overcome this inflexibility?

....

This inflexibility can be dealt with in two ways: rolling budgets and flexible budgets. With rolling budgets the budget is updated every month. There is then a new twelve-month budget. The problem with rolling budgets is that it takes a lot of time and effort to update budgets regularly. Flexible budgets attempt to deal with inflexibility by setting a range of budgets with different activity levels. So a company might budget for servicing 100,000, 150,000 or 200,000 customers. In this case, there would, in effect, be three budgets for three different levels of business activity.

They are similar in that both the cash budget and cash flow statement chart the flows of cash within a business. The differences arise in that the cash flow statement is normally prepared in a standardised format in accordance with accounting regulations and looks backwards in time. By contrast, the cash budget is not in a standardised format and looks forward in time.

Essentially, the cash budget looks into the future. Figure 17.4 gives the format of the cash budget. We start with the opening cash balance. Receipts are then recorded, for example, cash received from cash sales, from debtors or from the sale of fixed assets. Cash payments are then listed, for example, cash purchases of goods, payments to creditors or expenses paid. Receipts less payments provide the monthly cash flow. Opening cash and cash flow determine the closing cash balance.

Figure 17.4   The Format of a Cash Budget

	Jan. £	Feb. £	March £	April £	May £	June £	Total £
Opening cash	X	X	X	X	X	X	X
Add *Receipts*							
Debtors	X	X	X	X	X	X	X
	X	X	X	X	X	X	X
Less *Payments*							
Payments for goods	X	X	X	X	X	X	X
Expenses	X	X	X	X	X	X	X
Other payments	X	X	X	X	X	X	X
	X	X	X	X	X	X	X
Cash flow	Y	Y	Y	Y	Y	Y	Y
Closing cash	X	X	X	X	X	X	X

In Figure 17.5, we show an actual example of how in practice a cash budget is constructed.

Figure 17.5   Illustrative Example of a Cash Budget

Jason Chan has £12,000 in a business bank account. His projections for the first six months trading are as follows.
(i)   Credit sales will be: January £8,800, February £8,800, March £9,000, April £12,500, May £20,200, June £30,000. Debtors pay in the month following sale.
(ii)   Goods supplied on credit will be: January £7,000, February £10,000, March £9,800, April £10,400, May £7,000, June £8,000. Creditors are paid one month in arrears.
(iii)   Loan receivable 1 March £4,000 to be repaid in full plus £400 interest on 1 June.
(iv)   Drawing £500 per month.
Prepare the cash budget.

	Jan. £	Feb. £	March £	April £	May £	June £	Total £
Opening cash	12,000	11,500	12,800	15,100	13,800	15,400	12,000
Add *Receipts*							
Debtors		8,800	8,800	9,000	12,500	20,200	59,300
Loan received			4,000				4,000
	–	8,800	12,800	9,000	12,500	20,200	63,300
Less *Payments*							
Payments for goods		7,000	10,000	9,800	10,400	7,000	44,200
Loan repayment						4,400	4,400
Drawings	500	500	500	500	500	500	3,000
	500	7,500	10,500	10,300	10,900	11,900	51,600
Cash flow	*(500)*	*1,300*	*2,300*	*(1,300)*	*1,600*	*8,300*	*11,700*
Closing cash	11,500	12,800	15,100	13,800	15,400	23,700	23,700

Helpnotes:
(i) The receipts from debtors and payments by creditors are thus running one month behind actual sales and actual purchases, respectively. Thus, for example, the debtors will pay the £30,000 of sales made in June in July and they are, therefore, not recorded in this budget.
(ii) The cash flow column is simply total receipts less total payments. Cash outflows (where receipts are less than payments) are recorded in brackets.

Other Budgets

A business may have numerous other budgets. Indeed, each department of a large business is likely to have a budget. In this section, we will look at three key budgets common to many businesses: sales budget; debtors budget and creditors budget.

In the next section, we will look at three additional budgets that are commonly found in manufacturing businesses: raw materials budget, finished goods budget and production cost budget. Finally, we will bring the budgets together in a comprehensive example.

(i) Sales Budget

The sales budget is determined by examining how much the business is likely to sell during the forthcoming period. Figure 17.6 provides an example. Sales budgets like many other budgets can be initially expressed in units before being converted to £s. In many businesses, the sales budget is the key budget as it determines the other budgets. The sales budget is, therefore, often set first.

Figure 17.6   Example of a Sales Budget

A business has two products, Alpha and Omega. It is anticipated that sales of the Alpha will run at 500 units throughout January to June. However, the Omega will start at 1,000 units and rise by 100 units per month. Each Alpha sells at £35, each Omega sells at £50. Prepare the sales budget.

	Jan. £	Feb. £	March £	April £	May £	June £	Total £
Alpha	17,500	17,500	17,500	17,500	17,500	17,500	105,000
Omega	50,000	55,000	60,000	65,000	70,000	75,000	375,000
Total sales	67,500	72,500	77,500	82,500	87,500	92,500	480,000

(ii) Debtors Budget

The debtors budget begins with opening debtors (often taken from the opening balance sheet) to which are added credit sales (often taken from the sales budget). Cash receipts are then deducted, leaving closing debtors. An example of the format for a debtors budget is provided in Figure 17.7, while Figure 17.8 on the next page provides an illustrative example.

Figure 17.7   Format of a Debtors Budget

	Jan. £	Feb. £	March £	April £	May £	June £	Total £
Opening debtors	X	X	X	X	X	X	X
Credit sales	X	X	X	X	X	X	X
	X	X	X	X	X	X	X
Cash received from debtors	(X)	(X)	(X)	(X)	(X)	(X)	(X)
Closing debtors	X	X	X	X	X	X	X

Figure 17.8   Example of a Debtors Budget

Sara Peters has opening debtors of £800. Debtors pay one month in arrears. Sales are forecast to be £900 in January rising by £200 per month. Prepare the debtors budget.

	Jan. £	Feb. £	March £	April £	May £	June £	Total £
Opening debtors	800	900	1,100	1,300	1,500	1,700	800
Credit sales	900	1,100	1,300	1,500	1,700	1,900	8,400
	1,700	2,000	2,400	2,800	3,200	3,600	9,200
Cash received	(800)	(900)	(1,100)	(1,300)	(1,500)	(1,700)	(7,300)
Closing debtors	900	1,100	1,300	1,500	1,700	1,900	1,900

(iii) Creditors Budget

In many ways, the creditors budget is the mirror image of the debtors budget. It starts with opening creditors (often taken from the opening balance sheet), adds credit purchases and then deducts cash paid. The result is closing creditors. The format for the creditors budget is given in Figure 17.9, while Figure 17.10 provides an illustrative example.

Figure 17.9   Format of a Creditors Budget

	Jan. £	Feb. £	March £	April £	May £	June £	Total £
Opening creditors	X	X	X	X	X	X	X
Credit purchases	X	X	X	X	X	X	X
	X	X	X	X	X	X	X
Cash paid to creditors	(X)	(X)	(X)	(X)	(X)	(X)	(X)
Closing creditors	X	X	X	X	X	X	X

Figure 17.10   Example of a Creditors Budget

Jon Matthews has opening creditors of £1,200. Creditors are expected to pay one month in arrears. In January, purchases are forecast to be £9,000 rising by £100 per month. Prepare the creditors budget.

	Jan. £	Feb. £	March £	April £	May £	June £	Total £
Opening creditors	1,200	9,000	9,100	9,200	9,300	9,400	1,200
Credit purchases	9,000	9,100	9,200	9,300	9,400	9,500	55,500
	10,200	18,100	18,300	18,500	18,700	18,900	56,700
Cash paid	(1,200)	(9,000)	(9,100)	(9,200)	(9,300)	(9,400)	(47,200)
Closing creditors	9,000	9,100	9,200	9,300	9,400	9,500	9,500

Manufacturing Budgets

Manufacturing companies normally hold more stock than other businesses. It is, therefore, common to find three additional budgets: a production cost budget; a raw materials budget; and a finished goods budget. Often these budgets are expressed in units, which are then converted into £s. For ease of understanding, we express them here only in financial terms.

(i) Production Cost Budget

The production cost budget, as its name suggests, estimates the cost of production. This involves direct labour, direct materials and production overheads. There may often be sub-budgets for each of these items. The production cost format is shown in Figure 17.11, while Figure 17.12 shows an example. Once the production cost is determined, the finished goods budget can be prepared. It is important to realise that the budgeted production levels are generally determined by the amount the business can sell.

Figure 17.11   Format of a Production Cost Budget

	Jan. £	Feb. £	March £	April £	May £	June £	Total £
Direct materials	X	X	X	X	X	X	X
Direct labour	X	X	X	X	X	X	X
Production overheads	X	X	X	X	X	X	X
	X	X	X	X	X	X	X

Figure 17.12   Example of a Production Cost Budget

Ray Anderson has the following forecast details from his production department. Direct materials are £6 per unit, direct labour is £8 per unit and production overheads are £4 per unit. 1,000 units will be made in January rising by 100 units per month. Prepare the production cost budget.

	Jan. £	Feb. £	March £	April £	May £	June £	Total £
Direct materials	6,000	6,600	7,200	7,800	8,400	9,000	45,000
Direct labour	8,000	8,800	9,600	10,400	11,200	12,000	60,000
Production overheads	4,000	4,400	4,800	5,200	5,600	6,000	30,000
	18,000	19,800	21,600	23,400	25,200	27,000	135,000
Units	1,000	1,100	1,200	1,300	1,400	1,500	7,500

(ii) Raw Materials Budget

The raw materials budget is particularly useful as it provides a forecast of how much raw material the company needs to buy. This can supply the purchases figure for the creditors budget. The raw materials budget format is shown in Figure 17.13. It starts with opening stock of raw materials (often taken from the opening balance sheet); purchases are then added. The amount used in production is then subtracted, arriving at closing stock. An example is shown in Figure 17.14.

Figure 17.13   Format of a Raw Materials Budget

	Jan. £	Feb. £	March £	April £	May £	June £	Total £
Opening stock of raw materials	X	X	X	X	X	X	X
Purchases	X	X	X	X	X	X	X
	X	X	X	X	X	X	X
Used in production	(X)	(X)	(X)	(X)	(X)	(X)	(X)
Closing stock of raw materials	X	X	X	X	X	X	X

Figure 17.14   Example of a Raw Materials Budget

Dai Jones has opening raw materials stock of £1,200. Purchases of raw materials will be £600 in January, increasing by £75 per month. Production will be 400 units per month using £2 raw material per unit. Prepare the raw materials budget.

	Jan. £	Feb. £	March £	April £	May £	June £	Total £
Opening stock of raw materials	1,200	1,000	875	825	850	950	1,200
Purchases	600	675	750	825	900	975	4,725
	1,800	1,675	1,625	1,650	1,750	1,925	5,925
Used in production	(800)	(800)	(800)	(800)	(800)	(800)	(4,800)
Closing stock of raw materials	1,000	875	825	850	950	1,125	1,125

(iii) Finished Goods Budget

The finished goods budget is similar to the raw materials budget except it deals with finished goods. As Figure 17.15 shows, it starts with the opening stock of finished goods (often taken from the balance sheet), the amount produced is then added (from the production cost budget). The cost of sales (i.e., cost of the goods sold) is then deducted. Finally, it finishes with the closing stock of finished goods. The finished goods budget is useful for keeping a check on whether the business is producing sufficient goods to meet demand. Figure 17.16 gives an example of a finished goods budget.

Figure 17.15   Format of a Finished Goods Budget

	Jan. £	Feb. £	March £	April £	May £	June £	Total £
Opening stock of finished goods	X	X	X	X	X	X	X
Produced	X	X	X	X	X	X	X
	X	X	X	X	X	X	X
Cost of sales	(X)	(X)	(X)	(X)	(X)	(X)	(X)
Closing stock of finished goods	X	X	X	X	X	X	X

Figure 17.16   Example of a Finished Goods Budget

Ranjit Patel has £8,000 of finished good stocks in January. 1,000 units per month will be produced at a product cost of £10 each. Sales will be £10,000 in January rising by £1,000 per month. Gross profit is 25% of sales. Prepare the finished goods budget.

	Jan. £	Feb. £	March £	April £	May £	June £	Total £
Opening stock of finished goods	8,000	10,500	12,250	13,250	13,500	13,000	8,000
Produced	10,000	10,000	10,000	10,000	10,000	10,000	60,000
	18,000	20,500	22,250	23,250	23,500	23,000	68,000
Cost of sales*	(7,500)	(8,250)	(9,000)	(9,750)	(10,500)	(11,250)	(56,250)
Closing stock of finished goods	10,500	12,250	13,250	13,500	13,000	11,750	11,750
*Cost of sales is 75% of sales	10,000	1,000	12,000	13,000	14,000	15,000	75,000

Comprehensive Budgeting Example

Once all the budget have been prepared, it is important to gain an overview of how the business is expected to perform. Normally, a budgeted trading and profit and loss account and budgeted balance sheet are drawn up. This is often called a master budget. The full process is now illustrated using the example of Jacobs Engineering (see Figure 17.17), a manufacturing company. A manufacturing company is used so as to illustrate the full range of budgets

Figure 17.17   Comprehensive Budgeting Example

Jacobs Engineering is a small manufacturing company. There are the following forecast summarised details.

Jacobs Engineering Ltd
Balance Sheet (Abridged) as at 31 December 2009

	£	£	£
Fixed Assets			100,000
Current Assets			
Debtors (Nov. £13,000, Dec £14,000)	27,000		
Stock of raw materials	10,000		
Stock of finished goods	15,000	52,000	
Current Liabilities			
Creditors (Nov. £12,000, Dec. £13,000)	(25,000)		
Bank overdraft	(7,000)	(32,000)	
Net current assets			20,000
Total net assets			120,000

	£
Share Capital and Reserves	
Share Capital	
Ordinary share capital	90,000
Reserves	
Profit and loss account	30,000
Total shareholders' funds	120,000

Notes:

1. Depreciation is 10 % straight line basis per year.
2. Purchases will be £10,000 in January, increasing by £300 per month. They are payable two months after purchase.
3. Sales will be 450 units of product A at average production cost plus 25 % and 500 units of product B at average production cost plus 20 %. Debtors will pay two months in arrears.
4. Average production cost *per unit* remains the same as last year and is the same for product A and product B. It consists of direct materials £10, direct labour £7, production overheads £3. Both direct labour and production overheads will be paid in the month used. Production 1,000 units per month.
5. Non-production expenses are £4,000 per month, and will be paid in the month incurred.

Required: Prepare the sales budget, cash budget, debtors budget, creditors budget, production cost budget, finished goods budget, raw materials budget, budgeted trading, profit and loss account and budgeted balance sheet for six months ending 30 June, 2010.

Figure 17.17   Comprehensive Budgeting Example (*continued*)

Sales Budget

	Jan. £	Feb. £	March £	April £	May £	June £	Total £
Product A*	11,250	11,250	11,250	11,250	11,250	11,250	67,500
Product B**	12,000	12,000	12,000	12,000	12,000	12,000	72,000
	23,250	23,250	23,250	23,250	23,250	23,250	139,500

* (450 units × (£20 average production cost, i.e. direct materials £10, direct labour £7 and production overheads £3) plus 25 %

** (500 units × (£20 average production cost, i.e. direct materials £10, direct labour £7 and production overheads £3) plus 20 %

Cash Budget

	Jan. £	Feb. £	March £	April £	May £	June £	Total £
Opening cash	(7,000)	(20,000)	(33,000)	(33,750)	(34,800)	(36,150)	(7,000)
Add Receipts							
Debtors	13,000	14,000	23,250	23,250	23,250	23,250	120,000
	13,000	14,000	23,250	23,250	23,250	23,250	120,000
Less Payments							
Payment for goods	12,000	13,000	10,000	10,300	10,600	10,900	66,800
Non-production expenses	4,000	4,000	4,000	4,000	4,000	4,000	24,000
Direct labour	7,000	7,000	7,000	7,000	7,000	7,000	42,000
Production overheads	3,000	3,000	3,000	3,000	3,000	3,000	18,000
	26,000	27,000	24,000	24,300	24,600	24,900	150,800
Cash flow	(13,000)	(13,000)	(750)	(1,050)	(1,350)	(1,650)	(30,800)
Closing cash	(20,000)	(33,000)	(33,750)	(34,800)	(36,150)	(37,800)	(37,800)

Debtors Budget

	Jan. £	Feb. £	March £	April £	May £	June £	Total £
Opening debtors	27,000	37,250	46,500	46,500	46,500	46,500	27,000
Credit sales	23,250	23,250	23,250	23,250	23,250	23,250	139,500
	50,250	60,500	69,750	69,750	69,750	69,750	166,500
Cash received	(13,000)	(14,000)	(23,250)	(23,250)	(23,250)	(23,250)	(120,000)
Closing debtors	37,250	46,500	46,500	46,500	46,500	46,500	46,500

Figure 17.17   Comprehensive Budgeting Example (*continued*)

Creditors Budget

	Jan. £	Feb. £	March £	April £	May £	June £	Total £
Opening creditors	25,000	23,000	20,300	20,900	21,500	22,100	25,000
Credit purchases	10,000	10,300	10,600	10,900	11,200	11,500	64,500
	35,000	33,300	30,900	31,800	32,700	33,600	89,500
Cash paid	(12,000)	(13,000)	(10,000)	(10,300)	(10,600)	(10,900)	(66,800)
Closing creditors	23,000	20,300	20,900	21,500	22,100	22,700	22,700

Production Cost Budget

	Jan. £	Feb. £	March £	April £	May £	June £	Total £
Direct materials	10,000	10,000	10,000	10,000	10,000	10,000	60,000
Direct labour	7,000	7,000	7,000	7,000	7,000	7,000	42,000
Production overheads	3,000	3,000	3,000	3,000	3,000	3,000	18,000
	20,000	20,000	20,000	20,000	20,000	20,000	120,000

Finished Goods Budget

	Jan. £	Feb. £	March £	April £	May £	June £	Total £
Opening stock of finished goods	15,000	16,000	17,000	18,000	19,000	20,000	15,000
Produced	20,000	20,000	20,000	20,000	20,000	20,000	120,000
	35,000	36,000	37,000	38,000	39,000	40,000	135,000
Cost of sales*	(19,000)	(19,000)	(19,000)	(19,000)	(19,000)	(19,000)	(114,000)
Closing stock of finished goods	16,000	17,000	18,000	19,000	20,000	21,000	21,000

*(950 units × £20)

Raw Materials Budget

	Jan. £	Feb. £	March £	April £	May £	June £	Total £
Opening stock of raw materials	10,000	10,000	10,300	10,900	11,800	13,000	10,000
Purchases	10,000	10,300	10,600	10,900	11,200	11,500	64,500
	20,000	20,300	20,900	21,800	23,000	24,500	74,500
Used in production*	(10,000)	(10,000)	(10,000)	(10,000)	(10,000)	(10,000)	(60,000)
Closing stock of raw materials	10,000	10,300	10,900	11,800	13,000	14,500	14,500

*1,000 units per month × £10 direct materials.

Figure 17.17   Comprehensive Budgeting Example (*continued*)

Jacobs Ltd Engineering
Budgeted Trading and Profit and Loss Account
for Year Ending 30 June 2010

	£	£	Source budget
Sales		139,500	Sales
Less *Cost of Sales*		114,000	Finished goods
Gross Profit		25,500	
Less *Expenses*			
Depreciation	10,000		–
Expenses	24,000	34,000	
Net Loss		(8,500)	–

Jacobs Ltd Engineering
Budgeted Balance Sheet as at 30 June 2010

	£ Cost	£ Accumulated depreciation	£ Net book value	Source Budget
Fixed Assets	100,000	(10,000)	90,000	
Current Assets				
Debtors	46,500			Debtors
Stock of raw materials	14,500			Raw materials
Stock of finished goods	21,000	82,000		Finished goods
Current Liabilities				
Creditors	(22,700)			Creditors
Bank overdraft	(37,800)	(60,500)		Cash
Net current assets			21,500	
Total net assets			111,500	
Share Capital and Reserves				
Share Capital			£	Opening balance
Ordinary share capital			90,000	sheet
Reserves				
Opening profit and loss account		30,000		Opening balance sheet
Less: Loss for year		(8,500)	21,500	Trading and
Total shareholders' funds			111,500	profit and loss account

discussed in this chapter. An overview of the whole process is presented in Figure 17.18. It must be appreciated that Figure 17.18 does not include all possible budgets (for example, many businesses have labour, selling and administration budgets). However, Figure 17.18 does give a good appreciation of the basic budgetary flows.

Figure 17.18   Budgeting Overview

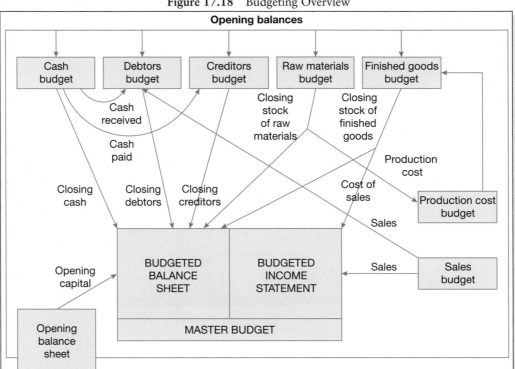

After the budgetary period, the actual results are compared against the budgeted results. Any differences between the two sets of results will be investigated and action taken, if appropriate. This basic principle of investigating why any variances have occurred is common in both budgeting and standard costing.

Behavioural Aspects of Budgeting

It is important to realise that there are several, sometimes competing, functions of budgets, for example, planning, coordinating, motivation and control. Budgeting is thus a mixture of technical (planning and coordinating) and behavioural (motivation and control) aspects. In short, budgets affect the behaviour of individuals within firms.

The budgetary process is all about setting targets and individuals meeting those targets. The problem is that an optimal target for the business is not necessarily optimal for the individual employee. Conflicts of interest, therefore, arise between the individual and the company. It may, for example, be in a company's interests to set a very demanding budget. However, it is not necessarily in the employee's interests. Budgets can, therefore, have powerful motivational or demotivational effects. For employees, in particular, budgets are often treated with great suspicion. Managers often use budgets deliberately as a motivational tool (see Real-Life Nugget 17.2).

REAL-LIFE NUGGET 17.2

Budgetary Optimism

Where senior managers and accountants use a single budget and are reluctant to relinquish it as a motivational tool, which they often are, the problem gives rise to the 'bottom drawer phenomenon'. The main budget is designed to include some reflection of aspired performance levels, but the senior accountants keep another version in the bottom drawer of their desks which tries to make some allowance for the prevailing corporate optimism. Sometimes this merely takes the form of an overall 5 per cent or 10 per cent, but in other organisations, it is done on a departmental basis, with 5 per cent off Fred's budget and possibly 15 per cent off Joe's, depending on estimates of the aspirational element in each case. This is obviously done because senior management required a more realistic statement of expected performance for decision and planning purposes.

Source: A. Hopwood (1974), *Accounting and Human Behaviour*, p. 63

To demonstrate the behavioural impact of budgeting, we look below at three behavioural practices associated with budgeting: spending to budget; padding the budget; and creative budgeting.

SOUNDBITE 17.2

Spending to Budget

'People spend what's in a budget, whether they need it or not.'

George W. Sztykiel, *Fortune* (December 28, 1992)

Source: *The Wiley Book of Business Quotations* (1998), p. 90

(i) Spending to Budget

Many companies allocate their expense budget for the year. If the budget is not spent, then the department loses the money. This is a double whammy as often next year's budget is based on this year's. So an underspend this year will also result in less to spend next year. It is in managers' individual interests (but not necessarily in the firm's interests) to avoid this. Managers, therefore, will spend money at the last-minute on items such as recarpeting of offices. This is the idea behind the cartoon at the start of this chapter!

PAUSE FOR THOUGHT 17.3

Spending to Budget

Jane Morris has a department and was allocated £120,000 to spend for year ended 31 December 2005. In 2006, the budget is based on the 2005 budget plus 10% inflation. She spends prudently so that by 1 December she has spent £90,000. Normal expenditure would be a further £10,000. Thus, she would have spent £100,000 in total. What might she do?

Well, it is possible she might give the £20,000 unspent back to head office. However, this will result in only £110,000 (£100,000 + 10%) next year. More likely she will try to spend the surplus. For example, buy

- a new computer
- new office furniture
- new carpets

REAL-LIFE NUGGET 17.3

Padding the Budget

Managers seek out and receive facts and opinions in order to arrive at an estimate of what they should ask for in the light of what they can expect to get and then, with due '*padding*' made to allow for anticipated cuts, they seek to market their budgetary demands. As in the initial example, the support of other parties can be actively canvassed and demands packaged in the most appealing form. Tangible results can be given undue weight and complex activities described in either the simplest or the most complex of terms ... Emphasis can be placed on the qualitative rather than measurable advantages, the forthcoming rather than current results, and the procedures rather than the outcome.

Source: A. Hopwood (1974), *Accounting and Human Behaviour*, p. 56

(ii) Padding the Budget

Budgets are set by people. Therefore, there is a great temptation for individuals to try to create slack in the system to give themselves some leeway. For example, *you might think* that your department's sales next year will be £120,000 and the expenses will be £90,000. Therefore, you think you will make £30,000 profit. However, at the budgetary committee *you might argue* that your sales will be only £110,000 and your expenses will be £100,000. You are, therefore, attempting to set the budget so that your profit is £10,000 (i.e., £110,000 – £100,000). You have, therefore, built in £20,000 budgetary slack (£30,000 profit [true position] less £10,000 profit [argued position]). Real-Life Nugget 17.3 demonstrates the negotiating process involved in padding the budget.

(iii) Creative Budgeting

If departmental managers are rewarded on the basis of the profit their department makes, then they may indulge in creative budgeting. Creative budgeting may, for example, involve deferring expenditure planned for this year until next year (see, for example, Figure 17.19).

Figure 17.19   Creative Budgeting

Jasper Grant gets a bonus of £1,000 if he meets his budgeted profit of £100,000 for the year ending in December. At the end of November, he has the following information.

	£
Sales commission to date	200,000
Extra sales commission for December	25,000
Expenses to date	97,000
Expenses to be incurred	
: Weekly press advertising	3,000
: Repairs	8,000
: Necessary expenses	25,000

How can Jasper meet budget?

At the moment, Jasper's situation is as follows:

	£
Sales commission (£200,000 + £25,000)	225,000
Less: *Expenses* (£97,000 incurred + £36,000 anticipated)	133,000
Actual Profit	92,000
Budgeted Profit	100,000
Budgetary Shortfall	(8,000)

Jasper would, therefore, fail to meet his budgeted profit.

However, if the advertising and repairs were deferred until the next period, Jasper would make the budget. So he might be tempted to defer them.

	£
Sales commission	225,000
Less: Expenses to date	97,000
Necessary expenses	25,000
Actual Profit	103,000
Budgeted Profit	100,000
Surplus over Budget	3,000

Jasper would, therefore, gain his bonus as he would meet his target. However, what is good for Jasper is not necessarily good for his firm. By not advertising or having repairs done quickly it is likely that the long-term productivity of the firm will suffer.

Responsibility Accounting

The behavioural aspects of budgeting can be utilised when designing responsibility accounting systems. In such systems, organisations are divided into budgetary areas, known as responsibility centres. Managers are held accountable for the activities within these centres. As Figure 17.20 shows there are different sorts of responsibility centre.

Figure 17.20   Responsibility Centres and Managerial Accountability

Responsibility Centre	Managerial Accountability
Revenue Centre	Revenues
Cost Centre	Costs
Profit Centre	Revenues, costs and thus profits
Investment Centre	Revenues and costs (i.e., profits) and investment

Managers of investment centres thus have more responsibility than those of profit centres who in turn have more responsibility than managers of cost or revenue centres. A key aspect of responsibility accounting is that the manager is responsible for controllable costs, but not uncontrollable costs. Controllable costs are simply those costs that a manager can be expected to influence.

Responsibility accounting is a way of monitoring the activities of managers and judging their performance. The budgeted costs, revenues and profits are compared with the actual results. Managers can be rewarded or penalised accordingly often by the payment or non-payment of bonuses.

Investment centres are often evaluated using specific performance measures. Three of the most common are Return on Investment (ROI), Residual Income (RI) and Return on Sales (ROS). These three ratios are outlined in Figure 17.21.

Figure 17.21   Three Performance Measures

Ratio	Definition	Comments
i. Return on Investment (ROI)	$\dfrac{\text{Income}}{\text{Investment}}$	Simple, but often investment difficult to determine. Does not take size into account. Similar to return on capital employed.
ii. Residual Income (RI)	Income − (required rate of return × investment)	Quite simple; can use quite an arbitrary rate of return.
iii. Return on Sales (ROS)	$\dfrac{\text{Operating profit}}{\text{Sales}}$	Quite simple. Definition of profit may be difficult. Similar to net profit ratio.

Below, in Figure 17.22, is an example of how these particular measures may be used in practice. The example of three divisions of an international car hire firm is used, HireCarCo. These are based in London, Paris and Berlin.

Figure 17.22   Performance Measures for Three Divisions

HireCarCo has three operating divisions in London, Paris and Berlin. Each acts as a broadly independent investment centre. The key figures are set out below

	London	Paris	Berlin
	£m	£m	£m
Investment	1,000,000	800,000	600,000
	£m	£m	£m
Sales	500,000	350,000	200,000
Costs	(300,000)	(180,000)	(120,000)
Operating profit	200,000	170,000	80,000

Required:

Calculate   a) Return on Investment (ROI)
b) Residual Income (RI) – assuming the required rate of return is 10 %
c) Return on Sales (ROS)

	London	Paris	Berlin
i) Return on Investment			
$\dfrac{\text{Income}}{\text{Investment}}$	$\dfrac{£200,000}{£1,000,000} = 20\%$	$\dfrac{£170,000}{£800,000} = 21.2\%$	$\dfrac{£80,000}{£600,000} = 13.3\%$
ii) Residual Income			
Income – (Required Rate of Return × Investment)	£200,000 – (£1,000,000 × 10%) = £100,000	£170,000 – (£800,000 × 10%) = £90,000	£80,000 – (£600,000 × 10%) = £20,000
iii) Return on Sales			
$\dfrac{\text{Operating Profit}}{\text{Sales}}$	$\dfrac{£200,000}{£600,000} = 33.3\%$	$\dfrac{£170,000}{£350,000} = 48.6\%$	$\dfrac{£80,000}{£200,000} = 40\%$

From the results, it can be seen that measured by return on investment and return on sales the manager of the Paris branch would be judged to be performing the best. However, in absolute terms, the London manager has done best having the highest residual income.

Conclusion

Budgeting is planning for the future. This is important as a business needs to compare its actual performance against its targets. Most businesses prepare a cash budget and large businesses often prepare a complex set of interlocking budgets which culminate in a budgeted trading and profit and loss account and a budgeted balance sheet. Budgets have a human as well as a technical side. As well as being useful for planning and coordination, budgets are used to motivate and monitor individuals. Budgets are often used as the basis for performance evaluation. Sometimes, therefore, the interests of individuals and businesses may conflict.

Q&A   Discussion Questions

Questions with numbers in blue have answers at the back of the book.

Q1 What are the advantages and disadvantages of budgeting?

Q2 Why do some people think that the cash budget is the most important budget?

Q3 The behavioural aspects of budgeting are often overlooked, but are extremely important. Do you agree?

Q4 State whether the following statements are true or false? If false, explain why.
   (a) The four main aspects of budgets are planning, coordinating, control and motivation.
   (b) The commonest limiting factor on the budgeting process is production.
   (c) A master budget is formed by feeding in the results from all the other budgets.
   (d) Depreciation is commonly found in a cash budget.
   (e) Spending to budget, padding the budget and creative budgeting are all common behavioural responses to budgeting.

Q&A   Numerical Questions

Questions with numbers in blue have answers at the back of the book.

Q1 Jill Lee starts her business on 1 January with £15,000 in the bank. Her plans for the first six months are as follows.
   (a) Payments for goods will be made one month after purchase:

January	February	March	April	May	June
£21,000	£19,500	£18,500	£23,400	£25,900	£31,100

(b) All sales will be cash sales:

January	February	March	April	May	June
£25,200	£27,100	£21,200	£20,250	£48,300	£37,500

(c) Expenses will be £12,000 in January and will rise by 10 % per month. They will be paid in the month incurred.

Required: Prepare Jill Lee's cash budget from 1 January to 30 June.

Q2   John Rees has the following information for the six months 1 July to 31 December.
(a) Opening cash balance 1 July £8,600
(b) Sales at £25 per unit:

	April	May	June	July	Aug.	Sept.	Oct.	Nov.	Dec.
Units	100	130	150	180	200	210	220	240	280

Debtors will pay two months after they have bought the goods.
(c) Production in units:

	April	May	June	July	Aug.	Sept.	Oct.	Nov.	Dec.	Jan.
Units	140	140	140	180	200	190	200	210	260	200

(d) Raw materials costing £10 per unit are delivered in the month of production and will be paid for three months after the goods are used in production.
(e) Direct labour of £6 per unit will be payable in the same month as production.
(f) Other variable production expenses will be £6 per unit. Two-thirds of this cost will be paid for in the same month as production and one-third in the month following production.
(g) Other expenses of £200 per month will be paid one month in arrears. These expenses have been at this rate for the past two years.
(h) A machine will be bought and paid for in September for £8,000.
(i) John Rees plans to borrow £4,500 from a relative in December. This will be banked immediately.

Required: Prepare John Rees's cash budget from 1 July to 31 December.

Q3   Fly-by-Night plc has the following sales forecasts for two products: the Moon and the Star.
(a) The Moon will sell at 1,000 units in January, rising by 50 units per month. From January to March each Moon will sell at £20, with the price rising to £25 from April to June.
(b) The Star will sell 2,000 units in January rising by 100 units per month. Each Star will sell at £10.

Required: Prepare the sales budget for Fly-by-Night from January to June.

Q4   David Ingo has opening debtors of £2,400 (November £1,400, December £1,000). The debtors will pay two months in arrears. Credit sales in January will be £1,000 rising by 10 % per month.

Required: Prepare D. Ingo's debtors budget for January to June.

Q5   Thomas Iger has opening creditors of £2,900 (£400 October, £1,200 November, £1,300 December). Creditors will be paid three months in arrears. Credit purchases in January will be £2,000 rising by £200 per month until March and then suffering a 10 % decline in April and remaining constant.

Required: Prepare T. Iger's creditors budget for January to June.

Q6   Brenda Ear will have production costs per unit of £5 raw materials, £5.50 direct labour and £2 variable overheads. Production will be 700 units in January rising by 50 units per month.

Required: Prepare B. Ear's production cost budget for January to June.

Q7   Roger Abbit has £1,000 opening stocks of raw materials. Purchases will be £900 in January rising by £200 per month. Production will be 240 units from January to March at £4 raw materials per unit, rising to 250 units per month at £5 raw materials per unit from April to June.

Required: Prepare R. Abbit's raw materials budget for January to June.

Q8   Freddie Ox has £9,000 of opening finished goods stocks. In July, 1,500 units will be produced at a production cost of £10 each. Production will increase at 100 units per month; production cost remains steady. Sales will be £15,000 in July rising by £1,500 per month. Gross profit is 20 % of sales.

Required: Prepare F. Ox's finished goods budget for July–December.

Q9   Asia is a small non-listed manufacturing company. There are the following details.

Asia Ltd
Abridged Balance Sheet as at 31 December 2005

	£	£	£
Fixed Assets			99,500
Current Assets			
Debtors (Nov. £10,000, Dec. £11,000)	21,000		
Stock (raw materials)	10,000		
Stock (finished goods)	9,500	40,500	
Current Liabilities			
Creditors (Nov. £3,500, Dec. £3,500)	(7,000)		
Bank	(8,000)	(15,000)	
Net current assets			25,500
Total net assets			125,000
Share Capital and Reserves			£
Share Capital			
Ordinary share capital			103,000
Reserves			
Profit and loss account			22,000
Total shareholders' funds			125,000

Notes

1. Fixed assets are at cost. Depreciation is at 10 % straight line basis per year.
2. Purchases will be £4,800 in January increasing by £200 per month. They will be paid two months after purchase.
3. Sales will be £15,000 in January increasing by £400 per month. Debtors pay two months in arrears. They will be based on market price with no formal mark-up from gross profit.
4. Production cost per unit will be: direct materials £12; direct labour £10; production overheads £2 (direct labour and production overheads will be paid in the month incurred). Production 400 units per month. Sales 380 units per month.
5. Expenses will run at £6,000 per month. They will be paid in the month incurred.

Required: Prepare sales budget, cash budget, debtors budget, creditors budget, production cost budget, raw materials budget, finished goods budget, trading and profit and loss account and balance sheet for six months ending 30 June 2005.

Q10   Peter Jenkins manages a department and has the following budget for the year.

	£	£
Sales	100,000	
Discretionary costs:		
Purchases	(20,000)	
Advertising	(10,000)	
Training	(8,000)	
Repairs	(19,000)	(57,000)
		43,000
Non-discretionary costs:		
Labour (split equally throughout the year)		(18,000)
Profit		25,000

Peter receives a budget of 10 % of profit for any quarter in which he makes a minimum profit of £8,000. If he makes less than £8,000 profit, he receives no bonus. Any quarter in which he makes a loss he will earn no profit, but will not incur a penalty.

Required: Calculate the maximum and minimum bonuses Peter could expect. Assume Peter has *complete discretion* about when the sales will be earned and when the discretionary costs will be incurred.

Q11   All Sunshine Enterprises runs a hire car service in three locations: London, Oslo and Stockholm. The three operating divisions have the following results for the year.

	London	Oslo	Stockholm
	£m	£m	£m
Investment	2,000,000	1,000,000	500,000
	£m	£m	£m
Sales	1,500,000	800,000	300,000
Costs	(800,000)	(400,000)	(135,000)
Operating profit	700,000	400,000	165,000

Required:
Calculate   a) Return on Investment (ROI)
b) Residual Income (RI) – assuming the required rate of return is 12 %
c) Return on Sales (ROS)

Which is the best relative measure for each division?

Chapter 18

"No amount of planning will ever replace dumb luck."

Anonymous

Source: *The Executive's Book of Quotations* (1994), p. 217

Annual Standard Setting

Head Office intends to keenly monitor our actual against our budgeted performance.

We either set strenuous, motivational standards or easy-to-meet laid back ones.

Shall we order the deckchairs now then?

©MMI Mike Jones

Learning Outcomes

After completing this chapter you should be able to:

✔ Explain the nature and importance of standard costing.

✔ Outline the most important variances.

✔ Calculate variances and prepare a standard costing operating statement.

✔ Interpret the variances.

Planning, Control and Performance: Standard Costing

In a Nutshell

- *Costing, and planning, control and performance are the two main branches of cost accounting.*

- *Standard costing, along with budgeting, is one of the key aspects of planning, control and performance.*

- *Standard costing is a sophisticated form of budgeting based on predetermined costs for cost elements such as direct labour or direct materials.*

- *There are sales and cost variances.*

- *Variances are deviations of the actual results from the standard results.*

- *Standard cost variances can be divided into quantity variances and price variances.*

- *There are direct materials, direct labour, variable overheads and fixed overheads cost variances.*

- *Standard cost variances are investigated to see why they have occurred.*

Introduction

Cost accounting has two main branches: costing, and planning, control and performance. Standard costing, along with budgeting, is one of the two parts of planning, control and performance. Standard costing can be seen as a more specialised and formal type of budgeting. A particular feature of standard costing is the breakdown of costs into various cost components such as direct labour, direct materials, variable overheads and fixed overheads. In standard costing, **expected (or standard) sales or costs are compared against actual sales or costs**. Any differences between them (called **variances**) are then investigated. Variances are divided into those based on quantity and those based on prices. Standard costing, therefore, links the future (i.e., expected costs) to the past (i.e., costs that were actually incurred). Standard costing has proved a useful planning and control tool in many industries.

Nature of Standard Costing

Standard costing is a sophisticated form of budgeting. Standard costing was originally developed in manufacturing industries in order to control costs. Essentially, standard costing involves investigating, often in some detail, the distinct costing elements which make up a product such as direct materials, direct labour, variable overheads and fixed overheads. After this investigation the costs which should be incurred in making a product or service are determined. For example, a table might be expected to be made using eight hours of direct labour and three metres of wood. These become the standard quantities for making a table.

DEFINITION 18.1

Standard Cost

Working definition
A predetermined calculation of the costs that *should* be incurred in making a product.

Formal definition
'The planned unit cost of the products, components or services produced in a period. The standard cost may be determined on a number of bases. The main uses of standard costs are in performance measurement, control, stock valuation and in the establishment of selling prices.'

Source: Chartered Institute of Management Accounting (2000), *Official Terminology*

After a table is made the direct labour and direct materials actually used are compared with the standard. For example, if nine hours are taken rather than eight, this is one hour worse than standard. However, if two metres of wood rather than three metres are used, this is one metre better than standard.

These differences from standard are called variances, which may be favourable (i.e., we have performed better than expected) or unfavourable (i.e., we have performed worse than expected). Unfavourable variances are sometimes called adverse variances. The essence of a good standard costing system is to establish the reason for any variances. Although standard costing is associated with manufacturing industry, it can be adopted in other industries, such as hotel and catering.

Setting standards involves making a decision about whether you are aiming for ideal, attainable or normal standards. They are all different. As Real-Life Nugget 18.1 shows, there is no such thing as a perfect standard. Ideal standards are those which would be attained in an ideal world. Unfortunately, the real world differs from the ideal world. Attainable standards are more realistic and can be reached with effort. Normal standards are those which a business usually attains. Attainable standards are the standards most often used by organisations.

REAL-LIFE NUGGET 18.1

A Manager under Pressure

'We had unrealistic production allowances in the budget last year, but I got them adjusted a bit. It's done by the industrial engineers and the accountants, but I have a bit of a say in it. Some are too slack now, but they are very workable. There is never a perfect standard. The industrial engineers are back in the caveman era. Well, if there is going to be some imperfections, why not have them in my favour? We can modify them and we have done quite well. Why should I beat myself'

Source: A. Hopwood, *Accounting and Human Behaviour* (1974), p. 82

Standards are usually set by industrial engineers in conjunction with accountants. This often causes friction with the workers who are actually monitored by the standards. Real-Life

Nugget 18.2 gives a flavour of these tensions.

REAL-LIFE NUGGET 18.2

Setting the Standards

'Remember those bastards are out to screw you, and that's all they got to think about. They'll stay up half the night figuring out how to beat you out of a dime. They figure you're going to try to fool them, so they make allowances for that. They set [rates] low enough to allow for what you do. It's up to you to figure out how to fool them more than they allow for....'

Source: W.P. Whyte, *Money and Motivation* (1955), pp. 15–16, as quoted in A. Hopwood, *Accounting and Human Behaviour* (1974), p. 6

Standard Cost Variances

In order to explain how standard costing works, the illustration of manufacturing a table is continued. In a succession of examples, more detail is gradually introduced. Figure 18.1 introduces the basic overview information for Alan Carpenter who is setting up a furniture business. In May, he makes a prototype table. To simplify the presentation in the figures *favourable* variances are shorted to 'Fav'. and *unfavourable* variances to 'Unfav'.

Figure 18.1   Overview of Standard Costs for Alan Carpenter for May

	Standard £	Actual £	Variance £	
Sales	30	33	3	Fav.
Costs	20	22	(2)	Unfav.
Profit	10	11	1	Fav.

Before the prototype table was actually made, Alan Carpenter thought it would cost £20 and that he could sell it for £30. He, therefore, anticipated a profit of £10. In actual fact, the table was sold for £33. Carpenter thus made £3 more sales than anticipated. However, the table cost £22 (£2 more than anticipated). Overall, therefore, actual profit is £11 rather than the predicted standard profit of £10. Carpenter benefits £3 from selling well, but loses £2 through excessive costs. There is an overall favourable sales variance of £3, and an overall unfavourable cost variance of £2 which gives a £1 favourable profit variance.

We now expand the example and look at Alan Carpenter's operations for June. In June he anticipates making and selling 10 tables. In actual fact, he makes and sells only 9 tables (see Figure 18.2).

Figure 18.2   Standard Costs for Alan Carpenter for June

	Budget 10 Tables £	Actual 9 Tables £
Sales	300	290
Costs	200	170
Profit	100	120

Calculation of variances

i. Flex the Budget

	Budget 10 Tables £	Flexed Budget 9 Tables £	Actual 9 Tables £	Variance £	
Sales	300	270	290	20	Fav.
Costs	200	180	170	10	Fav.
Profit	100	90	120	30	Fav.

ii. Calculate Variances

	£	
Budgeted Profit	100	
Sales quantity variance (1 table at £10 profit)	(10)	Unfav.
Budgeted profit for actual production	90	
Sales price variance	20	Fav.
Cost variance	10	Fav.
Actual Profit	120	

Before calculating the variances, we must flex the budget. Flexing the budget simply means adjusting the budget to take into account the *actual quantity produced*. We need to do this because we need to calculate the costs *which would have been incurred if we actually made* nine tables. If we made only nine tables, we would logically expect to incur costs for nine rather than ten tables. In addition, we would expect to sell nine not ten tables. The budget must, therefore, be calculated on the basis of the nine actual tables made rather than the ten predicted.

By making nine rather than ten tables, the profit for one table is lost. This was £10 (as there was £100 profit for ten tables). There is thus a £10 drop in profits. This is called a **sales quantity variance**. (Note that we are *assuming*, at this stage, that all the *costs will vary in direct relation to the number of tables*.)

We can now compare the sales and costs actually earned and incurred for nine tables with those that were expected to be earned and incurred. As Figure 18.2 shows, the nine tables were expected to sell for £270, but were actually sold for £290. In other words, we received £20 more than we had anticipated for our tables. This was the **sales price variance**. Note that the sales quantity variance is caused by lost profit. By contrast, the sales price variance is caused by the fact we are selling the tables for more than we anticipated. There is thus a **favourable sales price variance** of £20.

The budgeted cost for nine tables was £180. However, the actual cost incurred is only £170. There is thus a favourable cost variance of £10. The difference between the budgeted profit of £100 and the actual profit of £120 can be explained by these three variances (unfavourable sales quantity variance (£10), favourable sales price variance (£20), and favourable cost variance (£10)).

So far, we have seen that it is important to flex the budget, and looked at the sales volume variance and the sales price variance. It is now time to look in more detail at the cost variances. When looking at cost variances, it is important to distinguish between variable and fixed costs. As we saw in Chapter 15, variable costs are those costs that directly vary with a product or service (for example, direct materials, direct labour or production overheads). The more products made, the more the variable costs. Thus, if it costs £20 to make one table, it will cost £200 to make ten tables. Fixed costs, however, do not vary. You will pay the building's insurance of £10 per month whether you make one table or 100 tables. In continuing the Alan Carpenter example, the costs are now divided into fixed and variable.

Essentially, *all the variable costs* (direct materials, direct labour, and variable overheads) *have two elements – price and quantity*. For example, when making a table we might predict using the following standard prices and standard quantities:

	Price		*Quantity*
Direct labour	£5 per hour	for	2 hours
Direct materials	£1 per metre	for	5 metres of wood
Variable overheads (incurred on basis of direct labour hours)	£2.0 per hour	for	2 hours

When our actual price and actual quantity vary from standard, we will have price and quantity variances. In other words, the overall cost variances for direct labour, direct materials and variable overheads can be divided into a quantity and a price variance. **Price variances** are caused when the **standard price** of a product *differs* from the **actual price. Quantity variances** are caused when the **standard quantity** *differs* from the **actual quantity**. These differences between the standard and the actual quantity when multiplied by standard price will give us the overall quantity variance. Favourable variances are where we have done better than expected; unfavourable variances are where we have done worse than expected. For fixed overheads, which do not vary with production, we compare the actual fixed overheads incurred with the standard. We call this difference, the fixed overheads quantity variance.

An overview of all these variances is given in Figure 18.3 and in Figure 18.4 the main elements of all the variances are summarised. For simplification, this book uses the terms price and quantity variances throughout. Often, however, more technical terminology is used (these alternative technical terms are shown in the second column of Figure 18.4).

Figure 18.3   Diagram of Main Variances

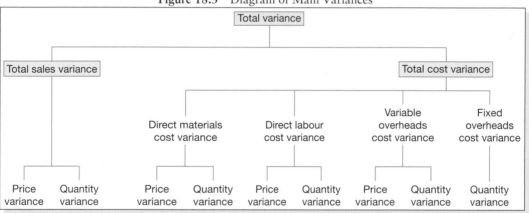

Figure 18.4   Calculation of the Main Variances

Variances	Technical Name	Calculation
i. SALES (a) Overall Variance	Sales	Not usual to calculate an overall sales variance
(b) Price	Price	(Standard price per unit – actual price per unit) × actual quantity of units sold
(c) Quantity	Volume	(Standard quantity of units sold – actual quantity of units sold) × standard contribution per unit

Figure 18.4   Calculation of the Main Variances (*continued*)

ii. COSTS **Direct Materials** *(a) Overall Variance*	Cost	Standard cost of materials for actual production less actual cost of materials used in production
(b) Price	Price	(Standard price per unit of material – actual price per unit of material) × actual quantity of materials used.
(c) Quantity	Usage	(Standard quantity of materials for actual production – actual quantity of materials used) × standard material price per unit of materials
Direct Labour *(a) Overall Variance*	Cost	Standard cost of labour for actual production less actual cost of labour used in production
(b) Price	Rate	(Standard price per hour – actual price per hour) × actual quantity of labour hours used
(c) Quantity	Efficiency	(Standard quantity of labour hours for actual production – actual quantity of labour hours used) × standard labour price per hour
Variable Overheads *(a) Overall Variance*	Cost	Standard cost of variable overheads for actual production less actual cost of variable overheads for production
(b) Price	Efficiency	(Standard variable overhead price per hour – actual variable overheads prices per hour) × actual quantity of labour hours used
(c) Quantity	Expenditure	(Standard quantity of labour hours for actual production – actual quantity of labour hours used) × standard variable overheads price per hour
Fixed Overheads *(a) Quantity*	Spending	(Standard fixed overheads – actual fixed overheads)

Figure 18.4 Calculation of the Main Variances (*continued*)

Helpnote

At first sight this table looks daunting. However, in essence the way we calculate all the overall variances, price variances and quantity variances is remarkably similar. The key essentials are explained below. *Note that in standard costing, standard refers to the budget.*

i. Overall Variances

Here we are interested in comparing the budgeted cost of the actual items we produce **(standard cost of actual production)** with the actual cost of items we produce **(actual cost of production).** The only variation is whether we are talking about direct materials, direct labour or variable overheads. The overall variance can be split into **price and quantity variances.** There is no overall variance for sales or fixed overheads. It is important to realise that, in practice, the **overall variance is normally calculated just by flexing the budget.** The difference between the flexed budget and the actual results gives the overall variance.

ii. Price Variances

Here we are interested in comparing the **standard price for the actual quantity used or sold** with the **actual price for the actual quantity used or sold.** The only variation is whether we are relating this to sales, direct materials, direct labour, or variable overheads. For variable overheads we use the actual quantity of labour hours used, as we are recovering variable overheads using labour hours. There is no price variance for fixed overheads. The standard formula is:

(Standard price – actual price) × *actual quantity used or sold*

iii. Quantity Variances

In this case, we are interested in comparing the budgeted cost of the actual items produced or sold **(standard cost of actual production or standard quantity for sales)** with the actual quantity produced or sold **(actual quantity used or sold).** This gives us the quantity difference. This is then multiplied by the standard contribution per item for the sales variance and by the standard price per unit **(normally, metres or hours)** for the other variances. The only variation is whether we are considering the standard price of direct materials, direct labour or variable overheads, or the standard selling price. For variable overheads, we use the standard quantity of labour hours and the actual quantity of labour hours used as we are recovering variable overheads using labour hours. The standard formula is:

Standard quantity of actual production (or, for sales, standard quantity for sales) less actual quantity used (or, for sales, actual quantity sold) × *standard price (or, for sales, standard contribution per item)*

For fixed overheads, the quantity variance is simply standard fixed overheads less actual fixed overheads.

In order to see how these variances all interlock, we now expand the Alan Carpenter example (see Figure 18.5).

Figure 18.5   Worked Example: Alan Carpenter's Standard Costs for June

i. Standard Cost per Table	£	£
Selling Price		30
Direct materials: 5 metres of wood at £1 per metre	(5)	
Direct labour: 2 hours at £5 per hour	(10)	
Variable overheads (recovered on labour hours):		
2 hours at £2 per hour	(4)	
Fixed overheads: £10 in total divided by 10 tables	(1)	(20)
Budgeted Profit		10

ii. Budgeted (i.e. standard) Results for June: 10 Tables	£	£
Selling Price		300
Direct materials: 50 metres of wood at £1 per metre	(50)	
Direct labour: 20 hours at £5 per hour	(100)	
Variable overheads: 20 hours at £2 per hour	(40)	
Fixed overheads	(10)	(200)
Budgeted Profit		100

iii. Actual Results for June: 9 Tables	£	£
Selling Price		290
Direct materials: 44 metres of wood at £1.20 per metre	(52.80)	
Direct labour: 16 hours at £4.50	(72.00)	
Variable overheads	(33.00)	
Fixed overheads	(12.20)	(170)
Actual Profit		120

Using Figure 18.5, we now calculate the variances in two steps: flexing the budget and calculating the individual variances.

Flexing the Budget

Note that fixed overheads are not flexed! This is because by their very nature they do not vary with production. The flexed budget is used in the calculation of variances so that the levels of activity are the same and can be used as a basis for meaningful comparisons.

	Budget (i.e., standard) 10 Tables		Flexed Budget (i.e., standard quantity of actual production) 9 Tables		Actual Results 9 Tables		Overall Variances
	£	£	£	£	£	£	£
Sales		300		270		290.00	20.00 Fav.
Direct materials	(50)		(45)		(52.80)		(7.80) Unfav.
Direct labour	(100)		(90)		(72.00)		18.00 Fav.
Variable overheads	(40)	(190)	(36)	(171)	(33.00)	(157.80)	3.00 Fav.
Contribution*		110		99		132.20	
Fixed overheads		(10)		(10)		(12.20)	(2.20) Unfav.
Profit		100		89		120.00	

*This is sometimes known as profit before fixed overheads.

By flexing the budget, *we have automatically calculated (1) the sales price variance, and (2) the overall cost variances* for direct materials, direct labour and variable overheads. It is important to note that the *flexed budget gives us the standard quantity of the actual production.* The cost variances will then be broken down into the individual price and quantity variances (see Figure 18.6). However, *first* we need to calculate the sales quantity variance.

Calculating Individual Variances

(a) Sales Quantity Variance

$$\begin{array}{ccccc} \text{Standard quantity} & & & & \\ \text{of units sold} & - & \text{actual quantity of units sold} & \times & \text{contribution*} \\ 10 & - & 9 & \times & £11^{**} \quad = £\,11 \text{ Unfav.} \end{array}$$

Notes:

* This is budgeted profit before fixed overheads (£110) divided by the budgeted number of tables (10). Therefore, we have, £110 ÷ 10 = £11. Note that this is calculated *before* fixed overheads. This is because fixed overheads will remain the same whatever the value of sales. They must be excluded from the calculation and their variance calculated separately.
** This represents the difference between the budgeted profit (£100) less the flexed budget (£89). *In practice, this is the easiest way to calculate this variance.*

(b) Individual Price and Quantity Variances

When we calculate the price and quantity variances based on our flexed budget, we can use the standard price and quantity formulas given below (see Figure 18.6). We then need to remember that the standard price for sales is the standard selling price per unit, for direct materials it is the price per unit of direct materials used and so on. For quantity we need to remember that we are concerned with the standard quantity of materials, labour, etc. Figure 18.6 is based on Figure 18.5 and our flexed budget.

Figure 18.6   Calculation of Individual Price and Quantity Variances for Alan Carpenter

Overall Variance =	Price Variance +	Quantity Variance
	(standard price – actual price sold or used) × actual quantity sold or used	*(standard quantity of actual production – actual quantity used) × standard price*

	Price calculations · **Notes**	**Quantity calculations** · **Notes**
(a) *Sales* i. *Sales price* *Note the sales price variance is automatically given by flexing the budget*	(£30 – £32.22*) × 9 tables = £20 Fav. **(1)** *£290 sold ÷ 9 tables sold = (£32.22)	ii. *Sales quantity* See calculation above (2a) for **(2)** sales quantity variance
(b) *Direct Materials* **Overall (£7.80) Unfav.**	(£1– £1.20 × 44 metres = (£8.80) Unfav. **(3)** = (£8.80) Unfav. +	(45 metres – 44 metres) × £1 = £1 Fav. **(4)** £1 Fav.
(c) *Direct Labour* **Overall £18 Fav**	(£5 – £4.50) × 16 hours = £8 Fav. **(5)** = £8 Fav. +	(18 hours – 16 hours) × £5 = £10 Fav. **(6)** £10 Fav.
(d) *Variable Overheads* **Overall £3 Fav.**	(£2.00 – £2.06*) × 16 hours = (£1) Unfav. **(7)** *£33 actual at 16 hours = £2.06 per hour = (£1) Unfav. +	 (18 hours – 16 hours) × £2 = £4 Fav. **(8)** £4 Fav.
(e) *Fixed Overheads* **Overall (£2.20) Unfav.**	 =	Standard less actual £10 – £12.20 = (£2.20) Unfav. **(9)** (£2.20) Unfav.

Notes:
1. **Sales Price Variance:** The standard selling price is £30 per unit. However, we sell at £32.22 per table (£290 ÷ 9). Therefore, overall, across the nine tables, we make £20 (9 × £2.22) more than we expected.
2. **Sales Quantity Variance:** The standard quantity expected to be sold was ten tables. We actually sold nine tables. Therefore, we lose the contribution on one table of £11. This was the overall contribution expected of £110 divided by the standard quantity of ten tables.
3. **Direct Materials Price Variance:** The standard price (£1.00) per metre is less than the actual price (£1.20) paid per metre by £0.20 pence per metre. As 44 metres were used this results in an unfavourable variance of £8.80.
4. **Direct Materials Quantity Variance:** The standard quantity to make nine tables is 45 metres. However, only 44 were actually used. As the standard price was £1 per metre, Alan Carpenter gains £1, which is a favourable variance.
5. **Direct Labour Price Variance:** The standard price (£5.00) per labour hour is greater than the actual price paid (£4.50). As 16 labour hours were used, the result is an £8 favourable variance.
6. **Direct Labour Quantity Variance:** The standard quantity to make nine tables is 18 hours. Alan Carpenter has taken 16 hours. As the standard price per labour hour is £5, there is a £10 favourable variance.
7. **Variable Overhead Price Variance:** The standard recovery rate is £2.00 per hour. However, Alan Carpenter has recovered £33 in the 16 hours actually worked (i.e., £2.0625 per hour). Given the 16 hours worked, this results in an overall over-recovery of £1 (i.e. 16 × £0.0625). In other words, we expected to recover £32, but we actually recovered £33 (16 hours × £2.06). We thus recovered £1 more than expected, which is unfavourable.
8. **Variable Overheads Quantity Variance:** It was anticipated that 18 hours would be used to recover variable overheads. In actual fact, 16 hours were used. Since £2 per hour is recovered, there is an under-recovery of £4. This is favourable.
9. **Fixed Overhead Volume Variance:** The fixed overhead was expected to be £10. In fact, it was £12.20. This is £2.20 more than expected. Therefore, we have a £2.20 unfavourable variance.

We can now draw up a standard cost reconciliation statement. This statement reconciles the budgeted profit of £100 to the actual profit of £120.

Alan Carpenter: Standard Cost Reconciliation Statement for June				
	£	£	£	
Budgeted Profit			100	
Sales quantity variance			(11)	Unfav.
Budgeted Profit at Actual Sales			89	
	Fav.	Unfav.		
Variances	£	£		
Sales price	20			
Direct materials price		8.80		
Direct materials quantity	1			
Direct labour price	8			
Direct labour quantity	10			
Variable overhead price		1.00		
Variable overhead quantity	4			
Fixed overhead variance		2.20		
	43	12.00	31	Fav.
Actual Profit			120	

Interpretation of Variances

A key aspect of both budgeting and standard costing is the investigation of variances. In Figure 18.7 we look at some possible reasons for variances.

Figure 18.7 Possible Causes of Variances

Variance	Favourable	Unfavourable
1. Sales Quantity	We sell more than we expect because of • good market conditions • good marketing.	We sell less than we expect because of • poor market conditions • bad marketing.
2. Sales Price	We sell at a higher price than expected because of • unexpected market demand • good economy.	We sell at a lower price than expected because of • tough competition • poor economy.
3. Direct Materials Quantity	We use more material than expected because of • poor-quality material • sloppy production.	We use less material than expected because of • high-quality material • efficient production.
4. Direct Materials Price	Our material costs are more than expected because of • a price rise.	Our material costs are less than we expect because • we find an alternative cheaper supplier.
5. Direct Labour Quantity	We use more labour than we expected because of • inefficient cheaper workers who take longer • labour problems.	We use less labour than expected because of • efficient workers who are quicker.
6. Fixed Overheads	The overall costs are more than expected because of • inflation.	The overhead costs are less than expected because • we change to a cheaper source.

These variances represent differences in what actually happened to what we expected to happen. It must be remembered that variances are only as good as the original budgets or standards that are set. Therefore, if unrealistic, incorrect or unattainable standards are set, this will create misleading variances. As we saw earlier, setting the original standards can often cause severe tensions between the standard setters and the employees. In standard costing a more sophisticated, systematic approach is taken to the investigation of variances than in budgeting.

The nature of variable overheads means that these variances are tied into the basis of absorption (for example, direct labour hours). The causes for the variable overhead variances will, therefore, tend to reflect those for the direct labour hours. It is not, therefore, particularly meaningful to investigate the reasons for these variances separately. Variable overheads have, therefore, been excluded from Figure 18.7.

SOUNDBITE 18.1

Behavioural Aspects of Standards

'All persons concerned with setting standards are striving to gain some measure of personal control over factors which are important in their organisational lives.'

Source: A. Hopwood, *Accounting and Human Behaviour* (1974), pp. 6–7

PAUSE FOR THOUGHT 18.2

Compensating Variances

Why might there be compensating variances? For example, an unfavourable material quantity variance, but a favourable material price variance.

....

Sometimes the quantity and price variances are interconnected. For example, we plan to make a product and we budget for a high quality material. If we then substitute a low quality material, it will be likely to cost less. However, we will need to use more. Therefore, we would have an unfavourable material quantity variance, but a favourable price variance.

Conclusion

Standard costing is a sophisticated form of budgeting. It was originally used in manufacturing industries, but is now much more widespread. Standard costing involves predetermining the cost of the various elements of a product or service (such as selling price, direct materials, direct labour and variable overheads). These standard costs are then compared with the actual costs and any differences, called variances, investigated. These variances are split into price and quantity variances. Standard costing allows costs to be monitored very closely. In many businesses, it is thus a very useful form of planning, control and performance.

Q&A Discussion Questions

Questions with numbers in blue have answers at the back of the book.

Q1 'Setting the standards is the most difficult part of standard costing.'
What considerations should be taken into account when setting standards?

Q2 'Standard costing is good for planning and control, but unless great care is taken can often be very demotivational.' Discuss.

Q3 Standard costing is more about control than motivation. Do you agree with this statement?

Q4 'The key to standard setting is providing a good, fair initial set of standards.' Discuss.

Q5 State whether the following statements are true or false. If false, explain why.
(a) Favourable cost variances are where actual costs are less than standard costs.
(b) Flexing the budget means adjusting the budget to take into account the actual prices incurred.
(c) Price and quantity variances are the main constituents of the overall cost variances.
(d) The direct materials price variance is: (standard price per unit of material – actual price per unit of material) × actual quantity of materials used.
(e) The direct labour quantity variance is: (standard price of labour hours for actual production – actual price of labour hours used) × standard labour price per hour.

Q&A Numerical Questions

Questions with numbers in blue have answers at the back of the book.

Q1 Stuffed restaurant has the following results for May 2010

	Budget	Actual
Number of meals	10,000	12,000
	£	£
Price per meal	10.00	10.60
Food cost	30,000	37,200
Labour cost	35,000	36,000
Variable overheads	5,000	6,000
Fixed overheads	3,000	3,100

Required:

(a) Calculate the flexed budget.

(b) Calculate the sales price variance.

(c) Calculate the overall cost variances for materials, labour, variable overheads and fixed overheads (note: you do not have enough information to calculate the more detailed price and quantity variances).

(d) Calculate the sales quantity variance.

(e) Discuss the variances. In particular, highlight what extra information might be needed.

Q2 Engines Incorporated, a small engineering company, has the following results for April 2006 for its product, the Widget. It budgeted to sell 12,500 widgets at £9.00 each. However, 16,000 widgets were actually sold at £8.80 each. The budgeted and actual costs are given below.

	Budget	Actual
Number of widgets	12,500	16,000
	£	£
Price per widget	9.00	8.80
Direct materials	40,000	42,000
Labour cost	32,000	29,000
Variable overheads	6,000	8,000
Fixed overheads	8,000	10,000

Required:

(i) Calculate the flexed budget.

(ii) Calculate the sales price and sales quantity variances.

(iii) Calculate the overall cost variances for materials, labour, variable overheads and fixed overheads (note: you do not have enough information to calculate the more detailed price and quantity variances).

(iv) Discuss the variances. In particular, highlight what extra information might be needed.

Q3 Birch Manufacturing makes bookcases. The company has the following details of its June production.

	Estimated	Actual
Number of bookcases	10,000	11,000
Metres of wood	100,000	120,000
Price per metre	0.50p	0.49p

Required: Calculate the:

(i) overall direct materials cost variance

(ii) direct materials price variance

(iii) direct materials quantity variance.

Q4   Sweatshop has the following details of direct labour used to make tracksuits for July.
     (a) Standard: 550 sweatshirts at 2 hours at £5.50 per hour.
     (b) Actual production: 500 sweatshirts at 1,050 hours for £5,880.

     Required: Calculate the:
       (i) overall direct labour cost variance
      (ii) direct labour price variance
     (iii) direct labour quantity variance.

Q5   Toycare manufactures puzzlegames. It has the following details of its March production.

	Estimated	Actual
Number of puzzlegames	11,000	12,000
Kilos of raw materials	5,500	4,800
Price per kilo	0.45p	0.46p
Direct labour (hours)	6,600	4,800
Direct labour price per hour	£5.50	£5.30

     Required: Calculate the:
       (i) overall direct materials cost variance
      (ii) direct materials price variance
     (iii) direct materials quantity variance
      (iv) overall direct labour cost variance
       (v) direct labour price variance
      (vi) direct labour quantity variance.

Q6   Wonderworld has the following details for its variable overheads for August for its
     Teleporter. Each Teleporter is expected to take two labour hours and variable overheads
     are expected to be £2.50 per labour hour. Wonderworld expects to make 100,000
     teleporters. In actual fact, it makes 110,000 teleporters using 230,000 labour hours. Its
     budgeted fixed overheads were £10,000. However, it actually spends £9,800 on fixed
     overheads. Actual variable overheads are £517,500.

     Required: Calculate the:
       (i) overall variable overheads cost variance
      (ii) variable overheads price variance
     (iii) variable overheads quantity variance
      (iv) fixed overheads variance.

Q7   Special Manufacturers has the following details for its variable overheads for July on its Startrek product. Each Startrek is expected to take three labour hours and variable overheads are expected to be £4.25 per labour hour. The firm expects to make 200,000 Startreks. In actual fact, it makes 180,000 Startreks using 630,000 labour hours. Its budgeted fixed overheads were £25,000. However, it actually spends £23,000 on fixed overheads. Actual variable overheads are £2,800,000.

Required: Calculate the:
  (i) overall variable overheads cost variance
 (ii) variable overheads price variance
(iii) variable overheads quantity variance
(iv) fixed overheads variance.

Q8   Peter Peacock plc manufactures a subcomponent for the car industry. There are the following details for August.
  (a) *Budgeted data*
      Sales: 200,000 subcomponents at £2.80 each
      Direct labour: 40,000 hours at £7.25 per hour
      Direct materials: 100,000 sheets of metal at £1.25 each
      Variable overheads: £40,000 recovered at £1.00 per direct labour hour
      Fixed overheads: £68,000
  (b) *Actual data*
      220,000 subcomponents were actually sold and produced
      Sales: 220,000 subcomponents at £2.78 each
      Direct labour: 43,500 hours at £7.30 per hour
      Direct material: 125,000 sheets of metal at £1.20
      Variable overheads: £42,500
      Fixed overheads: £67,000

Required:
  (i) Calculate the flexed budget and overall variances.
 (ii) Calculate the individual price and quantity variances.
(iii) Calculate a standard cost reconciliation statement for August.
(iv) Comment on the results.

Q9 Supersonic plc manufactures an assembly mounting for the aircraft industry. In July, it was expected that 80,000 assembly mountings would be sold at £18.80 each. In actual fact, 76,000 assembly mountings were sold for £20.00 each. The cost data are provided below.

	Budgeted data	*Actual data*
Direct materials	200,000 sheets of metal at £2.10 each	150,000 sheets of metal at £2.20 each
Direct labour	50,000 hours at £8.00 per hour	51,000 hours at £7.50 per hour
Variable overheads	£45,000 recovered at £0.90 per direct labour hour	£41,000
Fixed overheads	£78,000	£80,000

Required:
  (i) Calculate the flexed budget and overall variances.
 (ii) Calculate the individual price and quantity variances.
(iii) Calculate a standard cost reconciliation statement for July.
(iv) Comment on the results.

Chapter 19

"So there I was, fresh from the annual meeting of the Society for Judgement and Decision Making, and behaving like Buridan's Ass – the imaginary creature which starved midway between two troughs of hay because it couldn't decide which to go for."

Ditherer's Dilemma, Peter Aytan, *New Scientist*, 12 February 2000, p. 47

Learning Outcomes

After completing this chapter you should be able to:

✔ **Explain the nature of short-term business decisions.**

✔ **Understand the concept of contribution analysis.**

✔ **Investigate some of the decisions for which contribution analysis is useful.**

✔ **Draw up break-even charts and contribution graphs.**

Short-Term Decision Making

In a Nutshell

- *In business, decision making involves choosing between alternatives and involves looking forward, using relevant information and financial evaluation.*

- *Businesses face a range of short-term decisions such as how to maximise limited resources.*

- *It is useful to distinguish between costs that vary with production or sales (variable costs) and costs that do not (fixed costs).*

- *Sales less variable costs equals contribution.*

- *Contribution less fixed costs equals net profit.*

- *Contribution and contribution per unit are useful when making short-term business decisions.*

- *Contribution analysis can help determine which products or services are most profitable, which are making losses, whether to buy externally rather than make internally and how to maximise the use of a limited resource.*

- *Throughput accounting attempts to remove bottlenecks from a production system; it treats direct labour and variable overheads as fixed.*

- *Break-even analysis shows the point at which a product makes neither a profit nor a loss.*

- *Both break-even charts and contribution graphs are useful ways of portraying business information.*

Introduction

Businesses, like individuals, are continually involved in decision making. A decision is simply a choice between alternatives. It is forward looking. Business decisions may be long-term strategic ones about raising long-term finance or capital expenditure. Alternatively, the decisions may be short-term, day-to-day, operational ones, such as whether to continue making a particular product. This particular chapter looks at short-term decisions. When making short-term decisions, it is important to consider only factors relevant to the decision. Depreciation, for example, will not generally change whatever the short-term decision. It is not, therefore, included in the short-term decision-making calculations.

Decision Making

Individuals make decisions all the time. These may be short-term decisions: Shall we go out or stay in? If we go out, do we go for a meal, to the cinema or to a pub? Or long-term decisions: Shall we get married? Shall we buy a house? These decisions involve choosing between various competing alternatives.

Managers also make continual decisions about the short-term and long-term future. Shall we make a new product or not? Which product shall we make: A or B? Figure 19.1 gives some examples of short-term business decisions.

Figure 19.1   Some Short-Term Managerial Decisions

- Which products should the business continue to make this year?
- Which departments should the business close down this year?
- How should the business maximise limited resources this year?
- At what level of production does the business currently break even?
- How can the business maximise current profits?

Whatever the nature of the decision, informed business decision making will share certain characteristics, such as being forward-looking, using relevant information and involving financial evaluation.

(a) Forward-looking

Decisions look to the future and, therefore, require forward-looking information. Past costs that have no ongoing implications for the future are irrelevant. These costs are sometimes known as **sunk costs** and should be *excluded from decision making*.

(b) Relevant Information

When choosing between alternatives, we are concerned only with information which is relevant to the particular decision. For example, after arriving in the centre of town by taxi, you are trying to choose between going to the cinema or pub. The taxi fare is a sunk cost which is not relevant to your decision. You cannot alter the past. *Relevant costs and revenues are, therefore, those costs and revenues that will affect a decision. Sunk costs are non-relevant costs.*

To make an informed decision only relevant information is needed. This information may be financial or non-financial. The non-financial information will normally, however, have indirect financial consequences. For example, a drop in the birthrate may have financial consequences for suppliers of baby products.

(c) Financial Evaluation

In business, effective decision making will involve financial evaluation. This means gathering the relevant facts and then working out the financial benefits and costs of the various alternatives. There are a variety of techniques available to do this, which we will be discussing in subsequent chapters.

Decisions may have **opportunity costs**. *Opportunity costs are the potential benefit lost by rejecting the best alternative course of action.* If you work in the union bar at £7 per hour and the next best alternative is the university bookshop at £5 per hour, then the opportunity cost is £5 per hour. This is because you forgo the chance of working in the bookshop at £5 per hour.

However, from the above, it should not be assumed that business decision making is always wholly rational. As we all know, many factors, not all of them rational, enter into real-life decision making (see Real-Life Nugget 19.1).

REAL-LIFE NUGGET 19.1

Decision Making

The upshot? Although you might think that asking what you want should be the flip-side of asking what you don't want, it isn't. When you reject something you focus more on the negative features; when you select something you're focusing on the positive. So whether it's an ice cream or a prospective employee, deciding what (or who) you want by a process of rational elimination may not actually give you what you want. There is no simple panacea to ease the pain of choice other than passing the buck, of course (hence the irksome cliché: 'No, you decide').

As for you sadistic purveyors of all this choice, don't get too smug. When Sheena Sethi-Iyengar, from the Massachusetts Institute of Technology, set up a tasting counter for exotic jams in a grocery, she found that too much choice can be bad for business. More customers stopped to sample from a 24-jam counter than from a 6-jam counter. But only 3 per cent bought any jam when 24 were on offer, compared with 30 per cent when there were 6 to choose from.

Source: Ditherer's Dilemma, Peter Aytan, *New Scientist*, 12 February 2000, p. 471

Contribution Analysis

When making short-term decisions, a technique called contribution analysis has evolved. This technique has several distinctive features (see Figure 19.2).

Figure 19.2 Key Features of Contribution Analysis

- Distinction between those costs that are the same whatever the level of production or service (*fixed costs*) and those that vary with the level of production or service (*variable costs*).
- Profit is no longer the main criterion by which decisions are judged. The key criterion becomes *contribution to fixed costs*.
- Calculations are often performed on the basis of *unit costs* rather than in total.
- Contribution analysis focuses on the *extra cost of making an extra product* or providing an extra unit of service.

It is now important to look more closely at the key elements of contribution analysis: fixed costs, variable costs and contribution. The analysis and interaction of these elements is sometimes called cost-profit-volume analysis. In this book, the term contribution analysis is used because it is considered easier to understand and more informative.

PAUSE FOR THOUGHT 19.1

Fixed Costs

In the long run all fixed costs are variable. Why do you think this is so?

....

This is because at some stage the underlying conditions will change. For example, at a certain production level it will be necessary to buy extra machines, this will necessitate extra depreciation and insurance both normally fixed costs. Alternatively, if a factory closes then even the fixed costs will no longer be incurred.

(i) Fixed Costs

Fixed costs *do not change* if we sell more or less products or services. **They are thus irrelevant for short-term decisions.** For a business, fixed costs might be business rates, depreciation, insurance or rent. On a normal household telephone bill, for example, the fixed cost is the amount of the rental. It should be stressed that fixed costs will not change over the short term, but over the long term all costs will change (see Pause for Thought 19.1).

(ii) Variable Costs

These costs *do vary* with the level of production or service provided. **They are thus relevant for short-term decisions.** If we take a business, variable costs might be direct labour, direct materials, or overheads directly linked to service or production.

In practice, it may be difficult to ascertain which costs are fixed and which are variable. In addition, some costs will have elements of both a fixed and variable nature. For example, an electricity bill has a fixed standing charge and then an amount per unit of electricity used. However, to simplify matters, we shall treat costs as either fixed or variable.

(iii) Contribution

Contribution to fixed overheads, or contribution in short, is simply sales less variable costs. If sales are greater than variable costs, it means that for each product made or service provided the business contributes to its fixed overheads. Once a business's fixed overheads are covered, a profit will be made.

Contribution, as we shall see, is a very useful technique which enables businesses to choose the most profitable goods and services. Contribution analysis is sometimes called **marginal costing**. This comes from economics where a marginal cost is the *extra cost or 'incremental' cost needed to produce one more good or service*. Figure 19.3 demonstrates how contribution analysis works.

Figure 19.3   Demonstration of Contribution Analysis

Clueless has two products (X and Y) and the following abridged trading and profit and loss account.

	£	£
Sales		100,000
Less: *Costs*		
Direct materials	25,000	
Direct labour	35,000	
Overheads	20,000	80,000
Net Profit		20,000

Which of the two products is the most profitable?

To answer this question, we need additional information about X and Y and about which costs are fixed and which are variable. We can then use contribution analysis.

Additional information	**X**	**Y**
Sales units	1,000	2,000
	£	£
Sales	50,000	50,000
Direct materials	15,000	10,000
Direct labour	20,000	15,000
Variable overheads	7,000	3,000
Fixed overheads	10,000	

Contribution Analysis

	X (1,000 units)				**Y (2,000 units)**			
	Per unit		Total		Per unit		Total	
	£	£	£	£	£	£	£	£
Sales		50		50,000		25		50,000
Less: *Costs*								
Direct materials	15		15,000		5.0		10,000	
Direct labour	20		20,000		7.5		15,000	
Variable overheads	7	42	7,000	42,000	1.5	14	3,000	28,000
Contribution		8		8,000		11		22,000
X's contribution								8,000
Total Contribution								30,000
Fixed overheads								(10,000)
Net Profit								20,000

We can thus see that:
1. X make a contribution of £8 per unit, while Y makes a contribution of £11 per unit.
2. X contributes £8,000 to fixed overheads, while Y contributes £22,000 to fixed overheads.

The contribution data in Figure 19.3 can be used to answer a series of 'what if' questions, varying the levels of sales for X and Y. Contribution analysis is thus very versatile (as Figure 19.4 shows).

Figure 19.4   'What if' Questions for Products X and Y

(i) What if sales of X and Y double?
(ii) What if sales of X and Y halve?

(i) If sales of X and Y double, the contribution would double. Thus,

	£
X (Existing contribution £8,000)	16,000
Y (Existing contribution £22,000)	44,000
	60,000
Fixed overheads	(10,000)
Net Profit	50,000

(ii) If sales of X and Y halve the contribution will halve. Thus

	£
X (Existing contribution £8,000)	4,000
Y (Existing contribution £22,000)	11,000
	15,000
Fixed overheads	(10,000)
Net Profit	5,000

Helpnote:
The net profit (originally £20,000) increases and decreases by more than the direct increase or decrease in sales units. The contribution varies in line with sales, but fixed overheads do not vary. The overall net profit, in turn, therefore does not alter in direct proportion to the change in sales or contribution.

Decisions, Decisions

Contribution analysis can be used in a range of possible situations. All these involve the basic business questions:

- Are we maximising the firm's contribution by producing the most profitable products?
- Is the product making a positive contribution to the firm? If not, cease production.
- Should we make the products in house?
- Are we making the most of limited resources?

Although the decisions are different, the basic approach is the same (see Helpnote 19.1).

HELPNOTE 19.1

Basic Contribution Approach to Decision Making

1. Separate the costs into fixed and variable.
2. Allocate sales and costs to different products.
3. Calculate contribution (sales less variable cost) for each product:
   (a) in total
   (b) where appropriate, per unit or per unit of limiting factor.

It is important to realise that contribution analysis provides a rational approach to decision making. However, it should not be seen as providing a definitive answer. In the end, making the right decision will also involve an element of judgement. This is the sentiment expressed in Soundbite 19.1.

SOUNDBITE 19.1

Decision Making as an Art

'Management is more art than science. No one can say with certainty which decisions will bring the most profit, any more than they can create instructions over how to sculpt a masterpiece. You just have to feel it as it goes.'

Richard D'Aveni, *Financial Times* (September 1, 1992)

Source: *The Wiley Book of Business Quotations* (1998), p. 311

(i) Determining the Most Profitable Products

If a company makes a range of products or services, we can use contribution analysis to see which are the most profitable (see Figure 19.5).

Figure 19.5   Determining the Most Profitable Products or Services

A garage provides its customers with three services: the basic service, the deluxe service and the superdeluxe service. It has the following details.

	Selling price £	Direct labour £	Direct materials £
Basic	75	35	10
Deluxe	95	45	12
Superdeluxe	120	65	14

Variable overheads are 50% direct labour. Fixed overheads are £1,000 per month. Which services are the most profitable?

. . . .

We need to calculate *per unit*	Basic £	£	Deluxe £	£	Superdeluxe £	£
Sales Price		75.00		95.00		120.00
Less: *Variable costs*						
Direct materials	10.00		12.00		14.00	
Direct labour	35.00		45.00		65.00	
Variable overheads	17.50		22.50		32.50	
Total variable costs		62.50		79.50		111.50
Contribution		12.50		15.50		8.50
Ranked by profitability		2		1		3

The deluxe service is the most profitable (£15.50 contribution per unit), followed by the basic service (£12.50 contribution per unit) and the superdeluxe (£8.50 contribution per unit). Note that we do not take fixed costs into account. This is because they are irrelevant to the decision.

(ii) Should We Cease Production of Any Products?

The key here is to see whether or not any products or services are making a negative contribution.

PAUSE FOR THOUGHT 19.2

Negative Contribution

Why should we discontinue any product or service with a negative contribution?

. . . .

Products and services with negative contribution are bad news. This means that every extra product or service makes no contribution to our fixed costs. In actual fact, the more products or services we provide the greater our loss. This is because our variable costs per unit are greater than the selling price per unit.

Let us take the example in Figure 19.6.

Figure 19.6 Dropping Loss-Making Products

We have the following information for Dolly, which makes three sweets: the mixtures, the sweeteners and the gobsuckers.

Current Sales	£	£
Mixtures (100,000 at 50p)		50,000
Sweeteners (200,000 at 20p)		40,000
Gobsuckers (400,000 at 10p)		40,000
		130,000
Less: Costs		
Direct materials	50,000	
Direct labour	40,000	
Variable overheads	20,000	
Fixed overheads	10,000	
Total costs		120,000
Net Profit		10,000

The variable costs are split between the products: 50% to mixtures, 25% to sweeteners and 25% to gobsuckers.
Are all these products profitable? If not, what is the effect on profit of dropping the unprofitable one?

We need to rearrange our information to identify contribution per sweet.

		Mixtures		Sweeteners		Gobsuckers
	£	£	£	£	£	£
Sales		50,000		40,000		40,000
Less: Variable costs:						
Direct materials	25,000		12,500		12,500	
Direct labour	20,000		10,000		10,000	
Variable overheads	10,000	55,000	5,000	27,500	5,000	27,500
Contribution		(5,000)		12,500		12,500
Total Contribution ((£5,000) + £12,500 + £12,500)						20,000
Fixed overheads						(10,000)
Net Profit						10,000

Sweeteners and gobsuckers thus make positive contributions of £12,500 each and are therefore profitable. By contrast, mixtures makes a negative contribution of £5,000. If we drop mixtures, profit increases by £5,000, we can see this below.

	£
Sweeteners	12,500
Gobsuckers	12,500
Total Contribution	25,000
Less: Fixed overheads	(10,000)
Net Profit	15,000

(iii) The Make or Buy Decision

Here we need to compare the cost of providing goods or services internally with the cost of buying in the goods or services. We compare the variable costs of making them internally with the external costs. Businesses often outsource (i.e., buy in) their non-essential activities. In Real-Life Nugget 19.2 British Airways has outsourced its engineering and IT services.

REAL-LIFE NUGGET 19.2

British Airways and Outsourcing

At the height of its prosperity in the mid-1990s, BA brought in an ambitious plan to cut £1 billion off its £8 billion annual costs. So far it has found savings of about £700m; it hopes to hack out the other £300 m by March. A cull of 1,000 middle managers should lop a further £225 m off costs. This was proclaimed as a precautionary measure to prepare BA for the next downturn, when price competition was bound to intensify. BA also started to outsource as much as it could, getting rid of such services as engineering, IT and catering. Its bosses talked of 'a virtual airline', one that concentrated only on selling seats and operating flights. Analysts noted approvingly that BA had been the first international airline to emerge smiling from the 1990–91 slump, thanks to similar prompt action.

Source: Diving for Cover, *The Economist*, 16 October 1999

This sort of decision is also often faced by local governments in tendering or contracting out services such as cleaning (see Figure 19.7).

Figure 19.7   The Make or Buy Decision

A local government is looking at a particular cleaning contract. One of the existing local government departments has bid for a particular contract, with the following costs.

	£
Direct materials	28
Direct labour, 25 hours at £5.10	
Variable overheads	12

Speedyclean, a private company, has offered to do the contract for £165, should we accept?

Internally	£
Direct materials	28.00
Direct labour (25 hours at £5.10)	127.50
Variable overheads	12.00
	167.50
Externally	165.00

Yes, on pure cost grounds it should be awarded externally to Speedyclean.

(iv) Maximising a Limiting Factor

Businesses often face a situation where one of the key resource inputs is a limiting factor on production. For example, the quantity of direct materials may be limited or labour hours may be restricted. The basic idea, in this case, is to **maximise the contribution of the limiting factor**. Figure 19.8 demonstrates this concept for a hotel which has three restaurants, but a limited amount of direct labour hours.

Figure 19.8   Maximising Contribution per Limiting Factor

A hotel has three restaurants (Snack, Bistro and Formal). There are only 1,150 labour hours available at £10 per hour. If the restaurants opened normally for the coming week then 1,300 hours would be used: 400 hours for Snack, 500 hours for Bistro and 400 hours for Formal. Under normal opening you expect the following:

	Snack		Bistro		Formal	
Customers	2,000		3,000		2,000	
	£	£	£	£	£	£
Sales		10,000		12,000		16,000
Less: *Costs*						
Direct materials	2,000		2,500		7,500	
Direct labour	4,000		5,000		4,000	
Variable overheads	1,000		1,250		2,000	
Fixed overheads*	2,000	9,000	3,000	11,750	2,000	15,500
Net Profit		1,000		250		500

*Allocated by number of customers

You are required to maximise profit.

Figure 19.8   Maximising Contribution per Limiting Factor (*continued*)

To maximise profit, we need to **maximise our contribution per unit of limiting resource,** i.e., labour hours. We need to maximise this as *labour is limited to 1,150 hours.* We must, therefore, first determine our overall contribution and the contribution per labour hour.

		Snack 400		Bistro 500		Formal 400
Labour hours						
	£	£	£	£	£	£
Sales		10,000		12,000		16,000
Less: *Variable costs*						
Direct materials	2,000		2,500		7,500	
Direct labour	4,000		5,000		4,000	
Variable overheads	1,000	7,000	1,250	8,750	2,000	13,500
		3,000		3,250		2,500
Contribution						

Contribution per labour hour:

Contribution	£3,000		£3,250		£2,500	
Hours	400 hours	= £7.50	500 hours	= £6.50	400 hours	= £6.25

Above, we have divided the coming week's contribution by the number of labour hours available. We ought, therefore, to use our labour first in the Snack, then in the Bistro, and only, lastly, on the Formal restaurant. This is because our contribution is greatest for the Snack at £7.50 per hour, next for the Bistro at £6.50 per hour and least for the Formal at £6.25 per hour. Our maximum profit (to the nearest £) is therefore:

		£
Snack 400 hours (i.e. the Snack's capacity) × £7.50		3,000
Bistro 500 hours (i.e. the Bistro's capacity) × £6.50		3,250
Formal 250 hours (i.e. the balance) × £6.25		1,563
1150 hours		7,813
Less: Fixed costs		(7,000)
Net Profit		813

Any other allocation would result in less profit. For example, if we allocated the hours according to *maximum contribution per customer* (i.e., in the order Snack, Formal, Bistro).

		£
Snack	400 hours (i.e. Snack's capacity) × £7.50	3,000
Formal	400 hours (i.e. Formal's capacity) × £6.25	2,500
Bistro	350 hours (i.e. Balance) × £6.50	2,275
	1150 hours	7,775
Less: Fixed costs		(7,000)
Net Profit		775

Throughput Accounting

Throughput accounting is a relatively new approach to production management, and uses a variant of contribution per limiting factor. This approach looks at a production system from the perspective of bottlenecks. It essentially asks what are a system's main bottlenecks? For instance, is it shortage of machine hours in a certain department? Every effort is then made to eliminate the bottlenecks. Goldratt and Cox in *The Goal* (1992) look at throughput contribution (defined as sales less direct materials) as a key measure. Interestingly, therefore, all other costs are treated as fixed. Thus, direct labour and variable overheads are seen as fixed overheads in this system. Figure 19.9 provides an example of a throughput operating statement. The throughput contribution is £40,000 (i.e., sales of £105,000 less direct materials at £65,000).

Figure 19.9   Throughput Accounting

Sanderson Engineering has the following details from its accounting records for May 2006.

	£000		£000
Sales	105,000	Production overheads	10,000
Direct materials	65,000	Administrative expenses	6,000
Direct labour	18,000	Selling and distribution expenses	5,000

Prepare a throughput accounting statement.

Sanderson Engineering Throughput Accounting Statement for May 2006.

	£000	£000
Sales		105,000
Direct materials		(65,000)
Throughput Contribution		40,000
Direct labour	(18,000)	
Production overheads	(10,000)	
Administrative expenses	(6,000)	
Selling and distribution expenses	(5,000)	(39,000)
Net Profit		1,000

Break-Even Analysis

The contribution concept is particularly useful when determining the break-even point of a firm. The break-even point is simply that point at which a firm makes neither a profit nor a loss. A firm's break-even point can be expressed as follows:

$$\text{Sales} - \text{Variable costs} - \text{Fixed costs} = 0$$

Figure 19.10   The Essentials of Break-Even Analysis

Break-Even Point	Contribution	Break-Even Point in Units
The point at which a business makes neither a profit or a loss	Sales – Variable costs	$\dfrac{\text{Fixed costs}}{\text{Contribution per unit}}$

In other words, the break-even point is the point where contribution equals fixed costs. We can find the break-even point in units by dividing fixed costs by contribution per unit. Figure 19.11 shows how the break-even point works.

Figure 19.11   An Example of Break-Even Analysis

A restaurateur, William Bunter, has expected sales of 15,000 meals at £20 each. His variable costs are £8 per meal. If the fixed costs are £120,000, what is the break-even point? What is sales revenue at break-even profit?

We, therefore, have

$$\frac{\text{Fixed costs}}{\text{Contribution per unit (i.e. meal)}} = \frac{£120,000}{£20 - £8} = \frac{£120,000}{£12} = 10,000 \text{ meals}$$
(sales – variable cost per unit (i.e. meal))

Sales revenue at break-even is thus $10,000 \times £20 = £200,000$.

Assumptions of Break-Even Analysis

The beauty of break-even analysis is that it is comparatively straightforward. However, break-even analysis is underpinned by several key assumptions. Perhaps the main one is **linearity**. Linearity assumes that the behaviour of the sales and costs will remain constant despite increases in the level of sales. Sales and variable costs are assumed always to be strictly variable and fixed costs are assumed to be strictly fixed. For instance, in Figure 19.11 it is assumed that sales will remain at £20 per meal, variable costs will remain at £8 per meal and fixed costs will remain at £120,000, whether we sell 1,000 meals, 10,000 meals or 100,000 meals. In practice, it is more likely that these costs will be fixed or variable within a particular range of activity (often called the **relevant range**). The break-even point also implies a precision which is perhaps unwarranted. A better description might be the break-even area.

Other Uses of Break-Even Analysis

Break-even analysis can also form the basis of more sophisticated analyses such as (i) calculating the margin of safety, (ii) the basis for 'what-if' analysis, or (iii) the basis for graphical analysis.

(i) Margin of Safety

Bunter may wish to calculate how much he has sold over and above the break-even point. This is called the margin of safety. Bunter's margin of safety is calculated using a general formula:

$$\frac{\text{Actual units sold} - \text{units at break-even point}}{\text{Actual units}}$$

The break-even point can be calculated in either (a) units (i.e., in this case, meals) or (b) in money. Therefore,

(a) Bunter's margin of safety (units) $= \dfrac{15{,}000 - 10{,}000}{10{,}000} = 50\,\%$

(b) Bunter's margin of safety (£s) $= \dfrac{£300{,}000 - £200{,}000}{£200{,}000} = 50\,\%$

(ii) What-if Analysis

The break-even point can also be used as a basis for 'what-if' analysis. For instance, we know that each unit sold in excess of the break-even point adds one unit's contribution to profit. Similarly, each unit less than the break-even point creates a loss of one unit's contribution. So, we can easily answer questions such as 'what is the profit or loss if Bunter sells (a) 8,000 meals or (b) 13,000 meals?'

(a) **8,000 meals.** This is 2,000 meals less than the break-even point of 10,000 meals. The loss is, therefore, 2,000 meals × contribution per meal. Thus,

2,000 meals × £12 contribution per meal = £24,000 loss

(b) **13,000 meals.** This is 3,000 meals more than the break-even point of 10,000 meals. The profit is thus.

3,000 meals × £12 contribution per meal = £36,000 profit

The break-even point is a very flexible concept and provides potentially rewarding insights into business.

(iii) Graphical Break-Even Point

Another benefit of break-even analysis is that it can be shown on a graph (see Figure 19.12).

Figure 19.12   Graphical Break-Even Point

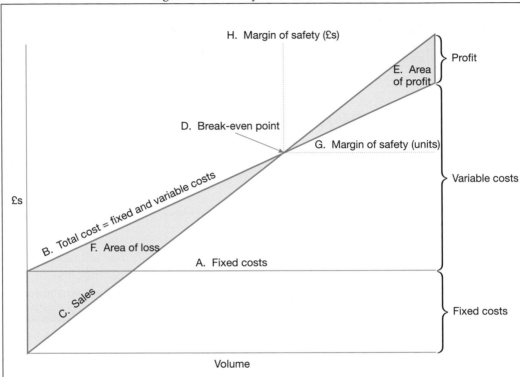

On the graph, it is important to note the following points:

A. **Fixed costs.** This is a straight horizontal line.

B. **Variable costs (total cost).** This is a straight line which starts on the vertical Y axis and 'piggybacks' the fixed cost line.
   Effectively, the variable cost line also represents the **total cost (fixed cost plus variable costs).**

C. **Sales.** The sales line starts at the origin and then climbs steadily.

D. **Break-even point.** This is the point where the sales line (C) and the total cost line (B) (i.e., variable costs line) cross.

E. **Area of profit.** This is where the sales line (C) is higher than the total cost line (B). A profit is thus being made.

F. **Area of loss.** This is where the sales line (C) is lower than the total cost line (B). There is thus a loss.

G. **Margin of safety (units).** This is the difference between current sales and the sales needed to break even in units.

H. **Margin of safety (£s).** This is the difference between current sales and the sales needed to break even in £s.

Figure 19.13 is the graph for William Bunter. Sales are set at four levels: 0 meals; 5,000 meals; 10,000 meals; and 15,000 meals. Break-even point is 10,000 meals.

Figure 19.13 Bunter's Break-Even Chart

First, we need to work out the figures to graph.
Remember: each sale is £20, variable costs are £8 and fixed costs are £120,000.

Number of Meals	Fixed Costs	Variable Costs	Total Costs	Sales	Profit (Loss)
£	£	£	£	£	£
–	120,000	–	120,000	–	(120,000)
5,000	120,000	40,000	160,000	100,000	(60,000)
10,000	120,000	80,000	200,000	200,000	–
15,000	120,000	120,000	240,000	300,000	60,000

Now, we can draw the break-even chart.

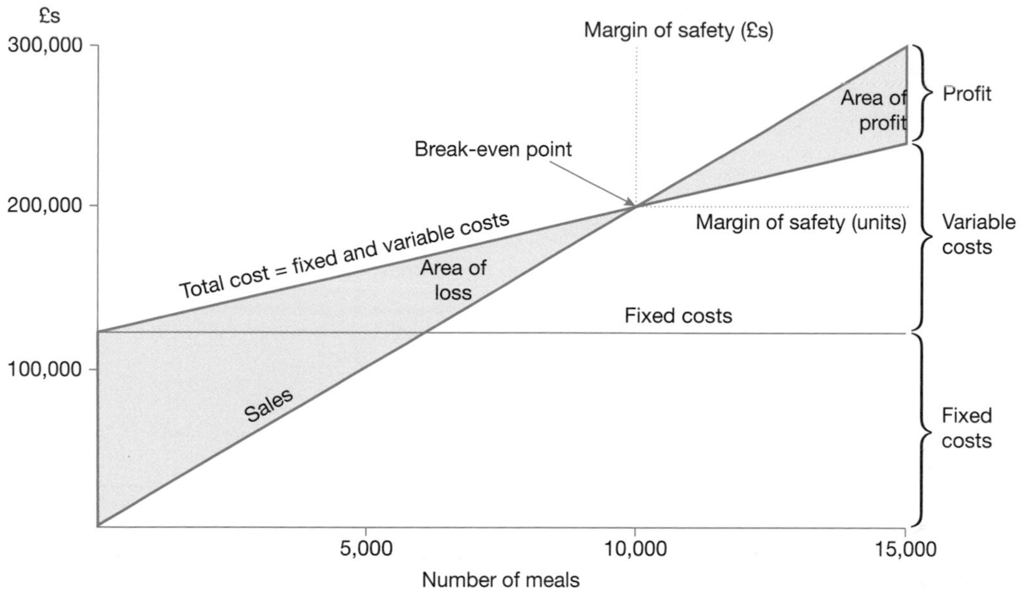

Contribution Graph

A further limitation of the break-even chart is that it can be used for only one product. This disadvantage is overcome by using a contribution graph (see Figure 19.14). This is sometimes called a *profit/volume chart*. However, in this book we use the term contribution graph as it is easier to understand. A contribution graph looks a bit like a set of rugby posts! It is based on the idea that each unit sold generates one unit's contribution. Initially, this contribution covers fixed costs and then generates a profit. The horizontal line represents level of sales (either in units or £s). Above the horizontal line is profit, while below the line is loss. The diagonal line represents contribution. In effect, it is the cumulative profit or loss plotted against cumulative sales. So when sales are zero there is a loss (point A). This loss is, in effect, the total fixed costs. The company then breaks even at point B. At this point contribution equals fixed costs. Above point B each unit sold adds one unit of contribution to the company's profit. Finally, point C represents maximum cumulative sales and maximum contribution.

Figure 19.14   Contribution Graph

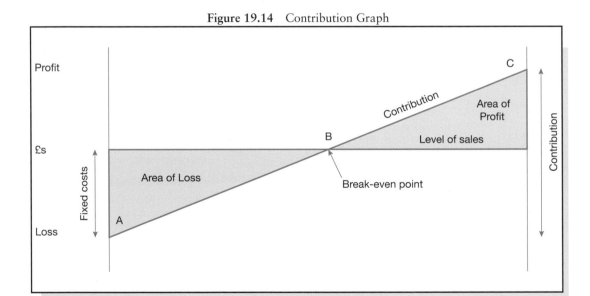

The relationship between contribution and sales is defined as $\frac{\text{Contribution}}{\text{Sales}}$. Sometimes this is known as the profit/volume ratio.

This ratio provides an easy way of comparing the contributions of different products. We take, as an example, a department store which has three departments: toys, clothes and records (see Figure 19.15).

Figure 19.15 Contribution Graph for a Department Store

Department	Sales	Variable Costs	Contribution	Contribution/Sales Ratio		Ranking
	£	£	£	%		
Toys	20,000	10,000	10,000	50	(£10,000/£20,000)	1
Clothes	40,000	30,000	10,000	25	(£10,000/£40,000)	3
Records	60,000	40,000	20,000	33	(£20,000/£60,000)	2
Total	120,000	80,000	40,000	33	(£40,000/£120,000)	
Fixed costs			(20,000)			
				33⅓		
Net Profit			20,000			
				33⅓		

Using this information draw a contribution graph.

First we draw up a cumulative profit/loss table ranked by the highest contribution/sales ratio. The cumulative profit/loss is simply cumulative contribution less fixed costs.

	Cumulative Sales	Cumulative Contribution	Cumulative Profit/(Loss)
	£	£	£
Fixed costs			(20,000)
Toys	20,000	10,000	(10,000)
Records	80,000	30,000	10,000
Clothes	120,000	40,000	20,000

We are now in a position to draw up a graph.

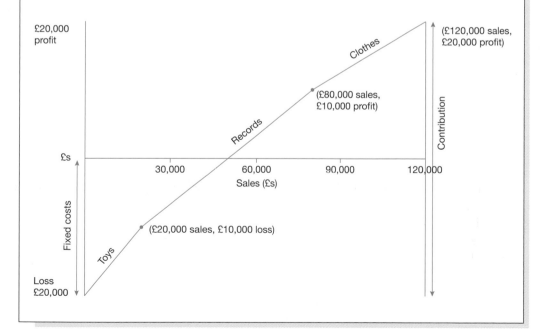

In many industries, there are substantial fixed costs. In the retail industry, for example, as Real-Life Nugget 19.3 shows, the concept of break-even becomes very important.

REAL-LIFE NUGGET 19.3

Fixed Costs and Supermarkets

The question is of particular interest in Britain, where the competition authorities are investigating newspaper claims that the big four supermarket chains Tesco, J. Sainsbury, Asda and Safeway are making excessive profits.

In recent years these four chains have tried to avoid price wars because price-slashing makes little sense in markets where a few big operators with similar cost structures operate.

The reason is that each has substantial fixed costs, making a profit by driving more than enough volume through its stores to cover its overheads. If one operator cuts prices, the others are compelled to follow for fear of seeing their own volumes fall below the break-even point. So nobody gains market share, and everybody's profits fall.

Source: Marketing Value for Money, Richard Tomkins, *Financial Times*, 14 May 1999

Conclusion

Businesses constantly face short-term decisions such as how to maximise a limited resource. When making these decisions it is useful to distinguish between fixed and variable costs. Fixed costs do not, in the short run, change with either production or sales (for example, insurance or depreciation). Variable costs, by contrast, do change when the production volume or sales volume changes (examples are direct materials and direct labour). Sales less variable costs gives contribution. Contribution is a useful accounting concept. By calculating contribution we can, for example, determine which products are the most profitable. Break-even analysis is another useful concept that builds on contribution analysis. The break-even point is the point at which a business makes neither a profit or a loss. It is determined by dividing fixed costs by the contribution per unit. The break-even chart shows the break-even point graphically. The contribution graph is a useful way of graphing the profit or loss of one or more products.

Discussion Questions

Questions with numbers in blue have answers at the back of the book.

Q1   Distinguish between fixed and variable costs. Why are fixed costs irrelevant when making a choice between certain alternatives such as whether to produce more of product A or of product B?

Q2 What is contribution per unit and why is it so useful in short-term decision making?

Q3 What are the strengths and weaknesses of break-even analysis?

Q4 State whether the following statements are true or false? If false, explain why.
 (a) Fixed costs are those that do not vary with long-term changes in the level of sales or production.
 (b) Contribution is sales less variable costs.
 (c) Break-even point is $\frac{\text{Variable costs}}{\text{Contribution per unit}}$
 (d) Contribution/sales ratio is $\frac{\text{Profit}}{\text{Sales}}$
 (e) Non-financial items are not important in decision making.

Q&A Numerical Questions

Questions with numbers in blue have answers at the back of the book.

Q1 Jungle Animals makes 10 model animals with the following cost structure.

	Selling Price £	Direct Labour £	Direct Materials £	Variable Overheads £
Alligators	1.00	0.50	0.20	0.35
Bears	1.20	0.60	0.10	0.30
Cougars	1.10	0.66	0.15	0.33
Donkeys	1.15	0.60	0.18	0.30
Eagles	1.20	0.56	0.12	0.28
Foxes	0.90	0.50	0.10	0.25
Giraffes	1.05	0.40	0.25	0.20
Hyenas	1.25	0.56	0.10	0.28
Iguanas	0.95	0.40	0.12	0.20
Jackals	0.80	0.40	0.13	0.20

Required:
 (i) Calculate the contribution per toy.
 (ii) Calculate the contribution/sales ratio per toy.
 (iii) Which two toys bring in the greatest contribution?
 (iv) Which three toys have the highest contribution/sales ratio?
 (v) Which two toys would you not manufacture at all?

Q2 An insurance company, Riskmore, has four divisions: car, home, personal and miscellaneous. These four divisions account, respectively, for 40 %, 30 %, 20 % and 10 % of sales and 25 % each of the variable costs. Riskmore has the following summary profit and loss account.

	£
Sales	200,000
Less: *Costs*	
Variable costs	100,000
Fixed costs	50,000
Net Profit	50,000

Required: Calculate the profitability of the divisions.

Q3 Scrooge Ltd is looking to outsource its accounts department. Ghost Ltd, has approached Scrooge and offered to provide the service for £160,000. Scrooge Ltd ascertains the following costs are involved internally.

Clerical labour	10,000 hours at £5
Supervisory labour	6,000 hours at £10
Direct materials	£25,000
Variable overheads	£3 per clerical labour hour
Fixed overheads	£8,000

Required: Calculate whether or not Scrooge Ltd should accept Ghost's bid. State any assumptions you have made and other factors you might take into account.

Q4 A large hotel, The Open Umbrella, has two kiosks. One sells sweets and is open 35 hours per week. The second sells newspapers and magazines and is open 55 hours per week. Unfortunately, next week labour is restricted to 70 hours. Labour is £5 per hour. Last week's results when both were fully open and 90 labour hours were available are set out below.

	Kiosk 1 (Sweets)		Kiosk 2 (Newspapers)	
	£	£	£	£
Sales		900		1,200
Less: *Costs*				
Direct labour	175		275	
Direct materials	600		700	
Variable overheads	70	845	110	1,085
Contribution		55		115

Required: How would you maximise the profits using the 70 labour hours available?

Q5 Globeco makes four geographical board quiz games: France, Germany, UK and US. Globeco has the following recent results.

	France		Germany		UK		US	
Units sold	1,000		1,500		4,000		6,000	
	£	£	£	£	£	£	£	£
Sales		2,000		3,000		12,000		24,000
Less: *Variable Costs*								
Direct labour	800		1,350		6,000		15,600	
Direct materials	200		300		1,300		1,400	
Variable overheads	80		135		600		1,560	
Fixed overheads (equal allocation)	1,000		1,000		1,000		1,000	
		2,080		2,785		8,900		19,560
Net Profit (loss)		(80)		215		3,100		4,440

For next year, there are only 3,000 direct labour hours available. Last year's results used 4,750 direct labour hours. Direct labour is paid at £5 per hour. The maximum sales (in units) are predicted to be 2,000 France, 3,500 Germany, 6,000 UK and 8,000 US.

Required: Calculate the most profitable production schedule, given that direct labour hours, the limiting factor, are restricted to 3,000 hours.

Q6 Freya manufactures heavy-duty hammers. They each cost £4 in direct materials and £3 in variable expenses. They sell for £10 each. Fixed costs are £30,000. Currently 20,000 hammers are sold.

Required:
  (i) What is the break-even point?
  (ii) What is the profit if the number of hammers sold is:
     (a) 4,000   (b) 14,000?
  (iii) What is the current margin of safety in (a) units and (b) £s?
  (iv) Draw a break-even chart.

Q7 Colin Xiao runs a restaurant which serves 10,000 customers a month. Each customer spends £20, variable costs per customer are £15. Fixed costs are £10,000.

Required:
  (i) What are the current break-even point and margin of safety in £s?
  (ii) Calculate the new break-even point and margin of safety in £s if the average spend per customer is:
     (a) £17   (b) £19   (c) £25
     Assume all other factors remain the same.

Q8 A computer hardware distributor, Modem, has three branches in Cardiff, Edinburgh and London. It has the following financial details.

	Sales	Direct Labour	Other Variable Overheads
	£	£	£
Cardiff	200,000	60,000	105,000
Edinburgh	300,000	80,000	150,000
London	1,000,000	350,000	520,000

Head office fixed overheads are £150,000.

Required:
 (i) Calculate the contribution/sales ratios.
(ii) Draw the contribution graph.

Chapter 20

"Today's management accounting information, driven by the procedures and cycle of the organisation's financial reporting system, is too late, too aggregated, and too distorted to be relevant for managers' planning and control decisions."

H.T. Johnson and R.S. Kaplan (1987), *Relevance Lost: The Rise and Fall of Management Accounting*, p. 1

Learning Outcomes

After completing this chapter you should be able to:

✔ Explain the nature and importance of strategic management accounting.

✔ Understand and explain techniques used to assess the current position of the business.

✔ Appreciate the techniques of SWOT analysis, balanced scorecard and benchmarking.

✔ Discuss the strategic choices facing companies.

Strategic Management Accounting

In a Nutshell

- *Strategic management accounting is externally orientated and concerns a business's future long-term strategy.*

- *Strategic management accounting is a relatively new topic.*

- *The three stages of strategic management accounting are (i) assessment of the current position of the business, (ii) appraisal of the current position of the business, and (iii) strategic choice of future direction of the business.*

- *The assessment of the current position of the business is concerned with both the external and internal environment and may use techniques such as value chain analysis, life cycle analysis and the product portfolio matrix.*

- *The appraisal of the current position of the business may use SWOT (strengths, weaknesses, opportunities and threats) analysis, the balanced scorecard and benchmarking.*

- *Strategic choice may involve exploiting inherent strengths such as the business's products or customer base and/or external diversification through acquisition or merger.*

Introduction

Strategic management accounting attempts to involve management accountants in wider business strategy. It concerns a business's future, long-term direction. As Soundbite 20.1 shows, essentially strategy is concerned with where a business is now and where it wants to be in the future. Strategic management accounting is thus an attempt by management accountants to move away from a narrow, functional specialism towards full participation in the long-term strategic planning of businesses. In a sense, this continues a long historical process whereby management accountants have consistently widened the scope of their activities, for example, from costing to management accounting. It also meets the criticism that management accounting has failed to respond to changing environmental circumstances and focuses too much on a business's internal activities and too little on a business's external environment. In short, traditional management accounting is criticised for being too narrow. Strategic management accounting is a very contentious topic. For some, it represents the next stage in the evolution of the management accounting profession. For others, it is seen as a step too far, an unsuitable activity for management accountants.

SOUNDBITE 20.1

Strategy

'There's no rocket science to strategy . . . you're supposed to know where you are, where your competition is, what your cost position is, and where you want to go. Strategies are intellectually simple, their execution is not.'

Lawrence A. Bossidy, *Harvard Business Review*, March–April, 1995

Source: *The Wiley Book of Business Quotations* (1998), p. 88

Nature of Strategic Management Accounting

Strategic management accounting is relatively new. It dates from the 1980s. At this time, considerable concern was expressed that management accounting had lost its way. Johnson and Kaplan capture this concern in a book entitled *Relevance Lost: The Rise and Fall of Management Accounting*. They argue that conventional management accounting has failed to adapt to a changing industrial environment, that traditional product costing systems are increasingly inappropriate, that financial accounting dominates management accounting and that management accounting needs to reflect the external environment (see Real-Life Nugget 20.1).

REAL-LIFE NUGGET 20.1

Criticisms of Traditional Management Accounting

'Most [of today's] accounting and control systems have major problems: they distort product costs; they do not produce the key financial data required for effective and efficient operations; and the data they do produce reflect external reporting requirements far more than they do the reality of the new manufacturing environment.'

Source: Yesterday's Accounting Undermines Production', R.S. Kaplan, *Harvard Business Review*, 1984, p. 95

Strategic management accounting is one response to these criticisms. It attempts to involve management accountants in strategic business decisions and in the planning of a business's future long-term direction. The exact nature and extent of strategic management accounting is still, however, somewhat vague. In Definition 20.1, we provide a working definition and the Chartered Institute of Management Accountants' formal definition.

DEFINITION 20.1

Strategic Management Accounting

Working definition
A form of management accounting which considers both an organisation's internal and external environments.

Formal definition
'A form of management accounting in which emphasis is placed on information which relates to factors external to the firm as well as non-financial information and internally-generated information.'

Source: Chartered Institute of Management Accountants (2000), *Official Terminology*

This book takes strategic accounting to be a form of management accounting, which emphasises the external and future environment of the business, but also takes into account

Figure 20.1 Overview of Strategic Management Accounting

the internal environment of a business. In essence, it is the way in which a business seeks to implement its long-term strategic objectives, such as to be the world's leading supplier of a particular good or service. Figure 20.1 shows the three main stages of strategic management accounting. These stages are outlined briefly here and then discussed in more detail in the following section.

(i) Assessment of current position of the business

This is essentially an information gathering stage. Information is gathered on the current internal and external environment of the business.

(ii) Appraisal of current position of the business

This involves a hard look at the current position of the business investigating its strengths, weaknesses and competitiveness.

(iii) Strategic choice of future direction of the business

Once the current position of the business has been identified and appraised, it is time to choose the future direction of the business. This may involve diversification into new areas or the fuller exploitation of old areas.

It is important to appreciate that these strategic management activities are ongoing, not one-off. A well-run business will continually be assessing and appraising its current position and looking at its strategic choices. Assessment and appraisal are not distinct activities, but overlap. However, it is useful here to deal with them separately. As Soundbite 20.2 shows, it is harder to implement than plan business strategy.

SOUNDBITE 20.2

Implementation of Strategy

'Strategy is easy, implementation is hard . . . [O]nly the superb companies actually find a way to do what they say they're going to do.'

Raymond Smith, Speech (1 November 1995)

Source: *The Wiley Book of Business Quotations* (1998) p. 88

Assessment of Current Position of the Business

The first step in strategic management accounting is an assessment of the current position of the business. In essence, this is an information-gathering exercise. Information is gathered about the national and international external environment and the business's internal environment. Figure 20.2 outlines some of the issues that might be covered.

Figure 20.2   Information Useful in Assessment of Current Position

External Environment	Internal Environment
Political and legal environment Economic environment Social and cultural environment Technological change Interest and pressure groups Environmental issues Competitors	Resources Current products Operating systems Internal organisation Customers Sources of finance

External Environment

The seven factors listed in Figure 20.2, and discussed briefly below, serve as a basis for assessing both the current national and international environment. The importance of each factor varies from business to business.

Political and Legal Environment

This may involve the legal framework, national and international laws, and government policy. For example, privatised utilities in the UK, such as the water companies, are subject to a complex regulatory system.

Economic Environment

The economy is a key consideration for any business. Indeed, correctly assessing the current and future state of the economy is probably the most important external factor in business success.

PAUSE FOR THOUGHT 20.1

Economic Environment

What are some of the considerations which a business might take into account when assessing the economy?

....

These are varied, but they include:

- current economic indicators (such as economic growth, inflation, interest rates, taxation and unemployment) at the regional, national and international level
- stage in economic cycle (boom or slump)
- long-term trends (such as towards a knowledge-based economy)
- government economic policy (such as spending, subsidy, privatisation)
- international trade (different economic conditions in different countries, exchange rates).

Social and Cultural Environment

Society continually evolves. For example, in developed countries there are increasing numbers of retired people and single-person households. These long-term demographic trends need to be matched to a company's products and services.

Technological Change

A business needs to look closely at technological change. Well-positioned businesses are best-placed to exploit social trends such as the use of mobile phones or laptop computers.

Interest and Pressure Groups

It is important to realise that a business operates within society not outside society. Businesses must, therefore, keep an eye on public opinion, which is often manifested in pressure groups. For example, mutual building societies often face pressure from groups wishing to abolish their mutual status and turn them into publicly listed companies.

Environmental Issues

Nowadays, environmental issues are critically important for businesses. Companies must increasingly take on board environmental concerns. Indeed, many businesses have separate environmental departments. Some companies, such as Body Shop, have built their businesses upon a strong environmental ethic.

Competitors

A business needs to be aware of its competitors and the competitive environment in which it operates. Both customers and suppliers have potential power over a business. Businesses must also be aware of potential entrants to an industry as well as potential substitute products. For example, the entry of the US supermarket chain Wal-Mart into the UK caused repercussions for UK companies such as Sainsbury and Tesco.

Internal Environment

A business's internal environment, like its external environment, varies from business to business. The six factors listed in Figure 20.2 (resources, current products, operating systems, internal organisation, customers and sources of finance) are reviewed below. We will then look at three techniques useful in assessing the internal environment: value chain analysis, product life cycle and the product portfolio matrix.

Resources

The resources potentially important in an internal assessment include materials, management, fixed assets, working capital, human resources, brands and other intangibles, and intellectual capital. Nowadays, in an increasingly knowledge-driven society, the last three resources are becoming ever more important. An important element of the resource assessment is the determination of any limiting factors or bottlenecks which will stop a business fulfilling its plans.

Current Products

It is important for a company to review its current product mix. This may include its current competitiveness, a product life cycle analysis, a product profitability review and an analysis of its customers.

Operating Systems

Operating systems are those information systems that form the backbone of a company, such as the sales invoicing system or the payroll system. Their effectiveness needs to be carefully assessed.

Internal Organisation

The effectiveness of the organisational structure of a business, such as the relationship between the head office and the department, needs to be carefully examined.

Customers

A key element of any internal assessment is the customer base. There is a need to gather data and profile customers, for example, by age, ethnicity, sex and social class.

Sources of Finance

It is useful to assess the sources of short-term and long-term capital and the mix between debt and equity. This important topic will be covered in more detail in Chapter 22.

Three techniques potentially useful in the internal assessment are now discussed: the value chain, the product life cycle and the product portfolio matrix.

(i) Value chain analysis

Value chain analysis was devised by Porter (1985). It represents a systematic way of looking at a business. Porter's idea is that each business has a value chain consisting of primary activities and support activities. The primary activities represent a set of value-creating activities from the handling of the raw materials (receiving goods) to after-sales service (service). These primary activities are supported by a set of support activities such as the personnel department (human resource management) or computer department (technology department) (see Figure 20.3).

Figure 20.3   Value Chain Analysis

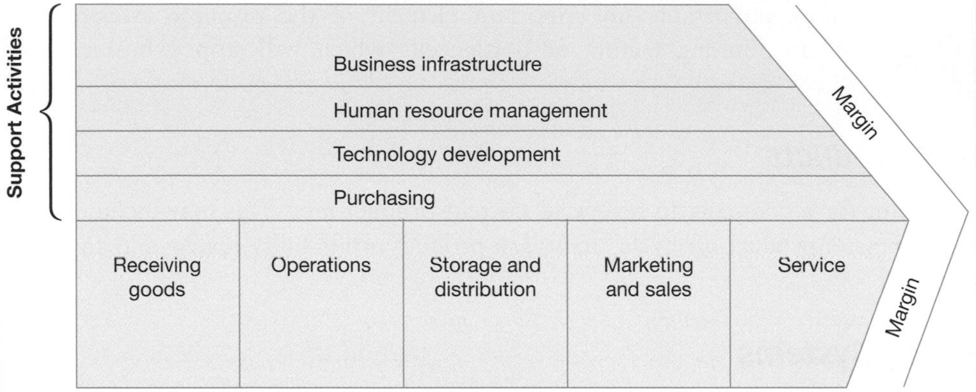

Source: Adapted from M.E. Porter (1985), *Competitive Advantage: Creating and Sustaining Superior Performance*, p. 37. Some of the terminology has been changed to aid understanding.

In Figure 20.4 we set out a value chain for a retail computer superstore.

Figure 20.4   Value Chain for a Retail Computer Superstore

Activity	*Definition*	*Example*
A. Primary Activities		
1. *Receiving goods*	Activities of receiving, handling inputs	Warehousing, transport, stock control
2. *Operations*	Conversion of inputs to outputs	Preparing computers for sale, service staff
3. *Storage and distribution*	Activities concerned with storing and distributing the product	Packaging, warehousing, delivery
4. *Marketing and sales*	Activities which inform and persuade customers	T.V. advertising campaigns
5. *Service*	After sales	Computer helplines
B. Support Activities		
1. *Purchasing*	Acquisition of resources	Computers for resale
2. *Technology development*	Techniques and work organisation	New computer system
3. *Human resources management*	Recruiting, training, developing and rewarding people	Induction course, computer training course
4. *Business infrastructure*	Information and planning systems	Sales invoicing system, budgetary system

The cost of these activities is determined by certain cost drivers (i.e., factors which determine the cost of each activity) such as location. Once these cost drivers have been established, then the management accountant can work out the organisation's sustainable competitive advantage. This involves reducing the costs of each activity while increasing the final sales.

PAUSE FOR THOUGHT 20.2

Value Chain Cost Drivers

Porter identified 10 possible cost drivers. How many can you identify?

....

- **Location**. Is the business in the correct geographical location?
- **Economies of scale**. For example, often the greater the amount purchased, the cheaper the cost per unit.
- **Learning curve**. How experienced is the company at delivering its product or service?
- **Capacity utilisation**. Is the company fully utilising its production capacity?
- **Linkages**. How well are business linkages utilised, such as relationships with suppliers?
- **Interrelationships**. How good are the relations with other units within the group?
- **Timing**. Does the business buy and sell (assets, for example) at the right time?
- **Integration**. How well are the business's individual departments integrated?
- **Discretionary policies**. For example, has the business chosen the optimal computer operating systems?
- **Institutional factors**. Are the business's organisational structures (for example, its management structures) optimal?

(ii) Product life cycle analysis

Most products have a life cycle. Just as with human beings, this involves birth (known as introduction), growth, maturity, decline and senility (known as withdrawal). The key point is that each of these stages is associated with a certain level of sales and profit. Essentially, a product will make a profit once it becomes established. A period of growth will follow in both sales and profits. A period of maturity will then exist and, in this period, profitability will be maximised. The product's sales and profits will then decline and, finally, the product will be withdrawn.

A life cycle analysis graph is shown in Figure 20.5. It is important to realise that for some products, such as the latest children's toy, the product life cycle is short. On the other hand, for certain products, such as a prestige car, the life cycle is very long.

Figure 20.5   Life Cycle Analysis

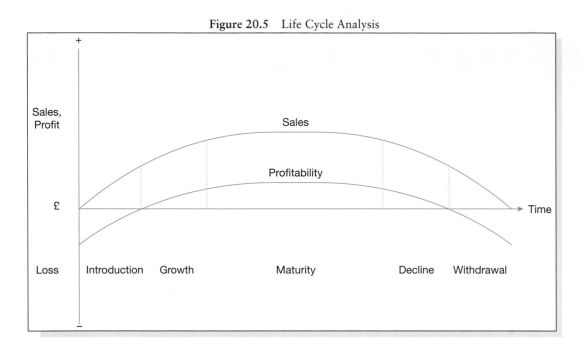

PAUSE FOR THOUGHT 20.3

Product Life Cycles

Are product life cycles today longer or shorter than in the past? If so, what are the consequences for a business?

It is difficult to give a definitive answer. However, the expectation would be shorter. Technology and society are changing at an ever-faster pace, with new technology flourishing. Consumers also, in general, become rich with greater spending power. You would, therefore, expect fashion, styles and products to change more rapidly. Most products thus have shorter life cycles.

The consequences are that businesses need to invest more resources into product development and associated activities such as research and development. If they don't they will not keep pace with the changing market. In addition, it is likely that they will have to relaunch existing products and spend more on advertising and marketing.

Businesses will obviously try, through advertising and other means, to prolong the length of their product life cycle, especially in its mature phase. However, whatever the length of the product's life cycle, a business needs to develop new products for the eventual replacement of the existing product. Just as products have life cycles, it is also true that industries have life cycles (see, for example, Real-Life Nugget 20.2).

REAL-LIFE NUGGET 20.2

Industry Life Cycle

Industries are born, grow, mature and die, and for investors the most spectacular gains are to be had when an industry breaks through from immaturity to growth. This may seem a simple-minded truism to rank alongside "buy low, sell high" but, according to research by the investment bank Schroder Salomon Smith Barney, plotting the position of each sector on the growth/decline curve is fiendishly tricky.

The reason? Industries simply do not behave as they should.

On paper it looks straightforward, with the life-cycle of an industry resembling a motorway flyover. There is an up ramp (immaturity and growth), a flat stretch (maturity) and a down ramp (decline). Salomon is too delicate to include the final stage, but, as Edward G Robinson said in Double Indemnity: "The last stop's the cemetery."

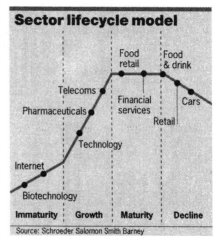

Source: Dead but Refusing to Lie Down, Don Atkinson, *The Guardian*, 7 June 2000, p. 27. © Guardian Newspapers Limited 2000

(iii) The product portfolio matrix

The Boston Consulting Group (BCG) developed a product portfolio matrix based partially on the ideas behind the product life cycle. There are four major categories of products: stars, cash cows, question marks and dogs.

(a) **Stars**. Stars are characterised by high market growth and high market share. Perhaps the mobile phone in its developmental stage. Stars may be cash earners or cash drains, requiring heavy capital expenditure.

(b) **Cash cows**. Cash cows are a company's dream product. They are well-established products which require little capital expenditure, but generate high returns.

(c) **Question marks**. They have low market share, but are in high market growth industries. So the potentially difficult problem for businesses is should they invest in marketing, advertising or capital expenditure in order to gain market share? Alternatively, should they completely withdraw from the market?

(d) **Dogs**. Dogs are cash traps with low market growth and low market share. Dogs tie up capital and often should be 'withdrawn'.

The product portfolio matrix is set out in Figure 20.6.

Figure 20.6   Boston Consulting Group's Product Portfolio Matrix

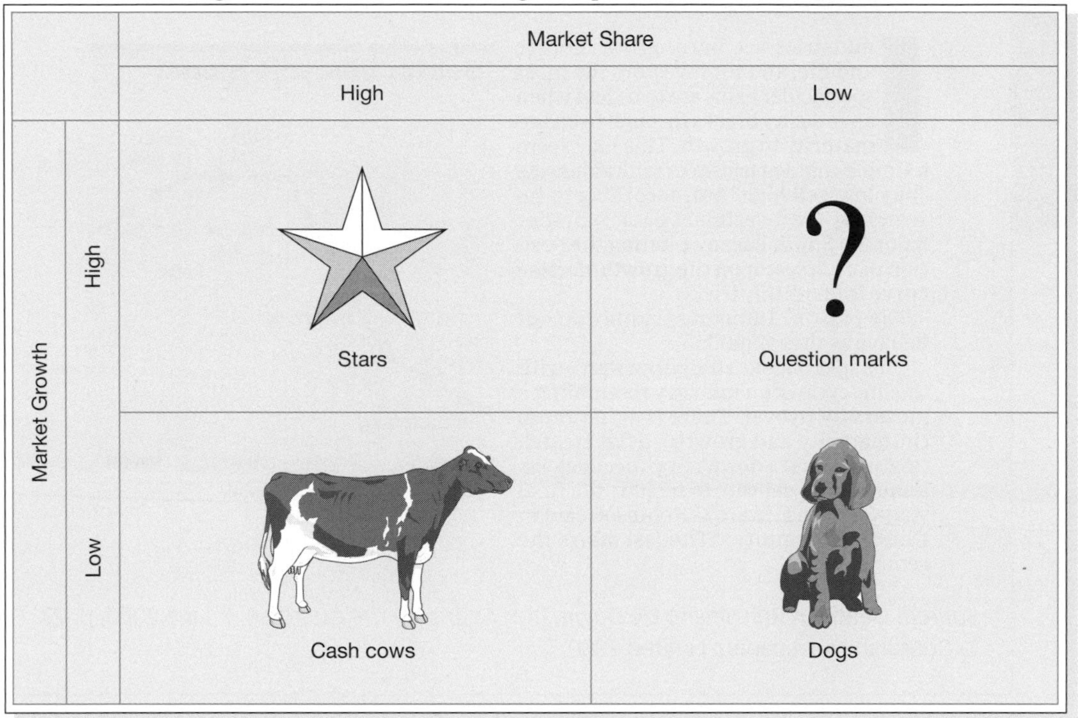

Appraisal of Current Position of the Business

Once the current position of the business has been assessed, it needs to be appraised. We focus here on three major appraisal methods: SWOT analysis; the balanced scorecard; and benchmarking. These appraisal methods take both financial and non-financial factors into account. The appraisal of a business also includes ratio analysis (see Chapter 9).

(i) SWOT Analysis

SWOT analysis is a way of critically assessing a business's strengths and weaknesses, opportunities and threats. SWOT analysis is thus wide-ranging and looks at internal and external factors. As Figure 20.7 shows, SWOT analysis embraces the whole business and might include marketing, products, finance, infrastructure, management, organisational structure and resources. This list is illustrative rather than exhaustive. SWOT analysis involves the management accountant in detailed financial analysis using quantitative and qualitative data.

Figure 20.7   Typical Factors included in SWOT Analysis

(i) Marketing
- What is our market share?
- Are advertising campaigns effective?
- Are customers happy?

(ii) Products
- Is the branding strong?
- Do we have cash cows or dogs?
- Where are the products in their life cycle?

(iii) Finance
- Are the accounting ratios healthy?
- What is the contribution per product?
- Are the sources of finance secure?
- What is the product cost structure?
- Are we profitable and liquid?
- Do we have optimal gearing?

(iv) Infrastructure
- What is the age of our fixed assets?
- What is the market value of the assets?
- Have we sufficient space for expansion?

(v) Management
- What is the age spread?
- Have we training programmes in place?
- Do we have an appropriate skills base?

(vi) Organisational Structure
- Is our organisational structure appropriate?
- Is there a clear command structure?
- Is the management style appropriate?

(vii) Resources
- Are our sources of supply secure?
- Have we any resource bottlenecks?
- Have we good stock control?

Once the strengths and weaknesses of the business are identified, we can investigate the potential opportunities and threats. Major strengths are matched with profitable opportunities and major weaknesses with potential threats. For example, if a particular product is selling well in Italy [strength], we may decide to market it in Spain [opportunity]. Or if an advertising campaign has gone wrong [weakness], a potential competitor might see a chance to launch a new competing product [threat].

So how does this analysis work in practice? Figure 20.8 attempts to answer this question. A SWOT analysis is conducted for a sweet manufacturer.

Figure 20.8   Illustration of SWOT Analysis

A major national company, Sweetco, has conducted an internal and external assessment of its products. It establishes the following:

- two products the Guzzler and the Geezer are only marketed in the UK
- the Guzzler is selling very well; the Geezer is struggling for sales, with many complaints, and is at the end of its product life
- long-term loan: repayment date is approaching
- computer system needs replacing
- management training is poor
- supplies of basic materials for products are running out.

Prepare a SWOT analysis

SWOT Analysis

Strengths	Weaknesses
Guzzler is a cash cow	Geezer is a dog Long-term loan Poor management training Lack of raw materials
Opportunities	**Threats**
Expand Guzzler into Europe Bring out a similar product to Guzzler Renegotiate a cheaper long- term finance package Introduce effective training programmes	Supplies of raw materials will run out Without loan, cash flow position is unhealthy. Geezer will tie up resources.

In this case, therefore, the Guzzler is clearly a strength, but the Geezer is a weakness. Sweetco, therefore, needs to focus on exploiting the Guzzler and minimising the problems caused by the Geezer.

(ii) Balanced Scorecard

The balanced scorecard attempts to look at a business from multiple perspectives. Definition 20.2 shows a working definition and the formal CIMA definition.

DEFINITION 20.2

The Balanced Scorecard

Working definition
A system of corporate appraisal which looks at financial and non-financial elements from a financial, customer, internal business and innovation perspective.

Formal definition
'An approach to the provision of information to management to assist strategic policy formulation and achievement. It emphasises the need to provide the user with a set of information which addresses all relevant areas of performance in an objective and unbiased fashion. The information provided may include both financial and non-financial elements, and cover areas such as profitability, customer satisfaction, internal efficiency and innovation.'

Source: Chartered Institute of Management Accountants (2000), *Official Terminology*

The balanced scorecard takes a strategic, holistic view of an organisation. It combines both financial and non-financial information to provide a multi-perspective view of the organisation's activities. The balanced scorecard was adapted by Norton and Kaplan (1992) from the practice of some US companies. To Kaplan's credit, it seeks to address Kaplan's earlier criticisms of management accounting (such as lack of external focus) which were expressed in Real-Life Nugget 20.1. The balanced scorecard is a way of appraising a business's performance from four perspectives: *a financial perspective* (e.g., how profitable is it?), *a customer perspective* (e.g., how good is the after-sales service?), *an internal business perspective* (e.g., how efficient is our manufacturing process?), and *an innovation and learning perspective* (e.g., how many new products do we produce?). In essence, each perspective is set goals and then a set of performance measures devised. Thus, from the financial perspective the goals may be survival and profitability. These might be measured using cash flow and return on capital employed. As Soundbite 20.3 shows, a balanced scorecard is concerned with implementing rather than formulating strategy.

SOUNDBITE 20.3

The Balanced Scorecard

'The [balanced] scorecard is not a way of formulating strategy. It's a way of understanding and checking what you have to do throughout the organization to make your strategy work.'

David Norton and Robert Kaplan, quoted in *Financial Times* (1 April 1997)

Source: The Wiley Book of Business Quotations (1998), p. 295

Businesses such as Apple Computers have successfully used the balance scorecard. Figure 20.9 gives an example of a balanced scorecard.

Figure 20.9   Illustration of the Balanced Scorecard

Financial Perspective		Customer Perspective	
Goals	*Measures*	*Goals*	*Measures*
Survival	Cash flow	Quality product	Defect rate
Profitability	Return on capital employed	Good after-sales service	Response time

Internal Business Perspective		Innovation and Learning Perspective	
Goals	*Measures*	*Goals*	*Measures*
Managerial efficiency	Throughput of products	Continual improvement	Number of employee suggestions
Advertising success	Increase in customer spend	Develop new products	Number of new product launches

The balanced scorecard thus looks at a business in a comprehensive way. It devises goals and then seeks to measure them. Finally, it combines financial and non-financial measures. One problem with the balanced scorecard is that by taking a multiple-perspective view, no single goal is overriding. It is, therefore, difficult to prioritise the goals. In addition, the appropriate selection of a balanced set of measures may prove difficult, in practice.

(iii) Benchmarking

Benchmarking measures a business against its competitors. The concept is easy – find the best and compare oneself against them across a series of performance indicators. These might be, for example, customer service, number of complaints, or debtors collection period.

DEFINITION 20.3

Benchmarking

Working definition
The comparison of a business with its direct competitors or industry norms.

Formal definition
'The establishment, through data gathering, of targets and comparators, through whose use relative levels of performance (and particularly areas of underperformance) can be identified. By the adoption of identified best practices it is hoped that performance will improve.'

Chartered Institute of Management Accountants (2000), *Official Terminology*

By benchmarking, companies aim to improve their own performance by comparing themselves against their competitors. The problem is that the most effective comparison is to competitors in the same industry. These competitors will be reluctant to provide the data. Benchmarking is thus more usually conducted against industry norms. A practical example of benchmarking is given in Real-Life Nugget 20.3.

REAL-LIFE NUGGET 20.3

Benchmarking in the Dairy Industry

Farmers generally supply their milk to local, regionalised dairies. These dairies may take the milk of, say, 20–30 farmers. Every month the dairy provides these farmers with a printout of how they are doing in comparison with the other farmers. This printout might contain, for example, milk yield per cow in litres, cows per hectare, yield from grazing, litres per cow. From this printout, the individual farmers can judge their relative productivity. The printouts are anonymous so that the farmers can only identify themselves. An extract from a printout is given below.

ANNUAL ROLLING RESULTS TO: August 2000

STOCK		MILK		FEED			FORAGE
Cows in herd	Cows/ hectare	Milk price pence	Yield litres/ cow	All concs tonnes/ cow	Av concs price £/tonne	All bought feed costs pence per litre	Yield from grazing litres/cow
133	2.75	16.19	7022	1.35	95	1.88	–
87	3.46	17.33	5836	1.06	108	1.97	3065
99	1.91	18.57	8005	1.35	106	2.04	2742
175	2.43	18.46	6707	1.59	95	2.24	–
99	2.49	15.42	7870	1.57	111	2.31	2181

Source: By kind permission of *Promar International*

Strategic Choice of Future Direction

Once the current position has been assessed and appraised, there is a need to plan for future strategy. In essence, there are two main directions. A business can either exploit its inherent strengths, for example, by expanding its product range or by more effectively utilising its customer base. Or alternatively, a business can diversify externally, for example, by acquiring another business. We explore these two directions briefly below.

(i) Exploit Inherent Strengths

If a particular product or service is successful, a business may consider expanding its range to similar, but as yet untapped, markets. For instance, if the product is selling well in Brazil, the company might expand its sales to other South American countries.

PAUSE FOR THOUGHT 20.4

Exploiting a Product's Strength

Can you think of any ways other than exploiting new geographical markets in which you could use an existing product's strength?

It might be possible to do the following:

....

- target existing buyers to buy more
- target a new market segment, such as a new age range (e.g., market a child's book to adults, such as the Harry Potter series) or social group
- sell other products in association with the main product (e.g., the range of Barbie products with the Barbie doll).

An alternative to expanding its geographical range is for the business to exploit its customer base more fully. In order to gain relevant information, market research may be carried out. This may seek to ascertain the size of the customer base, the contribution of each sales item, product market share, sales growth and product demand.

Another technique is customer profitability analysis. In essence, this involves a detailed analysis of revenue looking at customer profitability and customer mix. To do this the customers are analysed by characteristics such as age, sex, spending power or social class. The aim is to focus on the most profitable customers.

Various techniques are now available which facilitate customer profitability analysis. Database mining, for example, enables a sales database to be critically examined for trends and other useful information. Interestingly, the findings from using these techniques are not always obvious, as Real-Life Nugget 20.4 shows.

REAL-LIFE NUGGET 20.4

Database Mining

A telecommunications company analysed its database using database mining. The customers were rated as low, medium and high spenders. The initial reason for the investigation was to maximise sales by encouraging the low spenders to spend more. In actual fact, the company found that the way to maximise sales was quite the reverse. The big spenders could easily be encouraged to spend still more.

(ii) External Diversification

A business may grow internally, acquire or merge with another business or cooperate with other businesses through a joint venture. This section concentrates on the acquisition/merger alternative. An acquisition is where one business takes over another (i.e., acquires more than 50 % of another company's shares), whereas a merger is where two businesses combine their resources to form a new company. From an accounting perspective, mergers have the advantage that a business's profits are pooled and available for distribution to shareholders. In acquisitions not only are profits not available for distribution, but goodwill is created (see Chapter 12 for a more detailed discussion of goodwill).

Businesses seek mergers/acquisitions because they are a quick way of growing and also there may be certain operating advantages such as economies of scale. Vodafone, for example, acquired Mannesmann, a German company, so that it could extend its mobile phones into the European and, in particular, the German market. There are also other more specific reasons. For example, a manufacturing company's SWOT analysis might indicate a shortage of raw materials. To safeguard its supplies, the company might then purchase a key supplier.

Conclusion

Strategic management accounting attempts to overcome the inward-looking nature of management accounting. It is concerned with the long-term strategy of a business. Strategic management accounting is still evolving and is an elusive concept. However, three stages are identifiable. First, an assessment of the current position of a business. This involves an audit of a company's external environment (for example, political, legal and economic environment) and internal environment (for example, resources and current products). The techniques of value chain analysis, life cycle analysis and the product portfolio matrix are sometimes used. The second stage involves an appraisal of the business's current position. This may use SWOT analysis (strengths, weaknesses, opportunities and threats), the balanced scorecard (using financial and non-financial performance measures in a multi-perspective context) and benchmarking against competitors. And, lastly, there is the strategic choice of future direction. This may involve focusing internally on finding new product markets or more fully exploiting the customer database. Alternatively, a business may choose to diversify externally through a merger or acquisition.

Selected Reading

Johnson, H.T. and R.S. Kaplan (1987), *Relevance Lost: The Rise and Fall of Management Accounting*, Harvard University Press.
   A ground-breaking book which re-examined the history of management accounting and argued it was out of touch with contemporary business needs.

Kaplan, R.S. (1984), 'Yesterday's accounting undermines production', *Harvard Business Review*, July/August, pp. 95–101.

In the same vein as *Relevance Lost*. It argues management accounting has not kept sufficiently up-to-date.

Kaplan, R.S. and D.P. Norton (1992), 'The Balanced Scorecard: measures that drive performance', *Harvard Business Review*, January–February, pp. 71–9.

Offers an alternative to the perceived inadequacies of management accounting.

Porter, M.E. (1985), *Competitive Advantage: Creating and Sustaining Superior Performance*, New York, Free Press.

A well-respected book which looks at how businesses can gain competitive advantage through techniques such as value chain analysis.

Q&A Discussion Questions

Questions with numbers in blue have answers at the back of the book.

Q1 What is strategic management accounting and how does it address some of the limitations of traditional management accounting?

Q2 Management accountants and strategy do not mix very well. Management accountants should, therefore, not involve themselves in strategic management accounting. Discuss the main arguments for and against this view.

Q3 Briefly outline the nature of the following techniques and then discuss their strengths and weaknesses:
(a) value chain analysis
(b) life cycle analysis
(c) the product portfolio matrix
(d) SWOT analysis
(e) the balanced scorecard
(f) benchmarking

Q4 Is growth through exploiting the internal resources of a company better than growth through acquisition/merger?

Q5 State whether the following statements are true or false. If false, explain why.
(a) Strategic management accounting looks at both the internal and external environments of a business.
(b) The cost of activities in value chain analysis is determined by key cost drivers.
(c) The product portfolio matrix consists of dogs, cats, cows and horses.
(d) The balanced scorecard uses only financial information.
(e) SWOT analysis stands for strengths, weaknesses, openings and threats.

Q&A   Numerical Questions

Questions with numbers in blue have answers at the back of the book.

Q1   You have the following details for three products (the maxi, mini and midi) for five years.

	Maxi		Mini		Midi	
Year	Sales	Profits (losses)	Sales	Profits (losses)	Sales	Profitability
	£	£	£	£	£	£
1	8,000	(3,000)	100,000	33,000	–	–
2	25,000	4,000	60,000	18,000	1,000	(3,000)
3	100,000	25,000	30,000	6,000	25,000	8,000
4	110,000	26,000	10,000	(3,000)	50,000	18,000
5	60,000	13,000	1,000	(4,000)	55,000	26,000

Required: In Year 3, state at which stage of their life cycle you would anticipate the products to be (introduction, growth, maturity, decline or withdrawal)?

Q2   Four products (the apple, orange, pear and banana) have the following financial profiles.

	Market Share	Market Growth
Apple	70 %	80 %
Orange	15 %	70 %
Pear	80 %	10 %
Banana	20 %	15 %

Required: Classify the products into either stars, cash cows, question marks or dogs. Explain if you would expect them to be profitable.

Q3   You have the following details about Computeco, a computer games manufacturer and distributor. An internal and external audit establishes the following details of two products, the Kung and the Fu.

	Market Share	Market Growth	Sales (000's)	Contribution (000's)
Kung	70 %	80 %	£10,000	£10,000
Fu	18 %	20 %	£3,000	£500

The Kung is currently marketed only in the UK; the Fu is marketed throughout the world. The product life cycles are five years. The Kung is 18 months old; the Fu is 4-years-old. The top developmental programmer has just left. Computeco has just installed a state-of-the-art computer system. The company is small, friendly and well-connected. A Japanese company has just approached Computeco asking it to market their product.

Required: Prepare a SWOT analysis stating your recommendations to management for the future.

Q4 You have gathered the following information for a regional railway company.
(a) The mission statement of the company is to survive, be profitable, be safe, give customers good service, run an efficient service, maintain a good infrastructure, and constantly improve.
(b) The main financial indicators are cash flow, return on capital employed and return on investment.
(c) The company has recently offered full-ticket refunds to customers who are unhappy with the service provided or where trains are more than 10 minutes late.
(d) The company publishes monthly details of accidents.
(e) The company aims to use staff more efficiently and maximise the train operating times.
(f) The company operates a continual improvement programme based on staff suggestions.
(g) A new capital expenditure programme has expanded considerably the rolling stock.

Required: From this information, prepare a balanced scorecard.

Q5 You sell the Feelgood, a health cushion, to 100,000 customers. Each cushion costs £25. You obtain the following breakdown of sales by customer category.

Sales Matrix

Age	Sales £	Geographical Location	Sales £	Sex	Sales £	TV Viewing	Sales £	Newspaper	Sales £
0–20	10,000	South	150,000	Male	50,000	BBC	200,000	Mail	150,000
21–40	50,000	Midland	20,000	Female	200,000	ITV	20,000	Sun	10,000
41–60	80,000	North	70,000			Sky	30,000	Telegraph	20,000
60+	110,000	Overseas	10,000					Times	10,000
								Express	60,000
	250,000		250,000		250,000		250,000		250,000

Required:
(i) Using this customer matrix, state which customers you might target.
(ii) State whether you need any further information.
(iii) State where you might target your advertising campaign.

Chapter 21

"There are no maps to the future."

A.J.P. Taylor

Learning Outcomes

After completing this chapter you should be able to:

✔ Introduce and explain the nature of capital investment.

✔ Outline the main capital investment appraisal techniques.

✔ Appreciate the time value of money.

✔ Explain the use of discounting.

Long-Term Decision Making: Capital Investment Appraisal

In a Nutshell

■ *Capital investment decisions are long-term, strategic decisions, such as building a new factory.*

■ *Capital investment decisions involve initial cash outflows and then subsequent cash inflows.*

■ *Many assumptions underpin these cash inflows and outflows.*

■ *There are four main capital investment techniques. Two (payback and accounting rate of return) do not take into account the time value of money. Two do (net present value and internal rate of return).*

■ *Payback is the simplest method. It measures how long it takes for a company to recover its initial investment.*

■ *The accounting rate of return uses profit not cash flow and measures the annual profit over the initial capital investment.*

■ *Net present value discounts estimated future cash flows back to today's values.*

■ *Internal rate of return establishes the discount rate at which the project breaks even.*

■ *Sensitivity analysis is often used to model future possible alternative situations.*

Introduction

Management accounting can be divided into cost recovery and control, and decision making. In turn, decision making consists of short-term and long-term decisions. Whereas strategic management sets the overall framework within which the long-term decisions are made, capital investment appraisal involves long-term choices about specific investments in future projects. These projects may include, for example, investment in new products or new infrastructure assets. Without this investment in the future, firms would not survive in the long term. However, capital investment decisions are extremely difficult as they include a considerable amount of crystal ball gazing. This chapter looks at four techniques (the payback period, the accounting rate of return, net present value and the internal rate of return) which management accountants use to help them peer into the future.

Nature of Capital Investment

Capital investment is essential for the long-term survival of a business. Existing fixed assets, for example, will wear out and need replacing. The capital investment decision operationalises the strategic, long-term plans of a business. As Figure 21.1 shows, long-term capital expenditure decisions can be distinguished from short-term decisions by their time span, topic, nature and level of expenditure, by the external factors taken into account and by the techniques used.

Figure 21.1   Comparison of Short-Term Decisions and Long-Term Capital Investment Decisions

Characteristic	Short-Term	Long-Term
1. Time Span	Maximum 1 to 2 years, mostly present situation	Upwards from 2 years
2. Topic	Usually concerned with current operating decision, e.g., discontinue present product	Concerned with future expenditure decisions, e.g., build new factory
3. Nature	Operational	Strategic
4. Level of Expenditure	Small to medium	Medium to great
5. External Factors	Generally not so important	Very important, especially interest rate, inflation rate
6. Sample Techniques	Contribution analysis, break-even analysis	Payback, accounting rate of return, net present value, and internal rate of return

Capital investment decisions are thus usually long-term decisions, which may sometimes look 10 or 20 years into the future. They are often the biggest expenditure decisions that a business faces. Some examples of capital investment decisions might be deciding whether or not to build a new factory or whether to expand into a new product range. A football club, such as Manchester United, for example, might have to decide whether or not to build a new stadium. A common capital expenditure decision will involve choosing between alternatives. For example, which of three particular stadiums should we build? Or which products should we currently develop for the future? These decisions are particularly important given the fast-changing world (see for example, Soundbite 21.1).

A key problem with any capital investment decision is taking into account all the external factors and correctly forecasting future conditions. As the quotation by A.J.P. Taylor at the start of the chapter stated: 'There are no maps to the future'. In Real-Life Nugget 21.1 Peter Aytan wonders why everything takes longer to finish and costs more than originally budgeted.

REAL-LIFE NUGGET 21.1

Forecasting the Future

Trouble ahead

WHY does everything take longer to finish and cost more than we think it will?

The Channel Tunnel was supposed to cost £2.6 billion. In fact, the final bill came to £15 billion. The Jubilee Line extension to the London Underground cost £3.5 billion, about four times the original estimate. There are many other examples: the London Eye, the Channel Tunnel rail link.

This is not an exclusively British disease. In 1957, engineers forecast that the Sydney Opera House would be finished in 1963 at a cost of A$7 million. A scaled-down version costing A$102 million finally opened in 1973. In 1969, the mayor of Montreal announced that the 1976 Olympics would cost C$120 million and 'can no more have a deficit than a man can have a baby'. Yet the stadium roof alone – which was not finished until 13 years after the games – cost C$120 million.

Source: Peter Aytan, *New Scientist*, 29 April 2000, p. 43

The basic decision is simply whether or not a particular capital investment decision is worthwhile. In business, this decision is usually made by comparing the initial cash out-flows associated with the capital investment with the later cash inflows. We can distinguish between the initial investment, net cash operating flows for succeeding years and other cash flows.

PAUSE FOR THOUGHT 21.1

A Football Club's New Stadium

A football club is contemplating building a new stadium. What external factors should it take into account?

....

There are countless factors. Below are some that might be considered.

- How much will the stadium cost?
- How many extra spectators can the new stadium hold?
- How much can be charged per spectator?
- How many years will the stadium last?
- What is the net financial effect when compared with the present stadium?
- How confident is the club about future attendance at matches?

(i) Initial Investment

This is our initial capital expenditure. It will usually involve capital outflows on infrastructure assets (for example, buildings or new plant and machinery) or on working capital. This initial expenditure is needed so that the business can expand.

(ii) Net Cash Flows

These represent the operating cash flows expected from the project once the infrastructure assets are in place. Normally, we talk about annual net cash flow. This is simply the cash inflows less the cash outflows calculated over a year. For convenience, *cash flows are usually assumed to occur at the end of the year*.

(iii) Other Flows

These involve other non-operating cash flows. For example, the taxation benefits from the initial capital expenditure or the cash inflow from scrap.

PAUSE FOR THOUGHT 21.2

Assumptions in Capital Investment Decisions

A big problem in any capital investment decision is the assumptions that underpin it. Can you think of any of these?
....

- Costs of initial outlay
- Tax effects
- Cost of capital
- Inflation
- Cash inflows and outflows over period of project. These, in turn, may depend on pricing policy, external demand, value of production etc.

Capital Investment Appraisal Techniques

The four main techniques used in capital investment decisions are payback period, accounting rate of return, net present value and internal rate of return. An overview of these four techniques is presented in Figure 21.2. These techniques are then discussed below.

Figure 21.2   Four Main Types of Investment Appraisal Techniques

Feature	Payback	Accounting Rate of Return	Net Present Value	Internal Rate of Return
Nature	Measures time period in which *cumulative cash inflows* overtake *cumulative cash outflows*	Assesses *profitability* of initial investment	*Discounts* future cash flows to present	Determines the *rate of return* at which a project *breaks even*
Ease of use	Very easy	Easy	May be difficult	Quite difficult
Takes time value of money into account	No	No	Yes	Yes
Main assumptions	Value and volume of cash flows	Reliability of annual profits	Value and volume of cash flows, cost of capital	Value and volume of cash flows, cost of capital
Focus	Cash flows	Profits	Cash flows	Cash flows

It is important to realise that the payback period and the accounting rate of return take into account only the *actual* cash inflows and outflows. However, net present value and accounting rate of return take into account the *time value of money*.

Time Value of Money

Why do you think it is important to take into account the time value of money?

There is an old saying that time is money! In the case of long-term capital investment decisions, it certainly is. Would you prefer £100 now or £100 in 10 years time? That one is easy! But what about £100 now or £150 in five years time? There is a need to standardise money in today's terms. To do this, we need to attribute a time value to money. In practice, we take this time value to be the rate at which a company could borrow money. This is called the cost of capital. If our cost of capital is 10%, we say that £100 today equals £110 in one year's time, £121 in 2 years time and so on. If we know the cost of capital of future cash flows we can, therefore, discount them back to today's cash flows.

As Real-Life Nugget 21.2 shows, amounts spent yesterday can mean huge sums today. Compounding is the opposite of discounting! If we discounted the $136,000,000,000 dollars back from 1876 to 1607 using a 10 % discount rate we should arrive at one dollar.

Compound Growth

Compound Interest

From a speech in Congress more than 100 years ago:

It has been supposed here that had America been purchased in 1607 for $1, and payment secured by bond, payable, with interest annually compounded, in 1876 at ten percent, the amount would be – I have not verified the calculation – the very snug little sum of $136,000,000,000; five times as much as the country will sell for today. It is very much like supposing that if Adam and Eve have continued to multiply and replenish once in two years until the present time, and all their descendants had lived and had been equally prolific, then, saying nothing about twins and triplets, there would now be actually alive upon the earth, a quantity of human beings in solid measure more than thirteen and one-fourth times the bulk of the entire planet.

Source: Peter Hay (1988), *The Book of Business Anecdotes*, Harrap Ltd, London, p. 10

Each of the four capital investment appraisal techniques is examined using the information in Figure 21.3.

Figure 21.3 Illustrative Example of a Financial Service Company Wishing to Invest in a New On-Line Banking Service

The Everfriendly Building Society is contemplating launching a new on-line banking service, called the Falcon. There are three alternative approaches, each involving £20,000 initial outlay. In this case, cash inflows can be taken to be the same as profit. Cost of capital is 10%.

Projects

Year	A	B	C
Cash flows	£	£	£
0 (i.e. now)	(20,000)	(20,000)	(20,000)
1	4,000	8,000	8,000
2	4,000	6,000	8,000
3	8,000	6,000	6,000
4	6,000	3,000	6,000
5	6,000	2,000	3,000

Helpnote: The cash outflow is traditionally recorded as being in year 0 (i.e., today) in brackets. The cash inflows occur from year 1 onwards and are conventionally taken at the end of the year. To simplify matters, in this example, cash inflows have been taken to be the same as net profit. Finally, cost of capital can be taken as the amount that it cost the Everfriendly Building Society to borrow money.

Payback Period

The payback period is a relatively straightforward method of investment appraisal. It simply measures the cumulative cash inflows against the cumulative cash outflows until the project recovers its initial investment. The payback method is useful for screening projects for an early return on the investment. Ideally, it should be complemented by another method such as net present value.

DEFINITION 21.1

Payback Period

The payback period simply measures the cumulative cash inflows against the cumulative cash outflows. The point at which they coincide is the payback point.

Specific advantages

1 Easy to use and understand.
2 Conservative.

Specific disadvantages

1 Fails to take into account cash flows after payback.
2 Does not take into account the time value of money.

Taking Everfriendly Building Society's Falcon project, when do we recover the £20,000? Figure 21.4 shows this is after 3.67 years for project A, 3 years for project B and 2.67 years for project C.

Figure 21.4   Payback Using Everfriendly Building Society

	Projects		
	A	**B**	**C**
Year	£	£	£
0 (i.e. now) Cash outflows	(20,000)	(20,000)	(20,000)
Cumulative cash inflows			
1	4,000	8,000	8,000
2	8,000	14,000	16,000
3	16,000	**20,000**	**22,000**
4	**22,000**	23,000	28,000
5	28,000	25,000	31,000
Payback year	3.67 years*	3 years	2.67 years*

*For these two projects, payback will be two-thirds of the way through a year. This is because (taking project A to illustrate) after three years our cumulative inflows are £16,000 and after four years they are £22,000. Assuming, and it is a big assumption, a steady cash flow, we reach payback point after two-thirds of a year (i.e., £4,000 needed for payback, divided by £6,000 cash inflows).

Payback is a relatively straightforward investment technique. It is simple to understand and apply and promotes a policy of caution in the investment decision. The business always chooses the investment, which pays off the initial investment the most quickly. However, although useful, payback has certain crucial limitations.

PAUSE FOR THOUGHT 21.4

Limitations of Payback

Can you think of any limitations of payback?

Two of the most important limitations of payback are that it ignores both cash flows after the payback and the time value of money. Thus, a project may have a slow payback period, but have substantial cash flows once it is established. These will not be taken into account. In addition, cash flows in later years are treated as being the same value as cash flows in early years. This ignores the time value of money and may distort the capital investment decision.

Accounting Rate of Return

This method, unlike the other three methods, focuses on the profitability of the project, rather than its cash flow. Thus it is distinctly different in orientation from the other methods. The basic definition of the accounting rate of return is:

$$\text{Accounting rate of return} = \frac{\text{Average annual profit}}{\text{Capital investment}}$$

However, once we look more closely we run into potential problems. What exactly do we mean by 'profit' and 'capital investment'? For profit, do we take into account interest, taxation and depreciation? For capital investment, do we take the initial capital investment or the average capital employed over its life? Different firms will use different versions of this ratio. In this book, profit before interest and taxation, and initial capital investment are preferred (see Definition 21.2). This is because it is similar to conventional accounting ratios and seems logical! The accounting rate of return is easy to understand and use. Its main disadvantages are that profit and capital investment have many possible definitions and, like payback, the accounting rate of return does not take into account the time value of money.

DEFINITION 21.2

Accounting Rate of Return

Accounting rate of return is a capital investment appraisal method which assesses the viability of a project using annual profit and initial capital invested. We can define it as:

$$\frac{\text{Average annual profit before interest and taxation}}{\text{Initial capital investment}}$$

Specific advantages

1 Takes the whole life of a project.
2 Similar to normal accounting ratios.

Specific disadvantages

1 Many definitions of profit and capital investment possible.
2 Does not consider the time value of money.

The accounting rate of return is applied to the Everfriendly Building Society in Figure 21.5.

Figure 21.5   Accounting Rate of Return Using Everfriendly Building Society

	Project Cash Flows		
	A	**B**	**C**
Year	£	£	£
0 (i.e. now) Cash outflows	(20,000)	(20,000)	(20,000)
Net cash inflows (note)			
1	4,000	8,000	8,000
2	4,000	6,000	8,000
3	8,000	6,000	6,000
4	6,000	3,000	6,000
5	6,000	2,000	3,000
Total	28,000	25,000	31,000
Average profit	£28,000	£25,000	£31,000
	5 years	5 years	5 years
	= 5,600	= 5,000	= 6,200
Our accounting rate of return is therefore:	£5,600	£5,000	£6,200
	£20,000	£20,000	£20,000
	= 28%	= 25%	= 31%

We would, therefore, choose project C because its accounting rate of return is the highest.

Note: In this case, cash inflow equals net profit. This will not always be the case.

Returns on investment are treated very seriously by businesses. In Real-Life Nugget 21.3, Vodafone has a projected rate of return of at least 15 % on its capital investment. However, it is not absolutely clear from the press extract whether it has used the accounting rate of return.

REAL-LIFE NUGGET 21.3

Rates of Return

Vodafone AirTouch yesterday gave the first indication of how much money it expects to make from third generation mobile networks during the release of better-than-expected full-year results.

Key Hydon, finance director, said that the projected rate of return on the large capital investment required for licences and infrastructure was at least 15 per cent.

Although the £6 bn cost of Vodafone's new UK licence will be spread over its 20-year lifespan, most of the estimated £4 bn network spending and handset subsidy will be required in the first four or five years.

This implies that the company is projecting potential operating profits of about £75 m above its existing performance.

Source: Telecommunications group releases internal targets to counter criticism it overpaid for licence, Dan Roberts, *Financial Times*, 31 May 2000

Net Present Value

The net present value and internal rate of return can be distinguished from the payback period and accounting rate of return because they take into account the time value of money. Essentially, time is money. If you invest £100 in a bank or building society and the interest rate is 10 %, the £100 is worth £110 in one year's time (100×1.10), and £121 in two year's time (100×1.10^2, or 110×1.10).

We can use the same principle to work backwards. If we have £110 in the bank in a year's time with a 10 % interest rate, it will be worth £100 today (£110 × 0.9091, i.e. 100 ÷ 110). Similarly, £121 in two years' time would be worth £100 today (£121 × 0.8264, i.e. 100 ÷ 121).

PAUSE FOR THOUGHT 21.5

Discounting

You are approached by your best friend, who asks you to lend her £1,000. She promises to give you back £1,200 in two years' time. Your money is in a building society and earns 6 %. Putting friendship aside, do you lend her the money?

To work this out, we need to compare like with like. We could either work forwards (i.e., multiplying £1,000 by the 6 % earned over two years (1.06^2) = £1, 123.60). £1,000 today is worth £1,123.60 in two years' time. Or more conventionally, we work back from the future using the time value of money, in this case 6 %.

Thus, £1,200 in one year's time = £1,200 × (100/106, i.e., 0.9434)

$$= £1,132.08 \text{ today}$$

While £1,200 in two years' time = £1,200 × (100/112.36, i.e., 106 × 1.06)

$$= £1,200 \times 0.8900$$

$$= £1,068 \text{ today}$$

Therefore, as £1,200 in two year's time is the equivalent of £1,068 today you should accept your friend's offer as this is £68 more than you currently have.

Fortunately, we do not have to calculate discount rates all the time! We use discount tables (see Appendix 21.1 at the end of this chapter). So to obtain a 10 % interest rate in two year's time, we look up the number of years (two) and the discount rate (10 %). We then find a discount factor of 0.8264!

As Definition 21.3 shows, net present value uses the discounting principle to work out the value in today's money of future expected cash flows. It uses the cost of capital as the discount rate. Conventionally, the cost of capital is taken as the rate at which the business can borrow money. However, the estimation of the cost of capital can be quite difficult. In Chapter 22 we look in more detail at how companies can derive their cost of capital. Cost of capital is a key element of capital investment appraisal. Essentially, a business is seeking to earn a higher return from new projects than its cost of capital. If this is achieved, the projects will be viable. If not, they are unviable.

DEFINITION 21.3

Net Present Value

Net present value is a capital investment appraisal technique which discounts future expected cash flows to today's monetary values using an appropriate cost of capital.

Specific advantages

1 Looks at all the cash flows.
2 Takes into account the value of money.

Specific disadvantages

1 Estimation of cost of capital may be difficult.
2 Assumes all cash flows occur at end of year.
3 Can be complex.

Behavioural factors can also play their part in making a decision. This is shown in Real-Life Nugget 21.4.

REAL-LIFE NUGGET 21.4

Behavioural Implications of Cost of Capital

If a company decides it will only go ahead with projects that show a discounted return on investment of better than 15 per cent, anyone putting forward a project will ensure that the accompanying figures indicate a better than 15 per cent return. If the criterion is raised to 20 per cent, the figures will be improved accordingly. And there is no way in which the person analysing the project can contest those figures – unless he can find a flaw in the performance of the projection rituals.

Source: Graham Cleverly (1971), *Managers and Magic*, Longman Group Ltd, London, p. 86

Figure 21.6 applies net present value to the Everfriendly Building Society.

Figure 21.6   Net Present Value as Applied to the Everfriendly Building Society

	Project Cash Flows			Discount Rate	Discounted Cash Flows		
	A	B	C	10%	A	B	C
Year	£	£	£		£	£	£
0 (i.e. now)	(20,000)	(20,000)	(20,000)	1	(20,000)	(20,000)	(20,000)
1	4,000	8,000	8,000	0.9091	3,636	7,273	7,273
2	4,000	6,000	8,000	0.8264	3,306	4,958	6,611
3	8,000	6,000	6,000	0.7513	6,010	4,508	4,508
4	6,000	3,000	6,000	0.6830	4,098	2,049	4,098
5	6,000	2,000	3,000	0.6209	3,725	1,242	1,863
Total discounted cash flows					20,775	20,030	24,353
Net Present Value (NPV)					775	30	4,353

All three projects have a positive net present value and, therefore, are worth carrying out. However, project C has the highest NPV and thus should be chosen if funds are limited.

When using the net present value, it is useful to follow the steps laid out in Helpnote 21.1.

HELPNOTE 21.1

Calculating Net Present Value

1. Calculate initial cash flows.

2. Choose a discount rate (usually given), normally based on the company's cost of capital.

3. Discount original cash flows using discount rate.

4. Match discounted cash flows against initial investment to arrive at net present value.

5. Positive net present values are good investments. Negative ones are poor investments.

6. Choose the highest net present value. This is the project that will most increase the shareholders' wealth.

PAUSE FOR THOUGHT 21.6

Discount Tables

Using the discount tables given in Appendix 21.1, what are the following discount factors:

(i) 8 % at 5 years, (ii) 12 % at 8 years, (iii) 15 % at 10 years, (iv) 20 % at 6 years, and (v) 9 % at 9 years.

. . . .

From Appendix 21.1, we have
(i) 0.6806; (ii) 0.4039; (iii) 0.2472; (iv) 0.3349; (v) 0.4604.

In practice, calculating net present values becomes very complicated. For example, you have to take into account taxation, inflation, etc. However, net present value is a very versatile technique, allowing you to determine which projects are worth investing in and to choose between competing projects.

Internal Rate of Return (IRR)

The internal rate of return is a more sophisticated discounting technique than net present value. As Definition 21.4 shows, it can be defined as the rate of discount required to give a net present value of zero. Another way of looking at this is the maximum rate of interest that a company can afford to pay without suffering a loss on the project. Projects are accepted if the company's cost of capital is less than the IRR. Similarly, projects are rejected if the company's cost of capital is higher than the IRR. The advantages of the internal rate of return are that it takes into account the time value of money and calculates a break-even rate of return. However, it is complex and difficult to understand.

DEFINITION 21.4

The Internal Rate of Return

The internal rate of return represents the discount rate required to give a net present value of zero. It pays a company to invest in a project if it can borrow money for less than the IRR.

Specific advantages
1 Uses time value of money.
2 Determines the break-even rate of return.
3 Looks at all the cash flows.

Specific disadvantages
1 Difficult to understand.
2 No need to select a specific discount rate.
3 Complex, often needing a computer.
4 In certain situations, gives misleading results (for example, where there are unconventional cash flows).

The relationship of the internal rate of return to net present value is shown in Figure 21.7 and the internal rate of return is then applied to the Everfriendly Building Society in Figure 21.8.

Figure 21.7 Relationship Between the Net Present Value and Internal Rate of Return

A project has the following net present values (NPVs).

£2,000 NPV at 10% discount rate.
(£1,000) NPV at 15% discount rate.
What is the internal rate of return?

We can find the internal rate of return either (i) *diagrammatically* or (ii) *mathematically* by a process called interpolation.

(i) Diagrammatically

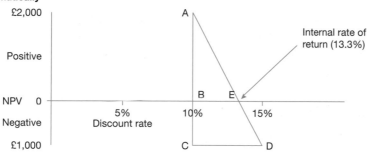

A = Discount rate 10%, £2,000 NPV
D = Discount rate 15%, (£1,000) NPV
E = Internal rate of return (13.3%)

(ii) Mathematically

We need to find point E. To do this, we can find the distance from B to E using the principles of similar triangles from mathematics:

$$\frac{BE}{CD} = \frac{AB}{AC}$$

$$\therefore \frac{BE}{5} = \frac{2,000}{3,000}$$

$$\therefore \frac{BE}{5} = \frac{10,000}{3,000} = 3.3\%$$

$$\therefore IRR = 10\% + 3.33\% = 13.3\%$$

This can be re-written as follows:

IRR = Lowest discount rate + difference in discount rates × $\dfrac{\text{lowest discount rate NPV}}{\text{difference in NPVs}}$

$$13.3\% = \quad 10\% \quad + \quad 5\% \quad \times \quad \frac{2,000}{3,000}$$

It is this formula that we will use from now on.

Figure 21.8   Internal Rate of Return as Applied to the Everfriendly Building Society

From Figure 21.6, we know that at 10% our net present values are all positive, A £775, B £30 and C £4,353. To solve the problem mathematically, we need to ascertain a negative present value for each project. So, first of all, we try 15%.

Year	Project Cash Flows A £	Project Cash Flows B £	Project Cash Flows C £	Discount Rate 15%	Discounted Cash Flows (DCF) A £	Discounted Cash Flows (DCF) B £	Discounted Cash Flows (DCF) C £	Discount Rate 20%	DCF C £
0	(20,000)	(20,000)	(20,000)	1	(20,000)	(20,000)	(20,000)	1	(20,000)
1	4,000	8,000	8,000	0.8696	3,478	6,957	6,957	0.8333	6,666
2	4,000	6,000	8,000	0.7561	3,024	4,537	6,049	0,6944	5,555
3	8,000	6,000	6,000	0.6575	5,260	3,945	3,945	0.5787	3,472
4	6,000	3,000	6,000	0.5718	3,431	1,715	3,431	0.4823	2,894
5	6,000	2,000	3,000	0.4972	2,983	994	1,492	0.4019	1,206
Total discounted cash inflows					18,176	18,148	21,874		19,793
Net Present Value (NPV)					(1,824)	(1,852)	1,874		(207)

15% produced A (£1,824), B (£1,852) and C £1,874 in net present values. We still need a negative value for C. So above we also ran a higher discount rate 20% for C. This gives us a negative NPV of (£207).

To solve this we can now use our formula.

$$\text{IRR} = \text{Lowest discount rate} + \text{difference in discount rates} \times \frac{\text{lowest discount rate NPV}}{\text{difference in NPVs}}$$

$$\text{A. } 10\% + (15 - 10\%) \times \frac{£775}{£775 + £1,824} = 10\% + (5\% \times 0.2982) = 11.5\%$$

$$\text{B. } 10\% + (15 - 10\%) \times \frac{£30}{£30 + £1,852} = 10\% + (5\% \times 0.01594) = 10.1\%$$

$$\text{C. } 10\% + (20 - 10\%) \times \frac{£4,353}{£4,353 + £207} = 10\% + (10\% \times 0.9546) = 19.6\%$$

Our ranking for the IRR method is thus project C, then A and, finally, B. As all projects have IRRs which exceed our cost of capital of 10% all three projects are potentially viable. However, for project B the IRR is only marginally greater than the cost of capital.

When calculating the IRR, there are four main steps. These are shown in Helpnote 21.2.

The IRR can be a very useful technique. However, the complexity is often off-putting. In practice, students will be pleased to learn that the calculations to arrive at the IRR are generally done using a computer program. Normally, the results from NPV and IRR will be consistent. However, in some cases, such as projects with unconventional cash flows (e.g., alternating cash inflows and outflows), the NPV and IRR may give different results. In these cases, NPV is probably the most reliable.

If there was a clash between the results from the different methods then it would be difficult to choose. Different businesses will prefer different methods depending on their priorities. I would probably choose net present value as the superior method. This is because it takes into account the time value of money, is more reliable, and is easier to understand and use than the internal rate of return.

Now that we have calculated the results for the Everfriendly Building Society using all four methods, we can compare them (see Figure 21.9). Project C is clearly the superior method.

> ## HELPNOTE 21.2
>
> # Calculating the Internal Rate of Return (IRR)
>
> 1. Calculate a positive NPV for all projects.
> 2. Calculate a negative NPV for all projects. Use trial and error. The higher the discount rate, the lower the NPV.
> 3. Calculate out the IRR using the formula:
>   IRR = Lowest discount rate + difference in discount rates $\times \dfrac{\text{lowest discount rate NPV}}{\text{difference in NPVs}}$
> 4. Choose the project with the highest IRR. When evaluating a single project, the project will be chosen when its IRR is higher than the company's cost of capital.

Figure 21.9 Comparison of the Projects for Everfriendly Building Society Using the Four Capital Appraisal Methods

	Projects		
	A	**B**	**C**
Payback Period	3.67 years	3 years	2.67 years
Ranking	3	2	1
Accounting Rate of Return	28%	25%	31%
Ranking	2	3	1
Net Present Value	£775	£30	£4,353
Ranking	2	3	1
Internal Rate of Return	11.5%	10.1%	19.6%
Ranking	2	3	1

Project C is the superior project using all methods, so we could choose project C.

Before we leave the capital investment appraisal techniques, it is important to reiterate that the results achieved will only be as good as the assumptions that underpin them. This is powerfully expressed in Real-Life Nugget 21.5.

REAL-LIFE NUGGET 21.5

Investment Appraisal Techniques

But where the very existence of angels is in doubt, debating how many of them can dance on a pin seems a sterile exercise. Where the validity of one's original information is suspect, performing ever more sophisticated calculations seems pointless. Nonetheless, there can hardly be a company in which new projects are not required to be subjected to a ritual calculation of the 'internal rate of return', 'net present value', 'payback period' or some other criterion of profitability. And yet most of the time the performers themselves are not convinced of the validity of the material information they are manipulating.

Source: Graham Cleverly (1971), *Managers and Magic*, Longman Group Ltd, London, p. 86

Other Factors

There are many other factors that affect capital investment appraisal. Below we discuss three of the most important: sensitivity analysis, inflation and taxation.

1. Sensitivity analysis

The assumptions underpinning the capital investment decision mean that it is often sensible to undertake some form of **sensitivity analysis**. Sensitivity analysis involves modelling the future to see if alternative scenarios will change the investment decision. For example, a project's estimated cash outflow might be £10 million, its estimated inflows might be £6 million and its cost of capital might be 10%. All three of these parameters would be altered to assess any impact upon the overall results.

2. Inflation

The effects of inflation should also be included in any future capital investment model. Inflation means that a pound in a year's time will not buy as much as a pound today, as the price of goods will have risen. Therefore, we need to adjust for inflation. This can be done in two ways.

1 *By adjusting future cash flow*. Under this method, we increase the future cash flows by the expected rate of inflation. If inflation was 3 % over a year we would, therefore, increase an expected cash flow of £100 million by 3 % to £103 million. We would then discount these adjusted flows as normal.

2 *By adjusting the discount rate*. If we were using a discount rate of 10 %, we would deduct the inflation rate. If inflation was 3 %, we would then discount the future cash flows at 7 %.

3. Taxation

As we saw in Chapter 8 cash flow and profit are distinctly different. Discounted cash flows are based on cash flows not on accounting profit. In order to arrive at forecast cash flows from forecast profit we must, therefore, adjust the profit for non cash-flow items. In particular, we need to add back depreciation (disallowed by taxation authorities) and deduct any capital allowances. Capital allowances are allowed by the taxation authorities as a replacement for depreciation. They can be set off against taxable profits. Capital allowances, thus, reduce cash outflows. Normally, companies will pay their taxation nine months after their year end.

Conclusion

Capital investment appraisal methods are used to assess the viability of long-term investment decisions. Capital investment projects might be a football club building a new stadium or a company building a new factory. Capital investment decisions are long-term and often very expensive. It is, therefore, very important to test their viability. Four capital investment appraisal methods are commonly used: payback period; accounting rate of return; net present value; and internal rate of return. Unlike the last two, the first two do not take into account the time value of money. The payback period simply assesses how long it takes a company's cumulative cash inflows to outstrip its initial investment. The accounting rate of return assesses the profitability of a project using average annual profit over initial capital investment. Net present value discounts back estimated future cash flows to today's values using cost of capital as a discount rate. Finally, internal rate of return establishes the discount rate at which a project breaks even. All four appraisal methods are based on many assumptions about future cash flows. These assumptions are often tested using sensitivity analysis.

Q&A   Discussion Questions

Questions with numbers in blue have answers at the back of the book.

Q1   (a) Why do you think capital investment is necessary for companies?
      (b) What sort of possible capital investment might there be in:
      (i) the shipping industry?
      (ii) the hotel and catering industry?
      (iii) manufacturing industry?

Q2   Discuss the general assumptions that underpin capital investment appraisal.

Q3   Briefly outline the four main capital investment appraisal techniques and then discuss the specific advantages and disadvantages of each technique.

Q4   Why is time money?

Q5   State whether the following statements are true or false. If false, explain why.
      (a) The four main capital investment appraisal techniques are payback period, accounting rate of return, net present value and internal rate of return.
      (b) The payback period and net present value techniques generally use discounted cash flows.
      (c) The accounting rate of return is the only investment appraisal technique that focuses on profits not cash flows.
      (d) The discount rate normally used to discount cash flows is the interest rate charged by the Bank of England.
      (e) Sensitivity analysis involves modelling future alternative scenarios and assessing their impact upon the results of capital investment appraisal techniques.

Q&A   Numerical Questions

Questions with numbers in blue have answers at the back of the book.

These questions gradually increase in difficulty. Students may find question 6, in particular, testing.

Q1   What are the appropriate discount factors for the following:

(i)   5 years at 10 % cost of capital   (iv) 4 years at 12 % cost of capital
(ii) 6 years at 9 % cost of capital   (v) 3 years at 14 % cost of capital
(iii) 8 years at 13 % cost of capital   (vi) 10 years at 20 % cost of capital

Q2   A company, Fairground, has a choice between investing in one of three projects: the Rocket, the Carousel or the Dipper. The cost of capital is 8 %. There are the following cash flows.

	Rocket £	Carousel £	Dipper £
Initial outlay	(18,000)	(18,000)	(18,000)
Cash inflow			
Year 1	8,000	6,000	10,000
Year 2	8,000	4,000	6,000
Year 3	8,000	14,000	5,000

Required: An evaluation of Fairground using:
 (i) the payback period
 (ii) the accounting rate of return (assume cash flows are equivalent to profits)
 (iii) net present value
 (iv) the internal rate of return.

Q3   Wetday is evaluating three projects: the Storm, the Cloud, and the Downpour. The company's cost of capital is 12 %. These projects have the following cash flows.

	Storm £	Cloud £	Downpour £
Year			
0 (Initial outlay)	(18,000)	(12,000)	(13,000)
Cash inflow			
1	4,000	5,000	4,000
2	5,000	2,000	4,000
3	6,000	3,000	4,000
4	7,000	2,500	4,000
5	8,000	3,000	4,000

Required: Calculate
 (i) the payback period
 (ii) the accounting rate of return (assume cash flows equal profits)
 (iii) the net present value
 (iv) the internal rate of return.

Q4 A company, Choosewell, has £30,000 to spend on capital investment projects. It is currently evaluating three projects. The initial capital outlay is on a piece of machinery that has a four-year life. Its cost of capital is 9 %.

	Ready		Steady		Go	
	£		£		£	
Initial capital outlay	(30,000)		(15,000)		(15,000)	
	Inflows	Outflows	Inflows	Outflows	Inflows	Outflows
Year	£	£	£	£	£	£
1	36,000	24,000	25,000	16,000	16,000	8,000
2	36,000	14,000	18,000	11,000	13,000	6,500
3	32,000	26,000	17,000	12,000	12,000	6,000
4	4,000	5,000	3,000	4,000	6,000	6,000

Required: Calculate
  (i) the payback period
 (ii) the accounting rate of return
(iii) the net present value
(iv) the internal rate of return.

Q5 A football club, Manpool, is considering investing in a new stadium. There are the following expected capital outlays and cash inflows for two prospective stadiums.

	Bowl	Superbowl
Year	£000	£000
Outlays		
0	(1,000)	(1,000)
1	(1,000)	(1,000)
Net inflows		
1	50	300
2	100	300
3	150	300
4	200	300
5	250	300
6	300	300
7	350	300
8	400	300
9	450	300
10	500	300

Assume the football club can borrow money at respectively

(a) 5 %   (b) 8 %   (c) 10 %

Required:
  (i) Calculate which stadium should be built and at which rate using net present value?
  (ii) What is the internal rate of return for the two stadiums?

Q6 A company, Myopia, has the following details for its new potential product, the Telescope.

Year	Capital Outlay	Capital Inflow	Sales	Interest	Expenses (Excludes Depreciation)	Taxation
	£	£	£	£	£	£
0	(700,000)	–	–	–	–	–
1			340,000	20,000	(40,000)	–
2			270,000	20,000	(130,000)	(4,500)
3			320,000	20,000	(160,000)	(18,375)
4			345,000	20,000	(185,000)	(24,281)
5			430,500	20,000	(205,000)	(48,361)
6			330,300	20,000	(160,300)	(35,033)
7			200,600	20,000	(100,100)	(16,825)
8			145,300	20,000	(46,500)	(18,034)
9			85,200	20,000	(28,100)	(6,925)
10		5,000	38,600	20,000	(8,300)	–

Myopia's cost of capital is 10 %. The capital outlay is for the Jodrell machine which will last 10 years. The capital inflow of £5,000 is the scrap value after 10 years.

Required: Calculate
  (i) the payback period
  (ii) the accounting rate of return
  (iii) the net present value
  (iv) the internal rate of return.

Helpnote. In this question, which has a different format from those encountered so far, it is first necessary to calculate *profit before interest and tax* (i.e., sales less expenses and depreciation). After this we need to adjust for interest, taxation, depreciation (based on the initial capital outlay) and other cash flows to arrive at a final cash flow figure.

Appendix 21.1 Present Value of £1 at Compound Interest Rate (1 + r)

Years (n)	Interest rates (r)										
	1 %	2 %	3 %	4 %	5 %	6 %	7 %	8 %	9 %	10 %	
1	0.9901	0.9804	0.9709	0.9615	0.9524	0.9434	0.9346	0.9259	0.9174	0.9091	1
2	0.9803	0.9612	0.9426	0.9246	0.9070	0.8900	0.8734	0.8573	0.8417	0.8264	2
3	0.9706	0.9423	0.9151	0.8990	0.8638	0.8396	0.8163	0.7938	0.7722	0.7513	3
4	0.9610	0.9238	0.8885	0.8548	0.8227	0.7921	0.7629	0.7350	0.7084	0.6830	4
5	0.9515	0.9057	0.8626	0.8219	0.7835	0.7473	0.7130	0.6806	0.6499	0.6209	5
6	0.9420	0.8880	0.8375	0.7903	0.7462	0.7050	0.6663	0.6302	0.5963	0.5645	6
7	0.9327	0.8706	0.8131	0.7599	0.7107	0.6651	0.6227	0.5835	0.5470	0.5132	7
8	0.9235	0.8535	0.7894	0.7307	0.6768	0.6274	0.5820	0.5403	0.5019	0.4665	8
9	0.9143	0.8368	0.7664	0.7026	0.6446	0.5919	0.5439	0.5002	0.4604	0.4241	9
10	0.9053	0.8203	0.7441	0.6756	0.6139	0.5584	0.5083	0.4632	0.4224	0.3855	10

Years (n)	Interest rates (r)										
	11 %	12 %	13 %	14 %	15 %	16 %	17 %	18 %	19 %	20 %	
1	0.9009	0.8929	0.8850	0.8772	0.8696	0.8621	0.8547	0.8475	0.8403	0.8333	1
2	0.8116	0.7972	0.7831	0.7695	0.7561	0.7432	0.7305	0.7182	0.7062	0.6944	2
3	0.7312	0.7118	0.6931	0.6750	0.6575	0.6407	0.6244	0.6086	0.5934	0.5787	3
4	0.6587	0.6355	0.6133	0.5921	0.5718	0.5523	0.5337	0.5158	0.4987	0.4823	4
5	0.5935	0.5674	0.5428	0.5194	0.4972	0.4761	0.4561	0.4371	0.4190	0.4019	5
6	0.5346	0.5066	0.4803	0.4556	0.4323	0.4104	0.3898	0.3704	0.3521	0.3349	6
7	0.4817	0.4523	0.4251	0.3996	0.3759	0.3538	0.3332	0.3139	0.2959	0.2791	7
8	0.4339	0.4039	0.3762	0.3506	0.3269	0.3050	0.2848	0.2660	0.2487	0.2326	8
9	0.3909	0.3606	0.3329	0.3075	0.2843	0.2630	0.2434	0.2255	0.2090	0.1938	9
10	0.3522	0.3220	0.2946	0.2697	0.2472	0.2267	0.2080	0.1911	0.1756	0.1615	10

Helpnote: This table shows what the value of £1 today will be in the future, assuming different interest rates. Therefore, £1 today will be worth 90.91 pence in one year's time if the interest rate is 10 %. If you are given cash flows at a future time you need to use the interest rates in the table to adjust them to today's monetary value. Thus, if we have £5,000 in five years' time and our interest rate is 10 %, then, using the table, this will be worth £5,000 × 0.6209 or £3,104 in today's money.

Chapter 22

"It doesn't take very long to screw up a company. Two, three months should do it. All it takes is some excess inventory [stock], some negligence in collecting, and some ignorance about where you are."

Mary Baechler in *Inc.*, October (1994) quoted in *The Wiley Book of Business Quotations* (1998), p. 86

Learning Outcomes

After completing this chapter you should be able to:

✔ **Explain the nature and importance of sources of finance.**

✔ **Discuss the nature of short-term financing.**

✔ **Analyse the ways in which the long-term finance of a company may be provided.**

✔ **Understand the concept of the cost of capital.**

The Management of Working Capital and Sources of Finance

In a Nutshell

- *Sources of finance are vital to the survival and growth of a business.*

- *There are internally and externally generated sources of finance.*

- *Sources of finance can be short-term or long-term.*

- *Short-term and long-term sources of finance are normally matched with current assets and long-term, infrastructure assets, respectively.*

- *Short-term internal sources of finance concern the more efficient use of cash, debtors and stock.*

- *Techniques for the internal management of working capital involve the debtors collection model, the economic order quantity and just-in-time stock management.*

- *Short-term external sources of finance include a bank overdraft, a bank loan, debt factoring, invoice discounting, and the sale and buy back of stock.*

- *Retained profits are where a company finances itself from internal funds.*

- *Three major sources of external long-term financing are leasing, share capital and long-term loans.*

- *Leasing involves a company using, but not owning, an asset.*

- *Share capital is provided by shareholders who own the company and receive dividends.*

- *Loan capital providers do not own the company and receive interest.*

- *Cost of capital is the effective rate at which a company can raise finance.*

Introduction

Sources of finance are vital to a business. They allow it to survive and grow. Sources of finance may be raised internally and externally. The efficient use of working capital is an important internal, short-term source of funds, while retained profits can be an important internal, long-term source. External funds may also be short-term or long-term. Bank loans and debt factoring are examples of external short-term finance. External long-term sources allow businesses to carry out their long-term strategic aims. Share capital and loan capital are examples of long-term finance. Every business aims to optimise its use of funds. This involves minimising short-term borrowings and financing long-term infrastructure investments as cheaply as possible.

Nature of Sources of Finance

Sources of finance may be generated internally or raised externally. These sources of finance may be short-term or long-term. If short-term, they will typically be associated with operational activities involving the financing of working capital (such as stock, debtors or cash). If long-term, they will typically be associated with funding longer-term infrastructure assets, such as the purchase of land and buildings.

Normally, it is considered a mistake to borrow short and use long (e.g., use bank overdrafts for long-term purposes). For instance, if a bank overdraft was used to finance a new building, then the company would be in trouble if the bank suddenly withdrew the overdraft facility.

As Figure 22.1 shows, *internal* sources of finance may be generated over the *short term* through the efficient management of working capital, or over the *long term* by reinvesting retained profits.

Figure 22.1   Overview of Sources of Finance

	Short-term (less than 2 years)	*Long-term (over 2 years)*
Internal (within firm)	(a) Efficient cash management (b) Efficient debtors management (c) Efficient stock management	(a) Retained profits
External (outside firm)	(a) Bank overdraft (b) Bank loans (c) Invoice discounting (d) Debt factoring (e) Sale and leaseback	(a) Leasing (b) Share capital (c) Long-term borrowing

External sources of capital may be raised in the *short term* by cash overdrafts, bank loans, invoice discounting, debt factoring or sale and leaseback. Over the *longer term* the three most important external sources of finance are leasing, share capital and long-term borrowing. Although 'short-term' is defined as less than two years, this is, in fact, very arbitrary. For example, some leases may be for less than two years while bank overdrafts and bank loans will sometimes be for more than two years. However, this division provides a useful and convenient simplification.

Short-Term Financing

Short-term financing is often called the management of working capital (current assets less current liabilities). One of the main aims is to reduce the amount of short-term finance that companies need to borrow for their day-to-day operations. The more money that is tied up in current assets, the more capital is needed to finance those current assets. Essentially, as well as using its working capital as efficiently as possible, a company may use short-term borrowings to finance its stock, debtors or cash needs.

Figure 22.2 provides an overview of a company's short-term sources of finance. This includes *internal* management techniques for the efficient management of working capital (for example, debtor collection model and economic order quantity) and the main *external* sources of funds.

Figure 22.2 Overview of Short-Term Sources of Finance

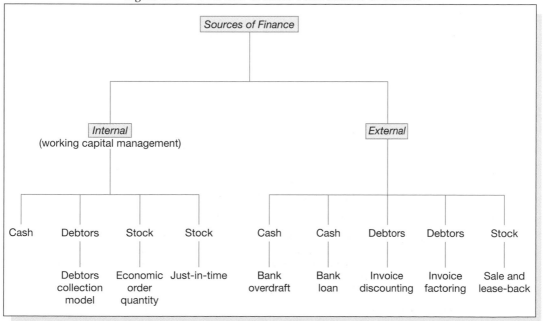

Internal Financing

Companies will try to minimise their levels of working capital so as to avoid short-term borrowings. In this section, we look at the main elements of efficient working capital management and three important techniques used to control working capital levels. In Chapter 5, we looked at the working capital cycle.

(a) Cash

As we saw in Chapter 8, cash is the lifeblood of a business. Companies need cash to survive. Businesses will try to keep enough cash to manage their day-to-day business operations (e.g., purchase stock and pay creditors), but not to maintain excessive amounts of cash. Businesses prepare cash budgets (see Chapter 17), which enable them to forecast the levels of cash that they will need to finance their operations. They may also use the liquidity and quick ratio to assess their level of cash (see Chapter 9). If despite careful cash management the business's short-term cash requirements are insufficient then the business will have to borrow.

(b) Debtors

Debtors management is a key activity within a firm. It is often called credit control. Debtors result from the sale of goods on credit. There is, therefore, the need to monitor carefully the receipts from debtors to see that they are in full and on time.

There will often be a separate department of a business concerned with credit control. The credit control department will, for example, establish credit limits for new customers, monitor the age of debts and chase up bad debts. In particular, they may draw up a debtors age schedule. This will profile the age of the debts and allow old debts to be quickly identified.

Debtors Collection Model   A useful technique designed to maintain the most efficient level of debtors for a company is the debtors collection model. A debtors collection model balances the extra revenue generated by increased sales with the increased costs associated with extra sales (i.e., credit control costs, bad debts and the delay in receiving money). The model assumes that the more credit granted the greater the sales. However, these extra sales are offset by increased bad debts as the business sells to less trustworthy customers. Whether the delay in receipts means that the business receives less interest or pays out more interest depends on whether or not the bank account is overdrawn. Usually, the cost of capital (i.e., effectively, the company's borrowing rate: see later in this chapter) is used to calculate the financial costs of the delayed receipts. Figure 22.3 illustrates the debtors collection model.

Figure 22.3   Debtors Collection Model

Bruce Bowhill is the finance director of a business with current sales of £240,000. If credit rises, so do bad debts. The contribution is 20%, the cost of capital is 15%, the credit control costs are £10,000 per annum at all levels of sales.

Credit	Annual sales	Bad Debts
Nil	£240,000	–
1 month	£320,000	1%
2 months	£500,000	5%
3 months	£650,000	10%

What is the most favourable level of sales?

We need to balance the increased contribution earned by increased sales with the increased costs of easier credit (i.e., credit control, bad debts and cost of capital).

	Nil credit £	1 month £	2 months £	3 months £
Sales	240,000	320,000	500,000	650,000
Contribution 20%	48,000	64,000	100,000	130,000
Cost of credit control		(10,000)	(10,000)	(10,000)
Bad debts 1% sales		(3,200)		
5% sales			(25,000)	
10% sales				(65,000)
Cost of capital relating to delay in payment: 15% of average debtors*		(4,000)	(12,500)	(24,375)
Revised Contribution	48,000	46,800	52,500**	30,625

*Average debtors per month
= £26,667   (£320,000 ÷ 12) (1 month)
= £83,333   (£500,000 ÷ 6) (2 months)
= £162,500 (£650,000 ÷ 4) (3 months)

**The optimal level is thus two months as it has the highest revised contribution.

(c) Stock

For many businesses, especially for manufacturing businesses, stock is often an extremely important asset. Stock is needed to create a buffer against excess demand, to protect against rising prices or against a potential shortage of raw materials and to balance sales and production.

Stock control is concerned not primarily with valuing stock (see Chapter 16), but with protecting the stock physically and ensuring that the optimal level is held. Stock may be stolen or may deteriorate. For many businesses such as supermarkets the battle against theft and deterioration is never-ending. A week-old lettuce in a supermarket is not a pleasant asset!! For supermarkets, stock can also be a competitive advantage (see Real-Life Nugget 22.1).

REAL-LIFE NUGGET 22.1

Stock

A Way to Look at It

When F.W. Woolworth opened his first store, a merchant on the same street tried to fight the new competition. He hung out a big sign: 'Doing business in this same spot for over fifty years'. The next day Woolworth also put out a sign. It read: 'Established a week ago; no old stock'.

Source: Peter Hay (1988), *The Book of Business Anecdotes*, Harrap Ltd, London, p. 275

Two common techniques associated with efficient stock control are the economic order quantity model and just-in-time stock management.

(i) Economic Order Quantity (EOQ)   The EOQ model seeks to determine the optimal order quantity needed to minimise the costs of ordering and holding stock. These costs are the costs of placing the order and the carrying costs. Carrying costs are those costs incurred in keeping an item in stock, such as insurance, obsolescence, interest on borrowed money or clerical/security costs. The costs of ordering stock are mainly the clerical costs. The EOQ can be determined either graphically or algebraically. Figure 22.4 on the next page demonstrates both methods. A key assumption underpinning the EOQ model is that the stock is used in production at a steady rate.

Figure 22.4   Economic Order Quantity

Tree plc has the following information about the Twig, one of its stock items. The Twig has an average yearly use in production of 5,000 items. Each Twig costs £1 and the company's cost of capital is 10% per annum. For each Twig, insurance costs are 2p per annum, storage costs are 2p per annum and the cost of obsolescence is 1p. The ordering costs are £60 per order.

i. Graphical Solution
We must first compile a table of costs at various order levels. For example, at an order quantity of 500, Tree needs 10 orders per annum (i.e., to buy 5,000 Twigs) which would give a total order cost of £600. The average quantity in stock (250) will be half the order quantity (500). If it costs 15 pence to carry an item, the total carrying cost will be £37.50 (i.e., 250 × 15p). Finally, the total cost will be £637.50 (total order cost £600 plus total carrying cost £37.50).

Order quantity (Q)	Average number or orders per annum	Order cost	Total order cost	Average quantity in stock	Carrying cost per item of stock	Total carrying cost	Total cost
			(1)	(2)	(3)	(4)	(5)
		£	£		£	£	£
500	10	60	600	250	0.15	37.50	637.50
1,000	5	60	300	500	0.15	75.00	375.00
2,000	2.5	60	150	1,000	0.15	150.00	300.00
2,500	2	60	120	1,250	0.15	187.50	307.50
5,000	1	60	60	2,500	0.15	375.00	435.00

Notes from table:
(1) Number of orders per annum multiplied by order cost.
(2) This represents half the order quantity. It assumes steady usage and instant delivery of stock.
(3) Cost of capital 10p (10% × £1), insurance 2p, storage 2p, obsolescence 1p. All per item.
(4) Average quantity in stock (2) multiplied by the carrying cost of £0.15 (3).
(5) Total order cost (1) and total carrying cost (4).

The graph can now be drawn with order quantity on the horizontal axis and annual costs along the vertical axis. The intersection of carrying cost and ordering cost represents the optimal re-order level. The optimal order quantity is thus close to 2,000.

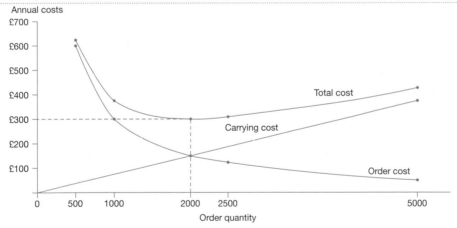

ii. Algebraic Solution
Fortunately, there is no need to know how to derive this formula, just apply it.

$$Q = \sqrt{\frac{2AC}{i}}$$ where Q = economic order quantity
A = average annual usage
C = cost of each order being placed
i = carrying cost per unit per annum

$$\therefore Q = \sqrt{\frac{2 \times 5,000 \times 60}{0.15}} = 2,000 \text{ Twigs}$$

(ii) Just-in-Time   Just-in-time was developed in Japan, where it has proved an effective method of stock control. It seeks to minimise stock holding costs by the careful timing of deliveries and efficient organisation of production schedules. At its best, just-in-time works by delivering stock just before it is used. The amount of stock is thus kept to a minimum and stock holding costs are also minimised. In order to do this, there is a need for a very streamlined and efficient production and delivery service. The concept behind just-in-time has been borrowed by many UK and US firms. Taken to its logical extreme, just-in-time means that no stocks of raw materials are needed at all. One potential problem with just-in-time is that if stock levels are kept at a minimum there is no stock buffer to deal with unexpected emergencies. For example, in the fuel blockade of Autumn 2000 in the UK, many supermarkets ran out of food because they had kept low levels of stock in their stores.

External Financing
(a) Cash

If a company is not generating enough cash from trading it may need to borrow. The most common method of borrowing is via a bank overdraft or a bank loan. Bank overdrafts are very flexible. Most major banks will set up an overdraft facility for a business as long as they are sure the business is viable. A bank overdraft is a good way to tackle the fluctuating cash flows experienced by many businesses.

PAUSE FOR THOUGHT 22.1

Bank Overdrafts

A bank overdraft represents a flexible way for a business to raise money. Can you think of drawbacks?

Overdrafts usually carry relatively high rates of interest. Overdrafts often carry variable rates of interest and are subject to a limit, which should not be exceeded without authorisation from the bank. They can be withdrawn at very short notice and are normally repayable on demand. Generally, interest is determined by time period and security. The shorter the time period, the higher the interest rate typically paid. In addition, if the loan is not secured on an asset (i.e., is unsecured) the rate of interest charged will once again be higher. Small businesses without a track record may often find it difficult to get a bank overdraft. Even when an overdraft is granted, the bank may insist that it is secured against the company's assets.

An alternative to a bank overdraft is a bank loan. The exact terms of individual bank loans will vary. However, essentially a loan is for a set period of years and this may well be more than two years. The rate of interest on a loan will normally be lower than on a bank overdraft. Loans may be secured on business assets, for example specific assets, such as stock or motor vehicles.

(b) Debtors

Since debtors are an asset, it is possible to raise money against them. This is done by debt factoring or invoice discounting.

(i) Debt factoring   Debt factoring is, in effect, the subcontracting of debtors. Many department stores, for example, find it convenient to subcontract their credit sales to debt factoring companies. The advantage to the business is twofold. First, it does not have to employ staff to chase up the debtors. Second, it receives an advance of money from the factoring organisation. There are, however, potential problems with factoring. The debt factoring company is not a charity and will charge a fee, for example 4 % of sales, for its services. In addition, the debt factoring company

SOUNDBITE 22.1

Debt Factoring

'Handing over your sales ledger to a factor was once viewed in the same league as Dr Faustus flogging his soul off to the devil – a path of illusory rides that would lead only to inevitable business ruin and damnation.'

Jerry Frank, *No Longer a Deal with the Devil*

Source: *Accountancy Age*, 18 May 2000, p. 27

will charge interest on any cash advances to the company. Finally, the company will lose the management of its customer database to an external party. As Soundbite 22.1 shows, debt factoring has traditionally been viewed with some suspicion.

(ii) Invoice discounting   Invoice discounting, in effect, is a loan secured on debtors. The financial institution will grant an advance (for example, 75 %) on outstanding sales invoices (i.e., debtors). Invoice discounting can be a one-off, or a continuing, arrangement. An important advantage of invoice discounting over debt factoring is that the credit control function is not contracted out. The company, therefore, keeps control over its records of debtors. Figure 22.5 compares debt factoring with invoice discounting.

Figure 22.5   Comparison of Debt Factoring and Invoice Discounting

Element	Debt Factoring	Invoice Discounting
Loan from financial institution	Yes	Yes
Sales ledger (i.e., keeping records of debtors)	Management by financial institution	Managed by company
Time period	Continuing	Usually one-off, but can be continuing

The aim of debtors management is simply to collect money from debtors as soon as possible. For an optimal cash balance, with no considerations of fairness, a business will benefit if it can accelerate its receipts and delay its payments. Receipts from customers and payments to suppliers are measured using the debtors/creditors collection period ratio (see Chapter 9).

(c) Stock

As with debtors, it is sometimes possible to borrow against stock. However, the time period is longer. Stock needs to be sold, then the debtors need to pay. Stock is not, therefore, such an attractive basis for lending for the financial institutions. However, in certain circumstances, financial institutions may be prepared to buy the stock now and then sell it back to the company at a later date.

PAUSE FOR THOUGHT 22.2

Sale and Buy Back of Stock

Can you think of any businesses where it may take such a long time for stock to convert to cash that businesses may sell their stock to third parties?

....

The classic example of sale and buy back occurs in the wine and spirit business. It takes a long time for a good whisky to mature. A finance company may, therefore, be prepared to buy the stock from the whisky distillery and then sell it back at a higher price at a future time. In effect, there is a loan secured against the whisky.

Another example might be in the construction industry. Here the financial institution may be prepared to loan the construction company money in advance. The money is secured on the work-in-progress which the construction company has already completed. The construction company repays the loan when it receives money from the customers.

Long-Term Financing

There are potentially four main sources of long-term finance: retained profits; leasing; share capital; and loan capital (see Figures 22.6 and 22.7).

Figure 22.6   Overview of Sources of Long-Term Finance

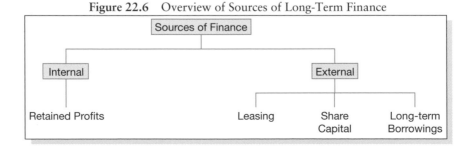

Figure 22.7   Sources of Long-Term Finance

(i) Internal Sources	*Main Features*
Retained profits	The company reinvests the profits it has made back into the business. It does not have to pay interest.
(ii) External Sources	
Leasing	A lessor leases specific assets to a company, such as a train or a plane. The company makes lease payments to the lessor.
Share capital	Money is raised from shareholders. Company pays dividends.
Long-term loan	Money is borrowed from banks or debt holder. Company repays interest.

For long-term finance, there is a need to raise money as cheaply and effectively as possible. Long-term finance is usually used to fund long-term infrastructure projects and can often be daunting, given the huge sums involved (see Soundbite 22.2).

Internal Sources

Retained Profits

Retained profits (or revenue reserves) represent an alternative to external financing. In effect, the business is financing itself from its past successes. Instead of distributing its profits as dividends, the company invests them for the future. Shareholders thus lose out today, but hope to gain tomorrow. As the company grows using its retained profits, it will in the future make more profits, distribute more dividends and then have a higher share price. In theory, that is!

In many businesses, retained profits represent the main source of long-term finance. It is important to realise that retained profits, themselves, are not directly equivalent to cash. However, indirectly they represent the cash dividends that the company could have paid out to shareholders. Retained profits are particularly useful in times when interest rates are high.

> **SOUNDBITE 22.2**
>
> ## Finance
>
> 'What is high finance? It's knowing the difference between one and ten, multiplying, subtracting and adding. You just add noughts. It's no more than that.'
>
> John Bentley, *Sunday Mirror*, 8 April 1973
>
> *Source*: *The Book of Business Quotations* (1991), p. 156

Retained Profits

What might be a limitation of using only retained funds as a source of long-term finance?

....

Retained profits are an easy resource for a company to draw upon. There is, however, one major limitation: a company can only grow by its own efforts and when funds are available. Therefore, growth may be very slow. The situation is similar to buying a house, you could save up for 25 years and then buy a house. Or you could buy one immediately by taking out a mortgage. Most people, understandably, prefer not to wait.

External Sources

(a) Leasing

In principle, the leasing of a company's assets is no different to an individual hiring a car or a television for personal usage. The property, initially at least, remains the property of the lessor. The lessee pays for the lease over a period of time. Depending on the nature of the property, the asset may eventually become the property of the lessee or remain, forever, the property of the lessor.

The main advantage of leasing is that the company leasing the asset does not immediately need to find the capital investment. The company can use the asset without buying it. This is particularly useful where the leased asset will directly generate revenue which is then used to pay the leasing company. Many of the tax benefits of leasing assets have now been curtailed. However, leasing remains an attractive way of financing assets such as cars, buses, trains or planes. Normally, leasing is tied to specific assets.

In the end, the company leasing the assets will pay more for them than buying them outright. The additional payments are how the leasing companies make their money. Leases are usually used for medium or long-term asset financing. Hire purchase or credit sales, which share many of the general principles of leases, are sometimes used for medium to short-term financing.

Strictly, leasing is a source of assets rather than a source of finance. It does not result in an inflow of money. However, it is treated as a source of finance because if the asset had been bought outright, not leased, the business would have needed to fund the original purchase. Long-term leasing can be considered equivalent to debt. The asset is purchased by the lessor, but used and paid for by the lessee, including an interest payment. Long-term leases must be disclosed on the balance sheet. There is a recent trend where businesses that own property portfolios sell them for cash. They then lease back the original properties. This is the strategy being considered by Marks & Spencer in Real-Life Nugget 22.2.

REAL-LIFE NUGGET 22.2

Sale and Leaseback

Marks & Spencer, the troubled retail group, is poised to sell up to 40 of its high street stores across the country in a bid to raise up to £250 m.

M&S, whose chief executive Peter Salsbury is conducting a strategy review to reverse the group's slump in profits, is said to be in talks with a select band of property investors. Under the proposals being considered, M&S would lease back the stores which are all understood to be prime sites and could include Oxford Circus, one of the retailer's larger London flagship stores.

Source: M&S £250 m Stores Sale, Doug Morrison, *The Sunday Telegraph*, 21 March 1999

(b) Share Capital

Apart from reserves, there are two main types of corporate long-term capital: share capital and loan capital. Share capital is divided into ordinary shares and preference shares. Both sets of shareholders are paid dividends. However, while ordinary shareholders are owners, preference shareholders are not (Chapter 9 provides a fuller discussion of these issues).

When a company wishes to raise substantial sums of new money, the normal choice is either raising share capital or loan capital. Freeserve, the Internet service provider, for example, chose a stock market flotation raising an anticipated £1.9 billion from shares (see Real-Life Nugget 22.3).

REAL-LIFE NUGGET 22.3

Stock Market Flotations

Freeserve, the free internet access service launched last September by Dixons Group, the electrical retailer, is likely to be valued at £1.9 billion or £1,500 per subscriber, when it comes to the stock market. A flotation is likely to take place next month.

Details of the float, disclosed yesterday, emerged at a turbulent time for Internet stocks in the US, and are likely to cause controversy in the City.

Freeserve's value on a 'per subscriber' basis will be similar to that of BSkyB, the satellite broadcaster, 40 per cent owned by News International.

Source: Freeserve plans £1.9bn float, Chris Ayres, *The Times*, 16 June 1999, p. 25

There are three main methods by which a company may raise share capital: rights issue, public issue and placing. The main features of these alternatives are listed in Figure 22.8.

Figure 22.8   Types of Share Issue

Type	Main Feature
Rights Issue	Existing shareholders can buy more shares in proportion to their existing holdings.
Public Issue	Company itself directly offers shares to the public. A prospectus containing the company's details is issued. The shares may be issued at a fixed price or open to tender (i.e., bidding). A variation on the public issue is the offer for sale. The company sells the new issue of shares to a financial institution which then issues them on the company's behalf.
Placing	A company coming to the market for the first time may allow underwriters to 'place' shares with certain financial institutions. These institutions will then hold them or sell them.

A **rights issue** is therefore an issue to existing shareholders. In June 2001, for example, British Telecom asked its *existing* shareholders for £5.9 billion extra cash. By contrast, **public issues** and **placings** involve new shareholders. The public issue is distinguished from the placing chiefly by the fact that the shares are 'open' to public purchase rather than being privately allocated. In all three types of share issue, the company receives the amount that the shareholders pay for the shares. This money can then be used to finance expansion or on any other corporate activity. Stock market issues can make entrepreneurs potentially very rich, as happened to the creators of Lastminute.com (see Real-Life Nugget 22.4), although this wealth is dependent upon them selling their shares!

REAL-LIFE NUGGET 22.4

Getting Rich Quick

Yesterday's frenzied debut for Lastminute.com once again raises a question that may never be properly answered: how much is an internet company really worth?

To many people a share is worth what the financial markets think it is, no more and no less. That would make Lastminute 'worth' every penny of the £800 m at which the total value of its shares were trading at one point yesterday. And no one can say investors were hoodwinked. They flocked to buy the shares despite the descant sung by analysts that they were overvalued.

Source: Watch out for those last minute lemmings, Victor Keegan, *The Guardian*, 15 March 2000, p. 26. © Guardian Newspapers Limited 2000

(c) Loan Capital

Loan capital is long-term borrowing. The holders of the loans are paid loan interest. Loan capital can chiefly be distinguished from ordinary share capital by four features. First, loan interest is a *deduction* from profits *not*, like dividends, a *distribution* of profits. Second, loan capital, unlike ordinary share capital, is commonly repaid. Third, unlike ordinary shareholders, the holders of loan capital do not own the company. And, finally, most loans will be secured either on the general assets of the company or on specific assets, such as land and buildings. In other words, if the company fails, the loan holders have first call on the company's assets. They will be able to sell the assets of the company to recover their loans. Sometimes convertible loans are issued which may be converted into ordinary shares at a specified future date. Loans and debt have always attracted humourists, as Real-Life Nuggets 22.5 and 22.6 show.

REAL-LIFE NUGGET 22.5

Loans

The Importance of Being Seen

Around the turn of the century a speculator by the name of Charles Flint got into financial difficulties. He had a slight acquaintance with J.P. Morgan, Sr., and decided to touch him for a loan. Morgan asked him to come for a stroll around the Battery in lower Manhattan. The two men discussed the weather in some detail, and other pressing matters, when finally, after about an hour or so, the exasperated Flint burst out: 'But Mr. Morgan, how about the million dollars I need to borrow?'

Morgan held out his hand to say goodbye: 'Oh, I don't think you'll have any trouble getting it now that we have been seen together.'

Peter Hay (1988), *The Book of Business Anecdotes*, Harrap Ltd, London, p. 5

REAL-LIFE NUGGET 22.6

Debt

Stratagem

A moneylender complained to Baron Rothschild that he had lent 10,000 francs to a man who had gone off to Constantinople without a written acknowledgement of his debt.

'Write to him and demand back 50,000 francs,' advised the baron.

'But he only owes me 10,000,' said the moneylender.

'Exactly, and he will write and tell you so in a hurry. And that's how you will have acknowledgement of his debt.'

Peter Hay (1988), *The Book of Business Anecdotes*, Harrap Ltd, London, p. 5

As we saw in Chapter 9, the relationship between ordinary share capital and a company's fixed interest funds (long-term loans and preference shares) is known as gearing. Gearing is particularly important when assessing the viability of a company's capital structure.

Cost of Capital

From the details of a company's different sources of finance, it is possible to determine its cost of capital. In essence, the cost of capital is simply the cost at which a business raises funds. The two main sources of funds are debt (from long-term loans) and equity (from share capital). Normally, debt finance will be cheaper than equity. As Soundbite 22.3 below shows, it is an important business concept. Each source of finance will have an associated cost of capital. However, it is important to calculate the business's overall cost of capital (known as the **weighted average cost of capital** or WACC). WACC is the cost of capital normally used as the discount rate in capital investment appraisal (see Chapter 21).

SOUNDBITE 22.3

Cost of Capital

'Business is the most important engine for social change in our society ... And you're not going to transform society until you transform business. But you're not going to transform business by pretending it's not a business. Business means profit. You've got to earn your cost of capital. They didn't do it in the former Soviet Union, that's why it's former.'

Lawrence Perlman, *Twin Cities Business Monthly* (November 1994)

Source: *The Wiley Book of Business Quotations* (1998), p. 69

The same principles can be adopted for personal finance and for business. We take the examples of Deborah Ebt, a student, in Figure 22.9 and Costco plc in Figure 22.10 (both overleaf).

Figure 22.9   Calculation of Cost of Capital for a Student, D. Ebt

D. Ebt finances her college course as follows:

General expenses, by credit card	£3,000 at 25% interest per annum
Accommodation, by bank loan	£4,000 at 10% interest per annum
Car, by loan from uncle	£3,000 at 5% interest per annum

What is D. Ebt's overall weighted average cost of capital?

Source of Finance	Proportion		Cost of Capital	Weighted Average Cost of Capital (WACC)
	£	%	%	%
Credit card	3,000	30	25	7.5
Bank loan	4,000	40	10	4.0
Personal loan	3,000	30	5	1.5
	10,000	100		13.0

Helpnote
The weighted average cost of capital is the proportion of total debt financed by loan source multiplied by interest rate. Therefore, for credit cards (£3,000/£10,000) × 25% = 7.5%. The cost of capital for each source of finance is simply the interest rate.

Figure 22.9 thus shows that overall the weighted average cost of capital is 13% for D. Ebt. The most expensive source of finance was the credit card and the cheapest was the personal loan.

Figure 22.10   Example of a Company's Cost of Capital

Costco plc has 800,000 £1 ordinary shares currently quoted on the stock market at £2.50 each. It pays a dividend of 20p per share. Costco also has £200,000 worth of debt capital currently worth £1,000,000 on the stock market. The loan interest payable is 60,000.

Calculate Costco plc's weighted average cost of capital.

Source of Finance	Market Value	Proportion %	Cost of capital	Weighted Average Cost of Capital (WACC)
Equity	£2,000,000	66.67	8% (£0.20 ÷ £2.50)	5.3%
Debt	£1,000,000	33.33	6% (£60,000 ÷ £1,000,000)	2.0%
	£3,000,000	100.00		7.3%

The cost of capital is thus 7.3%.

Helpnote
We need to take the *market value* of the capital, not the original nominal value of the capital, as this is the value that the capital is *currently worth*. The cost of equity capital is simply the dividend divided by the share price and the cost of debt capital is the interest payable divided by the market price of the debt.

Figure 22.10 thus indicates that overall the weighted average cost of capital is 7.3 %. The equity capital constitutes most of this (i.e. 5.3 %).

The cost of capital is a potentially complex and difficult subject. However, the basic idea is simple, the company is trying to find the optimal mix of debt and equity which will enable it to fund its business at the lowest possible cost. Investors show great interest in a company's cost of capital (see Real-Life Nugget 22.7).

REAL-LIFE NUGGET 22.7

Railtrack's Cost of Capital

As for cost of capital, it's a matter of guesswork – or the capital-asset pricing model – to calculate the figure in the first place. However, the rail regulator reckons that Railtrack's cost of capital is close to 7.5 per cent before both tax and inflation. For investors, that figure looks pretty generous. Here's why: Railtrack will pay little tax in the coming years so, assuming inflation averages 2.5 per cent a year, the regulator is allowing Railtrack a post-tax return on its capital of nearly 10 per cent. That's approaching growth stock status and – using another branch of the capital-asset pricing model – means that investors could expect a total return from owning Railtrack shares of 10 per cent plus their current dividend yield, which is 2.8 per cent.

Source: Playing Monopoly, Bearbull, *The Investors Chronicle*, 4 August 2000, p. 18

Conclusion

Sources of finance are essential to a business if it is going to grow and survive. We can distinguish between short-term and long-term sources of finance. Short-term financing concerns the management of working capital: cash, debtors and stock. This may involve the more efficient use of working capital using various techniques such as the debtors collection model and the economic order quantity model. Alternatively, it may involve raising loans from the bank by an overdraft, or loans secured on debtors by debt factoring, or by the sale and leaseback of stock. Long-term sources of capital are used to fund the long-term activities of a business. The four main sources are an internal source (retained profits) and three external sources (leasing, share capital and loan capital). Retained profits are not borrowings but, in effect, represent undistributed profits ploughed back into the business. Leasing involves a company using an asset, but not owning it. Shareholders own the company and are paid dividends. Loan capital providers do not own the company and are paid loan interest. A key function of managing long-term finance is to minimise a company's cost of capital which is the effective rate at which a company can raise funds.

Q&A   Discussion Questions

Questions with numbers in blue have answers at the back of the book.

Q1   Why are the sources of finance available to a firm so important? What are the main sources of finance and which activities of a business might they finance?

Q2   What is working capital and how might a company try to manage it?

Q3   What are the advantages and disadvantages of retained funds, debt and equity as methods of funding a business?

Q4   What is the weighted average cost of capital and why is it an important concept in business finance?

Q5   State whether the following statements are true or false. If false, explain why.
   (a) Long-term sources of finance are usually used to finance working capital.
   (b) A debtors collection model seeks the efficient management of debtors by balancing the benefits of extra credit sales against the extra costs of those sales.
   (c) Two common techniques of stock control are the economic order quantity model and the just-in-time approach.
   (d) There are four external long-term sources of finance: retained profits, leasing, share capital and loan capital.
   (e) A rights issue, a public issue and a placing are three major ways in which a company can raise share capital.

Q&A   Numerical Questions

Questions with numbers in blue have answers at the back of the book.

Q1   Lathe plc is a small manufacturing firm. It buys in a subcomponent, the Tweak, for £1.50. The cost of insurance and storage per Tweak are £0.40, and £0.50 per item per year, respectively. It costs £25 for each order. The annual quantity purchased is 20,000.

   Required:
   (i) What is the economic order quantity? Solve this (a) graphically and (b) algebraically.
   (ii) What are the total costs per annum at this level?

Q2   A bookshop, Bookworm, buys 2,500 copies of the book, *Deep Heat*, per year. It costs the bookshop £0.80 per annum to carry the book in stock and £20 to prepare a new order.

Required:
(i) The total costs if orders are 1, 2, 5, 10 and 20 times per year.
(ii) The economic order quantity. An algebraic solution only is required.

Q3   Winter Brollies wishes to revise its credit collection policy. Currently it has £500,000 sales, a credit policy of 25 days and an average collection period of 20 days. 1 % of debtors default. Credit control costs are £5,000 for 25 days and 30 days; £6,000 for 60 days and 90 days. There is the following potential sales forecast.

Credit Period (Days)	Average Collection Period (Days)	New Annual Sales (£)	Bad Debts (%)
30	25	600,000	2
60	55	700,000	4
90	85	800,000	8

The cost of capital is 10 % and the average contribution is 20 % on selling price. Assume 360 days in year.

Required: Advise Winter Brollies whether or not it should revise its credit policy.

Q4   Albatross plc has the following information about its capital.

Source of Finance	Current Market Value £million	Present Cost of Capital %
Ordinary shares	4	12
Preference shares	1	10
Long-term loan	3	8

Required: What is Albatross's weighted average cost of capital?

Q5   Nebula plc is looking at its sources of finance. It collects the following details. Currently, there are 500,000 ordinary shares in issue, with a market price of £1.50 and a current dividend of £0.30. The number of preference shares in issue is 300,000, with a market price of £1.00 and a dividend of 15p. There are £200,000 of long-term debentures carrying 12 % interest. These are currently trading at £220,000.

Required: Calculate Nebula's weighted average cost of capital.

Further Reading

In this book, I have tried to give non-specialist readers a comprehensive introduction to accounting. Most accounting textbooks are designed for accounting students and, therefore, often focus on demonstrating and explaining technical issues. These books must, therefore, be used by non-specialists with care.

In Section B, I have listed a considerable number of books and articles to supplement the theoretical chapters which deal with the conceptual and regulatory frameworks, measurement systems, the annual report, creative accounting and international accounting. Readers are referred back to these individual chapters.

Below, I detail some further reading which students may find useful for Section A on Financial Accounting and Section C on Management Accounting. There are separate references at the end of Chapter 20 on Strategic Management Accounting in Section C. There is, in fact, a much greater choice for Section A on Financial Accounting than for Section C on Management Accounting.

Section A: Financial Accounting

Alexander D. and A. Britton (2004) *Financial Reporting*, Thomson Business Press.
This book provides an in-depth look at financial accounting for those who have mastered the basics.

Edwards J.R. and J.R. Mellett (2001) *Introduction to Accounting*, Paul Chapman Publishing.
This book is pitched at a reasonable introductory level, but aimed at students specialising in accounting. Provides a good background supplemental text.

Elliott, B. and J. Elliott (2003) *Financial Accounting and Reporting*, Financial Times/Prentice Hall.
A book to be used with care. Provides in-depth coverage for those who have mastered the basics.

Gillespie, I. and R. Lewis (2004) *Principles of Financial Accounting*, Prentice Hall.
This introductory text is aimed at first year students. It provides a good supplemental text. The spread-sheet approach may take some getting used to.

Horngren C.T. (2005) *Introduction to Financial Accounting*, Prentice Hall.
This is a heavy-weight US text. Its in-depth approach and use of US terminology may make this book less accessible to UK students.

Section C: Management Accounting

Arnold, J. and S. Turley (1996) *Accounting for Management Decisions*, Prentice Hall.
Provides a reasonable coverage of many of the key issues. At times may be too complex for non-specialist, first year students.

Drury C. (2005) *Management and Cost Accounting*, Thomson Business Press.
Provides a comprehensive coverage of management accounting for those who have grasped the basics.

Horngren C.T., G.L. Sundem and W.O. Stratton (2004) *Introduction to Management Accounting*, Prentice Hall.
A heavy-weight US text which mirrors the similar text on financial accounting. The in-depth approach and use of US terminology may make this book less accessible to UK students.

Weetman P. (2002) *Financial and Management Accounting: An Introduction*, Financial Times/Prentice Hall.
An accessible text for students who wish to rehearse their knowledge of the basics.

Glossary of Key Accounting Terms

This glossary contains most of the key accounting terms that students are likely to encounter. Words highlighted in bold are explained elsewhere in the glossary.

Absorption costing
The form of costing used for valuing stock for external financial reporting. All the overheads which can be attributed to a product are recovered. Unlike **marginal costing** which can sometimes be used for stock valuation, absorption costing includes both fixed and variable production overheads.

Acid test ratio
See **quick ratio**

Accounting
The provision of information to managers and owners so they can make business decisions.

Accounting concept
A principle underpinning the preparation of accounting information.

Accounting equation
The basic premise that **assets** equals **liabilities**.

Accounting period
The time period for which the accounts are prepared. Audited financial statements are usually prepared for a year.

Accounting policies
The specific accounting methods selected and followed by a company in areas such as sales, foreign currencies, stocks, goodwill and pensions.

Accounting rate of return
A method of **capital investment appraisal** which assesses the viability of a project using annual profit and initial capital invested.

Accounting standards
Accounting pronouncements which set out the disclosure and measurement rules businesses must follow to give a **true and fair view** when drawing up accounts.

Accounting Standards Board (ASB)
The Accounting Standards Board sets the UK's **accounting standards**.

Accruals
The amounts owed to the suppliers of services at the balance sheet date, for expenses such as telephone or light and heat.

Accruals concept
See **matching concept**

Accumulated depreciation
The total depreciation on **tangible fixed assets** including this year's and prior years' depreciation.

Activity-based costing
A cost recovery technique which identifies key activities and key activity **cost drivers**

Annual report
A report produced annually by **companies** comprising both financial and non-financial information.

Appropriation account
The sharing out of partners' profit after net profit has been calculated in the **profit and loss account.**

Asset turnover ratio
A ratio which compares sales to total assets employed.

Assets
Essentially, items owned or leased by a business. Assets may be tangible or intangible, current or fixed. Assets bring economic benefits through either sale (for example, stock) or use (for example, a car).

Associated company
A company in which 20–50 % of the shares are owned by another company or in which another company has a significant influence.

Attainable standard cost
A **standard cost** which can be reached with effort.

Auditors

A team of professionally qualified accountants *independent* of a company. Appointed by the **shareholders** on the recommendation of the **directors**, the auditors check and report on the accounts prepared by the directors.

Auditors' report

A statement in a company's **annual report** which states whether the financial statements present a '**true and fair view**' of the company's activities over the previous financial year.

Authorised share capital

The amount of **share capital** that a company is *allowed* to issue to its shareholders.

Average cost (AVCO)

A method of stock valuation where stock is valued at the average purchase price (see also **first-in-first-out** and **last-in-first-out**).

Bad debts

Those debts that will definitely not be paid. They are an **expense** in the **profit and loss account** and are written off **debtors** in the **balance sheet**.

Balance off

In **double-entry bookkeeping,** the accounts are balanced off and, the figures for **assets** and **liabilities** are carried forward to the next period. In effect, this signals the end of an **accounting period**.

Balance sheet

A financial statement which is a snapshot of a business at a particular point in time. It records the **assets, liabilities** and **capital** of a business. Assets less liabilities equals capital. Capital is the owners' interest in the business.

Balanced scorecard

In **management accounting,** the balanced scorecard looks at a business from multiple perspectives such as financial, customer, internal business, and innovation and learning perspectives.

Bank overdraft

A business or individual owes the bank money.

Batch costing

A number of items of a similar nature are processed and costed together (e.g., baking bread).

Benchmarking

In **management accounting,** benchmarking measures a business against its competitors across a series of performance indicators (e.g., customer service or number of complaints).

Bookkeeping

The preparation of the basic accounts. Monetary transactions are entered into the books of account. A **trial balance** is then extracted, and a **profit and loss account** and a **balance sheet** are prepared.

Break-even analysis

Break-even analysis involves calculating the point at which a product or service makes neither a profit nor a loss. **Fixed costs** are divided by the contribution per unit giving the **break-even point.**

Break-even point

The point at which a firm makes neither a profit nor a loss. A firm's break-even point can be expressed as: Sales – variable costs – fixed costs = 0.

Budget

A future plan which sets out a business's financial targets.

Budgeting

Budgeting involves setting future targets. Actual results are then compared with budgeted results. Any **variances** are then investigated.

Called-up share capital

The amount of **issued share capital** that is fully paid up by **shareholders**. For example, a share may be issued for £1.50 and paid in three equal instalments. After two instalments the called-up share capital is £1.

Capital

Capital represents the owner's interest in the business. In effect, capital is a liability as it is owed by the business to the owner (e.g., **sole trader**, partner or **shareholder**). Capital is the assets of a business less its liabilities to third parties. Capital is accumulated wealth and is increased by profit, but reduced by losses. For listed companies capital is known as **equity**.

Capital expenditure

A payment to purchase an **asset** with a long life such as a **fixed asset**.

Capital expenditure and financial investment

In a **cash flow statement,** cash flows relating to the purchase and sale of **fixed assets** and **investments.**

Capital investment appraisal

A method of evaluating long-term **capital expenditure decisions.**

Capital investment decisions

Usually long-term decisions (such as building a new factory).

Capital maintenance concept
A way of determining whether the 'capital' of a business has improved, deteriorated or stayed the same over a period of time. There is both **financial** and **physical capital maintenance**.

Capital reserves
Reserves not distributable to shareholders as dividends (e.g., the **share premium account** or **revaluation reserve**).

Carriage inwards
The cost of delivering raw materials. Refers to the days when goods were delivered by horse-and-carriage.

Carriage outwards
The cost of delivering the finished goods. Refers to the days when goods were delivered by horse-and-carriage.

Carrying costs
Costs such as insurance, obsolescence, interest on borrowed money or clerical/security costs incurred in holding stock.

Cash and bank
The actual money held by the business either at the business as cash or at the bank.

Cash at bank
Money deposited with a bank.

Cash book
In large businesses, a separate book which records cash and cheque transactions.

Cash budget
This budget records the projected inflows and outflows of cash.

Cash cows
An element in the **product portfolio matrix**. Cash cows are a company's dream product. They are well-established, require little capital expenditure, but generate high returns.

Cash flow statement
A financial statement which shows the cash inflows and outflows of a business.

Chairman's statement
A statement in a company's **annual report** which provides a personalised overview of the company's performance over the past year. It generally covers strategy, financial performance and future prospects.

Companies Acts
Acts of Parliament which lay down the legal requirements for companies including accounting regulations.

Company
A business enterprise where the **shareholders** have **limited liability**.

Conceptual framework
A coherent and consistent set of accounting principles which underpin the preparation and presentation of financial statements.

Consistency concept
An accounting principle which states similar items should be treated similarly from year to year.

Contract costing
A form of **costing** in which costs are allocated to contracts (i.e., usually big jobs which occur in construction industries such as shipbuilding). A long-term contract extends over more than one year and creates the problem of when to take profit.

Contribution
Contribution to fixed overheads, or contribution in short, is **sales** less **variable costs**.

Contribution analysis
A technique for short-term decision making where **fixed costs, variable costs** and **contribution** are analysed. The objective is to maximise a company's contribution (and thus profit) when choosing between different operating decisions.

Contribution graph
A graph which plots cumulative contribution against cumulative sales. Also called a profit/volume graph.

Controllable cost
A cost that a manager can influence and that a manager can be held responsible for.

Corporate governance
The system by which companies are directed and controlled. The financial aspects of corporate governance relate principally to internal control and the way in which the board of directors functions and reports to the shareholders on the activities and progress of the company.

Cost
An item of expenditure (planned or actually incurred).

Cost accounting
Essentially, **costing** and **planning and control**.

Cost allocation
The process by which **indirect costs** are recovered into total cost or into stock.

Cost centre
In **responsibility accounting**, where a manager is held responsible for costs.

Cost driver
In **activity-based costing**, a factor causing a change in an activity's costs.

Cost minimisation
Minimising cost either by tight budgetary control or cutting back on expenditure.

Cost recovery
The process by which costs are recovered into a product or service to form the basis of pricing or stock valuation.

Cost of capital
The interest rate at which a business raises funds.

Cost of sales
Essentially the cost of directly providing the sales.

Cost-volume-profit analysis
A **management accounting** technique which looks at the effect of changes in fixed costs, variable costs and sales on profit. Also called **contribution analysis**.

Costing
Recovering **costs** as a basis for pricing and stock valuation.

Creative accounting
Using the flexibility within accounting to manage the measurement and presentation of the accounts so that they serve the interests of the preparers.

Credit
An entry on the right-hand side of a 'T' account. Records principally increases in **liabilities**, **capital** or **income**. May also record decreases in **assets** or **expenses**.

Credit control
Controlling **debtors** by establishing credit limits for new customers, monitoring the age of debts and chasing up **bad debts**.

Creditors
Amounts owed to trade suppliers for goods supplied on credit, but not yet paid. Known as **trade payables** for listed companies.

Creditors budget
This **budget** forecasts the level of future creditors. It keeps a running balance of creditors by adding purchases and deducting cash payments.

Creditors collection period
Measures how long a business takes to pay its **creditors** by relating creditors to cost of sales.

Current assets
Those **assets** (e.g., **stocks, debtors** and cash) that a company uses in its day-to-day operations.

Current liabilities
The liabilities that a business uses in its day-to-day operations (e.g., **creditors** (**trade payables**)).

Current purchasing power
A **measurement system** where historical cost is adjusted by general changes in the purchasing power of money (e.g., inflation), often measured using the retail price index (RPI).

Current ratio
A short-term test of liquidity which determines whether short-term **assets** cover short-term **liabilities**.

Debenture
Another name for a **long-term loan**. Debentures may be **secured** or **unsecured loans**.

Debit
An entry on the left-hand side of a 'T' **account**. Records principally increases in either **assets** or **expenses**. May also record decreases in **liabilities, capital** or **income**.

Debt factoring
Where the **debtors** are subcontracted to a third party who are paid to manage them.

Debtors
When sales are made on credit, but the customers have not yet paid. Known as **trade receivables** for **listed companies**.

Debtors age schedule
A credit control technique which profiles the age of the debts and allow old debts to be quickly identified.

Debtors budget
This **budget** forecasts the level of future debtors. It keeps a running balance of debtors by adding sales and deducting cash received.

Debtors collection model
A technique for managing **working capital** which seeks to maintain the most efficient level of debtors for a company. It balances the extra revenue generated by increased sales with the increased costs associated with extra sales (e.g., credit control costs, bad debts and the delay in receiving money).

Debtors collection period
A ratio which measures how long customers take to pay their debts by relating debtors to sales.

Decision making in management accounting
The choice between alternatives. Only **relevant costs and revenues** should be considered.

Decision-making objective of financial reporting
Providing users, especially shareholders, with financial information so that they can make decisions such as whether to buy or sell shares.

Depreciation
Depreciation attempts to match a proportion of the original cost of the **fixed assets** to the **accounting period** in which the fixed assets were used up as an annual expense.

Direct costs
Costs directly identifiable and attributable to a product or service (e.g., the amount of direct labour or direct materials incurred). Sometimes called *product costs*.

Direct labour overall variance
Standard cost of labour for actual production less actual cost of labour used in production.

Direct labour price variance
(Standard price per hour – actual price per hour) × actual quantity of labour used.

Direct labour quantity variance
(Standard quantity of labour hours for actual production – actual quantity of labour hours used) × standard labour price per hour.

Direct materials overall variance
Standard cost of materials for actual production less actual cost of materials used in production.

Direct materials price variance
(Standard price per unit of material – actual price per unit of material) × actual quantity of materials used.

Direct materials quantity variance
(Standard price per unit of material – actual price per unit of material) × actual quantity of materials used.

Direct method of preparing cash flow statement
Classifies *operating* cash flows by function or type of activity (e.g., receipts from customers).

Directors
Those responsible for running the business. Accountable to the **shareholders** who, in theory, appoint and dismiss them.

Directors' remuneration report
A statement in an **annual report** in which companies include details of their directors' pay.

Directors' report
A narrative statement in an **annual report**. It supplements the financial information with information considered important for a full appreciation of a company's activities.

Discount allowed
A reduction in the selling price of a good or service allowed by the business to customers for prompt payment. Treated as an **expense**.

Discount factor
A factor by which future cash flows are discounted to arrive at today's monetary value.

Discount received
A reduction in the purchase price of a good or service granted to a business from the supplier for paying promptly. Treated as an **income**.

Discounted cash flow
The future expected cash inflows and outflows of a potential project discounted back to their present value today to see whether or not proposed projects are viable.

Dividend cover
A ratio showing how many times profit available to pay ordinary dividends covers actual dividends.

Dividend yield
A ratio showing how much dividend ordinary shares earn as a proportion of market price.

Dividends
A cash payment to shareholders rewarding them for investing money in a company.

Dogs
An element in the **product portfolio matrix**. Dogs are cash traps with low market growth and low market share.

Double-entry bookkeeping

A way of systematically recording the financial transactions of a company so that each transaction is recorded twice.

Doubtful debts

Debts which may or may not be paid. Usually, businesses estimate a certain proportion of their debts as doubtful.

Drawings

Money which a **sole trader** or partner takes out of a business as living expenses. It is, in effect, the owner's salary and is really a withdrawal of capital.

Earnings per share (EPS)

A key ratio by which investors measure the performance of a company.

Economic order quantity (EOQ)

A technique for managing **working capital**. The optimal EOQ is calculated so as to minimise the costs of ordering and holding stock.

Efficiency ratios

Ratios which show how efficiently a business uses its assets.

Entity concept

A business has a distinct and separate identity from its owner. This is obvious in the case of a large limited company where **shareholders** own the company and managers manage the company. However, there is also a distinction between a **sole trader's** or **partnership's** personal and business assets.

Equity

The term used for **capital** for a listed company.

Equivalent units

In **process costing**, partially finished units are converted to fully completed equivalent units by estimating the percentage of completion.

Expenses

The day-to-day **costs** incurred in running a business, e.g., telephone, business rates and wages. Expenses are expenses even if goods and services are consumed, but not yet paid. Expenses are, therefore, different from cash paid.

Financial accounting

The provision of financial information on a business's financial performance targeted at external users, such as shareholders. It includes not only **double-entry bookkeeping**, but also the preparation and interpretation of the financial accounts.

Financial capital maintenance concept
This concept is primarily concerned with *monetary measurement*, in particular, the measurement of the net assets.

Financial Reporting Council (FRC)
A UK supervisory body which ensures that the overall accounting standard-setting system is working.

Financial Reporting Review Panel (FRRP)
The FRRP investigates contentious departures from accounting standards and is part of the UK's standard-setting regime.

Financing cash flows
In a **cash flow statement**, they relate to the issuing or buying back of shares or loan capital.

Finished goods stock
The final stock after the manufacturing process is completed, for example, finished tables. The cost includes materials and other manufacturing costs (e.g., labour and manufacturing overheads).

First-in-first-out (FIFO)
A method of stock valuation where the stock bought first is the first to be sold. See also **average cost** and **last-in-first-out**.

Fixed assets
Infrastructure assets used to run the business long-term and *not* used in day-to-day production. Includes **tangible fixed assets** (e.g., motor vehicles, land and buildings, fixtures and fittings, plant and machinery) and **intangible fixed assets** (e.g., goodwill). Fixed assets are known as **property, plant and equipment** for a listed company.

Fixed costs
Costs that *do not vary* with production or sales (for example, insurance) in an **accounting period** and are not affected by short-term decisions. Often called fixed overheads.

Fixed overheads
See **fixed costs**.

Fixed overheads quantity variance
(Standard fixed overheads – actual fixed overheads).

Flexing the budget
Adjusting the **budget** to account for the *actual quantity produced*.

Gearing
The relationship between a company's ordinary shareholders' funds and the debt capital.

General reserve
A **revenue reserve** created to deal with general, unspecified contingencies such as inflation.

Going concern concept
The business will continue into the foreseeable future. **Assets, liabilities, incomes** and **expenses** are measured on this basis.

Goodwill
In takeovers, the purchase price less the amount paid for the net assets. It represents the value placed on the earning power of a business over and above its **net asset** value.

Gross profit
Sales less **cost of sales.**

Gross profit ratio
This ratio relates the profit earned through trading to sales.

Historical cost
A **measurement system** where monetary amounts are recorded at the date of original transaction.

Historical cost convention
The amount recorded in the accounts will be the *original* amount paid for a good or service.

Horizontal analysis
A form of ratio analysis which compares the figures in the accounts across time. It is used to investigate trends in the data.

Ideal standards
In **standard costing,** standards attained in an ideal world.

Impression management
Managers try to influence the financial reporting process in their own favour. Includes both **creative accounting** and **narrative enhancement.**

Income
The revenue earned by a business, e.g., **sales.** Income is income, even if goods and services have been delivered but customers have yet to pay. Income thus differs from cash received.

Income receivable
Receivable by the business from a third party, e.g., **dividends** receivable (from companies) or interest receivable (from the bank).

Income statement
The term used in **listed companies** for the **profit and loss account.**

Indirect costs
Those costs *not* directly identifiable *nor* attributable to a product or service, e.g., administrative, and selling and distribution costs. These costs are totalled and then recovered indirectly into the product or service. Also called *indirect overheads* or *period costs.*

Indirect method of preparing cash flow statement
Operating cash flow is derived from the **profit and loss account** and **balance sheet** and not classified directly by function (such as receipts from sales).

Indirect overheads
See **indirect costs.**

Intangible assets
Fixed assets one cannot touch, unlike **tangible fixed assets** (such as land and buildings). Most common in **companies.**

Interest cover
A ratio showing the amount of profit available to cover the **interest payable** on long-term borrowings.

Interest payable
An expense related especially to bank loans. When paid becomes interest paid.

Internal rate of return (IRR)
A **capital investment appraisal** technique. The internal rate of return represents the discount rate required to give a **net present value** of zero. It pays a company to invest in a project if it can borrow money for less than the IRR.

International Accounting Standards Board (IASB)
An international body founded in 1973 to work for the improvement and harmonisation of accounting standards worldwide. Originally called the International Accounting Standards Committee.

Interpretation of accounts
The evaluation of financial information, principally from the **profit and loss account** and **balance sheet,** so as to make judgements about profitability, efficiency, liquidity, gearing, cash flow, and the success of a financial investment. Sometimes called **ratio analysis.**

Inventory
The term used for **stock** in a **listed company.**

Investment Centre

In **responsibility accounting**, where a manager is held responsible for the revenues, costs (i.e., profits) and investment.

Investment ratios

Measures the returns to the shareholder (**dividend yield, earnings per share** and **price/earnings ratio**) or the ability of a company to sustain its dividend or interest payments (**dividend cover** and **interest cover**).

Investments

Assets such as stocks and **shares**.

Invoice discounting

The sale of debts to a third party for immediate cash.

Issued share capital

The share capital *actually* issued by a **company**.

Job costing

The recovery of costs into a specific product or service.

Just-in-time

A method of stock control developed in Japan. It seeks to minimise stock holding costs by the careful timing of deliveries and efficient organisation of production schedules. At its best, just-in-time delivers stock just before it is used.

Last-in-first-out (LIFO)

A method of stock valuation where the last stock purchased is the first sold. See also **average cost** and **first-in-first-out**.

Leasing

Where the **assets** are owned by a third party which the business pays to use them.

Liabilities

Amounts the business owes (e.g., creditors, bank loan). They can be short-term or long-term, third party liabilities or capital (i.e., liability owed by the business to the owner).

Limiting factor

Where production is constrained by a particular shortage of a key element, e.g., a restricted number of labour hours.

Limited liability

Shareholders are only liable to lose the amount of money they initially invested.

Liquidity ratios
Ratios derived from the **balance sheet** that measure how easily a firm can pay its debts.

Listed company
A **company** quoted on a stock exchange.

Loan capital
Money loaned to a company by third parties who do not own the company and are entitled to interest *not* dividends.

Loans
Amounts borrowed from third parties, such as a bank.

Long-term creditors
Amounts borrowed from third parties and repayable after a year. The most common are **long-term loans**. Known as **non-current liabilities** for **listed companies**.

Long-term loan
A loan, such as a bank loan, not repayable within a year. Sometimes called a **debenture**.

Management accounting
The provision of both financial and non-financial information to managers for **cost accounting, planning, control and performance, and decision making**. It is thus concerned with the internal accounting of a business.

Management accounting control system
An assemblage of management control techniques which enable a business to plan, monitor and control ongoing financial activities. In addition, management control systems facilitate performance evaluation. **Budgeting** and **standard costing** are examples of management accounting control systems.

Margin of safety
In **break-even analysis**, the difference between current sales and break-even sales.

Marginal costing
Marginal costing excludes fixed overheads from the costing process. It focuses on **sales, variable costs** and **contribution. Fixed costs** are written off against contribution. It can be used for decision making or for valuing stock. When valuing stock only variable production overheads are included in the stock valuation.

Market value
The value shares fetch on the open market, i.e., their trading value. This may differ significantly from their **nominal value**.

Master budget
The overall budgeted **balance sheet** and **profit and loss account** prepared from the individual **budgets**.

Matching concept
Recognises **income** and **expenses** when accrued (i.e., earned or incurred) rather than when money is received or paid. Income is matched with any associated expenses to determine the appropriate profit or loss. Also known as the accruals concept.

Materials requirement planning (MRP) system
An MRP system is based on sales demand and coordinates production and purchasing to ensure the optimal flow of raw materials and optimal levels of **raw material stocks**.

Measurement systems
The processes by which the monetary amounts of items in the financial statements are determined. Such systems are fundamental to the determination of **profit** and to the measurement of **net assets**. There are five major measurement systems: **historical cost, current purchasing power, replacement cost, realisable value** and **present value.**

Monetary measurement convention
Only items measurable in financial terms (for example, pounds or dollars) are included in the accounts. Atmospheric pollution is thus excluded, as it has no measurable financial value.

Narrative enhancement
Managers use the narrative parts of the **annual report** to convey a more favourable impression of performance than is actually warranted, e.g., by omitting key data or stressing certain elements.

Net assets
Total assets less **long-term loans** and **current liabilities**.

Net book value
The cost of **tangible fixed assets** less accumulated depreciation.

Net cash flow from operating activities
In a **cash flow statement**, cash flows from the normal trading activities of a business.

Net present value
A **capital investment appraisal** technique which discounts future expected cash flows to today's monetary values using an appropriate cost of capital.

Net profit
Sales less **cost of sales** less **expenses**.

Net profit ratio
A ratio which relates **profit** after **expenses** (i.e., **net profit**) to **sales**.

Nominal value
The face value of the shares when originally issued.

Non-current liabilities
The term used for **long-term creditors** in a **listed company**.

Normal standards
In **standard costing**, standards which a business usually attains.

Note on historical cost profits and losses
A statement in the **annual report** which records any differences caused by departures from the **historical cost convention** (e.g., revaluation and subsequent depreciation of fixed assets).

Notes to the accounts
In a company's **annual report,** they provide additional information about items in the accounts.

Objective of financial statements
To provide information about the financial position, performance and changes in financial position of an enterprise useful to a wide range of **users** in making decisions.

Operating and financial review
A statement in a company's **annual report** which enables companies to provide a formalised, structured and narrative explanation of financial performance. It has two parts. First, the operating review covers items such as a company's operating results, profit and dividends. Second, the financial review discusses items such as capital structure and treasury policy.

Operating cash flow
In a **cash flow statement**, operating profit adjusted for movements in **working capital** and non-cash flow items such as **depreciation**.

Operating profit
Net profit before taxation adjusted for interest paid and interest received.

Opportunity cost
The potential benefit lost by rejecting the best alternative course of action.

Ordinary (equity) share capital
Share capital issued to the **shareholders,** who own the company and are entitled to ordinary **dividends**.

Overall variances
In **standard costing**, the budgeted cost of the actual items produced (*standard cost of actual production*) is compared with the actual cost of items produced (*actual cost of production*).

Overheads
See **indirect costs**.

Padding the budget
In **budget** setting, where individuals try to create slack to give themselves some room for manoeuvre.

Partnership
Business enterprises run by more than one person, whose liability is normally unlimited.

Partnership capital accounts
The long-term capital invested into a partnership by the individual partners.

Partnership current accounts
The partners' share of the profits of the business. The main elements are the opening balances, salaries, profit for year, drawings and closing balances.

Patents
An **intangible asset** resulting from expenditure to protect rights to an invention.

Payback method
A method of **capital investment appraisal** which measures the cumulative cash inflows against the cumulative cash outflows to determine when a project will pay for itself.

Performance evaluation
The monitoring and motivation of individuals often in **responsibility accounting** systems.

Period costs
See **indirect costs**.

Periodicity convention
Accounts are prepared for a set period of time, i.e., an accounting period.

Physical capital maintenance concept
This concept is concerned with maintaining the physical productive capacity (i.e., operating capacity) of the business.

Planning, control and performance
The planning and control of future costs as well as the evaluation of performance using **budgeting** and **standard costing**. An abbreviated form of planning, control and performance evaluation.

Preference share capital
Share capital issued to **shareholders** who are *not* owners of the company and who are entitled to fixed dividends.

Prepayment
The amount paid in advance to the suppliers of services, e.g., prepaid insurance.

Present value
A **measurement system** where future cash inflows are discounted back to present-day values.

Price/earnings ratio
A ratio which measures **earnings per share** against share price.

Price variances
In **standard costing,** the *standard* price for the *actual* quantity used or sold is compared with the *actual* price for the *actual* quantity used or sold.

Prime cost
Direct materials, direct labour and direct expenses totalled.

Private limited company
A company where trading in shares is restricted.

Process costing
Used in industries with a continuous production process (e.g., beer brewing) where products progress from one department to another.

Product costs
See **direct costs.**

Product life cycle analysis
In **management accounting,** the analysis of product life cycles. The five stages of birth (known as introduction), growth, maturity, decline and senility (known as withdrawal) are associated with a certain level of sales and profit.

Product portfolio matrix
A strategic way of looking at a company's products and dividing them into **cash cows, dogs, question marks** and **stars.**

Production cost budget
This **budget** estimates the future cost of production, incorporating direct labour, direct materials and production overheads.

Production departments
Where products are manufactured.

Profit
Sales less purchases and **expenses.**

Profit and loss account
A financial statement which records the **income** and **expenses** of a business over the **accounting period,** normally a year. **Income** less **expenses** equals **profit.** By contrast, where expenses are greater than income, losses will occur. The balance from the profit and loss account is transferred annually to the **balance sheet** where it becomes part of **revenue reserves.** The term **income statement** is used for a listed company.

Profit centre
In **responsibility accounting,** where a manager is held responsible for the revenues and costs and thus profits.

Profitability ratios
They establish how profitably a business is performing.

Profit/volume chart
See **contribution graph.**

Property, plant and equipment
The term used for **fixed assets** in a **listed company.**

Provision for doubtful debts
Those debts a business is dubious of collecting. Deducted from **debtors** in the **balance sheet.** Only *increases* or *decreases* in the provision are entered in the **profit and loss account.**

Prudence concept
Income and **profit** should only be recorded in the books when an inflow of cash is certain. By contrast, any **liabilities** should be provided as soon as they are recognised even though the amount may be uncertain. Introduces an element of caution into accounting.

Public limited company
A **company** where shares are bought and sold by the general public.

Quantity variances
The budgeted cost of the actual items produced or sold (*standard cost of actual production* or *standard quantity sold*) is compared with the actual quantity produced or sold (*actual quantity used or sold*).

Question marks
An element of the **product portfolio matrix**. Question marks have low market share, but high market growth.

Quick ratio
Measures extreme short-term liquidity, i.e., **current assets** (excluding stock) against **current liabilities**. Sometimes called the 'acid test ratio'.

Ratio analysis
See **interpretation of accounts**.

Raw material stock
Stock purchased and ready for use, e.g., a carpenter with wood awaiting manufacture into tables.

Raw materials budget
This **budget** forecasts the future quantities of raw materials required. May supply the purchases figure for the **creditors budget**.

Realisable value
A **measurement system** where assets are valued at what they would fetch in an orderly sale. Also known as net realisable value.

Reconciliation of movements in shareholders' funds
A financial statement in the **annual report** which highlights major changes to the wealth of shareholders such as profit (or loss) for the year, annual dividends and new share capital.

Reducing balance method of depreciation
A set percentage of **depreciation** is written off the **net book value** of **tangible fixed assets** every year.

Regulatory framework
The set of rules and regulations which govern accounting practice, mainly prescribed by government and the accounting standard-setting bodies.

Relevance
Relevant information affects **users'** economic decisions. Relevance is a prerequisite of usefulness and, for example, helps to predict future events or to confirm or correct past events.

Relevant costs and revenues
Costs that will affect a decision (as opposed to non-relevant costs, which will not).

Reliability
Reliable information is free from material error and is unbiased.

Replacement cost
A **measurement system** where assets are valued at the amounts needed to replace them with an equivalent asset.

Reserves
The accumulated profits (**revenue reserves**) or capital gains (**capital reserves**) to shareholders.

Residual Income
A ratio often used in **performance evaluation** in which a required rate of return on investment is deducted from income.

Responsibility accounting systems
Where an organisation is divided into budgetary areas for which individuals are held responsible. The budgetary areas may be known as **revenue centres, cost centres, profit centres,** or **investment centres.**

Retained profits
The **profit** a company has not distributed via **dividends**. An alternative to external financing. In effect, the business finances itself from its past successes.

Return on capital employed
A ratio looking at how effectively a company uses its capital. It compares **net profit** to capital employed. The most common definition measures **profit** before tax and **debenture** interest against long-term capital (i.e., **ordinary share capital** and **reserves, preference share capital, long-term loans**).

Return on investment
A ratio often used in **performance evaluation** which relates income to investment.

Return on sales
A ratio often used in **performance evaluation** which relates operating profit to sales.

Returns on investments and servicing of finance
In a **cash flow statement,** cash received from investments or paid on loans.

Revaluation reserve
A **capital reserve** created when **fixed assets** are revalued to more than the original amount for which they were purchased. The revaluation is a gain to the shareholders.

Revenue centre
In **responsibility accounting,** where a manager is held responsible for the revenues.

Revenue expenditure
Payments for a current year's good or service such as purchases for resale or telephone expenses.

Revenue reserves
Reserves potentially distributable to shareholders as **dividends,** e.g., the **profit and loss account, general reserve.**

Review of operations
In a company's **annual report,** a narrative where the chief executive reviews the individual business operations.

Rights issue
Current **shareholders** are given the right to subscribe to new shares in proportion to their current holdings.

Sale and leaseback
Companies sell their **tangible fixed assets** to a third party and then lease them back.

Sales
Income earned from selling goods.

Sales budget
This **budget** estimates the future quantity of sales.

Sales price variance
(Standard price per unit – actual price per unit) × actual quantity of units sold.

Sales quantity variance
(Standard quantity of units sold – actual quantity of units sold) × standard contribution per unit.

Secured loans
Loans guaranteed (i.e., secured) by the **assets** of the company.

Securities Exchange Commission (SEC)
An independent regulatory institution in the US with quasi-judicial powers. US **listed companies** must file a detailed annual form, called the 10–K, with the SEC.

Sensitivity analysis
Involves modelling the future to see if alternative scenarios will change an investment decision.

Service costing
Service costing concerns specific services such as canteens run as independent operations. The cost of a particular service is the total costs for the service divided by the number of service units.

Service delivery departments
Departments in service industries that deliver the final service to customers.

Service support departments
Departments that supply support activities such as catering, administration, or selling and distribution.

Share capital
The total capital of the business is divided into shares. Literally a 'share' in the capital of the business.

Share options
Directors or employees are allowed to buy shares at a set price. They can then sell them for a higher price at a future date if the share price rises.

Share premium account
A **capital reserve** created when new shares are issued for more than their **nominal value**. For example, for shares issued for £150,000 with a nominal value of £100,000, the share premium account is £50,000.

Shareholders
The owners of the company who provide share capital by way of shares.

Social and environmental accounting statement
A voluntary statement produced by companies in their **annual report** dealing with social and environmental issues such as sustainable development.

Sole trader
A business enterprise run by a sole owner whose liability is unlimited.

Spending to budget
Departments ensure they spend their allocated **budgets**. If they do not the department may lose the money.

Standard cost
A standard cost is the individual cost elements of a product or service (such as direct materials, direct labour and variable overheads) that are estimated in advance. Normally, the quantity and the price of each cost element are estimated separately. Actual costs are then compared with standard costs to determine **variances**.

Standard costing
A standardised version of **budgeting**. Standard costing uses preset costs for direct labour, direct materials and overheads. Actual costs are then compared with the standard costs. Any **variances** are then investigated.

Stars

An element of the **product portfolio matrix**. Stars are characterised by high market growth and high market share. Stars may be cash earners or cash drains requiring heavy capital expenditure.

Statement of changes in equity

An alternative term to the **statement of total recognised gains and losses** and reconciliation of **movements in shareholders' funds** as produced by a listed company.

Statement of directors' responsibilities for the financial statements

A statement in a company's **annual report** where directors spell out their responsibilities including (i) keeping proper accounting records; (ii) preparing financial statements in accordance with the Companies Act 1985; (iii) applying appropriate accounting policies; and (iv) following all applicable accounting standards.

Statement of total recognised gains and losses (STRGL)

A financial statement in the **annual report** which attempts to highlight all shareholder gains and losses and not just those from trading. The STRGL begins with the **profit** from the **profit and loss account** and then adjusts for *non-trading gains and losses*.

Stewardship

Making individuals accountable for **assets** and **liabilities**. Stewardship focuses on the physical monitoring of assets and the prevention of loss and fraud rather than evaluating how efficiently the assets are used.

Stock

Goods purchased and awaiting use (**raw materials**) or produced and awaiting sale (**finished goods**). **Inventory** is the term used for stock in a **listed company**.

Stock turnover ratio

Measures the time taken for stock to move through a business.

Straight-line method of depreciation

The same amount of **depreciation** is written off the **tangible fixed assets** every year.

Strategic management accounting

A form of **management accounting** which considers an organisation's internal and external environments.

Subsidiary company

A **company** where more than half of the shares are owned by another company or which is effectively controlled by another company, or is a subsidiary of a subsidiary.

Sunk cost

A past cost with no ongoing implications for the future. It should thus be *excluded from decision making* as it is a non-relevant cost.

SWOT analysis
A strategic way of critically assessing a business's strengths and weaknesses, opportunities and threats.

'T' account (ledger account)
Each page of each book of account has a **debit** side (left-hand side) and a **credit** side (right-hand side). This division of the page is called a 'T' account.

'T' Account (ledger account)

Assets and expenses on the left-hand side DEBIT	Incomes, liabilities and capital on the right-hand side CREDIT

Tangible fixed assets
Fixed assets one can touch (e.g., land and buildings, plant and machinery, motor vehicles, fixtures and fittings). Tangible fixed assets are known as **property, plant and equipment** in **listed companies**.

Target costing
A price is set with reference to market conditions and customer purchasing patterns. A target profit is then deducted to arrive at a target cost.

Third party liabilities
Amounts owing to third parties. They can be short-term (e.g., **creditors**, bank overdraft) or long-term (e.g., a bank loan).

Throughput accounting
This uses a variant of contribution per limiting factor to determine a production system's main bottlenecks (e.g., shortage of machine hours in a certain department).

Total absorption costing
Both **direct costs** and **indirect costs** are absorbed into a product or service so as to recover the total costs in the final selling price.

Total shareholders' funds
The **share capital** and **reserves** owned by both the ordinary and preference shareholders.

Trade payables
The term used for **creditors** in a **listed company**.

Trade receivables
The term used for **debtors** in a **listed company**.

Trading and profit and loss account
The formal name for the full profit and loss account prepared by a **sole trader**.

Trading and profit and loss and appropriation account
The formal name for the profit and loss account prepared by a **company** or a **partnership**.

Trial balance
A listing of debit and credit balances to check the correctness of the **double-entry bookkeeping** system.

True and fair view
Difficult to define but, essentially, a set of financial statements which faithfully, accurately and truly reflect the underlying economic transactions of the organisation.

Uncontrollable cost
A cost that a manager cannot influence and that the manager cannot be held responsible for.

Unsecured loans
Loans which are not guaranteed (i.e., secured) by a company's **assets**.

Urgent Issues Task Force (UITF)
The UITF is part of the UK's standard-setting process. It makes recommendations to curb undesirable interpretations of existing accounting standards or prevent accounting practices which the **Accounting Standards Board** considers undesirable.

Users
Those with an interest in using accounting information, such as shareholders, lenders, suppliers and other trade creditors, customers, government, the public, management and employees.

Value chain analysis
In **management accounting**, a strategic way of determining a value chain for a business consisting of primary activities (e.g., receiving goods) and support activities (e.g., technology development).

Variable costs
These costs vary with production and sales (for example, the metered cost of electricity). Short-term decision making is primarily concerned with variable costs.

Variable overheads overall variance
Standard cost of variable overheads for actual production less actual cost of variable overheads for production.

Variable overheads price variance
(Standard variable overheads price per hour – actual variable overheads price per hour) × actual quantity of labour hours used.

Variable overheads quantity variance
(Standard quantity of labour hours for actual production – actual quantity of labour hours used) × standard variable overheads price per hour.

Variance
The difference between the budgeted costs and the actual costs in both **budgeting** and **standard costing**.

Vertical analysis
In **ratio analysis,** vertical analysis is where key figures in the accounts (such as sales, balance sheet totals) are set to 100 %.

Work-in-progress stock
Partially completed stock (sometimes called stock in process) which is neither **raw materials** nor **finished goods**.

Working capital
Current assets less **current liabilities** (in effect, the operating capital of a business).

Zero-based budgeting
A **budget** based on the premise that the activities are being incurred for the first time.

Appendix: Answers

Chapter 1: Discussion *Answers*

The answers provide some outline points for discussion.

A1 Accounting is important because it is the language of business and provides a means of effective and understandable business communication. The general terminology of business is thus accounting-driven. Concepts such as profit and cash flow are accounting terms. In addition, accounting provides the backbone of a business's information system. It provides figures for performance measurement, for monitoring, planning and control and gives an infrastructure for decision making. It enables businesses to answer key questions about past business performance and future business policy.

A3 There are many differences. The six listed below will do for starters!
   (a) Financial accounting is designed to provide information on a business's recent financial performance and is targeted at external users such as shareholders. However, the information is also often used by managers. By contrast, management accounting is much more internally focused and is used solely by managers.
   (b) Financial accounting operates within a regulatory framework set out by accounting standards and the Companies Acts. There is no such framework for management accounting.
   (c) The main work of financial accounting is preparing financial statements such as the balance sheet and profit and loss account (income statement). By contrast, management accounting uses a wider range of techniques for planning, control and performance, and for decision making.
   (d) Financial accounting is based upon double-entry bookkeeping, while management accounting is not.
   (e) Financial accounting looks backwards, while management accounting is forward-looking.
   (f) The end product of financial accounting is a standardised set of financial statements. By contrast, management accounting is very varied. Its output depends on the needs of its users.

Chapter 2: Discussion *Answers*

The answers provide some outline points for discussion.

A1 Financial accounting is essentially the provision of financial information to users for decision making. More formally:

> 'The objective of financial statements is to provide information about the financial position, performance and changes in financial position of an enterprise that is useful to a wide range of users in making economic decisions.'
>
> International Accounting Standards Board (2000), *Framework for the Preparation and Presentation of Financial Statements.*

In other words, financial accounting provides financial information (such as assets, liabilities, capital, expenses and income) to users (such as management and shareholders). This is useful because they can assess how well the managers run the company. On the basis of their assessment of the stewardship of management, they can make business decisions, for example, shareholders can decide whether or not to keep or sell their shares.

Financial accounting is central to any understanding of business. It provides the basic language for assessing a business's performance. Unless we understand financial accounting, it is difficult to see how we can truly understand business. It would be like trying to drive a car without taking driving lessons. For non-specialists, a knowledge of financial accounting will help them to operate effectively in a business world.

A5 True or false?
  (a) *True.* Assets show what a business owns, while liabilities show what a business owes.
  (b) *False.* The profit and loss account does show income earned and expenses incurred. However, net assets are the assets less liabilities which are shown in the balance sheet. Income less expenses equals profit.
  (c) *False.* Stewardship used to be the main objective up until about the 1960s. However, now decision making is generally recognised as the main objective.
  (d) *True.* This is because of the entity concept where the business is separate from the owner. Therefore, business assets, liabilities, income and expenses must be separated from private ones.
  (e) *True.* This is because the matching concept seeks to match income and expenses to the accounting period in which they arise. There is thus accounting symmetry. By contrast, prudence dictates that income should be matched to the year in which it is earned; any liabilities should be taken as soon as they are recognised. This means that if it is known that a liability would be incurred, say, in three years' time it would be included in the current accounting period. There is thus accounting asymmetry. The two principles thus clash.

Chapter 2: Numerical *Answers*

A1 Sharon Taylor   **Profit and Loss Account**

	£	£
Sales		8,000
Less *Expenses*		
General expenses	4,000	
Trading expenses	3,000	7,000
Net Profit		1,000

Balance Sheet

	£
Assets	15,000
Liabilities	(3,000)
Net assets	12,000

	£
Opening capital employed	11,000
Add Profit	1,000
Closing capital employed	12,000

Cash Flow Statement

	£
Cash inflows	10,000
Cash outflows	(12,000)
Net cash outflow	(2,000)

Chapter 3: Discussion *Answers*

The answers provide some outline points for discussion.

A1 Double-entry bookkeeping is the essential underpinning of accounting. It provides an efficient mechanism by which organisations can record their financial transactions. For instance, large companies, such as Tesco or British Petroleum, may have millions of transactions per year. Double-entry bookkeeping provides a useful way of consolidating these. In a sense, therefore, the double-entry process permits organisations to make order from chaos. Double-entry bookkeeping enables the preparation of a trial balance. This, in turn, permits the construction of a profit and loss account and a balance sheet.

A6 True or false?

(a) *True*.

(b) *False*. We credit the sales account with sales, but debit the purchases account with purchases.

(c) *True*.

(d) *True*.

(e) *False*. Sales and capital are credits, but rent paid is a debit.

Chapter 3: Numerical *Answers*

A1 (i)   Assets $=$ Liabilities

$£25,000 = £25,000$

(ii)   Assets $=$ Liabilities $+$ Capital

$£25,000 = £15,000 + £10,000$

(iii)   Assets $=$ Liabilities $+$ Capital $+$ Profit

$£40,000 = £15,000 + £10,000 + £15,000$

(iv)   Assets $=$ Liabilities $+$ Capital $+$ (Income $-$ Expenses)

$£40,000 = £15,000 + £10,000 + (£60,000 - £45,000)$

(v)   Assets $+$ Expenses $=$ Liabilities $+$ Capital $+$ Income

$£40,000 + £45,000 = £15,000 + £10,000 + £60,000$

(vi)

'T' Account		'T' Account	
Assets + Expenses	Liabilities + Capital + Income	$£40,000 + £45,000$ $= £85,000$	$£15,000 + £10,000 +$ $£60,000 = £85,000$

A2	*Account*	*Debit*	*Account*	*Credit*
(a)	Wages	Increases an expense	Bank	Decreases an asset
(b)	Bank	Increases an asset	Capital	Increases capital
(c)	Hotel	Increases an asset	Bank	Decreases an asset
(d)	Electricity	Increases an expense	Bank	Decreases an asset
(e)	Bank	Increases an asset	Sales	Increases income
(f)	Purchases	Increases an expense	A. Taylor (creditor)	Increases a liability

A3 A. Bird

(i) Ledger accounts

Sales

	£		£
		6 June Thrush	4,000
		6 June Raven	7,000
7 June Bal. c/f	17,000	6 June Starling	6,000
	17,000		17,000
		7 June Bal. b/f	17,000

Purchases

	£		£
1 June Robin	8,000		
1 June Falcon	6,000		
1 June Sparrow	5,000	7 June Bal. c/f	19,000
	19,000		19,000
7 June Bal. b/f	19,000		

Sales returns

	£		£
7 June Starling	1,000	7 June Bal. c/f	1,000
	1,000		1,000
7 June Bal. b/f	1,000		

Purchases returns

	£		£
7 June Bal. c/f	3,000	4 June Robin	1,000
		4 June Falcon	2,000
	3,000		3,000
		7 June Bal. b/f	3,000

Thrush (debtor)

	£		£
6 June Sales	4,000	7 June Bal. c/f	4,000
	4,000		4,000
8 June Bal. b/f	4,000		

Raven (debtor)

	£		£
6 June Sales	7,000	7 June Bal. c/f	7,000
	7,000		7,000
8 June Bal. b/f	7,000		

Starling (debtor)

	£		£
6 June Sales	6,000	7 June Sales Rets.	1,000
		7 June Bal. c/f	5,000
	6,000		6,000
8 June Bal. b/f	5,000		

Robin (debtor)

	£		£
4 June Purchases Rets.	1,000	1 June Purchases	8,000
7 June Bal. c/f	7,000		
	8,000		8,000
		8 June Bal. b/f	7,000

Falcon (creditor)

	£		£
4 June Purchases Rets.	2,000	1 June Purchases	6,000
7 June Bal. c/f	4,000		
	6,000		6,000
		8 June Bal. b/f	4,000

Sparrow (creditor)

	£		£
7 June Bal. c/f	5,000	1 June Purchases	5,000
	5,000		5,000
		8 June Bal. b/f	5,000

Note. To aid understanding the balancing off process is italicised.

A6 Katherine Jones: (i) Ledger accounts

Capital

	£		£
7 July Bal. c/f	195,000	1 July Bank	195,000
	195,000		195,000
		8 July Bal. b/f	195,000

Bank

	£		£
1 July Capital	195,000	2 July Premises	75,000
7 July Edwards	5,000	2 July Office	9,000
7 July Smith	4,500	equipment	
7 July Patel	3,500	2 July Purchases	7,000
		5 July Wages	4,000
		5 July Electricity	2,000
		5 July Telephone	1,000
		7 July Johnston	1,250
		7 July Singh	500
		7 July Bal. c/f	108,250
	208,000		208,000
8 July Bal. b/f	108,250		

Sales

	£		£
		3 July Edwards	10,000
		3 July Smith	9,000
7 July Bal. c/f	26,000	3 July Patel	7,000
	26,000		26,000
		7 July Bal. b/f	26,000

Purchases

	£		£
2 July Bank	7,000		
2 July Johnston	3,000		
2 July Singh	1,000	7 July Bal. c/f	11,000
	11,000		11,000
7 July Bal. b/f	11,000		

Telephone

	£		£
5 July Bank	1,000	7 July Bal. c/f	1,000
	1,000		1,000
7 July Bal. b/f	1,000		

Purchases returns

	£		£
7 July Bal. c/f	500	4 July Johnston	500
	500		500
		7 July Bal. b/f	500

Electricity

	£		£
5 July Bank	2,000	7 July Bal. c/f	2,000
	2,000		2,000
7 July Bal. b/f	2,000		

Wages

	£		£
5 July Bank	4,000	7 July Bal. c/f	4,000
	4,000		4,000
7 July Bal. b/f	4,000		

Premises

	£		£
2 July Bank	75,000	7 July Bal. c/f	75,000
	75,000		75,000
8 July Bal. b/f	75,000		

Office equipment

	£		£
2 July Bank	9,000	7 July Bal. c/f	9,000
	9,000		9,000
8 July Bal. b/f	9,000		

A6 Katherine Jones (*continued*)

Edwards (debtor)	£		£
3 July Sales	10,000	7 July Bank	5,000
		7 July Bal. c/f	5,000
	10,000		10,000
8 July Bal. b/f	5,000		

Smith (debtor)	£		£
3 July Sales	9,000	7 July Bank	4,500
		7 July Bal. c/f	4,500
	9,000		9,000
8 July Bal. b/f	4,500		

Patel (debtor)	£		£
3 July Sales	7,000	7 July Bank	3,500
		7 July Bal. c/f	3,500
	7,000		7,000
8 July Bal. b/f	3,500		

Johnston (creditor)	£		£
4 July Purchases Rets.	500	2 July Purchases	3,000
7 July Bank	1,250		
7 July Bal. c/f	1,250		
	3,000		3,000
		8 July Bal. b/f	1,250

Singh (creditor)	£		£
7 July Bank	500	2 July Purchases	1,000
7 July Bal. c/f	500		
	1,000		1,000
		8 July Bal. b/f	500

(ii) Trial balance

Katherine Jones
Trial Balance as at 7 July

	£	£
Capital		195,000
Bank	108,250	
Sales		26,000
Purchases	11,000	
Purchases returns		500
Telephone	1,000	
Electricity	2,000	
Wages	4,000	
Premises	75,000	
Office equipment	9,000	
Edwards (debtor)	5,000	
Smith (debtor)	4,500	
Patel (debtor)	3,500	
Johnston (creditor)		1,250
Singh (creditor)		500
	223,250	223,250

A8 Jay Shah

Jay Shah
Trial Balance as at 31 December

	Debit £	Credit £	Type
Capital		45,300	Capital
Motor car	3,000		Asset
Building	70,000		Asset
Office furniture	400		Asset
A. Smith (debtor)	250		Asset
J. Andrews (creditor)		350	Liability
T. Williams (creditor)		550	Liability
G. Woolley (debtor)	150		Asset
Purchases returns		500	Income*
Bank	3,600		Asset
Electricity	1,400		Expense
Business rates	1,800		Expense
Rent	1,600		Expense
Wages	3,500		Expense
Long-term loan		9,000	Liability
Sales		100,000	Income
Purchases	70,000		Expense
	155,700	155,700	

*An income because it reduces the expense of purchases.

A10 Rajiv Sharma

Rajiv Sharma
Trial Balance as at 31 December

	Debit £	Credit £
Shop	55,000	
Machinery	45,000	
Car	10,000	
Sales	135,000	
Purchases	80,000	
Opening stock	15,000	
Debtors	12,000	
Creditors		8,000
Long-term loan		16,000
General expenses	300	
Telephone	400	
Light and heat	300	
Repairs	400	
Capital		59,400
	218,400	218,400

Chapter 4: Discussion *Answers*

The answers provide some outline points for discussion.

A1 The profit and loss account is used by a variety of users for a variety of purposes. Sole traders and partnerships use it to determine how well they are doing. They will want to know if the business is making a profit. This will enable them to make decisions such as how much they should take by way of salary (commonly called drawings). Similarly, the tax authorities will use the profit and loss account as a starting point to calculate the tax that these businesses owe the government.

For the shareholders of a limited company, profit enables them to assess the performance of the company's management. Shareholders can then make decisions about their investments. Company directors, on the other hand, may use profits to work out the dividends payable to shareholders, or to calculate their own profit-related bonuses. In short, profit has multiple uses.

A5 True or false?
(a) *False*. Profit is income earned less expenses incurred.
(b) *True*.
(c) *False*. Sales returns are returns by customers.
(d) *True*.
(e) *True*.

Chapter 4: Numerical *Answers*

A1 Joan Smith

Joan Smith
Trading and Profit and Loss Account Year Ended 31 December 2009

	£	£
Sales		100,000
Less *Cost of Sales*		
Opening stock	10,000	
Add Purchases	60,000	
	70,000	
Less Closing stock	5,000	65,000
Gross Profit		35,000
Less *Expenses*		
General expenses	10,000	
Other expenses	8,000	18,000
Net Profit		17,000

A2 Dale Reynolds

Dale Reynolds
Trading Account Year Ended 31 December 2009

	£	£	£
Sales			50,000
Less Sales returns			1,000
			49,000
Less *Cost of Sales*			
Opening stock		5,000	
Add Purchases	25,000		
Less Purchases returns	2,000		
	23,000		
Add Carriage inwards	1,000	24,000	
		29,000	
Less Closing stock		8,000	21,000
Gross Profit			28,000

Chapter 5: Discussion *Answers*

The answers provide some outline points for discussion.

A1 The balance sheet and profit and loss (or income statement in the case of a listed company) are indeed complementary. Both are prepared from a trial balance. The balance sheet takes the assets, liabilities and capital, and arranges them into a position statement. By contrast, the profit and loss account takes the income and expenses and arranges them into a performance statement. The balance sheet represents a snapshot of the business at a certain point in time. The profit and loss account represents a period, usually a month or a year. The balance sheet deals with liquidity, while the profit and loss account deals with performance. Both together, therefore, provide a complementary picture of an organisation both at a particular point in time and over a period.

A5 True or false?
  (a) *True.*
  (b) *False.* Stock and bank are indeed current assets, but creditors are current liabilities.
  (c) *False.* Total net assets are fixed assets and current assets less current liabilities, but also less long-term creditors.
  (d) *True.*
  (e) *False.* An accrual is an expense owing, for example, an unpaid telephone bill. An amount prepaid (for example, rent paid in advance) is a prepayment.

Chapter 5: Numerical *Answers*

A1 Jane Bricker

Jane Bricker
Capital Employed as at 31 December 2009

	£
Opening capital	5,000
Add Profit	12,000
	17,000
Less Drawings	7,000
Closing capital	10,000

A2 Alpa Shah

Alpa Shah
Total Net Assets as at 30 June 2009

	£	£
Fixed Assets		100,000
Current Assets	50,000	
Current Liabilities	(30,000)	
Net current assets		20,000
Total assets less current liabilities		120,000
Long-term Creditors		(20,000)
Total net assets		100,000

Chapter 6: Discussion *Answer*

The answer provides some outline points for discussion.

A1 A sole trader is where only one person owns the business. For example, a retailer, such as a baker, might be a sole trader. It is important for sole traders to prepare accounts for several reasons. First, as a basis for assessing their own financial performance. This indicates whether they can take out more wages (known as drawings), whether they can expand or pay their workers more. Second, the tax authorities need to be assured that the profit figure, which is the basis for assessing tax, has been properly prepared. And, third, if any loans have been borrowed, for example, from the bank, then the bankers will be interested in assessing performance.

Chapter 6: Numerical *Answers*

A1 M. Anet

M. Anet

Trading and Profit and Loss Account for Year Ended 31 December 2009

	£	£
Sales		25,000
Less *Cost of Sales*		
Purchases		15,000
Gross Profit		10,000
Less *Expenses*		
Electricity	1,500	
Wages	2,500	4,000
Net Profit		6,000

M. Anet

Balance Sheet as at 31 December 2009

	£	£	£
Fixed Assets			
Hotel			40,000
Van			10,000
			50,000
Current Assets			
Bank	8,000		
A. Brush (debtor)	400	8,400	
Current Liabilities			
A. Painter (creditor)	(500)	(500)	
Net current assets			7,900
Total assets less current liabilities			57,900
Long-term Creditors			–
Total net assets			57,900
Capital Employed			£
Opening capital			51,900
Add Net Profit			6,000
Closing capital			57,900

A2 P. Icasso

P. Icasso
Trading and Profit and Loss Account for Year Ended 31 March 2009

	£	£
Sales		35,000
Less Sales returns		3,000
		32,000
Less *Cost of Sales*		
Purchases	25,000	
Less Purchases returns	4,000	21,000
Gross Profit		11,000
Less *Expenses*		
Electricity	1,000	
Advertising	800	1,800
Net Profit		9,200

P. Icasso
Balance Sheet as at 31 March 2009

	£	£	£
Fixed Assets			
Hotel			50,000
Van			8,000
			58,000
Current Assets			
Bank	9,000		
Shah (debtor)	1,250		
Chan (debtor)	2,250	12,500	
Current Liabilities			
Jones (creditor)	(1,250)	(1,250)	
Net current assets			11,250
Total assets less current liabilities			69,250
Long-term Creditors			–
Total net assets			69,250

	£
Capital Employed	
Opening capital	60,050
Add Net Profit	9,200
Closing capital	69,250

A3 R. Ubens

R. Ubens

Trading and Profit and Loss Account for Year Ended 31 December 2009

	£	£	£
Sales			88,000
Less Sales returns			800
			87,200
Less *Cost of Sales*			
Opening stock		3,600	
Add Purchases	66,000		
Less Purchases returns	1,200	64,800	
		68,400	
Less Closing stock		4,000	64,400
Gross Profit			22,800
Less *Expenses*			
Electricity		1,500	
Advertising		300	
Printing and stationery		50	
Telephone		650	
Rent and rates		1,200	
Postage		150	3,850
Net Profit			18,950

R. Ubens

Balance Sheet as at 31 December 2009

	£	£	£
Fixed Assets			
Building			20,400
Motor van			3,500
			23,900
Current Assets			
Stock	4,000		
Bank	4,400		
Debtors	2,600	11,000	
Current Liabilities			
Creditors	(3,800)	(3,800)	
Net current assets			7,200
Total assets less current liabilities			31,100
Long-Term Creditors			–
Total net assets			31,100
Capital Employed			£
Opening capital			19,950
Add Net Profit			18,950
			38,900
Less Drawings			7,800
Closing capital			31,100

A4 C. Onstable

Trading and Profit and Loss Account (extracts)	Balance Sheet (extracts)
Expenses	**Current liabilities**
Rent £2,880 (i.e., 12 × £240)	Prepayments £840*
Insurance £360 (£480 − £120)	*(Rent 3 × £240 = £720; Insurance £120)

A5 V. Gogh

V. Gogh
Trading and Profit and Loss Account Year Ended 31 December 2009

	£	£	£
Sales			40,000
Less Sales returns			500
			39,500
Less *Cost of Sales*			
Opening stock		5,500	
Purchases	25,000		
Less Purchases returns	450	24,550	
		30,050	
Less Closing stock		9,000	21,050
Gross Profit			18,450
		£	£
Less *Expenses*			
Business rates		1,000	
Rent		400	
Telephone		450	
Insurance		750	
General expenses		150	
Electricity		700	
Wages		10,500	13,950
Net Profit			4,500

A5 V. Gogh (*continued*)

V. Gogh
Balance Sheet as at 31 December 2009

	£	£	£
Fixed Assets			
Shop			9,000
Motor car			8,500
			17,500
Current Assets			
Stock	9,000		
Bank	1,300		
Debtors	3,500		
Prepayments	200	14,000	
Current Liabilities			
Creditors	(1,500)		
Accruals	(350)	(1,850)	
Net current assets			12,150
Total assets less current liabilities			29,650
Long-term Creditors			(3,700)
Total net assets			25,950
Capital Employed			£
Opening capital			34,350
Add Net profit			4,500
			38,850
Less Drawings			12,900
Closing capital			25,950

A6 L. Da Vinci

L. Da Vinci
Trading and Profit and Loss Account Year Ended 30 September 2009

	£	£	£
Sales			105,000
Less Sales returns			8,000
			97,000
Less *Cost of Sales*			
Opening stock		6,500	
Add Purchases	70,000		
Less Purchases returns	1,800		
	68,200		
Add Carriage inwards	250	68,450	
		74,950	
Less Closing stock		7,000	67,950
Gross Profit			29,050
Less *Expenses*			
Discounts allowed		300	
Electricity		2,025	
Telephone		500	
Wages		32,500	
Insurance		200	
Rent		1,000	
Business rates		1,000	37,525
Net loss			(8,475)

A6 L. Da Vinci (*continued*)

L. Da Vinci
Balance Sheet as at 30 September 2009

Fixed Assets	£	£	£
Business premises			18,000
Motor van			7,500
Computer			1,500
			27,000
Current Assets			
Stock	7,000		
Debtors	12,000		
Bank	1,800		
Prepayments	275	21,075	
Current Liabilities			
Creditors	(13,000)		
Accruals	(1,375)	(14,375)	
Net current assets			6,700
Total assets less current liabilities			33,700
Long-term Creditors			(6,600)
Total net assets			27,100

Capital Employed	£
Opening capital	44,075
Less Net loss	8,475
	35,600
Less Drawings	8,500
Closing capital	27,100

A7 H. Ogarth

H. Ogarth
Trading and Profit and Loss Account year ended 31 December 2009 (extracts)

Expenses	£
Depreciation on buildings	10,000
Depreciation on machinery	3,000
Depreciation on motor van	2,000
	15,000

Balance Sheet (extracts) Fixed assets	£ Cost	£ Accumulated depreciation	£ Net book value
Buildings	100,000	(10,000)	90,000
Machine	50,000	(3,000)	47,000
Motor van	20,000	(2,000)	18,000
	170,000	(15,000)	155,000

Chapter 7: Discussion *Answers*

The answers provide some outline points for discussion.

A1 These three forms of business enterprise fit various niches. The sole trader form is good for very small businesses, such as a window cleaner, carpenter or small shopkeeper. There is a limited amount of capital needed and the individual can do most of the work. The accounting records needed for this type of business are not extensive. Partnerships are useful where the business is a little more complicated. They are suitable for situations where more than one person work together. There is then a need to sort out each partner's share of capital and profits. Companies are useful where a lot of capital is needed. Thus, they are particularly suitable for medium-sized and large businesses. They are particularly appropriate when raising money externally because of the concept of limited liability. As shareholders are only liable for the amount of their initial investments, they will be keener to invest as their potential losses will be limited.

A5 True or false?
(a) *False.* Drawings are withdrawal of capital by the partners, they are found in the partners' current accounts.
(b) *True.*
(c) *False.* Nominal value is the face value of the shares, normally the amount the shares were originally issued at. Market value is their stock-market value.
(d) *False.* Unsecured loans are secured on the general assets of the business. It is secured loans which are attached to specific assets.
(e) *False.* Reserves are accumulated profits and cannot directly be spent. Only cash can be spent.

Chapter 7: Numerical *Answers*

A1 Tom and Thumb

Tom and Thumb
Trading, Profit and Loss and Appropriation Account for Year Ended
31 December 2009

		£	£
Net Profit before Appropriation			100,000
Less Salaries:			
Tom		10,000	
Thumb		30,000	40,000
			60,000
Profits:			
Tom	3	45,000	
Thumb	1	15,000	60,000

A1 Tom and Thumb (*continued*)

Tom and Thumb
Balance Sheet as at 31 December 2009

Capital Employed	£	£	£
	Tom	Thumb	
Capital Accounts	8,000	6,000	14,000
Current Accounts			
Opening balances	3,000	(1,000)	
Add:			
Salaries	10,000	30,000	
Profit share	45,000	15,000	
	58,000	44,000	
Less Drawings	25,000	30,000	
Closing balances	33,000	14,000	47,000
Total partners' funds			61,000

A2 J. Waite and P. Watcher

J. Waite and P. Watcher
Trading, Profit and Loss and Appropriation Account for Year Ended
30 November 2009

		£	£
Sales			350,000
Less Cost of Sales			
Opening stock		9,000	
Add Purchases		245,000	
		254,000	
Less Closing stock		15,000	239,000
Gross Profit			111,000
Less *Expenses*			
Depreciation:			
Land and buildings		2,000	
Motor vehicles		3,000	
Electricity		3,406	
Wages		14,870	
Rent and business rates		6,960	
Telephone		1,350	
Interest on loan		2,800	
Other expenses		5,500	39,886
Net Profit before Appropriation			71,114
Less Salaries:			
Waite		18,000	
Watcher		16,000	34,000
			37,114
Profits:			
Waite	3	22,268	
Watcher	2	14,846	37,114

A2 J. Waite and P. Watcher (*continued*)

J. Waite and P. Watcher
Balance Sheet as at 30 November 2009

	£ Cost	£ Accumulated depreciation	£ Net book value
Fixed Assets			
Land and buildings	166,313	(2,000)	164,313
Motor vehicles	65,000	(3,000)	62,000
	231,313	(5,000)	226,313
Current Assets			
Stock	15,000		
Debtors	12,000		
Bank	6,501	33,501	
Current Liabilities			
Creditors	(18,500)		
Accruals	(300)	(18,800)	
Net current assets			14,701
Total assets less current liabilities			241,014
Long-term Creditors			(28,000)
Total net assets			213,014

	Waite £	Watcher £	£
Capital Employed			
Capital Accounts	88,000	64,000	152,000
Current Accounts			
Opening balances	(2,500)	12,000	
Add:			
Salaries	18,000	16,000	
Profit share	22,268	14,846	
	37,768	42,846	
Less Drawings	13,300	6,300	
Closing balances	24,468	36,546	61,014
Total partners' funds			213,014

A5 **Red Devils Ltd**   **Red Devils Ltd**
Profit and Loss Account for the Year Ended 30 November 2009 (unpublished)

	£	£
Sales	[As per Accounts of Sole	
Less Cost of Sales	Trader or Partnership]	
Gross Profit		150,000
Less *Expenses*		
Debenture interest	14,000	
General expenses	22,100	
Directors' fees	19,200	
Auditors' fees	7,500	62,800
Profit before Taxation		87,200
Taxation		(17,440)
Profit after Taxation		69,760
Proposed dividends on ordinary shares	(25,000)	
Proposed dividends on preference shares	(9,000)	
Transfer to general reserve	(3,500)	(37,500)
Retained Profit		32,260

Red Devils Ltd
Balance Sheet as at 30 November 2009

	£	£	£
Fixed Assets			680,900
Current Assets			
Stock	105,000		
Debtors	4,700		
Bank	5,300	115,000	
Current Liabilities			
Creditors	(12,200)		
Taxation	(17,440)		
Dividends (ordinary £25,000,			
preference £9,000)	(34,000)		
Auditors' fees	(7,500)		
Debenture interest	(14,000)	(85,140)	
Net current assets			29,860
Total assets less current liabilities			710,760
Long-term Creditors			(200,000)
Total net assets			510,760
Share Capital and Reserves			
Share Capital		Authorised	Issued
Ordinary share capital (£1 each)		400,000	250,000
6 % preference shares		150,000	150,000
		550,000	400,000

A5 Red Devils Ltd (*continued*)

	£	£	£
Reserves			
Capital reserves			
Share premium account			55,000
Other reserves			
Opening general reserve	11,000		
Transfer for year	3,500		
Closing general reserve		14,500	
Opening profit and loss account	9,000		
Retained profit for year	32,260		
Closing profit and loss account		41,260	55,760
Total shareholders' funds			510,760

A6 Superprofit Ltd

Superprofit Ltd

Trading, Profit and Loss and Appropriation Account for the Year Ended 31 December 2009

	£000	£000	£000
Sales		351	
Less *Cost of Sales*			
Opening stock		23	
Add Purchases		182	
		205	
Less Closing stock		26	179
Gross Profit			172
Less *Expenses*			
Depreciation:			
Land and buildings		18	
Motor vehicles		7	
Auditors' fees		2	
Loan interest		4	
Electricity		12	
Insurance		3	
Wages		24	
Light and heat		8	
Telephone		5	
Other expenses		26	109
Profit before Taxation			63
Taxation			(13)
Net Profit after Taxation			50
Ordinary dividends		(9)	
Preference dividends		(3)	(12)
Retained Profit			38

A6 Superprofit Ltd (*continued*)

Superprofit Ltd
Balance Sheet as at 31 December 2009

	£000 Cost	£000 Accumulated depreciation	£000 Net book value
Fixed Assets			
Intangible Assets			
Patents			12
Tangible Assets			
Land and buildings	378	(18)	360
Motor vehicles	47	(7)	40
	425	(25)	400
Total fixed assets			412
Current Assets			
Stock	26		
Debtors	18		
Bank	31	75	
Current Liabilities			
Creditors	(33)		
Taxation payable	(13)		
Dividends payable	(12)		
Other accruals (see note below)	(6)	(64)	
Net current assets			11
Total assets less current liabilities			423
Long-term Creditors			(32)
Total net assets			391
Share Capital and Reserves			
Share Capital		Authorised	Issued
Ordinary share capital		250	210
Preference share capital		50	25
		300	235
Reserves			
Capital reserves			
Share premium account		40	
Other reserves			
Revaluation reserve		35	
General reserve		15	
Opening profit and loss account	28		
Retained profit for year	38		
Closing profit and loss account		66	156
Total shareholders' funds			391

Note: Loan interest (£4) and auditors' fees (£2).

A9 Stock High plc

Stock High plc
Profit and Loss Account for the Year Ended 31 March 2010

	Notes	£000
Sales		1,250
Cost of Sales		(400)
Gross Profit		850
Administrative expenses		(216)
Distribution expenses		(230)
Profit before Taxation		404
Taxation		(94)
Profit for year		310

Stock High plc
Balance Sheet as at 31 March 2010

ASSETS	Notes	£000
Non-current Assets		
Property, Plant and Equipment	2	814
Intangible Assets	1	50
		864
Current Assets		
Inventory		20
Trade Receivables		100
Bank		22
		142
Total Assets		1006
LIABILITIES		
Current Liabilities	3	(20)
Non-Current Liabilities		(60)
Total Liabilities		(80)
Net Assets		926
EQUITY		£000
Capital and Reserves	4	
Called-up share capital	5	550
Share premium account		25
Other reserves	6	55
Profit and loss account	7	296
Total Equity		926

A9 Stock High plc (*continued*)

Notes:

1. Property, Plant and Equipment

	£000 Cost	£000 Accumulated depreciation	£000 Net book value
Land and buildings	800	(156)	644
Motor vehicles	400	(230)	170
	1,200	(386)	814

2. Intangible Assets

Patents	50
	50

3. Current Liabilities

Creditors	12
Taxation	8
	20

4. Authorised Share Capital

Ordinary share capital (£1)	600
Preference share capital (£1)	150
	750

5. Called-up Share Capital

Ordinary share capital	450
Preference share capital	100
	550

6. Other Reserves

	£000
Revaluation reserve	30
General reserve	25
	55

7. Profit and Loss Account

Balance as at 1 April 2009	36
Retained profit for year	310
Less: Dividends	(50)
Balance as at 31 March 2010	296

Chapter 8: Discussion *Answers*

The answers provide some outline points for discussion.

A1 Cash is king because it is central to the operations of a business. Unless you generate cash you cannot pay employees, suppliers or expenses, or buy new fixed assets. The end result of a lack of cash is the closure of a business. Cash is also objective. There is very little subjectivity involved in estimating cash. Either you have cash or your don't! With profits, however, there is much more subjectivity. Often one can alter the accounting policies of a business, for example, use a different rate of depreciation and thus alter the amount of profit. It is not as easy to manipulate cash.

A5 **True or false?**
- (a) *False.* It is true that both items are non-cash flow items and that depreciation is added back to operating profit. However, profit from sale of fixed assets is deducted from operating profit.
- (b) *False.* Stock and debtors are items of working capital. However, fixed assets are not.
- (c) *True.*
- (d) *True.*
- (e) *False.* It is much more commonly used than the direct method.

Chapter 8: Numerical *Answers*

A1 **Bingo**

Included in profit and loss account	Included in cash flow statement
(a) Yes as part of charge for year	No
(b) No	Yes, financing
(c) Yes	No
(d) Yes	Yes, net cash outflow from operating activities
(e) No	Yes, capital expenditure and financial investment
(f) No	Yes, capital expenditure and financial investment
(g) No	Yes, returns on investments and servicing of finance
(h) Yes, part of charge for year	No
(i) No	Yes, financing
(j) Yes	Yes, returns on investments and servicing of finance.

A2 Peter Piper

Peter Piper
Cash Flow Statement for Year Ended 31 December 2009

	£	£
Net Cash Inflow From Operating Activities		
Receipts from customers	250,000	
Payments to suppliers	(175,000)	
Payments to employees	(55,000)	
Expenses	(10,000)	10,000
Returns on Investments		
and Servicing of Finance		
Interest received	1,150	
Interest paid	(350)	800
Capital Expenditure and Financial Investment		
Sale of property	25,000	
Purchase of office equipment	(15,000)	10,000
Financing		
Loan repaid	(25,000)	(25,000)
Decrease in Cash		(4,200)

A4 D. Rink

D. Rink
Reconciliation of Operating Profit to Operating Cash Flow
Year Ended 31 December 2009

	£	£
Operating Profit		95,000
Add:		
Decrease in stock	3,000	
Decrease in prepayments	1,500	
Increase in creditors	300	
Increase in accruals	250	
Depreciation	8,000	13,050
Deduct:		
Increase in debtors	(1,150)	
Profit on sale of fixed assets	(3,500)	(4,650)
Net Cash Inflow from Operating Activities		103,400

A6 Grow Hire Ltd

Grow Hire Ltd
Reconciliation of Operating Profit to Operating Cash Flow
Year Ended 31 December 2009

	£	£
Operating Profit (Note)		105,500
Add:		
Decrease in stock	2,000	
Decrease in debtors	7,000	
Increase in accruals	1,000	
Depreciation (£44,000 – £28,000)	16,000	26,000
Deduct:		
Decrease in creditors	25,000	25,000
Net Cash Inflow from Operating Activities		106,500

	£
Note:	
Net Profit before Taxation	112,000
Add: Interest paid	6,500
Deduct: Interest received	(13,000)
Operating Profit	105,500

Grow Hire Ltd
Cash Flow Statement for Year Ended 31 December 2009

	£	£
Net Cash Inflow from Operating Activities		106,500
Return on Investments and Servicing of Finance		
Interest received	13,000	
Interest paid	(6,500)	6,500
Taxation		
Taxation paid	(33,600)	(33,600)
Capital Expenditure and		
Financial Investment		
Patents purchased	(34,200)	
Land and buildings purchased	(20,000)	(54,200)
Equity Dividends Paid	(35,800)	(35,800)
Financing		
Increase in long-term creditors	12,000	
Increase in share capital	1,600	13,600
Increase in Cash		3,000

	£
Opening Cash	7,000
Increase in cash	3,000
Closing Cash	10,000

A8 Expenso plc

Expenso plc
Reconciliation of Profit before Taxation to Operating Cash Flows for
the Year Ended 30 September 2009

	£000	£000
Net Profit before Taxation		10,017
Add:		
Interest paid	85	
Increase in trade payables	400	
Depreciation	2,500	2,985
Deduct:		
Interest received	(868)	
Decrease in accruals	(50)	
Increase in inventory	(3,600)	
Increase in accounts receivable	(1,300)	(5,818)
Operating Cash Flows		7,184

Expenso plc
Cash Flow Statement for the Year Ended 30 September, 2009

	£000	£000
Net Cash Inflow from Operating Activities		
Operating cash flows	7,184	
Interest paid	(85)	
Taxation paid	(4,005)	3,094
Cash Flows from investing activities	–	
Interest received	868	
Land and buildings purchased	(6,000)	
Plant and machinery purchased	(5,000)	
Patents purchased	(500)	(10,632)
Cash Flows from Financing Activities		
Equity dividends paid	(4,105)	
Increase in Non-current liabilities	405	
Increase in share capital	3,938	238
Decrease in Cash		(7,300)

	£000
Opening Cash	8,800
Decrease in cash	(7,300)
Closing Cash	1,500

Note: We needed to calculate taxation paid (in £000s).

Helpnote: An alternative form of presentation, following Figure 8.10, would have been to adjust the Net Profit Before Taxation in the Cash Flow Statement itself.

A8 Expenso plc (*continued*)

Opening accrual + Profit and loss account − Amount paid = Closing accrual

i, Taxation   £4,200   +   £3,005   −   £4,005   =   £3,200

Or alternatively,

Taxation paid

	£		£
Paid	4,005	Bal. b/f	4,200
Bal. c/f	3,200	Profit and loss	3,005
	7,205		7,205

Chapter 9: Discussion *Answers*

The answers provide some outline points for discussion.

A1 Ratio analysis is simply the distillation of the figures in the accounts into certain key ratios so that a user can more easily interpret a company's performance. Ratio analysis is also known as financial statement analysis or the interpretation of accounts. There are traditionally thought to be six main types of ratios:
   (a) *Profitability ratios*: Generally derived from the profit and loss account (income statement), they seek to determine how profitable the business has been. Main ratios: return on capital employed, gross profit, net profit.
   (b) *Efficiency ratios*: Compare the profit and loss account (income statement) to key balance sheet figures. Try to work out how efficiently the company is utilising its assets and liabilities. Main ratios: debtor collection period, creditors collection period, stock turnover and asset turnover ratio.
   (c) *Liquidity*: Assesses the short-term cash position of the company. They are derived from the balance sheet. Main ratios: current ratio and quick ratio.
   (d) *Gearing*: Looks at the relationship between the owners' capital and the borrowed capital. This ratio is derived from the balance sheet.
   (e) *Cash flow*: This ratio seeks to measure how the company's cash inflows and cash outflows compare. The cash flow ratio, unlike the other ratios, is derived from the cash flow statement.
   (f) *Investment ratios*: These ratios are used by investors to determine how well their shares are performing. They generally compare share price with dividend or earnings information. The five main ratios are: dividend yield, dividend cover, earnings per share, price/earnings ratio and interest cover.

A5 True or false?

(a) *True.*

(b) *False.* More usually: Net profit $= \dfrac{\text{Net profit before taxation}}{\text{Sales}}$

(c) *False.* Current ratio $= \dfrac{\text{Current assets}}{\text{Current liabilities}}$. The ratio given was the quick ratio.

(d) *True.*

(e) *False.* This is actually the fixed assets turnover ratio.

Asset turnover ratio $= \dfrac{\text{Sales}}{\text{Total assets}}$

(f) *False.* Dividend yield $= \dfrac{\text{Dividend per ordinary share}}{\text{Share price}}$

(g) *True.*

Chapter 9: Numerical *Answers*

A1 John Parry

The ratios below are calculated in £s.

(a) Return on capital employed $\quad = \quad \dfrac{\text{Net profit}^*}{\text{Capital employed}^{**}}$

$$= \quad \dfrac{50,000}{(300,000 + 500,000) \div 2} \quad = \quad 12.5\,\%$$

*For sole traders, tax is not an issue.
**We take average for year.

(b) Gross profit ratio $\quad = \quad \dfrac{\text{Gross profit}}{\text{Sales}} = \dfrac{80,000}{150,000} \quad = \quad 53.3\,\%$

(c) Net profit ratio $\quad = \quad \dfrac{\text{Net profit}^*}{\text{Sales}} = \dfrac{50,000}{150,000} \quad = \quad 33.3\,\%$

*For sole traders, tax is not an issue

(d) Debtors collection period $\quad = \quad \dfrac{\text{Average debtors}}{\text{Credit sales per day}}$

$$= \quad \dfrac{(18,000 + 19,000) \div 2}{150,000 \div 365} \quad = \quad 45\,\text{days}$$

(e) Creditors collection period $\quad = \quad \dfrac{\text{Average creditors}}{\text{Credit purchases per day}}$

$$= \quad \dfrac{(9,000 + 10,000) \div 2}{75,000 \div 365} \quad = \quad 46\,\text{days}$$

A1 John Parry (*continued*)

(f) Stock turnover ratio $= \dfrac{\text{Cost of sales}}{\text{Average stock}}$

$\qquad\qquad = \dfrac{70,000}{(25,000 + 30,000) \div 2} = 2.5 \text{ times}$

(g) Asset turnover ratio $= \dfrac{\text{Sales}}{\text{Average total assets}}$

$\qquad\qquad = \dfrac{150,000}{(50,000 + 60,000) \div 2} = 2.7 \text{ times}$

A2 Henry Mellett

(a) Current ratio $= \dfrac{\text{Current assets}}{\text{Current liabilities}} = \dfrac{£\ 31,903}{14,836} = 2.2 \text{ times}$

(b) Quick ratio $= \dfrac{\text{Current assets–stock}}{\text{Current liabilities}} = \dfrac{31,903 - 18,213}{14,836} = 0.9 \text{ times}$

(c) Gearing ratio $= \dfrac{\text{Long-term borrowings}}{\text{Total long-term capital}^*} = \dfrac{30,000}{150,000 + 30,000} = 16.7\%$

*Remember, total net assets are equivalent to shareholders' funds.

A3 Jane Edwards

	Cash inflows £	Cash outflows £
Customers	125,000	
Issue of shares	29,000	
Sale of fixed assets	35,000	
Employees		18,300
Suppliers		9,250
Buy back loan		8,000
Dividends		8,000
Taxation		16,000
Purchase of fixed assets		80,000
	189,000	139,550

Cash flow ratio $= \dfrac{\text{Total cash inflows}}{\text{Total cash outflows}} = \dfrac{£189,000}{£139,550} = 1.35$

A4 Clatworthy plc

£000*

(a) Dividend yield $= \dfrac{\text{Dividend per ordinary share}}{\text{Share price (in £s)}} = \dfrac{40 \div 500}{1.25} = 6.4\%$

(b) Dividend cover $= \dfrac{\text{Profit after tax and preference dividends}}{\text{Ordinary dividends}} = \dfrac{580}{40} = 14.5 \text{ times}$

(c) Earnings per share $= \dfrac{\text{Profit after tax and preference dividends}}{\text{Number of ordinary shares}} = \dfrac{580}{500} = £1.16$

(d) Price/earnings ratio $= \dfrac{\text{Share price}}{\text{Earnings per share}} = \dfrac{1.25}{1.16} = 1.08$

*Except for price/earnings ratio.

(e) Interest cover $= \dfrac{\text{Profit before tax and loan interest}}{\text{Loan interest}} = \dfrac{790}{40} = 19.8 \text{ times}$

A7 Anteater plc

The ratios below are calculated from the accounts. There is insufficient information to average return on capital employed and the efficiency ratios. The closing year figure is, therefore, taken from the balance sheet. This is indicated by a single asterisk. Except where indicated, calculations are in £000s.

(a) **Profitability ratios**

	Ratio	Calculations (£000s)	
Return on capital employed	Net profit before tax and loan interest/Average capital employed*	(100 + 3)/500* * = 300 + 20 + 10 + 70 + 100	= 20.6%
Gross profit ratio	Gross profit/Sales	250/1,000	= 25%
Net profit ratio	Net profit before tax/Sales	100/1,000	= 10%

(b) **Efficiency ratios**

Accounts receivable collection period	Average receivables*/ Credit sales per day	50/(1,000 ÷ 365)	= 18.3 days
Accounts payable collection period	Average payables*/ Credit purchases per day (cost of sales taken)	40/(750 ÷ 365)	= 19.5 days
Inventory turnover ratio	Cost of sales/Average inventory*	750/40	= 18.8 times
Asset turnover ratio	Sales/Average total assets*	1,000/(420 + 120)	= 1.8 times

A7 Anteater plc (*continued*)

	Ratio	Calculations (£000s)	
(c) Liquidity ratios			
Current ratio	Current assets/Current liabilities	120/40	= 3.0
Quick ratio	Current assets – inventory/ Current liabilities	(120 – 40)/40	= 2.0
(d) Gearing ratio			
Gearing	Long-term borrowings/Total long-term capital	(100 + 20)/ (400 + 100)	= 24 %
(e) Investment ratios			
Dividend yield	Dividend per ordinary share/ Share price (in £s)	(40 ÷ 300)/2.00	= 6.7 %
Dividend cover	Profit after tax and preference dividends/Ordinary dividends	70/40	= 1.8
Earnings per share	Profit after tax and preference dividends/Number of ordinary shares	70/300	= 23.3p
Price/earnings ratio [+]Calculation in pence.	Share price/Earnings per share[+]	200/23.3	= 8.6
Interest cover	Profit before tax and loan interest/ Loan interest	103/3	= 34.3

Chapter 10: Discussion *Answers*

The answers provide some outline points for discussion.

A1 The role of the three is complementary.
(a) The directors run the business and prepare the accounts. They invest their labour and are rewarded, for example, by salaries and bonuses.
(b) The shareholders own the business and make decisions partly on the basis of the accounts they receive. They invest their capital and are rewarded, hopefully, by dividends and an increase in share price.
(c) The auditors check that the directors have prepared accounts that provide a 'true and fair' view of the company's performance over the year. They invest their labour and are rewarded by the auditors' fees. They are independent of the directors and, in theory, are responsible to the shareholders.

A2 The decision-making model is concerned with communicating economic information to users so that they can make decisions. Or more formally:

'The objective of financial statements is to provide information about the financial position, performance and changes in financial position of an enterprise that is useful to a wide range of users in making decisions' (*Framework for the Preparation and Presentation of Financial Statements*, International Accounting Standards Board, 1999, para. 12).

There are a variety of users. The International Accounting Standards Board, for example, identified shareholders, suppliers and other trade creditors, employees, customers, government and its agencies, and the general public. We can also add academics, management, analysts and advisers, and pressure groups. These users have a variety of different information needs, such as profitability (the shareholders) or future employment prospects (the employees). They also will want to make different decisions. For example, the shareholder will want to buy and sell shares whereas the employee may be wondering whether or not to change jobs. The financial information provided (i.e., income, expenses, assets, capital and liabilities) is normally provided in the form of the profit and loss account (income statement), balance sheet or cash flow statement.

This appears reasonable as far as it goes. However, critics argue that the decision-making model has several flaws. First, it assumes that one set of financial statements is appropriate for all users. Second, what is appropriate for shareholders is assumed to be appropriate for all users. Third, the focus on decision making neglects other important aspects such as stewardship. And, finally, and most radically, the decision-making model focuses on financial information, thus ignoring non-financial aspects such as the environment.

Chapter 11: Discussion *Answers*

The answers provide some outline points for discussion.

A1 An accounting measurement system is a method of determining the monetary amounts in the accounts. Different measurement systems will result in different valuations for net assets. This in turn will cause profit to be different. The measurement of assets and the determination of profit is key to the preparation of accounts. However, different accounting measurement systems can cause wide variation in both net assets and net profit. Thus, it is probably not unreasonable to call accounting measurement systems the skeleton that underpins the accounting body. The accounting measurement systems will determine the basic parameters of the accounting results.

A2 Historical cost is still widely used internationally. Indeed, it is certainly much more popular than the alternative measurement bases. However, historical cost has been widely criticised. In particular, there is concern that it fails to reflect changing asset values resulting from inflation or technological change. There has, therefore, been extensive debate over alternative measurement systems, most obviously by the Financial Accounting Standards Board in the US, the Accounting Standards Board in the UK and the International Accounting Standards Board. All these bodies have wrestled with alternative measurement systems, seeing them as essential to framing a successful conceptual theory for accounting.

So far, there has been little agreement on an alternative system. The first reason is that historical cost is widely used, easy to understand and objective. Users are, therefore, reluctant to abandon it. This is particularly true when the alternatives are often not easy to understand or use and are often subjective. In addition, the main incentive to change was the high level of inflation in the Western world, particularly in the UK and the US in the 1970s. However, more recently inflation rates have fallen and with them interest in alternatives to historical cost.

Chapter 12: Discussion *Answers*

The answers provide some outline points for discussion.

A1 The annual report plays a central role in corporate governance. Essentially, it is a key mechanism by which the directors report to the shareholders and other users on their stewardship of the company. The directors prepare the financial statements, which provide information on income and expenses, assets, liabilities and capital, so that shareholders can monitor the activities of the directors. This monitoring allows the shareholders to see that the managers are not abusing their position, for example, by paying themselves great salaries at the expense of the shareholders. In order to ensure that the accounts are true and fair, the auditors audit the financial statements. These financial statements will be included in an annual report along with other financial and non-financial information. The annual report itself is often prepared by design consultants.

A2 These three roles have the following functions
  (i) *Stewardship and accountability*
      The directors provide information to the shareholders so that they can monitor the directors' activities. This has grown out of ideas of accountability (i.e., the control and safeguarding of corporate assets). The idea has been extended to corporate governance, in particular, the monitoring of directors' remuneration.
  (ii) *Decision making*
      The decision-making aim is 'to communicate economic measures of, and information about, the resources and performance of the reporting entity useful to those having reasonable rights to such information' (*The Corporate Report*, 1975). The aim, therefore, in essence, is to provide users, such as shareholders, with information so that they can make decisions, such as buying or selling shares.
  (iii) *Public relations*
      The public relations objective of the annual report is simply recognising the incentives that management has to use the annual report to show the results in a good light. It is often associated with the idea of the annual report as a marketing tool.
        The clash between these three objectives is that while the first two (accountability and decision making) are based on the idea of a true and fair view, public relations

is not about truth and fairness. Public relations attempts to depart from truth and fairness to show the company in the best possible light.

Chapter 13: Discussion *Answers*

The answers provide some outline points for discussion.

A1 Creative accounting is using the flexibility within accounting to manage the measurement and presentation of the accounts so that they serve the interests of the managers. These interests may be to smooth profits, to increase profits or reduce gearing. The essential point of creative accounting is that it serves the interests of the preparers not the users. In particular, creative accounting may clash with the basic requirement that the financial statements should give a true and fair view of the company's financial position and financial performance. This is because creative accounting puts the interests of preparers first. The regulatory framework specifies that accounting should be unbiased and neutral and should faithfully represent the economic reality of the company. Accounting cannot do this if it is managed creatively for the benefit of the preparers.

A2 Creative accounting can exist, and indeed thrive, particularly in countries such as the UK where accounting is valued for its flexibility. The basic idea is that accounting professionals should be free to choose accounting policies which give a true and fair view. In other words, accounting should not be governed by a set of inflexible and constraining rules, as are found in some other countries, such as Germany.

However, the flexibility that allows accounting to present a 'true and fair view' is also the same flexibility that enables accounting to be used creatively. Indeed, it is all a matter of degree and intention. Creative accounting is when accounting policies are chosen to serve the managers' interests rather than to give a 'true and fair' view. However, in reality, it is extremely difficult for outsiders to distinguish between the two. This is especially true as there is generally more than one possible 'true and fair' view.

Chapter 14: Discussion *Answers*

The answers provide some outline points for discussion. However, they should not be taken as exhaustive or prescriptive. International accounting is a topic that is very fluid and open to interpretation.

A2 There are potentially eight divergent forces: objectives, users, sources of finance, regulation, taxation, the accounting profession, spheres of influence and culture. In their own way, they are all important. They are also interrelated. It is, therefore, very difficult to sort out the most important. Different individuals will legitimately have different views.

In my opinion, the most important divergent forces are the sources of finance, regulation, taxation and the accounting profession. This is because:

- Sources of finance provide the basic funding for industry (either debt or equity finance); they thus orientate the accounting system towards a balance sheet or a profit and loss account (income statement) focus.
- Regulation determines the backbone of the accounting system, setting out the detailed rules and regulations.
- Taxation is one of the main drivers of financial accounting in some countries, such as Germany and France. Companies comply with taxation requirements which then dictate financial accounting practices.
- The accounting profession because qualified accountants provide the judgement and interpretation in countries such as the UK and US, which enable the achievement of a 'true and fair' view.

However, it must be stressed that this is just my opinion. Other viewpoints are equally justifiable.

A3 These two systems are distinguishable in many ways. In essence, the Anglo-American system is followed by countries such as the US and the UK, and is often termed a 'micro' system. By contrast the continental accounting system is followed by countries such as France and Germany and is often termed a 'macro' system. The main differences are as follows:

- **Objectives**. The Anglo-American system favours the true and fair/present fairly objective of financial reporting designed to show economic reality. The continental system is more about planning and control.
- **Users**. In the Anglo-American model, these are primarily shareholders; in the continental model, they are the government, the banks, and the tax authorities.
- **Sources of Finance**. In the Anglo-American model, shareholders provide risk capital; whereas in the continental model, banks provide loan capital.
- **Regulation**. In the Anglo-American model, standards are very important. In addition, in the UK, the Companies Acts provide detailed regulation, while in the US listed companies supply a detailed 10-K to the Securities Exchange Commission (an independent regulatory commission). In the continental model, detailed regulation generally comes from the government. In European countries, International Financial Reporting Standards are now increasingly important in the UK, France and Germany.
- **Taxation**. In the Anglo-American model, taxation is not an important driver of the financial accounts. In the continental model, taxation drives financial accounting.
- **Accounting Profession**. This is strong and influential in the Anglo-American model, comparatively weak and uninfluential in the continental model.

Chapter 15: Discussion *Answers*

The answers provide some outline points for discussion.

A1	*Branches*	*Functions*

(1) Cost Accounting

   (i) Costing — To recover costs as a basis for pricing and for stock valuation.

   (ii) Planning, Control and Performance

     (a) Budgeting — To plan and control future costs and engage in performance evaluation through budgeting.

     (b) Standard costing — To plan and control future costs and engage in performance evaluation through standard costing.

(2) Decision Making

   (i) Short-term Decisions — To make short-term decisions (such as whether to make a product) using techniques such as contribution analysis and break-even analysis. In addition, to minimise the cost of working capital.

   (ii) Long-term Decisions

     (a) Strategic management — To make decisions of a strategic nature such as whether or not to diversify the business.

     (b) Capital budgeting — To make decisions about whether or not to invest in long-term projects such as a new product or service.

     (c) Sources of finance — To make decisions about whether to raise new finance via share or loan capital.

A6 True or False?

  (a) *True.*

  (b) *False.* Total absorption costing is where all the costs incurred by a company are totalled so that they can be recovered into the product or service's final selling price.

  (c) *True.*

  (d) *False.* Strategic management accounting is concerned with the long-term strategic direction of a firm.

  (e) *True.*

Chapter 16: Discussion *Answers*

The answers provide some outline points for discussion.

A1 Costing is the process of recording, classifying, allocating and then absorbing costs into individual products and services. Costing is particularly important for two main reasons: stock valuation and pricing. In stock valuation, the aim is to recover the costs incurred in producing a good. The costs of stock valuation thus include direct materials, direct labour, direct expenses and appropriate production overheads. In absorption costing, we include all production overheads, both fixed and variable. In marginal costing, we include only variable production overheads. In effect, financial accounting drives the stock valuation process. This is because external reporting regulations allow attributable production overheads (i.e., allow absorption costing) to be included in stock. For pricing, all the overheads (i.e., total absorption costing) are included in the cost before a percentage is added for profit. Thus the total cost may include direct materials, direct labour, direct expenses, production and non-production overheads. Nowadays, with the decline of manufacturing industry, there has been a decline in the importance of direct costs and an increase in the importance of indirect costs or overheads.

A5 True or False?
- (a) *False.* It is true that a cost can be an actual past expenditure. However, it is important to appreciate that a cost can also be an estimated, future expenditure.
- (b) *True.*
- (c) *False.* We identify activity cost drivers in activity-based costing.
- (d) *True.*
- (e) *False.* No, in financial reporting we use absorption costing.

Chapter 16: Numerical *Answers*

A1 *Sorter*

(i) Direct materials	*c* (purchase of raw materials)
(ii) Direct labour	*a* (machine workers' wages)
(iii) Production overheads	*b* (cost clerk's wages)* Assumes cost clerks are based in factory, *d* (machine repairs), *m* (depreciation on machinery), *o* (electricity for machines)
(iv) Administrative expenses	*e* (finance director's salary), *f* (office cleaners), *h* (managing director's car expenses), *i* (depreciation on office furniture), *j* (computer running expenses for office), *k* (loan interest), *l* (auditors' fees), *p* (bank charges)
(v) Selling and distribution costs	*g* (delivery van staff's wages), *n* (advertising costs)

A2 Costa

Costa
Costing Statement for Costa

	£	£	£
Direct materials			320,000
Direct labour			200,000
Royalties			3,600
(i) Prime Cost			523,600
Production Overheads			
Factory supervisors' wages		120,000	
Depreciation (£8,000 + £5,000)		13,000	
Computer overheads		6,000	
Other overheads		70,000	209,000
(ii) Production Cost			732,600
Other Costs			
Administrative Expenses			
Administrative salaries	90,800		
Depreciation (£4,200 + £2,500)	6,700		
Computer overheads	3,000		
Interest on loans	3,000	103,500	
Selling and Distribution Costs			
Wages	18,300		
Marketing salaries	25,000		
Commission	1,200		
Depreciation (£3,500 + £2,500)	6,000	50,500	154,000
(iii) Total Cost			886,600

A3 Makemore

Makemore
Overhead Allocation Statement

	Total £	Ratio Split	A £	B £	C £
Supervisors' salaries	25,000	1,000:2,000:500	7,143	14,286	3,571
Computer advisory	18,000	1,000:2,000:500	5,143	10,286	2,571
Rent and business rates	20,000	10,000:6,000:4,000	10,000	6,000	4,000
Depreciation	21,000	30,000:15,000	14,000	7,000	–
Repairs	4,000		2,800	1,100	100
Allocated	88,000		39,086	38,672	10,242
Reallocation of service support department			60 %	40 %	(100 %)
C's costs			6,145	4,097	(10,242)
Total Allocation	88,000		45,231	42,769	–
			80,000	40,000	
(i) Labour hours					
Rate per hour			£0.57	£1.07	
(ii) Machine hours			100,000	200,000	
Rate per hour			£0.45	£0.21	

A8 Serveco
Calculate activity-cost driver rates

Activity	Spare Parts Installed	Technical Support	Service Documentation
Cost	£100,000	£125,000	£300,000
Cost driver	150,000 parts	175,000 minutes	125,000 units
Cost per unit of Cost driver	£0.667	£0.7143	£2.4

Costs absorbed to services				Total cost
Basic	50,000 × £0.667 = £33,333	75,000 × £0.7143 = £53,572	100,000 × £2.4 = £240,000	£326,905
Enhanced	100,000 × £0.667 = £66,667	100,000 × £0.7143 = £71,428	25,000 × £2.4 = £60,000	£198,095
Total costs	£100,000	£125,000	£300,000	£525,000

Total overhead costs	Total overheads	Call outs	Overheads per call out
Basic	£326,905	50,000	£6.54
Enhanced	£198,095	10,000	£19.81

Call Out Cost/Charge

	Basic £		Enhanced £	
Labour hours (including travelling time)	20.00	$\dfrac{(25{,}000 + 25{,}000) \times £20}{50{,}000 \text{ call outs}}$	106.25	$\dfrac{(37{,}500 + 5{,}000) \times £25}{10{,}000 \text{ call outs}}$
Overheads	6.54		19.81	
Total Cost	26.54		126.06	
Profit: 25% mark-up on cost	6.63		31.51	
Call out Charge	33.17		157.57	

Note: Some of the calculations have been rounded in this answer.

Chapter 17: Discussion *Answers*

The answers provide some outline points for discussion.

A1 A major advantage of budgeting is that it requires you to predict the future in economic terms. You can plan ahead and buy in extra resources and schedule workloads. In addition, budgeting enables you to predict your future performance. You can then tell how well or how badly you are actually doing against your predicted budget. Finally, budgeting has an important responsibility and control function. You can put somebody in charge of the budget, make them responsible and so control future activities. Variances from budget can thus be investigated.

The major disadvantages of budgets are that they may be constraining and dysfunctional to the organisation. The constraint is caused by the budget perhaps setting a straitjacket which inhibits innovation and the adoption of flexible business policies. The dysfunctional nature of budgeting is that the objectives of the individual may not necessarily be the same as that of the organisation. Individuals may, therefore, seek to 'pad' their budgets or manage them to their own personal advantage.

A4 True or False?
(a) *True.*
(b) *False.* Although sometimes production is a limiting factor, the commonest limiting factor is sales.
(c) *True.*
(d) *False.* Depreciation is never found in a cash budget as it does not represent a cash flow.
(e) *True.*

Chapter 17: Numerical *Answers*

A1 Jill Lee

Jill Lee
Cash Budget for Six Months Ending June

	Jan.	Feb.	March	April	May	June	Total
	£	£	£	£	£	£	£
Opening cash	15,000	28,200	21,100	8,280	(5,942)	1,389	15,000
Add *Receipts*							
Sales	25,200	27,100	21,200	20,250	48,300	37,500	179,550
	25,200	27,100	21,200	20,250	48,300	37,500	179,550
Less Payments							
Goods	–	21,000	19,500	18,500	23,400	25,900	108,300
Expenses	12,000	13,200	14,520	15,972	17,569	19,326	92,587
	12,000	34,200	34,020	34,472	40,969	45,226	200,887
Cash flow	13,200	(7,100)	(12,820)	(14,222)	7,331	(7,726)	(21,337)
Closing cash	28,200	21,100	8,280	(5,942)	1,389	(6,337)	(6,337)

A3 Fly-by-Night

Fly-by-Night
Sales Budget for Six Months Ending June

	Jan. £	Feb. £	March £	April £	May £	June £	Total £
Moon (1)	20,000	21,000	22,000	28,750	30,000	31,250	153,000
Star (2)	20,000	21,000	22,000	23,000	24,000	25,000	135,000
	40,000	42,000	44,000	51,750	54,000	56,250	288,000
(1) Moon (units)	1,000	1,050	1,100	1,150	1,200	1,250	6,750
(2) Star (units)	2,000	2,100	2,200	2,300	2,400	2,500	13,500

Helpnote: Multiply the units by the price per unit.

A4 D. Ingo

D. Ingo
Debtors Budget for Six Months Ending June

	Jan. £	Feb. £	March £	April £	May £	June £	Total £
Opening debtors	2,400	2,000	2,100	2,310	2,541	2,795	2,400
Credit sales	1,000	1,100	1,210	1,331	1,464	1,610	7,715
	3,400	3,100	3,310	3,641	4,005	4,405	10,115
Cash received	(1,400)	(1,000)	(1,000)	(1,100)	(1,210)	(1,331)	(7,041)
Closing debtors	2,000	2,100	2,310	2,541	2,795	3,074	3,074

A6 B. Ear

B. Ear
Production Cost Budget Six Months Ending June

	Jan. £	Feb. £	March £	April £	May £	June £	Total £
Raw materials	3,500	3,750	4,000	4,250	4,500	4,750	24,750
Direct labour	3,850	4,125	4,400	4,675	4,950	5,225	27,225
Variable overheads	1,400	1,500	1,600	1,700	1,800	1,900	9,900
	8,750	9,375	10,000	10,625	11,250	11,875	61,875
Units	700	750	800	850	900	950	4,950

A7 R. Abbit

R. Abbit
Raw Materials Budget Six Months Ending June

	Jan. £	Feb. £	March £	April £	May £	June £	Total £
Opening stock	1,000	940	1,080	1,420	1,670	2,120	1,000
Purchases	900	1,100	1,300	1,500	1,700	1,900	8,400
	1,900	2,040	2,380	2,920	3,370	4,020	9,400
Used in production	(960)	(960)	(960)	(1,250)	(1,250)	(1,250)	(6,630)
Closing stock	940	1,080	1,420	1,670	2,120	2,770	2,770

A11 All Sunshine Enterprises

	London	Oslo	Stockholm

i, Return on Investment

$$\frac{\text{Income}}{\text{Investment}}$$

London	Oslo	Stockholm
$\dfrac{£700,000}{£2,000,000} = 35\%$	$\dfrac{£400,000}{£1,000,000} = 40\%$	$\dfrac{£165,000}{£500,000} = 33\%$

ii, Residual Income

Income − (Required rates of return × investment)

London	Oslo	Stockholm
£700,000 − (12 % × £2,000,000)	£400,000 − (12 % × £1,000,000)	£165,000− (12 % × £500,000)
= £460,000	= £280,000	= £105,000

iii, Return on Sales

	London	Oslo	Stockholm
$\dfrac{\text{Operating profit}}{\text{Sales}}$	$\dfrac{£700,000}{£1,500,000}$	$\dfrac{£400,000}{£800,000}$	$\dfrac{£165,000}{£300,000}$
	= 46.7 %	= 50 %	= 55 %

Therefore, Return on Investment gives Oslo 40 % and is its best relative measure. Residual Income gives Madrid £460,000 and is its best relative measure. Return on Sales gives Stockholm 55 % and is its best relative measure.

Chapter 18: Discussion *Answers*

The answers provide some outline points for discussion.

A1 Setting the standards involves first of all making a decision about whether one is aiming for ideal, attainable or normal standards. Ideal standards are those that can be reached if everything goes perfectly. Attainable standards are those that can be reached with a little effort. Normal standards are those that are based on past experience and that the business normally meets. Attainable standards are probably the best because they include a motivational element.

The two main elements of a standard are quantity (i.e., hours, materials) and price (i.e., hourly rate, price per kilo). It follows, therefore, that we need to consider the factors that influence quantity and price. These might be based on past experience, prevailing market conditions and future expectations. For instance, if a firm were setting labour standards it might base its labour quantity standard on the hours taken in the past less an improvement element. The labour price standard might be based on the prevailing wage rate with an amount built in for any wage increases.

A5 True or False?
  (a) *True.*
  (b) *False.* Flexing the budget means adjusting the budget to take into account the actual quantity produced.
  (c) *True.*
  (d) *True.*
  (e) *False.* The direct labour quantity variance is: (standard *quantity* of labour hours for actual production – actual *quantity* of labour hours used) × standard labour price per hour.

Chapter 18: Numerical *Answers*

A1 Stuffed (i–iii)	*Budget*	*Flexed Budget*	*Actual*	*Sales Price and Overall Cost Variances**	
Number of customers	10,000	12,000	12,000		
	£	£	£	£	
Sales	100,000	120,000	127,200	7,200	Fav.
Food cost					
(i.e., materials cost)	(30,000)	(36,000)	(37,200)	(1,200)	Unfav.
Labour cost	(35,000)	(42,000)	(36,000)	6,000	Fav.
Variable overheads	(5,000)	(6,000)	(6,000)	–	
Contribution	30,000	36,000	48,000	12,000	Fav.
Fixed overheads	(3,000)	(3,000)**	(3,100)	(100)	Unfav.
Profit	27,000	33,000	44,900	11,900	Fav.

Helpnotes
*The sales price variance is £7,200 Fav. The overall cost variances are food cost (i.e., direct materials) variance £1,200 Unfav., labour cost variance £6,000 Fav., zero overall variable overheads cost variance, and £100 Unfav. fixed overhead variance.

**Remember, fixed costs remain unchanged whatever the level of activity. We do not, therefore, flex these.

A1 Stuffed (*continued*)

(iv) *Sales Quantity Variance* = (standard quantity of meals sold – actual quantity of meals sold) × standard contribution per unit = $10,000 - 12,000 \times (£30,000 \div 10,000)$ = £6,000 Fav.

Note this is simply the flexed profit (£33,000) less the original budget (£27,000) = £6,000 Fav.

(v) (a) *Sales Variances*. Both are favourable. 2,000 more customers visited the restaurant than anticipated. They paid £0.60 more per meal than expected.

(b) *Material Cost*. We paid £1,200 more than expected. This may be due to increased prices or increased quantity used. We need more information on this.

(c) *Labour Cost*. We paid £6,000 less than expected. Either we paid less per hour or we used fewer hours than expected. We need more information.

(d) *Variable Overheads*. These were as budgeted.

(e) *Fixed Overheads*. These were slightly more (£100 more) than expected.

A3 Birch Manufacturing

	£	
(i) Overall Direct Materials Variance		
Standard cost of materials for actual production		
(10 metres of wood* at 50p × 11,000)	55,000	
Actual cost of materials used in production		
(120,000 metres × 0.49 pence)	58,800	
	(3,800)	Unfav.

*Each bookcase is estimated to take 10 metres of wood (100,000 metres ÷ 10,000 bookcases)

	£	
(ii) Direct Materials Price Variance		
(standard price per unit of material – actual price per unit of material) × actual quantity of materials used		
= (50p – 49p) × 120,000 metres	1,200	Fav.

(iii) Direct Materials Quantity Variance		
(standard quantity of materials for actual production – actual quantity of materials used) × standard material price per unit		
= (11,000 × 10 metres – 120,000 metres) × 0.50p	(5,000)	Unfav.
	(3,800)	Unfav.

A4 Sweatshop

	£	
(i) Overall Direct Labour Variance		
Standard cost of labour for actual production		
(500 sweatshirts at 2 hours) × £5.50	5,500	
Actual cost of labour used in production	5,880	
	(380)	Unfav.

A4 Sweatshop (*continued*)

(ii) Direct Labour Price Variance   £

(standard labour price per hour − actual price per hour)
   × actual quantity of labour used

    = (£5.50 − £5.60*) × 1,050 hours   (105) Unfav.

*£3,780 labour cost divided by 1,050 hours

(iii) Direct Labour Quantity Variance

(Standard quantity of labour hours for actual production −
   actual quantity of labour hours used)
   × standard labour price per hour

    = (2 hours × 500 sweatshirts − 1,050 hours) × £5.50 per hour   (275) Unfav.

                                                        (380) Unfav.

A6 Wonderworld

(i) Overall Variable Overheads Cost Variance

Standard cost of variable overheads for actual production   £

(110,000 teleporters at 2 labour hours at £2.50)   550,000

Actual cost of variable overheads for production   517,500

                                                          32,500 Fav.

(ii) Variable Overheads Price Variance

(standard variable overheads price per hour −
   actual variable overheads price per hour) ×
   actual quantity of labour hours used   £

    = (£2.50 − £2.25)* × 230,000   57,500 Fav.

*variable overheads £517,500 ÷ 230,000 actual labour hours

(iii) Variable Overheads Quantity Variance

(standard quantity of labour hours for actual production −
   actual quantity of labour hours used) × standard variable
   overheads price per hour

    = (110,000 × 2 hours − 230,000 hours) × £2.50   (25,000) Unfav.

                                                          32,500 Fav.

(iv) Fixed Overheads Variance

Standard fixed overheads less actual fixed overheads   £

    = £10,000 − £9,800   200 Fav.

A8 Peter Peacock plc
August's results

(i) Flexed budget

	Budget (i.e., standard)	Flexed Budget (i.e., standard quantity of actual production)	Actual	Sales Price and Overall Cost Variances	
Volume	200,000	220,000	220,000		
	£	£	£	£	
Sales	560,000	616,000	611,600	(4,400)	Unfav.
Direct materials	(125,000)	(137,500)	(150,000)	(12,500)	Unfav.
Direct labour	(290,000)	(319,000)	(317,550)	1,450	Fav.
Variable overheads	(40,000)	(44,000)	(42,500)	1,500	Fav.
Contribution	105,000	115,500	101,550	(13,950)	Unfav.
Fixed overheads	(68,000)	(68,000)	(67,000)	1,000	Fav.
Profit	37,000	47,500	34,550	(12,950)	Unfav.

(ii) Individual Variances: Sales

Sales Quantity Variance
(Standard quantity of units sold – actual quantity of units sold) × standard contribution

$$£$$
$(200,000 - 220,000) \times 0.525^* = 10,500$ Fav.**

$$\frac{^*\text{Contribution}}{\text{Budgeted sales volume}} = \frac{105,000}{200,000}$$

**Represents budgeted profit £37,000 – flexed budget profit £47,500

Sales Price Variance
This can be taken direct from the flexed budget, or it can be calculated as follows:
(standard selling price – actual selling price per unit) × actual quantity of units sold
$(£2.80 - £2.78) \times 220,000 = (£4,400)$ Unfav.

A8 Peter Peacock plc (*continued*)
Costs

Price	Quantity
(standard price − actual price per unit) × actual quantity	*(standard quantity of actual production − actual quantity) × standard price*

Direct Material Variances

(£1.25 per sheet − £1.20 per sheet) × 125,000 sheets = £6,250 Fav.

(220,000 subcomponents × 0.50 sheets per subcomponent* gives 110,000 sheets − 125,000 sheets) × £1.25 = (£18,750) Unfav.
*100,000 sheets ÷ 200,000 subcomponents. This gives the amount of material per subcomponent.

Direct Labour Variances

(£7.25 per hour − £7.30 per hour) × 43,500 hours = (£2,175) Unfav.

(220,000 subcomponents × 0.20 hours* gives 44,000 hours − 43,500 hours) × £7.25 = £3,625 Fav.
*40,000 hours ÷ 200,000 subcomponents. This gives the amount of the labour per subcomponent

Variable Overhead Variances

(£1.00 per hour − £0.977 per hour)* × 43,500 hours = £1,000 Fav.
*£42,500 variable overheads ÷ 43,500 hours

(220,000 subcomponents × 0.20 hours* gives 44,000 hours − 43,500 hours) × £1.00 = £500 Fav.
*40,000 hours ÷ 200,000 subcomponents. This gives the amount of labour per subcomponent and we are recovering our variable overheads on the labour hours.

Fixed Overheads

£68,000 standard fixed overheads − £67,000 actual fixed overheads = £1,000 Fav.

(iii)

Peter Peacock plc
Standard Cost Reconciliation Statement for August

	£	£	£	
Budgeted Profit			37,000	
Sales quantity variance			10,500	Fav.
Budgeted profit at actual sales			47,500	
Variances	*Fav.*	*Unfav.*		
Sales price		4,400		
Direct materials price	6,250			
Direct materials quantity		18,750		
Direct labour price		2,175		
Direct labour quantity	3,625			
Variable overheads price	1,000			
Variable overheads quantity	500			
Fixed overheads variance	1,000			
	12,375	25,325	(12,950)	
Actual Profit			34,550	

(iv) The actual profit for Peacock is £2,450 less than budgeted (£37,000 − £34,550). Peacock has actually sold 20,000 more units than anticipated, creating a favourable sales quantity variance of £10,500. However, it has done this by reducing the price slightly so there is an unfavourable sales price variance.

On the cost variances, there is a favourable direct materials price variance (£6,250) as the sheets are cheaper than anticipated. However, more sheets were used than anticipated, possibly because they were poorer quality. There is thus an unfavourable quantity variance of £18,750. The labour price variance of £2,175 is unfavourable since Peacock paid £7.30 per hour rather than the budgeted £7.25. However, perhaps because a better quality of labour was used, less hours were used creating a favourable quantity variance of £3,625. For variable overheads, less overheads than anticipated were incurred creating a favourable price variance of £1,000. Also because of the fewer hours used, less overheads were recovered into the product causing a favourable quantity variance. Finally, fixed overheads were less than anticipated.

Chapter 19: Discussion *Answers*

The answers provide some outline points for discussion.

A1 Fixed costs are those costs, like depreciation or insurance, which do not vary with production or sales. They remain fixed whatever the level of production or sales. This is not universally true as at a certain point, such as acquiring a new machine, fixed costs will vary. However, it is a reasonable working assumption.

Variable costs, by contrast, are those costs that do vary with production or sales. If we make more products or provide more services, then our variable costs will increase. Conversely, if we make fewer products or provide fewer services, then our variable costs will decrease.

Fixed costs are irrelevant for decision making because they will be incurred whatever the decision. They are fixed within the relevant range of activity. For example, insurance and depreciation will not vary whether we choose to produce more of product A or more of product B. We should, therefore, ignore these costs when making decisions.

A4 True or False?
   (a) *False.* Wrong time horizon. Fixed costs do *not* vary with short-term changes in the level of sales or production.
   (b) *True.*
   (c) *False.* Wrong numerator. Break-even point is $\dfrac{\text{Fixed costs}}{\text{Contribution per unit}}$
   (d) *False.* Contribution/sales ratio is $\dfrac{\text{Contribution}}{\text{Sales}}$
   (e) *False.* Non-financial items do not feature directly in the calculations, but they are extremely important.

Chapter 19: Numerical *Answers*

A1 Jungle Animals

(i), (ii)	Selling Price £	Variable Costs £	Contribution £	Contribution/ Sales Ratio %
Alligators	1.00	1.05	(0.05)	(5.0)
Bears	1.20	1.00	0.20	16.7
Cougars	1.10	1.14	(0.04)	(3.6)
Donkeys	1.15	1.08	0.07	6.1
Eagles	1.20	0.96	0.24	20.0
Foxes	0.90	0.85	0.05	5.6
Giraffes	1.05	0.85	0.20	19.0
Hyenas	1.25	0.94	0.31	24.8
Iguanas	0.95	0.72	0.23	24.2
Jackals	0.80	0.73	0.07	8.8

(iii) The two toys with the highest contribution are Hyenas (£0.31 contribution) and Eagles (£0.24 contribution).

(iv) The three toys with the highest contribution/sales ratio are Hyenas (24.8 %), Iguanas (24.2 %) and Eagles (20 %).

(v) Alligators and Cougars have a negative contribution so we would not make them.

A3 Scrooge

Internal bid:	£
Clerical labour	50,000
Supervisory labour	60,000
Direct materials	25,000
Variable overheads	30,000
	165,000
External bid	(160,000)
Thus saving by buying in	5,000

So on the straight accounting calculation Scrooge would outsource. The chief assumption is that all the labour is indeed variable and can be laid off or redeployed easily. Other factors are the impact upon industrial relations, long-term implications and confidentiality. The outside bid is marginally superior. However, when these other factors are taken into account it may be better to go with the status quo.

A6 Freya

(i) Contribution per hammer

	£	£
Sales		10
Less: *Variable Costs*		
Direct materials	4	
Variable expenses	3	7
Contribution		3

$$\text{Break-even point: } \frac{\text{Fixed costs}}{\text{Contribution per unit}} = \frac{£30,000}{£3} = 10,000 \text{ hammers}$$

(ii) (a) If 4,000 sold

Contribution (4,000 × £3) =	£12,000
Fixed costs	(£30,000)
Loss	(£18,000)

(b) If 14,000 sold

Contribution (14,000 × £3) =	£42,000
Fixed costs	(£30,000)
Profit	£12,000

(iii) Current margin of safety

(a) Units (i.e. Hammers):

$$\frac{\text{Actual hammers sold} - \text{hammers at break-even}}{\text{Hammers at break-even}}$$

$$= \frac{20,000 - 10,000}{10,000} = 100\,\%$$

(b) £s:

$$\frac{\text{Actual sales} - \text{sales at break-even}}{\text{Sales at break-even}}$$

$$= \frac{200,000 - 100,000}{100,000} = 100\,\%$$

(iv) Break-even chart

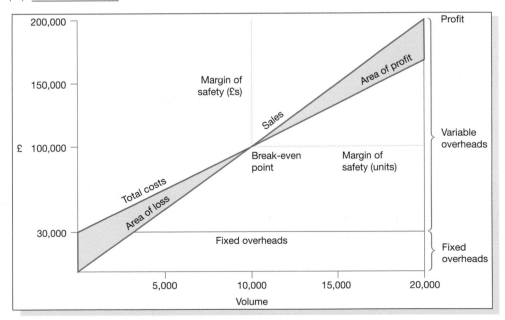

A8 Modem

(i)

Branch	Sales £	Variable Costs £	Contribution £	Contribution/ Sales Ratio %	Ranking
Cardiff	200,000	165,000	35,000	17.5 (£35,000/£200,000)	2
Edinburgh	300,000	230,000	70,000	23.3 (£70,000/£300,000)	1
London	1,000,000	870,000	130,000	13.0 (£130,000/£1,000,000)	3
	1,500,000	1,265,000	235,000		
Fixed costs			(150,000)		
Net Profit			85,000		

(ii) Cumulative profit table in contribution/sales ratio ranking:

	Cumulative Sales £	Cumulative Contribution £	Cumulative Profit/Loss £
Fixed costs			(150,000)
Edinburgh	300,000	70,000	(80,000)
Cardiff	500,000	105,000	(45,000)
London	1,500,000	235,000	85,000

Modem's Contribution/Sales Graph

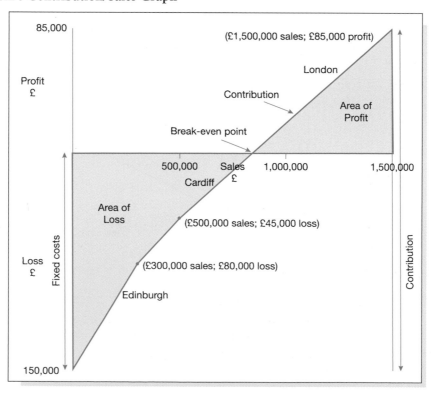

Chapter 20: Discussion *Answers*

The answers provide some outline points for discussion.

A1 Strategic management accounting is a relatively new branch of management accounting. It is concerned with a business's strategic future, long-term direction. A working definition of strategic management accounting is a form of management accounting which considers both an organisation's internal and external environments. Strategic management accounting comprises three main stages. First, an assessment of the current position of a business, which seeks to establish the internal and external elements of the business's environment. Second, an appraisal of the current position of the business. This establishes the current strengths and weaknesses. Finally, strategic management accounting looks at the possible strategic choices of the business, such as product diversification or mergers/acquisitions.

Strategic management accounting grows out of a concern with the traditional role of the management accountant. Traditionally, management accounting has been criticised as inward-looking and failing to respond to the external environment. Strategic management accounting attempts to lift management accountants out of this, traditionally fairly narrow, functional specialism. There is an emphasis on long-term strategic thinking embracing the whole business.

A5 True or False?
   (a) *True.*
   (b) *True.*
   (c) *False.* No, the four components are stars, question marks, cash cows and dogs.
   (d) *False.* The balanced scorecard uses a mixture of financial and non-financial performance indicators.
   (e) *False.* Almost right. SWOT analysis stands for strengths, weaknesses, *opportunities* and threats.

Chapter 20: Numerical *Answers*

A1 Maxi, Mini, Midi

In year 3		
	Maxi – high sales, high profitability, thus	**Maturity**
	Mini – sales declining, profits declining thus	**Decline**
	Midi – sales growing fast, profitability growing, thus	**Growth**

A2 Apple, Orange, Pear and Banana

Apple:	Star (high market share; high market growth)
Orange:	Question mark (low market share; high market growth)
Pear:	Cash cow (high market share; low market growth)
Banana:	Dog (low market share; low market growth)

The pears are cash cows and likely to be profitable, whereas the bananas are dogs and probably unprofitable. The situation with apples and oranges is more complex. The apples are stars and it depends on the current capital expenditure. If low they would be profitable, but if high they might not be. The oranges are question marks and are probably unprofitable at the moment. They leave the company with the difficult question of whether to invest more resources or whether to pull out of the market.

Chapter 21: Discussion *Answers*

The answers provide some outline points for discussion.

A1 (a) Capital investment is necessary for the development of a company's infrastructure. Companies also expand or reorientate their strategic direction. Therefore, they need to invest in infrastructure assets, such as factories or plant and machinery. Essentially, in a competitive business world companies will either grow or stagnate. If they stagnate they will be likely to be taken over.

(b) (i) Ships or equipment for making ships such as dry docks, cranes, heavy equipment etc.

(ii) New hotels or refurbishment of old ones.

(iii) New factories, plant and machinery, computer technology.

A5 **True or False?**
(a) *True.*
(b) *False.* Net present value and the internal rate of return use discounted cash flows. The payback period generally does not use discounted cash flows. It is, however, possible to incorporate them into payback models.
(c) *True.*
(d) *False.* The discount rate normally used for discounting cash flows is the company's weighted average cost of capital.
(e) *True.*

Chapter 21: Numerical *Answers*

A1 (i) 0.6209
(ii) 0.5983
(iii) 0.3762
(iv) 0.6355
(v) 0.6750
(vi) 0.1615

A2 Fairground

	Rocket	*Carousel*	*Dipper*

(i) Payback

Rocket	*Carousel*	*Dipper*
£16,000 +	£10,000 +	£16,000 +
(£2,000/£8,000)	(£8,000/£14,000)	(£2,000/£5,000)
= 2.25 years	= 2.57 years	= 2.4 years

(ii) Accounting rate of return

	Rocket	*Carousel*	*Dipper*
Annual average profit/	(£24,000 ÷ 3)/	(£24,000 ÷ 3)/	(£21,000 ÷ 3)/
Initial investment	£18,000	£18,000	£18,000
	= 44.4 %	= 44.4%	= 38.9%

(iii) Net present value

Year	Rocket £	Carousel £	Dipper £	Discount Rate 8 %	Rocket £	Carousel £	Dipper £
0	(18,000)	(18,000)	(18,000)	1	(18,000)	(18,000)	(18,000)
1	8,000	6,000	10,000	0.9259	7,407	5,555	9,259
2	8,000	4,000	6,000	0.8573	6,858	3,429	5,144
3	8,000	14,000	5,000	0.7938	6,350	11,113	3,969
Net Present Value (NPV)					2,615	2,097	372

So on (i)–(iii) we would choose the Rocket on all criteria as our project.

(iv) Internal rate of return (IRR): choose 18 % to achieve a negative NPV

Net present value Year	Rocket £	Carousel £	Dipper £	Discount Rate 18 %	Rocket £	Carousel £	Dipper £
0	(18,000)	(18,000)	(18,000)	1	(18,000)	(18,000)	(18,000)
1	8,000	6,000	10,000	0.8475	6,780	5,085	8,475
2	8,000	4,000	6,000	0.7182	5,746	2,873	4,309
3	8,000	14,000	5,000	0.6086	4,869	8,520	3,043
Net Present Value (NPV)					(605)	(1,522)	(2,173)

Therefore, calculate IRR using formula:

$$\text{IRR} = \text{Lowest discount rate} + \text{difference in discount rates} \times \frac{\text{lowest discount rate NPV}}{\text{difference in NPVs}}$$

$$\text{Rocket} \quad = \quad 8\% \quad + \quad \left(10\% \times \frac{£2,615}{£2,615 + £605}\right) \quad = \quad 16.1\%$$

$$\text{Carousel} \quad = \quad 8\% \quad + \quad \left(10\% \times \frac{£2,097}{£2,097 + £1,522}\right) \quad = \quad 13.8\%$$

$$\text{Dipper} \quad = \quad 8\% \quad + \quad \left(10\% \times \frac{£372}{£372 + £2,173}\right) \quad = \quad 9.5\%$$

A2 Fairground (*continued*)

Therefore, as our cost of capital (8 %) is less than the IRR, we could potentially undertake all the projects. We would choose to invest in Rocket because it has the highest IRR. Rocket is the preferred project under all four methods.

A3 Wetday

	Storm	Cloud	Downpour
(i) Payback	£15,000 +	£10,000 +	£12,000 +
	(£3,000/£7,000)	(£2,000/£2,500)	(£1,000/£4,000)
	= 3.43 years	= 3.8 years	= 3.25 years

(ii) **Accounting rate of return**

	Storm	Cloud	Downpour
Average annual profit/	£6,000/£18,000	£3,100/£12,000	£4,000/£13,000
Initial investment	= 33.3 %	= 25.8%	= 30.8%

(iii) **Net present value**

Year	Storm £	Cloud £	Downpour £	Discount Rate 12 %	Storm £	Cloud £	Downpour £
0	(18,000)	(12,000)	(13,000)	1	(18,000)	(12,000)	(13,000)
1	4,000	5,000	4,000	0.8929	3,572	4,464	3,572
2	5,000	2,000	4,000	0.7972	3,986	1,594	3,189
3	6,000	3,000	4,000	0.7118	4,271	2,135	2,847
4	7,000	2,500	4,000	0.6355	4,449	1,589	2,542
5	8,000	3,000	4,000	0.5674	4,539	1,702	2,270
Net Present Value (NPV)					2,817	(516)	1,420

Therefore, depending upon the criteria, we will choose a different project. Downpour has the quickest payback; Storm the highest accounting rate of return and NPV. Probably, therefore, we will choose Storm. We will definitely not choose Cloud, because of its negative NPV.

(iv) **Internal rate of return (IRR)**. Choose 20 % for Storm and Downpour to get a negative NPV. However, choose 8 % for Cloud to get a positive NPV.

Year	Storm £	Cloud £	Downpour £	Discount Rate 20 % £	Discount Rate 8 % £	Storm (20%) £	Cloud (8%) £	Downpour (20%) £
0	(18,000)	(12,000)	(13,000)	1	1	(18,000)	(12,000)	(13,000)
1	4,000	5,000	4,000	0.8333	0.9259	3,333	4,629	3,333
2	5,000	2,000	4,000	0.6944	0.8573	3,472	1,715	2,778
3	6,000	3,000	4,000	0.5787	0.7938	3,472	2,381	2,315
4	7,000	2,500	4,000	0.4823	0.7350	3,376	1,837	1,929
5	8,000	3,000	4,000	0.4019	0.6806	3,215	2,042	1,608
Net Present Value (NPV)						(1,132)	604	(1,037)

A3 Wetday (*continued*)

Calculate IRR, using formula

$$IRR = \text{Lowest discount rate} + \text{difference in discount rates} \times \frac{\text{lowest discount rate NPV}}{\text{difference in NPVs}}$$

$$\text{Storm} \quad = \quad 12\% \quad + \quad \left(8\% \times \frac{£2,817}{£2,817 + £1,132}\right) \quad = \quad 17.7\%$$

$$\text{Cloud} \quad = \quad 8\% \quad + \quad \left(4\% \times \frac{£604}{£604 + £516}\right) \quad = \quad 10.2\%$$

$$\text{Downpour} \quad = \quad 12\% \quad + \quad \left(8\% \times \frac{£1,420}{£1,420 + £1,037}\right) \quad = \quad 16.6\%$$

As our cost of capital is 12 %, we could potentially undertake Storm or Downpour. Storm has the highest IRR and we would choose this project if funds were limited. As Storm has the highest accounting rate of return, NPV and IRR, this is our preferred project.

Chapter 22: Discussion *Answers*

The answers provide some outline points for discussion.

A1 Firms are in some ways like living things. They need energy to survive and grow. In the case of living things, the energy is provided by sunlight. For firms, the energy is supplied by sources of finance. These may be short-term, like a bank overdraft, or long-term, like a long-term loan. These sources of finance enable a firm to buy stock, carry out day-to-day operations and expand by the purchase of new fixed assets. In essence, short-term finance should be used to sustain the firm's working capital, while long-term finance should fund the company's infrastructure. Some of the major sources of finance and the activities financed are outlined below:

Source of finance	*Activities financed*
Bank overdraft	Working capital, day-to-day operations
Debt factoring	Debtors
Invoice discounting	Debtors
Sale and buy back of stock	Stock
Leasing	Leased assets
Retained profits	Infrastructure assets, e.g., fixed assets
Share capital	Infrastructure assets, e.g., fixed assets
Long-term loan	Infrastructure assets, e.g., fixed assets

A5 True or False?

(a) *False.* They are normally used to finance long-term infrastructure assets.

(b) *True.*

(c) *True.*

(d) *False.* Retained profits is an internal, not an external, source of long-term finance.

(e) *True.*

Chapter 22: Numerical *Answers*

A1 Lathe

   (i) (a) **Graphical Solution**

Order Quantity Q	Number of Orders per annum	Order Cost	Total Order Cost	Average Quantity in Stock	Carrying Cost	Total Carrying Cost	Total Cost
		£	£	£	£	£	£
250	80	25	2,000	125	0.90	112.50	2,112.50
500	40	25	1,000	250	0.90	225.00	1,225.00
1,000	20	25	500	500	0.90	450.00	950.00
1,500	13.33	25	333	750	0.90	675.00	1,008.00
2,000	10	25	250	1,000	0.90	900.00	1,150.00

Graphical solution: Optimal order quantity about 1,000

A1 Lathe (*continued*)

(i) (b) Algebraic solution:

Economic order quantity formula

$$Q = \sqrt{\frac{2AC}{i}}$$

where:

Q = Economic order quantity
A = Average annual usage
C = Cost of each order being placed
i = Carrying cost per unit per annum

$$Q = \sqrt{\frac{2 \times 20,000 \times 25}{0.90}} = 1,054 \text{ Tweaks}$$

(ii) Total costs per annum

		£
Costs of purchase	£1.50 × 1,054	1,581
Order costs	$\dfrac{20,000}{1,054} \times £25$	474
Holding costs	$\dfrac{1,054}{2} \times 0.90$	474
Total costs		2,529

A4 Albatross

Source of Finance	Current Market Value		Present Cost of Capital	Weighted Average Cost of Capital
	£ million	%	%	%
Ordinary shares	4	50.0	12	6.00
Preference shares	1	12.5	10	1.25
Long-term loan	3	37.5	8	3.00
	8	100.0		10.25

Index